Examining the Rapid Advance of Digital Technology in Africa

Lloyd G. Adu Amoah
University of Ghana, Ghana

A volume in the Advances in IT Standards and
Standardization Research (AITSSR) Book Series

Published in the United States of America by
  IGI Global
  Engineering Science Reference (an imprint of IGI Global)
  701 E. Chocolate Avenue
  Hershey PA, USA 17033
  Tel: 717-533-8845
  Fax: 717-533-8661
  E-mail: cust@igi-global.com
  Web site: http://www.igi-global.com

                    Library of Congress Cataloging-in-Publication Data

Names: Amoah, Lloyd G. Adu, 1973- editor.
Title: Examining the rapid advance of digital technology in Africa / edited
  by Lloyd G. Adu Amoah.
Description: Hershey, PA : Engineering Science Reference, 2024. | Includes
  bibliographical references and index. | Summary: "This book seeks to
  expand the frontiers of the understanding of Africa's digitalization
  from an empirical and theoretical standpoint to the extent that it
  engages directly with expressions of this ever-evolving phenomenon in a
  continent that cannot be ignored in the global political economy"--
  Provided by publisher.
Identifiers: LCCN 2023038640 (print) | LCCN 2023038641 (ebook) | ISBN
  9781668499627 (hardcover) | ISBN 9781668499672 (ebook)
Subjects: LCSH: Information technology--Economic aspects--Africa. |
  Information technology--Technological innovations--Africa. |
  Technological innovations--Economic aspects--Africa. |
  Cyberinfrastructure--Africa.
Classification: LCC HC800.Z9 I55473 2024 (print) | LCC HC800.Z9 (ebook) |
  DDC 303.48/33096--dc23/eng/20230822
LC record available at https://lccn.loc.gov/2023038640
LC ebook record available at https://lccn.loc.gov/2023038641

This book is published in the IGI Global book series Advances in IT Standards and Standardization Research (AITSSR) (ISSN: 1935-3391; eISSN: 1935-3405)

British Cataloguing in Publication Data
A Cataloguing in Publication record for this book is available from the British Library.

For electronic access to this publication, please contact: eresources@igi-global.com.

Advances in IT Standards and Standardization Research (AITSSR) Book Series

Kai Jakobs
RWTH Aachen University, Germany

ISSN:1935-3391
EISSN:1935-3405

MISSION

IT standards and standardization are a necessary part of effectively delivering IT and IT services to organizations and individuals, as well as streamlining IT processes and minimizing organizational cost. In implementing IT standards, it is necessary to take into account not only the technical aspects, but also the characteristics of the specific environment where these standards will have to function.

The **Advances in IT Standards and Standardization Research (AITSSR) Book Series** seeks to advance the available literature on the use and value of IT standards and standardization. This research provides insight into the use of standards for the improvement of organizational processes and development in both private and public sectors.

COVERAGE

- Standards and Technology Transfer
- Analyses of Standards-Setting Processes, Products, and Organization
- Case Studies on Standardization
- Standardization for Organizational Development
- Emerging roles of formal standards Organizations and consortia
- Open source and standardization
- User-Related Issues
- Conformity assessment
- Standardization and Public Policy Formation
- Descriptive Theory of Standardization

IGI Global is currently accepting manuscripts for publication within this series. To submit a proposal for a volume in this series, please contact our Acquisition Editors at Acquisitions@igi-global.com or visit: http://www.igi-global.com/publish/.

Titles in this Series

For a list of additional titles in this series, please visit:
http://www.igi-global.com/book-series/advances-standards-standardization-research/37142

Modernizing Enterprise IT Audit Governance and Management Practices
Manish Gupta (University at Buffalo, SUNY, USA) and Raj Sharman (University at Buffalo, SNY, USA)
Engineering Science Reference • © 2023 • 318pp • H/C (ISBN: 9781668487662) • US $250.00

Handbook of Research on Evolving Designs and Innovation in ICT and Intelligent Systems for Real-World Applications
Kandarpa Kumar Sarma (Gauhati University, India) Navajit Saikia (Assam Engineering College, India) and Mridusmita Sharma (Gauhati Universit, India)
Engineering Science Reference • © 2022 • 312pp • H/C (ISBN: 9781799897958) • US $380.00

Digital Transformation for Promoting Inclusiveness in Marginalized Communities
Munyaradzi Zhou (Midlands State University, Zimbabwe) Gilbert Mahlangu (Midlands State University, Zimbabwe) and Cyncia Matsika (Midlands State University, Zimbabwe)
Engineering Science Reference • © 2022 • 311pp • H/C (ISBN: 9781668439012) • US $260.00

The Strategies of Informing Technology in the 21st Century
Andrew Targowski (Independent Researcher, USA)
Engineering Science Reference • © 2022 • 557pp • H/C (ISBN: 9781799880363) • US $240.00

Developing Countries and Technology Inclusion in the 21st Century Information Society
Alice S. Etim (Winston Salem State University, USA)
Information Science Reference • © 2021 • 318pp • H/C (ISBN: 9781799834687) • US $205.00

IT Auditing Using a System Perspective
Robert Elliot Davis (Walden University, USA)
Information Science Reference • © 2020 • 260pp • H/C (ISBN: 9781799841982) • US $215.00

Handbook of Research on the Evolution of IT and the Rise of E-Society
Maki Habib (The American University in Cairo, Egypt)
Information Science Reference • © 2019 • 602pp • H/C (ISBN: 9781522572145) • US $245.00

Global Implications of Emerging Technology Trends
Francisco José García-Peñalvo (University of Salamanca, Spain)
Information Science Reference • © 2018 • 323pp • H/C (ISBN: 9781522549444) • US $185.00

701 East Chocolate Avenue, Hershey, PA 17033, USA
Tel: 717-533-8845 x100 • Fax: 717-533-8661
E-Mail: cust@igi-global.com • www.igi-global.com

Table of Contents

Detailed Table of Contents

Chapter 1
Lloyd G. Adu Amoah, University of Ghana, Ghana

Cyberization has become the new inescapable reality of contemporary life. Cyberization points to the ways in which daily living in the last thirty years has become decidedly entangled in digital artifacts, infrastructure, and networks. The recent COVID-19 pandemic provides the most recent empirical, incontrovertibly global, and demonstrable snapshot of this reality. This chapter concerns itself with what all this means for Africa's place in the scheme of global power mediated by the era of cyberization. Using Ghana's attempt at scientific and technological advance under President Kwame Nkrumah and its cyberization experience in the era of neoliberal capitalism as a case study, and drawing insights from the fields of techno-politics, science and technology studies (STS), development studies and international relations, the chapter offers some conceptual building blocks wound around the idea of digital imperialism as a starting point for catalyzing theorizing about Africa and the power dynamics of the cyberization turn in the global political economy.

Chapter 2
Wei Ye, The Chinese University of Hong Kong, Shenzhen, China

This chapter examines the trajectory and effectiveness of Africa-China digital talent development cooperation by investigating university-industry-government relations. Based on participant observation conducted in China from 2017 to 2019 and fieldwork in Ethiopia from 2019 to 2020, it identifies a typology of four collaboration types based on the nature of initiators and the partnership modes. Ethiopia is selected as an information-rich case due to its diverse typology variations. Each collaboration type addresses specific digital education needs in Ethiopia, including equipping education officials and professionals with digital knowledge in higher education, providing digital skills training for pre-service and in-service teachers, and empowering youth through digital innovation and entrepreneurship. This chapter uncovers the interactions among universities, industry, and governments in digital talent development between Africa and China. It argues that African governments should take a more proactive role in facilitating effective university-industry linkages.

Chapter 3

Lloyd G. Adu Amoah, University of Ghana, Ghana
Eyram Tawia, Leti Arts, Ghana

This chapter provides a state-of-the art account(their creation, logics and play) of video games in Africa by explicating its ties, tensions and possibilities vis-à-vis the wider global video games industry. This explanation is rendered through a critical examination of vital elements such as policies, key actors, knowledge capabilities, institutions, investments, history, business, technology, and cultural economy by drawing on the evolution and growth of the African video games space in the last twenty years.

Chapter 4

Josephine Aboagye, University of Cape Coast, Ghana
Isaac Nunoo, University of Cape Coast, Ghana

This chapter examines the practice of digital diplomacy in Ghana during the COVID-19 pandemic. The chapter analyses how diplomatic activities were conducted, the challenges encountered during the pandemic and what the future looks like for digital diplomacy in Ghana. The study also tests whether COVID-19 increased the use of technology and digital diplomacy in Ghana. Using the mixed method approach, the findings reveal that COVID-19 increased digital diplomacy and the use of digital platforms in Ghana. Some of the challenges encountered were institutional challenges, internet issues and lack of privacy. The study also reveals that the future of digital diplomacy in Ghana is promising and a combination of traditional and digital diplomacy would enhance Ghana's diplomacy.

Chapter 5

Getachew H. Mengesha, Addis Ababa University, Ethiopia
Elefelious Getachew Belay, Addis Ababa Institute of Technology, Ethiopia
Rachel Adams, Research ICT Africa, South Africa

This study explores technical considerations for designing, developing, adopting, and using AI-based systems in Africa. Africa did not benefit as intended from the first three industrial revolutions. Cognizant of this fact, the continent is now expected to be aware of and ready to tap into the opportunities created by AI and the Fourth Industrial Revolution to fix chronic problems connected to efficiency while minimizing the unintended consequences AI might pose. Data for the study was gathered through focus group discussion (FGD), key informant interview (KII), and document review. The outcome of the study reveals that AI model adoption issues, AI biases, AI data availability, security, and privacy, AI model accuracy and quality, and AI resources have emerged as major technical considerations for adopting and using AI in the African context. The chapter provides valuable insights that would serve as input for policy formulation and AI capacity development endeavors.

    Margaret Richardson Ansah, University of Ghana, Ghana
    Hannah Chimere Ugo, Afe Babalola University, Nigeria
    Isaac Adjaye Aboagye, University of Ghana, Ghana
    Nii Longdon Sowah, University of Ghana, Ghana
    Gifty Osei, University of Ghana, Ghana
    Srinivasan S. Balapangu, University of Ghana, Ghana
    Samuel Kojo Kwofie, University of Ghana, Ghana

As the application of artificial intelligence (AI) expands across various fields of practice including health its deployment, regulation, acceptability, preparedness challenges, and ethical concerns in Africa requires a critical look. The chapter's primary objective is to provide a comprehensive understanding of how AI can positively affect health outcomes in Africa. The authors explored the potential for AI to transform and improve healthcare in low-resource areas like Africa and reviewed the current state of how AI algorithms can be used to improve diagnostics, treatment, and disease monitoring, as well as how AI can help with pandemic preparedness. The chapter also highlights the challenges and ethical considerations that need to be addressed when deploying AI in Africa. The chapter concludes that AI is poised to assist countries in improving the quality of health service delivery through innovation using telemedicine-assisted approaches and that there is a need to deploy new technologies and share lessons and experiences among countries on the African continent to help improve healthcare in Africa.

    Wasswa Shafik, School of Digital Science, Universiti Brunei Darussalam, Brunei & Dig
      Connectivity Research Laboratory (DCRLab), Kampala, Uganda

Artificial intelligence (AI) and robotics are becoming more popular globally, which makes Africa a potential hub for innovation and development in these fields. However, for the full benefits of these technologies to be realized, it is vital to understand and deal with the unique challenges and barriers that make it hard for them to be used and integrated in Africa. This chapter presents an overview of the current state of robotics and AI in Africa and explores the challenges associated with their adoption, including infrastructure limitations, inadequate technical expertise, and ethical considerations. It further discusses potential strategies for overcoming these challenges, such as investment in infrastructure and education, international collaboration, and the development of ethical frameworks for AI. Finally, the chapter suggests some future directions for continued attention and investment in the responsible and equitable development of AI and robotics in Africa to benefit stagnant and slow-growing African economies.

    Gideon Mensah Anapey, University of Ghana, Ghana

Regardless of the imperatives of the COVID-19 pandemic and the increasing adoption of artificial intelligence (AI) in higher education to meet learning outcomes, little is known about its integration in dialogic learning outcomes in the post-COVID 19 era. From the learning sciences perspective, this chapter explores faculty members' adoption of AI resources for dialogic pedagogy using a participatory research design and social-constructivism theory. Interview data was obtained from 6 faculty members of two of Ghana's teacher education universities. Manual coding in Microsoft Excel yielded themes from the participants' narrative data with voices embedded. The results suggest that generic computer training, social media and internet exposure, data analytics, multimedia capacity, and digital pedagogy are the leading skills required for AI integration for dialogic learning goals among faculty members. In conclusion, capacity building for faculty to effectively deploy AI resources in students' dialogic learning goals requires learning scientists' effort and inputs.

Chapter 9

The purpose of this research was to examine how banking digitalisation acts as a catalyst for money transfers and economic development between countries of origin and country of labour migration in Africa. This chapter used desktop research to understand how improvements in banking digitalisation using different platforms is transforming African movement of money and saving money senders a lot of money and time in inter account transfers. M-PESA; Mukuru, supermarket money market transfers, bank transfers have been dominant FinTech innovations transforming and improving quality of life and fostering financial inclusion within the African continent and diaspora. This chapter aids in understanding how digitalisation assists ordinary citizens, especially the poor who need to save every rand or dollar that they can save in order to make meaningful change in their lives and the lives of their loved ones anywhere in Africa and the world under these trying post-COVID 19 economic conditions.

The adoption of digital payments presents new opportunities for enhancing public sector service delivery. However, little coherent literature exists on the diffusion of public-sector digital payments, including deployment challenges and successes. This chapter reviews the evidence on the evolution of digital payments in Ghana's public sector. It draws upon stakeholder theory to analyze the diffusion of digital payments for public service delivery in Ghana. This chapter gathered qualitative evidence through expert interviews to map the evolution of public sector digital payments. The findings of this chapter reveal that Ghana's public sector finances are digititalized, leading to a significant reduction in the use of physical cash. Government entities are empowered to access public finance data in real time, supporting better revenue collection, disbursement, and judicious utilization of financial resources. This chapter highlights the need to improve stakeholder engagement as a prerequisite to ensuring increased usage of public sector digital payments.

Chapter 11

Fintech infrastructure in Africa has continued to evolve towards more resilient digital forms over the past decade. The chapter reviews various stages of the Ghanaian journey and the disaggregation into the pillars of innovation that the chapter identifies. Fintech is considered as only one of such pillars. The discussion touches briefly on AI, Big Data, Blockchain and other generic elements, which can be considered as arrowheads of change. The conclusion is that Platform Play is enabled by stitching together the various axes and multifaceted domains of digital and other forms of knowledge.

    Eli Fianu, Ghana Communication Technology University, Ghana
    Stephen Boateng, University of Mines and Technology, Ghana
    Zelda Arku, University of Mines and Technology, Ghana

The chapter attempts to unravel the factors that influence citizens' usage of an e-government location-based service, the Ghana Post GPS. The research model comprises a set of relationships between constructs from UTAUT (effort expectancy, performance expectancy, and social influence; age and gender as moderating variables), the model of PC utilization (complexity and affect towards use), TAM2 (output quality, intention to use, and actual usage). A quantitative research design was used for the study. The sample consisted of three hundred and thirty-seven (337) respondents. Data was analysed using PLS-SEM (partial least squares structural equation modelling) via SmartPLS 3. Twelve (12) hypotheses were tested; eight (8) were rejected while four (4) were accepted. The results are thoroughly discussed, and relevant recommendations made.

    Emmanuel de-Graft Johnson Owusu-Ansah, Kwame Nkrumah University of Science and
        Technology, Ghana
    Richard Kodzo Avuglah, Kwame Nkrumah University of Science and Technology, Ghana
    Yaa Adwubi Kyere, Kwame Nkrumah University of Science and Technology, Ghana

This chapter explores how the COVID-19 pandemic affected technology in Africa, focusing on technological innovations and uptake. The COVID-19 pandemic has encouraged industrial innovation and digital transformation in Africa. The COVID-19 pandemic has shown that traditional methods are ineffectual, and technology is needed. African nations need digital technology to improve healthcare, education, e-commerce, and governance. Technology narrows the digital divide by improving productivity, access to critical services, and promoting economic development. Telemedicine, e-learning, digital payments, and remote working made Africa resilient in the face of the pandemic. The chapter evaluates African technical problems and potential. Poor infrastructure, internet connectivity, high fees, and digital illiteracy are critical issues that need to be addressed. The chapter suggests that government, industry, and international organizations work together to solve these problems. COVID-19 might boost African technology. Technology may boost African economies and living standards through digital transformation if the aforementioned critical issues are overcome.

Chapter 14

Williams Kennedy George, Department of Technical Education, Akwa Ibom State College of Education, Nigeria
Edidiong Isonguyo Silas, Department of Technical Education, Akwa Ibom State College of Education, Nigeria
Digvijay Pandey, Department of Technical Education, India
Binay Kumar Pandey, Department of Information Technology, College of Technology,
 Govind Ballabh University of Agriculture and Technology, Pantnagar, India

Technical and vocational education and training (TVET) play a pivotal role in preparing the Nigerian workforce for the demands of a rapidly evolving digital economy. In the wake of the Fourth Industrial Revolution 4.0, the integration of digital competencies in TVET programs has become imperative. This chapter explores the strategies and approaches to foster digital competencies in Nigeria's TVET by leveraging Industrial Revolution 4.0 as an enabling technology. The chapter presents the context of the historical evolution of industry 4.0, its components, design principles, main characteristics, and the TVET approach in Nigeria. Emphasizing the urgency of aligning TVET programs with Industrial Revolution 4.0 requirements, the chapter presents best practices that illustrate successful models of incorporating digital competencies into vocational training. The chapter examines the existing challenges and gaps in integrating digital skills into TVET curriculum in Nigeria, addressing issues related to infrastructure, funding, policy frameworks, and inclusivity. The chapter discusses the role of stakeholders such as government bodies, educational institutions, industry partners, and international organizations in facilitating the implementation of Industrial Revolution 4.0-driven initiatives in Nigerian TVET. Furthermore, the chapter offers actionable recommendations for policymakers, educators, and stakeholders to collaboratively design and implement strategies for integrating Industrial Revolution 4.0 technologies into Nigeria's TVET landscape. By doing so, it advocates for a more agile and future-ready workforce capable of harnessing the transformative power of digital technologies in the Nigerian context.

Chapter 15

 William Chakabwata, University of South Africa, South Africa

The chapter assesses the state of digital technology in Africa as a catalyst for economic growth and development. The chapter also appraises the state of higher education on the continent in order to determine its preparedness to produce professionals who can function in a digital economy. A number of technological diffusion models which include diffusion of innovation (DIO), theory of reasoned action, and technology adoption model (TAM) were used to explore the diffusion of innovation to Africa from developed countries. Although there is a rapid growth in technological penetration in Africa impacting sectors such as agriculture, education, and finance, more investment in technology is still needed to power strides towards optimum levels of economic development. Africa, with its rapidly growing population and ever expanding market, is perceived as the next economic frontier after Asia. Higher education through curriculum models such as Education 5.0 can lead the way to make Africa the next economic frontier.

Foreword

Africa is at a critical conjuncture. There is not much reasonable debate when the assertion that as yet, the continent has under-delivered on the bright promise of independence is made. Too many people continue to wallow in mass misery of various descriptions on the continent.

The most urgent task for the continent at this stage therefore is to improve the living conditions of the broad masses of its people. This is the focus of development and of democracy, or should be; to guarantee dignity to everyone. In the 21st century a discussion about development will necessarily involve leveraging digital technology, as it is now a pervasive aspect of human existence.

If it is pervasive, digital technology discussions are sometimes also characterized by wild speculation and, to use Samir Amin's expression, tend to promise too many miracles that lead nowhere. Too many people claim to understand the subject while hanging in mid-air and making very superficial analysis that necessarily result in irrelevant prescriptions. This is the curse of the neoliberal embrace and shoddy intellectualism.

This book is written by people with deep and relevant experience of both technology and multiple perspectives of development. That makes it holistic and diverse in the way it searches for solutions. There is conceptual clarity in the distillation of the problems and opportunities, while the contributors show abundant evidence of understanding real life situations.

It is an extensive and expansive coverage of the area. In one book, the following areas are covered among others: Artificial Intelligence, Development in Africa, Digital infrastructure, Global Political-Economy, Implications of Technology Advancements in Africa, Socio-Economic Transformation, Pedagogy and Video Games.

The contributors approach their areas from varied but coherent perspectives, given they spring from many disciplines. This is a great strength of the book.

Development is understood properly as how to reorder the social relations around the means of production to achieve shared dignity and shared prosperity. Democracy is defined to benefit the people and to exist for the people.

Both democracy and development are seen as means not ends in themselves. It is understood within this context that digital technologies are also a means and not an end. So is the market, also a means not an end or a deity to be worshipped on its own.

Digital technologies can play a vital role in liberating the productive forces on the African continent to drive prosperity and improve livelihoods of the masses of our compatriots. That is a conclusion one inescapably comes to reading this book. More importantly suggestions are made on how to do this.

Wherever you fit on the development spectrum of discourse about Africa, if you are serious about plumbing new ideas with a view to obtaining real and practical ideas to improve society, this is a book for you.

It is hoped that policy makers in Africa and new scholars will delve into the conversation it contributes to with much seriousness. The contributors deserve congratulations.

Yaw Nsarkoh
Former Senior Vice President Unilever, UK

Yaw Nsarkoh *is a veteran of the consumer goods industry, having worked across many geographies, functions, and categories. He has a strong affinity to multi-stakeholder approaches to business and to development. Believing strongly that the purpose of both should first be to secure the long-term welfare or health of society. Yaw studied chemical engineering at University of Science and Technology. He then studied Management at the Henley Management College, UK. He has been certified as a professional coach by the University of Cambridge, UK. He is known for his eclectic and multidisciplinary perspectives on development and governance. Yaw is an outspoken critic of neoliberal capitalism. He has experience of working with communities on all inhabited continents of the earth and has watched digital strategies evolve in many parts of the world over the last three decades. Yaw loves to remind people he started his professional career in the same week the first SMS was sent in the world. He is a committed Pan Africanist.*

Preface

The last decade has been marked by far-reaching advances in digitalization. The emergence of quantum computing (New Scientist, 2016) is one such advance. In responding to the problem of collective action, scholars are pointing to the rise and centrality of algorithmic regulation and governance (Yeung and Lodge, 2019). When the COVID-19 pandemic struck, Zoom and Microsoft Teams showed how critical digital infrastructure is for maintaining a semblance of normal life in moments of crises. South Korea, a highly informatized society was one of the first to devise a testing regimen for COVID-19. As digital technology has advanced in recent times, Africa has been attracting the attention of some of the leading digital technology companies on the globe. Huawei has been building the digital infrastructure of African countries (Moore, 2023; Schindler et al, 2023). Alphabet Inc. set up an artificial intelligence research office in Ghana. Uber, the taxi hailing app, is available in more than 61 cities across seven countries in sub-Saharan Africa, namely South Africa, Ghana, Nigeria, Ivory Coast, Kenya, Uganda, and Tanzania. Africa is increasingly being considered as one of the key frontiers for any large scale phenomenal socio-economic transformation on the back of digitalization. Is this view a realistic and realizable one given the example of the Asian continent and countries within it like Japan, Singapore, Taiwan, China and Korea? In ideational and practical terms what does this view and belief mean for African countries such as Ghana, Kenya, Senegal, and Rwanda among others which are seriously considering such an option? What implications, potential and real, would result from the focused pursuit of the digitalization path to Africa's rapid socio-economic transformation? Embodying what has come to be described as datafied existence (Sadowski, 2019) writ large across the globe what do these developments mean for the African continent which provides its own unique experiences and empirics of what is still an evolving and complex digitalization process sweeping the entire world? It is crucial for the field of science and technology studies and its linkages with socio-economic impacts and transformation that Africa's experiences of and contribution to digitalization are tracked, analyzed, understood, and critiqued. This book through its chapters seeks to contribute to such an effort. The fifteen chapters in this book are grouped under three sections which specify the research foci and interests of their authors. Methodologically the chapters employed quantitative, qualitative, and mixed methods approaches.

Section 1(Chapters1-4) is concerned with the implications for Africa-at the levels of theory and practice-of a world in which life is increasingly suffused and conditioned by digital technology. In a digitalized world undergirded by dominant technical standards, norms, and rationalities (Adams, 2021) should Africa be engaged as a benign pliant consumer or as an active self-reflexive participant helping to shape the technical and non-technical values and ideals of this brave new world? On these broad questions which Section 1 grapples with recent scholarship on Africa and the latest developments in digital technology (artificial intelligence to be specific) has begun to tackle these issues (Jecker, Atuire and Ajei, 2022). The chapters in this section weigh in as well.

Amoah (Chapter 1) takes on the emergent literature on the geopolitics and geoeconomics of digital technology and Africa's place within it. Using the Nkrumah years and the politics of atomic physics as a key analytical framework as well drawing on data related to building and maintenance of the internet, the chapter argues that countries like Ghana in the Global South have become relatively passive in shaping the technical, ideational, and financial architecture of the contemporary digital age. The chapter suggests that the upshot of this situation is the emergence of digital imperialism which conceptually better captures Africa's experience of contemporary digital technology. The chapter argues for more conceptual and theoretical clarity and coherence for understanding Africa's place in the political economy of digitalization and offers digital imperialism as a critical focal idea for consideration.

Wei (Chapter 2) is interested in how given the worlding of digital technology, African countries can utilize their relations with international organizations and technologically advanced countries like China to build up technological capacity and talent. Focusing on Africa-China relations, the chapter exposes the complexity attending claims of digital support in official Chinese narratives within the context of the Forum on China-Africa Co-operation (FOCAC) and makes the case that in typological terms African governments(while taking the initiative on building digital infrastructure, making policy and providing constant power supply among other things) must prioritize engaging Chinese ICT firms such as Huawei for their national digital talent development needs.

In Chapter 3, Amoah and Akofa focus on the global video games industry and Africa's links with it. The chapter attempts to provide a state-of-the art account of games and gamification in Africa by explicating on the continent's ties, the attendant tensions, and possibilities vis-à-vis the wider global games industry. This explication is rendered through a critical examination of vital issues such as the history of video games, policies, key actors, knowledge capabilities, institutions, investments, technology, and cultural economy and drawing on the evolution and growth of the African video games space in the last twenty years. The chapter argues that video games by virtue of being toyetic have among other impacts society shaping influence via players' identity formation as well presenting huge economic possibilities that African countries should not ignore. The chapter rounds off by offering some suggestions on how African countries can build their video games industry.

Aboagye and Nunoo (Chapter 4) discuss the idea of what they describe as "digital diplomacy" occasioned by the strains and stresses of the COVID-19 pandemic. The chapter argues that the practise of Ghana's diplomacy during the pandemic exemplified the practice of digital diplomacy. The chapter analyses how diplomatic activities were conducted, the challenges encountered during the pandemic and what the future looks like for digital diplomacy in Ghana. The chapter underscores the ways in which the worlding of technology remakes the conduct of diplomacy in the African context.

Section 2(Chapters 5-8) takes on the Artificial Intelligence (AI) revolution the world is currently experiencing as exemplified in the launch on November 30, 2022, of Chat Generative Pre-Trained Transformer (ChatGPT), a chatbot developed by the company, OpenAI, and the AI race this has unleashed, especially in technologically advanced societies. The chapters in the section grapple with how African countries can successfully partake in the AI revolution and handle the impacts this portends.

Mengesha, Belay and Adams (Chapter 5) provide compelling ideas (technical and policy) on how African countries can build their AI systems. The authors provide their prescriptions because in their view "more advanced AI technology emerged before the continent could optimally use the conventional ICTs to improve the backbone telecom infrastructure and develop the necessary human resources." In other words, AI has creeped upon a continent that has not taken full advantage of prior existing technologies which reality poses grave challenges that it must overcome.

Richardson, Ugo, Aboagye, Sowah, Osei, Balanpagu and Koffie(Chapter 6) are interested in the the ways in which AI finds uptake in Africa's health sector. The authors therefore focus on offering a comprehensive understanding of how AI can positively affect health outcomes in Africa. The value of Chapter 6 is that it moves beyond the broad issues of building systems that Chapter 5 was concerned with and narrows down on AI application in a given sector. In doing this the chapter points out the value of deploying AI for healthcare (and the potential ethical challenges this entails) in low resource and income countries for improving diagnostics, treatment, and disease monitoring, as well pandemic preparedness.

Shafik (Chapter 7) continues in the same vein as Chapter 6 but is more interested in how linkages may be forged between AI and robotics on the African continent. The value of this chapter lies in the explicit ways in which it draws attention to the robotics-AI combine and thus "explores the main factors hindering the deployment and adoption of robotics and AI in Africa, including infrastructure constraints, the lack of technical expertise, and ethical considerations."

Anapey (Chapter 8) continues with the sectoral applications of AI in Africa that Chapter 7 pursued. Chapter 8 is interested in the pedagogical impact of AI adoption. The chapter draws timely attention to the pedagogical potential of AI adoption in education in Africa which may be realised via generic computer, social media, internet, analytics, multimedia, and digital pedagogical training.

Section 3(Chapters 9-15) grapples with the variegated ways in which digital technology has come to be ensconced in the policy sphere in Africa in recent times. Gwala and Mashau (Chapter 9) hold forth on the penetration of digital technology in Africa's financial sector. Focusing on indigenous innovations in the fintech space in Africa, the chapter underscores the value of digital innovations derived from the Africa context in general and more specifically the potential this has for digitalized financial intermediation for especially the poorest of the poor on the continent.

In Chapter 10, Ahiabenu brings the practitioner-scholar's voice to the literature on the public sector and digitalization (Amoah, 2014; Mager, 2012, Yeung, 2010) with a specific focus on Africa. While digital payments tend to be highlighted and examined in the financial sector as Chapter 9 does, Chapter 10 switches the focus onto the public sector. Using Ghana's public sector as a case study, Chapter 10, shows that digital payments are increasing becoming standard fare in Africa, but this tendency may be hampered without intentional stakeholder buy-in and interest.

In Chapter 11, Nsarkoh also brings on board a practitioner's perspective. Nsarkoh's focus is on the rise of platforms in Ghana's fintech space. Drawing on his experience participating in and leading major digitalization drives in the Ghana fintech arena, Nsarkoh reviews various stages of the Ghanaian digitalization journey and its disaggregation into key pillars of innovation of which fintech is one. The chapter draws attention to the idea of Platform Play (the seamless interaction of various fintech platforms) which is argued can only be enabled by the meshing together of the various axes and multifaceted domains of knowledge.

Ghana embarked on an aggressive and ambitious digitalization drive under the presidency of Nana Akufo-Addo. Vice-President Bawumia is the one who led the process and indeed championed it. One of the key policies of this digitalization was the provision of digitalized address system (given the non-existent physical address system) for homes and properties in Ghana. This system is known as national digital property address system (NDPAS) and also referred to as Ghana-Post GPS because it is tied to the Ghana Post Office system. In Chapter 12, Fianu, Boateng and Arku attempt to unpack the factors that influence the uptake of this novel address system and in so doing alert policymakers and benchmark some of the important issues to think through when rolling out such digital policies.

Owusu-Ansah, Avuglah and Kyere in Chapter 13 provide their lucubration on the spread of digital technology in various areas of African life triggered in the main by the COVID-19 pandemic. Focusing on a continental scale on areas such as healthcare, education, e-commerce, and governance, the chapter suggests that government, industry, and international organizations need to work together to tackle problems such as poor infrastructure, erratic internet connectivity, high fees, and digital illiteracy that hamper Africa's uptake of digital technology.

In Chapter 14, George, Silas, Pandey, and Pandey reflect on digitalization and pedagogy in Africa with a focus on Nigeria. The authors are interested in how digital technology may be fully integrated into technical and vocational education to power Africa's industrialization drive in the 21ˢᵗ century.

In Chapter 15, Chakabwata explores through desktop research filtered through three theoretical frameworks the rapid expansion of technology in Africa focusing on the challenges and opportunities for higher education. The chapter is keen to show how digital technology is increasingly becoming integrated into higher education in Africa to create a creative learner at home with this technology and the attendant challenges and opportunities.

This book seeks to contribute to expanding the frontiers of the understanding of Africa's digitalization from the empirical and theoretical standpoints to the extent that it interrogates varied expressions of this ever-evolving phenomenon in a continent that is being tightly wound up in the global digital political economy.

Lloyd G. Adu Amoah
University of Ghana, Ghana

REFERENCES

Adams, R. (2021). Can artificial intelligence be decolonized? *Interdisciplinary Science Reviews*, *46*(1-2), 176–197. doi:10.1080/03080188.2020.1840225

Amoah, L. G. A. (2014). *Impacts of the knowledge society on economic and social growth in Africa*. IGI Global. doi:10.4018/978-1-4666-5844-8

Jecker, N. S., Atiure, C. A., & Ajei, M. O. (2022). The moral standing of social robots: Untapped insights from Africa. *Philosophy & Technology*, *35*(34), 1–22. doi:10.1007/s13347-022-00531-5

Mager, A. (2012). Algorithmic ideology. *Information Communication and Society*, *15*(5), 769–787. doi:10.1080/1369118X.2012.676056

Moore, S. G. (2023). Huawei, Cyber-Sovereignty and Liberal Norms: China's Challenge to the West/Democracies. *Journal of Chinese Political Science*, *28*(1), 151–167. doi:10.1007/s11366-022-09814-2 PMID:35693300

New Scientist (2016). The Quantum World. *New Scientist*, *3*(3),1-128.

Sadowski, J. (2019). When data is capital: Datafication, accumulation, and extraction. *Big Data & Society*, *6*(1), 1–12. doi:10.1177/2053951718820549

Schindler, S., Alami, I., DiCarlo, J., Jepson, N., Rolf, S., Bayırbağ, M. K., Cyuzuzo, L., DeBoom, M., Farahani, A. F., Liu, I. T., McNicol, H., Miao, J. T., Nock, P., Teri, G., Vila Seoane, M. F., Ward, K., Zajontz, T., & Zhao, Y. (2023). The Second Cold War: US-China Competition for Centrality in Infrastructure, Digital, Production, and Finance Networks. *Geopolitics*, 1–38. doi:10.1080/14650045.2023.2253432

Yeung, K. (2010). The Regulatory State. In R. Baldwin, M. Cave, and M. Lodge (Eds.), The Oxford Handbook of Regulation. Oxford Academic. doi:10.1093/oxfordhb/9780199560219.003.0004

Yeung, K., & Lodge, M. (2019) Algorithmic Regulation. Oxford Academic. doi:10.1093/oso/9780198838494.001.0001

Acknowledgment

As a lad I gave my parents quite some undeserved grief for dismantling all the toys they bought for me. I remember one in particular: a model train. It went the way of all the others immediately I set my hands on it. My Dad surely burnt through his earnings in the employ of the Ghanaian Republic as a diplomat purchasing these toys. On hindsight this tendency of mine reflected a yearning to understand how things work which has undergirded my interest in technology and the ways it shapes society and with it the power dynamics that is often ignored. I must acknowledge here my primary school, Morning Star School in Accra, Ghana. There I was exposed to digital technology through the video games classmates brought to school especially my close buddy, Kweku Amoh; my gratitude is eternal. This work is a sequel to the first one I edited in 2014 titled *Impacts of the Knowledge Society on Economic and Social Growth in Africa* and acknowledges its debt to all those scholars across the world who have tried to understand and unpack the poetics of technology and dedicated intellectual effort to this over a lifetime.

This is for my dearest Sylvia for all those highbrow chats that allowed me to test and frame better my rough ideas on digital technology and Africa. This work is also dedicated to our children Kwame Adjei and Akua Otwiwa and their generation in Africa in the hope that they will engage technology beyond the lure of its consumption value and thereby grasp more acutely its politics to aid the necessary transition to creation and production. And this work is also in eternal debt to Akwasi Larbi and Felix Kwei-Kuma for their bankable "technology" of support in my family's life; Seth Adjei(my former student and mentee) for his constant diligent editorial assistance and my beloved mother, Mrs. Abigail Ama Otwiwa Amoah for all the lessons of life imparted. I will be remiss not to acknowledge the role of the Katekisama Project(involving scholars of the Universities of Ghana, Bonn and Basel) and the seminars and conferences on digital technology held under its auspices which helped me ponder and think through the emerging digital technology issues of our times.

Lloyd G. Adu Amoah
University of Ghana, Ghana

Chapter 1
Digital Imperialism and the Cyberization of Contemporary Life:
A Ghanaian Perspective

Lloyd G. Adu Amoah
University of Ghana, Ghana

ABSTRACT

Cyberization has become the new inescapable reality of contemporary life. Cyberization points to the ways in which daily living in the last thirty years has become decidedly entangled in digital artifacts, infrastructure, and networks. The recent COVID-19 pandemic provides the most recent empirical, incontrovertibly global, and demonstrable snapshot of this reality. This chapter concerns itself with what all this means for Africa's place in the scheme of global power mediated by the era of cyberization. Using Ghana's attempt at scientific and technological advance under President Kwame Nkrumah and its cyberization experience in the era of neoliberal capitalism as a case study, and drawing insights from the fields of techno-politics, science and technology studies (STS), development studies and international relations, the chapter offers some conceptual building blocks wound around the idea of digital imperialism as a starting point for catalyzing theorizing about Africa and the power dynamics of the cyberization turn in the global political economy.

Across the parapet......I can see springing up cities of Africa becoming the metropolis of science and learning and architecture and philosophy.

-Kwame Nkrumah (1976)

If we have not learned anything in the past century, it is that technology confers power, but that the consequences of that power are anything but predictable.

-Headrick (1991, p.3)

DOI: 10.4018/978-1-6684-9962-7.ch001

INTRODUCTION

Cyberization has become the new inescapable reality of contemporary life. Indeed, existence in the last thirty years has become decidedly entangled in the artifacts, infrastructure, and networks of information communication technology. The recent COVID-19 pandemic provides the most recent empirical, incontrovertibly global, and demonstrable snapshot of this reality. This chapter concerns itself with what all this means for Africa's place in the scheme of global power mediated by the era of cyberization. Using Ghana's attempt at scientific and technological advance under President Kwame Nkrumah and its cyberization experience in the era of neoliberal capitalism as a case study, and drawing insights from the fields of techno-politics, Science and Technology Studies(STS), development studies and international relations, the chapter offers some conceptual building blocks as a needed starting point for catalyzing theorizing about Africa and the power dynamics of the cyberization turn in the global political economy. In this regard the chapter argues preliminarily that the digital era heralds the rise of digital imperialism which countries like Ghana in the Global South need to come to terms with and speedily.

NKRUMAH'S SCIENTIFIC AND TECHNOLOGICAL VISION FOR GHANA

The Saint Lucian economist, Arthur Lewis, who eventually went on to win the Nobel Memorial Prize in Economics in 1979 was appointed Chief Economic Advisor in the year (1957) Ghana gained her independence from colonialism. He left that position in 1958, following policy differences (Tignor, 2006) between him and then Ghanaian President Kwame Nkrumah. The differences stemmed from the irreconcilable views the two had on industrial policy. Nkrumah was interested in heavy industries. Lewis, on his part, felt that Ghana should concentrate more on light industries and the agriculture sector. While this, on the surface, was a worldview clash between a politician and an economist, it was deeply revelatory of the role of science and technology in the nation building efforts of former colonies. The Nkrumah era, and Ghana's scientific endeavours under him, elicit even closer scrutiny because they represent a paradigm case of the global politics of science and technology in the global South that has scarcely been thoroughly analysed (Amoah, 2014; Mayer, Carpes and Knoblich, 2014). Given that Ghana was the first country in Black Africa to gain her independence, its experiences navigating the complex and ever shifting terrain of global science and technology merit scholarly attention for useful lessons.

Nkrumah considered the big push for Ghana's rapid industrialization, the most visible and eloquent evidence of Africa's full utilization of its technological and scientific capabilities and prowess and a sure basis for engaging a doubting world on an equal footing. For Nkrumah, industrialization which turned on specialized knowledge, was very much linked to the place of Ghana and Africa in the global power equation. In other words, those nations with knowledge had industrialized and dominated the world. In that sense, in his mind, a modern state propped essentially on agriculture and primary products was bound to be dominated by industrialized ones. Thus, he made the point incessantly that "returns on the export of primary products from mining, agriculture and forestry" could not "provide to any important extent the looked-for capital for investing in industrial foundation." (Nkrumah, 2004, p. 234).

Nkrumah's "Cult of Science"

Nkrumah's Seven-year Development Plan (1963/64-1969/70) revealed the central place of science and technology in Ghana's postcolonial future. In the foreword to the document on the Plan, Nkrumah (n.d., p. v) indicated that the plan was a "programme of social and economic development based on the use of *science and technology* to revolutionize our agriculture and industry" (author's emphasis). Nkrumah, therefore set about not just building the institutions for generating scientific know-how and expertise but embarking as well on projects that showcased science and technology in action. The noted Ghanaian scientist (the first Ghanaian woman to obtain a degree in Zoology and earn a doctorate generally and specifically in science), Letitia Obeng(2018, p.107), echoes this fixation on science when she avers that "the first President, Dr. Kwame Nkrumah, though not a scientist, believed in the absolute relevance of science and technology to the development programme that he intended for his new country, Ghana". Osseo-Asare (2019, p.6) described this interest as Nkrumah's introduction of the "cult of science" into Ghana. The votaries as it were of this cult were to be initiated into the mysteries of pure science and its application. In this regard Nkrumah was clear in his mind that

Ghana's need for scientists, engineers, architects, and skilled men generally is great. If we are to sustain our industrial and agricultural revolution, and contribute significantly to the progress of the African continent, it must be our duty to accelerate our pace many times over and improve existing training facilities for science and technical education. (Obeng, 2009, p.73)

Under Nkrumah, the Ghana Academy of Learning (the first of its kind in post-independence Africa) was set up in 1959 to promote learning in the sciences and humanities. In 1961 there was a name change of the Ghana Academy of Learning to the Ghana Academy of Sciences which was then merged with the National Research Council of Ghana. The Ghana Academy of Sciences had specialized research institutes under it such as the Cocoa Research Institute, National Institute of Health and Research, Building Research Institute, and the Agricultural Research Institute. Nkrumah instituted a comprehensive scheme to train Ghanaian manpower in science and technology. University intake of science students for example, was pegged at 60% and 40% for the arts. Scholarships were awarded to train Ghanaian scientists all over the world.

THE POLITICS OF NUCLEAR IMPERIALISM

Within this "cult of science" acquiring expertise on the atom and the implications of harnessing its power loomed large for Nkrumah. Promising Ghanaian students were sent to the then Union of Soviet Socialist Republics (USSR) to study atomic and nuclear physics. By 1964 some of these students had completed their studies and were roped in to push Nkrumah's vision for nuclear power for Ghana and Africa. Indeed, on February 25, 1964, the foundation stone was laid for Ghana's Atomic Reactor Centre at Kwabenya, a town north-east of the capital Accra, close to the University of Ghana. The reactor and the centre were part of what Nkrumah described as "the Ghana Atomic Energy Programme [hereafter GAEP]" (Nkrumah,1956). The Ghana Atomic Energy Commission (GAEC) had already been established by an Act of Parliament, Act 204 of 1963, as the sole entity in Ghana responsible for all matters relating to peaceful uses of atomic energy.

Nkrumah was a modernizer (Allman, 2013; Evan, 2003; Holden, 2013). The GAEP was part of his modernizing agenda and thus for him the "decision to build the centre, which you now see, rising before you, is to enable Ghana to take every advantage of the *decisive methods of research and development*, which mark our modern world" (Nkrumah, 1964; author's emphasis). This bent of his made industrialising Ghana a central feature of his statecraft (Amoah, 2020). But the key question to ask is this: industrialisation for what? Nkrumah felt that Ghana was economically too far behind Western industrialised nations like the United States (U.S.) and Britain. Ghana had to catch up by doing in a generation what they did over a hundred years (Nkrumah,1973) by industrializing (Nkrumah, 2004), and quickly. Nuclear energy was to be called upon to power the rapid industrialisation of Ghana: "Certainly, the foundations for the effective and rapid industrialisation of our country must rest on the provision of cheap and abundant power" (Nkrumah, 1964). Ghana's industrialisation had another critical rationale. Nkrumah, like other post-colonial leaders (Westad, 2007), felt that Ghana was weak, and industrialisation was therefore a sure route to build a strong Ghanaian state. A deliberate and conscious acquisition of scientific and technological know-how as exemplified in the GAEP was therefore necessary in a world in which strong states exploited and bullied weaker ones. These were the key tendencies Nkrumah was trying to balance when Ghana under him was drawn into the politics of nuclear power.

In the nineteenth and early decades of the twentieth century, leading opinion on the Gold Coast (as Ghana was then known as a British colony) was seized with the economic, political, and cultural issues in Asia (Casely-Hayford, 2014; Danquah, 1997). The nuclear bombardment of Hiroshima and Nagasaki in 1945 attracted banner headline coverage in the Gold Coast dailies such as the *Gold Coast Independent*, an Accra weekly. The world had entered the atomic age and Africa, and other developing regions of the world were keenly observing. Indeed, the Conference of Afro-Asian States held in 1955 in Bandung, Indonesia, mentioned in the final communiqué (issued on 24th April 1955) the word nuclear and its cognates nine times. It is instructive to quote in full what the leaders felt then about nuclearisation:

The Asian-African Conference emphasized the particular significance of the development of nuclear energy for peaceful purposes, for the Asian-African countries. The Conference welcomed the initiative of the Powers principally concerned in offering to make available information regarding the use of atomic energy for peaceful purposes; urged the speedy establishment of the International Atomic Energy Agency which should provide for adequate representation of the Asian-African countries on the executive authority of the Agency; and recommended to the Asian and African Governments to take full advantage of the training and other facilities in the peaceful uses of atomic energy offered by the countries sponsoring such programmes. (European Navigator, p.10)

Two tendencies stand out in the carefully couched diplomatic language: defensive and offensive. The African and Asian states gathered in Bandung realised their technological and military vulnerabilities in sharp contrast to that of the imperial powers. They sought solace in a defensive tendency in which these weaker countries tried to act in concert against nuclear tests (atmospheric and oceanic) and nuclear weapons. The offensive tendency involved taking full interest and part in the global regulatory processes on nuclearisation and acquiring technological know-how on same. The Ghanaian diplomat Armah's (2004) phrase "peace without power" captures rather well what the African and Asian nations sought to do from a position of relative weakness. These tendencies arguably framed Nkrumah's anti-nuclear imperialism. Classical imperialism (Brewer, 1980) as expounded by Hilferding (1970), Bukharin (1972) and Lenin (1950) was embodied and corporealized in transnational monopoly and finance capital (in the form of companies, especially the joint-stock company) and its territory dominating concerns. Nuclear imperialism evinced the same cross border attributes and domination concerns but in relatively more particulate (the atom and its components), dematerialized and invisibilized form and revealed rather starkly more than ever before the very technological nature of imperialism more broadly understood. In other words, nuclearisation conferred on dominant nations even more technological power as a prop for their economic and political dominance.

Ghana's anti-nuclear imperialism policy clearly showed the two tendencies referred to above and truly swung into action once France made clear its intentions to conduct its first atomic tests in Reganne, Algeria in early 1959. The authorization for these tests was given by Charles De Gaulle during a Defence Council meeting held on June 17, 1958. In 1959, Ghana took a series of measures aimed at pressuring France to abandon its planned tests in the Sahara Desert. These measures involved those that Ghana undertook in a solo fashion using the political, diplomatic, and economic means at its disposal and in concert with other governments and non-state actors. On the latter measures, Nkrumah cleverly internationalized the issue. Ghana recognized the Provisional Algerian Government and decided to send fighters to assist in their war of liberation against France. France considered it a direct attack on its colonial interests and recalled its ambassador to Ghana.

In October 1959, Nkrumah demanded that the major world powers ''stop all nuclear tests, stop research on, and manufacturing of nuclear weapons, destroy all existing stocks of atomic and hydrogen bombs and dismantle all rocket bases. . ..'' (Allman, 2008, p.87). Ghana joined other countries in the United Nations (O'Driscoll, 2009) to demand France's cessation of any nuclear tests in Reganne. On 20th November 1959, at the 840th plenary meeting of the UN General Assembly, Resolution 1379 XIV (the Moroccan text) was passed by 51 to 16, with 15 abstentions. Despite French, British, Italian, Belgian, and American votes against the resolution it earned the requisite two-thirds majority needed for approval. This resolution marked the first time that the General Assembly endorsed nuclear disarmament as part of the more comprehensive goal of general and complete disarmament under effective international control. In December of 1959, the Ghana Council for Nuclear Disarmament joined forces with known activists such as Bill Sutherland and Bayard Rustin on what was known as the "Sahara Protest Team." Funded by the Government of Ghana, the group tried to raise local and international awareness on France's planned atomic explosions by trying to reach Reganne overland through Upper Volta (now Burkina Faso). Despite all these protests France went ahead to explode its first nuclear bomb codenamed "Gerboise Bleue" (Blue Desert Rat) on 13th February 1960, in Reganne, Algeria. On that same day Nkrumah froze all the assets of French companies in Ghana (pending a clarification on the effects on the blasts on Ghana). France exploded a second bomb in April 1960. Nkrumah ratcheted up his government's response: "The government then suspended diplomatic relations with France, recalled J.E. Jantuah, the Ambassador to France, refused visas to French citizens, and froze all assets and properties of French citizens residing within Ghana's borders" (Allman, 2008, p.93).

Ghana continued to use the UN as a forum for making a strident case for cessation of nuclear tests by France on African soil. Ghana presented a draft resolution on the matter to the United Nations for consideration on December 1, 1960. The tone of the first draft was so expansive for it made a case for Africa as a nuclear free zone as well the removal of foreign military bases (Osseo-Asare, 2019). The draft resolution was fine-tuned (in the final text military bases were allowed so long as they were not employed for nuclear testing ends) and eventually passed by the UN General Assembly on November 24, 1961, as Resolution 1652(XVI). The focus on military bases is telling for it reveals Nkrumah's trepidation about the tremendous military power that nuclear bombs conferred on the Western powers and what this meant for the new African and Asian nations in the new-fangled international political economy and its trenchant ideological divisions at the time. This clearly recalls the ways in which advanced military technology in particular and technology more generally had aided quite profoundly the Western colonization project in Africa and Asia (Aboagye, 2010; Headrick, 1981). Nuclearisation was the most starkly evident and topical form of "the invisible weapon" to borrow the words of Headrick (1992) in Nkrumah's era. The foregoing explications clearly reveal Nkrumah's defensive tendency which was crafted to turn international opinion against nuclearisation and make the case for the Africa as a nuclear-free zone.

His offensive tendency was marked by making Ghana a part of the global regulatory framework for nuclearisation and instituting measures for acquiring, to some extent, nuclear technology know-how for peaceful purposes. Peaceful ends were the only necessary end for any other option -the military one to be precise- could not even be contemplated within the existing global hierarchy of power. It is instructive to note that the British who played a key role in building the knowledge infrastructure for the atomic bomb-and took full part in the Manhattan project in Los Alamos-were not in full possession of all the information on the bomb but could conceive of building the absolute weapon(Fehner, 1986).Ghana and Senegal were among the first African countries south of the Sahara to join the International Atomic Energy Commission in 1960.By the time Nkrumah laid the foundation for the Ghanaian atomic reactor in 1964 at Kwabenya, Ghanaians had a talented crop of scientists who had trained in nuclear and atomic physics especially in the USSR; "Nkrumah's elite" as Katsakioras(2020) described them. The University of Ghana had set up a world class radioisotope unit at the Department of Physics. After inaugurating the Volta Dam (Ghana's key means to the industrialization) and the GAEP (the key conduit for participation in the nuclear age), Nkrumah was deposed as president of Ghana. Ironically in the post-Nkrumah years, the atom has emerged as a critical factor in international politics. Here the significance of the atom lay not in the harnessing of its energy but in its value in the transmission of electrical impulses: electronics. Nkrumah broached the subject by pointing to how "Automation and the use of electronics are fast spreading and in America taking hold wherever large-scale production finds it more profitable to replace human labour by push-button thinly manned mechanisms" (Nkrumah, 2004, p.228). On the wider African continent, one of the leading African scientists, Cheikh Anta Diop, of Senegal had been mulling over nuclearisation and the imminent electronics revolution. Diop had worked at the frontiers of nuclear physics at the laboratory of Frédéric Joliot-Curie — the leading nuclear physicist in France at the time Diop was studying there (Spady, 1989). Joliot-Curie was the son-in-law of Madame Marie Curie who, along with her husband Pierre, discovered Radium. It is instructive to note that Joliot-Curie was High Commissioner of the French Atomic Energy Commission. Like Nkrumah, Diop framed these issues in terms of Africa's political, economic, and military weakness relative to the former imperial powers. On the military aspects, he observed quite perspicaciously, that no African country had:

.... attempted without delay to set up a powerful modern army with a properly equipped air force, civilian-trained, unsuited to putsches common in Latin America and **capable of measuring up on short notice to the historical tasks we might find facing us.** *On the contrary, we risk having nothing more than embryo armies with outmoded equipment, no air force, no ballistic missiles, yet counterbalanced by ultramodern dictatorial police forces (Diop, 1987, p.25; emphasis mine).*

Again, like Nkrumah, Diop envisaged some form of federated Africa to make the continent powerful "A federated Black Africa has the potential to become both industrially and politically powerful as either the USSR or the United States" (Diop, 1987, p.87). Diop construed the realization of this potential in unmistakably technological terms and suggested the setting up of six institutes (Diop, 1987, p.86) the top of the list of which were those on "nuclear chemistry and physics" and "electronics." We turn in the next section to how Ghana fared in the electronics age.

GHANA AND THE POLITICS OF DIGITAL IMPERIALISM (DI)

The Rise of Digital Imperialism

Three years after Nkrumah was overthrown a significant event took place which transformed the world. This event took place in the United States and laid the basis for the global dominance of that country of modern information technology. The science of electronics in shaping the era of bits and bytes was made possible by the construction of the open network architecture which the work of the Advanced Research Project Agency (ARPA) came to typify. ARPA was mandated to secure communications between the US government and the military in case a nuclear war broke out; clearly nuclear politics and therefore national security concerns led to the emergence of the internet. APRANET sought to ensure that boffins working on ARPA matters could tap into the processing power of the different computers under use. Initially a closed network, computers outside the system notably those of research centres at University of California at Los Angeles (UCLA), Stanford, University of California at Santa Barbara, and the University of Utah were added and thus was born the Internet. To be sure, this networking of computers goes as far back as the 1950s (and even further back to the age of the telegraph) and involved projects (commercial and non-commercial) outside of the US. We point this out because we take seriously the need to correct the erroneous view that "From a tiny acorn planted in 1969, we now have the giant oak of the global Internet. But a tree is the wrong metaphor" (Campbell-Kelly and Garcia-Swartz, 2013, p.18). In this sense the choice of the year 1969 is about a critical not a defining moment. Campbell-Kelly and Garcia-Swartz (2013, p.18) makes the case far better:

When the Internet took off in the early 1990s the world was covered by thousands of isolated networks and the integration of these networks into a global entity was likely to happen, whether ARPANET existed or not. A better metaphor is that the networked world was like a super-saturated salt solution. It just needed a single crystal of salt to make the whole change its state. As it happens, that crystal was the ARPANET's Transmission Control Protocol (TCP)/Internet Protocol (IP). But there were other protocols and technologies that could have established an internet.

The Internet allowed digitized information to be transmitted (based on specific protocols) using packets (by packet switching technology made possible by the work of Paul Baran and Daniel Davies) rather than by circuits. With this technological breakthrough, the next frontiers involved building the infrastructure that would allow more computers to be linked to each other and the emergence of interested players who would maintain, extend, and provide content for the technology. In the advanced industrialised countries, this infrastructure was built in the main by government led initiatives that roped in the private sector and academia. In the US (1987) for example, International Business Machines (IBM) and MCI were called upon by the National Science Foundation (NSF) to build a new internetwork backbone anchored in the TCP/IP protocol that had overtaken the Open Systems Interconnection (OSI) standards. France laid the basis for its backbone through its a national Videotex system, Télétel, which was sourced through Minitel (Fletcher, 2002, p.103–107). Ultimately this infrastructure merged computing, telecommunications and media; as Request for Comment(RFC) 828 put it "formerly distinct technologies of computing and telecommunications......converged"(1982,p.1).The international phone network which was delicately composed of this invisible combination of "electro-mechanical and solid-state switches, repeaters and multiplexers, copper wire and optical pipes, and submarine and satellite links"(Campbell-Kelly and Garcia-Swartz, 2013, p.24) had taken on a new also invisible plumbing of protocols, hardware and software.

This turn to hypermedia as has been shown was essentially fostered and engineered-institutionally, financially, technically, and politically- in the US and the former modern imperial centres of power in Europe. ARPA had access to a \$3.2billion annual budget from the Federal Government. The Internet Configuration Control Board (ICCB)-which was later transformed into the Internet Architectural Board (IAB) was central to this process. It is instructive[1] to note the IAB was born after a meeting of the ICCB in 1984 at the now defunct Royal Signals and Radar Establishment (RSRE) at Malvern in Worcestershire, England. The IAB was propped by 10 key research taskforces[2] that essentially laid down the technical blueprint for the infrastructure of the internet. As Braman (2012) points out, the decade,1969-1979, was crucial for the internationalization of the internet as countries engaged each other over the technical and geopolitical challenges that the internet presented. The key question to pose here is this: what were Ghana and other African countries up to as this whole critical process unfolded beginning in 1969? These "internet management structures" (Campbell-Kelly and Garcia-Swartz, 2013, p.28) essentially concentrated enormous financial, political, technical, and cultural power of global proportions in the hands of those who were driving the process. This process can be compared to the Berlin Conference of 1884 except that it was the world outside the US that was being divvied up not just Africa.

For Powers and Jablonskiv (2015, pp.51-73) a veritable Information-Industrial Complex (IIC) was the ultimate outcome and replaced the Military-Industrial Complex (MIC). For Purcell (1972) the MIC was about i) a coalition of groups in a society fully invested materially, psychologically, and morally in producing and maintaining high levels of weaponry ii) this coalition was possessed of a militaro-strategic conception of internal affairs and iii) the preservation of colonial markets. In the IIC, these key elements remain except that the colonial markets (now technically defunct) are better characterised as neo-colonial markets and the production of weaponry takes on a focused interest in the transmission of information (all that is embedded in it such as power, economic advantage, cultural domination etc) by wires and radio. Brutton (1988, p.600) points to the defining capital accumulation rationale of the state in the MIC; the IIC maintains this. Both Complexes are anchored in a clever if poorly masked, to borrow the words of Guerin (1973) anti-capitalist capitalism in which in sharp contradistinction to the capitalist logic of the free and unfettered market, the state is brazenly and openly interventionist.

Missing the Plot: From a "cult of science to a "market of science"?

What is interesting and disturbing as well is that this far-reaching technological shift with its rather grave geo-political portends did not seem to register and therefore generate in Ghana the kind of response that Nkrumah had offered on such shifts. This arguably can be linked to the kind of leadership that emerged in the post-Nkrumah years and the political economy context they had to operate in. In the main, a succession of military leaders took power after Nkrumah, unleashing in the process a long spell of political instability that scarcely lent itself to a heightened awareness of and responsiveness to the informational geo-political shifts underway. To be sure, there was push back in the 1970s and 1980s against the military and communication infrastructures set up by the industrialized nations in what came to be known as the New World Information and Communication Order (NWICO). The United Nations Educational, Scientific and Cultural Organization (UNESCO) became the forum for this concerted response by developing countries led by USSR, Cuba, Iran, and the Non-Aligned Movement. NWICO sought an alternative communication paradigm which focused on cultural identity, independence, and self-reliance (Zehle, 2012) in direct opposition to the free flow of information approach promoted by the US and its allies. This clash of views led ultimately to the US and Britain leaving UNESCO in 1984 and 1985 respectively with it their critical funding of the organisation. It is instructive to note there that Africa's activism on this critical issue was at best lukewarm and at worst nonchalant. No African leader emerged with the vision and perspicacity to actively promote this alternative vision on the world stage like Nkrumah had done with the nuclear issue. In any event in the Ghanaian context, political instability and economic collapse had dulled the appetite of its leaders (even if they were possessed of it) for the high global politics that marked the Nkrumah era. This came to frame the African response too more generally as subsequent events revealed. Though UNESCO became partial to the NWICO project and set up the International Programme for the Development of Communication (IPDC) to operationalize the NWICO, it was dogged by financial constraints and did not quite succeed. By the 1980s, the World Summit on Information Society (WSIS) had been set-up under the aegis of the International Telecommunications Union (ITU). The WSIS was dominated by the neoliberal view of internet governance (Pickard, 2007) which considered information a commodity to be produced, stored, and distributed by corporations within the context of the US's (and its Western allies) understanding of free flow of information. Packard (2007) refers to the discursive tropes of the US and its Western allies in the NWICO and WSIS contexts as tactics calculated at the final analysis as a cover for operations of U.S. power and sustenance for a prevailing status quo:

These tropes still constitute a central piece of the debate but are now less visible and refolded into emancipatory rhetoric that ultimately argues for commercial interests to operate unimpeded. The increasingly corporate-dominated Internet arguably represents a major triumph of this view. In this way, liberal rhetoric and good intentions have been co-opted repeatedly to cover the goals and manoeuvres of the U.S. state and transnational corporation. (p.133)

In this WSIS world, Ghana's elite seemed to have been fully enlisted and incorporated into the neoliberal vision of internet governance and scarcely paid the required attention to the "emergence of microprocessor-based computer networking technologies, their significance for the development of ICT industries, and the profound influence these have exerted on US economic and foreign policies," nor with it the " continuing dominance of US corporate power, of US-based transnational corporations (TNCs) and, among them, of ICT industries, within the global economy"(Boyd-Barret, p.21). Amoah (2019) has described statecraft in Ghana in post1980s as Neoliberal Developmentalist Statecraft (NDS) characterized by "a managerialist process aimed at creating a market economy and society....driven in the main by heavy budgetary reliance on foreign aid" (p.160).

The construction of a liberalised telecommunications sector was pursued under what was known as the Accelerated Developmental Plan (ADP) which took off in 1994. In a report, the Ghanaian journalist Asare (1996) indicated that the ADP sought to "increase the density of phone services in the country, allow private participation in some sectors of the industry, … permits other network operators to have the same rights and privileges as Ghana Telecommunications (GT)[3], including the right to install nationwide networks." The Government of Ghana (GoG) then led by President Kufuor proceeded to sell off 30% of its stake in GT for US$38 million to Telecom Malaysia (which acquired board and management control as well) while GOG retained 70% shares without decision making powers. This sale was mired in political and legal controversies and ultimately the GoG sold off its 70% stake to Vodafone. This liberalisation policy has ensured that as of March 2022, Ghana's telecommunications sector was dominated by multinational telcos namely MTN Ghana, Vodafone Ghana and AirtelTigo (renamed on June 22, 2023, as AT). The Ghanaian population is dependent on US social media platforms such as Google and Facebook. In the financial sector, Ericsson provides the platform for mobile money transactions in partnership with the telcos. As a consequence it seems that Ghana has become an exemplar of ongoing macro-structural communication trends emanating from the US and the West as spelt out by Boyd-Barrett(2006) such as: " 'Americanization' (adaptation of American business and content models);commercialization, impacting both market-driven and public sphere media; 'competitivization' – a cycle in which market opportunities are created by regulatory change or technological innovation, generating spurts of intense competition succeeded by consolidation; concentration of ownership within media markets…"(p.21). Arguably Ghana has therefore lost sight of the power of domination inherent in the technologies that drive the internet industries, and which is turning Ghanaians into hapless consumers locked into the least valuable part of the value chain.

The triumph of the free flow of information paradigm of internet governance led to the creation of key institutions to consolidate and reproduce it such as the Internet Architecture Board (IAB), International Corporation of Assigned Names and Number (ICANN), and the Internet Engineering Task Force (IETF). The IAB handles the core technical issues concerning the internet. The IETF oversees the everyday short-term issues of engineering and standards making as these relate to management and development of the Internet Protocol Suite, which includes the TCP and the IP- the very technical core of the internet. The membership of the IAB and the venues and participation record of IETF meetings is revelatory of the hegemony of the US and its Western allies when it comes to the engineering blueprint of the internet and with it the non-technology driven interest in internet governance by Ghana and other African countries. The IAB's own record shows (see Table 1) that no African has ever chaired it before, and the chairs have all come from leading tech companies in the US and Western Europe.

The IAB membership at its topmost echelons tells the same story; no African has been a member of the board of the IAB from its inception up till now (see Table 2). IETF meetings have been held mainly in North America, Europe and recently Asia. Of the 113 meetings (see Table 3) held thus far, 100 of those have been held in North America and Europe (88.5%), while 11(9.73%) have been held in Asia. Only 2 meetings (1.76%) have been held in Australia (which belongs to the Western Core anyway) and South America. None of these meetings have been held in Africa even when these were hosted virtually because of COVID-19 restrictions.

Attendance data (attendance [whether country A was present or not at a meeting] and number of attendees) at all 113 meetings paint an equally grim picture for Ghana and Africa. Attendance data is critical because these express the attitudinal posture regarding the policy value attached to matters of internet governance and the necessary proximity to high-level decision-making arenas to make a difference. By 2008 Neoliberal Capitalism (NC) had become well entrenched and seemingly unassailable as the dominant global ideology. In Ghana, almost a generation had passed since the neoliberal inflected structural adjustment policies were introduced by the WB and the IMF. The year 2008 is therefore also very instructive because the IETF provides data which allows a view into the thinking of the elites of Ghana and Africa on internet governance. As Table 4 shows Ghana attended just 10 of the 42 meetings (total number of attendees was just 14); posting an attendance average of only 0.238 in the period in ques-

Table 1. IAB Chairs* from its inception to the present time

Member	Organization (at time of service)	From	To
Dave Clark	MIT	1981	July 1989
Lyman Chapin	Data General, BBN	July 1991	March 1993
Christian Huitema	INRIA	March 1993	July 1995
Brian Carpenter	IBM	July 1995	March 2000
Leslie Daigle	Verisign, Cisco	March 2002	March 2007
Olaf Kolkman	NLNetlabs	March 2007	March 2011
Russ Housley	Vigil Security	March 2013	March 2015
Andrew Sullivan	Dyn, Inc.	March 2015	March 2017
Ted Hardie	Google	March 2017	March 2020
Mirja Kühlewind	Ericsson	March 2020	Present

* https://www.iab.org/ accessed 30/03/2022.

tion. The available data on IETF attendance on a continental scale shows that Africa is ranked among the lowest with other continents such as Oceania and South America. The data suggests that Africa's elites seem to have succumbed to the still inadequately and insufficiently contested view that the contemporary era of big data, artificial intelligence, social media, block chain and platforms is simply about technical matters (finance and engineering) and has nothing to do with power and domination. As a corollary, the cyberization of contemporary life- the myriad ways in which through network protocols, computers and various terminal devices at different locations are interlinked and how all this is shaping and reshaping contemporary life(Zhou *et al*, 2020)- is seen through the cheery lens of utilising information and communication technologies as benign harmless tools for the promotion of economic growth, social welfare enhancement and the entrenchment of the putative politically normatively superior liberal values. Zhou *et al* capture the life encompassing reality of cyberization by pointing out that it has "greatly improved the practical utility of computers and has been widely applied in transportation, finance, business management, education, telecommunications, commerce, and so on in our daily life (2021, p.1090). Of course, the political economy questions are not broached and thus the "real cyber war" (Powers and Jablonski, 2015)-the contest over who controls core information and communication technology and at what cost for whom-has been parsed for Africa into questions of cybersecurity, cyberwar, the digital divide, digital authoritarianism, digital access and the like.

Ultimately what is clear for Ghana and Africa is that the Nkrumahist vision of science and technology that was underpinned by a rather keen sense of its political economy ramifications has given way to a naïve one that seems unconcerned about or is oblivious of the power dynamics. If the Ghanaian cult of science was defined by a national geopolitical vision, I submit that the emergent free market of science that has supplanted it promotes with relish an individuated pursuit of profit. Science and

Table 2. IAB Board Members from its inception to the present times[1]

Member	Organization (at time of service)	From	To
Dave Clark	MIT	1983	?
Vint Cerf	Corporation for National Research Initiatives (CNRI)	1986	1993
Stephen Kent	BBN	1983	1995
Bob Braden	UCLA	1981	1994
Dave Mills	Linkabit	1984?	?
Bob Thomas	BBN	1984?	?
Ray McFarland	U.S. Department of Defense (DoD)	1984?	?
Rob Cole	UCL	1984?	?
Jim Mathis	SRI	1984?	1988
Dave Hartman	Mitre	1984?	?
Ed Cain	Defense Communications Engineering Center (DCEC) (part of DCA)	1984?	?
Doug Comer	Purdue University	1986	1989
Lyman Chapin	Data General, BBN	1989	1993
Hans-Werner Braun	Merit, San Diego Supercomputer Center (SDSC)	1990?	1994
Anthony Lauck	DEC	1990	1994
Barry Leiner	RIACS, Advanced Decision Systems (ADS), University Space Research Association (USRA)	1990?	1994
Keith Lantz	Olivetti Research	1989	?
Deborah Estrin	USC	1989	?
Dan Lynch	Interop	1990?	1994
Jon Postel	USC Information Sciences Institute (ISI)	1990?	1993
Elise Gerich	Merit	1993	1997
Jun Murai	WIDE	1993	1995
Yakov Rekhter	IBM Research	1993	1997
John Romkey	ELF Communications	1993	1995
Dave Sincoskie	Bellcore	1993	1995
Mike St Johns	ARPA	1993	1995
Phill Gross	CNRI	1994	1996
Christian Huitema	INRIA	1991	1996
Bernard Aboba	Microsoft	2003	2007
Jun-ichiro Itojun Hagino	IIJ	2003	2005
Mark Handley	ICIR, UCL	2003	2005
Patrik Fältström	Cisco	2003	2006
Bob Hinden	Nokia	2004	2006
Pete Resnick	Qualcomm	2004	2006
Jonathan Rosenberg	dynamicsoft, Cisco	2004	2006
Loa Andersson	Acreo	2005	2009
Kurtis Lindqvist	Netnod	2005	2009
David Meyer	Cisco / University of Oregon	2005	2007
Pekka Nikander	Ericsson / Helsinki University of Technology	2005	2006
David Oran	Cisco	2006	2010
Olaf Kolkman	NLnet Labs	2006	2012
Kevin Fall	Intel	2006	2008
Elwyn Davies	Folly Consulting	2006	2008
Dave Thaler	Microsoft	2006	2017
Barry Leiba	IBM	2007	2009
Danny McPherson	Arbor Networks, Verisign	2007	2013
Gonzalo Camarillo	Ericsson	2008	2010
Stuart Cheshire	Apple	2008	2010
Gregory Lebovitz	Juniper	2008	2010
Andrew Malis	Verizon	2008	2010
Marcelo Bagnulo	University Carlos III of Madrid	2009	2011
Vijay Gill	Google	2009	2010
John Klensin	Independent	2009	2011
Jon Peterson	Neustar	2009	2013
Bernard Aboba	Microsoft	2010	2014
Ross Callon	Juniper	2010	2014
Spencer Dawkins	Huawei	2010	2013
Andrei Robachevsky	RIPE / ISOC	2010	2012
Hannes Tschofenig	Nokia Siemens Networks	2010	2014
Alissa Cooper	Center for Democracy and Technology	2011	2014
Joel Halpern	Ericsson	2011	2015
David Kessens	Nokia Siemens Networks	2011	2013
Jari Arkko	Ericsson	2012	2013
Marc Blanchet	Viagenie	2012	2016
Russ Housley	Vigil Security	2013	2017
Eliot Lear	Cisco	2013	2015
Xing Li	Tsinghua University/CERNET Center	2013	2015
Andrew Sullivan	Dyn, Inc	2013	2017
Erik Nordmark	Cisco Systems, Arista, Zededa	2013	2020
Mary Barnes	Independent	2014	2016
Ted Hardie	Google	2014	2020
Joe Hildebrand	Cisco, Mozilla	2014	2018
Brian Trammell	ETH Zurich, Google	2014	2020
Ralph Droms	Cisco, Independent	2015	2017
Robert Sparks	Oracle, Independent	2015	2019
Suzanne Woolf	Independent	2015	2019
Lee Howard	Time Warner Cable, Independent	2016	2018
Martin Thomson	Mozilla	2016	2020
Jari Arkko	Ericsson	2017	present (***)
Gabriel Montenegro	Microsoft	2017	2019
Mark Nottingham	Akamai Technologies, Fastly	2017	2021
Jeff Tantsura	Futurewei, Nuage Networks, Apstra	2017	2021
Christian Huitema	Independent	2018	2020
Melinda Shore	Fastly	2018	2020
Stephen Farrell	Trinity College Dublin	2019	2021
Wes Hardaker	USC/ISI	2019	present (***)
Zhenbin Li	Huawei	2019	present (***)
Ben Campbell	Independent Consultant	2020	2022
Cullen Jennings	Cisco Systems	2020	present (**)
Mirja Kühlewind	Ericsson	2020	present (**)
Jared Mauch	Akamai Technologies	2020	2022
Tommy Pauly	Apple	2020	present (**)
Jiankang Yao	CNNIC China Internet Network Information Center	2020	present (**)
David Schinazi	Google	2021	present (***)
Deborah Brungard	AT&T	2021	present (***)
Russ White	Juniper	2021	present (***)
Mallory Knodel	Center for Democracy and Technology	2022	present (**)
Qin Wu	Huawei Technologies	2022	present (**)
Robert Elz	University of Melbourne	1994	1998
Brian Carpenter	IBM	1994	2002
Lixia Zhang	Xerox PARC	1994	1996
	UCLA	2005	2009
Steve Crocker	USC	1994	1996
J. Allard	Microsoft	1995	1997
Robert Moskowitz	Chrysler	1995	1999
Erik Huizer	SURFnet	1995	1999
Chris Weider	Microsoft	1995	1997
Steve Bellovin	AT&T	1996	2002
Jon Crowcroft	UCL, Cambridge	1996	2002
John Klensin	MCI, MCI Worldcom, AT&T	1996	2002
Radia Perlman	Sun Microsystems	1996	1998
Steve Deering	Cisco	1997	2002
Tony Hain	Microsoft	1997	2001
Cyndi Jung	3Com	1997	1999
Charlie Perkins	Sun	1997	1999
Ned Freed	Innosoft	1998	2000
Tim Howes	Netscape	1998	2000
Harald Alvestrand	Cisco	1999	2001
Ran Atkinson	Extreme Networks	1999	2003
Rob Austein	Integrated Systems, Internetshare, Grunchweather Associates, Internet Systems Consortium	1999	2005
Geoff Huston	Telstra, APNIC	1999	2005
Henning Schulzrinne	Columbia University	2000	2002
Leslie Daigle	ThinkingCat Enterprises, Verisign, Cisco, Internet Society	2000	2008
Fred Baker	Cisco	2001	2003
Sally Floyd	ACIRI, ICIR	2001	2005
Ted Hardie	Nominum, Qualcomm	2002	2003
Charlie Kaufman	IBM, Microsoft	2002	2004
James Kempf	NTT	2002	2004
Eric Rescorla	RTFM	2002	2006
Mike St Johns	Network Associates, Nominum	2002	2004

§ https://www.iab.org/ accessed 30/03/2022

** Term ends 2024

*** Term ends 2023

Table 3. Meetings and Venues of IETF Meetings (1986-2022)*

IETF Meetings held over a 34-year period			
Years	**Continents**	Frequency of Meetings	% share of meeting venues by Continents
1986-1996	North America	35	**67.26% of all meetings held in North America.**
	Europe	2	
	Africa	0	
	Australia/Oceania	0	
	Asia	0	**21.23% of all meetings held in Europe (EU block).**
	South America	0	
1997-2007	North America	24	
	Europe	6	
	Africa	0	
	Australia/Oceania	1	
	Asia	2	**11.50 % of all meetings held in Asia, Oceania and South America.**
	South America	0	
2008-2018	North America	14	
	Europe	11	
	Africa	0	
	Australia/Oceania	0	
	Asia	7	**0% of all meetings held in Africa.**
	South America	1	
2019-2022	North America	3	
	Europe	5	
	Africa	0	
	Australia/Oceania	0	
	Asia	2	
	South America	0	

* Data drawn from IETF website https://datatracker.ietf.org/stats/meeting/overview/ and accessed on April 5, 2022. Calculations by author.

technology in the post-Nkrumah years has become bereft of global political concern spawning in the process (in sharp contrast to the nationalistic Ghanaian science state of affairs Osseo-Asare [2019] points to in the Nkrumah years) non-nationalistic scientists content to operate within a global free market of science in which they readily and freely pawn their skills to the highest bidder with no questions asked. For the cyberization context, the politics has either been ignored or there subsists a blissful ignorance about it. Nkrumah wanted Ghana to participate at the highest levels of atomic and nuclear physics for the country's economic benefit, but he made it a point to highlight the geopolitical implications of nuclearisation for Ghana and the global South. One is thus hard-pressed to make a case for better understanding this new reality. In the next section I try to engage this question from a theoretical angle and sketch in the process some conceptual possibilities for grasping the political realities of cyberization for Ghana and Africa.

Table 4. Ghana's Attendance of IETF meeting (2008-2022)*

Republic of Ghana, West Africa		
Years and Months	**Venue (Country)**	**Attendees**
2008	Ireland, USA, USA§	0
2009	USA, Sweden, Japan	0
2010-July	Netherlands	1
2010-September	China	0
2011	Czechoslovakia, Taiwan, Canada	0
2012	France, Canada, USA	0
2013-March	USA	0
2013-July	Germany	0
2013-November	Canada	1
2014-March	UK	1
2014-July	Toronto	0
2014-November	USA	0
2015	USA, Czechoslovakia, Japan	0
2016	Argentina, South Korea	
2016-July	Germany	1
2017	USA, Czechoslovakia, Singapore	0
2018-July	Canada	1
2018	UK, Thailand	0
2019-March	Czechoslovakia	2
2019	Canada, Thailand	0
2020-March(Virtual)	Canada	2
2020-Virtual	Spain, Thailand	0
2021-March(Virtual)	Czechoslovakia	2
2021-July(Virtual)	USA	1
2021-November(Virtual)	Spain	2
2022	Vienna	0
Total Number of Meetings held = 42		**Total Number of Attendees = 15** **Total Number of meetings attended=10(23.8%)** **Average number of meetings attended = 4.2meetings**

* Data drawn from IETF website https://datatracker.ietf.org/stats/meeting/overview/ and accessed on April 4, 2022. Calculations by author.

§Venues represent the frequency of meeting. USA appearing twice means meetings were held twice in the USA. In a year meetings are held more than once.

AFRICA IN THE GLOBAL POWER STRUCTURE IN THE AGE OF DIGITAL CAPITALISM (DC): NEW UNDERSTANDINGS?

In my view the pressing issue in the age of DC for Ghana and Africa is better unpacking what accounts for the palpable de-politicization of the global spread of information and communication technologies in the last 30 odd years. I aver that clarity on this must necessarily be tied to existing theoretical insights which allow us to appreciate and better understand from a systemic and dynamic perspective, the historical continuities, and complications in the current global political economy. Dependency Theory (DT) provides such insights because it sheds critical light on the flow/eddies and socio-spatial trajectory of capital accumulation on a worldwide scale and its polarising effects (Kvangraven, 2020). Indeed, the intensifying and pervasive reach of contemporary global capital accumulation has inspired a welcome revival of DT over the last two decades. The *Cambridge Review of International Affairs*, for example, published one special issue (Special Issue on Uneven and Combined Development [UCD]) and a forum (UCD and International Political Economy [IPE]) on DT in 2020 and 2021 respectively. In one of these articles, Oatley (2021) insisted that "Mainstream American international political economy (IPE) has gradually lost relevance as a framework for understanding developments in the global political economy. It offers little help for understanding the impact of the China Shock, the development and consequences of the Global Financial Crisis, or the anti-system politics that began to emerge in 2016" and suggests as a panacea "the development of theoretical frameworks that are intrinsically systemic and dynamic" such as "the Uneven and Combined Development, and the Political Economy of Complex Interdependence, perspectives, supplemented by greater attention to system parameters, provide a strong foundation upon which to build such frameworks"(p. 318).

With his characteristic insight Amin (1974) recognized the current centrality of advanced technology (AT) in the era of monopoly capitalism (post-1945) both as a means to respond to the tendency of the profit rate to fall and reconfiguring core-periphery economic and power relations. AT, in the Amin framework, is controlled by transnational corporations and linked to the fields of space research, atomic power and electronics. Today Transnational Technology and Telecommunications Corporations (TTTC) like Vodafone, Google, Facebook, Huawei, Tiktok, Nvidia, X, Amazon among others embody the apotheosis of such AT and in their interminable search for profits across the world underline global capitalism's age old dynamic of UCD and with it Unequal exchange (Bieler and Morton, 2014) which is in full evidence in Africa and thereby incorporates the continent into the hierarchical and exploitative system of DC (Schiller, 1999). Historically this incorporation, driven by technology, has been imperialistic in character (Headrick, 1981; Kiely, 2010) and continues apace anchored in AT (Schiller, 1975; Schiller, 2001; Boyd-Barrett, 2006). Schiller (1999, p. xiv) underscores this in his claim that "the Internet and, indeed, the greater telecommunications system with which the Internet has intertwined comprise a leading edge of this epic transnationalization of economic activity"; for Schiller the "internet comprises nothing less than the central production and control apparatus of an increasingly supranational market system." Hong (2015) provides a lucid historicized account of this contemporary process in the Chinese case on which I draw for its compelling explanatory value for the Ghanaian example.

NC, the current instantiation of global capitalism, ensured especially through the World Trade Organization, that any protective barriers against finance capital inflows to Ghana as a market were totally removed or so lowered as to be redundant. Indeed, Ghana was one of the 69 countries to sign the World Trade Organization's 1997 Agreement on Telecommunication Services (Fourth Protocol to the General Agreement on Trade in Services [GATS]). As in the China case, with this breach firmly set in placed, the TTTCs establish a beachhead in the urban areas in a process which revealed the socio-spatial logic of Ghana's rural-urban divide, underdevelopment, and peripheral status. Ghana's elites were and remain key actors in this process (reflecting as Yu [2015] argues the two way and complicated nature of imperialism) as they manage the country's regulatory infrastructure to ensure unfettered access for global capital and low wages for its labour force. The reality that Ghana's elites made their nation a key player in the GATS processes evidences their internalization of the non-political and therefore imperialistically benign conception of internet governance. Ghana's elite undoubtedly accepted the economistic, humanitarian and therefore utopic non-political view of Renato Ruggiero (then WTO Director-General) when the 1997 deal was signed that "The telecoms deal will contribute to lower costs for consumers, and the price reductions will be very significant. This is good news for firms, which in the aggregate spend more on telecommunications services than they do on oil. It is also good news for families that in today's world are so often separated by physical distance" (WTO, 1997, p.2). Within such an understanding the presence of Google - it set up its first African AI centre in Accra in 2019) - and Twitter (now known as X announced that it had established its Africa headquarters in Ghana in 2021) in Ghana makes sense. Twitter reportedly chose Ghana because the West African country supports "free speech, online freedom, and the open internet"(Ndukwe, 2021). X, a barely disguised globally powerful economic force, clearly utilizes in a classical fashion the rhetoric of freedom as a carefully spun semantic strategy to rationalize its physical profit seeking presence in Africa and deflect in the process any critical political economy questioning that this may generate. This has been the gambit employed to devastating effect by the TTTCs and their originating country backers to make hegemonic inroads in developing countries without any significant push back in policy or critique. How can all this change?

The (Critical) Political Economy of Digital Imperialism (DI)

Scholars in the periphery and elsewhere need to lead the way by taking a number of key steps directed at fleshing out, conceptually and theoretically, the political economy of DI of which I preliminarily elaborate a few. DC must be brought to the fore more markedly in the analysis of the activities and presence of TTTCs in Africa. DC, and the technology driving it, must be understood as an epoch defining phenomenon (Innis, 1950; McLuhan, 1954; Postman, 1993; 1994). Tied to the DC and serving as its progenitor is NC. NC must be considered antecedent to DC and in a manner of speaking the battering ram that paved the way for DC by means of war (Woods,2005), regulatory manipulation and rhetoric. NC and DC therefore subsist in a dialectical relationship of sustenance in which both feed off each other; NC makes DC possible and through DC, NC reproduces itself globally on the back of AT.

In tandem, NC and DC, make DI plausible and possible. By DI it is meant the ways in which by means of the internet which serves as "the central production and control apparatus of an increasingly supranational market system (Schiller, 1999, p. xiv)" dominant countries, corporations, and institutions, impose their economic, technological, cultural, and political power and influence on other countries. In recent times the literature (Jutel, 2021, Howson, 2020; Kwet, 2019, Coleman, 2019) has been marked by analyses that gesture towards DI in peripheral countries. While these works provide useful explications on DI, there is obvious obfuscation over which of the two concepts, DI and Digital Colonialism (DCo) is central to the analyses. DCo seems to have been privileged in the literature. It is worth noting though that arguably Gajjala and Birzescu(2011) must be credited with making one of the earliest explicit ties between DI and DC if not coining the phrase DI. Kwet (2019) whose work is one of the most cited on the subject is clearly seized with "imperial control" (p.3). He uses DI three times and "colonialism" once in his abstract but settles on DCo as opposed to DI as the key concept in his conceptual framework on the subject. In all the cited works, the idea canvassed is control of data and other resources digital or otherwise for profit through exploitative means at a masked remove; what Rose and Miller (1992, p.173) describe as "technologies for 'governing at a distance.'" The works in effect point to imperialism at work without the complications of direct formal territorial control. This kind of new imperial control is about "manipulating the economic mechanisms of capitalism" (Woods, 2005, p. x); a manipulation made increasingly possible by AT. A clear focus on imperialism which tends to be territorial (colonizing) or otherwise is conceptually far useful for understanding the impact of DC on peripheral countries. For conceptual clarity, consistency, continuities, and departures in the literature on imperialism I propose that DI is a far better conceptual choice than DCo. The conscious adoption of DI by scholars would cure a lot of conceptual confusion and slippages as is presently the case wherein attempts at describing the imperialism in the digital age is made equivalent to colonization properly understood as the imposition of the formal rule of an alien state. As Mills (2013, p.77) shows naming a phenomenon and properly makes it real. Adopting DI provides the means to then engage the bewildering array of ways in which DC feeds capitalistic imperial control via infrastructure(platform) control, surveillance, crypto-currency etc without the added confounding phrasal neologisms such as "Blockchain imperialism," "Data imperialism," "Crypto-Colonialism," and "Platform Imperialism" which stretch concepts as to make them distorted if not confusing. After all, all these spring from one antecedental fount: the digitization or cyberization of contemporary life of which binary logic (which is lately routed through qubits) is at the core. The network of networks is what has made all these issues of critical concern even if these aggregate into platforms (Jin,2015) and so why not tie our conceptual formations to it and unambiguously so in DI?

There is the other pressing matter of unit of analysis. Woods (2007) and Harvey (2007) locked intellectual horns over the state versus non-state entities as units of analysis in the analysis of new imperialism. To cement the place of DI in digital political economy research, more work will be needed on the unit of analysis questions. Woods (2005; 2007) provides a lucid account of how the state by providing the stability and thriving for "anarchic capitalism" (Wood, 2007, p.155) allows global capital to go about capital accumulation safely and soundly. Harvey (2007) accepts Woods' view on the state and imperialism but correctly adds that the state "now nestles within a newly constructed hierarchy of institutional arrangements that have much to do with how the 'new' imperialism is being constructed. Put bluntly, the state may be fundamental, but its sovereign powers have changed along with the range over which state effects are felt" (p.67). More work on these issues related to the Global South and DI need to be undertaken to tease out the specificities, trajectories, dynamics, loci, logics as well as what all this will mean for anti-systemic (im) possibilities. Related to the matter of unit analysis is the need for tracking and unpacking how advanced capitalist states and emergent ones such as China, Turkey and Korea relate with each other and international organizations and global regulatory frameworks on DI and with it the role of these emergent states in peripheral regions. Of course, in all this the critical role of DT cannot be under-emphasised. Indeed, contrary to the claim by Mayer et al (2014, p.10) that "…. controversies mirroring the typical North-South divide for decades have increasingly faded" I insist on a resurgence of the core-periphery/North-South divide-while conscious of the complications raised in the literature- on account of DI and thus echo Wood's(2007) view that "The national economies of advanced capitalist societies will continue to compete with one another, while 'global capital' (always based in one or another national entity) will continue to profit from uneven development, the differentiation of social conditions among national economies, and the preservation of exploitable low-cost labour regimes, which have created the widening gap between rich and poor so characteristic of 'globalization"(p.156). In a rather adumbrated, if sketchy fashion, I have tried to make a call drawing on the quite extensive work already undertaken for a more conscious DI research program anchored on concept formation awareness and clarity.

CONCLUSION

As canvassed in this work, cyberization is the new inescapable reality of contemporary life. Existence in the last thirty years has become decidedly entangled in the artifacts, infrastructure and networks of information and communication technology. The recent COVID-19 pandemic provides the most recent incontrovertibly global and demonstrable snapshot of this reality. This chapter has grappled with what all this means for Africa's place in the scheme of global power mediated by the era of cyberization. In Ghana, the government introduced an e-levy in the 2021 Budget which has proved controversial. Cyberization has made this unthinkable reality possible: taxing citizens for moving money in cyberspace. The cyberization focus in this work is critical given the ways in which information and technology are catalyzing the exercise of unprecedented power on a global scale at a remove; a reality that has not been given the needed intellectual attention regarding African societies. Using Ghana's attempt at scientific and technological advance under President Kwame Nkrumah in the 1960s and its cyberization experience in the era of neoliberal capitalism as a comparative case study and drawing insights from especially the idea of UCD and unequal exchange, this chapter has tried to offer some conceptual clarity to catalyze more active theoretical engagement of the African cyber terrain within a global framework. Ultimately this work challenges the dubious equality of states that Eurocentric liberal internationalism has both foisted on and promoted in Africa in recent decades by showing that cyberization exposes the poverty of this dominant paradigm by pointing up the worsening peripheralization and with it increasing deterioration in the living and welfare of circumstanced societies. Exploring such questions as has been attempted here is useful for theorizing about Africa and the power dynamics of the cyberization turn in the global political economy.

REFERENCES

Allman, J. (2008). Nuclear imperialism and the Pan-African struggle for peace and freedom: Ghana 1959-1962. *Souls*, *10*(2), 83–102. doi:10.1080/10999940802115419

Allman, J. (2013). Phantoms of the archive: Kwame Nkrumah, a Nazi pilot named Hanna, and the contingencies of postcolonial history-writing. *The American Historical Review*, *118*(1), 104–129. doi:10.1093/ahr/118.1.104

Amoah, L. G. A. (2014). *Impacts of the knowledge society on economic and social growth in Africa*. IGI Global. doi:10.4018/978-1-4666-5844-8

Amoah, L. G. A. (2019). Six decades of Ghanaian statecraft and Asia relations: strategies, strains and successes. In J. R. Ayee (Ed.), *Politics, governance, and development in Ghana* (pp. 147–166). Lexington Books.

Armah, K. (2004). *Peace without power: Ghana's foreign policy 1957-1966*. Ghana Universities Press.

Asare, K. (1996). Ghana communications: private players push slowly into the market. *ISP News*. http://www.ipsnews.net/1996/08/ghana-communications-private-players-push-slowly-into-the-market/

Braman, S. (2012). Internationalization of the internet by design: The first decade. *Global Media and Communication*, *8*(1), 27–45. doi:10.1177/1742766511434731

Brunton, B. G. (1988). Institutional Origins of the Military-Industrial Complex. *Journal of Economic Issues*, *22*(2), 599–606. doi:10.1080/00213624.1988.11504790

Bukharin, N. (1972). *Imperialism and world economy*. Merlin.

Campbell-Kelly, M., & Garcia-Swartz, D. D. (2013). The history of the internet: The missing narratives. *Journal of Information Technology*, *28*(1), 18–33. doi:10.1057/jit.2013.4

Casely-Hayford, J. E. (2004). *Ethiopia Unbound*. Lushena Books.

Coleman, D. (2019). Digital colonialism: The 21st century scramble for Africa through the extraction and control of user data and the limitations of data protection laws. *Michigan Journal of Race & Law*, *24*(24.2), 417–439. doi:10.36643/mjrl.24.2.digital

Danquah, J. B. (1997). *The Ghanaian Establishment*. Ghana Universities Press.

European Navigator. (n.d.). *Final communiqué of the Asian-African conference of Bandun*. ENA. https://www.ena.lu/final_communique_asian_african_conference_bandung_24_april_ 1955-2-1192.

Fehner, T. R. (1986). *National responses to technological innovations in weapons systems, 1815 to the present*. Booz- Allen and Hamilton Incorporated. doi:10.21236/ADA268480

Fletcher, A. (2002). France enters the information age: A political history of Minitel. *History and Technology*, *18*(2), 103–107. doi:10.1080/07341510220150315

Gajjala, R. and Birzescu, A. (2011). Digital imperialism through online social/financial networks. 46(13), 95-102.

Government of Ghana (n.d.) *Seven-Year Development Plan for national reconstruction and development*. Office of the Planning Commission: Accra.

Guerin, D. (1973). *Fascism and Big Business*. Pathfinder Press.

Headrick, D. (1991). *The invisible weapon: telecommunications and international politics, 1851-1945*. Oxford University Press. doi:10.1093/oso/9780195062731.001.0001

Headrick, R. D. (1981). *The tools of empire: technology and European imperialism in the nineteenth century*. Oxford University Press.

Hilferding, R. (1981). *Finance capital: a study of the latest phase of capitalism*. Routledge and Kegan Paul Ltd.

Holden, P. (2004). Modernity's body: Kwame Nkrumah's Ghana. *Postcolonial Studies*, *7*(3), 313–332. doi:10.1080/1368879042000311106

Hong, Y. (2015). Colonial legacies and peripheral strategies: Social-spatial logic of China's communications development since 1840. *Global Media and Communication*, *11*(2), 89–102. doi:10.1177/1742766515588415

Howson, P. (2020). Climate crises and crypto-colonialism: Conjuring value on the blockchain frontiers of the Global South. *Front. Blockchain*, *3*, 22. doi:10.3389/fbloc.2020.00022

Innis, H. (1950). *Empire and communication*. Clarendon Press.

Jin, D.J. (2013). The construction of platform imperialism in the globalization era. *triple*, *11*(1), 145-172.

Jin, D. J., & Curan, J. (2015). *Digital platforms, imperialism, and political culture*. Routledge.

Jutel, O. (2021). Blockchain imperialism in the Pacific. *Big Data & Society*, *8*(1), 1–14. doi:10.1177/2053951720985249

Katsakioris, C. (2021). Nkrumah's Elite: Ghanaian students in the Soviet Union in the Cold War. *Paedagogica Historica, 57*(3), 260–276. doi:10.1080/00309230.2020.1785516

Kiely, R. (2010). *Rethinking imperialism.* Palgrave, Macmillan. doi:10.1007/978-1-137-08870-3

Kvangraven, I. H. (2020). Beyond the stereotype: Restating the relevance of the Dependency Research Programme. *Development and Change, 52*(1), 76–112. doi:10.1111/dech.12593

Lenin, V. I. (1950). *Imperialism, the highest stage of capitalism.* Foreign Languages Publishing House.

Mayer, M., Carpes, M., & Knoblich, R. (2014). The global politics of science and technology: an introduction. In M. Mayer, M. Carpes, & R. Knoblich (Eds.), *The global politics of science and technology* (Vol. 1, pp. 1–35). Springer. doi:10.1007/978-3-642-55007-2_1

McLuhan, M. (1964). *Understanding media.* Routledge & Kegan Paul.

Ndukwe, I. (2021). *Ghana basks in Twitter's surprise choice as Africa HQ.* BBC. https://www.bbc.com/news/world-africa-56860658

Ndukwe, I. (2022). *Twitter lays off staff at its only Africa office in Ghana.* BBC. https://www.bbc.com/news/world-africa-63569525

Nkrumah, K. (1964). *Laying of the foundation stone of Ghana's Atomic Reactor: speech delivered by Kwame Nkrumah on the occasion of the laying of the foundation stone of Ghana's Atomic Reactor at Kwabenya.* Ministry of Information and Broadcasting. https://www.ghanaweb.com/GhanaHomePage/NewsArchive/Nkrumah-lays-foundation-for-atomic-reactor-in-1964-122255

Nkrumah, K. (2004). *Neo-colonialism: the last stage of imperialism.* Panaf.

O'Driscoll, M. (2009). Explosive challenge. *Journal of Cold War Studies, 11*(1), 28–56. doi:10.1162/jcws.2009.11.1.28

Obeng, L. E. (2018). *Anthology of a lifetime.* Goldsear.

Obeng, S. (2009). *Selected speeches of Kwame Nkrumah.* Afram Publications.

Osseo-Asare, A. D. (2019). *Atomic Junction: nuclear power in Africa after independence.* Cambridge University Press. doi:10.1017/9781108557955

Pickard, V. (2007). Neoliberal visions and revisions in global communications policy from NWICO to WSIS. *The Journal of Communication Inquiry, 31*(2), 118–139. doi:10.1177/0196859906298162

Postman, N. (1994). *The disappearance of childhood.* Vintage.

Powers, S. M., & Jablonski, M. (2015). The Real Cyber War: the Political Economy of Internet Freedom. Urbana, Chicago, and Springfield: University of Illinois Press. doi:10.5406/illinois/9780252039126.001.0001

Pursell, C. (1972). *The military–industrial complex.* Harper & Row Publishers.

Rose, N., & Miller, P. (1992). Political power beyond the state: Problematics of government. *The British Journal of Sociology, 43*(2), 173–205. doi:10.2307/591464 PMID:20092498

Schiller, D. (1999). *Digital capitalism: networking the global market system*. The MIT Press. doi:10.7551/mitpress/2415.001.0001

Schiller, D. (2001). World communications in today's age of capital. *Emergences*, *11*(1), 51–68. doi:10.1080/10457220120044666

Schiller, H. I. (1975). Genesis of the free flow of information principles: The imposition of communication domination. *Instant Research on Peace and Violence*, *5*(2), 75–86.

Spady, J. G. (1989). Dr. Cheikh Anta Diop and the background of scholarship on Black interest in Egyptology and Nile Valley civilizations. *Presence Africaine (Paris, France)*, (149/150), 292–312. doi:10.3917/presa.149.0292

Tignor, R. L. (2006). *Arthur Lewis and the birth of development economics*. Princeton University Press. doi:10.1515/9780691204246

Westad, O. A. (2007). *The global Cold War third world interventions and the making of our times*. Cambridge University Press.

White, E. (2003). Kwame Nkrumah: Cold war modernity, Pan-African ideology and the geopolitics of development. *Geopolitics*, *8*(2), 99–124. doi:10.1080/714001035

Woods, E. M. (2005). *Empire of capital*. Verso.

Woods, E. M. (2007). A reply to critics. *Historical Materialism*, *15*(3), 143–170. doi:10.1163/156920607X225915

Zehle, S. (2012). New world information and communication order. In G. Ritzer (Ed.), *The Wiley-Blackwell Encyclopedia of Globalization* (pp. 1–4). Wiley Blackwell. doi:10.1002/9780470670590.wbeog426

ADDITIONAL READING

Aboagye, F. B. (2010). Indigenous African warfare: its concepts and art in the Gold Coast, Asante and the Northern territories up to early 1900s. Pretoria: Ulinzi Africa Publishing (UAP) Solutions.

Amoah, L. G. A. (2014). *Impacts of the knowledge society on economic and social growth in Africa*. IGI Global. doi:10.4018/978-1-4666-5844-8

Austen, R. A., & Headrick, D. (1983). The role of technology in the African past. *African Studies Review*, *26*(3/4), 163–184. doi:10.2307/524168

Chinweizu (2023). *432 centuries of recorded science and technology in Black Africa*. Serujta ebooks.

Headrick, D. (1991). *The invisible weapon: telecommunications and international politics, 1851-1945*. Oxford University Press. doi:10.1093/oso/9780195062731.001.0001

Headrick, R. D. (1981). *The tools of empire: technology and European imperialism in the nineteenth century*. Oxford University Press.

Kokas, A. (2023). *Trafficking data: how China is winning the battle for digital sovereignty*. Oxford University Press.

Mayer, M., Carpes, M., & Knoblich, R. (Eds.). The global politics of science and technology: Vol. 1. *Concepts from International Relations and other disciplines*. Springer.

Mayer, M., Carpes, M., & Knoblich, R. (Eds.), *The global politics of science and technology, Vol. 2-Perspectives, Cases and Methods*. Springer.

Powers, S. M., & Jablonski, M. (2015). The Real Cyber War: the political economy of internet freedom. Urbana, Chicago, and Springfield: University of Illinois Press. doi:10.5406/illinois/9780252039126.001.0001

KEY TERMS AND DEFINITIONS

Cyberization: The constant reshaping of contemporary life conditioned by the myriad ways in which through network protocols, computers and various terminal devices at different locations are interlinked.

Digital Imperialism: The contemporary instantiation of imperialism afforded by the internet and wider globe spanning telecommunications infrastructure which are increasingly unchallengeably employed by powerful states and corporations-on account of their inventing them and holding the intellectual proprietary rights- in the Global North and richer parts of Asia as the core instruments of production, distribution, consumption, control, power, hegemony and domination.

ENDNOTES

[1] The Americans were collaborating with Western European nations, notably Britain and Norway, on the architecture of the network. These two countries were the first countries outside the US to be hooked to the APRANET.

[2] These where the groups: Gateway Algorithms, New End-to-End Service, Applications Architecture and Requirements, Privacy, Security Interoperability, Robustness and Survivability, Autonomous Systems, Tactical Internetting, Testing and Evaluation.

[3] This company was formed when the Posts and Telecommunications Department was split.

Chapter 2
Digital Talent Development Cooperation Between China and Africa

Wei Ye

ⓘ https://orcid.org/0000-0002-7902-2354

The Chinese University of Hong Kong, Shenzhen, China

ABSTRACT

This chapter examines the trajectory and effectiveness of Africa-China digital talent development co-operation by investigating university-industry-government relations. Based on participant observation conducted in China from 2017 to 2019 and fieldwork in Ethiopia from 2019 to 2020, it identifies a typology of four collaboration types based on the nature of initiators and the partnership modes. Ethiopia is selected as an information-rich case due to its diverse typology variations. Each collaboration type addresses specific digital education needs in Ethiopia, including equipping education officials and professionals with digital knowledge in higher education, providing digital skills training for pre-service and in-service teachers, and empowering youth through digital innovation and entrepreneurship. This chapter uncovers the interactions among universities, industry, and governments in digital talent development between Africa and China. It argues that African governments should take a more proactive role in facilitating effective university-industry linkages.

INTRODUCTION

Digital transformation is crucial for Africa's socio-economic development, for its potential to drive economic growth, create new jobs, and solve development challenges to fulfill Agenda 2063 of the African Union (AU). The COVID-19 pandemic has further underscored the importance of digital transformation in the African context. As per the United Nations Economic Commission for Africa (UNECA), sub-Saharan Africa (SSA) encountered its first economic recession in 25 years in 2020 (UNECA,2021). While the pandemic severely damaged the continent's economy and public health, it also shed light on the significance of digital technologies and expedited the adoption of digital solutions. In response to

DOI: 10.4018/978-1-6684-9962-7.ch002

lockdowns and social distancing measures, numerous African nations have embraced digital solutions in areas like payments, trade, education, and healthcare. Consequently, digital transformation has emerged as a vital catalyst for Africa's post-COVID-19 economic recovery and sustainable development. Nurturing a skilled digital workforce is thus an imperative prerequisite for unlocking the full potential of digital transformation in Africa.

Developing a digital economy and fostering compatible talent has emerged as a new priority within the Forum on China-Africa Cooperation (FOCAC), building upon existing foundations. Chinese companies have actively contributed to the development of Information and Communication Technologies (ICT) infrastructure in Africa over the past two decades, with Chinese ICT now reaching 92% of the African population (Wang et al., 2020). The advent of cloud computing, big data, and Artificial Intelligence (AI) in the last decade has expanded the scope of digital cooperation between China and Africa. During the China-Africa Internet Development and Cooperation Forum in August 2021, Assistant Minister Deng Li of China's Ministry of Foreign Affairs (MFA) proposed a digital innovation partnership program known as the "China-Africa Digital Innovation Partnership" in discussions with African countries (MFA, 2021). The Dakar Action Plan (2022-2024) further underscores the importance of digital cooperation and human resource development in key digital sectors such as ICT, fintech, e-commerce, cloud computing, big data, and cyberspace security (MFA, 2021).

However, the trajectory of digital talent development cooperation within the FOCAC exhibits ambiguity and fragmentation. On the one hand, it aligns with the conventional discourse of capacity building through educational programs and human resource development initiatives within FOCAC. On the other hand, it encompasses technology transfer and youth entrepreneurship via talent exchanges and training in the field of science and technology cooperation. Notably, the practices of Chinese companies in cultivating digital talent in Africa outpace the policy framework set by Beijing. While providing a guiding framework for digital partnership, the digital talent-related aspects within the "China-Africa Digital Innovation Partnership" and the Dakar Action Plan primarily present a concise overview of the ongoing practices. This phenomenon is consistent with the overarching trend of Chinese digital engagements in Africa that preceded Beijing's targeted digital initiatives, including the Digital Silk Road (DSR) of the Belt and Road Initiative (BRI) (Tugendhat and Voo, 2021) and the "China-Africa Digital Innovation Partnership." Consequently, it raises questions regarding China's specific trajectory for developing digital talent in Africa and the role played by various actors, particularly Chinese enterprises. What actions have these actors undertaken in digital talent development and to what extent are they (in)effective?

Cooperation in digital talent development between China and Africa remains underexplored since it is a relatively new priority in the FOCAC. Discussions on the China-Africa digital partnership briefly touch upon digital talent development cooperation, emphasizing capacity building for the digital economy and alignment of technological and business innovation strategies (Eguegu, 2022). Existing literature on China-Africa higher education cooperation acknowledges this as a new direction and suggests specific areas, such as open distance learning, for further expansion (Zhu and Chikwa, 2021). However, there is limited research on ongoing practices and a comprehensive understanding of the overall trajectory of digital talent development cooperation between China and Africa. In the African context, developing digital talent serves the dual mission of cultivating a skilled workforce and promoting national innovation, and necessitating university-industry linkages. Nevertheless, the existing literature on university-industry linkages in Africa is insufficient in uncovering the interactions among foreign affiliates, universities, domestic industry, and governments in facilitating knowledge and technology transfer.

To fill these gaps, this chapter explores the typology of China-Africa cooperation on digital talent development and examines its trajectory and effectiveness by investigating university-industry-government relations in the cooperation. Ethiopia is selected as an information-rich case for its central role in the Belt and Road Initiative (BRI) and its wide engagement in bilateral, multilateral, and non-governmental cooperation with China. It is one of the eight initial partners in the China Funds-in-Trust (CFIT) project with the United Nations Educational, Scientific and Cultural Organization (UNESCO) and a pioneer of digital economy cooperation with China (UNESCO-China Funds-in-Trust Project, n.d.). Therefore, it presents diverse typology variations in terms of digital and educational cooperation with China. As an information-rich case, it is expected to generate an in-depth understanding rather than empirical generalization (Patton, 2002; Miles et al., 2020; Liamputtong, 2019). The research generates qualitative data through participant observation as a project officer at the International Centre for Higher Education Innovation under UNESCO (UNESCO-ICHEI), focusing on capacity-building seminars on ICT in higher education from 2017 to 2019. Fieldwork on China-Ethiopia educational cooperation conducted in Addis Ababa and Bahir Dar in 2019 and 2020 is also included. This chapter identifies a typology of four collaboration types based on the nature of initiators and the partnership modes. Findings suggest that Chinese companies' practices are intertwined with the government's policy directions in the FOCAC while outpacing policy. Enterprises demonstrate stronger motivation and effectiveness in digital talent development cooperation with Africa. In contrast, development aid and the entrepreneurial academic paradigm are partially constrained by local conditions. The research underscores the need for African governments to take a more proactive role in facilitating effective university-industry linkages.

The subsequent sections of this chapter are organized as follows. Firstly, it examines Africa's demand for digital talent and situates it in the theoretical ground of university-industry linkages. In this regard, it also traces the discussions on university-industry linkages in the context of the evolving missions of universities and the triple helix model in response to the knowledge economy and how it is applied in the African context. Secondly, it reviews the evolution of China-Africa digital cooperation and the newfound emphasis on the digital economy to present the policy context for digital talent cooperation. Thirdly, it reveals a typology of China's approach to developing digital talent in Ethiopia through four illustrative case studies. Following the case studies, it further discusses how foreign affiliates, universities, industry, and governments interact to facilitate knowledge and technology transfer in each case and evaluate the effectiveness accordingly. Lastly, the chapter concludes by highlighting the need for African governments to take the lead in facilitating effective university-industry linkages.

THE DEMAND FOR DIGITAL TALENT IN AFRICA AND THE UNIVERSITY-INDUSTRY LINKAGES

The COVID-19 pandemic has highlighted the importance of digital technologies and accelerated the adoption of digital solutions in key sectors, such as education, healthcare, and business, in Africa. Capitalizing on digital technologies presents opportunities to unleash the potential of Africa's digital economy in the post-COVID-19 era. However, the development of a thriving digital economy hinges upon a skilled digital workforce, informed customers, and empowered citizens. A joint report from the World Bank suggests a $130 billion gap, covering the need of some 650 million people for digital skills in sub-Saharan Africa through 2030 (International Finance Corporation and L.E.K Consulting, 2019).

The gap between the demand and supply of the labor force with digital skills favored by employers in Africa, nearly 3.0, is significantly lower than the global average of 6.0 (Digital Skills Gap Index 2021, n.d.). Insufficient human capacity with digital competencies hinders the utilization of existing infrastructure and impedes the creation of a conducive digital environment. The discrepancy in the mastery of digital skills also leads to divergent opportunities in education, economic activities, and healthcare which will exacerbate social inequality.

In 2020, the AU introduced the Digital Transformation Strategy for Africa (DTSfA) to foster an inclusive digital society and economy. Developing digital skills and human capacity is among the four pillars (enabling environment, policy and regulation; digital infrastructure, digital skills and human capacity; and digital innovation and entrepreneurship) (AU, 2020). Following the DTSfA, the AU further launched its Digital Education Strategy and Implementation Plan (DESIP) in 2022 to echo the demand for digital skills and human capacity in Africa's digital transformation. The DESIP prioritizes the adoption of digital technologies in education, digital literacy, skills for all, and digital infrastructure (AU, 2022). These priorities highlight the interconnectedness of developing digital talent with digital infrastructure, the economy, and the broader social environment in Africa. This interconnectedness implies the necessity to facilitate closer university-industry linkages.

University-industry linkages play a critical role in facilitating technology and knowledge transfer between higher learning institutions and industries and fostering innovation. Researchers classify various modes of university-industry linkages according to different criteria, including organizational forms (Bonaccorsi and Piccaluga, 1994), the duration of relationships (Chen, 1994), channels (Arza, 2010; Nsanzumuhire et al, 2021), and functions (Santoro and Gopalakrishnan, 2000; D'Este and Patel, 2007; Kruss and Visser, 2017; Nsanzumuhire et al, 2021). Educational collaboration, research engagement, and academic entrepreneurship are typical modes of university-industry linkages (Nsanzumuhire et al, 2021). This classification is closely related to the traditional functions of universities, i.e., teaching and research, and the "third mission," i.e., economic development (Etzkowitz et al., 2000). Under the "third mission" thesis, Leydesdorff and Etzkowitz (1996) and Etzkowitz and Leydesdorff (2000) coin a triple helix model of university-industry-government relations as an analytic framework to address new dynamics in the knowledge-based economy. Acknowledging the increasing relevance between academia, political and economic infrastructures, this model proposes an entrepreneurial academic paradigm that emphasizes the commercialization of knowledge and technology incubation. It argues that universities, enterprises, and governments should jointly engage in innovation planning through a bottom-up approach (Etzkowitz and Leydesdorff, 2000).

However, existing literature on university-industry linkages is largely based on the experience of developed and emerging economies and pays insufficient attention to the context of African countries (Teixeira and Mota, 2012; Zavale and Langa, 2018). The intimate academia-industry linkages in developed and emerging economies are implicitly based on established infrastructure and industrial, educational, and social foundations. By contrast, the academia-industry linkages in African countries are relatively weak (Zavale and Macamo, 2016; Zavale and Schneijderberg, 2021; Nsanzumuhire et al., 2021; 2023). This is attributable to historical factors (Mpehongwa, 2013), the differentiated nature of universities (Kruss and Visser, 2017), and insufficient infrastructure, inadequate human capital, and poor institutional support (Kruss et al., 2012; Egbetokun, 2015; Nsanzumuhire et al., 2021). Therefore, university-industry linkages in African countries face the dual challenge of catching up with global technology and addressing the shortage of qualified labor force. This is particularly the case in Africa's digital transformation in which the leapfrogging opportunities and insufficient infrastructure, digital literacy, and labor force coexist. Creating a qualified labor force and facilitating national innovation are dual goals of developing digital talent. How national governments develop and integrate their innovation, industry, and education policies to facilitate closer university-industry linkages is crucial in achieving the dual goals.

Further, university-industry-government relations are not merely domestic but an issue in the global economy (Audretsch et al., 2014). Foreign direct investment (FDI) and development aid are significant channels in global technology transfer that contribute to local economic development in host countries (Acs and Preston, 1997; Saggi, 2002). This is particularly the case in Africa. For instance, foreign affiliates maintain stronger linkages with academia and the government, in contrast to the weak university-industry linkages, in Tanzania (UNCTAD, 2002; Mpehongwa, 2013). Nevertheless, how foreign affiliates, universities, (domestic) industry, and governments interact to facilitate knowledge and technology transfer, as well as the effectiveness of different modes, remain unveiled. Focusing on the case of Ethiopia, this chapter explores the typology of China-Africa cooperation on digital talent development to shed light on the modes and effectiveness of the interactions between foreign affiliates, universities, (domestic) industry, and the government.

CHINA-AFRICA DIGITAL COOPERATION AND THE ROLE OF TALENT DEVELOPMENT

China-Africa cooperation in the field of ICT dates back to the 1990s when Chinese ICT firms ZTE and Huawei entered into the African market. The timing was contemporaneous with both China's "going out" policy and the opening and growth of telecommunications in many African countries (Agbebi, 2022). Over time, this cooperation has gained significant momentum. Since its establishment in 2000, the FOCAC has gradually integrated ICT cooperation into its framework, as evident in the action plans. In 2003, the Addis Ababa Action Plan of the FOCAC stated the consensus to develop infrastructure in Africa in which Chinese companies' engagement in telecommunication is highlighted as one of the key sectors (MFA, 2009). Building upon this, the Beijing Action Plan of 2006 further outlined collaboration in information infrastructure construction, ICT applications and services, cyber security, and human resource development. The overarching goal was to bridge the digital divide and foster the development of an information society in Africa (MFA, 2006).

Digital transformation holds immense potential for achieving leapfrog development in Africa, as evident from the DTSfA and the integration of digital agendas within national and sectoral development plans across many African countries (Abimbola, et al., 2021). The COVID-19 pandemic has further underscored the significance of digital transformation in Africa and created a conducive environment for accelerating digital cooperation between Africa and China. This crisis has not only propelled digital policies in Africa but also facilitated deeper economic interdependence between Africa and China (UNDP, 2021), paving the way for enhanced collaboration in the digital economy. The Joint Statement of the Extraordinary China-Africa Summit on Solidarity Against COVID-19 in June 2020 expressed a shared commitment to expedite the digital economy and foster digital cooperation, particularly in ICT, health, education, 5G, and big data (MFA, 2020). In January 2021, Chinese Foreign Minister Wang Yi reaffirmed Beijing's commitment to digital cooperation and proposed joint efforts to build "Digital Africa" during his African visits (Zhang, 2021).

With this shared commitment, developing a digital economy has become a new priority in China-Africa cooperation in the post-COVID-19 era. This new priority is manifested in China's subsequent policy initiatives. In August 2021, Beijing held the inaugural China-Africa Internet Development and Cooperation Forum, launching the "China-Africa Initiative to Build a Community of Shared Future in Cyberspace." Additionally, the proposal to jointly establish the "China-Africa Digital Innovation Partnership Program" with Africa was put forward. During the forum, Chinese Assistant Foreign Minister Deng Li outlined six pillars of the program, encompassing digital infrastructure, digital economy, digital education, digital inclusiveness, digital security and governance, and platforms (MFA, 2021). The Dakar Action Plan in November 2021 included the digital economy as a new item within the section on economic cooperation (MFA, 2021). The digital economy in this context encompasses various aspects, such as the application of new digital technologies, smart cities, digital infrastructure, technology transfer and innovation, talent development, and e-commerce.

Talent development plays a crucial role in fostering China-Africa digital cooperation, serving two main purposes. Firstly, the sustained collaboration between China and Africa in ICT sectors heavily relies on the cultivation of digital talent, considering the prominent position held by Chinese ICT companies in Africa's digital landscape. This is closely linked to the trajectory of Chinese enterprises in Africa's ICT sectors and the accelerated digital transformation witnessed across African countries. Chinese ICT companies have evolved from infrastructure builders and product manufacturers to become providers of applications, platforms, and solutions (Agbebi, 2022). The rapid digital transformation in Africa presents opportunities not only in terms of infrastructure, such as 5G and data centers, but also in the digitalization of various sectors, including smart cities, healthcare, education, and fintech. Local talent support is imperative to ensure the continuity of this business transformation.

Secondly, empowering local talent in Africa with digital skills is essential for facilitating the new priority of the digital economy. The pursuit of a digital economy is driven by the recognition of digital technology's role in socioeconomic development and poverty reduction at the governmental level. Beyond aspirations and government initiatives, the success of the digital economy also hinges on a skilled workforce, adaptable customers, and innovative talent at the societal level. Consequently, equipping talent with digital skills is critical to creating an enabling social environment in Africa for a wide range of digital economy activities, encompassing digital applications in various sectors, e-commerce, and digital innovation.

Despite the digital economy being a recent addition to the FOCAC agenda, China has not yet developed a well-established strategy for digital cooperation and talent development with Africa. The policy framework for digital cooperation within the FOCAC displays a fragmented landscape, intertwined with the government's responses and policy directions. The digital Silk Road under the BRI largely represents a rebranding of existing practices (Tugendhat and Voo, 2021). Consequently, Beijing's initiatives for digital talent development in Africa assume a subordinate role in digital cooperation, scattered throughout discussions on science and technology cooperation, as well as education and human resource development.

In the inaugural China-Africa Internet Development and Cooperation Forum in August 2021, Chinese Assistant Foreign Minister Deng Li highlighted the Talented Young Scientist Program and the International Youth Innovation and Entrepreneurship Program (known as the Vine Program) within the education pillar of the China-Africa digital partnership (MFA, 2021). These programs were initially launched for science and technology cooperation within the BRI (Talented Young Scientist Program, 2015) and have now been extended to the FOCAC context, building on the science and technology partnership established in 2009 (Beijing International Studies University, 2018). Additionally, the Dakar Action Plan emphasizes the development of new capacity-building programs in ICT, fintech, digital economy, e-commerce, cloud computing, big data, and cybersecurity within the realm of education and human resource development (MFA, 2021).

However, the absence of a well-established strategy does not imply a lack of practical initiatives. In line with the overall trajectory of digital cooperation between China and Africa, the development of digital talent has been underway prior to the formulation of specific policies. To shed light on this trajectory, the subsequent section examines the practices of digital talent development between China and Africa, focusing on the case of Ethiopia.

A TYPOLOGY OF CHINA-AFRICA COOPERATION IN DIGITAL TALENT DEVELOPMENT: THE CASE OF ETHIOPIA

China-Ethiopia digital talent development cooperation stems from the dual context of evolving priorities of the FOCAC and Ethiopia's domestic development. As discussed in the general context of China-Africa digital cooperation, from the Chinese side, digital talent development cooperation with Ethiopia appears as an extension of human resources development, as well as science and technology cooperation, within the FOCAC to serve the digital economy. In practice, it has been an outcome of Chinese ICT companies' presence in Ethiopia during the past decades. From the Ethiopian side, the cooperation is situated in Ethiopia's domestic development, particularly the sectoral development of telecommunications and the aspiration for digital transformation. Telecommunication reform in Ethiopia began in the late 1990s (Adam, 2010) and has witnessed significant growth based on subsequent regulatory and policy development (Mammo, 2016). Since the 2010s, ICT has increasingly been prioritized in Ethiopia's national development strategies. In the national digital transformation strategy, digital skills are considered crucial enablers for access to e-government, e-commerce, social media, job creation, and innovation (Ministry of Innovation and Technology [MInT], 2020). Therefore, digital talent development cooperation becomes a shared interest of the two sides to sustain Chinese ICT companies' business and facilitate digital transformation in Ethiopia.

The collaboration can be classified into four types based on the actors involved and the modes of partnership: government cooperation in human resources development under the FOCAC framework, multilateral cooperation through international organizations, initiatives undertaken by Chinese enterprises, and programs initiated by the Ethiopian government. These categories cater to diverse needs in digital talent development in Ethiopia, encompassing the enhancement of ICT knowledge among officials and professionals in the education system, equipping pre-service and in-service teachers with digital skills for basic education, and empowering the youth through digital innovation and entrepreneurship. The subsequent section delves into four representative cases from each category to examine the trajectory and effectiveness of digital talent development.

Governmental Cooperation

Case One: Capacity-Building Seminars on ICT in Higher Education

Governmental cooperation on digital talent is situated in the framework of FOCAC. As discussed previously, ICT cooperation in the FOCAC has highlighted human resource development since the mid-2000s.

In this context, human resource development encompasses the cultivation of talent for the ICT sectors and the empowerment of the education system in terms of digital literacy and talent development to meet future demands. The Human Resource Development Program of China's foreign aid is characterized by a cascade training approach, which entails the training of trainers (Ye, 2023). In this specific case, it is manifested in the selection of participants. Within the broader scope of this program, training on ICT in education specifically caters to policymakers in the education system, college teachers and administrators, and both pre-service and in-service teachers. This approach is adopted to facilitate the dissemination of knowledge, skills, and ideas learned by participants to a broader audience, including their students, pupils, subordinates, and peers. Such dissemination is also expected to foster digital transformation in participants' home countries, which may offer potential business opportunities for Chinese companies (Anonymous, 2019).

Under the Human Resource Development Program sponsored by China's Ministry of Commerce, UNESCO-ICHEI and the Southern University of Science and Technology co-organized four capacity-building seminars on ICT in Higher Education for African countries between 2017 and 2019 (Capacity Building Seminar, n.d.). These seminars specifically target officials and technicians from the education governing bodies, as well as university instructors and administrators, in African countries. Leveraging China's expertise in higher education development and Shenzhen's ICT advantage, the seminars focus on key areas such as massification of higher education, digital transformation in education, online learning, artificial intelligence, big data, and cloud computing. A notable aspect of these seminars is the reciprocal nature of participation, where attendees serve as both recipients and contributors to jointly design UNESCO-ICHEI's projects in Africa with instructors based on participants' experiences. The course design incorporates practical projects from UNESCO-ICHEI in Africa, allowing for the direct application of seminar content within African countries.

In the case of Ethiopia, the capacity-building seminars on ICT in Higher Education play a vital role in providing intellectual support for the development of digital education projects. This support encompasses two key dimensions. Firstly, the seminars offer participants access to cutting-edge ICT knowledge, including Huawei's certified courses on artificial intelligence, big data, and cloud computing, the operation of multifunctional smart classrooms for interactive learning, and the application of virtual reality in scientific experiments and vocational education. Such knowledge aids the realization of their aspirations for digital transformation within the education system (Anonymous, 2020). Secondly, the seminars equip participants with the necessary skills, including operating smart classrooms and producing Massive Open Online Courses (MOOCs), to enhance their ICT competence. Notably, some participants have become instrumental in facilitating UNESCO-ICHEI's smart classroom project at Addis Ababa University. However, the current level of ICT application in higher education in Ethiopia remains relatively low. While existing "smart" classrooms at Addis Ababa University generally refer to classrooms equipped with computers and projectors for slide presentations, UNESCO-ICHEI's smart classroom emphasizes multimedia interaction for online and interactive education. The full integration of ICT in higher education across Ethiopia hinges upon the improvement of national infrastructure, including electricity and internet connectivity, as well as enhancing the ICT literacy of university teachers and students.

Multilateral Cooperation

Case Two: CFIT

Launched in 2012, the CFIT project was initiated by the Chinese government's annual financial contribution of $2 million US dollars to support educational development in Africa (UNESCO, 2018). Thus far, the CFIT has completed two phases focused on teacher education and has commenced its third phase centered on higher technical education in 2021 (UNESCO, 2021). The initial two phases of the project aimed to enhance the capacity of educational institutions and provide training for pre-service and in-service teachers in basic education through the integration of ICT. From 2012 to 2018, a total investment of $12 million US dollars was allocated to the project, benefiting ten African countries including Ethiopia, Namibia, Côte d'Ivoire, Democratic Republic of Congo, Congo, Liberia, Uganda, Tanzania, Togo, and Zambia.

The CFIT teacher education program in Ethiopia is implemented at Bahir Dar University in the north and Hawasa Teachers College in the south, with UNESCO-IICBA providing coordination based on the principle of country ownership (UNESCO, 2018). The project has established multimedia classrooms equipped with video conferencing devices at these institutions and developed various courses, including ICT literacy, for pre-service teachers. Additionally, each institution collaborates with five regional central schools, aiming to extend the training to in-service teachers from primary and middle schools in the entire region in a cascade approach. The CFIT teacher education project has achieved significant success at the college level, prompting the Ministry of Education of Ethiopia to integrate ICT literacy courses into the primary school teacher training framework. Furthermore, the curriculum content developed by the project has been widely disseminated to other universities and colleges across Ethiopia (UNESCO, 2018).

Despite its success in higher education, the implementation of the CFIT program in basic education faces constraints due to local political and economic conditions. At Tana Haik Secondary School, a partner school of Bahir Dar University, the video conferencing device provided by the CFIT project was put on hold due to the school's inability to cover internet fees. As a result, the plan for in-service teacher training through the central school became unsustainable. Unlike federally funded higher learning institutions such as Bahir Dar University, primary and secondary schools funded by local state governments receive less funding. Initially, the CFIT project covered the cost of internet access, with an agreement that the local government would bear this cost in the later stages. However, under the federal system, the local government has the freedom to allocate finances internally and is unwilling to cover the internet access fee for Tana Haik Middle School (Anonymous, 2020). Furthermore, the lack of electricity presents a greater challenge than the direct cost of internet access. Many universities have power generators to sustain daily teaching operations amid a nationwide power shortage, while primary and secondary schools rely solely on the national electricity infrastructure. Bahir Dar University's ICT equipment remains functional during insufficient city power supply, whereas the utilization of ICT equipment at Tana Haik Middle School is limited.

Enterprise Cooperation

Case Three: Huawei's Education Programs

Huawei, a prominent player in Ethiopia's ICT sector, is renowned for its contributions to infrastructure development and digital solutions. However, its significant involvement in the education sector has often been neglected. Leveraging its industrial and technological expertise, Huawei has been actively engaged in school-enterprise cooperation on a global scale since the 2010s. Starting in 2015, the company has established numerous ICT academies aimed at nurturing industry-relevant and innovative talents. Additionally, Huawei organizes annual ICT competitions that encourage the integration of innovation and practical skills, fostering a favorable ecosystem for ICT industry talent development. The comprehensive ICT Academy curriculum encompasses Huawei-certified professional courses in areas such as artificial intelligence, cloud computing, big data, Internet of Things, data transfer and storage, and cyber security. To date, Huawei has established over 1,500 ICT academies in more than 90 countries worldwide, including many African nations, and annually trains over 60,000 students (Huawei, n.d.).

Huawei's presence in Ethiopia's education sector includes the establishment of its first ICT academy in 2018 and extensive collaboration with 36 universities. Through the Huawei ICT Academy, local students have the opportunity to gain ICT skills at a minimal cost, as Huawei provides vouchers for completing ICT courses. Additionally, Huawei's commitment to corporate social responsibility is demonstrated through initiatives such as "Seeds for the Future," which offers international learning opportunities to local students. The company actively organizes job fairs, contributing to employment prospects for Ethiopian youth. In 2021, Huawei invested $2.1 million US dollars to establish an ICT practice center at Addis Ababa University, focusing on teacher training and providing scholarships for graduate students (Huawei, AUU launch, 2021). Interviews in 2019 and 2020 highlight Huawei's reputation as an ideal employer among Ethiopian youth (Anonymous, 2019; Anonymous, 2020). On the one hand, programs like the ICT Academy offer learning opportunities and enhance employment competitiveness for young individuals. On the other hand, these programs underpin Huawei's global talent ecosystem strategy by serving as a platform to promote its products and technologies among future engineers and attract young talent to work for Huawei (Anonymous, 2020).

Huawei's involvement in digital talent development in Ethiopia is rooted in local circumstances. Firstly, Huawei has astutely recognized the core issue in Ethiopian education. Higher education in the country has been disconnected from industry realities, resulting in an oversupply of graduates who lack the skills demanded by the job market. Since 2008, Ethiopia has implemented a four-to-six ratio, allocating a higher quota for natural science students compared to social science students in universities. The majority of university students, around 60%, pursue broad natural science majors, with engineering disciplines, including information and communication engineering, being predominant. However, due to the disparity between the growing number of graduates and the limited job market capacity, coupled with the mismatch between the curriculum and industry requirements, a large proportion of engineering graduates struggle to find employment. Huawei ICT Academy addresses the limitations of conventional university education by providing skills from the industry. Secondly, Huawei has identified the needs of Ethiopia's national digital transformation. The Ethiopian Ministry of Innovation and Technology has set an ambitious target to improve ICT literacy among 70% of the country's population by 2025 (MInT, 2020). In 2021, Huawei signed an agreement with the Ministry of Science and Higher Education of Ethiopia to extend their collaboration in talent development to include vocational and technical education, aligning with the country's strategic objectives in talent training (Ethiopian Monitor, 2021).

Notably, Huawei's engagement in digital talent development in Ethiopia is facilitated by its advantageous position in the ICT industry. This advantage manifests in two key aspects. Firstly, Huawei's industrial expertise equips it with the knowledge and skills to complement university education. Secondly, its industry foothold and market presence enable the company to provide resources that enhance students' employability. Huawei ICT Academy offers certification courses that are based on Huawei's products and technologies, serving as valuable knowledge products. Huawei's local market presence further strengthens the relevance of this knowledge to work practices. By leveraging its industrial advantages, Huawei plays a crucial role in supplementing university education and enhancing students' readiness for the job market. This strategic partnership between academia and industry not only enriches students' skill sets but also fosters a seamless transition from education to employment. Simultaneously, Huawei's significant role in enhancing the talent ecosystem not only contributes to a broader advancement but also elevates the visibility of its technology and production among the younger generation. This talent ecosystem strategy is expected to bolster Huawei's future market presence in Ethiopia.

Ethiopian Initiative

Case 4: Designed in Ethiopia: A National Electronics and Hardware Design Competition

Most research on the cooperation between Africa and China tends to adopt a China-centric perspective, inadvertently disregarding the agency of African countries. This phenomenon is influenced by two main factors. Firstly, it is shaped by the focus of research, which primarily revolves around China-Africa relations or Africa-China relations, and is influenced by Beijing's significant proactive initiatives within this partnership. Secondly, it is attributable to researchers neglecting the initiatives initiated by African countries in the same relationship. This is also the case in digital talent development cooperation between China and Ethiopia. Although not numerous in quantity, there are indeed Ethiopia-initiated initiatives in existence.

In 2018, the former Ministry of Science and Technology of Ethiopia collaborated with Shenzhen Open Innovation Laboratory and a local AI company in Ethiopia to organize a national electronic hardware design competition named "Designed in Ethiopia." Emulating the open innovation model of Silicon Valley and Shenzhen, this project aims to foster economic development and industrialization in Ethiopia through nurturing talents in ICT innovation and entrepreneurship. Its objective is to establish a platform for youth innovation and electronic hardware prototyping, aiming to position Ethiopia as a technological innovation hub in East Africa. The competition attracted 200 teams nationwide, from which 50 contestants were selected for the final round. International experts were invited to provide training on prototyping skills, resulting in the selection of the top 10 projects for mass production in Shenzhen and subsequent introduction to the Ethiopian market (Mo, 2018).

Diverging from preceding cases, this project combines international cutting-edge expertise in technology and innovation with the local context, with the overarching objective of fostering innovation and entrepreneurial endeavors to achieve leapfrog development. An international expert engaged in this competition indicated that the project embraces the non-hierarchical and flattened structures inherent in the technological domain. Given the non-linear nature of technological advancements, rapid obsolescence occurs as short-term gaps are overcome through innovation (Anonymous, 2021). Nonetheless, the sustainability of this ICT innovation approach encounters limitations imposed by two factors. Firstly, Ethiopia's local manufacturing capacity imposes constraints on hardware design, particularly in cases where the production of fundamental electronic components is not viable locally (Anonymous, 2021). Secondly, the sustainability of this project is hindered by the instability prevalent within domestic political dynamics, government structure, and policy formulation and implementation in Ethiopia. Consequently, the project was halted in 2019 following the transition from the former Ministry of Science and Technology to the newly established Ministry of Innovation and Technology.

DISCUSSION

The four cases listed serve as an illustrative selection rather than an exhaustive representation of the diverse types and specific activities involved in China-Ethiopia cooperation for developing digital talent. This typology, however, serves the purpose of exploring the trajectory of such cooperation. Despite the distinct focuses within each type, the typology reveals a trajectory that involves the engagement of the governments, industry, and education system in digital talent development within Ethiopia and between China and Ethiopia.

The Chinese government's engagement in digital talent development with Ethiopia is primarily through development aid. The bilateral human resource development programs are reciprocal for they facilitate the transfer of knowledge, skills, and ideas to participants, as well as foster potential business opportunities and policy environment for Chinese companies. To some extent, this approach projects China's experience of reform and opening up in the late 1970s and 1980s when elites developed their aspiration for further transformation through overseas learning. Such learning might not necessarily facilitate substantial technology transfer to participants, but further extend their aspirations by broadening their horizons with new knowledge and ideas. However, it is worth noting that overseas learning in China's case was proactively organized by policymakers in Beijing rather than external development partners.

The Ethiopian case shows that the effectiveness of bilateral development partners' initiatives is constrained by local conditions, particularly infrastructure and policy environment. This is also the case in multilateral development aid. Compared to bilateral development aid, the Chinese government is less visible in the CFIT project through UNESCO. This is due to the project's principle of emphasizing host countries' ownership and management mechanisms of international organizations. Particularly, the intention to facilitate business opportunities for Chinese companies is not found. For instance, field observations show that the ICT equipment of the CFIT project at Bahir Dar University and Tana Haik Middle School is primarily provided by LG, a Korean company, rather than Chinese ICT companies. Nevertheless, the CFIT case also shares the same feature of local constraints, including insufficient electricity, poor internet connectivity, and bureaucratic politics. These findings echo the conclusion of Zavale and Macamo (2016) based on the case of Mozambique. Thus, the African governments should take the lead in facilitating effective university-industry linkage.

Compared to development aid, FDI is a more effective channel to facilitate technology transfer between industry and universities and between Chinese ICT companies and Ethiopia. The case of Huawei shows that it is more effective in digital talent development than other Chinese actors, owing to three distinct factors. Firstly, its urgent demand for digital talent serves as a strong motivation to engage the education system in Ethiopia. Secondly, its industry advantages provide it with more relevant knowledge for cultivating digital talent. Thirdly, its market presence offers practical scenarios for digital talent to apply their skills. Furthermore, the Ethiopian government's aspiration to engage also contributes to effective role Huawei plays in the education sector of Ethiopia. Through effective engagement with Ethiopia's education sector, Huawei resolves the dilemma of local talent shortage and nurtures its future market and users in Ethiopia.

The "Designed in Ethiopia" case implies the unsatisfactory effectiveness of the entrepreneurial academic paradigm. Nevertheless, it does not necessarily imply the infeasibility of such a paradigm in Ethiopia. As revealed in the case, the paradigm is hindered by Ethiopia's poor infrastructure, insufficient local manufacturing capacity, policy inconsistency, and instability. This once again highlights the crucial role of the government in university-industry linkage. Conventional discussions on the triple helix model of university-industry-government relations are largely university-centered. Because this model is based on the implicit condition of developed and emerging economies with (at least partially) free markets and adequate infrastructure. However, in the Ethiopian context, the government should take the lead in developing national infrastructure, maintaining stability, planning digital industry policy, and coordinating industry policy with education policy to create the initial foundation for university-industry interactions.

Among the four types of cooperation mentioned above, with the exception of innovation and entre-preneurship projects initiated by the former Ethiopian Federal Ministry of Science and Technology, the other types are widely implemented in various African countries,[1] such as Kenya, Uganda, Namibia, Nigeria, South African, and Egypt, beyond Ethiopia. Therefore, the case of Ethiopia holds significant implications for comprehending "Digital talent development cooperation between China and Africa".

CONCLUSION

China-Africa cooperation in digital talent development serves as an extension of human resources development, as well as science and technology cooperation, within the FOCAC. It reveals the combi-nation of evolving priorities of the FOCAC and African countries' domestic development aspirations. This topic is under-researched as the practices outpace the policy frameworks. This chapter fills the gap by presenting a typology of China-Africa cooperation in digital talent development based on the case of Ethiopia. It examines the trajectory and effectiveness of different types of cooperation by explor-ing university-industry-government relations. According to the nature of initiators and the partnership modes, it identifies governmental cooperation, multilateral cooperation, enterprise cooperation, and the Ethiopian initiative in typology. Each collaboration type addresses specific digital education needs in Ethiopia, including equipping education officials and professionals with up-to-date ICT knowledge in higher education, providing digital skills training to pre-service and in-service teachers in basic educa-tion, and empowering youth through digital innovation and entrepreneurship.

As an outcome of Chinese ICT companies' presence in Africa, China-Africa cooperation in digital talent development follows the trajectory of ICT collaboration between China and Africa. Thus, Chinese companies' practices are intertwined with the government's responses and policy directions within the framework of the FOCAC, while the enterprises outpace policy in this regard. Enterprises exhibit stronger motivation and greater effectiveness in digital talent development cooperation with Africa. The effective-ness is also based on their industrial advantages, market presence, and business ambition, as well as the Ethiopian government's aspiration to engage higher education with the industry. By contrast, develop-ment aid provides a less direct solution to meeting Africa's talent demand due to the cascade approach in both bilateral and multilateral channels and local constraints in Africa. Local constraints, including poor infrastructure, insufficient local manufacturing capacity, policy inconsistency, and instability also hinder the Ethiopian government's initiative based on the entrepreneurial academic paradigm.

The findings of this chapter make it clear that the African governments should further take the lead in facilitating effective university-industry linkage. Conventional discussions on the triple helix model of university-industry-government relations are largely based on the implicit condition of developed and emerging economies with (at least partially) free markets and adequate infrastructure. However, in the Ethiopian (as well as in African countries) context, the government should take the lead in developing national infrastructure, maintaining stability, planning digital industry policy, and coordinating industry policy with education policy to create the initial foundation for university-industry interactions.

REFERENCES

Abimbola, O., Aggad, F., & Ndzendze, B. (2021). What is Africa's Digital Agenda?. *Africa Policy Research Institute (APRI), 23.*

Acs, Z. J., & Preston, L. (1997). Small and medium-sized enterprises, technology, and globalization: Introduction to a special issue on small and medium-sized enterprises in the global economy. *Small Business Economics*, *9*(1), 1–6. doi:10.1023/A:1007945327618

Adam, L. (2010). *Ethiopia ICT sector performance review 2009/2010?* (Policy Paper No.9). Research ICT Africa. https://www.researchictafrica.net/publications/ICT_Sector_Performance_Reviews_2010/Vol%202%20Paper%209%20-%20Ethiopia%20ICT%20Sector%20Performance%20Review%202010.pdf

African Union. (2020). *Digital transformation strategy for Africa (2020-2030)*. African Union. https://au.int/sites/default/files/documents/38507-doc-dts-english.pdf

African Union. (2022). *Digital education strategy and implementation plan*. African Union. https://au.int/en/documents/20221125/digital-education-strategyand-implementation-plan

Agbebi, M. (2022, February 1). China's Digital Silk Road and Africa's technological future. *Council on Foreign Relations*. https://www.cfr.org/sites/default/files/pdf/Chinas%20Digital%20Silk%20Road%20and%20Africas%20Technological%20Future_FINAL.pdf

Arza, V. (2010). Channels, benefits and risks of public-private interactions for knowledge transfer: Conceptual framework inspired by Latin America. *Science & Public Policy*, *37*(7), 473–484. doi:10.3152/030234210X511990

Audretsch, D. B., Lehmann, E. E., & Wright, M. (2014). Technology transfer in a global economy. *The Journal of Technology Transfer*, *39*(3), 301–312. doi:10.1007/s10961-012-9283-6

Beijing International Studies University. (2018, April 28). *Beijing International Studies University held the 2018 International Youth Innovation and Entrepreneurship Program (known as the Vine Program) international student internship and the African session*. BISU. UNESCO. https://www.bisu.edu.cn/art/2018/4/28/art_1424_173269.html

Bonaccorsi, A., & Piccaluga, A. (1994). A theoretical framework for the evaluation of university-industry relationships. *R & D Management*, *24*(3), 229–247. doi:10.1111/j.1467-9310.1994.tb00876.x

Capacity Building Seminar. (n.d.). *International Centre for Higher Education Innovation under the Auspices of UNESCO*. UNESCO. https://en.ichei.org/dist/index.html#/buildingIntro

Chen, E. Y. (1994). The evolution of university-industry technology transfer in Hong Kong. *Technovation*, *14*(7), 449–459. doi:10.1016/0166-4972(94)90003-5

D'Este, P., & Patel, P. (2007). University-industry linkages in the UK: What are the factors underlying the variety of interactions with industry? *Research Policy*, *36*(9), 1295–1313. doi:10.1016/j.respol.2007.05.002

Digital Skills Gap Index 2021: Your tool to determine global digital skills levels. (n.d.). John Wiley & Sons, Inc. https://dsgi.wiley.com/

Egbetokun, A. A. (2015). Interactive learning and firm-level capabilities in latecomer settings: The Nigerian manufacturing industry. *Technological Forecasting and Social Change*, *99*, 231–241. doi:10.1016/j.techfore.2015.06.040

Eguegu, O. (2022). The Digital Silk Road: Connecting Africa with new norms of digital development. *Asia Policy*, *29*(3), 30–39. doi:10.1353/asp.2022.0049

Etzkowitz, H., & Leydesdorff, L. (2000). The dynamics of innovation: From National Systems and "Mode 2" to a Triple Helix of university-industry-government relations. *Research Policy*, *29*(2), 109–123. doi:10.1016/S0048-7333(99)00055-4

Etzkowitz, H., Webster, A., Gebhardt, C., & Terra, B. R. C. (2000). The future of the university and the university of the future: Evolution of ivory tower to entrepreneurial paradigm. *Research Policy*, *29*(2), 313–330. doi:10.1016/S0048-7333(99)00069-4

Huawei. (2021, June 1). AUU launch the first Huawei ICT Practice Center in Ethiopia. *Addis Standard*. https://addisstandard.com/2021/news-huawei-aau-launch-the-first-huawei-ict-practice-center-in-ethiopia/

Huawei. (2021, June 8). Ministry extend agreement to open more ICT academies. *Ethiopia Monitor*. https://ethiopianmonitor.com/2021/06/08/huawei-ministry-extend-agreement-to-open-more-ict-academies/#:~:text=Huawei%2C%20Ministry%20Extend%20Agreement%20to%20Open%20More%20ICT,industry%2C%20and%20the%20nurturing%20of%20highly%20skilled%20labor

International Finance Corporation and L.E.K Consulting. (2019). *Digital skills in Sub-Saharan Africa spotlight on Ghana*. IFC. https://www.ifc.org/wps/wcm/connect/ed6362b3-aa34-42ac-ae9f-c739904951b1/Digital+Skills_Final_WEB_5-7-19.pdf?MOD=AJPERES

Kruss, G., Adeoti, J., & Nabudere, D. (2012). Universities and knowledge-based development in sub-Saharan Africa: Comparing university-firm interaction in Nigeria, Uganda and South Africa. *The Journal of Development Studies*, *48*(4), 516–530. doi:10.1080/00220388.2011.604410

Kruss, G., & Visser, M. (2017). Putting university-industry interaction into perspective: A differentiated view from inside South African universities. *The Journal of Technology Transfer*, *42*(4), 884–908. doi:10.1007/s10961-016-9548-6

Leydesdorff, L., & Etzkowitz, H. (1996). Emergence of a Triple Helix of university—industry—government relations. *Science & Public Policy, 23*(5), 279–286.

Leydesdorff, L., & Etzkowitz, H. (1996). Emergence of a Triple Helix of university-industry-government relations. *Science & Public Policy, 23*(5), 279–286.

Liamputtong, P. (2019). *Qualitative research methods.* Oxford University Press.

Mammo, Y. (2016). Analysis of Ethiopia's national ICT policy and strategy: Insights into policy issues and policy goals. *Ethiopian Journal of Education and Sciences, 11*(2), 75–89.

Miles, M. B., Huberman, A. M., & Saldaña, J. (2020). *Qualitative data analysis: A methods sourcebook* (4th ed.). Sage.

Ministry of Foreign Affairs. (2006, November 16). *Forum on China-Africa Cooperation-Beijing Action Plan.* Ministry of Foreign Affairs. http://www.focac.org/eng/zywx_1/zywj/200611/t20061116_7933564.htm

Ministry of Foreign Affairs. (2009, September 25). *Forum on China-Africa Cooperation-Addis Ababa Action Plan.* Ministry of Foreign Affairs. http://www.focac.org/eng/zywx_1/zywj/200909/t20090925_7933568.htm

Ministry of Foreign Affairs. (2020, June 17). *Joint Statement of the Extraordinary China-Africa Summit on Solidarity Against COVID-19.* Ministry of Foreign Affairs. https://www.fmprc.gov.cn/eng/wjdt_665385/2649_665393/202006/t20200617_679628.html

Ministry of Foreign Affairs. (2021, August 24). *China will work with Africa to formulate and implement a China-Africa partnership plan on digital innovation.* Ministry of Foreign Affairs. https://www.fmprc.gov.cn/mfa_eng/wjbxw/202108/t20210825_9134687.html

Ministry of Foreign Affairs. (2021, December 22). *Forum on China-Africa Cooperation Dakar Action Plan (2022-2024).* FOCAC. http://www.focac.org/eng/zywx_1/zywj/202201/t20220124_10632444.htm

Ministry of Innovation and Technology. (2020). *Digital Ethiopia 2025: A digital strategy for Ethiopia inclusive prosperity.* Government of Ethiopia.

Mo, Z. (2018, October 12). Shenzhen boosts Ethiopia's entrepreneurs. *China Daily.* https://global.chinadaily.com.cn/a/201810/12/WS5bc0115aa310eff303282044.html

Mpehongwa, G. (2013). Academia-industry-government linkages in Tanzania: trends, challenges and prospects. *Global Journal of Education Research, 1*(1), 084-091.

Nsanzumuhire, S. U., Groot, W., Cabus, S. J., & Bizimana, B. (2021). Understanding the extent and nature of academia-industry interactions in Rwanda. *Technological Forecasting and Social Change, 170,* 120913. doi:10.1016/j.techfore.2021.120913

Nsanzumuhire, S. U., Groot, W., Cabus, S. J., Ngoma, M. P., & Masengesho, J. (2023). Assessment of industry's perception of effective mechanisms to stimulate academia-industry collaboration in sub-Saharan Africa. *Industry and Higher Education, 37*(3), 409–432. doi:10.1177/09504222221131695

Patton, M. Q. (2002). Qualitative research and evaluation methods. *Sage (Atlanta, Ga.).*

Saggi, K. (2002). Trade, foreign direct investment, and international technology transfer: A survey. *The World Bank Research Observer*, *17*(2), 191–235. doi:10.1093/wbro/17.2.191

Santoro, M. D., & Gopalakrishnan, S. (2000). The institutionalization of knowledge transfer activities within industry-university collaborative ventures. *Journal of Engineering and Technology Management*, *17*(3-4), 299–319. doi:10.1016/S0923-4748(00)00027-8

Talented Young Scientist Program. (2015, November 24). *China Science and Technology Exchange Center*. CISTC. http://www.cistc.gov.cn/scientist/details.asp?column=919&id=89345

Teixeira, A. A. C., & Mota, L. (2012). A bibliometric portrait of the evolution, scientific roots and influence of literature on university-industry links. *Scientometrics*, *93*(3), 719–743. doi:10.1007/s11192-012-0823-5

Tugendhat, H., & Voo, J. (2021). *China's Digital Silk Road in Africa and the future of internet governance* (Working Paper No. 2021/50). China Africa Research Initiative (CARI). https://static1.squarespace.com/static/5652847de4b033f56d2bdc29/t/61084a3238e7ff4b666b9ffe/1627933235832/WP+50+-+Tugendhat+and+Voo+-+China+Digital+Silk+Road+Africa.pdf

UNESCO-China Funds-in-Trust Project. (n.d.). Harnessing technology for quality teacher training in Africa" phase I conclusion and phase II launch meeting. *United Nations Educational, Scientific and Cultural Organization*. UNESCO. https://en.unesco.org/events/unesco-china-funds-trust-project-harnessing-technology-quality-teacher-training-africa-phase

United Nations Conference on Trade and Development (2002). *Investment policy review: Tanzania*. United Nations.

United Nations Development Program. (2021). *Analyzing long-term socioeconomic impacts of COVID-19 across diverse African contexts*. UNDP Regional Bureau for Africa. https://www.undp.org/sites/g/files/zskgke326/files/migration/africa/f5a32ba0e2fb380796e3596e0857ab63f2acb1300c5b-b17aad9847e13f941c43.pdf

United Nations Economic Commission for Africa. (2021). *Building forward for an African green recovery*. United Nations Economic Commission for Africa. https://hdl.handle.net/10855/43948

United Nations Educational, Scientific and Cultural Organization. (2018). *Improving the quality of teacher education in Sub-Saharan Africa: Lessons learned from a UNESCO-China Funds-in-Trust project*. UNESCO.

United Nations Educational, Scientific and Cultural Organization. (2023, July 24). *China Funds-in-Trust phase III (CFIT III) in higher education*. UN. https://www.unesco.org/en/articles/china-funds-trust-phase-iii-cfit-iii-higher-education

Wang, R., Bar, F., & Hong, Y. (2020). ICT aid flows from China to African countries: A communication network perspective. *International Journal of Communication*, *14*, 1498–1523.

Ye, W. (2023). *China's education aid to Africa: Fragmented soft power*. Routledge. doi:10.4324/9781003361961

Zavale, N. C., & Langa, P. V. (2018). University-industry linkages' literature on Sub-Saharan Africa: Systematic literature review and bibliometric account. *Scientometrics*, *116*(1), 1–49. doi:10.1007/s11192-018-2760-4 PMID:29527070

Zavale, N. C., & Macamo, E. (2016). How and what knowledge do universities and academics transfer to industry in African low-income countries? Evidence from the stage of university-industry linkages in Mozambique. *International Journal of Educational Development*, *49*, 247–261. doi:10.1016/j.ijedudev.2016.04.001

Zavale, N. C., & Schneijderberg, C. (2021). Academics' societal engagement in ecologies of knowledge: A case study from Mozambique. *Science & Public Policy*, *48*(1), 37–52. doi:10.1093/scipol/scaa055

Zhang, Y. (2021, January 11). State Councilor and Foreign Minister Wang Yi's media interview upon concluding his visit to five African countries. *China Daily*. https://cn.chinadaily.com.cn/a/202101/11/WS5ffba980a3101e7ce973a014.html

Zhu, X., & Chikwa, G. (2021). An exploration of China-Africa cooperation in higher education: Opportunities and challenges in open distance learning. *Open Praxis*, *13*(1), 7–19. doi:10.5944/openpraxis.13.1.1154

ADDITIONAL READINGS

African Union Commision and Organisation for Economic Co-operation and Development. (2021). *Africa's Development Dynamics 2021: Digital Transformation for Quality Jobs*. OECDiLibrary. doi:10.1787/0a5c9314-en

Etzkowitz, H., & Dzisah, J. (2008). Rethinking development: Circulation in the triple helix. *Technology Analysis and Strategic Management*, *20*(6), 653–666. doi:10.1080/09537320802426309

Large, D. (2022). China, Africa and the 2021 Dakar FOCAC. *African Affairs*, *121*(483), 299–319. doi:10.1093/afraf/adac014

KEY TERMS AND DEFINITIONS

Digital Divide: The digital divide in this chapter refers the gaps between Africa and other regions of the world, different countries within Africa, rural and urban areas in Africa, as well as gender disparities in Africa, in terms of the access to ICT.

Digital Silk Road (DSR): DSR refers to the digital component of the BRI, which involves the development of digital infrastructure, connectivity, and cooperation between China and participating countries along the BRI routes.

Triple Helix: The Triple Helix model refers to the interaction and collaboration between academia, industry, and government in facilitation innovation and development. Entrepreneurial Academic Paradigm The entrepreneurial academic paradigm refers to the new universities and academic institutions' mission, in collaboration with the industry, of fostering entrepreneurial mindsets and actions to serve regional development.

Forum on China-Africa Cooperation (FOCAC): FOCAC is a platform established in 2000 as a joint response of Africa and China to economic globalization. It facilitates economic, political, and cultural ties between China and African nations. China Funds-in-Trust (CFIT)

CFIT Initiative: The CFIT initiative was launched in 2012 as a collaborative effort between UNESCO and the Chinese government to enhance quality education in Africa. The first two phases focus on teacher education, while the third phase shifts to higher technical and vocational education.

Massive Open Online Courses (MOOCs): MOOCs are online educational courses that are designed to be accessible to unlimited number of learners worldwide. MOOCs provide open access to course materials, including lectures, videos, readings, and assessments, allowing learners to participate remotely.

ENDNOTES

[1]   Except for the CFIT project which was exclusively conducted in eight African countries in the first phase, extended to two more African countries in the second phase, and concentrated to six of the initial eight countries in the third phase. See https://www.unesco.org/en/higher-education/cfit-africa?TSPD_101_R0=080713870fab2000a9f1e528b2882a6154ce1fd407062bed9d936 fecab58376707538e2c4bd05d19088cfa736f14300029ed8181e48d86613 500f4e435fbc122cbecd7576f5cdbb9612e4980774fc6bbd99a447df28b6 08a8d4045e38123c131.

Chapter 3
Africa and the Global Video Games Industry:
Ties, Tensions, and Tomorrow

Lloyd G. Adu Amoah
University of Ghana, Ghana

Eyram Tawia
Leti Arts, Ghana

ABSTRACT

This chapter provides a state-of-the art account(their creation, logics and play) of video games in Africa by explicating its ties, tensions and possibilities vis-à-vis the wider global video games industry. This explanation is rendered through a critical examination of vital elements such as policies, key actors, knowledge capabilities, institutions, investments, history, business, technology, and cultural economy by drawing on the evolution and growth of the African video games space in the last twenty years.

Let the children play everyday

Momma come together

Papa come together

Let the children play everyday

-Lee Duodo (1984) on the track "Children's Song " on the George Darko album " Hi Life Time"

INTRODUCTION

In the quote above Ghanaian highlife maestro, George Darko, extols the value of play in a track off his second album on which his creative and music partner Lee Duodu was the vocalist. Play has always

DOI: 10.4018/978-1-6684-9962-7.ch003

been part of the African experience since antiquity (Crist, 2019). This is evident in African board games (Kyele, 2016; Townshend, 1979; Natsoulas, 1995; Pankhurst, 1971; Muller, 1930) such as *senet* (Third Dynasty, Ancient Egypt), *Bao* (Eastern Africa), *Warri* (played among the Yoruba in West Africa; also known as *oware* in Ghana) and *Morabaraba* (South Africa and Botswana). On *Bao*, Kyele (2019) reports that it is "the eastern African variant of the *mankala* group of games. The *mankala* are indigenous African mathematical strategy board games of skill and, perhaps, the prototype of other numerous board games including chess, pachisi and draughts" (p.93). Play and games in Africa were and are enjoyed by all classes, gender, and demographics.

Chess known as *säntäräj* in Ethiopia has been played there in all probability for over half a millennium and was reportedly the game of royalty and the nobility (Pankhurst, 1971). While adults amused themselves at play, children in Africa "in historical times, …. played jacks with rocks as they did in other countries and as they do today. There's a long history of games without any equipment at all. They ran races and played hide and seek. Kids scratched lines in the dirt to play jumping games like hopscotch. Or they got long vines or a rope to play jumprope" (Carr, 2017). George Darko and Lee Duodo broadcast this fascination with play through a genre known as Burgher Highlife. Highlife is a West African music genre that was cobbled together (with indigenous music) from a blend of foreign music such as Western classical and ballroom music, regimental brass-band music and jazz introduced into the region during the period of colonization (Collins, 1989). In the Ghana case, according to Collins (2005) "By the 1940's 'highlife' became the generic term for all these new forms of Ghanaian music, whether played by brass bands, guitar bands or dance orchestras" (p.17). Burgher Highlife was a spin-off of Highlife invented by Ghanaian musicians domiciled in Europe (Hamburg, Germany to be precise who became known as "burghers") in the 1980s with the aid of advances in electronics that impacted music technology. These advances in music technology led to the emergence of drum-machines and synthesizers which these creative musicians exploited. To be sure, this modern electronics revolution which influenced the evolution of Ghana music goes back to the 19th century in Western Europe and came to exert a profound impact on playing games and the kind of toys that accompanied this not only in Western Europe and North America but across the globe including Africa. The question to pose at this juncture is: just what is a toy?

THE CULTURAL ECONOMY AND SUBJECTIVITY OF TOYS AND PLAY

The preceding section brought into sharp focus the gamut of games that were played in Africa ranging from those that can be deemed serious to those for pure amusement. The jump rope exemplifies such amusement and brings right to the fore children and their natural need to be entertained. To play jump rope, a rope is needed and can thus be deemed to function as a toy. Toys thus clearly function classically as the equipment for amusement and entertainment for children and as we shall see increasingly for adults too. The emergence of toys can be traced to antiquity in all cultures:

There is a Mesopotamian model of a sheep dating from 2300 BC, and an Egyptian miniature tiger from about 1000 BC, both in the British Museum. Examples abound, in other words, of miniature replica animals, people and objects from many cultures and across thousands of years of history. Many clearly had ritual significance for adults; some were funerary offerings, as in the Egyptian tombs filled with models of daily life to give comfort to the journeying dead; while others were merely decorative. Some were play-things. The three-thousand-year old Egyptian wooden tiger had a hinged jaw that could be operated by pulling a string. Probably most of the playthings have been lost because they were in robust daily use, while ritual objects were carefully kept. (Fleming, 1996, p. 81)

In modern times, the toy conceptually took on certain characteristics tied to the evolution of the political economy anchored on technological changes and breakthroughs especially in Western Europe and later America. So, from the outset it is important to note that the concept of the toy tended to shift with major political and economic changes of the times. Within this overall shifting scheme, the toy as a concept has come to enact especially simulacrum, miniaturization and spectacularity. In England, these were embodied in what was called the English toy theatre originating from William West's ingenuity in the 19th century which attempted to essentially bring home to children the action and scenes of London theatres. Fleming draws our attention to why this was so in the England of the period: "For middle-class English children of the nineteenth century, evenings were often spent consigned to an austere 'playroom' by absent parents. Making and enacting miniature dramas of the kind the adults attended must have seemed a very appropriate way of spending the long evenings" (1996, p.83). The peep show continued to capture this enactment in Europe where by literally peeping into a contraption for a fee the dazzling use of drawings and perspectives allowed customers to see representations of say the Thames Tunnel, Arabian minarets or some such constructions from otherwise inaccessible or distant places. The advent of machines especially from the 1850s onwards impacted on toys as replica tinplate (steel coated with tin to prevention corrosion) cars and aircraft came to embody the power of technology and effectively acculturate children to the emergent capitalist and technological world. Toys effectively came to be increasingly manufactured and on a large scale as steam-powered metal tooling machinery proliferated ultimately underlying the fame and fortune of toy-making companies like Märklin (Germany), Martin (France) and Marx (USA) by turn of the 20th century. It comes as no surprise then that Märklin, for example, remains one of the leading metal toys makers in the 21st century and is currently the world leader in model railway gauges. Here it is important to note an important cultural development. While the advent of machines had initially focused on mechanizing toys, a new interest was added to this: representational accuracy of which the toy car was the most emblematic. These two tendencies merged in the emergence of constructional toys associated with companies like Meccano and Lego.

In all of this it is important to note that in the literature (Fleming, 1996; Provenzo,1991; Kline, 1993; Jameson, 1991) the toy lent itself to being narrativized and thus become a bearer of history and meanings in what Jameson (1991, pp.18-27) considers a particularly postmodern phenomenon and marker of late capitalism. In his signature ponderous style, Jameson describes this meaning making with reference to architecture "as the remarkable current intensification of an addiction to the photographic image... itself a tangible symptom of an omnipresent, omnivorous, and well-nigh libidinal historicism....'' He describes it further as a "gusto" which "cannibalizes all the architectural styles of the past and combines them in overstimulating ensembles" (1991, pp. 18-19). Jameson points rather elaborately to the intertextuality this narrativization feeds off as "as a deliberate, built-in feature of the aesthetic effect and as the operator of a new connotation of "pastness" and pseudohistorical depth, in which the history of aesthetic styles displaces "'real" history'' (1991, p.20). Logically for toys as for other ensembles, intertextual meaning does not emerge from a reclusive or isolated existence of these toys; on the contrary they emerge from placing these toys side by side with comic strips, films, pop groups, books, fashion and the like the proliferation of which and access to has been made possible by late capitalism's globe spanning vast manufacturing infrastructure that is today digitized.

How does this meaning play out then which is the point of this narrativization of the toy? Fleming (1996) offers for this work a compelling approach for this toy meaning making because he also looks at video games. His schema draws on (psycho-analysis *contra* Freud) object-relations theory in the work of Erikson (1977; 1978) and Miller (1987). In his schema, toys bear or better still make meaning by means of two layers for identity formation and therefore subject formation or subject-fixing to use his term. The first layer, the substrate, deals with gender roles and preparing the child for their place in the confusing vagaries of the capitalist political economy. Fleming (1996) however rejects any mechanistic view of this substrate for determining identity. He postulates convincingly instead a layer atop this substrate, the object-relational interpellation(s), which sit in dynamic and fluid tectonic alliance with the substrate, and which are also known as structures of subordination in each social formation. His view of the subject (derived from Althusser) is thus not one in which a "subjectivity is a position inscribed (and endlessly reinscribed) within structures of subordination that are produced (and endlessly reproduced) within a given social formation" (Fleming, 1996, p.196). In his scheme, Fleming (1996) suggests that toys as objects serve as "devices of enthrallment" and trigger effects which then battle endlessly the substrate for determination of what the subject becomes:

To suggest that some objects in the world hold us enthralled, not just because they are conduits for delivery of an ideological 'summons', a fix, but also because we summon forth from them a function as devices of enthrallment, is to propose a more interested role for the subject than has been allowed in most cultural studies to date (and evokes the notion from psychoanalytic object-relations theory that pleasure is not an end in itself but a 'signpost' to a meaningful object). We would have to accept that such attachments are not fully explained when we say that they are something like affective implants installed in us by the operation of ideology. (p. 196-197)

The kind of toy then determines the nature of this Flemingan subject formation. Fleming (1996) argues that video games are essentially toys which make this process portable and repetitive endlessly unlike other toys. Thrift (2003) rejects this Flemingan position by insisting that hand-held video games like Nintendo's *Game Boy* do not reconfigure the subject because "they tend to work to set scripts and so have little adaptive capacity" (2003, p.396). It bears pointing out though that it is precisely this "set script" that Fleming (1996) deploys to elucidate the subject forming power of video games which are set off anytime the player turns on the game through an opening and a stretched-out middle:

So what is emerging from this discussion is something like a substrate of subject-fixing processes on top of which a kind of opening and return, a prolonged 'middle' is operative. The former is the level of the drive towards closure, the end of the story, the drawing of everything into place — in a sense, then, also the place of sleep where all pretense of freedom and control is surrendered. The 'opening and return' is the postponing of sleep in the child's ramblings......, but also the place where playing supplements being a spectator, where stories supplant each other rather than ending, where metonymic elaborations are achieved and where identity-effects interact with other effects. (Fleming, 1996, p.177)

We have been painstaking here to show that producing and playing video games is not some benign process entirely and simply defined by the search for profits. Video games once they are properly understood as special toys sit comfortably within the Quaysonian (2021) structure of denominations in which case they are sign-posts which render history and psycho-existential meanings and are thus not

Table 1. Videogames and subjectivity

Sample of Classic Videogames	Fleming's Subject Making Processes through Effects
Donkey Kong, Super Mario Bros, Super Mario Bros 2 and 3, Super Mario Bros: The Lost Levels, Super Mario All Stars	First Level Effect: subject-fixing substrate drawn from societal gender roles and dominant ideology
	Second Level Effects: harmonising, relational, totemic, narrative, commodification, social-semiotic, textual

just about dry semiotics but have empirical/material import as well (already pointed out as money in the form of profits). Clearly then video games (the emergence of which we turn in the next section) are toys and much more because of their being toys of a special kind and must perforce matter for Africa.

THE RISE OF VIDEO GAMES

It was in America that the video games industry was birthed and spread from there to Japan and other Asian countries such as South Korea, Singapore and lately China. To be sure though Japan's post-war rise as an electronics global powerhouse did not leave the world including Africa untouched. The search for markets around the globe which was embedded in Japan's switch to Export Oriented Industrialization (EOI) brought an assortment of electronic goods into the African continent. The most visible and even beloved Japanese electronic items on the African market were calculators and watches (the calculator watch was a marvel) manufactured by Casio and Sharp. But there was another class of Japanese electronic goods that surely left its mark in Africa: the handheld video games. In Ghana for example, Nintendo handheld video games such as *Octopus*, *Donkey Kong* and *Super Mario* ruled the roost at private primary schools' (such as Morning Star School, Ghana International School, Christ the King School and Ridge Church School among others) playgrounds in the capital, Accra, in the 1980s. These were known as the Game and Watch Series which were developed, manufactured, released, and marketed by Nintendo from 1980 to 1991. How did video games themselves emerge and how did Japan become so central to and intimately involved in the making of video games? We provide an adumbrated narrative in the next section.

From the American Connection to Japan

The work of the German physicist Johann Geissler produced the Geissler tube which allowed the discovery of the electron and the invention of the Cathode Ray Tube (CRT). Without the CRT modern gadgets like the television and video game would certainly not have been invented for it allowed the electron to be manipulated for various purposes. After all a video game is that which provides or makes play possible by means of a television or television like screen. Though the manipulation of electrons is central to the emergence of video games, it must be noted that not all electronic games are video games. Ultimately video games emerged from the cross between computing power and television screens. War and the quest for precision firing (the need for firing tables [Polacheck,1997]) led to one of the first computers designed by Massachusetts Institute of Technology (MIT) alumnus, Vannevar Bush being built in 1931. The Electronic Numerical Integrator and Computer (ENIAC) (powered by 19468 vacuum tubes and descended from earlier vacuum tubes), was another computer built in 1945. ENIAC was then followed by the Electronic Discrete Variable Automatic Computer (EDVAC) which John von Neuman (1993) helped build by writing out the complex technical details thereby laying down the basis for computer architecture and video games. Two years after this breakthrough in computing, the Cathode Ray Amusement Device was built by Dumont Laboratories and emerged as the first video game in the long line of what came to be known in the literature as arcade games.

Over time these games improved as the technology developed. The first video games were technology wise rather simple compared with what are available today. They had black and white LCD screens; could not admit multiple players at a time even at one location let alone multi-sites and run on very low processing power. Higher computer processing power (that even allow sensations in games to be simulated in what is now known as Haptic Technology), high bandwidth and advances in game building technology have revolutionized games and gaming. The online gaming market was valued at US$56billion in 2021 and is set to grow in value even more in the coming years. Banfi's (2023) recent categorization (Gaming I, Gaming II and Gaming III) shows the shifts in game history from the earliest moments to date. Gaming I encompass the arcade and home system boom era in which Japan emerged as a powerful player in the global video games industry on the back of Nintendo Inc through the rare vision and drive of its president Hiroshi Yamauchi and its creative genius Shigeru Miyamoto. Nintendo guaranteed the place of Japan in gaming history through Gaming II (post-crash console era) to the current Gaming III (video game subscriptions era). While 90% of Nintendo's revenue reportedly come from its console business in the last decade it has been pursuing an Intellectual Property (IP) based transformation (to rival Disney) centred around its signature character the Mario Brothers spin-offs (Natsumi, 2023) such as merchandize, theme parks, movies, and convenience store snacks. The history and current video games environment clearly displays constant changes which Africa must respond to if it seeks to be a key player in that global space. We turn to this in the next section.

Figure 1. Mario Bros characters
Picture by authors, Narita Airport, Tokyo, Japan.

Figure 2. Nintendo Store
Picture by authors, Shibuya, Tokyo

Africa and Video Games: Tenuous Ties?

The Game Development industry is one that developing countries in Africa do not seem to have paid serious attention to. Working in the games industry is something that is considered rare and hardly seen as an occupation around the region. Presently in 2023, the global video game market is projected to reach revenues of over US$ 370billion.[1] It is instructive that in 2008, revenue value was around US$22 billion (conservative estimate) in the US and US$30 to US$42 billion globally. The projected revenue of US$370 in 2023 in just 15 years truly confirms the view that gaming could be the fastest growing component of the international media sector.

While many countries have seen an aggressive development of successful gaming industry as a part of an economic growth strategy there has been far too few attempts from the African perspective. Back in 2010, at the Games Development Conference (GDC 2010) held in San Francisco only one company from sub-Saharan Africa, Leti Games, was present in the game development space. Clearly, other attendees were surprised to see that such skill sets existed within sub-Saharan Africa and wondered which educational institutions offered game development courses. Eventually, this company attracted front page coverage in the business segment, of the San Jose *Mercury* newspaper where Leti Games showcased their latest game iWarrior.

Given the perceived development needs of many African countries it might at first seem strange to consider African gaming as a priority. This kind of thinking is based on a poorly informed Western view of African needs and abilities. Incomes across Africa are not evenly distributed with many urban areas leading a relatively developed lifestyle. Over a decade ago Aker and Mbiti (2010) reported a massive growth in mobile phone ownership with 60% of the population (477 million people) having mobile phone coverage by 2008. They also reported that mobile phone ownership has risen from 16 million in 2000 to 376 million in 2009 which vastly outstrips land-line development, effectively leap frogging Western developments. This data shows how games in Africa could find an available and fertile platform more than a decade ago.

Africa, Video Games, and the Possibilities of Ubiquitous Computing

The African context suggests that countries in sub-Saharan Africa have already entered the cyberage through ubiquitous computing (Bell and Dourish, 2006) rather than the established desktop computing model predominant in the West. Given the potential advantages and dare we claim lead that Africa has over the West back then and still has now, the question becomes, how does Africa take advantage of this?

Ubiquitous computing shows the future is already here; it is just not evenly distributed. Weiser (1991) anticipated a world in which computation would be embedded into our everyday worlds – not just physically embedded but also socially and procedurally embedded, becoming part and parcel of how we act in the world. In the African context the signs of this are more than evident. Mobile phones and PDAs are in widespread use throughout the continent and all classes of users enjoy this. The fascinating thing about this is both literates and illiterates know how to use these everyday gadgets which makes it very viable for services like gaming to spawn since they build on top of existing infrastructure. Data for 2022 and 2023 shows that mobile phones generated the highest game revenues of US$778.6million (out of total revenue of US$862.8million) and US$907.3million (out of a total revenue of US$998.1million) respectively.

Table 2. Video games revenue for Africa (2022 and 2023)

Segment	2022	2023
Total Revenues	US$862.8million	US$998.1million
PC Revenues	US$49.4million	US$53.2million
Mobile Revenues	**US778.6million**	**US$907.3million**
Apple AppStores Revenues	US$204.6million	US$245.6million
Android Stores Revenues	US$574.0million	US$661.7million
Console Revenues	US$34.8million	US$40.9million

In developed countries, where ubiquitous computing is also being realized, investors are reaping huge earnings from it. Africa is yet to reap such benefits. To be sure some puny infrastructure is being built and Telcos are increasing coverage gradually. This uneven distribution is getting even gradually which would form the basis of the gaming infrastructure. The messiness of ubiquitous computing however and with-it uneven distribution of IT infrastructure in Africa has left a vast vacuum for building a very important industry such as the video games one which can be a major contributor to African economies. The statistics cited earlier pertaining to the US show how much Africa is missing out. But then, trends show massive growth where ubiquitous computing is surfacing in Africa. This positive growth if properly harnessed can lay the foundation for Africa to benefit ideationally and monetarily from the video games industry in its different guises such as pc gaming, mobile gaming, mobile gaming advertising, web and console gaming which will improve the entertainment industry and inspire the use of entertainment as well in African education, edutainment.

Beyond the Tenuous Ties?

Africa is a late-comer to the global video game scene. The emergence and dominance of video games as a form of entertainment and industry took the world by storm, but Africa struggled to keep pace. The price paid by Africa for this delayed entry into the world of gaming was significant, and its response to this challenge has been a testament to its resilience and determination given that the pioneers virtually took off on their own with any direct government support or interest.

For years, Africa was largely absent from the global video game industry. Its lack of technological infrastructure, limited access to reliable internet connections, and the high cost of gaming consoles and software hindered the growth of the gaming market on the continent. As a result, African gamers faced numerous obstacles and were often left out of the global gaming conversation. The consequences of this exclusion were manifold. African gamers missed out on the social and cultural impact of video games, which became a vital part of the youth's identity and popular culture in other parts of the world. Additionally, the absence of a local gaming industry meant that Africa's creative talent was largely untapped, stifling the potential for economic growth and innovation.

However, despite these challenges, Africa refused to remain on the sidelines. As internet connectivity improved and technology became more accessible, African gamers started to make their presence felt. Online gaming communities began to emerge, connecting gamers from different parts of the continent and fostering a sense of camaraderie. In a lecture at GDC 2013 on the emerging landscape of African video game development, a comprehensive timeline of how games emerged on the continent was provided.[2] African game developers, fueled by passion and a desire to showcase their unique perspectives, also started to emerge. They found creative ways to overcome financial and infrastructural limitations. Mobile gaming became a popular avenue for African developers, as it required less powerful hardware and catered to the continent's growing smartphone market. The rise of mobile gaming in Africa brought about a renaissance of sorts. Local game studios began creating games that drew inspiration from African folklore, history, and culture. These games not only provided entertainment but also served as a means of preserving and celebrating Africa's rich cultural heritage. Titles like *Africa's Legends* from Leti Arts and *Aurion: Legacy of the Kori-Odan,* by Kiroo Games brought African narratives to the forefront of the global gaming scene, captivating players around the world. Initiatives aimed at supporting and nurturing Africa's gaming industry started to gain traction. Earlier in the history of the industry, organizations like the Meltwater Entrepreneurial School of Technology (MEST), British Council and International Games Development Association (IGDA) (through some local representatives) recognized the potential of the gaming industry as an economic driver and began providing funding, training, and mentorship opportunities mostly in the creative sector to established game developers who also helped extend this to aspiring game developers. This support paved the way for more African voices and stories to emerge in the gaming world.

The African gaming scene, while still in its early stages, is slowly gaining momentum. Esports tournaments are being organized, bringing together talented players from across the continent to compete on a global stage. Local gaming conventions and expos are growing in popularity, providing a platform for African game developers to showcase their creations and connect with a wider audience. In February 2022, the top ten studios in Africa formed a group (Makoni, 2022) known as the Pan Africa Gaming Group (PAGG). The PPAG aims to grow the industry by a factor of two annually and to put Africa "on the map of the global game industry."[3] The tenuous ties that once existed between Africa and video games are gradually being replaced by strong firm ones. The continent's journey to catch up with the rest of the world has been marked by perseverance, resourcefulness, and a deep passion for gaming. Africa's response to the challenges it faced demonstrates its ability to adapt and thrive in the face of adversity.

As the gaming landscape continues to evolve, Africa's role within it is poised for growth. With a growing market, a vibrant community of gamers, and a burgeoning game development scene, Africa has the potential to become a powerhouse in the global gaming industry. By nurturing local talent, fostering innovation, and addressing the infrastructure gaps that persist, Africa can establish itself as a force to be reckoned with. While the continent may have paid a price for its delayed entry, it is now embracing the opportunity to shape its own gaming narrative. As Africa's ties with video games strengthen, the world will witness the rise of a vibrant and unique gaming culture that draws inspiration from the continent's rich history and diverse cultural and artistic treasures.

AFRICAN VIDEO GAMES: STATE-OF-THE ART AND THE FUTURE

The African video game industry has been making significant strides in recent years, with key actors, games, new developments, and policies shaping the landscape. In this section we provide a snapshot of the exciting developments happening at the industry level in Africa, shedding light on the progress made and the emerging trends.

Key Actors

Several key actors have played pivotal roles in driving the growth of the video game industry in Africa. These include game developers, publishers, governments, and organizations supporting the gaming ecosystem.

Game Developers

African game developers have been instrumental in shaping the industry and showcasing African narratives and experiences through their creations. Studios such as Leti Arts (Ghana), Nyamakop (South Africa), Kiro'o Games (Cameroon), and Qene Technologies (Nigeria) have gained international recognition for their innovative games.

Publishers and Distributors

Publishers and distributors have played a crucial role in bringing African games to global audiences. Companies like Plug-In Digital, Devolver Digital, and Akamai Technologies have been actively involved in publishing and promoting African-developed games.

Governments

Governments across the continent have started-though belatedly- recognizing the potential of the gaming industry and have taken steps to support its growth. For instance, the South African Department of Trade and Industry has implemented programs to foster game development, while the Kenyan government launched the Video Games Bill to regulate and promote the industry. The interest of the South African government in video games is not strange given that as of 2022, 24million South Africans (half of the population) were playing games.

Gaming Organizations

Various organizations have emerged to support the African gaming ecosystem. The African Game Developers Association (AGDA) promotes collaboration and knowledge-sharing among game developers, while initiatives like AGW, Playtopia and A MAZE also contribute to this direction. African gaming events such as festivals and conferences are providing platforms for networking and showcasing African talent.

Key Games

Several notable games have emerged from Africa, capturing global attention and acclaim. These games reflect the diversity of African cultures, histories, and experiences, often challenging traditional gaming narratives. Here are a few examples:

Africa's Legends by Leti Arts (Ghana): This critically acclaimed game explores the spectrum of Africa's greatest set in a beautifully crafted world, drawing inspiration from African folklore and storytelling traditions.

Aurion: Legacy of the Kori-Odan by Kiro'o Games (Cameroon): This action Role-Playing Game (RPG) incorporates African mythology and culture, immersing players in a vibrant world inspired by Central African aesthetics.

Broforce by Freelives (South Africa): this is a platform-based game involving one of the players acting as a gender neutral "bro" (akin to popular culture figures such as Rambo) and rescuing other "bros" in dangerous terrain.

New Developments

The African video game industry continues to witness exciting new developments that contribute to its growth and recognition. Some noteworthy trends and advancements include:

Esports: Esports is gaining popularity in Africa, with tournaments and competitions being organized at both local and international levels. The Africa Esports Championship, for example, showcases the region's competitive gaming talent and provides opportunities for African gamers to excel on the global stage.

Virtual Reality (VR) and Augmented Reality (AR): African game developers are exploring VR and AR technologies to create immersive and interactive gaming experiences. This emerging trend opens new possibilities for storytelling and gameplay mechanics unique to the African context.

Mobile Gaming: Mobile gaming continues to dominate the African gaming market (as data cited earlier shows), thanks to the widespread availability of smartphones across the continent. This accessibility has allowed African game developers to reach a broader audience and create games specifically tailored for mobile platforms.

Policies and Support

Governments and organizations are recognizing the importance of establishing supportive policies and frameworks for the gaming industry. Some notable initiatives include:

Funding and Grants: Governments and organizations have initiated funding programs and grants to support African game developers. For instance, the Digital Lab Africa offers funding and mentorship for digital content creators, including game developers.

Skills Development and Training: Various institutions provide training programs and workshops to develop the skills of aspiring game developers. This includes coding boot camps, game development courses, and mentorship programs, equipping individuals with the necessary tools to enter the gaming industry.

Policy and Regulation: Governments are implementing policies and regulations to create a favorable environment for the gaming industry. This includes intellectual property protection, tax incentives, and the establishment of regulatory bodies to ensure responsible and sustainable growth.

The African video game industry is rapidly evolving, driven by passionate developers, supportive organizations, and the formulation and implementation of some of forward-thinking policies. With an ever-expanding catalog of unique games and increasing recognition on the global stage, Africa is establishing itself as an exciting hub of creativity and innovation within the world of video games. The key question to ask at this juncture is what must be done in the coming years to allow the African video game to be one of the most developed, profitable and recognized on the global stage.

Building the Future Today for Africa's Video Games

The trends in Africa for mobile telephony and internet services are very promising for the future of video games. As Africa seeks to further establish its presence in the global video game industry, it must embrace a forward-thinking approach and take strategic steps to position itself at the forefront of the evolving gaming landscape. While gaming may prove strategic for the African economy there are several barriers to its development. It is an industry where a lot is put in, with a high chance of very low revenue returns or failure. To secure a prominent role in the game, Africa must focus on several key areas to maximize its potential and drive growth.

Gaming is one aspect of the ICT industry that builds on top of other infrastructure. When there is development and infrastructure to support extra technology, innovation happens. For innovation to happen, the educational system becomes paramount. Game development is a technical undertaking which needs special attention, keen interest, passion and creative thinking minds in order to succeed in the field. Due to this, students in sciences are more likely to pursue careers in a field like this though gaming cuts across all skills-set. Obviously, interest in science related courses both in Africa and worldwide is a bit negative thus requiring some special attention to pedagogy in science programs to make it an attractive field. There is a need to build more interest in students to offer Science, Technology, Engineering and Mathematics (STEM) and Science, Technology, Engineering, Arts and Mathematics (STEAM) courses at the tertiary level. As Africa looks to the future and aims to establish itself as a significant player in the global video game industry, several key steps must be taken to ensure its success. By focusing on infrastructure development, fostering talent and innovation, and embracing emerging technologies, Africa can position itself at the forefront of the gaming landscape. Drawing on several years of direct experience in the African game we offer below some ideas on what needs to be done for Africa to truly get into the game.

Infrastructure Development

One of the primary areas Africa needs to address is infrastructure development. Reliable and affordable high-speed internet connectivity is essential for online gaming, esports, and digital distribution platforms. Governments and private entities should invest in expanding internet access and improving network infrastructure to ensure a seamless gaming experience for players and facilitate the growth of the gaming industry. Investments in high-speed broadband networks, data centers, and cloud computing infrastructure are essential to support online gaming platforms, game streaming services, and emerging technologies like virtual reality (VR) and augmented reality (AR). Collaborations with telecommunications companies and international partners can accelerate the development of robust infrastructure across the continent.

Education and Skill Development

To nurture a thriving gaming ecosystem, Africa must prioritize education and skill development in game development and related fields. Collaboration between educational institutions, industry professionals, and gaming organizations is crucial to establish programs that offer comprehensive training and support for aspiring game developers, designers, artists, and professionals. By providing accessible and quality education, Africa can build a highly skilled workforce capable of creating innovative and competitive games.

Nurturing local talent is vital for Africa's gaming industry to flourish. Steps should be taken to provide training and educational opportunities in game development, design, programming, and related fields. Partnerships between educational institutions, gaming studios, and industry experts can help establish game development programs and workshops. Furthermore, mentorship programs, game jams, and hackathons can encourage collaboration, innovation, and knowledge sharing within the gaming community. Platforms and initiatives should be created to highlight African game developers, providing them with exposure, support, and funding opportunities.

Supportive Policies and Incentives

Governments should formulate and implement supportive policies and incentives to attract investment in the gaming industry. This includes tax incentives, grants, and funding opportunities for game development studios, as well as streamlined regulations and intellectual property protection. By creating a conducive, facilitating, and attractive environment, Africa can encourage local and international game developers to establish a presence on the continent, fostering economic growth and job creation. Establishing gaming industry associations and councils can facilitate dialogue between the government, developers, and investors. Regular industry conferences and expos can also provide a platform for networking, knowledge exchange, and showcasing African gaming talent. The key question here is how African governments understand and play their role in the gaming environment. There exist best practices that African governments can learn from. In Singapore and Korea their governments got involved in video games in ways that suited their peculiar geoeconomic realities and allowed both nations to "exemplify two leading Asian tigers that are basking in the success of digital development'' (Chung, 2008, p.305). To be sure, for the

Asia- Pacific region as a whole "the gaming industry has facilitated the region's transformation of its economic and technological sectors into a global cultural capital as people are eager to adopt virtual life'' (Anh, 2021, p.174). African countries can benefit from the strategies used.

In Korea the approach to gaming involved a strategic move by the Korean government involving a sophisticated IT policy that invested heavily in dependable and fast IT infrastructure and allocated funds to internet service providers generating game playing outlets known as *bangs*. The overall strategy was to generate revenues within Korea to allow Korean gaming to be competitive enough to enter the global market. The Korean state also set up specific institutions that spearheaded this strategy such as the Ministry of Information and Communication (MIC) and the Ministry of Culture and Tourism (MCT). Korea's overseas gaming thrust was also aided by government agencies such as the Korea ICT International Cooperation Agency (KIICA) which provided marketing and technological support through the MIC by setting up offices in China, Singapore, Japan, Germany, and the USA. These processes led to the emergence of Korean gaming companies such as Nexon (now headquartered in Japan and which has published titles such as *MapleStory*, *Dungeon & Fighter*, *Sudden Attack*, and *KartRider*) and NCSoft (mainly known for the distribution of massively multiplayer online role-playing games (MMORPG) such as *Lineage* and *Guild Wars*). Through Nexon, Korea pioneered the world's first multiplayer online graphic game *Kingdom of the Winds*. That game invented a new massive global market, the Online Game Industry, which currently exceeds in size and growth most of the traditional entertainment markets, such as film or television.

In Singapore the approach was the reverse of what the Korean state did which we will describe as the *inward-outward-inward approach* (IOI). Singapore engaged in what we will describe as the *outward-inward-outward approach* (OIO) by which global gaming talent and capital was attracted into Singapore (to build and strengthen the local gaming industry) to make the city-state competitive regionally and globally. By 1985 Singapore had realized the importance of culture, art, creativity, and technology in its overall national development agenda (Kong, 2000). New institutions such as the National Art Council (NAC) and National Heritage Board (NHB) were set up. These new institutions worked hand in hand with already established ones such as the Media Development Authority (MDA), the Economic Development Board (EDB), and Information Development Authority of Singapore (IDA) to build a Singapore cultural economy anchored on technology through policy ideas such as *Design Singapore*, *Media 21* and *Renaissance City*. Through tax schemes and funding Singapore encouraged leading global interactive and digital media companies to set up offices in Singapore. The Singapore government also facilitated active collaboration between international and local game companies so industry networks could be forged quickly (Chung, 2008). In the Singaporean OIO, government ensured active and organic synergy between multinational gaming companies and local ones. Singapore provided more than US$360million to assist local game start-ups begin or complete projects. The effect of all this was that by 2008 major creative companies such as Lucas Films, Electronic Arts, Koei, Ubisoft, RealU and 10Tacle had set up offices in Singapore enabling local companies like Boomzap, Nexgen and Mikoishi to flourish and penetrate global and regional markets. Mikoishi for example completed the first made-in-Singapore video game *Dropcast* for Nintendo in 2007 while Japanese company Koei launched its first developed-in-Singapore MMORPG, *Romance of the Three Kingdoms On-line*, in 2008 (Chia, 2008). Korea and Singapore offer important and useful lessons for Africa's gaming future at the level of policy formation.

Collaboration and Networking

Africa must actively seek collaborations and networking opportunities within the global gaming industry. Establishing partnerships with international game development studios, publishers, and industry associations can facilitate knowledge exchange, resource sharing, and access to global markets. African game developers should also collaborate with local content creators, musicians, and artists to infuse unique African flavors into their games, enhancing cultural representation and authenticity.

Promoting Local Content and Narratives

To stand out in the global gaming market, Africa should focus on promoting and celebrating its rich cultural heritage and diverse narratives through games. Encouraging game developers to draw inspiration from African history, folklore, and contemporary experiences can create a distinctive gaming identity for the continent. This not only appeals to a global audience interested in diverse storytelling but also empowers African players to see themselves represented in the games they play. Africa's rich cultural heritage and diverse narratives provide a unique advantage in the gaming industry. African game developers should continue to draw inspiration from their local contexts, showcasing stories, folklore, and history that resonate with both local and global audiences.

Collaboration with storytellers, artists, musicians, historians, literary scholars, philosophers, and filmmakers can further enhance the storytelling aspect of African games. Emphasizing inclusivity and representation by featuring diverse characters and perspectives will help African games connect with players worldwide. African themed games can best present the African story especially as a response and antidote to the existing tendency in videogames production which seem geared at reinforcing the long modern history of denigrating, stereotyping and misrepresenting Africa and Africans. In the literature video games have been analyzed as socio-cultural artifacts in which representations of race, ethnicity and postcoloniality have been unpacked (LaPensée, 2012; Šisler,2008; Murkherjee, 2017,2018; Brock, 2011; Lallani, 2023). In a recent work Lallani (2023, p.541) is at pains to show how in the MMORPG, *Runescape* " colonial ways of possessing the resources of Others are important to the in-game advancement of *Runescape* players. In connecting virtual advancement of user accounts to performances of colonialism it is asserted that *Runescape* reproduces empire projects in which European powers commodified other societies to serve their own economic and cultural agendas." Clearly then video games of all kinds are a veritable battleground over signs and representation in which Africa gaming must participate to challenge stereotypes and accurately depict Africa and Africans.

Embracing Emerging Technologies

To stay ahead in the rapidly evolving gaming landscape, Africa must embrace emerging technologies. Virtual reality (VR), augmented reality (AR), and mixed reality (MR) offer new avenues for immersive gaming experiences. Collaboration between game developers, technology companies, and researchers can drive the adoption, adaptation, and even new inventions of these technologies in Africa. Additionally, exploring the potential of blockchain technology and decentralized gaming platforms can foster innovation, enhance player ownership of in-game assets, and create new economic opportunities within the gaming ecosystem.

Esports and Gaming Events

Africa should embrace the growing popularity of esports and gaming events. Organizing and hosting regional and international esports tournaments, conferences, and gaming festivals can attract global attention, generate revenue, and provide platforms for African gamers to showcase their skills. By nurturing a competitive esports scene and fostering a vibrant gaming community, Africa can become a hub for esports and gaming enthusiasts.

Accessibility and Inclusivity

Ensuring accessibility and inclusivity in gaming is paramount. Africa should prioritize initiatives that make gaming accessible to marginalized communities, individuals with disabilities, and people from various socioeconomic backgrounds. This includes developing localized content, supporting game accessibility features, and providing opportunities for underrepresented groups to participate in the industry.

By taking these proactive steps, Africa can overcome its current challenges and secure a prominent position in the global video game industry. The potential for economic growth, cultural preservation and dynamism, and technological innovation is immense. With a focus on infrastructure, talent development, government support, emerging technologies, and authentic representation, Africa can truly become a force to be reckoned with in the gaming world of tomorrow.

CONCLUSION

In this chapter we have attempted to provide a state-of-the art account of games and gaming in Africa by explicating the ties, tensions, and possibilities vis-à-vis the wider global games industry. This explication was rendered through a critical examination of vital elements such as policies, key actors, know-how, institutions, investments, history, business, technology, and cultural economy in the last twenty years. It is obvious that even though Africa as region has come to the game industry as a builder as a late-comer, game production has always representationally and ideationally engaged Africa. Regarding Africa as a game builder, we have shown that Africa can catch up given the great potential in countries like Ghana, South Africa, Kenya, and Nigeria. This catch-up clearly requires a strategy in which African governments recognize quickly the cultural, technological, and economic value of video games (as well as the potential problems that have afflicted leading gaming nations such as game addiction [King,Delfabbro and Griffiths, 2013]) in a post-COVID 19 world and draw in know-how, best practices and investments from the public and private sectors both at home and abroad. With respect to its representational and ideational aspects we have shown that video games are not merely inert, fanciful toys but culturally and psychologically significant and influential artifacts. If Quayson (2002) is correct that Africa has in modern times always been interpreted under a sign of crises, video games have come to play a part in this and can in equal measure ensure a reversal. Video games after all are about mammon, pleasure, the mind and more and Africa must pay attention.

REFERENCES

Aker, J. C., & Mbiti, I. M. (2010). Mobiles phones and economic development in Africa. *The Journal of Economic Perspectives*, *24*(3), 207–232. doi:10.1257/jep.24.3.207

Anh, P. Q. (2021). Shifting the focus to East and Southeast Asia: A critical review of regional game research. *Fudan Journal of the Humanities and Social Sciences*, *14*(2), 173–196. doi:10.1007/s40647-021-00317-7

Banfi, R. (2023). Gaming I, II, and III: Arcades, video game systems, and modern game streaming services. *Games and Culture*, *0*(0), 1–38. doi:10.1177/15554120231186634

Bell, G., & Dourish, P. (2006). Yesterday's tomorrows: Notes on ubiquitous computing's dominant vision. *Personal and Ubiquitous Computing*, *11*(2), 133–143. doi:10.1007/s00779-006-0071-x

Brock, A. (2011). "When Keeping it Real Goes Wrong": Resident Evil 5, Racial Representation, and Gamers. *Games and Culture*, *6*(5), 429–452. doi:10.1177/1555412011402676

Carr, K. (2017). *Early African Board Games and Toys – History of Games*. Quatr. https://quatr.us/history/african-games-history.htm

Chia, Y. M. (2008). Game Developer's Local Arm Launched Debut Title. *Strait Times*.

Collins, J. (1989). The early history of West African Highlife music. *Popular Music*, *8*(3), 221–230. doi:10.1017/S0261143000003524

Collins, J. (2005). A social history of Ghanaian popular entertainment since independence. *Transactions of the Historical Society of Ghana*, *9*, 17–40. https://www.jstor.org/stable/41406722

Cornelius, M. (1986). An historical background to some mathematical games. *Mathematics in School*, *15*(1), 47–49.

Crist, W. (2019). Passing from the Middle to the New Kingdom: A *Senet* Board in the Rosicrucian Egyptian Museum. *The Journal of Egyptian Archaeology*, *105*(1), 107–113. https://www.jstor.org/stable/26949436. doi:10.1177/0307513319896288

Fleming, D. (1996). *Toys as popular culture*. Manchester University Press.

King, D. L., Delfabbro, P. H., & Mark, D. Griffiths. (2013). Video Game Addiction. In P. M. Miller (Ed.), Principles of Addiction (pp. 819-825). London, San Diego and Massachusetts: Academic Press.

Kline, S. (1993). *Out of the Garden: Toys and Children's Culture in the Age of TV Marketing*. Verso.

Kong, L. (2000). Cultural policy in Singapore: Negotiating economic and socio-cultural agendas. *Geoforum*, *31*(4), 409–424. doi:10.1016/S0016-7185(00)00006-3

Kyule, M. (2016). The bao: a board game in Africa's antiquity. In A.-M. Deisser & M. Njuguna (Eds.), *Conservation of Natural and Cultural Heritage in Kenya: A Cross-Disciplinary Approach* (1st ed., pp. 93–107). UCL Press. doi:10.2307/j.ctt1gxxpc6.13

Lallani, S. S. (2023). Virtual empire: Performing colonialism in the MMORPG *Runescape*. *Games and Culture*, *18*(5), 539–558. doi:10.1177/15554120221109130

LaPensée, E. (2021). *When Rivers Were Trails*: Cultural expression in an indigenous video game. *International Journal of Heritage Studies*, *27*(3), 281–295. doi:10.1080/13527258.2020.1746919

Miedzian, M. (1992). *Boys Will Be Boys*. Virago.

Muller, H. R. (1930). Warri: A West African game of skill. *Journal of American Folklore*, *43*(169), 313–316. doi:10.2307/534943

Murkherjee, S. (2018). *Videogames and postcolonialism: empire plays back*. Springer.

Murkherjee, S. (2018). Playing subaltern: Video games and postcolonialism. *Games and Culture*, *13*(5), 504–520. doi:10.1177/1555412015627258

Natsoulas, A. (1995). The game of mancala with reference to commonalities among the peoples of Ethiopia and in comparison to other African peoples: Rules and strategies. *Northeast African Studies*, *2*(2), 7–24. doi:10.1353/nas.1995.0018

Natsumi, K. (2023). *Nintendo's Mario mission: grab IP limelight as Switch sales dim*. Nikkei.

Pankhurst, R. (1971). History and principles of Ethiopian chess. *Journal of Ethiopian Studies*, *9*(2), 149–172. https://www.jstor.org/stable/41967474

Polacheck, H. (1997). Before the ENIAC [weapons firing table calculations]. *IEEE Annals of the History of Computing*, *19*(2), 25–30.

Provenzo, E. F. (1991). Video Kids: Making Sense of Nintendo. Cambridge, Mass., Harvard: University Press. doi:10.4159/harvard.9780674422483

Quayson, A. (2002). Obverse denominations: Africa? *Public Culture*, *14*(3), 585-588.

Quayson, A. (2021). Tragedy and postcolonial literature. Cambridge, New York, Melbourne, New Dehli, Singapore: Cambridge University Press. doi:10.1017/9781108921992

Šisler, V. (2008). Digital Arabs: Representation in video games. *European Journal of Cultural Studies*, *11*(2), 203–220.

Thrift, N. (2003). Closer to the machine? Intelligent environments, new forms of possession and the rise of the supertoy. *Cultural Geographies*, *10*(4), 389–407. doi:10.1191/1474474003eu282oaa

Tylor, E. B. (1880). Remarks on the geographical distribution of games. *Journal of the Anthropological Institute of Great Britain and Ireland*, *9*, 23–30. doi:10.2307/2841865

Van Rheenen, D. (2012). A century of historical change in the game preferences of American children. *Journal of American Folklore*, *125*(498), 411–443. doi:10.5406/jamerfolk.125.498.0411

von Neuman, J. (1993). First draft of the report on EDVAC. *IEEE Annals of the History of Computing*, *15*(4), 27–43. doi:10.1109/85.238389

Weisser, M. (1991). The computer for the twenty-first century. *Scientific American, 265*(3), 94–104. doi:10.1038/scientificamerican0991-94

ADDITIONAL READING

Amoah, L. G. A. (2014). *Impacts of the knowledge society on economic and social growth in Africa.* IGI Global. doi:10.4018/978-1-4666-5844-8

Austen, R. A., & Headrick, D. (1983). The role of technology in the African past. *African Studies Review, 26*(3/4), 163–184. doi:10.2307/524168

Chinweizu (2023). *432 centuries of recorded science and technology in Black Africa.* Serujta ebooks.

Dennis, J. P. (2009). Gazing at the black teen: Con artists, cyborgs and sycophants. *Media Culture & Society, 31*(2), 179–195. doi:10.1177/0163443708098418

Headrick, D. (1991). *The invisible weapon: telecommunications and international politics, 1851-1945.* Oxford University Press. doi:10.1093/oso/9780195062731.001.0001

Headrick, R. D. (1981). *The tools of empire: technology and European imperialism in the nineteenth century.* Oxford University Press.

Hennessey, J. (2017). *The comic book story of video games: the incredible history of the electronic gaming revolution.* Potter/TenSpeed/Harmony.

Shoichi, S. (1986). The U.S. and the Japanese electronics industry: Competition and cooperation. *Issues in Science and Technology, 2*(3), 53–60.

Wataru, N., Boulton, W., & Pecht, M. (1991). *The Japanese electronics industry.* Chapman and Hall/CRC.

Wolf, P. (2001). *The medium of the video game.* University of Texas Press.

ENDNOTES

[1] https://www.dentons.com/en/insights/guides-reports-and-whitepapers/2023/april/17/video-games-industry-report#:~:text=The%20video%20game%20industry%20has,of%20over%20US%24370%20billion.

[2] https://www.gdcvault.com/play/1018024/The-Emerging-Landscape-of-African .

[3] https://peopleofcolorintech.com/front/10-game-development-studios-in-africa-have-come-together-under-one-umbrella-to-unify-the-continents-gaming-sector/

Chapter 4
COVID-19 and the Practice of Digital Diplomacy in Ghana

Josephine Aboagye
University of Cape Coast, Ghana

Isaac Nunoo
iD https://orcid.org/0000-0001-5759-3669
University of Cape Coast, Ghana

ABSTRACT

This chapter examines the practice of digital diplomacy in Ghana during the COVID-19 pandemic. The chapter analyses how diplomatic activities were conducted, the challenges encountered during the pandemic and what the future looks like for digital diplomacy in Ghana. The study also tests whether COVID-19 increased the use of technology and digital diplomacy in Ghana. Using the mixed method approach, the findings reveal that COVID-19 increased digital diplomacy and the use of digital platforms in Ghana. Some of the challenges encountered were institutional challenges, internet issues and lack of privacy. The study also reveals that the future of digital diplomacy in Ghana is promising and a combination of traditional and digital diplomacy would enhance Ghana's diplomacy.

INTRODUCTION

From the beginning of the twenty-first century, nations like the United States, the United Kingdom, Canada, and Australia have relied heavily on the use of the digital trend making it easier to perform diplomatic duties across the globe albeit with some challenges. COVID-19 constituted a historic global crisis (Adesina, 2022). No pandemic has had such an impact on the world since the Spanish Influenza of 1918. Technology has always had a profound impact on international relations, and digitalization is having a significant impact on diplomacy (Ozili & Arun, 2020). Diplomacy's reliance on modern communication technology extends right to its essential functions, such as negotiation, representation and communication. Studies acknowledge that almost every country on the globe has, in some way, imitated the use of technology in conducting diplomacy (Verrekia, 2017). However, several obstacles

DOI: 10.4018/978-1-6684-9962-7.ch004

arise, particularly in developing nations, making full implementation impossible. Global economies and communities were impacted by the COVID-19 pandemic, which could have long-lasting effects on social and political structures.

In the immediate aftermath of the pandemic, the World Health Organisation and some Western commentators were skeptical about the capacity of African countries south of the Sahara to contain the virus. This skepticism was also echoed internally due to Ghana's inadequate health infrastructure and personnel. However, the government of Ghana through the Ministries of Health and Information instituted some measures to contain the disease. In March 2020, the government announced several immediate measures to detect, contain, and stop the spread of the disease. These included closing schools, churches, mosques, and other places of worship on March 16; prohibiting entry for visitors from nations where there had been more than 200 confirmed cases of COVID-19 within the previous 14 days on March 17; requiring all visitors to the country to remain in quarantine for 48 hours (Kenu et al., 2020). Also, on the 22nd of March the government moved further to close the country's borders; and partially locked down Accra, Kasoa, and Kumasi on March 30, 2020 (Kenu et al., 2020).

Meanwhile, the steps taken to contain it have impacted our daily activities that attempt to maintain a work-life balance, and research practises. Consequently, long-planned intergovernmental gatherings were cancelled, transportation was suspended, and borders were closed. For instance, in Ghana, while there was a lockdown, all centres and venues where people massively gathered were closed temporarily. The COVID-19 epidemic in Ghana, in the same manner, caused alarm since it left millions of Ghanaians trapped around the world and prevented them from returning home. This made some embassies and consulates employ a lot of digital methods to communicate with them. Thus, the COVID-19 pandemic has highlighted the reliance of the modern world on digital tools and technology. The pandemic-related gathering restrictions forced diplomacy, to go online, with many activities being moved online. The disruptive aspect of the epidemic has, in many respects, contributed to the emergence of novel virtual decision-making processes. Traveling restrictions made platforms like Zoom, Google Meet, and others became crucial for international conferences, diplomatic meetings, and decision-making (Adesina, 2022). African nations have embraced digital diplomacy through these virtual methods during this turbulent time. In May 2020, the AU successfully conducted a three-week online seminar titled "Silencing the Guns" (Adesina, 2022). Also, during the pandemic, African leaders—such as President Cyril Ramaphosa of South Africa, the chairman of the African Union, have held many virtual meetings to discuss several topical continental issues with stakeholders.

In Ghana the president, Nana Akuffo Addo communicated via digital platforms such as YouTube, Facebook Live, and Twitter (now X) among others. These channels were used to spread information on repatriation, economic concerns, and health advisories. The government of Ghana also employed these digital platforms to express support for the populace that the global pandemic had forced indoors. These programmes contributed to improving ties between the public and the government. Embassy and foreign affairs organisations continued to face intense pressure to deliver precise and current data about the pandemic.

Individuals participated in public debate, and their replies to social media posts (in the form of likes, comments, shares/retweets, calls to action, and trending hashtags) were viewed as indicators of engagement and involvement. Several other diplomats and dignitaries even decided to address the people live on X and Facebook. As a result of the COVID-19 pandemic, digital diplomacy is now notably supporting states in conveying their foreign policies to domestic and international audiences (Bjola & Manor, 2018). However, before the worldwide pandemic, little thought was paid to the significance of 'Internet diplomacy.' With this analogue economic and administrative orientation, the sudden but mandatory digital switchover introduced a challenging operational environment for individuals in both private and public spheres. Today, digital diplomacy is critical to advancing a diplomatic agenda (Seib, 2013). A good illustration of this is the social media site X, which is particularly beneficial for communication and information sharing by diplomats, leaders of the state, and other people in prominent positions (Vadrot et al., 2021).

While there is no specific literature on Ghana emphasising its use of digital diplomacy during or in the post-COVID-19 era, this study however examines how state and non-state actors have employed digital diplomacy in the COVID-19 and post-COVID-19 eras. The argument is that although the Ghanaian population is still moving slowly towards a digital life, the necessities of the time forced a quick migration to what was previously seen as a distant goal. The study addresses three main objectives: first, to ascertain whether the COVID-19 pandemic increased digital diplomacy in Ghana. Second, to examine the impacts of the COVID-19 pandemic on the conduct of diplomacy in Ghana and thirdly, to assess the challenges and prospects of digital diplomacy in Ghana. Also, the researchers test for two hypotheses: COVID-19 increased the use of technology among Ghanaians and COVID-19 has increased the use of digital diplomacy in Ghana. The study proceeds by reviewing previous scholarship on digital diplomacy and diplomacy and the differences between public diplomacy and digital diplomacy. It continues by reviewing relevant studies of technology use and more recent studies explicitly focused on the benefits and challenges of digital diplomacy and the impacts of the COVID-19 pandemic on digital diplomacy. This is followed by a description of the research methodology. The next section presents the results and the discussion. This is followed by the conclusion and recommendations for supporting adaptation to virtual diplomacy and more hybrid engagement.

LITERATURE REVIEW

Diplomacy and Digital Diplomacy

Since digital diplomacy is relatively a new concept, there are not many studies that have been done on it, especially in Africa. Scholars such as Melissen (2013) and Roberts (2007), first explain the transformation from traditional diplomacy to public diplomacy. These sources highlight how public diplomacy reshaped foreign policy discussions from engaged only among elites to now occurring between government officials and foreign publics (Kluver & Banerjee, 2013). However, there is debate amongst scholars as to how new digital technologies are affecting public diplomacy. Scholars such as Hocking and Melissen (2015) and Kamen and Murray (2013) point out two different theories, with some scholars believing digitalisation enhances public diplomacy, and others claiming that it completely alters it into something new, known as digital diplomacy.

Diplomacy has developed over the years and is now assisted by technology. As a result, people now refer to digital diplomacy when discussing diplomacy in terms of vocabulary. This section will attempt to explore the concept of 'Digital Diplomacy,' which has been raised in the literature by numerous scholars. Researchers and practitioners have defined digital diplomacy in a variety of ways to mean various things relating to how countries communicate with one another in the realm of foreign policy formation and action (Sotiriu, 2015). Over time, diplomacy has changed to accommodate advancements in technology, global politics, and cultural values. In the past, city-states and empires have utilised diplomacy to settle disputes. Diplomacy in the ancient world was focused on close ties between messengers and monarchs. It was the primary tool used to carry out the broad tactics, plans, and objectives of foreign policy. In other words, it is the time-honoured method used by governments to protect specific or broader interests, such as the lowering of tensions between or within themselves (Cohen, 1998). It works to maintain peace and attempts to foster goodwill towards other nations and peoples to secure their collaboration or, in the absence of that, their neutrality (Adesina, 2017).

The concept of diplomacy has evolved from the traditional understanding of peaceable dialogue and dealings between political actors and institutions to modern diplomacy starting with "the so-called Westphalian state system" after the "Peace of Westphalia" in 1648. The concept now has a multilayered connotation representing a formulation and execution of external politics, tactics of foreign affairs, global negotiations and specialised activities being undertaking by the diplomats (Benk, 1997: 255-262; Nicolson, 1988/1939: 3-5, cited in Krajnc, 2004). Vukadinovic defines diplomacy as a key approach to realising foreign politics and serves as the normal avenue for global engagements (1994: 109). It is accountable for handling the interstate and other nonstate thespians interactions usually via the aid of "advice, design and realization of foreign politics, coordinating and ensuring specific and wide interests" (Barston, 1988, cited in Krajnc, 2004: 2). Diplomacy is an emollient that lubricates foreign politics (Olson, 1991: 60).

In addition to these conceptual studies, some scholars like Bjola and Manor (2018) have examined the use of digital diplomacy by various governments and organisations. For example, their work investigated the use of digital diplomacy by the British Council, a cultural organisation that promotes British culture worldwide. They discovered that the British Council uses digital diplomacy to strengthen its public diplomacy activities, particularly through engagement with young people and the promotion of cultural diversity and understanding. Adesina (2017) confirms that states now use digital diplomacy as a key weapon to advance their objectives and improve their standing abroad. States can influence public opinion abroad and connect directly with overseas audiences using digital diplomacy. Also, it gives states a way to interact with foreign publics in a two-way manner, which can promote mutual respect and understanding.

The inclusion of the general public in the diplomatic process, according to Sotiriu (2015), has increased the number of parties involved in international diplomacy, ranging from state-to-state relations to international organisations and non-governmental organisations. He adds that recently, this has extended to the general public, whom diplomats have sought to approach to strengthen communication or to elicit opposing viewpoints on a variety of problems (Sotiriu, 2015). This means that the management, analysis and dissemination of information of interest to foreign ministries has an impact on a variety of relationships that have been established between the government and various aspects of society. For minor governments and non-state entities, which can have constrained resources and diplomatic presence, digital diplomacy is especially crucial. They can get around some of the obstacles that traditional diplomacy faces and make a bigger effect on the world stage by utilising modern technologies. Small states, for instance, can interact with expatriate communities and promote their culture, tourism, and trade using social media platforms (Bennett & Segerberg, 2013).

Public Diplomacy and Digital Diplomacy

Public diplomacy and digital diplomacy are two terms that have gained increasing attention in the field of international relations and diplomacy. While there is some overlap between the two concepts, there are also some significant differences. Certain academic journals on public diplomacy highlight how public diplomacy has shifted foreign policy conversations away from elites and towards government officials and foreign audiences. Scholars disagree, however, on how new digital technologies are changing public diplomacy. Some researchers believe digitisation improves public diplomacy while others believe it entirely transforms it into something new called digital diplomacy (Verrekia, 2017). Public diplomacy, a type of diplomatic activity, has been defined as a 'tool used by nations to comprehend cultures, attitudes and behaviour; foster and oversee contacts; influence thoughts and mobilise actions to advance their interests and values' (Melissen, 2013, p. 436). Sotiriu (2015, p.36) believes that 'putting the public at large into the diplomatic equation has also enlarged the range of actors involved in global diplomacy, from state-to-state relations to international organisations and international non-governmental organisations.'

More recently, this has comprised average citizens, whom diplomats in most circumstances have relied on for their reinforcing, or differing views on several subjects (Sotiriu, 2015, p. 36). The efforts of governments and other entities to connect with and influence the foreign public to promote their own goals and values are referred to as public diplomacy. Public diplomacy encompasses the development and transmission of ideas, information, and culture in a way that impacts the views and behaviours of international partners and governments (Snow & Taylor, 2009). Digital diplomacy, on the other hand, is a more contemporary concept that refers to the use of digital technologies and social media platforms in diplomacy. Digital diplomacy is the use of digital technologies and communication tactics to advance foreign policy goals and impact international relations (Zaharna, 2010).

The fact that digital diplomacy is a subset of public diplomacy is one of the key distinctions between the two. Digital diplomacy, as opposed to public diplomacy, focuses exclusively on the use of digital technologies and social media platforms. Public diplomacy includes a variety of communication and cultural activities. Digital diplomacy has the potential to reach a bigger and more diversified audience than conventional means of public diplomacy, which is another significant difference. Internet diplomacy can provide direct, immediate, and unfiltered access to global audiences without the use of intermediaries or conventional censors (Seib, 2013). Moreover, digital diplomacy can encourage increased participation and two-way contact between governments and foreign publics. Digital diplomacy has the potential to increase chances for discussion, exchange, and collaboration between governments and civil society players in different parts of the world (Kluver & Banerjee, 2013).

Despite the considerable overlap, public diplomacy and digital diplomacy are separate ideas with different emphases and methodologies. While digital diplomacy focuses especially on the use of digital technology and social media platforms to practice diplomacy and communicate with foreign audiences, public diplomacy generally refers to a spectrum of communication and cultural events intended to influence the foreign public.

The Use of Digital Diplomacy by Non-State Actors

The exclusive domain of governments and state actors has long been held when it comes to digital diplomacy. The use of digital technology for diplomatic purposes by non-state actors, such as NGOs, civil society organisations, the media, academics, and private businesses, has increased recently. NGOs have been instrumental in using digital diplomacy to further their goals. The use of social media by NGOs as a diplomatic tool is one such example. NGOs have reportedly used social media platforms like X and Facebook to interact with their audiences, spread awareness of their causes, and promote policy change, according to Khamis et al. (2017). NGOs have used digital technology to engage in diplomatic activities like attending UN conferences and making written remarks to the UN (Khamis et al., 2017.

According to Bennett and Segerberg (2013), digital diplomacy has helped civil society organisations (CSOs) enhance their lobbying and advocacy in international affairs. Bennett and Segerberg (2013) found that civil society organisations have used social media and other digital platforms to amplify their voices, increase awareness of their causes, and connect with decision-makers in their study of civil society organisations and digital diplomacy.

Digital diplomacy has also been used by businesses to further their objectives in international relations. Adesina (2017) showed that firms use digital technology to engage with overseas markets, promote their brands, reach a wider customer audience, and affect policy results in a study of corporate diplomacy. Some multinational and private companies, for instance, use social media to advertise their goods and services in foreign and local markets, while business associations employ technology to advocate for favourable laws and regulations (Adesina, 2017). Thanks to digital diplomacy, businesses can now reach a wider audience globally and exert new types of influence over policy outcomes.

To be sure the use of digital technology in diplomacy by non-state actors has also presented several difficulties, such as establishing credibility and legitimacy and resisting restrictions and surveillance. Non-state actors must be proactive in addressing these challenges to ensure the effectiveness of digital diplomacy in the post-pandemic world.

Benefits and Risks of Digital Diplomacy

Postmodern diplomacy is nothing new. The idea of sending messengers to a foreign state is old and was common in many communities, however, it has taken on several forms in contemporary times (Chan, 2017). While digital diplomacy does not take the role of traditional diplomacy, it can effectively and quickly increase the state's involvement in international affairs. It is now a requirement for implementing foreign policy. Digital diplomacy is incredibly helpful in attaining foreign policy goals, expanding global alignment, and persuading people who have never visited any embassies throughout the world. Direct public interaction and the involvement of non-state actors urge nations to use social media and digital diplomacy as a way to build or strengthen alliances in a changing world while preserving their legitimacy (Deos, 2015). With the use of digital diplomacy, governments may interact and communicate more productively and effectively, lowering costs and improving results. Governments may engage and collaborate in real-time utilising digital tools such as instant messaging, email, and video conferencing, increasing efficiency. According to Hocking and Melissen's (2015) study, digital diplomacy enhances efficiency by promoting more effective communication and collaboration across nations, lowering costs and improving results. Governments, for example, can hold meetings via video conferencing instead of travelling, lowering expenses and increasing productivity.

Another benefit of digital diplomacy is enhancing fast and effective communication. The advancement of national interests may frequently be aided by a quick understanding of various events. Digital technologies are very helpful for acquiring and analysing information regarding diplomatic activity as well as for communicating quickly in emergencies (Adesina, 2017). Governments can use them to assess how global changes might impact their nation. For instance, during a crisis, embassies can create WhatsApp groups including the ambassador, consular officer, publicity secretary, employees who gather information on the internet; diplomats from the headquarters, and staff workers who respond to online questions from citizens. This team can function as a crisis management cell, gathering data in real-time, making choices, and sharing information. Digital technologies, on the other hand, enable the free expression of disagreements with certain issues and reduce authoritarianism for those who live under authoritarian regimes that seek to restrict their ability to communicate both domestically and internationally (McGlinchey, 2017). A study by Seib (2013) found that digital diplomacy improves engagement by enabling governments to communicate with their people and other governments, which fosters diplomacy and builds connections between nations. For instance, governments can interact with their citizens and other governments through social media. This fosters diplomacy and improves relations between nations (Seib, 2013).

Low cost is a vital element of digital diplomacy that has been covered in several areas of academic studies. For nations with limited resources or low budgets, using digital technology and social media platforms to reach broad audiences is an appealing alternative to using traditional diplomatic tactics (Adesina, 2017). The cost of using new technologies is continually declining because of ongoing technological advancements. International experience demonstrates that those who invest in digital diplomacy tools may benefit greatly from their effective use of them.

While digital diplomacy offers numerous advantages, it also comes with several risks that could have an impact on how diplomatic activities are conducted and how they turn out. The potential for misunderstandings and misinterpretations is one of the major risks connected to digital diplomacy (Rashica, 2018). A Pew Research Centre study found that face-to-face communication often has more complexity and context than digital communication channels like social media platforms (Hocking & Melissen, 2015). As a result, diplomatic statements sent via digital channels might be readily misunderstood, which can result in misunderstandings and even conflicts. For instance, North Korea mistook a tweet from US President Donald Trump in 2017 that threatened it with fire and fury as a declaration of war (Rashica, 2018). In terms of international affairs, such misunderstandings might have serious repercussions.

The loss of confidentiality and privacy is another problem posed by digital diplomacy (Bradshaw, 2015). When used for diplomatic purposes, digital tools like email and social media platforms run the risk of disclosing private data to unauthorised people and/or organisations. Sensitive material that affected the 2016 US presidential election was made public due to the hacking of the Democratic National Committee's email system (Nance, 2016). Similarly, using social media platforms for diplomatic purposes runs the risk of disclosing private data to foreign intelligence services and jeopardising national security. According to a report by the Brookings Institution, digital diplomacy has increased the potential of cyberattacks on diplomats, hence nations must invest in cybersecurity initiatives to mitigate this risk (Friedman, 2013). Digital diplomacy also carries the danger of relying too heavily on technology. The overreliance on technology that might result from using digital tools for diplomatic purposes is a false sense of security. This may lead to a failure to prepare for and respond to emergencies and other unforeseen occurrences that might call for human involvement.

Based on the above limitations, it is safe to conclude that digital diplomacy provides several advantages, including enhanced public participation abroad and remote diplomacy, but it also poses several difficulties or dangers to nations' diplomatic efforts.

THEORY

The COVID-19 epidemic has had a significant impact on how people interact, share information, and adjust to quickly changing situations worldwide. The increased reliance on social media platforms as instruments for information sharing, communication, and overcoming the problems provided by the epidemic has been a crucial component of this transition. The Technology Acceptance Model (TAM) is the theoretical framework that might be particularly helpful in understanding the dynamics of how people adopted and utilised social media platforms during the pandemic.

Since it was introduced more than 25 years ago, there has been a sizable amount of study on the technology acceptance model (TAM), which demonstrates the model's popularity in the industry. The TAM model, created by Davis in 1989 and based on psychology theories of planned behaviour and reasoned action, has become a crucial tool for comprehending the factors that determine whether or not people would embrace the use of emerging technologies (Gwala & Mashau, 2023). To create future understandings and include these new technologies, it is essential to theorise while understanding the perspectives of users and usage trends on social media websites like X, Facebook, Snapchat, Instagram and LinkedIn.

TAM should be revisited to address such studies on the factors impacting social media usage behaviour (Rauniar et al., 2014). According to TAM, perceived usefulness and simplicity of use are important elements that affect consumers' intentions to embrace and use a technology, which in turn affects actual utilisation. Although TAM has minimal explanatory value for purposes relating to specific systems, it has been routinely utilised to gauge consumer acceptance of broad technologies (Gwala & Mashau, 2023). The TAM model illustrates how people adopt and utilize technology. This theoretical foundation is based on the idea that when people are introduced to new technology, three main factors affect their choice of when and how to use the said technology (Mugo et al., 2017). The first determinant is its perceived usefulness, the second is the perceived ease of use, and the third determinant is user attitude towards usage (Mugo et al., 2017). The perceived usefulness is the degree to which a user believes that using a particular system would enhance his or her job performance. Conversely, perceived ease of use refers to how much a person feels that utilising a specific technology would need little effort. Alternatively, it refers to the extent to which users believe a particular technology to be superior to other alternatives (Mugo et al., 2017). In this case, the public's and diplomats' perception of a mobile and social media device's utility is based on how easily and quickly it can be used to acquire local and international news. TAM places strong emphasis on perceived utility, or people's expectations of how utilising technology would improve their lives. Social media platforms were essential for spreading updates on COVID-19, safety precautions and community support during the pandemic. Users found these platforms helpful for interacting with others who were going through similar problems, sharing their experiences, and getting access to real-time news. Social media platforms were widely adopted because of the idea that they provide useful and pertinent information.

The perception of social media platforms' usability was a key factor in their uptake during the COVID-19 pandemic. Lockdowns and other restrictions made it difficult for people to engage physically, so they looked for other ways to keep connected and informed. User-friendly and intuitive social media platforms like Facebook, Twitter, and Instagram become available resources for keeping in touch with loved ones and finding information. These networks were appealing in an uncertain period because of how easy it was to register, submit updates, and interact with content. The ease with which students can adopt and use electronic machine gadgets, for instance, will facilitate their use of digital information resources, make studying easier for them, and have an effect on their academic activities in daily life. In other words, employing technology to retrieve information automatically makes it simpler than doing it through more laborious manual means. Today, students receive lecture notes on their laptops, tablets, or even smartphones before the lecture rather than writing them down. Students save time since they can access their notes from anywhere, even if they are absent. Youths often absorb technology more quickly than adults do (Bjola & Manor 2022).

According to TAM, the ambition to utilise a technology precedes its actual application. People who believed social media to be simple to use and helpful for remaining updated and connected appeared more likely to make use of these platforms throughout the pandemic till the present. People read news items, shared updates, and participated in debates about the pandemic, showing that this objective was put into practice. As a result, TAM contributes to the explanation of the use of social media in pandemic-related contexts. The COVID-19 pandemic's effects drove many Ghanaians to adopt a digital lifestyle as a coping strategy. The argument is that although the Ghanaian population is still moving slowly towards a digital life, the necessities of the time forced a quick migration to what was previously seen as a distant goal. TAM aids in understanding the individual-level factors that affected the adoption and usage of social media.

The epidemic brought home the significance of technology in influencing human behaviour and society's capacity to respond to unanticipated problems. Social media, which was previously a tool for amusement and social engagement, became a vital source of knowledge, connections, and resilience. Researchers can develop a more nuanced understanding of the complicated interaction between individual choices and more general technical factors in times of crisis by considering TAM. This method adds to our understanding of technological adoption and societal change and provides insightful theoretical background for this study.

METHODOLOGY

The study adopted the mixed method approach, employing both quantitative (the administration of questionnaires) and qualitative (in-depth interviews) data. A direct comparison of the quantitative data with the qualitative findings was done to establish conformity and/or difference to gain a more realistic picture of any correlation between COVID-19 and the practice of digital diplomacy (Plano Clark & Ivankova, 2016). The study's population involved diplomats, academics, and entrepreneurs.

The quantitative method examined how Ghanaian non-state actors (Entrepreneurs and Academics) used technology in their daily affairs before, during and after the pandemic. This relates to the hypothesis of whether COVID-19 sparked the ardent use of technology or not and reinforces the broader picture of the challenges and prospects of the use of technology and digital diplomacy. The study population was chosen using a multi-stage sampling procedure for the quantitative data and the respondents were chosen at random. A total number of six hundred and eighty-eight (687) respondents (quantitative data) were chosen using the convenience sampling method. This was complemented by the qualitative method which employed the purposive sampling technique to select diplomats, and practitioners from embassies and consulars abroad, the Ministry of Foreign Affairs and Integration (MFARI), the Ministry of Information (MOI), and the Ministry of Parliamentary Affairs (MOPA), for in-depth interviews to know how diplomatic activities were conducted during the pandemic. Because there was no existing sampling frame for all academics and entrepreneurs in Ghana, the study employed the convenience sampling technique to select these respondents. However, to get a sample size quite representative enough, a total of six hundred and eighty-seven (687) respondents were selected. The study used 8 respondents in all for the qualitative data upon reaching a saturation. According to a study by Guillemin et al. (2015), a researcher reaches saturation when no new concepts or relevant information emerges with additional interviews. The study also examined the use of social media by these stakeholders during the initial COVID-19 epidemic and looked into whether the MFARI and diplomats interacted with the public at home and abroad using social media instead of just the latter. The study argued that even though diplomacy is frequently aimed at foreign people, COVID-19 fostered the former as well as the practice of domestic digital diplomacy (Bjola & Holmes, 2015). It also magnified the use of digital technology in Ghana in general on the part of both state and non-state actors.

The information acquired in the field were thoroughly assessed, processed, and analysed. SPSS version 23 was used to process the statistical data. The study employed descriptive and inferential analysis to learn about the respondents' characteristics and test the hypothesis. A content analysis technique was employed to reflect the research design, as frequency tables and graphs were used to depict some of the findings. The content analysis model entails incorporating and interpreting several data sources to derive meaning based on the study objectives (Yin, 2004).

The qualitative data were transcribed verbatim and arranged by themes such as the benefits, challenges, prospects and impacts of digital diplomacy in Ghana. These topics were explored based on the research objectives, and they served as the foundation for analysing field data. Thematic analysis is a technique for identifying, analysing, and reporting patterns within data, according to Braun and Clarke (2016). Theme analysis is more flexible and appropriate for the bulk of research and hypotheses, according to Braun and Clarke (2016). It is also suitable for inquiries that depend on people's perspectives or experiences. Data acquired from secondary sources, such as journals books, reports and newspapers were used to further define some of the study's research objectives and for comparative purposes.

Respondents' anonymity was duly respected. Moreover, the study adhered to all the ethical guidelines established by the University of Cape Coast, Ghana. The reliability and validity of the acquired data for the research relied on the audit trail methodology. Cassel et al. (2018) state that the audit trail approach requires the researcher to provide a detailed account of the procedures followed, starting from data collection, and continuing through to data analysis. The researcher also employed investigator triangulation to guarantee the validity of the obtained data. Triangulation, as described by Pansiri (2005), is a technique used to validate data by including multiple perspectives. These methods effectively eliminate any biases and inaccuracies during the data analysis process. In this work, the transcribed data and the generated themes were examined by colleagues to ensure that the analysis aligned with, rather than contradicting, the acquired data.

RESULTS AND DISCUSSION

Demographic Features

An examination of the information obtained from the respondents via a survey questionnaire and one-on-one interviews is presented in this section. The section provides demographic information on the respondents, as well as a descriptive analysis and data findings. To display the findings and explain the answers to the research questions posed, tables, bar graphs, and pie charts have been provided.

Analyzing the demographic features of respondents, the study first discussed the personal data of the respondents which comprise their gender, age, educational level, respondents' employment status, and area of expertise of respondents. Three hundred and eighty-five of the respondents, representing about 56% were males, whereas three hundred and two (44%) were females. The majority of the respondents, representing 31% of the respondents were between the twenty-six and thirty years inclusive. Approximately, only seven percent (7%) of the respondents were above forty-five years but none were above sixty years. This demonstrates that the youth were the majority who answered the questions showing that the use of digital platforms is mostly common among the younger generation. The majority of the respondents, three hundred and eighty-two, representing fifty-five percent (55%) were unemployed. Thirty-five percent were employed, and the other nine percent (9%) were self-employed. For those who were either employed or self-employed, the predominant work stated were Administrator, Teacher, Project manager, Banker, Accountant, fashion/event designer, and business (trade). Out of the six hundred and eighty-seven respondents who participated in the study, about seventy-three percent of the respondents were in academia whereas about twenty-seven percent (one hundred and eighty-seven of the respondents) were entrepreneurs. Out of the five hundred respondents who indicated that they were in academia, forty-five were lecturers whereas four hundred and fifty-five were students. The distribution of the platform used by the entrepreneurs is presented in Figures 1.

Figure 1. Platforms used by entrepreneurs

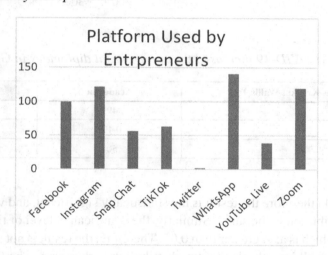

Figure 1 presents the platforms used by entrepreneurs. For the entrepreneurs, the predominant platforms used were WhatsApp, Instagram, Zoom and Facebook. X was the least utilized.

Figure 2 presents the platforms used by the academics. Zoom was the most utilized in the field of academia. Other platforms utilised by the academics are Microsoft Meet, Ulesson and Instative (see Figure 2).

COVID-19 and Digital Diplomacy in Ghana

The first objective of this study was to test the hypothesis that the Covid-19 pandemic increased the use of digital diplomacy. In other words, this section focused on examining the influence of the COVID-19 pandemic on the conduct of diplomacy in Ghana.

Table 1 presents the Kruskal-Wallis test result which sought to test the hypothesis that the distribution of "Covid-19 increased the use of digital diplomacy" is the same across categories. That is, each of the respondents in academia or entrepreneurship agrees that the COVID-19 pandemic necessitated the use of digital diplomacy. For those in academia, the significance level of the test statistics is 0.492

Figure 2. Platforms used by academics

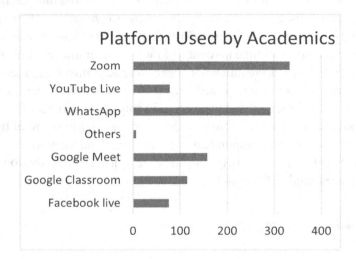

Table 1. Hypothesis test (COVID-19 increased the use of digital diplomacy in Ghana)

Independent Samples Kruskal-Wallis Test	Academia	Entrepreneurship
Test Statistic	499	186
Asymptotic Sig. (2-sided test)	0.492	0.486
Total Observation	500	187

which is greater than 0.05 therefore the result is not statistically significant, and we fail to reject the null hypothesis that the distribution is the same. Similarly, the significance level of the test statistics for the entrepreneurs is 0.486 which is also greater than 0.05. Therefore, the result is not statistically significant, and we fail to reject the null hypothesis that the distribution is the same. The findings reveal that the COVID-19 pandemic increased the use of technology in both academia and the entrepreneurial field. This is because, many persons encountered limits in their working practices, much like many people all around the world. Parents had to work from home while homeschooling their children as a result of the closure of schools and other services, and some company owners had to discover alternative ways to operate their companies. Many respondents including academics and businesspeople who were asked how COVID-19 affected their jobs noted how expensive but beneficial the situation was. This corroborates the findings of Vadrot et al. (2021) which assert that despite the difficulties that both state and nonstate players encountered during the lockdowns, they persisted in communicating with other actors by using various communication tools in place of face-to-face meetings. The results from the interview also corroborated similar results. The MFARI mentioned intimated that since the beginning of the pandemic, they continued to have online meetings with stakeholders.

Social media platforms have billions of active users worldwide, making them a powerful channel for diplomats to reach a broad and diverse audience. Because we had the systems already in place all we had to do was to get them running and make some few additions if countries did not have the kind of system.

So, during the pandemic, most of our meetings with other missions were on Zoom and Microsoft Teams and this helped us respond to the global demand easily. Diplomatic missions can disseminate information, share updates, and engage with citizens, foreign audiences, and the international community more effectively (Interviewee 8, 02/05/2023).

Also, respondent 2 stated that,

…the president used his social media pages (@NAkufoAddo) and other major news networks across the country to deliver messages or address the Ghanaian populace. Even now we see that whenever there is an issue, for example, the Russian-Ukraine crisis sparked, he used his social media platforms to address it. This shows that you do not have to be there in person to communicate your sentiments but can go through the digital system.' (Interviewee 7, 02/05/23).

Another respondent also intimated that:

These digital tools offer diplomats and governments several advantages that enhance their diplomatic efforts and communication with various stakeholders. Social media allows governments to promote their country's culture, values, and policies to a global audience. By sharing positive stories and engaging in public diplomacy efforts, diplomats can influence public opinion and build their country's soft power (Interviewee 2, 07/06/23).

Another respondent stated that several ministries, especially the tourism ministry had promotional videos of tourist attractions, festivals, and events posted on their websites so that people from all over may go there and watch them and get a sense of the Ghanaian culture. Additionally, they have developed pages for practically all of Ghana's tourist attractions. According to Cull (2020), digital diplomacy will remain crucial for fostering global collaboration and solving pandemics and climate change issues.

The study further adopted the Independent Samples Median test, Independent Samples Mann-Whitney U Test, and Independent Samples Kolmogrov-Smirnov Test to check the level of agreement in the response between those in academia and the entrepreneurs using the median of their ranks. The results are presented in Table 2. The test statistics for all the tests are statistically significant indicating that the two categories agree that the COVID-19 pandemic necessitated the use of digital diplomacy, which was made possible by an increase in the use of technology. This corroborates Seib's (2021) finding that the pandemic has disrupted traditional diplomatic procedures, such as face-to-face meetings, diplomatic banquets, and other types of traditional diplomacy.

Figure 3 presents the distribution of independent-sample median test

Figure 4 presents the distribution of independent-sample Mann-Whitney U test

Figure 5 presents the distribution of independent-sample Kolmogorov-Smirnov test

The null hypothesis for each of the tests states that the distribution or median is the same across the area of expertise. For each of the tests employed, the significance value obtained, that is, 0.73, 0.108 and 0.244 for the Independent Samples Median test, Independent Samples Mann-Whitney U Test, and Independent Samples Kolmogorov Smirnov Test respectively were greater than 0.05 (. This implies that the test result is not significant and we fail to reject the null hypothesis. The findings indicate that across all the areas of expertise (academia and entrepreneurship), Covid-19 increased digital diplomacy. These results are also highlighted in figures 3, 4 and 5.

Figure 3. Distribution of independent-sample median test

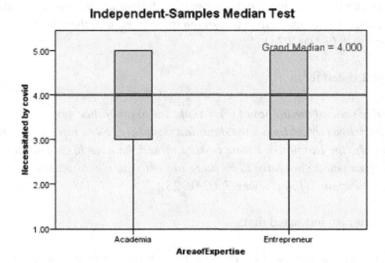

Figure 4. Distribution of independent-sample Mann-Whitney U test

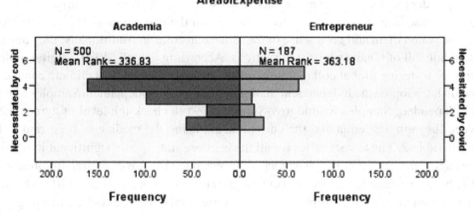

Covid-19 and the Use of Technology

The objective of this section was to test the hypothesis on whether or not the Covid-19 pandemic had an effect on the use of technology (i.e., hypothesis two).

The paired sample t-test presented in Table 3 was used to compare whether there was a statistical difference in the use of technology before the COVID-19 pandemic and after the COVID-19 pandemic. For each of the areas of experience, the significance level (0.00; 0.00) was less than 0.05, indicating that there was a statistical difference in the use of technology before and after the COVID-19 pandemic.

Figure 5. Distribution of independent-Sample Kolmogorov-Smirnov test

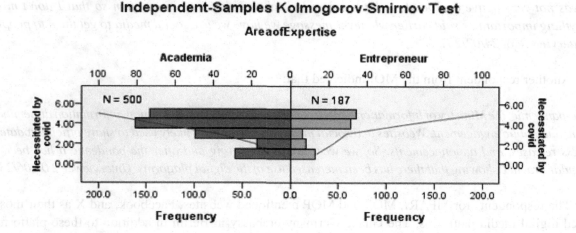

Table 2. Level of agreement in responses

	Independent Samples Median Test	Independent Samples Mann-Whitney U Test	Independent Samples Kolmogrov_Smirnov Test
Test Statistic	3.211	1.609	1.025
Asymptotic Sig. (2-sided test)	0.73	0.108	0.244
Total N	687	687	687

Table 3. Paired sample test (Covid-19 propelled the use of technology)

	Academia	Entrepreneurship
Test Statistic	-13.211	-9.358
Asymptotic Sig. (2-sided test)	0.00	0.00
Total N	500	187

Therefore, it can be concluded that COVID-19 had an effect on the use of technology among entrepreneurs and people in academia. This corresponds with the finding of Adesina (2017) who argues that firms use digital technology to engage with overseas markets, promote their brands, and affect policy results in a study of corporate diplomacy. Multinational companies, for instance, utilise social media to advertise their goods and services in foreign markets, while business associations employ technology to advocate for favourable laws and regulations (Adesina, 2017). Digital technologies have been embraced by non-state players, such as enterprises, people, and civil society organisations, to further their objectives in international relations. These actors may now reach a larger audience, make their views heard, and affect policy results in novel ways thanks to digital media. Also, for the state actors,

One respondent highlighted that:

I was not very active on social media but now I check the platforms more often so that I don't miss anything important as said earlier whatever message we have we use social media to get them to people (Interviewee 6, 24/02/23).

Another respondent from the MOI indicated that:

Pre-pandemic, the Ministry of Information likely used technology for communication, information dissemination, and public engagement. Websites and social media platforms were likely used to share official updates, press releases, and announcements. So, we were active but during and after the pandemic it has been a regular practice showing that there has been increased use of the digital platforms' (Interviewee 2 07/06/23).

The respondents for MFARI, MOI, and MOP mentioned websites, Facebook, and X as their most-used digital media platforms. The Ghana Germany embassy in Berlin in addition to these platforms used Instagram in their line of work. Also, the MOI used a YouTube channel when the trend demand was overwhelming. Newsletters and information regarding events and upcoming programs were sent via email. This agrees with the survey by (Bjola and Manor, 2022)), that SMEs impacted by the COVID-19 problem had a high awareness of social media and a strong inclination to embrace it as a channel for marketing their goods and engaging with consumers. The epidemic, according to Bjola and Manor (2022), has also compelled diplomats to rely increasingly on digital technologies for public diplomacy, negotiation, and communication.

The Challenges of Technology Usage and Digital Diplomacy

Figure 6 shows the overall distribution of challenges selected by respondents. 347 and 345 of respondents selected either 'It is costly', or 'Not effective (network problems)' respectively. This suggests that a

Figure 6. Challenges of digital diplomacy

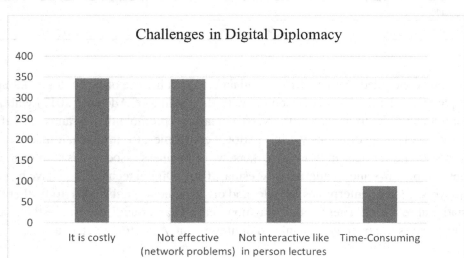

significant portion of respondents found this challenge to be noteworthy. While 201 and 89 respondents chose 'Not interactive like in-person lectures' and 'Time-consuming.'

From the figure, "costly, ineffective (network problems)", or both were the most frequently selected challenges, while all the challenges mentioned were chosen by the fewest respondents. This implies that the respondents face issues of finance (i.e., it is costly) and have network problems, which does not make it effective. Also, the entrepreneurs mentioned that they become victims of fraudulent acts on the said platform they ply their trade or ventures on, which does not make it effective. Furthermore, addiction to online platforms raises time management issues as compared to the traditional ways of plying their trades.

Objective three was to assess the challenges and prospects of the use of technology and digital diplomacy in Ghana. The data indicate that a substantial portion of respondents found cost and network problems to be significant challenges in the context of digital diplomacy and use of technology in general. Therefore, it serves as empirical evidence supporting the assessment of challenges that need to be evaluated in the broader discussion of the prospects and obstacles facing digital diplomacy and the use of technology in Ghana in general. The findings from the academics and the entrepreneurs reinforce the general problems associated with the use of technology in Ghana and thus, highlights the potential challenges of digital diplomacy in Ghana.

For the state actors, the major challenges were institutional factors, internet issues, online impersonation, and privacy invasion. For example, one of the respondents stated that:

Some of the old officers who did not grow up with computers went to the business secretariat where they were taught to use typewriters. However, when we phased out the traditional and manual way of doing things some of them found it difficult to adjust to the use of computers, so they still relied on human capacity. We also have other officers here who never bothered to learn the digitised systems, so they also struggled in delivering their duties. Consequently, some superiors preferred traditional media to digital media and therefore did not pay much attention to the work when it had to do with the use of technology (Interviewee 5, 2/06/23).

In corroboration, another official disclosed:

…sometimes too we have situations whereby when you are looking for information it doesn't come in fast due to slow internet services. when there is an urgent situation and our internet is down or information is not available, contacting the government for information becomes difficult (Interviewee 3, 01/05/23)

This was further accentuated by Interviewee 5 thus:

For instance, with our embassy in Ethiopia where the internet is very unstable, sometimes you would have to wait for a while when the internet went off. Due to that, when there was an emergency, it was difficult to immediately send mail across. We also have the challenge of electricity … Again, in Nigeria for instance, where they do not have a constant and reliable electricity supply what it means is that when the lights go off you would have to use a generator. Now between the time the lights go off and when the generator is put on if there is anything you are doing you could lose it or when transmitting any document, it might not go through. (Interviewed, 2/06/23).

Another respondent highlighted that numerous phoney accounts were impersonating their organisations, and occasionally spreading untrue information about them.

People impersonate the institutions and even some of the heads of institutions and ministries. The unfortunate thing is that they use such accounts to defraud people, kidnap people, collect money and even harm others. Some people sadly fall prey to these accounts. These days even verified accounts are sold so verification is a challenge too (Interviewee 3, 01/05/23).

...these fake accounts are created as representatives engaging on social media platforms and may inadvertently post content that is perceived as offensive or controversial by other nations or communities. Such incidents can lead to diplomatic crises and damage international relations (Interviewee 8, 02/05/2023).

It is also important to note that:

Scepticism about the authenticity and reliability of digital information can affect the credibility of diplomatic efforts conducted through online channels. For instance, during COVID-19, people were posting their own COVID-19 updates on social media which contradicted what the office of the president and Ghana Health Service were updating or posting on their pages (Interviewee 7, 02/05/23).

According to Interviewees 3 and 4,

The spread of fake news, misinformation, and disinformation can easily occur in the digital realm. False narratives and rumours can quickly go viral, leading to misunderstandings and diplomatic tensions (Interviewee 3, 01/05/23); sometimes you realise some people try to post unnecessary things on Facebook and will be tagging us making when there is no need (Interviewee 4, 10/7/23).

Thus, despite the numerous prospects of digital diplomacy, there are equally eminent challenges that plague its efficiency both in terms of technological determinism and technical know-how.

Future of Digital Diplomacy

Among the 687 respondents, 676 respondents projected the direction and fate of digital diplomacy in the future through the views they shared. The views were divided into positive and negative categories with a few having mixed or no views on the future of digital diplomacy. The majority of respondents gave an affirmative response, which implies that positivity is the dominant view among respondents. The high affirmative response indicates a high level of optimism among the surveyed individuals regarding the future of digital diplomacy. This suggests that the majority of respondents believe that digital diplomacy holds promising and potential benefits for the country or the international community. This agrees **with** Bjola and Manor's (2022) finding that with the ongoing development of technology, digital diplomacy has a bright future, opening up fresh opportunities for collaboration, diplomacy, and resolution of disputes in the twenty-first century. While the majority view is positive, it is important to note that some of the respondents gave a negative response. This minority group may have concerns, reservations, or scepticism such as fraud, cost, and internet issues among others about digital diplomacy. These concerns should not be dismissed and should be considered in the development and implementation of digital diplomacy strategies. State actors emphasised that traditional diplomacy cannot be eradicated with digital diplomacy. They were more disposed toward traditional in-person meetings.

Physical meetings are important because negotiations often take place on the sidelines of international gatherings, through impromptu discussions between global leaders at tea or lunch breaks, or a chance encounter in the corridor or rest room and so on. Also, physical meetings provide an opportunity for participants to observe and interpret the body language and emotions of the parties, which may help in decision making. As of now, traditional diplomacy cannot be discarded because that is what we know and have been using and I do not think digital diplomacy can fully overtake traditional diplomacy (Interviewee 8, 02/05/23).

Another reiterated:

When we have online meetings, people are not able to express their sentiments because they do not see yours. However, in my perspective, digital diplomacy has come to stay and will just help make traditional diplomacy easier, less costly and very quick (Interviewee 8, 02/05/23).

Furthermore, one respondent added:

Again, I was asked one day if I could have meetings at home then why travel and I mentioned that it makes a difference when diplomats make eye contact. When I negotiate with you, I don't just listen to you but look at your body language. I use some kind of intimidation to look at you because I kind of want to have the upper hand since it is a negotiation, so it is never the same when you have it virtually. However, for now, I think diplomats are trying to have a hybrid where you come together at the same venue while others may contribute virtually. But I tell you technology can never replace human-to-human contact (Interviewee 6, 24/02/23).

CONCLUSION

Technology's introduction to diplomacy has made it easier to negotiate agreements. Technological innovations like Emails, Skype, AI and cell phones, to name a few, have altered the nature of diplomacy and facilitated communication. The technology world changed, and so did the diplomatic procedure. This led to the development of new fields in diplomacy like electronic or digital diplomacy and the idea of e-governance, which was made feasible by the usage of digital media platforms like websites, Facebook, X, Instagram, YouTube, Google Meet, and WhatsApp among others.

This research highlighted the immense opportunities presented by digital diplomacy and the potential for social media platforms to enhance the goals of public diplomacy. It set out to assess how Ghana conducted its digital diplomacy during the COVID-19 pandemic and focused on the tactics, strategies and competencies of the MFAs, as well as the challenges that come with digital diplomacy and how the future is seen to determine whether Ghana's digital diplomacy during the pandemic was effective and efficient. According to the study, African governments like Ghana have not been left out of the development of digital diplomacy, which was first used in industrialised nations like the USA, the UK, and Russia among others to communicate with both local and foreign audiences. Ghana as a nation has acknowledged the value of technology. Ghanaian Ministries, States and Departments have also embraced digital media platforms and do have a presence there. The COVID-19 pandemic forced many nations, including Ghana, to seize the opportunity and aggressively pursue their foreign policy goals and opportunities for a positive outlook through the development of websites, blogs, and the use of social media platforms like Facebook, X, Instagram, YouTube, Zoom, Google plus and others. While the study focused on Ghana's digital diplomacy during the pandemic, it suggests that despite the great potential, Ghana's MFAs have to put in more effective strategies to help push its foreign policy goals. The study recommends that there should be proper education on the use of digital platforms and MFAs should be more proactive and innovative to help confront the many challenges that will come up in their application of digital diplomacy.

REFERENCES

Adesina, O. S. (2017). Foreign policy in an era of digital diplomacy. *Cogent Social Sciences*, *3*(1), 13. doi:10.1080/23311886.2017.1297175

Adesina, O. S. (2022). *Africa and the future of digital diplomacy*. Brookings Institution.

Bennett, W. L., & Segerberg, A. (2013). *The logic of connective action: Digital media and the personalization of contentious politics*. Cambridge University Press. doi:10.1017/CBO9781139198752

Bjola, C., & Holmes, M. (Eds.). (2015). *Digital Diplomacy: Theory and Practice*. Routledge. doi:10.4324/9781315730844

Bjola, C., & Manor, I. (2018). *From digital tactics to digital strategies: Practicing digital PD*. CPD Blog.

Bjola, C., & Manor, I. (2022). The rise of hybrid diplomacy: From digital adaptation to digital adoption. *International Affairs*, *98*(2), 471–491. doi:10.1093/ia/iiac005

Bradshaw, S. (2015). Digital diplomacy-# not diplomacy. *Canadá: Centre of international governance innovation*.

Braun, V., & Clarke, V. (2006). *Thematic Analysis*. Psych. http;//www.psych.auckland.ac.nz

Cassell, C. A., Drake, M. S., & Dyer, T. A. (2018). Auditor litigation risk and the number of institutional investors. *Audit.: J. Pract. Theory*, *37*(3), 71–90.

Chan, S. (2017). *Mediations on diplomacy: Comparative cases in diplomatic practice and foreign policy*. E-International Relations Publishing.

Cohen, R. (1998). *Reflections on the new global diplomacy* [Innovation in diplomatic practice, studies in diplomacy]. MacMillan Press Ltd.

Cole, B., & Wolfe. (2018). Twiplomacy Study 2018.

Cooper, A., Heine, J., & Thakur, R. (2013). Introduction: the challenges of 21st-century diplomacy.

Cull, N. J. (2020). The future of digital diplomacy after COVID-19. *Place Branding and Public Diplomacy*, *16*(3), 135–139.

Deos, S. A. (2015). *Digital diplomacy & social capital*. University of Otago.

Gwala, R. S., & Mashau, P. (2023). COVID-19 and SME adoption of social media in developing economies in Africa. In S. Qalati, D. Ostic, & R. Bansal (Eds.), *Strengthening SME performance through social media adoption and usage* (pp. 133–152). doi:10.4018/978-1-6684-5770-2.ch008

Hocking, B., & Melissen, J. (2015). *Diplomacy in the digital age. Clingendael*. Netherlands Institute of International Relations.

Holmes, M. (2015). *The future of digital diplomacy. Digital diplomacy: Theory and Practice*. Routledge.

Kamen, L. & A. (2013). The digital diplomacy potential. *KMWorld, 22*(6).

Kenu, E., Frimpong, J., & Koram, K. (2020). Responding to the COVID-19 pandemic in Ghana. *Ghana Medical Journal, 54*(2), 72–73. doi:10.4314/gmj.v54i2.1 PMID:33536675

Kluver, R., & Banerjee, I. (2013). *Digital diplomacy: Theory and practice*. Routledge.

Krajnc, P. K. (2004). Public Diplomacy: Basic Concepts and Trends. Teorija in praksa –. *Theory into Practice, 41*(3-4), 643–658.

McGlinchey, S. (Ed.). (2017). *International Relations*. E-International Relations Publishing.

Melissen, J. (2013). Public diplomacy. In A. Cooper, J. Heine, & R. Thakur (Eds.), *The oxford handbook of modern diplomacy* (pp. 436–452). Oxford University Press.

Mugo, D., Njagi, K., Chemwei, B., & Motanya, J. (2017). The technology acceptance model (TAM) and its application to the utilization of mobile learning technologies. *British Journal of Mathematics & Computer Science, 20*(4), 1–8. doi:10.9734/BJMCS/2017/29015

Nance, M. (2016). *The plot to hack America: How Putin's cyberspies and WikiLeaks tried to steal the 2016 election*. Simon and Schuster.

Olson, W. C. (1991). *The theory and practice of international relations*. Prentice Hall.

OziliP. K.ArunT. (2020). Spillover of COVID-19: Impact on the global economy. Available at SSRN 3562570. doi:10.2139/ssrn.3562570

Pansiri, J. (2005). Pragmatism: A methodological approach to researching strategic alliances in tourism. *Tourism and Hospitality Planning & Development, 2*(3), 191–206. doi:10.1080/14790530500399333

Plano C., V. L. & Ivankova, N. V. (2016). *Mixed methods research. A guide to the field*.

Rashica, V. (2018). The benefits and risks of digital diplomacy. *See Review, 13*(1), 75–89. doi:10.2478/seeur-2018-0008

Rauniar, R., Rawski, G., Yang, J., & Johnson, B. (2014). Technology acceptance model (TAM) and social media usage: An empirical study on Facebook. *Journal of Enterprise Information Management, 27*(1), 6–30. doi:10.1108/JEIM-04-2012-0011

Roberts, W. R. (2007). What is public diplomacy? Past practices, present conduct, possible future. *Mediterranean Quarterly, 18*(4), 36–52. doi:10.1215/10474552-2007-025

Seib, P. (2013). *Real-Time Diplomacy: Politics and power in the social media era*. Speech.

Snow, N., & Taylor, P. M. (2009). *Routledge handbook of public diplomacy*. Routledge.

Sotiriu, S. (2015). *Digital diplomacy: Between promises and reality. Digital diplomacy: Theory and practice*. Routledge.

Vadrot, A. B., Langlet, A., Tessnow-von Wysocki, I., Tolochko, P., Brogat, E., & Ruiz, S. C. (2021). Marine biodiversity negotiations during COVID-19: A new role for digital diplomacy? *Global Environmental Politics, 21*(3), 169–186. doi:10.1162/glep_a_00605

Verrekia, B. (2017). *Digital diplomacy and its effect on international relations*. Sage Publications.

Vukadinović, R. (1994). *Diplomacija. strategija političnih pogajanj (Diplomacy. strategy of political negotations)*. Arah Consulting.

Wekesa, B., Turianskyi, Y., & Ayodele, O. (2021). Introduction to the special issue: Digital diplomacy in Africa. *South African Journal of International Affairs, 28*(3), 335–339. doi:10.1080/10220461.2021.1961606

Yin, R. K. (2004). *Case Study Research: Design and Methods* (2nd ed.). Sage.

Zaharna, R. S. (2010). *Battles to bridges: US strategic communication and public diplomacy after 9/11*. Palgrave Macmillan. doi:10.1057/9780230277922

ADDITIONAL READINGS:

Aguirre, D., Manor, I., & Ramos, A. (2018). The digitalization of public diplomacy: towards a new conceptual framework. Revista *Mexicana de Política Exterior*, (113),7-13. https://revistadigital.sre.gob.mx/images/stories/numeros/n113/introduccion113.pd

Anderson, M. S. (1993). *The rise of modern diplomacy, 1450-1919*. Longman.

Bjola, C., & Manor, I. (2020b). *Digital diplomacy in the time of the coronavirus pandemic*. USC Center on Public Diplomacy. https://uscpublicdiplomacy.org/blog/digitaldiplomacy-time-coronavirus-pandemic

Manor, I., & Pamment, J. (2022). At a crossroads: Examining Covid-19's impact on public and digital diplomacy. *Place Branding and Public Diplomacy, 18*(1), 1–3. doi:10.1057/s41254-021-00249-9

Melissen, J., & Caesar-Gordon, M. (2016). Digital diplomacy and the securing of nationals in a citizen-wentric World. *Global Affairs, 2*(3), 321–330. doi:10.1080/23340460.2016.1239381

Sevin, E. (2018). Digital diplomacy as crisis communication: Turkish digital outreach after July 15. *Revista Mexicana de Politica Exterior, 113*(May–August), 1–14.

Wilder-Smith, A. (2021). COVID-19 in comparison with other emerging viral diseases: Risk of geographic spread via travel. *Tropical Diseases, Travel Medicine and Vaccines, 7*(3), 1–11. doi:10.1186/s40794-020-00129-9 PMID:33517914

KEY TERMS AND DEFINITIONS

COVID-19: Coronavirus disease 2019 (COVID-19) is an infectious disease caused by severe acute respiratory syndrome coronavirus 2 (also known as SARS-CoV-2).

Digital Diplomacy: The strategic use of digital technologies and communication tactics, including social media platforms to advance foreign policy goals and impact relations between governments and civil society across the globe.

Diplomacy: All forms of dialogue and relations between political actors, institutions as well as nonstate actors and nonpolitical institutions with the chief aim of advancing a nation's national interests; a group or institution's goal through either persuasive or coercive efforts or both.

Diplomat: A person appointed by a state or an intergovernmental institution to conduct diplomacy with both states and nonstate actors including international organizations.

Ghana: A west African country, located on the coast of the Gulf of Guinea

Non-State Actor: An individual or organization, not formally aligned with any state, yet wields substantial (political) influence.

Public Diplomacy: A type of diplomacy encapsulating strategic utilisation of cultures, attitudes and behaviour; encourage and superintend conducts; influence perceptions and assemble national resources to advance a nation's interests and values.

Technology Acceptance Model: An information systems theory that explains how people are encouraged to accept and utilize new technology.

Chapter 5
Technical Considerations for Designing, Developing, and Implementing AI Systems in Africa

Getachew H. Mengesha

https://orcid.org/0009-0007-0685-126X

Addis Ababa University, Ethiopia

Elefelious Getachew Belay

Addis Ababa Institute of Technology, Ethiopia

Rachel Adams

Research ICT Africa, South Africa

ABSTRACT

This study explores technical considerations for designing, developing, adopting, and using AI-based systems in Africa. Africa did not benefit as intended from the first three industrial revolutions. Cognizant of this fact, the continent is now expected to be aware of and ready to tap into the opportunities created by AI and the Fourth Industrial Revolution to fix chronic problems connected to efficiency while minimizing the unintended consequences AI might pose. Data for the study was gathered through focus group discussion (FGD), key informant interview (KII), and document review. The outcome of the study reveals that AI model adoption issues, AI biases, AI data availability, security, and privacy, AI model accuracy and quality, and AI resources have emerged as major technical considerations for adopting and using AI in the African context. The chapter provides valuable insights that would serve as input for policy formulation and AI capacity development endeavors.

DOI: 10.4018/978-1-6684-9962-7.ch005

INTRODUCTION

Nations around the world are showing a vested interest in tracking developments in AI and other emerging technologies. This is because AI and the associated technologies have the potential to disrupt and transform prevailing socio-economic activities. Scholars from around the world argue that AI would be a key driver of the fourth industrial revolution which is believed to be the next stage of socio-economic development. For various reasons, Africa could not benefit as intended from the first three industrial revolutions. A more advanced AI technology emerged before the continent could optimally use the conventional ICTs improve the backbone telecom infrastructure and develop the necessary human resources. In connection to this, Ade-Ibijola and Okonkwo (2023) point out that a lack of technical skills, uncertainty, lack of structured data, lack of government policies, ethics, and user attitude are likely to impede the adoption of AI-based technologies in Africa.

Artificial intelligence (AI) is a relatively new phenomenon in the socio-economic arena of Africa. As the continent is entangled with various challenges, rapidly emerging technologies like AI have grabbed less attention from policymakers in Africa. However, currently, a consensus seems to have been reached among the scientific community, policymakers, and African leaders recognizing that AI has enormous potential to fix some of Africa's chronic problems connected with efficiency and optimal use of resources. Among others, Africa's agricultural and healthcare sectors generate a huge amount of data that can be used to solve critical problems in these sectors.

Applications of AI that center on solving real-world problems affecting the lives of millions of ordinary people are supposed to bring about meaningful transformation in the continent (Nayebare, 2019). So far, most AI applications adopted in the cited sectors are developed in Western countries (Berhane, 2020). However, some initiatives are underway in different parts of the continent to foster local AI capacity development. For instance, Arakpogun et al. (2021) disclosed that inspired by AI Labs developed with the support of leading tech companies such as IBM in Kenya, Google Lab in Ghana and other labs established by initiatives of universities like the University of Cape Town and Makerere University, around 100 AI start-ups have emerged across Africa.

Although AI-related matters appear daunting to Africa given the current state of technological development and readiness to adopt such cutting-edge technologies, it is imperative to understand the potential impact of the technology and reduce potential marginalization that would occur because of disregarding this technology. To this end, studies have been undertaken to understand the current state of the continent in terms of adopting the technology. For instance, Baguma et al. (2022) propose an AI readiness index for Africa. The authors argue that the readiness index signals the continent's capacity to harness AI for socio-economic development. tied to the proposal of Baguma et al. (2022), other scholars such as (Arakpogun et al. 2021; Ade-Ibijola & Okonkwo 2023; Butcher et al. 2021) have expressed the challenges AI might pose in Africa and the opportunities the technology might bring to rectify the continent's persistent problems. These scholars contend that AI tends to amplify the historic structural inequalities among African citizens causing a disproportionate level of access to resources such as education, employment, healthcare services, etc., and eventually tends to transfer existing inequalities into a digital space and create a further digital divide. Particularly, Sub-Saharan African (SSA) countries are likely to encounter another round of digital divide due to inadequate telecom infrastructure, unreliable electric power, unaffordable smartphones, and a lack of digital skills (Arakpogun et al., 2021). AI involves the fusion of a range of technologies. This will entail another challenge of regulations and governance as most SSA governments lack the required institutional capacity, skills, and financial resources. The inability to regulate dynamic and complex AI technologies can lead to unintended consequences surrounding citizens' privacy and data security and eventually threaten national security (Arakpogun et al., 2021).

This chapter intends to shed light on major technical considerations for designing, developing, adopting, and using AI systems in Africa. To this end, first, an attempt has been made to highlight AI initiatives underway across the continent. The review we conducted revealed some promising achievements in terms of establishing ICT parks that would pave the way for innovation and investment in the sector. Second, lessons learned from the innovative use of mobile network systems to expand financial services and the huge data resources generated presents fertile ground to test AI technologies in the African financial sectors. Third, the study explored the overall technical capabilities and backbone infrastructural development across the continent and identified resource gaps, and pinpointed areas that need substantial improvement. Fourth, the study assessed the initiatives of the Ethiopian government, AI developers, and experts in the domain using Focus Group Discussion (FGD) and Key Informant Interviews (KII) and has identified major areas that need improvement to adopt and implement AI-based technologies.

The remaining part of the chapter is structured as follows. First, a review of related works is presented. Second, the study procedures, data collection, analysis techniques, and the main results of the study are presented. Third, discussion and reflection on the main findings of the study is provided. The fourth section provides concluding remarks of the study.

LITERATURE REVIEW

An extensive review of the literature was conducted to situate the chapter within the broader discussion of African place in the rapidly evolving AI global space. The chapter draws insights from the data collected in Ethiopia and from the African Observatory on Responsible AI project reports. The chapter employed the AI readiness index for Africa proposed by Baguma et al. (2023) together with AI challenges pointed out by Kiemde & Kora (2020) as a reference to validate the themes that emerged in this chapter. The readiness index sets out the following dimensions: Vision, Governance and Ethics, Digital Capacity, Size of the Technology Sector, Research and Development, Education, Infrastructure, Data Availability, employment in Data Science and AI roles, and Gross Domestic Product-Per Capita Purchasing Power Parity. Similarly, Kiemde and Kora (2020) identified access to large amounts of data, quality of data, data storage, and data regulation policy, broadband energy infrastructure, skilled workforce, and relevant education system as major challenges to AI adoption and use in Africa. This chapter reports six dimensions: AI model adoption, AI biases, AI data availability, AI security and privacy, AI model quality, and AI resources as salient technical considerations for the adoption and deployment of AI in Africa. These dimensions are fully congruent with the AI readiness index proposed by Baguma et al. (2023) and crucial factors identified by Kiemede and Kora (2020).

Existent literature by and large amplifies the significant impact of AI on global economic development and strongly insists Africa leverage this technology to tap opportunities being created and mitigate potential technological hazards that may arise. As Africa is battling with unique challenges historically rooted in the political and socioeconomic arena, the impact of AI on the continent needs to be framed and analyzed in the context of Africa (Wairegi, Omino, and Rutenberg, 2021). Other lines of inquiry magnify the infrastructural and technological impediments and advocate the establishment of an AI ecosystem that integrates AI resources across the continent (Arakpogun et al., 2021, Russo et al. 2021).

Although AI adoption and diffusion rates across Africa are slower, the past five years has have witnessed commendable initiatives for implementing AI in key economic sectors such as agriculture, health, finance, defense, environmental protection etc. Ade-Ibijola & Okonkwo (2023) cite several examples of AI adoption in Kenya, Nigeria, South Africa, Uganda, and Ethiopia for healthcare, agriculture, public transportation, government services, wildlife conservation, crop monitoring, financial services etc. Furthermore, Chat bots in Kenya and Nigeria have started providing healthcare services to people without the need to visit health facilities. In agricultural, sector interactive chat bots have started delivering real time insights to farmers (Francesc et al. 2019). In South Africa, Mama Money and Mukuru are used to swiftly transfer money across different parts of Africa. Innovative applications of Chat bots such as KUDI provide financial services to low-income people in Nigeria. Such innovative adoption of AI-based solutions is projected to increase in Africa and AI is the next technological wave that will garner wider acceptance and adoption (Ade-Ibijola & Okonkwo, 2023).

Despite all the observed initiatives and great optimism in AI, basic elements needed for AI adoption, use, and governance are still missing across most African countries (Hassan, 2023). In view of bridging the existing AI capacity gap, Hassan presents the African Master's in Machine Intelligence (AMMI) program at the African Institute for Mathematical Sciences (AIMS) as a commendable case. The author considers AMMI program as an important showcase for it focuses on developing AI talent and capacity within the continent bringing together various stakeholders to chart AI vision for Africa. In doing so, AMMI envisions scaling up the program to develop a pan-African AI program rooted in the African context.

While endeavors are underway to leverage AI solutions to realize socioeconomic developments, recently some African governments have shown interest in acquiring and using Unmanned Aerial Vehicles (UAV) commonly called drones to improve socioeconomic activities and enhance surveillance and military operations. Haula & Agbozo (2020) report on a few cases of drone adoption for agriculture, aerial photography, migration and border control, surveying and mapping, search and rescue missions, mail and parcel delivery, oil and gas exploration, inspections of public facilities, public safety, weather forecasting etc. Particularly, UAV use for military operations is garnering prominence in many African countries. Military Africa (2022) mentions Nigeria as one of the forerunners in terms of employing drones for surveillance and military operations against Boko Haram terrorist insurgents that are severely threatening Nigeria's national security. Military Africa (2022) reported that Nigeria has acquired several drones from China, Israel, and the United States and also attempted to develop its own drones. Capitalizing on the intensity of attacks Boko Haram is waging on Nigerian security forces and to thwart the massive atrocities it is committing on innocent civilians, Matthew et al. (2021) propose a more advanced UAV equipped with a neural network learning algorithm, infrared cameras, sensors, communication systems to effectively gather information and attack targets. Similarly, Agence France Presse (2022) reported that combat drones proved to be a decisive weapon which helped the Ethiopian government to turn the tide of the war against the Tigrayan People Liberation Front (TPLF).

Military Africa (2022) expresses the growing concern regarding the lack of transparency and accountability surrounding drone operations and the widespread reports of civilian casualties due to the inappropriate use of drones. Furthermore, as the technology evolves and matures many countries will decide to adopt combat drones, which is likely to escalate the arms race among African countries. To minimize the negative consequences of military drones, government entities, civil society groups, and international organizations need to work together to ensure transparency and accountability. Further, AI-powered technologies are being used to undertake a sophisticated cyber offense. To minimize the unintended consequences of AI technologies, Nobels (2023) suggests counter-offensive measures to thwart ever-increasing AI-based cyberattacks that target key business organizations and government entities. To this end, comprehensive ethical and legal frameworks are required to regulate the adoption and use of AI-based technologies.

In summary, AI adoption and use initiatives underway across Africa reveal favorable outcomes and AI is expected to yield major socioeconomic transformations in Africa. However, Africa is entangled with major capacity and infrastructural predicaments to ensure take full advantage of it. Country-wise socioeconomic disparities also exist among SSA countries with a corresponding different level of technology uptake. This calls for proactive measures from continental and regional organizations, like the African Union to examine the potential impact of AI, particularly on SSA countries. As a pivotal continental organization, the African Union should spearhead the process of developing relevant regulatory frameworks and AI policies that all member states adopt and comply with. Unfortunately, AU seems constrained by structural and capacity limitations and is not able to chart relevant digital policy for Africa (Yilma, 2023). The author further notes that the unprecedented pace of emerging digital technology has prompted AU to reimagine its role and reconstitute a dedicated body mandated to formulate a comprehensive digital policy for the continent.

METHODS AND KEY FINDINGS

The study aims to elicit relevant facts on ongoing initiatives regarding AI-based systems adoption, development, implementation, and use. Information for the study was gathered through Focus Group Discussion (FGD), Key Informant Interview (KII), comprehensive literature and policy document review, and workshop reports. A series of FGD and KII sessions were conducted with directors and department heads at Artificial Intelligence Services (AIS) and AI system developers in Addis Ababa, Ethiopia in a period ranging from July 8, 2021, to July 17, 2021. Moreover, relevant facts were drawn from HSRC/Facebook AI workshops held in Johannesburg, South Africa on April 7 and September 30, 2021, respectively. The two workshops brought together research teams from seven African countries including Egypt, Kenya, Nigeria, South Africa, Uganda, Ethiopia, and Zimbabwe. These teams have been conducting independent interdisciplinary academic research in the field of AI, ethics, and human rights with the funding support of Meta, former Facebook. A thematic analysis was conducted using Scribbr[1] thematic analysis approach. The study team members first conducted coding independently and presented the codes they came up with for discussion sessions. After an in-depth discussion, 239 initial codes were identified. The study team refined the codes through a series of discussion sessions and eventually about 64 themes emerged and categorized along four thematic areas: AI ethical principles and frameworks, AI policies and guidelines, psychosocial issues and AI design and adoption, and technical considerations for designing and implementing AI. This chapter focuses on technical considerations for designing and implementing AI. The themes that emerged regarding AI technical issues are summarized and presented in Table 1.

Table 1. AI technical issues

No	Themes	Descriptions
1	AI model adoption issues	This theme embraces various issues like the desire to adopt high-quality pre-trained models from around the world and introduce AI-based systems in critical economic sectors
2	AI biases	The theme refers to issues related to model explicability and testing.
3	AI data availability, security, and privacy	This theme relates to data acquisition or digitization, data access, sharing, and use of policy and procedures
4	AI model accuracy and quality	AI model quality and accuracy and strategies to reduce model biases. The theme also refers to model contextualization, quality, accuracy, & dynamism,
5	AI resources	The theme deals with backbone telecom infrastructure, hardware, and software technologies, data resources, and skills needed for the adoption and use of AI.

DISCUSSION

This chapter explores the quest surrounding the design and development of technically robust, acceptable, and legally compliant AI systems. Despite the widespread optimism regarding the potential impact of AI to transform the socioeconomic status of Africa and the rest of the world, enduring concerns related to the unintended consequences of AI are still a persistent political, legal, and human right discourse around the world. This section provides an in-depth discussion over the themes that emerged from the empirical data. The following themes have been considered as core technical dimensions for designing and implementing AI-based systems in Africa.

AI Resources

This thematic area involves infrastructural and data resources, human resources, ICT park development initiatives, and the need for the establishment of a digital ecosystem to speed up ICT developments in Ethiopia and other sub-Saharan African countries.

Infrastructural and Data Resources

Generally, Africa is labeled as a resource-short continent with poor basic infrastructures. Infrastructure development such as telecom, electric power, water supply, and transportation systems are deemed to be the top priorities for Africa (Calderón, Cantú, and Chuhan-Pole, 2018). A comparison of telecommunications density across regions shows that despite a surge, sub-Saharan Africa is still far behind other regions.

Modern technological innovation has provided other forms of telecommunications connectivity: the number of Internet users and fixed broadband subscriptions (both normalized by population) are proxies for telecommunications density other than phone lines. Internet density—as measured by the number of users per 100 people—in Sub-Saharan Africa in 2015 was only 16.7, less than that of any other benchmark region. Another indicator of Internet penetration is the number of fixed broadband subscriptions per 100 people. Over the past two decades, many improvements have been observed in mobile network coverage and Internet access throughout the continent. The global economic system is being transformed into a digital economy, where e-services are at the center of economic activities. Calderon et al. (2018) noted a positive association between infrastructure quality, data availability, Internet bandwidth, and per capita income.

AI and the associated machine learning systems require high-speed data communication systems and a robust backbone telecom infrastructure. So far, Internet bandwidth and data transmission capabilities are limited in many African countries. Still, most African countries are trailing with intermittent Internet connectivity and unstable power supply. Massive improvement of the backbone telecom Infrastructure is needed to successfully adopt and use AI systems in various spheres of economic activities. Kilaba and Manasseh (2020) note that the African telecom industry has witnessed exponential growth over the past few years. However, most population in rural areas is still covered by 2G signals with no access to broadband services, which is an important driving force for the development of the digital economy. This economic system is rapidly evolving around the world. Therefore, without high-quality network communication, competitive engagement in the digital economy is impossible.

Concerning the current status of mobile network communication systems, Kilaba and Manasseh (2020) state that although great strides have been observed with the subscription of the 4G network in Africa in the year 2018, 4G is not yet the dominant technology in Africa. They further recommend that telecom regulators in Africa should consider the timely release of the 700MHz digital dividend spectrum to extend high-speed mobile broadband coverage across urban and rural areas and keep an eye on the emerging 5G/6G networks that will likely arrive in Africa soon for its deployment will need a significant amount of contiguous spectrum blocks.

The telecommunications (hereafter telecom) infrastructure would continue to serve as a foundation for this emerging digital economic system. AI is supposed to play a significant role in this growing digital economic system. Both the digital economy and AI technologies presuppose the presence of sound telecom infrastructure. Africa is supposed to acquire state-of-the-art telecom infrastructure to take advantage of the emerging digital economy and rapidly evolving AI technologies. Therefore, Africa needs to set a strategy to bridge the broadband network coverage gaps by investing in the telecom sector over time (Kilaba, and Manasseh, 2020).

Similar to basic telecom infrastructure, data is a critical driver in AI-based innovations and technology platforms. Africa lacks well-refined and reliable quality data making difficult the deployment of efficient AI solutions (Gandomi and Haider, 2015). However, the current digital interactions demand an enormous amount of organized multimedia datasets. These authors further note that a clear regulatory framework that promotes sound data collection systems and appropriate use of data is missing in most African countries. This is likely to cause customers' privacy and security breaches when AI-based solutions are widely deployed.

AI systems require big data to extract important patterns and insights. Except for the agricultural, health, telecom, and financial sectors, big data is not readily available in African key socio-economic sectors. Related to the problems of data, Blackwell, Damena, and Tegegne (2022) posit that the absence of a big dataset affects the research outcome of Natural Language Processing (NLP) researchers in Ethiopia. The authors note that NLP researchers in Bahir Dar, Ethiopia create their own datasets, which tend to be small as compared with similar research being done in the English language with big datasets using deep learning methods. Therefore, the research outcome in Amharic language will remain incomparable with English particularly when identical algorithms are applied in both languages in an experimental machine learning research.

In recognition of infrastructural, data, and computing resource constraints, the Ethiopian government has embarked on various capacity development endeavors through the government agency it established to oversee, regulate, and support AI-related projects and initiatives. In this regard, respondents at Ethiopian Artificial Intelligence Service (AIS) stated the following:

AIS strives to rectify computational resource constraints by building AI infrastructure and data resources (Interview 1).

Further, respondents noted that AIS is attempting to pool together AI resources forging partnerships with private organizations, higher educational institutions, and overseas partner countries.

Human Resource Development

Advanced technologies like AI require well-trained skilled computer professionals. Skills gaps and a lack of infrastructure are deterring African countries from utilizing the potential of AI to improve public services, meaningfully contribute to AI development, and innovate AI-based goods and services (Sey and Mudongo, 2021). Technically well-versed interdisciplinary teams drawn from diverse fields of study such as social science, law, business, linguistics, etc. are highly needed to embark on socio-technical studies surrounding AI. Acknowledging relevant AI skill deficiencies in Africa, Butcher et al. (2021) suggest developing AI skills through formal education, on-job training, and through promoting the notion of independent and lifelong learning. They further note that revisiting African secondary and tertiary school curricula is imperative to build competencies in science, technology, mathematics, and critical thinking skills in humanities and social sciences.

Africa requires home-grown talent and professional AI developers to harness the technology to rectify the continent's chronic problems. However, many African countries still lack a sustainable supply of technical experts in the field (Sampene et al., 2022). Locally developed AI solutions are believed to be relevant in terms of solving local problems witnessed in a wide range of sectors. To this end, the continent needs to take advantage of its large youth population to build capacity in AI. This demands high-quality training in the field. Universities and colleges in Africa are expected to launch degree programs in AI and to include AI in the curriculum of basic sciences and technology disciplines. Nayebare (2019) has cited some AI capacity development endeavors across the continent. Among others, he cited Makerere University as an example for establishing AI labs. Concerning the general population's acquaintance with ICTs, Arakpogun et al. (2021) state that a lack of digital skills is one of the reasons for the occurrence of digital divides in Africa.

Global tech giants such as Google and Facebook have begun supporting local AI initiatives. For instance, Nayebare (2019) states that to provide developers with the tools they need to conduct their research and build solutions, Google has established an AI lab in Ghana. Similarly, the African Institute of Mathematical Sciences (AIMS) in Rwanda partnered with Facebook to start graduate studies in machine learning. Unless Africa develops the capacity to create AI rooted in local community needs and interests, it will remain dependent on foreign software and infrastructure (Birhane, 2020). Respondents echoed AI skill shortages during the FGD and KII sessions and suggested capacity development strategies. The AI system developers we interviewed made the following remark:

Ethiopia needs a comprehensive educational system overhaul to develop the analytical and problem-solving skills of students at all levels. He added that it is imperative to enhance the designing and problem-solving skills of young graduates in the computing domain instead of overly focusing on syntax or coding (FGD1).

Similarly, participants of the FGD have acknowledged AI skill shortages throughout Ethiopia and disclosed various strategies to enhance the capacity of AIS staff and contribute to capacity development initiatives at a national level. Accordingly, participants stated the following:

We have been running various on-job short pieces of training to develop the capacity of AIS experts. Furthermore, we are working with selected higher educational institutions in Ethiopia on curricula development to launch AI degree programs at undergraduate and graduate levels (FGD 2).

In summary, Africa requires a well-trained, technically and intellectually competent workforce capable of deploying the technology and equipped with the desired skill to critically assess the outputs of AI systems and knowledge to govern the deployment of AI-based systems. Moreover, AI and machine learning technologies are transforming the workplace and demanding new skill sets. Therefore, Africa needs to prepare its workforce for future work, in this globalized economic system, anticipating economic mobility opportunities for its citizens (Muhammad, Umar, & Adam, 2023). Potential job losses that may emanate with the wider deployment of AI appear a worrisome issue in the continent struggling to create job opportunities for millions of unemployed citizens. However, job losses could be compensated by investing in new skills needed to fill jobs created by AI technology (Sampene et al., 2022).

ICT Park Development Strategies

Silicon Valley modeled ICT park development initiatives are underway in many countries such as Nigeria, Kenya, and Ethiopia (Nayebare, 2019; Birhane, 2020). Furthermore, countries like Rwanda, Nigeria, and Ethiopia have recently exhibited commendable AI-related activities. For instance, Nigeria established a National Agency for Research in Robotics and Artificial Intelligence (NARRAI), whose focus is to train Nigerians to use skills in AI to quicken the country's economic growth (Nayebare, 2019). Similarly, Ethiopia has established ICT park and AI research development center that would spearhead innovations in AI by drafting relevant policies and putting in place infrastructure and varied platforms. On the other hand, Rwanda has managed to develop an AI national strategy, which is now publicly accessible.

Digital Ecosystems

Artificial Intelligence systems are powered by a fusion of ICTs that form a digital ecosystem, which is now lacking in Africa (Arakpogun et al., 2021). The absence of this important platform poses a considerable disadvantage for AI developers and users. A digital ecosystem is a digital environment populated by digital components or software components, applications, services, knowledge, etc. tied together and interact dynamically (Russo et al. 2021; Li et al., 2012). Artificial Intelligence and data analytics require interactions among different entities. ICT and Web 2.0 are meant to facilitate the development of complex, distributed, open, and holistic socio-technical environments (Russo et al. 2021; Li et al., 2012). The Digital Ecosystem has an infrastructure that supports the description, composition, evolution, integration, sharing, and distribution of its components. Undoubtedly, developing such a complex and dynamic environment is a challenging venture.

Africa needs to set a strategy that fosters the development of core ICT infrastructure like a digital ecosystem to support AI innovations and to enable digital resource sharing across the continent. During the FGD, participants stated the following:

The Ethiopian Artificial Intelligence Service was established in April 2020 and mandated to serve three main purposes: 1. to be an AI center of excellence backed by appropriate infrastructure, research, and development endeavors. 2. To draft relevant AI policy guidelines. 3. Create a platform and ecosystem for start-ups pooling together stakeholders and actors in the field (FGD 3).

Emphasizing the need to mobilize stakeholders, Schoeman et al. (2022) propose a solid ecosystem that embraces: (1). universities, (2) startups, (3) large companies, (4) policymakers, and (5) multi-stakeholder partnerships. The role of these five actors varies according to the context and the political culture of each country. Wang et al. (2022) state that digital ecosystem ideas are further developing into the notion of a Metaverse (digital universe) that integrates a range of the latest technologies and systems built on them as its basis. The potential vulnerabilities of these varieties of components and their intrinsic flaws coupled with the incidence of unfair outcomes of AI algorithms are raising issues regarding the safety of physical infrastructures and human bodies.

AI Data Availability, Security, and Privacy

During the FGD respondents stated that Ethiopian public institutions in the health, agriculture, manufacturing etc sectors did not develop a culture of storing data in an organized and systematic manner. For instance, in the health systems, hospitals in many places still handle paper-based patient data. In a handful of health institutions where automation took place, patient data is held in fragmented files. This problem is quite common in many Sub-Saharan African countries and is a real bottleneck for the advancement of AI in the continent.

Artificial Intelligence (AI) technologies are supposed to influence and reshape critical areas such as data usage and accessibility (Gaffley et al., 2022). AI systems' performance in terms of providing accurate suggestions for action hinges on the quality of data. Africa lacks a structured data ecosystem that is critical to machine learning and AI systems at large (Ade-Ibijola and Okonkwo, 2023). The presence of high-quality data in Africa would undoubtedly be helpful to generate useful information that would inform policy and decision-making. However, the observed high emphasis given to data acquisition from the human subject and the low regard for data privacy and security signals demeaning the person behind the data points. As data pertains to something (human or an object), not about the abstract entity, the collection, analysis, and manipulation of data potentially entail monitoring, tracking, and surveilling people (Birhane, 2020). Unlike the developed and other emerging nations, data privacy and security policies do not exist in many African countries. For instance, Arakpogun et al. (2021) note that only 19 of the 55 countries in Africa had enacted data security and privacy laws as of 2018. A comprehensive data management framework is needed to collect diverse datasets, store, safeguard, and avail accurate data for AI developers (Ade-Ibijola and Okonkwo, 2023).

AI systems could contain algorithms that reflect the prejudices and specific beliefs of the creators and tend to generate discriminatory results (Mahomed, 2018). Mahomed (2018) further notes that the

AI system itself can also be hacked, manipulated, or spammed with 'fake' data, and used maliciously to reveal sensitive personal information. Therefore, it is imperative to consider the ethical, legal, and social concerns while adopting and using AI systems.

Unless precautionary measures are sought proactively, the ever-increasing automation of socioeconomic activities tends to creep with perpetuating historical bias, discrimination, and injustice (Birhane, 2020). In this regard, Birhane (2020) cites the Kenyan Government's national biometric ID project temporarily suspended by the Supreme Court of Kenya as an example. This is because the court noted that the project risks excluding racial, ethnic, and religious minorities that have historically been discriminated against during enrollment on the national biometric ID given that the procedure requires documents such as a national ID card and birth certificate, which these minorities are historically deprived of acquiring. Moreover, the court raised its concern regarding the mode of securing, storing, accessing, and utilizing the sensitive data gathered about individuals in connection with the biometric project and eventually urged the government to put in place an appropriate regulatory framework.

Incidences of privacy and security breaches of AI are widely raised around the world. For instance, Murdoch (2021) disclosed the privacy challenges of AI by citing the following examples: 1. The DeepMind AI developed in partnership with the Royal Free London NHS was criticized on the ground that patients were not consulted over the use of their information. 2. The patient info was obtained based on an inappropriate legal basis. 3. AI algorithms may use the data in different ways than anticipated.

Financial Technology Ventures

With the advent of cell phones and their wider adoption in Africa, unprecedented financial transaction systems have emerged. This technological innovation has benefited millions of unbanked citizens in countries like Kenya who have gained access to financial services. For instance, Ahuja and Chan (2016) state that in Kenya the M-PESA mobile payment service helps to overcome the lack of physical banking branches by allowing people to use a simple SMS-based transaction system to send and receive digital currency. Furthermore, Orlikowski and Barrett (2014) disclose that more than two-thirds of the Kenyan adult population uses M-PESA and over 30% of Kenyan GDP flows through this system.

Applications like M-PESA and related financial technologies provide commendable services to most of the population. However, there is a growing concern that these systems behind the scenes continually capture high-volume data that could potentially be misused. For instance, as users transact with the system for a longer time, their digital activities and behavior can be monitored and easily traced. Based on their spending habits and location information, their creditworthiness and other loan-related affairs are surveyed and used by a third party to make decisions on issues that matter most in their lives.

Under the guise of preventing money laundering, government agencies implement various monitoring solutions, which tend to lead to multipurpose surveillance that infringes on individual privacy (Martin, 2019). With the advent of modern AI tools, the surveillance capabilities of government and nongovernmental agencies are expected to increase putting in question privacy, security, and human rights.

By and large, there is a growing belief that AI bolsters financial inclusion initiatives and support the finance sector transforming areas related to risk detection, addressing information asymmetry, improving customer support through Chat bots, and enhancing fraud detection and cybersecurity capabilities (Mhlanga, 2020). Nevertheless, liability issues issues persist; like who is responsible if something goes wrong? Dealing with compliance and meeting operational standards, comprehending AI's inherent risks, and the culture of the firm and regulatory requirements pose challenges to the large-scale adoption of AI in financial services (Mhlanga, 2020).

AI Pre-Trained Models Adoption Issues

Pre-trained language model systems learn universal language representations from a massive corpus and yield high generalizability capabilities. Guo et al. (2022) state that these models will be reused by fine-tuning with a small number of task-specific datasets. In doing so, they will be used for various downstream Natural Language Processing tasks such as text classification, question answering, and named entity recognition. This makes pre-trained models vulnerable to various attacks, planned or erroneously tampered with model parameters (Guo et al., 2022).

Modern Artificial intelligence systems have three basic components: user interface, models and inference engine, and database or repository systems. Generic models such as linear regression, logistic regression, neural networks, etc. are behind various AI algorithms. Further, big IT companies and research communities are also developing and deploying some domain-specific algorithms. For instance, Google has developed an image classification algorithm trained using flower image data and classifying flowers as lily, rose, daisy, tulip, sunflower, etc. Nelson (2019) states that such classification algorithm can be tweaked to read CT scans of patients with cancer. Countries with resource constraints are likely to adopt pre-trained AI models and tools from overseas. During the FGD session respondents stated that AIS targets adopting pre-trained models to deal with skill and computing resource constraints. In this regard, the FGD respondents stated that *"AIS has no intention to build models from scratch rather it plans to adopt retrained models"*. The respondent specifically noted the following:

Instead of battling to build our own models, we focus on retraining pre-trained models in four local languages: Amharic, Tigrigna, Afan Oromo, and Somali. Occasionally, we tweak models to fit the local context. For instance, in the healthcare system, skin disease detection models trained for white skin do not work as intended for black skin (FGD 4).

With the advent and success of large-scale models such as BERT and GPT, Han (2021) declares that the AI community has reached a consensus to adopt pre-trained models as a backbone for downstream tasks instead of training models from scratch. Considering recent developments in the field, African countries still need to thoroughly examine the appropriateness of pre-trained models to the local context.

Dealing With AI Bias

As a socio-technical system, ungoverned artificial intelligence (AI) might perpetuate bias (Nelson, 2019). AI systems, particularly the data and algorithms components could embed gender, racial, ethnic, and social status bias unless rigorous testing and validation is carried out before deploying them in real-life settings. Such biases might lead to a serious problem when they guide decisions that do not represent diversity and fails to consider the norm and values of a particular society (Castaneda et al., 2022). Castaneda et al., 2022 have provided several examples of bias discovered in speech recognition, facial recognition, and decision management AI systems. Regarding bias implicated in decision management systems, Dastin (2022) reveals that while a well-known hiring tool preferred male candidates over females, some credit services seemed to offer smaller credit lines to women than to men. The source of the cited biases boils down to the worldview and mindset of system developers and thr data used to train algorithms or it might occur without the intention and awareness of developers. In general, algorithms have the potential to duplicate or even amplify human errors. With the advent of Generative AI models, significant transformations have occurred in voice and facial recognition systems. Cloned AI applications that imitate public figures' and celebrities' voices and pictures have started releasing fake information through social media platforms for malicious purposes and are causing social unrest. For instance, a recently released burning video of the Pentagon has deceived mainstream Media and terrified the public for some time.

During the study, we noted the level of awareness of AIS experts and officers about the potential sources of AI bias and the mechanisms their organization is planning to put in place in order to counter some of these biases. In this regard, respondents in the FGD session state the following:

Considering the urgency of adopting AI-based technologies in critical economic sectors such as health, finance, metrology, transport, etc, and given the AI skill shortages in the country, our plan is to adopt pre-trained models elsewhere. We do not have a plan to build them from scratch. However, if we take the case in the health sector, there are pre-trained skin detection systems using white skin training data. This requires us to contextualize and update the model before adopting it locally (FGD 5).

Respondents further stated that over time, even a well-tested and contextualized AI model is likely to creep in bias and generate strange results as it operates for a longer time. Therefore, a periodic review and revisiting of AI models and algorithms are required to deal with the dynamism in the model and the datasets being used over time.

Parallel to this, Roselli, Matthews, and Talagala (2019) point out that as in the case of conventional software systems, AI algorithms may not be fully explainable even with a careful review of algorithms and datasets. To partly rectify this problem, they proposed a set of processes to mitigate and manage three general classes of bias: those related to mapping the business intent into the AI implementation, those that arise due to the distribution of samples used for training, and those that are present in individual input samples.

AI Model Accuracy and Quality

An enduring misconception surrounding computer system users is their belief that machines do not commit errors. As a result, less desire is observed to check the result delivered by the computer system. However, like any man-made system, computers are not free from errors. Acknowledging the possibility of fatal errors lingering in AI systems, respondents of the FGD and KII mentioned their concerns and disclosed the strategies AIS is attempting to pursue to ensure AI model quality and accuracy. In line with this, respondents stated that:

AIS fosters an open-door policy and platform where system developers and experts interact and promote a peer review and evaluation culture. In addition, domain experts, particularly from health and finance evaluate every single AI system and algorithm being developed or adopted. So far, we have been extensively employing peer and expert evaluation procedures. Further, AIS is committed to enforcing internationally accepted model evaluation and validation processes before any AI models are released and deployed (FGD 6).

Human decision-making suffers serious bias rooted in the individual personality or societal prejudice. Silberg and Manyika (2019) state that AI systems may provide two opportunities. The first is that AI can be used to identify and reduce human biases. The second is to improve AI systems themselves, from how they leverage data to how they are designed, developed, and used to prevent them from perpetuating human and societal biases. Historically rooted societal and systemic discrimination tend to manifest in AI systems and exacerbate and compound existing inequalities unless due consideration is given to thwart the prevailing stereotypes from being perpetuated in emerging digital technologies (Adams, 2021).

CONCLUSION

AI is not an entirely groundbreaking invention. In the first, second, and third industrial revolutions, several types of manufacturing machinery capable of executing various production processes with less human intervention were invented. However, AI has accelerated the speed and scope of transformation in the socioeconomic realm (Arakpogun et al., 2021). This study explored technical considerations to design, develop, adopt, and use regarding AI on the African continent. The study revealed that although some promising AI initiatives are underway across many African countries, policymakers and leaders of the continent need to draw up strategies to improve the backbone of telecom infrastructure and to start capturing relevant data across various African socio-economic sectors. Particularly, the continent should strive to formulate a strategy to enhance the broadband network coverage by fostering investments in the telecom sector through various stimulus schemes and policy support for potential investors.

Furthermore, the continent needs to start developing a comprehensive AI policy and guidelines to regulate the development and adoption of AI systems before the technology matures and causes unintended consequences. As a prominent continental organization, the African Union (AU) is supposed reimagine its roles and develop its internal capacity to spearhead the process of formulating the AI regulatory framework for Africa following the footsteps of its counterpart in Europe.

The study also revealed that instead of building AI models and systems from scratch locally, adopting pre-trained models from elsewhere is a viable strategy to quickly adopt AI systems to improve critical processes in key economic sectors. This requires proper contextualization, model evaluation, and validation strategies to avoid AI bias. In addition, African countries need to improve data-capturing capabilities and nurture digital culture to thrive. Africa is advised to undertake a comprehensive educational system overhaul to keep abreast of technological developments and to foster innovation. In addition to technical competence, AI-based technologies demand critical investigation of the intended and unintended consequences of these technologies. Therefore, AI developers are supposed to understand the ethical dimensions they need to address and be ready to assume professional responsibilities while developing and deploying AI systems (Borenstein and Howard, 2021). Furthermore, substantial improvement in the backbone of telecom infrastructure and AI human resource development is critical to tap opportunities created by AI and other emerging technologies. Any Artificial Intelligence system is powered by a fusion of ICTs that form a digital ecosystem. Therefore, Africa needs to come up with a strategy that fosters the development of core ICT infrastructure like a digital ecosystem to support AI innovations and to enable digital resource sharing across the continent.

In the end, we would like to proffer the following considerations as to how AI technologies ought to be designed, developed/adopted, implemented, and used in Africa. First, following the recommendations of Behrens (2013), Metz (2010), and other emerging works on African indigenous ethics, contextual AI ethical and regulatory framework should be developed to guide the development and adoption of AI-based technologies. Second, African nations need to get fully involved in aggressive AI capacity development campaign focusing special attention on human resource and telecom infrastructure development. Third, instead of adopting pre-trained AI models, concerted efforts by African countries is required to develop home-grown AI models. If adopting pre-trained models is deemed appropriate, African countries need to formulate model evaluation metrics to rigorously assess the relevance of the models to African context. Fourth, AU and other regional organizations should lay the groundwork for the development of digital ecosystems in Africa.

REFERENCES

Adams, R. (2021). Can artificial intelligence be decolonized? *Interdisciplinary Science Reviews*, *46*(1-2), 176–197. doi:10.1080/03080188.2020.1840225

Ade-Ibijola, A., & Okonkwo, C. (2023). Artificial Intelligence in Africa: Emerging Challenges. In D. O. Eke & ... (Eds.), *Responsible AI in Africa: Challenges and Opportunities* (pp. 101–117). Springer International Publishing. doi:10.1007/978-3-031-08215-3_5

Agance France Presse. (2022, June 06). *Ethiopia Shows off Combat Drone at Military Ceremony*. Garowe Online. https://www.garoweonline.com/en/world/africa/ethiopia-

Ahuja, S., & Chan, Y. E. (2016). Digital platforms for innovation in frugal ecosystems. In S. Tanja (Ed.), *Academy of management proceedings* (pp. 1700–17007). Academy of Management. doi:10.5465/ambpp.2016.17007abstract

Arakpogun, E. O., Elsahn, Z., Olan, F., & Elsahn, F. (2021). Artificial Intelligence in Africa: Challenges and Opportunities. In A. Hamdan, A. E. Hassanien, A. Razzaque, & B. Alareeni (Eds.), *The Fourth Industrial Revolution: Implementation of Artificial Intelligence for Growing Business Success. Studies in Computational Intelligence. 935* (pp. 375–388). Springer.

Baguma, R., Mkoba, E., Nahabwe, M., Mubangizi, M. G., Amutorine, M., & Wanyama, D. (2022). Towards an Artificial Intelligence Readiness Index for Africa. In: Ndayizigamiye, P., Twinomurinzi, H., Kalema, B., Bwalya, K., Bembe, M. (Eds.) *Digital-for-Development: Enabling Transformation, Inclusion and Sustainability Through ICTs. IDIA 2022. Communications in Computer and Information Science. 1774. International Development Informatics Association Conference* (pp. 285-303): Springer.

Birhane, A. (2020). Algorithmic colonization of Africa. *Script-ed*, *17*(2), 389–409. doi:10.2966/scrip.170220.389

Blackwell, A. F., Damena, A., & Tegegne, T. (2022). Inventing artificial intelligence in Ethiopia. *Interdisciplinary Science Reviews*, *46*(3), 363–385. doi:10.1080/03080188.2020.1830234

Borenstein, J., & Howard, A. (2021). Emerging challenges in AI and the need for AI ethics education. *AI and Ethics*, *1*(1), 61–65. doi:10.1007/s43681-020-00002-7

Butcher, N., Wilson-Strydom, M., & Baijnath, M. (2021). *Artificial intelligence capacity in sub-Saharan Africa: Compendium report*. Artificial Intelligence for Development Africa.

Calderon, C., Cantu, C., & Chuhan-Pole, P. (2018). Infrastructure development in Sub-Saharan Africa: a scorecard. *World Bank Policy Research Working Paper*, (8425), 1-47.

Castaneda, J., Jover, A., Calvet, L., Yanes, S., Juan, A. A., & Sainz, M. (2022). Dealing with gender bias issues in data-algorithmic processes: A social-statistical perspective. *Algorithms*, *15*(9), 1–16. doi:10.3390/a15090303

Dastin, J. (2022). Amazon scraps secret AI recruiting tool that showed bias against women. In *Ethics of data and analytics* (pp. 296–299). Auerbach Publications. doi:10.1201/9781003278290-44

Focus Group Discussion 1. (2021). Focus Group Discussion (FGD) with AIS team of experts. Addis Ababa, Ethiopia.

Focus Group Discussion 2. (2021). Focus Group Discussion (FGD) with AIS team of experts. Addis Ababa, Ethiopia.

Focus Group Discussion 3. (2021). Focus Group Discussion (FGD) with AIS team of experts. Addis Ababa, Ethiopia.

Focus Group Discussion 4. (2021). Focus Group Discussion (FGD) with AIS team of experts. Addis Ababa, Ethiopia.

Focus Group Discussion 5. (2021). Focus Group Discussion (FGD) with AIS team of experts. Addis Ababa, Ethiopia.

Focus Group Discussion 6. (2021). Focus Group Discussion (FGD) with AIS team of experts. Addis Ababa, Ethiopia.

Gaffney, M., Adams, R., & Shyllon, O. (2022). Artificial Intelligence. *African Insight*. A Research Summary of the Ethical and Human Rights Implications of AI in Africa. HSRC & Meta AI and Ethics Human Rights Research Project for Africa – Synthesis Report.

Guo, S., Xie, C., Li, J., Lyu, L., & Zhang, T. (2022). *Threats to pre-trained language models: Survey and taxonomy*.

Hassan, Y. (2023). Governing algorithms from the South: A case study of AI development in Africa. *AI & Society*, *38*(4), 1429–1442. doi:10.1007/s00146-022-01527-7

Haula, K., & Agbozo, E. (2020). A systematic review on unmanned aerial vehicles in Sub-Saharan Africa: A socio-technical perspective. *Technology in Society*, *63*, 1–17. doi:10.1016/j.techsoc.2020.101357

Interview 1. (2021). Field interview with Artificial Intelligence Service (AIS) expert. Addis Ababa, Ethiopia.

Kiemde, S. M. A., & Kora, A. D. (2020). The challenges facing the development of AI in Africa. In *2020 IEEE International Conference on Advent Trends in Multidisciplinary Research and Innovation (ICATMRI)* (pp. 1-6). IEEE.

Kilaba, E. J. M., & Manasseh, E. C. (2020). Telecom Revolution in Africa, The journey thus far and the journey ahead. *Africa and Middle East Journal*, *1*, 29–33.

Li, W., Badr, Y., & Biennier, F. (2012). Digital ecosystems: challenges and prospects. In proceedings of the international conference on management of Emergent Digital EcoSystems (pp. 117-122). doi:10.1145/2457276.2457297

Martin, A. (2019). Mobile money platform surveillance. *Surveillance & Society*, *17*(1/2), 213–222. doi:10.24908/ss.v17i1/2.12924

Matthew, U. O., Kazaure, J. S., Onyebuchi, A., Daniel, O. O., Muhammed, I. H., & Okafor, N. U. (2021). Artificial intelligence autonomous unmanned aerial vehicle (UAV) system for remote sensing in security surveillance. In *2020 IEEE 2nd International Conference on Cyberspace (CYBER NIGERIA)* (pp. 1-10). IEEE.

Metz, T. (2010). African and Western moral theories in a bioethical context. *Developing World Bioethics*, *10*(1), 49–58. doi:10.1111/j.1471-8847.2009.00273.x PMID:19961513

Mhlanga, D. (2020). Industry 4.0 in finance: The impact of artificial intelligence (AI) on digital financial inclusion. *International Journal of Financial Studies.*, *8*(45), 1–14. doi:10.3390/ijfs8030045

Military Africa. (2022, December 11). Military Drones in Africa: The New Arms Race. Military Africa. https://www.military.africa/2022/12/military-drones-in-africa-the-new-arms-race

Muhammad, A., Umar, U. A., & Adam, F. L. (2023). The Impact of Artificial Intelligence and Machine learning on workforce skills and economic mobility in developing countries: A case study of Ghana and Nigeria. *Journal of Technology Innovations and Energy*, *2*(1), 55–61. doi:10.56556/jtie.v2i1.466

Murdoch, B. (2021). Privacy and artificial intelligence: Challenges for protecting health information in a new era. *BMC Medical Ethics*, *22*(1), 1–5. doi:10.1186/s12910-021-00687-3 PMID:34525993

Nayebare, M. (2019). Artificial intelligence policies in Africa over the next five years. *XRDS: Crossroads. The ACM Magazine for Students.*, *26*(2), 50–54.

Nelson, G. S. (2019). Bias in artificial intelligence. *North Carolina Medical Journal*, *80*(4), 220–222. doi:10.18043/ncm.80.4.220 PMID:31278182

Nobles, C. (2023). Offensive Artificial Intelligence in Cybersecurity: Techniques, Challenges, and Ethical Considerations. In D. N. Burrell (Ed.), *Real-World Solutions for Diversity. Strategic Change, and Organizational Development: Perspectives in Healthcare, Education, Business, and Technology* (pp. 348–363). IGI Global. doi:10.4018/978-1-6684-8691-7.ch021

Orlikowski, W., & Barrett, M. (2014). Digital innovation in emerging markets: A case study of mobile money. *MIT Center for Information Systems, 14*(6). https://cisr.mit.edu/publication/2014_0601_DigitalInnovationVodafone

Roselli, D., Matthews, J., & Talagala, N. (2019). Managing bias in AI. In Liu & White (Eds) *Companion Proceedings of the 2019 World Wide Web Conference* (pp. 539–544). 10.1145/3308560.3317590

Russo Spena, T., Tregua, M., & Bifulco, F. (2021). Future Internet and Digital Ecosystems. In T. Russo Spena & F. Bifulco (Eds.), *Digital Transformation in the Cultural Heritage Sector* (pp. 17–38). Springer. doi:10.1007/978-3-030-63376-9_2

Sampene, A. K., Agyeman, F. O., Robert, B., & Wiredu, J. (2022). Artificial intelligence as a pathway to Africa's Transformation. [JMEST]. *Journal of Multidisciplinary Engineering Science and Technology*, *9*(1), 14939–14951.

Schoeman, W., Moore, R., Seedat, Y., & Chen, J. Y. J. (2021). Artificial intelligence: Is South Africa ready? Accenture, 1-22.

Sey, A., & Mudongo, O. (2021, July 20). *Case studies on AI skills capacity building and AI in workforce development in Africa*. Africa Portal. https://africaportal.org/publication/case-studies-ai-skills-capacity-building-and-ai-workforce-development-africa/

Silberg, J., & Manyika, J. (2019). Notes from the AI frontier: Tackling bias in AI (and in humans). *McKinsey Global Institute*, *1*(6), 1–8.

Wang, Y., Su, Z., Zhang, N., Xing, R., Liu, D., Luan, T. H., & Shen, X. (2022). A survey on metaverse: Fundamentals, security, and privacy. *IEEE Communications Surveys and Tutorials*, *25*(1), 319–352. doi:10.1109/COMST.2022.3202047

Yilma, K. (2023). In Search for a Role: The African Union and Digital Policies in Africa. *Digital Society: Ethics, Socio-Legal and Governance of Digital Technology*, *2*(2), 1–12. doi:10.1007/s44206-023-00047-1

ADDITIONAL READING

Ali, S. A., Khan, R., & Ali, S. N. (2023). The Promises and Perils of Artificial Intelligence: An Ethical and Social Analysis. In S. Charkraborty (Ed.), Investigating the Impact of AI on Ethics and Spirituality (pp. 1–24). IGI Global. doi:10.4018/978-1-6684-9196-6.ch001 doi:10.4018/978-1-6684-9196-6.ch001

Canca, C. (2020). Operationalizing AI ethics principles. Communications of the ACM, 63(12), 18–21. doi:10.1145/3430368 doi:10.1145/3430368

Lombardo, S. (2021). The Bad, the Good, and the Rebellious Bots: World's First in Artificial Intelligence. In H. T. Musiolik & A. D. Cheok (Eds.), Analyzing Future Applications of AI, Sensors, and Robotics in Society (pp. 221–237). IGI Global. doi:10.4018/978-1-7998-3499-1.ch013 doi:10.4018/978-1-7998-3499-1.ch013

Martínez-Fernández, S., Bogner, J., Franch, X., Oriol, M., Siebert, J., Trendowicz, A., & Wagner, S. (2022). Software engineering for AI-based systems: A survey. [TOSEM]. ACM Transactions on Software Engineering and Methodology, 31(2), 1–59. doi:10.1145/3487043 doi:10.1145/3487043

Munn, L. (2023). The uselessness of AI ethics. AI and Ethics, 3(3), 869–877. doi:10.1007/s43681-022-00209-w doi:10.1007/s43681-022-00209-w

Nobles, C. (2023). Offensive Artificial Intelligence in Cybersecurity: Techniques, Challenges, and Ethical Considerations. In D. N. Burell (Ed.), Bu Real-World Solutions for Diversity, Strategic Change, and Organizational Development: Perspectives in Healthcare, Education, Business, and Technology (pp. 348–363). IGI Global. doi:10.4018/978-1-6684-8691-7.ch021 doi:10.4018/978-1-6684-8691-7.ch021

Siau, K., & Wang, W. (2020). Artificial intelligence (AI) ethics: Ethics of AI and ethical AI. [JDM]. Journal of Database Management, 31(2), 74–87. doi:10.4018/JDM.2020040105 doi:10.4018/JDM.2020040105

Van de Poel, I. (2020). Embedding values in artificial intelligence (AI) systems. Minds and Machines, 30(3), 385–409. doi:10.1007/s11023-020-09537-4 doi:10.1007/s11023-020-09537-4

KEY TERMS AND DEFINITIONS

AI Algorithm: A computer program typically designed to perform high-level tasks such as prediction, classification, and revealing other interesting patterns from huge datasets.

AI bias: A scenario where a computer program carries an inherent human bias or bias created in the process of developing the computer algorithm, eventually leading the AI system to generate discriminatory and unbalanced results.

AI Model: A packaged computer program designed to learn from massive data sets and generate a pattern.

AI Resources: An infrastructure that includes database systems, hardware, software, communication systems, and essential procedures to develop, deploy, and set up AI-based technologies in a particular setting.

Artificial Intelligence (AI): A computer system that mimics a human being and performs some tasks which mainly used to be carried out typically by a human being such as decision-making and logical reasoning.

Digital Ecosystem: An integrated set of entities and components linked to interact, share

Machine Learning: A phenomenon where a computer program is designed to learn from huge datasets, sensors, and other data sources and generate interesting patterns, make a suggestion, or make relevant decisions.

resources: and reinforce each other in order to establish a robust self-regulating AI environment.

Trained Models: A set of computer programs that involve statistical models such as linear or logistic regressions, Neural Networks, or deep learning trained and validated using massive datasets and ready to be reused in other settings with or without fine tuning.

ENDNOTES

[1]   https://www.scribbr.com/methodology/thematic-analysis/

Chapter 6
Artificial Intelligence and Health in Africa:
Opportunities, Challenges, and Ethical Considerations

Margaret Richardson Ansah
(iD) https://orcid.org/0000-0002-8566-3297
University of Ghana, Ghana

Hannah Chimere Ugo
Afe Babalola University, Nigeria

Isaac Adjaye Aboagye
University of Ghana, Ghana

Nii Longdon Sowah
University of Ghana, Ghana

Gifty Osei
University of Ghana, Ghana

Srinivasan S. Balapangu
University of Ghana, Ghana

Samuel Kojo Kwofie
University of Ghana, Ghana

ABSTRACT

As the application of artificial intelligence (AI) expands across various fields of practice including health its deployment, regulation, acceptability, preparedness challenges, and ethical concerns in Africa requires a critical look. The chapter's primary objective is to provide a comprehensive understanding of how AI can positively affect health outcomes in Africa. The authors explored the potential for AI to transform and improve healthcare in low-resource areas like Africa and reviewed the current state of how AI algorithms can be used to improve diagnostics, treatment, and disease monitoring, as well as how AI can help with pandemic preparedness. The chapter also highlights the challenges and ethical considerations that need to be addressed when deploying AI in Africa. The chapter concludes that AI is poised to assist countries in improving the quality of health service delivery through innovation using telemedicine-assisted approaches and that there is a need to deploy new technologies and share lessons and experiences among countries on the African continent to help improve healthcare in Africa.

DOI: 10.4018/978-1-6684-9962-7.ch006

INTRODUCTION

Overview of AI Applications in African Healthcare

In Africa, where infectious and non-communicable diseases pose equal challenges, ensuring universal access to medications is paramount. However, numerous obstacles hinder access, including disease prevalence, limited pharmaceutical industry scale and costly raw materials, heavy reliance on foreign drug sources, weak supply chains, insufficient government investment, unfavorable manufacturing conditions, healthcare workforce shortages, inadequate health financing, infrastructure gaps, and limited investment in offshore initiatives (Adebisi et al., 2022).

Sub-Saharan Africa's healthcare systems confront a pressing crisis characterized by a severe shortage of healthcare personnel. In the face of this challenge, 57 nations grapple with a staggering deficit of 2.4 million doctors and nurses. This scarcity is compounded by the significant emigration of healthcare professionals, resulting in a stark imbalance, with only 2.3 healthcare workers per 1000 population in Africa compared to the Americas' 24.8 per 1000. Consequently, merely 1.3% of the world's healthcare workforce is left to address a substantial 25% of the global disease burden (Naicker et al., 2009).

This healthcare dilemma is further exacerbated by the continuous migration of medical experts from Africa to more affluent nations, intensifying the strain on already underfunded healthcare systems and hindering the delivery of even basic care standards. The relentless prevalence of diseases such as HIV/AIDS exacerbates this challenge, necessitating urgent measures to fortify the healthcare infrastructure. The global threat of emerging and re-emerging infectious diseases necessitates a robust pandemic preparedness approach. Artificial Intelligence (AI) emerges as a promising tool not only for pre-emptive action against such threats but also for understanding public behaviour and sentiments during epidemics. In a world characterized by interconnectedness, AI holds substantial potential to transform healthcare by enabling tailored interventions that save on treatment costs, improve access to health services, and foster individual health responsibility. (Ganasegeran & Abdulrahman, 2020).

Artificial Intelligence (AI) has the potential to revolutionize healthcare in Africa, addressing many of the unique challenges faced by the continent, such as a shortage of healthcare professionals, inadequate infrastructure, and a high burden of diseases. Here is an overview of AI applications in African healthcare:

Radiology automation: Mino Health AI Labs in Ghana is using deep learning and a convolutional neural network to automate radiology, improving the accuracy and efficiency of medical imaging analysis (Naicker et al., 2009; Owoyemi et al., 2020).

Diagnosis and treatment: AI mobile applications are being developed to diagnose birth asphyxia and malaria in rural areas of Africa (Adebisi et al., 2022; Owoyemi et al., 2020). AI-powered systems are providing faster and more accurate diagnoses, improving the quality of healthcare services in Africa (Kaur et al., 2023; Topol, 2019)

Data management: Proper digital infrastructure for storage of data from health facilities is essential for leveraging AI in healthcare. A strong data culture within health facilities that values data and makes tools and resources accessible to clinicians is also needed (Kaur et al., 2023; Naicker et al., 2009).

Supply chain management: AI can help manage supply chain processes, ensuring that healthcare facilities have precise medical supplies in stock, as demonstrated by Viebeg Technologies in Rwanda (Kaur et al., 2023; Topol, 2019).

Regulations and standards: Suitable regulations and standards for AI and data science are necessary to enable regulators to examine AI applications within health before their deployment (Kaur et al., 2023; Naicker et al., 2009).

While AI systems hold great promise for the future of healthcare in Africa, only a handful of African nations have embraced and pursued AI deployment in healthcare. These countries are notably Kenya, South Africa, and Rwanda (Ganasegeran & Abdulrahman, 2020; Mahomed, 2018). Barriers to adoption and utilization include a lack of data infrastructure, interconnectivity across healthcare systems, funding, and investment in AI technology and infrastructure (Adejoro et al., 2023; Mahomed, 2018).

The Health 4.0 paradigm is transforming healthcare, emphasizing patient and caregiver participation in value creation. This study, based on a project in Southern Italy, introduces a mobile clinical Decision Support System within Health 4.0, enhancing healthcare efficiency and quality, particularly in sensitive areas like home care for bedsores. Results suggest it not only improves service delivery but also empowers patients and caregivers, making them active value co-creators. This underscores the importance of integrating Health 4.0 into healthcare planning for economic and social sustainability (Ciasullo et al., 2022).

INTRODUCTION TO AI IN AFRICAN HEALTHCARE

Definition of AI and its Potential Impact on African Health Systems

Artificial intelligence, the field of science that enables computers to act intelligently and make predictions based on previously obtained data has gained much prominence in recent times. It is fast becoming the go-to model for developing computing systems due to its ability to bring meaning to data.

During the 1980s and 1990s, AI-based Machine learning algorithms were used to train and adapt to new data without being reprogrammed. This led to the development of programs that could analyze medical images, such as X-rays, to assist in the diagnosis of diseases. Some AI algorithms were also used for diagnosing, identifying, and analysing public health threats (Kaul et al., 2020).

More recently, improvements in natural language processing (NLP) have been used to understand and interpret human language. NLP techniques have been applied in healthcare to extract and analyze data such as electronic health records (EHRs), and medical images and assist with tasks (such as appointment scheduling and medication management). Due to an unprecedented increase in computing power, the availability of large amounts of data, and the rapid development of big data analytics, there has been an increase in AI applications. Deep learning (DL) machine learning technology, which involves training artificial neural networks (ANN) on large datasets, has been a major driver of recent AI advances. This has significantly influenced modernizing the global healthcare system to improve diagnosis and clinical care accuracy and efficiency. A convolutional neural network (CNN) is a type of DL algorithm that simulates the behaviour of interconnected neurons in the human brain (Kaul et al., 2020).

Different algorithms have been used to address different healthcare needs, such as Expert systems, machine learning, and deep learning. Although expert systems have been extensively, researched globally, little research has been conducted on its application in African healthcare systems. Expert systems can be beneficial, especially where scarcity of trained physicians and medical personnel exists, as is usually the case in African countries (Etori et al., 2023). Expert systems can help African healthcare systems diagnose patients and select treatment plans without extensively trained medical personnel, where a decision must be made quickly to save lives (Wahl et al., 2018). An example is where an expert system has been incorporated with fuzzy logic systems, to improve the diagnosis of chronic conditions like STDs, HIV/AIDS, cholera, abdominal pain, and diabetes decision support application in South Africa (Lee & Wang, 2010; Mburu et al., 2012; Thompson et al., 2017).

Natural language processing (NLP) has been used in developing a Medical Chatbot to diagnose patients in their early stages of the disease or to use social media data for surveillance and monitoring of infectious disease outbreaks (Abdelwahap et al., 2021; Gupta & Katarya, 2020). The use of NLP in African healthcare is still in its infancy stage. (Li et al (Li et al., 2020) conducted mental health condition research following the outbreak of coronavirus (COVID-19), using Twitter data from Nigeria and South Africa. Oyebode et al (Oyebode & Orji, 2018) demonstrated that Likita, a chatbot, could be used to diagnose common ailments and improve healthcare delivery in Africa.

Deep learning (DL) can process large amounts of data, such as images, and could potentially aid medical workers in decision-making, using an X-ray image to analyze multiple diseases. For instance, (Stephen et al. 2019) used X-ray images to classify Pneumonia with a validation accuracy of 93.73%. (Simi Margarat et al. 2022) also used X-ray data to diagnose early-stage Tuberculosis using a DL algorithm and achieved 99% accuracy. (Holbrook et al. 2021) used three pre-trained DL models (faster R-CNN, single-shot multi-box detector (SSD), and RetinaNet) for the microscopic diagnosis of malaria parasites, Malaria is one of the deadliest diseases in Sub-Sahara Africa in thick blood smears. The result found that a faster R-CNN has a higher accuracy than the other two models used in the study with an average precision of over 0.94. Hence this approach can improve the accuracy and efficiency of malaria diagnosis compared to traditional methods. ML models are used to predict and classify chronic diseases in Africa. They are gaining popularity for their simplicity and the availability of data in a few African countries

Akogo et al (Akogo et al., 2022) created two AI models to diagnose two chest conditions - pleural effusion and cardiomegaly. For both conditions, the best-performing AI model outperforms the best-performing radiologist by about 10%. These models will be of great utility in regions, like Sub-Saharan Africa, where there are scarce radiologists. To further ascertain the utility and performance of the AI models in regions like Ghana, the models were evaluated on a larger Ghanaian dataset.

The impact of AI on African healthcare systems is enormous. The many challenges faced in the African healthcare system will be greatly reduced if AI is adopted in many ways.

Overview of the Current State of AI Adoption in African Countries

There has been a lot of research on AI in healthcare, but there has been minimal discussion about AI in African healthcare. AI researchers have also found that there is a lack of diverse representation of AI models in healthcare particularly from African datasets. This has made it difficult to proceed with AI adoption in African countries. Various researchers are generating models that are more African-centered (Gupta & Katarya, 2020; Hagerty & Rubinov, 2019; Lee & Wang, 2010; Mburu et al., 2012; Thompson et al., 2017) in order to increase the acceptability of AI in African healthcare systems. They are plagued by various challenges in this quest.

The application of AI in the African healthcare system is still in its early stages. However, there is a growing interest and investment in the implementation of AI to improve different aspects of healthcare delivery in Africa. However, the implementation and acceptance of AI in Africa confronts many challenges (Owoyemi et al., 2020). Many African countries, for example, still have limited access to reliable electricity and to high-speed internet, making it challenging to implement and use AI systems. The successful implementation of AI in health care depends on the availability and dependability of the infrastructure (Mbunge et al., 2022).

For many years, African healthcare systems have had numerous challenges with adequate human resources, inadequate finances, lack of technical know-how, and an unstable political climate (Oleribe et al., 2019). Hence, most African countries are unable to meet the fundamental requirements for effective and reliable healthcare systems. Ineffective service integration is linked to poor governance, and human resource challenges (Nutbeam, 2000). The lack of basic access to healthcare makes it even harder to implement AI solutions (Tran et al., 2019).

The scarcity of trained professionals with expertise in AI in Africa is a major concern and a factor in deploying AI in the healthcare sector in Africa. Due to poor conditions of service in many healthcare facilities, they are struggling to meet the rising demand for services while also facing significant shortages of trained health workers and essential medicines (Guo & Li, 2018; Naicker et al., 2009). AI systems are quite new and quite expensive to develop or buy and coupled with inadequate funding in healthcare in Africa, most African countries rely heavily on developed nations for AI technologies to solve critical healthcare challenges (Guo & Li, 2018). Ethical considerations around the use of AI in healthcare in Africa, including issues related to data privacy and the potential for biased decision-making could contribute to slow AI implementation in the African region (Hagerty & Rubinov, 2019)

AI Applications in African Healthcare

AI has the potential to transform healthcare systems in Africa by addressing some of the major challenges they face, such as disease burden, human resource shortage, access barriers, and resource allocation (Owoyemi et al., 2020). One of the key applications of AI in African healthcare is to improve the diagnosis and early detection of diseases, especially in low-resource settings where laboratory facilities, diagnostic equipment, and trained personnel are scarce or unavailable. AI-powered algorithms can help diagnose diseases, such as cancer, malaria, tuberculosis, HIV, and eye disorders, using various modalities such as images, sounds, biosensors, and molecular tests (Ekekwe, 2018; Owoyemi et al., 2020; Sallstrom et al., 2019). For instance, Ubenwa is a start-up in Nigeria that uses machine learning and signal processing to enhance the detection of birth asphyxia in settings with limited resources (Onu et al., 2019). AI algorithms can learn to recognize patterns in medical images and data that show signs of disease, even when human experts may find it hard. For instance, a study by (Nwaneri & Ugo, 2022) created a graphical user interface (GUI) software based on a machine-learning model for early detection of chronic kidney disease (CKD). The machine-learning model achieved 95.83% accuracy. The GUI software was shown to be a point-of-care application for early CKD prediction. Another study (Gonsalves et al., 2019) showed that machine learning can predict coronary heart disease with high accuracy. The study used patient records from South Africa to train machine-learning models that could estimate the risk of coronary heart disease. The best model, with 82% accuracy, was chosen as a potential model for diagnosing coronary heart disease. This accuracy is much higher than the accuracy of traditional risk assessment methods. There are also other AI-based systems for diagnosing and detecting diseases such as CareAI, Ada Health, and Peek Vision among others. These AI-powered diagnostic tools can offer quick, precise, and cheap results that can help with prompt treatment and referral of patients. They can also lower the burden, mistakes of healthcare workers, and enhance the quality of care in settings with limited resources.

Another application of AI in African healthcare is to enable telemedicine and remote healthcare delivery, especially for rural and isolated populations who do not have access to quality healthcare services. Using AI, telemedicine tools can make diagnosis and treatment more accurate and reliable, as shown by (Alami et al., 2020; Owoyemi et al., 2020). These tools include virtual assistants, chatbots, robots, drones, and wearable devices that can link patients with health professionals and provide essential services such as consultations, prescriptions, referrals, follow-ups, education, counselling, and emergency response. AI-powered telemedicine tools can increase access to healthcare services for underserved communities and lower travel time and costs for patients and providers. Therefore, AI can enhance the way healthcare is provided and improve the health of patients through telemedicine.

AI has the potential to enhance health monitoring and disease surveillance in Africa, especially for chronic and infectious diseases that are prevalent on the continent. AI-powered data analytics, machine learning, and natural language processing can help collect, analyze, and interpret health-related data from various sources. For example, AI platforms can use electronic health records, mobile phones, social media, sensors, and satellites to estimate diabetes risk, forecast disease transmission, map disease vectors, detect disease outbreaks, and identify malnutrition. These AI tools can assist health decision-making and policy-making, and enable early detection and response to health emergencies.

A major challenge for African healthcare systems is the lack and unequal distribution of health workers. The World Health Organization (WHO) reports that Africa has only 2.3 health workers per 1,000 people, compared to the global average of 4.3 (Organization, 2016). This gap is likely to grow as the need for health services rises due to population growth, aging, urbanization, and epidemiological transitions. AI can help address this challenge by providing tools for human resource planning, such as predicting how long health workers might stay in public service, identifying factors that influence their retention and motivation, and optimizing their deployment and allocation. For instance, a system based on a multinomial logistic classifier is being used for human resource planning in South Africa, especially to estimate how long health workers might remain in public service (Moyo et al., 2018). The system analyzes data from a long-term survey of health workers to find out what factors influence their decision to stay or leave the public sector. The system then groups health workers into four types: stayers, leavers, undecideds, and returners. Policymakers can use this information to keep and attract health workers by implementing measures such as giving rewards, enhancing work environments, offering learning possibilities, and developing career prospects.

Challenges and Concerns of AI in African Healthcare

In the context of Africa, where healthcare challenges are particularly acute, the adoption of AI has the potential to be a game-changer. However, this promising journey also has challenges that necessitate careful examination. In this section, we explore some of these challenges such as data availability and quality in resource-constrained settings, limited infrastructure and connectivity, cultural diversity and the contextual adaptation of AI solutions and the profound impacts that these challenges may have on the healthcare professionals and workforce in Africa.

Limited Infrastructure and Connectivity Challenges

AI relies heavily on electricity and internet connectivity. The infrastructure that supports these must be present and reliable to support any substantial development and use of AI. In Africa, compared to the rest of the world, infrastructure to support AI is lacking. Nigeria and Kenya for example are some of the leading countries in AI development but their ranking on the 2023 Global AI index is low due to very low scores in infrastructure, operating environment, research, and development. Out of 62 countries, all five African countries included in the index: Egypt, South Africa, Tunisia, Morocco, Nigeria, Kenya, have low scores on infrastructure.

Electricity Infrastructure: A critical and often overlooked factor in the development and deployment of AI is electricity availability. AI, at its core, is a computational endeavor. It relies on vast amounts of data processing, complex algorithms, and machine learning models to make decisions and predictions. These computations demand substantial computational power, and that power is drawn from the electrical grid. Access to reliable electricity varies in Africa. Many regions still struggle with inconsistent power supply. Even in countries with comparatively robust electrical infrastructure like Ghana, Gabon, Botswana and South Africa, rural and remote areas may lack access to electricity. This limits the deployment of AI solutions in healthcare in these areas. According to a 2023 report by the United Nations Conference on Trade and Development (UNCTAD), 50% of the population in Sub Saharan Africa lack access to electricity. Nigeria, the largest economy in Africa continues to suffer from inadequate energy supply, load shedding, and power outages (Asumadu-Sarkodie & Owusu, 2016). The effect this has permeates several aspects of AI.

- AI Research and Development: Access to electricity directly affects AI research and development. Laboratories and institutions in areas with unstable power may face limitations in conducting experiments and training models.
- Deployment of AI Solutions: In sectors like healthcare, reliable electricity is essential for AI-powered diagnostic tools, telemedicine, and remote monitoring. Without a stable power supply, these solutions cannot function effectively.
- Economic Opportunities: The availability of electricity can determine whether startups and businesses can leverage AI for innovation and growth. In regions with consistent power, AI-driven enterprises have a competitive edge.
- Education and Training: Teaching AI concepts and programming often requires access to computers and the internet, both of which rely on electricity. Unequal access to electricity can exacerbate educational disparities.

There can be different possible solutions to the above-mentioned challenges. Some of which are:

- Renewable Energy Integration: Leveraging renewable energy sources, such as solar and wind power, can provide sustainable and reliable electricity for AI operations while minimizing environmental impact.
- Energy-Efficient Algorithms: Researchers are developing AI algorithms that are more energy-efficient, reducing the computational power required for AI tasks.
- Edge Computing: Edge AI, which processes data locally on devices, reduces the dependence on cloud-based data centres and can work effectively in areas with limited connectivity and electricity.
- Infrastructure Investment: Governments and organizations can invest in expanding and stabilizing electrical infrastructure to ensure widespread access to electricity.

Internet Connectivity: While some urban areas in Africa boast high-speed internet access and technology hubs, many rural and remote regions struggle with limited or no connectivity. Internet penetration rates in Africa have been steadily increasing, driven in part by the proliferation of mobile phones. According to the International Telecommunication Union (ITU), Africa's internet penetration rate in urban Africa stood at 28% in 2019, compared to just 4.5% in 2005, however, penetration in rural Africa was only 6% (ITU, 2019). AI requires a significant amount of data to operate, and the internet is the primary source of data for most AI systems. However, with only about 28% internet access in Africa, successful implementation and deployment of AI systems are negatively affected. The main hurdles to internet connectivity in Africa are infrastructure gaps and cost barriers. Expanding internet infrastructure to remote and underserved areas remains a formidable challenge. Many rural communities lack the necessary network infrastructure, such as fiber optic cables and cell towers. As most of the investment in this infrastructure comes from the private sector, profitability of such infrastructure expansions is of greater importance to investors. The cost of internet access is also often prohibitive for many Africans, particularly in low-income countries. High data prices and limited competition among service providers contribute to these cost barriers. High data prices can also be partly attributed to high telecommunication taxes especially in Tanzania, Sierra Leone, Democratic Republic of Congo and Mozambique which are higher than the global average (Lucini, 2016).

The lack of internet connectivity can significantly impact the development, deployment, and effectiveness of Artificial Intelligence (AI) in several ways:

- Limited Access to Data: AI algorithms rely on large and diverse datasets for training and continuous learning. Without internet connectivity, accessing and updating these datasets becomes challenging. In many AI applications, especially machine learning and deep learning, online learning is essential in maintaining model accuracy and relevance. A lack of connectivity can lead to outdated models.
- Reduced Interactivity and Real-time Capabilities: Real-time AI applications, such as natural language processing chatbots, which are frequently used to provide first-hand health information to users, require a constant internet connection to function effectively. A lack of connectivity limits the interactivity and responsiveness of these AI systems. In sectors like healthcare, AI-powered remote monitoring and control systems are invaluable. A lack of connectivity can impede these systems' ability to transmit critical data and receive commands in real-time.
- Inequality in Access to AI Benefits: Without internet connectivity, a section of the population misses the benefits of AI technologies, such as improved healthcare, this can contribute to inequality and disparities in development. Relatively better internet connectivity in urban Africa compared to rural Africa implies that the majority of AI research, development and application will be concentrated in urban areas, further deepening the digital divide that already exists.

Data Availability and Quality in Resource Constrained Settings

The successful application of AI in healthcare critically depends on the availability and quality of data. AI in healthcare relies on vast amounts of data, ranging from electronic health records (EHRs) to medical images, genomics, and patient-generated data. These datasets serve as the foundation upon which AI algorithms learn, analyze, and make informed decisions. However, in resource-constrained settings like Africa, access to quality and readily available healthcare datasets is a challenge.

Data silos and interoperability issues: Data fragmentation across different healthcare systems and providers creates silos, limiting the seamless exchange of information. Data silos refer to isolated repositories of data within organizations or systems that do not communicate or share information effectively with one another. In the context of AI in Africa, data silos often manifest as separate databases or systems maintained by different healthcare institutions or government bodies. This makes it difficult to create comprehensive patient histories. The situation is complicated by lack of standardized data formats and duplicated patient records across data silos making interoperability difficult. Even with access to different data silos, integrating data is complex and time-consuming, requiring significant resources and technical expertise due to different standards and data redundancy.

Data governance: Establishing clear data governance policies and guidelines is crucial to ensuring data quality and ethical use. In Africa, there are policies, processes, and practices that ensure data is managed, protected, and utilized effectively. The African Union (AU) data protection framework (Union, 2014) encourages collaboration between member states with regards to data governance. African sub regional organizations like the Economic Community of West African States (ECOWAS) and the East Africa Community (EAC) also have data protection and governance frameworks. These frameworks have guided the data protection policies available in member countries like Ghana, Kenya, Uganda, Nigeria, and Tanzania. However, these policies and frameworks do not explicitly specify how health data should be used in AI research and development. The focus of these frameworks has been on data protection and cybersecurity for electronic transactions, personal data, and mitigating cybercrimes. Frameworks for data governance specifically for AI should include personal data protection facilitation of open data access, direction for training, testing and validation datasets and most importantly standards for the verification of the accuracy and effectiveness of models (Townsend et al., 2023). Personal data protection frameworks aim to protect individuals' privacy and ensure that their personal data is collected, processed, and stored in a secure and transparent manner. Open data frameworks aim to promote the sharing and reuse of data to foster

innovation and economic growth. Perhaps, the best place to look for any form of data governance regarding the use of health data in AI development and use are digital health laws and not data protection frameworks and policies in general. The Inter-Governmental Authority on Development, made up of 8 East African countries, has developed a health data sharing plan (Hu et al., 2016) to foster cross border health data sharing which can significantly promote AI development. Ghana and Kenya have policies that allow e-prescription and e-dispensing. South Africa, Kenya, Zimbabwe, and Ghana have policies on telemedicine and informed consent is mandated in most countries for the carrying out of any health research and health data collection (Townsend et al., 2023). AI specific regulations are lacking in general in Africa. More effort must the made towards developing robust data governance frameworks for AI.

Cultural Diversity and Contextual Adaptation of AI Solutions

Cultural diversity and contextual adaptation are crucial considerations in the development and deployment of Artificial Intelligence (AI) systems. Artificial intelligence as a technology is considered as a western import, designed and developed first outside Africa, that has to be utilized in solutions that address the unique problems in Africa (Eke et al., 2023). Some challenges in AI in Africa pertaining to cultural diversity and contextual adaptation include lack of Afrocentric datasets, linguistic diversity, and high levels of digital illiteracy.

Datasets: The lack of Afrocentric datasets for training AI models is a significant challenge in the development of artificial intelligence that accurately represents and serves African populations and contexts. Afrocentric datasets, which include data points, related to African cultures, languages, demographics, and environments, are limited in comparison to datasets from other regions. Many NLP datasets used for tasks like sentiment analysis, chatbots, and language models primarily focus on English and a few other widely spoken languages. Afrocentric languages and dialects are under-represented in NLP datasets, hindering the development of NLP applications tailored to African linguistic diversity (Adebara & Abdul-Mageed, 2022). Speech recognition systems, which convert spoken language into text, will perform better in languages and dialects that have well-represented datasets. While datasets for English and other widely spoken languages are abundant, datasets for African languages and dialects are often scarce or incomplete (Hedderich et al., 2020). This limits the development of accurate speech recognition systems for African languages. Healthcare datasets used for AI applications, such as disease diagnosis, treatment recommendations and food recom-mendation systems, often lack representation of health conditions, genetic variations, and healthcare practices specific to African populations. Datasets from OpenAfrica and Zindi are available to ad-dress this gap, however, more effort and support is required.

Linguistic diversity: Africa is home to thousands of languages and dialects. Developing AI systems that cater to this linguistic diversity is a significant challenge but essential for acces-sibility. Apart from limited datasets on African languages, issues like tone, vowel harmony and ideophones are significant in the interpretation of a message (Adebara & Abdul-Mageed, 2022). There are about 2000 languages in Africa and some of the most widely spoken ones are Swahili, Hausa, Amharic, Yoruba, Igbo and Fula (Childs, 2003). Language translation is a major application of NLP and is important in the healthcare space for telemedicine and health chatbots and voice bots. Google Translate is arguably the largest language translation application and can translate over 100 languages. However, less than 20% of these languages are African. Other language translation applications including Yandex Translate and DeepL Translate have even fewer African languages. Applications like the Khaya Translator and ABENA, developed through GhanaNLP are focusing on developing Afrocentric translators with speech recognition capabilities. Apart from this, African researchers have also used neural machine translation to translate English to five official South African languages: Afrikaans, isiZulu, Northern Sotho, Setswana, Xitsonga and have made their dataset publicly available for other researchers (Martinus & Abbott, 2019). This shows the effort African researchers and startups are putting into catering for the linguistic diversity issue in Africa.

Digital literacy: Digital literacy is an essential skill that enables individuals to access informa-tion, communicate, and participate in the digital world. There are varied levels of digital literacy across Africa, and this is influenced by various factors. The continent comprises several nations with varying degrees of digital access, infrastructure, and educational resources. For instance, North African countries, such as Tunisia and Egypt, have relatively higher digital literacy rates due to better access to technology and educational opportunities. However, sub-Saharan Africa faces challenges that are more substantial. The low levels of digital literacy can be attributed to these regional variations, limitations with technology infrastructure as mentioned previously and educational limitations.

Impact on Healthcare Professionals and Workforce in Africa

While tremendous effort has been put into improving AI development and use in Africa, the challenges mentioned above still need to be overcome as they impact negatively on AI in the region. The numerous challenges also imply great opportunity for growth.

Positive Impacts: There is an opportunity for healthcare professionals and researchers to collaborate and develop even better AI models and applications by tapping into the immense knowledge available from several years of AI development from other parts of the world. Hence, costly mistakes that have been documented can be avoided. In addition, the challenges to AI that are peculiar to Africa, offer a chance to develop novel modelling techniques and applications that can be imported by the rest of the world.

Negative Impacts: Due to the lack of Afrocentric datasets, AI models that perform extremely well in other regions perform poorly in Africa. This makes it difficult for healthcare professionals to benefit from the potential of AI to augment disease-screening process or improve telemedicine through natural language models. A number of research that have tried to use Google translate to interpret certain medical phrases found that African languages had the lowest accuracies (Leite et al., 2016; Patil & Davies, 2014). This shows that these models are currently unreliable in the African context and cannot be trusted in healthcare settings. Our unreliable infrastructure also poses a risk to the adoption of AI in critical healthcare procedures like remote surgery procedures and telemedicine in general. If not handled properly, this may nurture distrust of AI systems among healthcare professionals.

Ethical Considerations in AI Adoption for African Health

One of the major concerns for the adoption of AI in Africa is ethical considerations. These considerations are mainly biases in the pipeline of AI from the creation of the dataset, formulation of the problem, processing of data to analysis of the data (Srinivasan & Chander, 2021). The authors developed a taxonomy of biases in AI, a structural organization of different forms of biases in the AI pipeline.

The implications of these biases could range from mild to severe or even fatal depending on the area of implementation. AI biases in healthcare defined as "the instances when the application of an algorithm compounds existing inequities in socioeconomic status, race, ethnic background, gender, religion, gender, disability or sexual orientation to amplify them and adversely impact inequities in health systems" (Panch et al., 2019) can be deadly.

Challenges in Ensuring Fairness and Transparency in AI Algorithms

There have been efforts to make AI algorithms fair and transparent however, these efforts are impeded by diverse challenges. Some of which are the lack of fairness standard, generalisation of application and in-transparent nature of deep learning (Chen et al., 2023).

Lack of Fairness Standard

Data used in developing algorithms are gathered from the world around us. The unavailability of a standardised quantitative metric for the evaluation of fairness, evaluations are subject to implicit biases.

Certain demographic groups can be over-represented while others are under-represented due to sampling and measurement biases leading to inequality (Norori et al., 2021; Panch et al., 2019). Practicing open science, code sharing and developing AI standard in healthcare will *eliminate unfairness in AI.*

Generalisation of Application

Individual differences in health, gender, genetics and environmental factors influences the health of different patient groups. Taking these factors into consideration during algorithm development is very critical but majority of AI algorithms ignore these factors (Cirillo et al., 2020). Diversity in health systems and lack of resources has made existing health dataset inequitable in representing all group. However, AI algorithms based on the skewed dataset applied generally to all patient groups, including those underrepresented in the dataset. This can lead to misdiagnosis and fatal consequences. Ensuring community engagement and cultural sensitivity in data acquisition and participatory science will elimi-nate deep-rooted societal biases (Norori et al., 2021).

Intransparent Nature of Deep Learning

In as much as deep learning algorithm is highly technical and cannot be easily understood by non-technical persons, transparency in dataset, algorithms and their parameters such as inputs and outputs to all parties from developer (data scientists), implementers (clinicians) to users (patients) will limit the both intended and unintended biases (Chen et al., 2023; Norori et al., 2021).

Case Studies and Best Practices

The onset of the fourth Industrial Revolution (4IR) is releasing a wave of technological advancements poised to reshape the trajectory of African progress. At the forefront of this transformative era is artificial intelligence (AI), a catalyst with the capacity to revolutionize multiple sectors and drive inclusive expansion. AI has seamlessly integrated into numerous aspects of daily life, spanning commerce, education, health, public services, communications, governance, agriculture, and manufacturing, highlighting its pervasive impact.

Furthermore, the transformative potential of AI is poised to reshape business operations, spur innovation, and uplift millions of lives across the African continent, aligning with the collective aspirations of the African Union's Agenda 2063. According to Lichtenthaler (Sallstrom et al., 2019), Artificial Intelligence (AI) has become a popular and rapidly advancing field of computer science, with the potential to transform many aspects of human life. By catalysing swift economic progress, expanding healthcare and education access, and promoting sustainable agriculture, AI emerges as a pivotal tool in addressing the continent's critical issues (de-Lima-Santos & Ceron, 2021).

Research ICT Africa, a non-profit think tank that conducts research on the digital economy, has launched an African Observatory on Responsible AI which was funded by the International Development Research Centre (IDRC) and the Swedish International Development Cooperation Agency (SIDA) under the AI4D programme. Developments in AI will drastically improved health services, diagnostics, and personalized medicine.

Various initiatives are already employing basic technology applications to provide essential healthcare services. These are particularly relevant in the context of African healthcare, where the technology in use currently can easily incorporate AI-based solutions. Presently, AI development in sub-Saharan Africa is hampered by poor infrastructure, the lack of skills and regulatory confusion. In spite of the aforementioned challenges, a handful of countries in the region, spurred by the demand for economic development and the need to combat COVID-19, are laying the groundwork for innovation in the technology. For example, Safermom is a Nigerian start-up that empowers pregnant women and new mothers to make informed decisions by using low-cost mobile technologies (two-way SMS, voice calling, and mobile apps) to transmit vital health information (Lunze et al., 2015).

Mauritius, South Africa, Seychelles, Rwanda and Senegal are making artificial intelligence a priority. Mauritius has built on its AI strategy launched in 2018, which spawned recommendations from the working group set out to research how AI could be integrated into national priorities and embedded in the business ecosystem. The island nation has created a Mauritius Artificial Intelligence Council, provides strong fiscal incentives for innovation-driven activities and has set up a National SME Incubator Scheme (NSIS). The country is the highest-ranked African nation on the Government AI Readiness Index.

Similarly, Rwanda has opted for a national strategy with the government looking to the Future Society, an independent, non-profit "think-and-do tank," for its AI strategy development. "A comprehensive national AI policy, AI ethical guidelines, and a practical implementation strategy fit for the local context can serve as a powerful roadmap to achieve Rwanda's national development and sustainable development goals," the government said in a statement.

Countries that stand out include South Africa, where examples of AI readiness adoption include the SARS e-filing and mobile app and the use of AI and machine learning bots improving service delivery and engagement with citizens. The Department of Health, for example, adopted a WhatsApp-based chatbot to help and support people with COVID-related health queries and direct them to where they could access accurate health information. AI technology is finding practical application in South Africa's healthcare domain for rapid HIV testing.

New AI and automation innovations have led to additional challenges such as big data requirements for the value of new technologies to be effectively shown. For future technology to learn from the challenges already faced, a comprehensive technology backbone needs to be built. Furthermore, organizations must have a longer-term vision of implementation rather than the need for immediacy and short-term gains. Ultimately, these technologies aim to create more intelligence in healthcare to better serve people. As AI and automation come into play, workforces fear employee levels will diminish, as roles become redundant.

While technology can take away specific jobs, it also creates them. In responding to change and uncertainty, technology can be a force for good and a source of considerable opportunity, leading to, in the longer term, more jobs for humans with specialist skill sets. While AI technologies and applications have the potential to address many of humanity's most pressing problems through, for example, fostering a world that is less sick, less hungry, more productive, better educated, and better prepared to thwart the effects of climate change—this promise comes with risks of entrenched and amplified social inequality (Hagerty & Rubinov, 2019).

AI grounded in non-representative or biased data can entrench existing social and economic inequities, with AI systems reproducing the representation gaps and biases of the data sets on which they are trained (Powles, 2018). AI can be used by already-dominant technology firms to further entrench their economic and social power, or by governments to violate the privacy and other human rights of citizens. AI's negative consequences can be compounded by a lack of transparency and accountability as such systems are scaled up (Koene et al., 2019). By combining the barriers that must be overcome by both humans and AI systems in the innovation process with the key activities of idea generation and development that need to be conducted, we can derive a framework of potentially creative application areas of AI within the innovation process.

To understand the possibilities of AI, we need to delineate where AI can assist and potentially replace human decision making in innovation management. Specifically, in developing ideas by overcoming information processing constraints, generating ideas by overcoming information processing constraints, developing ideas by overcoming local search routines, and generating ideas by overcoming local search routines. AI systems have different levels of sophistication in terms of their ability to augment and replace human managers in innovation processes. These levels of sophistication can be derived by looking at the kinds of capabilities that an information processing system must have in order to complete a function. For this, we will consider the 'innovation process' and the 'barriers to innovation' dimensions as the problem space and the solution space, respectively (Restrepo & Christiaans, 2004; Smith et al., 1998).

The first dimension, which describes the tasks in the innovation process (idea development and idea generation), can also be viewed as the problem space that is the subject of innovation. In line with an information processing perspective on the innovation process, the "problem space is the internal representation of the task environment" used by the subject being a human manager or an AI system (Newell & Simon, 1972). When going through the innovation process, an information processing system can either continue with its current definition of the problem space, which would correspond to simply developing a new idea or solution based on the problem space, or it could decide to include additional data, information, and/or knowledge, thereby redefining the problem space and opening up the ability to generate new ideas and solutions.

Another way to describe these two options would be to consider the former as the exploitation of an existing problem space and the latter as the exploration of a redefined, evolving, or different problem space. The second dimension, describing the barriers to be overcome in the innovation process (information processing constraints and ineffective or local search), may be interpreted as the ways in which the solution space for innovation can be altered. Overcoming information-processing constraints does not require any change in the specification of the solution space, since this barrier to innovation 'merely' indicates that the solution space is searched more efficiently and quickly. In other words, overcoming information-processing constraints indicates that the solution space is more effectively and efficiently exploited. In order to overcome local and inefficient search routines, however, it is necessary to explore the solution space so that more distant and creative solutions can be found.

To understand the capability levels of current AI systems in terms of assisting humans in the innovation process, it is important to understand some key technical features of these systems. Specifically, there are two key characteristics in most AI systems developed today that are constrained by human capabilities. First, human AI experts who collaborate with domain experts relying on their existing knowledge base train most current AI systems. This means that these AI systems should generally try to search a known, related knowledge base more extensively that is to say, most systems are limited in the extent which they can explore the problem space [10]. Second, state of the art AI systems are set up so that the learning process is optimized for a given objective function (Sejnowski, 2018). The human AI researchers implementing and training the system define this objective function.

Moreover, these objective functions are generally very sparse since the human researchers who are calibrating the systems cannot possibly know all possible objectives and, therefore, tend to fall short in their ability to provide an ideal objective function. Consequently, for most AI applications, the solution space is pre-defined by humans, and so current AI systems tend to have a very limited ability to explore the solution space autonomously. As a result, these two features of AI systems pose technical limitations on the systems' abilities to redefine and explore both the problem space and the solution space. Furthermore, most current AI systems are limited in their ability to generate or recognize ideas and opportunities and to overcome local search routines.

However, there have been some recent advancements suggesting that AI systems may indeed be able to overcome these limitations. Thus, we are able to derive a range of what we term 'information processing capability levels' for AI systems that indicate how likely AI systems are to replace and complement human decision making.

Despite its promising potential, AI presents significant challenges for African governments, authorities, and organizations, particularly in the realm of ethics. AI-driven technologies can amplify the effectiveness of hacking, digital surveillance, monitoring, and malicious software (Chan, 2018). The increasing reliance on AI systems has raised ethical concerns that need to be addressed. The development and deployment of AI systems need to be guided by ethical principles to ensure that they are used for the betterment of society. The use of AI in healthcare systems in Africa, in particular, can eliminate inefficiencies such as misdiagnosis, shortage of healthcare workers, and wait and recovery time. However, it is important to safeguard against issues such as privacy breaches, or lack of personalized care and accessibility. The central tenet of an AI framework must be ethics.

Globally, the most critical issue in healthcare is providing overarching and effective treatment options that improve standards of living. The World Health Organization (WHO) has developed a five-year strategic plan for reaching public health targets, as outlined in the Sustainable Development Goals (SDGs). In 2019, the WHO introduced the "triple billion" targets for global health, i.e. universal healthcare, health emergency protections, and overall better health outcomes for one billion people across the world (Chan, 2018). AI-centric solutions can help achieve these goals by increasing access, improving quality, and reducing costs. Despite countless benefits, however, the application of AI is vulnerable to pitfalls.

The current AI-powered health systems suffer from an absence of accurate datasets and the uneven management of sensitive health data. To be sure, the most significant ethical violations are not rooted in malicious intent, but in a lack of awareness of appropriate AI practices and safeguards. Stakeholders, including government and international organizations, are attempting to incorporate and implement safeguarding measures, with ethics as a central tenet of the AI framework. Accountability mechanisms when managing healthcare information can promote integrity and durability in AI systems.

By approaching AI systems with measured diffidence, a company can implement checks on the AI algorithm to reduce biases and promote holistic analyses. A study by the biopharmaceuticals company Syneos Health found one of the primary public concerns facing AI systems to be the "lack of human oversight and the potential for machine errors leading to mismanagement of their health" (Sallstrom et al., 2019). In 2018, the EU-backed EU High-Level Expert Group on Artificial Intelligence, which included industry professionals, non-governmental agencies, and scholars, released a guidance note concerning AI Ethics. The AI-HLEG is a European Commission-backed working group comprising representatives from industry, academia, and NGOs (Larsson, 2020). Entrepreneurs and major technology companies, such as Elon Musk, Peter Thiel, Sam Altman, Infosys, Microsoft, and Amazon, have created a joint non-profit AI research company called Open AI (de-Lima-Santos & Ceron, 2021). The International Telecommunication Union (ITU) and the WHO have collaborated to create a Focus Group on AI, aiming to establish standards and guidelines for AI-based methods in the healthcare sector. The ITU is an Africa-friendly forum, which may present opportunities for African AI researchers and innovators, as well as related healthcare experts (Sallstrom et al., 2019). In recent years, there has been increased global endeavour to establish basic principles of the ethical use of AI and accountability. However, current regulatory approaches to this field of technology remain mostly in the philosophical realm. Since this aspect of technology development is without precedent, there is little basis for formulating regulations.

Moreover, the need to strike a careful balance between allowing technology growth and ensuring accountability renders inadequate most of the current proposals. In collaboration with AI experts from across African Union (AU) Member States, the African Union High-Level Panel on Emerging Technologies (APET) is formulating an African Union – Artificial Intelligence Continental Strategy for Africa. To this end, APET has convened multiple consultative meetings with AI experts since 2021 to shape this continental strategy. In this strategy, APET underscores the importance of establishing ethical and legal frameworks to harness AI's potential while mitigating risks and emphasizing responsible data use. In addition to various other considerations, the AU-AI Continental Strategy encompasses promoting ethical AI practices, establishing consistent legal principles, and embracing pertinent treaties and guidelines. To achieve this, AU Member States are encouraged to establish regulatory bodies overseeing AI creation and usage, implement codes of ethics for AI stakeholders, and collaborate to create a pan-African AI legislative framework. Harmonizing AI legislation, defining guiding principles, and facilitating practical implementation are pivotal steps toward a unified and effective approach to AI development and utilization in Africa. This framework anticipates potential AI risks, facilitates the development of proactive safeguards, and establishes a robust strategy for fostering sustainable AI solutions across the continent.

CONCLUSION

An overview of specific areas of African healthcare where AI can have a transformative impact has been highlighted; including disease diagnosis, telemedicine, health monitoring, disease surveillance, and public health management. The effective AI efforts that have already been implemented in many African nations, their significance and advantages has also been presented. The lack and unequal distribution of health workers in the African healthcare systems, coupled with the unavailability of Afro-centric data and quality in resource-constrained settings in various health facilities in Africa may hinder the effective use of AI in African health care. AI also presents both opportunities and challenges that impact on healthcare professionals and workforce in Africa positively as well as negatively. In the positive sense, AI improves health care delivery and offer opportunities to develop new models that are Afrocentric. On the negative side, the lack of afro-centric data can lead to wrong diagnosis and workforce who do not upgrade their skills can become redundant. Highlighting successful AI initiatives in different African countries, which put South Africa, Mauritius, Rwanda and Nigeria as the countries that have developed framework to regulate the use of AI. The rest of the continent need to establish ethical AI practices in order to provide fair access, privacy protections, and responsible application of AI technology in Africa. A continental ethical guidelines, standard framework and regulatory body for AI in African healthcare must be developed harmony and easy transfer of technology.

CONTRIBUTION AND SIGNIFICANCE

By concentrating explicitly on the possibilities, difficulties, and ethical issues of AI in African healthcare, this chapter will significantly advance the literature. It will be a resource for policymakers, healthcare workers, researchers, and technology developers interested in utilizing AI to enhance health outcomes in Africa by addressing context-specific aspects.

REFERENCES

Abdelwahap, M., Elfarash, M., & Eltanboly, A. (2021). Applications Of Natural Language Processing In Healthcare Systems. *The International Undergraduate Research Conference*. Research Gate.

Adebisi, Y. A., Nwogu, I. B., Alaran, A. J., Badmos, A. O., Bamgboye, A. O., Rufai, B. O., Okonji, O. C., Malik, M. O., Teibo, J. O., Abdalla, S. F., Lucero-Prisno, D. E. III, Samai, M., & Akande-Sholabi, W. (2022). Revisiting the issue of access to medicines in Africa: Challenges and recommendations. *Public Health Challenges*, 1(2), e9. doi:10.1002/puh2.9

Akogo, D., Samori, I. A., Jimah, B. B., Anim, D. A., Mensah, Y. B., & Sarkodie, B. D. (2022). Mino-Health. AI: A Clinical Evaluation of Deep Learning Systems for the Diagnosis of Pleural Effusion and Cardiomegaly in Ghana, Vietnam, and the United States of America. *arXiv preprint arXiv:2211.00644*.

Alami, H., Rivard, L., Lehoux, P., Hoffman, S. J., Cadeddu, S. B. M., Savoldelli, M., Samri, M. A., Ag Ahmed, M. A., Fleet, R., & Fortin, J.-P. (2020). Artificial intelligence in health care: Laying the Foundation for Responsible, sustainable, and inclusive innovation in low-and middle-income countries. *Globalization and Health*, 16(1), 1–6. doi:10.1186/s12992-020-00584-1 PMID:32580741

Asumadu-Sarkodie, S., & Owusu, P. A. (2016). Forecasting Nigeria's energy use by 2030, an econometric approach. *Energy Sources. Part B, Economics, Planning, and Policy*, 11(10), 990–997. doi:10.1080/15567249.2016.1217287

Chan, M. (2018). *Ten Years in Public Health 2007-2017: Report by Dr Margaret Chan Director-General World Health Organization*. World Health Organization.

Chen, R. J., Wang, J. J., Williamson, D. F., Chen, T. Y., Lipkova, J., Lu, M. Y., Sahai, S., & Mahmood, F. (2023). Algorithmic fairness in artificial intelligence for medicine and healthcare. *Nature Biomedical Engineering*, 7(6), 719–742. doi:10.1038/s41551-023-01056-8 PMID:37380750

Childs, G. T. (2003). *An introduction to African languages* (Vol. 1). John Benjamins Publishing. doi:10.1075/z.121

Cirillo, D., Catuara-Solarz, S., Morey, C., Guney, E., Subirats, L., Mellino, S., Gigante, A., Valencia, A., Rementeria, M. J., Chadha, A. S., & Mavridis, N. (2020). Sex and gender differences and biases in artificial intelligence for biomedicine and healthcare. *NPJ Digital Medicine*, 3(1), 81. doi:10.1038/s41746-020-0288-5 PMID:32529043

de-Lima-Santos, M.-F., & Ceron, W. (2021). Artificial intelligence in news media: current perceptions and future outlook. *Journalism and media, 3*(1), 13-26.

Eke, D. O., Wakunuma, K., & Akintoye, S. (2023). Introducing Responsible AI in Africa. In *Responsible AI in Africa: Challenges and Opportunities* (pp. 1-11). Springer International Publishing Cham. doi:10.1007/978-3-031-08215-3_1

Ekekwe, N. (2018). How new technologies could transform Africa's health care system. *Harvard Business Review*, 6.

Etori, N., Temesgen, E., & Gini, M. (2023). What We Know So Far: Artificial Intelligence in African Healthcare. *arXiv preprint arXiv:2305.18302.*

Ganasegeran, K., & Abdulrahman, S. A. (2020). Artificial intelligence applications in tracking health behaviors during disease epidemics. *Human Behaviour Analysis Using Intelligent Systems,* 141-155.

Gonsalves, A. H., Thabtah, F., Mohammad, R. M. A., & Singh, G. (2019). Prediction of coronary heart disease using machine learning: An experimental analysis. Proceedings of the 2019 3rd International Conference on Deep Learning Technologies.

Gupta, A., & Katarya, R. (2020). Social media based surveillance systems for healthcare using machine learning: A systematic review. *Journal of Biomedical Informatics, 108,* 103500. doi:10.1016/j.jbi.2020.103500 PMID:32622833

Hagerty, A., & Rubinov, I. (2019). Global AI ethics: a review of the social impacts and ethical implications of artificial intelligence. *arXiv preprint arXiv:1907.07892.*

Hedderich, M. A., Lange, L., Adel, H., Strötgen, J., & Klakow, D. (2020). A survey on recent approaches for natural language processing in low-resource scenarios. *arXiv preprint arXiv:2010.12309.*

Hu, S., Zhou, L., Dong, N., Zhou, Y., Gao, Z., Xu, J., & Liang, Z. (2016). The design and implementation of the privacy protection system of a Regional Health Information Platform. *2016 IEEE International Conference on Bioinformatics and Biomedicine (BIBM).* IEEE.

Kaul, V., Enslin, S., & Gross, S. A. (2020). History of artificial intelligence in medicine. *Gastrointestinal Endoscopy, 92*(4), 807–812. doi:10.1016/j.gie.2020.06.040 PMID:32565184

Kaur, P., Mack, A. A., Patel, N., Pal, A., Singh, R., Michaud, A., & Mulflur, M. (2023). *Unlocking the Potential of Artificial Intelligence (AI) for Healthcare.* IEEE.

Koene, A., Clifton, C., Hatada, Y., Webb, H., & Richardson, R. (2019). *A governance framework for algorithmic accountability and transparency.*

Larsson, S. (2020). On the governance of artificial intelligence through ethics guidelines. *Asian Journal of Law and Society, 7*(3), 437–451. doi:10.1017/als.2020.19

Lee, C.-S., & Wang, M.-H. (2010). A fuzzy expert system for diabetes decision support application. *IEEE Transactions on Systems, Man, and Cybernetics. Part B, Cybernetics, 41*(1), 139–153. PMID:20501347

Leite, F. O., Cochat, C., Salgado, H., da Costa, M. P., Queirós, M., Campos, O., & Carvalho, P. (2016). Using Google Translate^© in the hospital: A case report. *Technology and Health Care, 24*(6), 965–968. doi:10.3233/THC-161241 PMID:27447408

Li, I., Li, Y., Li, T., Alvarez-Napagao, S., Garcia-Gasulla, D., & Suzumura, T. (2020). What are we depressed about when we talk about covid-19: Mental health analysis on tweets using natural language processing. *Artificial Intelligence XXXVII: 40th SGAI International Conference on Artificial Intelligence, AI 2020,* Cambridge, UK.

Lunze, K., Higgins-Steele, A., Simen-Kapeu, A., Vesel, L., Kim, J., & Dickson, K. (2015). Innovative approaches for improving maternal and newborn health-A landscape analysis. *BMC Pregnancy and Childbirth*, *15*(1), 1–19. doi:10.1186/s12884-015-0784-9 PMID:26679709

Mahomed, S. (2018). Healthcare, artificial intelligence and the Fourth Industrial Revolution: Ethical, social and legal considerations. *South African Journal of Bioethics and Law*, *11*(2), 93–95. doi:10.7196/SAJBL.2018.v11i2.664

Martinus, L., & Abbott, J. Z. (2019). A focus on neural machine translation for african languages. *arXiv preprint arXiv:1906.05685*.

Mbunge, E., Muchemwa, B., & Batani, J. (2022). Are we there yet? Unbundling the potential adoption and integration of telemedicine to improve virtual healthcare services in African health systems. *Sensors International*, *3*, 100152. doi:10.1016/j.sintl.2021.100152 PMID:34901894

Moyo, S., Doan, T. N., Yun, J. A., & Tshuma, N. (2018). Application of machine learning models in predicting length of stay among healthcare workers in underserved communities in South Africa. *Human Resources for Health*, *16*(1), 1–9.

Naicker, S., Plange-Rhule, J., Tutt, R. C., & Eastwood, J. B. (2009). Shortage of healthcare workers in developing countries—Africa. *Ethnicity & Disease*, *19*, 60–64. PMID:19484878

Newell, A., & Simon, H. A. (1972). *Human problem solving* (Vol. 104). Prentice-hall Englewood Cliffs.

Norori, N., Hu, Q., Aellen, F. M., Faraci, F. D., & Tzovara, A. (2021). Addressing bias in big data and AI for health care: A call for open science. *Patterns (New York, N.Y.)*, *2*(10), 100347. doi:10.1016/j.patter.2021.100347 PMID:34693373

Nutbeam, D. (2000). Health literacy as a public health goal: A challenge for contemporary health education and communication strategies into the 21st century. *Health Promotion International*, *15*(3), 259–267. doi:10.1093/heapro/15.3.259

Nwaneri, S., & Ugo, H. (2022). Development of a graphical user interface software for the prediction of chronic kidney disease. *Nigerian Journal of Technology, 41*(1), 175–183-175–183.

Oleribe, O. O., Momoh, J., Uzochukwu, B. S., Mbofana, F., Adebiyi, A., Barbera, T., Williams, R., & Taylor-Robinson, S. D. (2019). Identifying key challenges facing healthcare systems in Africa and potential solutions. *International Journal of General Medicine*, *12*, 395–403. doi:10.2147/IJGM.S223882 PMID:31819592

Onu, C. C., Lebensold, J., Hamilton, W. L., & Precup, D. (2019). Neural transfer learning for cry-based diagnosis of perinatal asphyxia. *arXiv preprint arXiv:1906.10199*. doi:10.21437/Interspeech.2019-2340

Organization, W. H. (2016). Health workforce requirements for universal health coverage and the sustainable development goals. *Human Resources For Health Observer, 17*.

Owoyemi, A., Owoyemi, J., Osiyemi, A., & Boyd, A. (2020). Artificial intelligence for healthcare in Africa. *Frontiers in Digital Health*, *2*, 6. doi:10.3389/fdgth.2020.00006 PMID:34713019

Oyebode, O., & Orji, R. (2018). Likita: a medical chatbot to improve healthcare delivery in Africa. *HCI Across Borders (HCIxB)*.

Panch, T., Mattie, H., & Atun, R. (2019). Artificial intelligence and algorithmic bias: Implications for health systems. *Journal of Global Health*, *9*(2), 010318. doi:10.7189/jogh.09.020318 PMID:31788229

Patil, S., & Davies, P. (2014). Use of Google Translate in medical communication: Evaluation of accuracy. *BMJ (Clinical Research Ed.)*, *349*(dec15 2), 349. doi:10.1136/bmj.g7392 PMID:25512386

Powles, J. (2018). *The seductive diversion of 'solving' bias in artificial intelligence.*

Restrepo, J., & Christiaans, H. (2004). Problem structuring and information access in design. *Journal of Desert Research*, *4*(2), 218–236. doi:10.1504/JDR.2004.009842

Sallstrom, L., Morris, O., & Mehta, H. (2019). Artificial intelligence in Africa's healthcare: Ethical considerations. *ORF Issue Brief,* (312).

Sejnowski, T. J. (2018). *The deep learning revolution.* MIT press. doi:10.7551/mitpress/11474.001.0001

Srinivasan, R., & Chander, A. (2021). Biases in AI systems. *Communications of the ACM*, *64*(8), 44–49.

Thompson, T., Sowunmi, O., Misra, S., Fernandez-Sanz, L., Crawford, B., & Soto, R. (2017). An expert system for the diagnosis of sexually transmitted diseases–ESSTD. *Journal of Intelligent & Fuzzy Systems*, *33*(4), 2007–2017. doi:10.3233/JIFS-161242

Topol, E. (2019). *Deep medicine: how artificial intelligence can make healthcare human again.*

Townsend, B. A., Sihlahla, I., Naidoo, M., Naidoo, S., Donnelly, D.-L., & Thaldar, D. W. (2023). Mapping the regulatory landscape of AI in healthcare in Africa. *Frontiers in Pharmacology*, *14*, 14. doi:10.3389/fphar.2023.1214422 PMID:37693916

Tran, B. X., Vu, G. T., Ha, G. H., Vuong, Q.-H., Ho, M.-T., Vuong, T.-T., La, V.-P., Ho, M.-T., Nghiem, K.-C. P., Nguyen, H. L. T., Latkin, C., Tam, W., Cheung, N.-M., Nguyen, H.-K., Ho, C., & Ho, R. (2019). Global evolution of research in artificial intelligence in health and medicine: A bibliometric study. *Journal of Clinical Medicine*, *8*(3), 360. doi:10.3390/jcm8030360 PMID:30875745

Union, A. (2014). African Union convention on cyber security and personal data protection. *African Union, 27*.

Wahl, B., Cossy-Gantner, A., Germann, S., & Schwalbe, N. R. (2018). Artificial intelligence (AI) and global health: How can AI contribute to health in resource-poor settings? *BMJ Global Health*, *3*(4), e000798. doi:10.1136/bmjgh-2018-000798 PMID:30233828

ADDITIONAL READING

Arakpogun, E. O., Elsahn, Z., Olan, F., & Elsahn, F. (2021). Artificial intelligence in Africa: Challenges and opportunities. *The fourth industrial revolution: Implementation of artificial intelligence for growing business success*, 375-388.

Bandyopadhyay, A. (2020). The multiplier effect of applied machine learning technology in modern healthcare. *International Journal of Information Science and Computing, 7*(1), 37–47. doi:10.30954/2348-7437.1.2020.4

Curiel-Lewandrowski, C., Novoa, R. A., Berry, E., Celebi, M. E., Codella, N., Giuste, F., & & Tschandl, P. (2019). Artificial intelligence approach in melanoma. *Melanoma*, 1-31.

Fruehwirt, W., & Duckworth, P. (2021). Towards better healthcare: What could and should be automated? *Technological Forecasting and Social Change, 172*, 120967. doi:10.1016/j.techfore.2021.120967

Kumar, A., Aelgani, V., & Vohra, R. (2023). *Artificial intelligence bias in medical system designs: a systematic review*. Multimed Tools Appl., doi:10.1007/s11042-023-16029-x

Mbunge, E., & Batani, J. (2023). Application of deep learning and machine learning models to improve healthcare in sub-Saharan Africa: Emerging opportunities, trends and implications. *Telematics and Informatics Reports*, 100097.

Naidoo, S., Bottomley, D., Naidoo, M., Donnelly, D., & Thaldar, D. W. (2022). Artificial intelligence in healthcare: Proposals for policy development in South Africa. *South African Journal of Bioethics and Law, 15*(1), 11–16. doi:10.7196/SAJBL.2022.v15i1.797 PMID:36061984

Njei, B., Kanmounye, U. S., Mohamed, M. F., Forjindam, A., Ndemazie, N. B., Adenusi, A., Egboh, S.-M. C., Chukwudike, E. S., Monteiro, J. F. G., Berzin, T. M., & Asombang, A. W. (2023). Artificial intelligence for healthcare in Africa: A scientometric analysis. *Health and Technology, 13*(6), 1–9. doi:10.1007/s12553-023-00786-8

Stacy, M. (2020). The ethical, legal and social implications of using artificial intelligence systems in breast cancer care. *The Breast, 49*, 25-32.

Woodman, R., & Mangoni, A. A. (2023). Artificial Intelligence and the Medicine of the Future. In *Gerontechnology. A Clinical Perspective* (pp. 175–204). Springer International Publishing. doi:10.1007/978-3-031-32246-4_12

Chapter 7
Navigating Emerging Challenges in Robotics and Artificial Intelligence in Africa

Wasswa Shafik

iD https://orcid.org/0000-0002-9320-3186

School of Digital Science, Universiti Brunei Darussalam, Brunei & Dig Connectivity Research Laboratory (DCRLab), Kampala, Uganda

ABSTRACT

Artificial intelligence (AI) and robotics are becoming more popular globally, which makes Africa a potential hub for innovation and development in these fields. However, for the full benefits of these technologies to be realized, it is vital to understand and deal with the unique challenges and barriers that make it hard for them to be used and integrated in Africa. This chapter presents an overview of the current state of robotics and AI in Africa and explores the challenges associated with their adoption, including infrastructure limitations, inadequate technical expertise, and ethical considerations. It further discusses potential strategies for overcoming these challenges, such as investment in infrastructure and education, international collaboration, and the development of ethical frameworks for AI. Finally, the chapter suggests some future directions for continued attention and investment in the responsible and equitable development of AI and robotics in Africa to benefit stagnant and slow-growing African economies.

INTRODUCTION

In the past few years, the robotics and artificial intelligence (AI) fields have grown and changed uniquely and impacted many industries and sectors worldwide (Bhagwan & Evans, 2023). These technologies can potentially revolutionize how we live and work, creating new opportunities for economic growth and development. However, as with any new technology, there are problems to solve, especially in places like Africa that are still developing (Ade-Ibijola & Okonkwo, 2023; Kamau & Ilamoya, n.d.). Even though the continent is quickly adopting new technologies, significant problems still make it hard for robots and AI to be widely used and integrated. In this situation, it is essential to figure out how to deal with

DOI: 10.4018/978-1-6684-9962-7.ch007

the problems and use the benefits of these technologies to support long-term growth and social progress (Nyholm, 2023; Shafik, 2024). Using a desktop research approach, this chapter critically engages the AI literature in order to examine some of the new problems that have arisen with the emergence of robotics and AI use in Africa and possible ways to solve them.

Before engaging the substantive issues for this chapter it important to provide a snapshot of the geography of the African continent. Africa is a continent that has 54 countries with an area of 30,370,000 km² and 1.4 billion individuals as of 2021, making 18% of the biosphere's people, subdivided into five major regions, like Northern Africa (with countries like Libya, Egypt, North Sudan, Algeria, Morocco, and Tunisia as demonstrated in Figure 1) inhabiting the northerly region of Africa. The most densely inhabited subregion of Africa is East Africa, with approximately 456 million people. There are two dependencies, and 18 countries which use the Swahili language as their eastern community language, with the majority practicing Islam and Christianity (Bainomugisha et al., 2023; Wang et al., 2023). These countries are Kenya, Madagascar, Mauritius, Zimbabwe, Malawi, Zambia, Comoros, Eritrea, Ethiopia, Djibouti, Mozambique, Uganda, Tanzania, Burundi, South Sudan, Somalia, Seychelles, and Rwanda, as demonstrated in Figure 2 as of the world atlas. Tanzania, Rwanda, South Sudan, Ethiopia, and Kenya are the fastest-growing nations due to AI and robotic involvement in economic and social well-being (Ruttkamp-Bloem, 2023).

Figure 1. North African countries

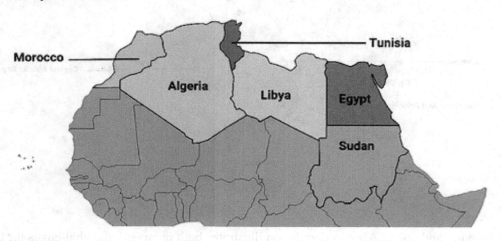

West Africa comprises of one dependency and 16 countries (Benin, Sierra Leone, Togo, Niger, Mali, Senegal, Nigeria, Mauritania, Cabo Verde, Guinea-Bissau, Burkina Faso, Ivory Coast, Guinea, Ghana, Gambia, Liberia), with Nigeria being the largest with the largest capital city. In this region, Burkina Faso, Niger, and Mali are landlocked countries; the geographical positions of these countries are illustrated in Figure 3. On the other hand, middle Africa is situated in the middle of Africa with nations like Sao Tome and Principe, Cameroon, the Democratic Republic of the Congo, Equatorial Guinea, Congo, the Central African Republic, Chad, Gabon, Angola, and South Africa situated in the southern part of the continent has countries South Africa, Eswatini, Botswana, Namibia, and Lesotho in Figure 4 and Figure 5, respectively.

Figure 2. East African countries

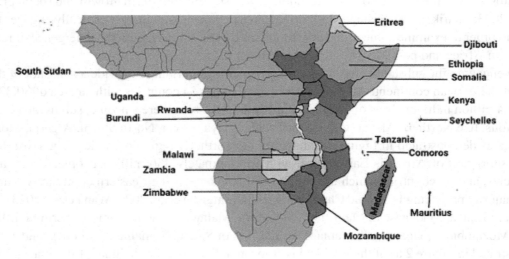

Figure 3. Middle African countries (Eq.= Equatorial and Rep = Republic, Dem. = Democratic)

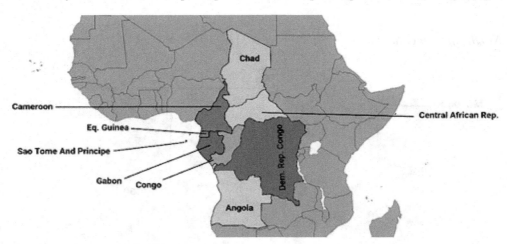

The growing and young African population illustrates both prospects and challenges for the growth of robotics and AI in the region. On the one hand, as the continent's economies and cities continue to grow, people are likely to want more automation and new technologies (Ramnund-Mansingh & Naidoo, 2023; Ruttkamp-Bloem, 2023). Also, there are concerns about the potential impact of automation on employment in sectors such as manufacturing and agriculture, which are essential sources of job opportunities for many Africans.

To simplify the technological concepts, robotics refers to the design, development, and operation of robots, which are machines capable of performing tasks autonomously or with minimal human input (Calabrese et al., 2023). Robotics involves using various high-tech devices, for example, controllers, actuators, and sensors, to enable robots to perceive and interact with the environment in which they operate. AI is simply the process of making computers that can do things that usually require human intelligence, like seeing, thinking, learning, and making decisions (Tsvetkova, 2023). AI uses algorithms, statistical

Figure 4. West African countries

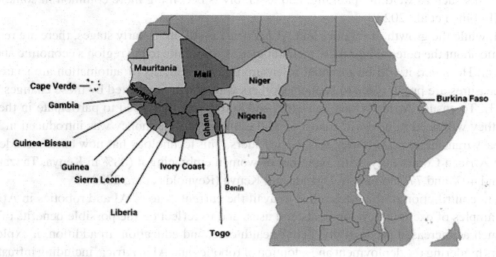

Figure 5. South African countries

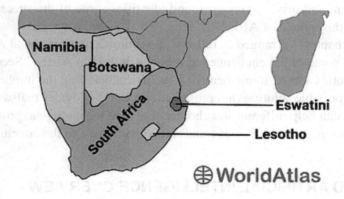

models, and machine learning to teach computers how to read and understand data, spot patterns, and make predictions or choices.

The market for robotics and AI in Africa is still relatively small, but it is predicted to grow in the coming generation. According to a report by Research & Markets, the AI market in Africa is anticipated to grow at a compound annual growth rate (CAGR) of 29.3% between 2020 and 2025 (Chauke et al., 2023; Shafik, 2024). The report notes that several factors are driving the growth of AI in Africa, including increased adoption of the Internet of Things (IoT), big data analytics, and cloud computing. IoTs are devices that connect to the internet mainly for resource sharing. Regarding robotics, the market in Africa is also expected to grow, particularly in healthcare, agriculture, and manufacturing (Foster et al., 2023; Yang et al., 2021; Shafik et al., 2020). For example, several startups in Africa are already developing robotic solutions for healthcare, such as autonomous drones for medical supply delivery and robotic exoskeletons for rehabilitation. In addition, the agriculture sector is showing a keen interest in using drones and other robotic systems for precision farming and crop monitoring. In manufacturing, using robots for tasks such as welding, painting, and assembly is becoming more common in some African countries (Lubinga et al., 2023).

Overall, while the growth of robotics and AI in Africa is still in its early stages, there are reasons to be optimistic about the potential for these technologies to contribute to the region's economic and social development. However, it will be essential to ensure that the benefits of automation are shared fairly and that measures are put in place to support workers who may be impacted by these changes (Ukoba et al., 2023). To ensure Africans have the skills and knowledge they need to participate in the digital economy, they will need to invest in education and training. Mobile money was introduced in Uganda to ensure easy transfer across different service providers. This technology has now been extended to the entire East African Community, with a number of women embracing it (88% in Kenya, Tanzania, and Uganda) and 40% and 77% in men in Uganda and Kenya (Reynolds et al., 2023).

The main contribution of this research is to avail the current state of AI and robotics in Africa, including examples of exciting developments and uses, and to reflect on the possible benefits of AI and robotics, such as increased productivity, better health care, and education. In addition, it explores the main factors hindering the deployment and adoption of robotics and AI in Africa, including infrastructure constraints, a lack of technical expertise, and ethical considerations (Kalinaki et al., 2024). Finally the chapter also analyzes the potential negative consequences of unchecked robotics and AI development, like job displacement and privacy concerns, and identifies some of the strategies for navigating these emerging issues in the context of Africa.

The rest of the chapter is arranged as follows. In section 2, a robotics and AI overview is presented. Section 3, explores some of the challenges of robotics and AI in Africa . Section 4 portrays emerging concerns about robotics and AI implementation in Africa, detailing the implications of the challenges, while in Section 5, possible solutions are presented. Section 6 provides real-world suggestions and recommendations that can help different stakeholders improve technological progress. Finally, Sections 7 and 8 hones in on future AI and robotics trends and directions, and the conclusion respectively.

ROBOTICS AND ARTIFICIAL INTELLIGENCE OVERVIEW

Robotics and AI are two of the most rapidly advancing fields in technology today. Regarding Africa, increasingly its people are using these technologies (Lubinga et al., 2023). These two fields have the potential to revolutionize how we consciously and subconsciously live and operate in our daily lives, demonstrating the sustainable, secure, and privacy-oriented global village of the future, as seen in some intelligent cities.

These robots can be programmed to do various jobs, from making things to going into space. Robotics has already made significant advancements in industries such as manufacturing, where robots are used to perform repetitive tasks with high precision and speed, reducing the need for human labor while increasing effectiveness (Baguma et al., 2023; Fahim et al., 2024). AI, on the other hand, involves the development of machines that can learn and perform tasks that typically require human intelligence. For example, AI systems can be trained to recognize patterns in data and make decisions based on that data. This technology has already been applied to various fields, including healthcare, finance, and transportation (Eke, Chintu, et al., 2023).

One of the most exciting research areas in robotics and AI is the development of autonomous systems. Self-driving robots and cars could change many industries, such as transportation and logistics. For example, autonomous vehicles could be used to transport goods and people more efficiently and safely (Bainomugisha et al., 2023; Chauke et al., 2023). This could significantly impact the environment, reducing traffic congestion and emissions. Humanoid robots that can interact with people naturally is another area of research in robotics and AI. These robots could be used in various settings, such as healthcare and education, to assist and support people.

The development of robotics and AI has also raised ethical concerns. For example, there are concerns about the impact of automation on jobs and the economy. As robots and AI systems improve, they might be able to do the jobs humans do now (Modiba, 2023; Shafik, 2023). This could lead to people losing their jobs. Moreover, because of the tested benefits, this industrial path is predicted to increase in growth and be seen in the next technological wave in Africa. There are also concerns about the impact of AI on privacy and security, as well as the potential for AI systems to be used in ways that are harmful to society (Aigbavboa et al., 2023; Shafik, 2023). However, robotics and AI are rapidly evolving and can potentially transform many aspects of our lives. Therefore, even though there are challenges and worries about these technologies, there is also much potential for them to help society if they are made and used responsibly.

Technically, robotics and AI are two closely related fields, and there is significant overlap between them even though a thin line exists between them. For instance, some similarities involve using computer software and hardware to accomplish tasks. Robotics is the study of designing, building, and using robots which can do tasks independently or with minimum human help (Stahl et al., 2023; Shafik, 2023). Conversely, AI is concerned with developing algorithms and software that can learn, reason, and make decisions similar to human beings. Both fields rely on sensors to gather information about the environment. In robotics, sensors like cameras, light detection and ranging (LIDAR), and proximity sensors are used to learn about the environment and move through it (Stahl et al., 2023). AI uses sensors such as microphones and cameras to perceive the environment and gather data for decisions.

Both fields require programming and algorithm design to accomplish tasks. In robotics, this involves programming the robot to perform tasks such as grasping objects, navigating through space, or performing a particular action (Aigbavboa et al., 2023; Stahl et al., 2023). AI involves designing algorithms that can process large amounts of data, learn from it, and make decisions based on that learning. AI and Roboticscan also be jointly used to achieve more complex tasks. For example, like a human, a robot can use AI to recognize and grasp objects, navigate through space, and perform a task in a human-like manner.

While there are many similarities between robotics and AI, some key differences can be noticed in terms of operational focus (Ndzendze & Marwala, 2023). For example, robotics focuses on designing, constructing, and operating physical machines that can perform tasks, while AI focuses on developing software algorithms that can learn, reason, and make decisions similar to humans. The target of robotics is to create machines that can perform tasks in place of humans or aid humans in performing tasks (Daniels et al., 2023; Alaziz et al., 2023). AI aims to make software that can mimic how people think and make decisions.

From a hardware and software perspective, robotics involves building and programming physical machines, while AI focuses entirely on software development. Given that sensing and perception require sensors, robotics requires sensors to perceive and interact with the physical world. While AI employs various data sources such as text, images, and audio to learn and make decisions for complexity; robotics tends to be more focused on specific tasks and requires a high degree of engineering expertise (Ndzendze & Marwala, 2023). AI can be applied to a broader range of problems and requires expertise in computer science, information technology, information systems, system engineering, computer engineering, mathematics, and other Science, Technology, Engineering, and Mathematics (STEM) disciplines. In summary, robotics is concerned with designing and building physical machines, while AI is concerned with developing intelligent software algorithms (Tompihe, 2023). While there are similarities between the two fields, their goals, foci, and methods are different.

ROBOTICS AND AI ACCEPTANCE EMERGING CHALLENGES

Emerging challenges of Africa's robotics and AI are seen to impact employment automation potentially. While robotics and AI can increase efficiency and productivity in many industries, they may also lead to job losses in Africa amidst an increased number of graduates from different arenas of endeavors, particularly in labor-intensive sectors, for instance, manufacturing and agriculture (Ade-Ibijola & Okonkwo, 2023; Stahl et al., 2023). This could the already the high unemployment rates in many African countries, creating social and economic challenges that must be addressed. Furthermore, there are ethical and regulatory challenges related to using robotics and AI in Africa. The increasing use of these technologies raises important questions about privacy, data protection, and accountability (Ndzendze & Marwala, 2023). The lack of clear legal frameworks and regulations for using robotics and AI systems could lead to potential abuses of these technologies, such as the spread of false information or the infringement of human rights, which are explored in the next section.

Insufficient Infrastructure

Infrastructure refers to standards that need to be available to implement AI and robotics in Africa. It impacts on development of AI and Robotics in some significant ways; for example, robots and AI systems require reliable and dependable power supply to function correctly (Daniels et al., 2023; Shafik et al., 2022). However, many developing countries in Africa and rural areas still experience regular power outages or have limited access to electricity. This can hinder the implementation of robotics and AI systems in these areas.

Network connectivity is necessary for AI and robotics systems to "talk" to each other and use cloud-based resources; such connectivity must be fast and reliable. In areas with poor network connectivity, this can lead to slow or disrupted communication, leading to degraded performance of AI and robotics systems (Foster et al., 2023). In addition adequate hardware infrastructure like sensors, processors, and storage devices is needed by AI and robotics to operate. In places where the hardware infrastructure is not good, it is difficult to get and keep these parts up to date, limiting what robots and AI systems can do.

Robotics and AI systems require skilled technicians and engineers to design, install, and maintain them. In areas with limited access to such skilled labor, it can be challenging to deploy and operate these systems effectively, especially in African countries that are affected by wars that are either political, tribal, or related. The communal and herder-farmer conflicts in Nigeria, the Somali Civil War in the Allied Democratic Forces insurgency, and the "Ituri" conflict, predominately in the Democratic Republic of Congo, war in Darfur, Sudan, M23 offensive, and Kivu conflicts in Congo, Rwanda, and Rwanda, are typical examples. Such conflicts, in most cases, hinder the uptake and growth of technology (Tsvetkova, 2023).

The lack of regulatory frameworks for the use of robotics and AI systems raises essential ethical and legal questions, and their deployment needs regulatory frameworks to ensure they are used safely and responsibly. In places where these frameworks do not exist or are not good enough, organizations may hesitate to use robotics and AI systems because they are worried about legal risks and ethical issues (Eke, Wakunuma, et al., 2023). So, a lack of both regulatory and physical infrastructure can make it hard for people to use robotics and AI, limiting their effectiveness and reach. These infrastructure-related problems must be fixed if these technologies are to be widely used and reach their full potential in Africa.

Network Connectivity

Network connectivity is crucial for the functioning of modern-day robots and AI systems. However, inadequate or unreliable network connectivity can severely hinder their adoption and performance. Regarding latency, robotics, and AI systems require low-latency network connections to respond quickly and accurately to the input they receive. High latency can cause delays and result in suboptimal performance, and for the bandwidth, robotics and AI systems generate large amounts of data, which need to be processed in real-time (Sanusi et al., 2023). Insufficient bandwidth can result in slow data transfer and processing, leading to system failures or errors.

From a security point of view, robotics and AI systems often interact with sensitive information. It would be best to have a secure network connection to keep this information safe from unauthorized access or hacking attempts (Zhao et al., 2023; Shokoor et al., 2022). Weak or unreliable network connectivity can result in security breaches and remote access. Many AI and robotics systems are made to work from afar, and they need to be connected to a network to "talk" to their operators or managers (Sanusi et al., 2023; Shava & Mhlanga, 2023). Remote access can be hard or even impossible when network connections are unreliable or limited. This makes it harder for these technologies to be used. Instant network connectivity is critical in the performance, security, and remote accessibility of robotics and AI systems (Stahl et al., 2023; Jun et al., 2021). Inadequate or unreliable network connectivity can severely hinder the adoption and effectiveness of robotics and AI in various fields, including healthcare, education, manufacturing, and transportation.

User Attitudes

User attitudes can significantly impact the adoption of robotics and AI technologies. Even if these technologies can potentially improve efficiency, productivity, and safety in many fields, they might not be used if people do not like them. One key User attitude that can hinder robotics and AI adoption is fear of job displacement. Some people fear that robots and AI will take over their jobs, leading to unemployment (Ma, 2023). This fear can lead to resistance and reluctance to adopt these technologies, even if they could benefit the workplace.

Users may not trust robotics and AI systems, mainly when new and unfamiliar. This lack of trust can lead to skepticism and resistance, making adopting and implementing these technologies challenging. Cultural attitudes towards technology and automation can also hinder robotics and AI adoption. Some cultures value traditional work methods and may be resistant to change. Robotics, and AI systems can be complex and challenging to understand, leading to a lack of confidence and a reluctance to use them (McCallum & Aziakpono, 2023). So, how people feel about robots and AI can significantly affect how they are used and how many people use them (Gyimah et al., 2023). To get people to adopt and use these technologies, dealing with these attitudes through education, communication, and training is essential.

Culture and Ethics

Different cultures have different values and beliefs, which can affect the acceptance of these technologies. Furthermore, ethical concerns surrounding the use of these technologies can also hinder their adoption (Daniels et al., 2023; Gyimah et al., 2023). The following examples depictways in which culture and ethics can hinder robotics and AI adoption.

Cultural differences: Automated, robotic, and AI technologies may be used differently in different cultures because of how people feel about them. Some cultures may be more open to these new technologies, while others may be more hesitant and stick to old ways.

Bias and discrimination:robotics and AI systems can reinforce existing biases and discrimination, which raises ethical questions. For example, people may be wrongly identified by facial recognition technology based on their race, which can lead to bias in law enforcement.

Privacy concerns: Robotics and AI systems may be able to collect and store sensitive information, which raises privacy concerns (Borokini et al., 2023). This can slow down adoption, especially in healthcare, where data privacy is paramount.

Safety concerns: Robotics and AI can pose safety risks, especially when interacting with people. This can raise ethical questions, which can slow down adoption in fields like transportation and healthcare. Concerns about culture and ethics can affect how robotics and AI are used and adopted (Borokini et al., 2023; Ruttkamp-Bloem, 2023). It is essential to deal with these worries to ensure that these technologies are built and used in a way that aligns with ethical values and principles in Africa and elsewhere.

Absence of Appropriate Government Policies on AI and Robotics

Culturale and ethical concerns can make it hard for robots and AI to be used because governments do not have the right policies. The lack of clear government policies on the ethical use of these technologies can create uncertainty and reluctance to adopt them. I discuss a few of the concerns regarding appropriate government policies below.

The lack of clear regulations on the use of robotics and AI technologies can lead to ethical concerns (Lauri et al., 2023). For example, there may be no guidelines on how to ensure the safety and security of these technologies or how to prevent bias and discrimination.

Uncertain liability and the lack of clear liability laws can make people less likely to use robotics and AI. This is particularly true regarding accidents or damages caused by these technologies.

Robotics and AI technologies require significant investment, and the lack of adequate funding can hinder their adoption (Mensah et al., 2023). Government policies that do not provide sufficient funding can limit the development and use of these technologies.

Robotics and AI technologies can be complex and require specialized skills to develop and use. The lack of educational programs and training opportunities can limit the adoption of these technologies (Mare et al., 2023)..

Uncertainty

Ambiguity can hinder the adoption of robotics and AI technologies. Because these technologies are new and could significantly affect society, knowing their benefits and risks can be challenging. Here are some ways in which uncertainty can hinder the adoption of robotics and AI technologies: Lack of trust and uncertainty about the benefits and risks of these technologies can lead to a lack of trust in them. Without trust, individuals and organizations may hesitate to adopt them (Uunona & Goosen, 2023). Fear of job loss: Robotics and AI technologies have the potential to automate many jobs, leading to concerns about job loss. This fear can make people not want to use these technologies, especially in fields where automation could significantly affect jobs.

Ethical concerns: people may be hesitant to use these technologies if they do not know what their ethical effects will be. People and organizations may hesitate to use these technologies because they worry about privacy, security, and bias. Lack of understanding: The complexity of robotics and AI technologies can make them challenging. This lack of understanding can create uncertainty about their benefits and risks, making individuals and organizations hesitant to adopt them (Baguma et al., 2023; McCallum & Aziakpono, 2023). Therefore, uncertainty can hinder the adoption of robotics and AI technologies. It is crucial to address concerns about trust, job loss, ethics, and understanding to promote the adoption of these technologies. Education, clear communication about benefits and risks, and ethical guidelines can help reduce uncertainty and increase adoption.

Addressing Emerging Challenges of Robotics and AI in Africa

The emerging challenges of robotics and AI in Africa can be addressed through various approaches. Here are some possible ways of addressing these challenges:

Education and Training

It requires education and training programs to increase the number of individuals with the necessary skills and knowledge to develop and use robotics and AI technologies in Africa. This could include trying to make technology education and training programs easier to get into, offering mentorship and internships, and supporting research and development in robotics and AI.

Collaboration and Partnerships

Ccollaboration and partnerships between African countries, international organizations, and private sector entities to foster innovation, knowledge-sharing, and resource mobilization is important. This could include technology transfer programs, cross-border research collaborations, and public-private partnerships to address societal needs and problems.

Policy and Regulatory Frameworks

Developing and implementing policies and regulatory frameworks that address emerging ethical, social, and legal concerns surrounding robotics and AI is a critical need. This could involve the creation of national AI and robotics strategies, data protection laws, and ethical guidelines that promote transparency, fairness, and accountability.

Infrastructure Development

Investing in physical infrastructure such as broadband connectivity, cloud computing services, and data centers to support the growth and development of robotics and AI technologies in Africa is important. This could be done through partnerships between the public and private sectors to make more resources available and improve connectivity and data management.

Investment in Research and Development

I Investment in research and development to promote the creation of locally relevant and culturally appropriate robotics and AI solutions cannot be emphasized enough. This could be done by forming partnerships between the business and academic worlds to encourage innovation and solve societal problems.

Awareness and Public Engagement Raising public awareness about the potential benefits and risks of robotics and AI technologies and engaging communities to understand that their needs and concerns can be addressed by these technologies is important. This could involve public outreach programs, workshops, and seminars to promote dialogue and collaboration.

Access to funding and Resources

The availability of venture capital funds, government-backed grants, and tax incentives would make it easier for African people to get the money and resources they need to develop and use robotics and AI technologies and encourage investment in the sector.

Addressing Infrastructure and Connectivity Gaps

Addressing infrastructure and connectivity gaps in Africa is key for developing and deploying robotics and AI technologies in remote and rural areas. This could mean putting money into the utilization of renewable energy sources (Shafik & Tufail, 2023), mobile technology, and new ways to store and manage data.

DISCUSSION ON ROBOTICS AND ARTIFICIAL INTELLIGENCE IN AFRICA

The emerging challenges of robotics and AI in Africa are significant, and addressing them will require a comprehensive approach that involves multiple stakeholders. These challenges include acquiring skills, appropriate government policy deficiencies, uncertainty, culture and ethics, network connectivity, and access to funding and resources (Turki et al., 2023). However, by investing in education and training, forging collaboration and partnerships, crafting policy and regulatory frameworks, infrastructure development, and promoting research and development, African countries can create an enabling environment for developing and adopting robotics and AI technologies (Tunjera & Chigona, 2023). Additionally, raising public awareness and engaging communities in the development process can ensure that these technologies are developed and deployed inclusively and sustainably to address societal challenges and create opportunities for economic growth (Ndhlovu & Goosen, 2023).

Even though robotics and AI have the potential to make significant changes in many fields, like healthcare, agriculture, and manufacturing, there are worries about how they might affect jobs and social equality. Because of this, it is essential to think about the ethical, social, and legal effects of these technologies and make sure they are made and used in fair and reasonable ways for everyone (Jide-Omole, 2023). Also, fixing infrastructure and connectivity problems is essential to ensure that these technologies can be used in all parts of Africa and help people living in remote or rural areas. Overall, governments, the private sector, and international organizations need to make a long-term commitment to support innovation, build capacity, and promote inclusive and sustainable development in Africa to deal with the new problems that robotics and AI pose (Uunona & Goosen, 2023).

Also, dealing with the new problems that robotics and AI will bring to Africa will require significant capital outlays especially for research and development. International collaborations and partnerships can be significant for accessing money, knowledge, and technology (Tunjera & Chigona, 2023). However, it is equally essential for African countries to develop their research and development capabilities to ensure that the solutions developed are relevant to their needs and challenges. Finally, addressing the acquisition of skills will be critical in ensuring that Africans are equipped with the knowledge and expertise necessary to participate in developing and deploying these technologies (Peter et al., 2023). This requires a focus on education and training programs tailored to local needs and challenges and can provide individuals with the skills required to create, use, and maintain robotics and AI technologies.

Furthermore, the issue of data privacy and security is of paramount importance in the context of Africa. As more organizations adopt robotics and AI, there is an increasing risk of data breaches and cyber-attacks (Shava & Mhlanga, 2023). Therefore, it is essential to prioritize cybersecurity measures and ensure that data privacy regulations are in place to protect the rights of individuals and businesses. While the challenges facing the adoption of robotics and AI in Africa are significant, they can be overcome with the right strategies and investment. There is a need for a concerted effort to create an environment that enables the development and adoption of these technologies in Africa (van Heerden & Mulumba, 2023). With the right approach, Africa has the potential to become a leader in the development and use of robotics and AI, driving economic growth and promoting sustainable development across the continent.

FUTURE ROBOTICS AND ARTIFICIAL INTELLIGENCE TRENDS

The field of robotics and AI is rapidly evolving, and several emerging trends are likely to shape the future of these technologies. Here are some of the most significant trends to watch for as it gets accepted in Africa:

Collaborative Robots (Cobots)

Cobots are robots designed to work alongside humans in a shared workspace, making it easier for humans and robots to work together. Cobots are becoming more common in manufacturing, healthcare, and other fields, and they are expected to be used even more in the future. Cobots, which stand for collaborative robots, are becoming increasingly popular in manufacturing, healthcare, and logistics fields.

Artificial General Intelligence (AGI)

AGI is a type of AI capable of performing any intellectual task that a human can. While current AI systems are specialized and focused on specific tasks, AGI is expected to be more versatile and adaptable. AGI is an AI that can perform any intellectual task that a human can. In the future, AGI could benefit people in numerous ways (Bhagwan & Evans, 2023). For example, AGI could help solve complex global challenges such as climate change, disease prevention, and poverty reduction. It could also be used to improve education by creating personalized learning experiences for students or to improve healthcare by assisting with diagnoses and treatments (Calabrese et al., 2023). Additionally, AGI could enhance safety and security by detecting and preventing crime and terrorism. However, there are also potential risks associated with AGI, such as job displacement and the potential for misuse or abuse, which must be carefully considered and addressed.

Autonomous Vehicles

Autonomous vehicles are vehicles that can operate without human intervention. In the future, autonomous vehicles are likely to revolutionize how people travel and commute, offering numerous benefits to individuals and society (Nyholm, 2023). For example, autonomous vehicles could significantly reduce the number of accidents caused by human error and reduce traffic congestion and travel times. They could also offer greater mobility to people who cannot drive, like the elderly or disabled. Additionally, autonomous vehicles could lead to greater efficiency in logistics and transportation, reducing costs and improving environmental sustainability (Ruttkamp-Bloem, 2023; Uunona & Goosen, 2023). However, there are also potential challenges and risks associated with autonomous vehicles, such as cybersecurity threats and the need for new infrastructure and regulations, which must be carefully addressed as these technologies become more prevalent. Self-driving cars and other autonomous vehicles will likely become more prevalent as technology improves and becomes more affordable.

Smart Homes and Cities

IoT and other smart technologies are making it possible to create homes and cities that are more connected and intelligent. Smart homes and cities are designed to be more efficient, convenient, and sustainable than traditional homes and cities (Daniels et al., 2023). In the future, these technologies could significantly improve people's quality of life by offering numerous benefits. For example, smart homes could allow residents to control and automate various systems, such as lighting, temperature, and security, improving comfort and energy efficiency. Similarly, smart cities could enable more efficient transportation, energy usage, and waste management, reducing costs and environmental impact (Forcucci, 2023). Additionally, these technologies could enhance public safety and security, with smart cameras and sensors helping to detect and prevent crime. However, there are also potential challenges and risks associated with smart homes and cities, such as the need for strong cybersecurity and data privacy protections, which must be carefully considered and addressed as these technologies become more prevalent.

Healthcare Robotics

Robots are increasingly being used in healthcare to assist with surgeries, provide patient care, and perform other tasks; this is now called the Internet of Medical Things (Nyholm, 2023). Healthcare robotics is a rapidly growing field that has the potential to revolutionize the way medical care is delivered. In the future, healthcare robotics could be used to improve patient outcomes, reduce costs, and enhance the efficiency of healthcare delivery. For example, robotic surgery could enable minimally invasive procedures with greater precision and accuracy, reducing the risk of complications and enabling faster recovery times. Similarly, robots could assist with patient monitoring and medication delivery, improving the quality of care for patients and reducing the burden on healthcare workers (Nyholm, 2023). In addition, healthcare robots could be used to enhance medical research and drug development, accelerating the pace of innovation and discovery in the field. However, there are also potential risks and challenges associated with healthcare robotics, such as the need for robust safety and regulatory frameworks.

Natural Language Processing (NLP)

NLP is a branch of AI that focuses on enabling machines to understand, interpret, and respond to human language. In the future, NLP will likely have a wide range of applications that could significantly improve people's daily lives. For example, NLP could enable more intuitive and natural interactions with virtual assistants and chatbots, enhancing the user experience and improving efficiency (Calabrese et al., 2023; Alnssyan et al., 2023). Similarly, NLP could be used to improve language translation, enabling more fantastic communication and collaboration across linguistic barriers. Additionally, NLP could be used to analyze and extract insights from vast amounts of text data, enabling more accurate and informed decision-making in fields such as finance, healthcare, and law (Ukoba et al., 2023).

Edge Computing

A distributed computing paradigm enables data processing to be performed closer to the data source, such as on the devices or sensors themselves, rather than relying on centralized cloud computing resources (Baguma et al., 2023; Eke, Chintu, et al., 2023). In the future, edge computing will likely have a wide range of applications that could benefit people. For example, edge computing could make games, virtual and augmented reality, and applications for self-driving cars faster and more responsive. Edge computing could also be used to improve healthcare by making it possible to monitor and analyze patient data in real-time (Modiba, 2023; Shafik, 2023). This would make it easier to diagnose and treat patients. Edge computing could also be used to improve industrial automation and IoT applications, making manufacturing, transportation, and other industries more efficient and safer. The future of robotics and AI will likely involve more collaboration between humans and machines, more advanced and flexible AI systems, and a greater focus on using these technologies to solve real-world problems in areas like healthcare, transportation, and the environment.

CONCLUSION

The emerging challenges of robotics and AI in Africa require a holistic and collaborative approach that involves multiple stakeholders, including governments, the private sector, academia, and civil society. Addressing these challenges must involve a focus on developing appropriate policies and regulatory frameworks, building infrastructure, promoting research and development, and investing in education and training programs. It is also essential to engage with communities to ensure that these technologies are developed and deployed equitably and inclusively, which benefits all. By addressing these challenges, Africa can harness the potential of robotics and AI to drive economic growth, improve social welfare, and address pressing societal challenges, such as healthcare, agriculture, and manufacturing, while ensuring that the benefits of these technologies are available to all..

REFERENCES

Ade-Ibijola, A., & Okonkwo, C. (2023). Artificial Intelligence in Africa: Emerging Challenges. In Responsible AI in Africa: Challenges and Opportunities (pp. 101–117). Springer International Publishing Cham.

Aigbavboa, C., Ebekozien, A., & Mkhize, N. (2023). A qualitative approach to investigate governance challenges facing South African airlines in the fourth industrial revolution technologies era. *Social Responsibility Journal*.

Alaziz, S. N., Albayati, B., El-Bagoury, A. A. A. H., & Shafik, W. (2023). Clustering of COVID-19 Multi-Time Series-Based K-Means and PCA With Forecasting. [IJDWM]. *International Journal of Data Warehousing and Mining*, *19*(3), 1–25. doi:10.4018/IJDWM.317374

Alnssyan, B., Ahmad, Z., Malela-Majika, J. C., Seong, J. T., & Shafik, W. (2023). On the identifiability and statistical features of a new distributional approach with reliability applications. *AIP Advances*, *13*(12), 125211. doi:10.1063/5.0178555

Baguma, R., Mkoba, E., Nahabwe, M., Mubangizi, M. G., Amutorine, M., & Wanyama, D. (2023). *Towards an Artificial Intelligence Readiness Index for Africa*. Digital-for-Development: Enabling Transformation, Inclusion and Sustainability Through ICTs: *12th International Development Informatics Association Conference, IDIA 2022*, Mbombela, South Africa.

Bainomugisha, E., Ujakpa, M. M., Nakatumba-Nabende, J., Lawrence, N., Kihoza, P., & Annette, I. (2023). *Computer Science Education in Selected Countries from Sub-Saharan Africa*.

Bhagwan, N., & Evans, M. (2023). A review of industry 4.0 technologies used in the production of energy in China, Germany, and South Africa. *Renewable & Sustainable Energy Reviews*, *173*, 113075. doi:10.1016/j.rser.2022.113075

Borokini, F., Wakunuma, K., & Akintoye, S. (2023). The Use of Gendered Chatbots in Nigeria: Critical Perspectives. In Responsible AI in Africa: Challenges and Opportunities (pp. 119–139). Springer International Publishing Cham.

Calabrese, A., Costa, R., Tiburzi, L., & Brem, A. (2023). Merging two revolutions: A human-artificial intelligence method to study how sustainability and Industry 4.0 are intertwined. *Technological Forecasting and Social Change, 188*, 122265. doi:10.1016/j.techfore.2022.122265

Chauke, K. R., Mamokere, J., & Mabeba, S. J. (2023). Reflection on the Proliferation of the Fourth Industrial Revolution and Its Implications on Rural Areas in South Africa. *International Journal of Social Science Research and Review, 6*(1), 214–226. doi:10.47814/ijssrr.v6i1.890

Daniels, C., Erforth, B., & Teevan, C. (2023). Digitalisation for Transformation: New Frontiers for Africa–Europe Cooperation. In Africa–Europe Cooperation and Digital Transformation (pp. 1–16). Routledge.

Eke, D. O., Chintu, S. S., & Wakunuma, K. (2023). Towards Shaping the Future of Responsible AI in Africa. In Responsible AI in Africa: Challenges and Opportunities (pp. 169–193). Springer International Publishing Cham. doi:10.1007/978-3-031-08215-3_8

Eke, D. O., Wakunuma, K., & Akintoye, S. (2023). Introducing Responsible AI in Africa. In Responsible AI in Africa: Challenges and Opportunities (pp. 1–11). Springer International Publishing Cham. doi:10.1007/978-3-031-08215-3_1

Fahim, K. E., Kalinaki, K., & Shafik, W. (2024). Electronic Devices in the Artificial Intelligence of the Internet of Medical Things (AIoMT). In *Handbook of Security and Privacy of AI-Enabled Healthcare Systems and Internet of Medical Things* (pp. 41–62). CRC Press.

Forcucci, L. (2023). Laser Nomad: Roadmaps for Art and Science Research into Ancestral Knowledge. *Leonardo, 56*(4), 1–10. doi:10.1162/leon_a_02354

Foster, L., Szilagyi, K., Wairegi, A., Oguamanam, C., & de Beer, J. (2023). Smart farming and artificial intelligence in East Africa: Addressing indigeneity, plants, and gender. *Smart Agricultural Technology, 3*, 100132. doi:10.1016/j.atech.2022.100132

Gyimah, P., Appiah, K. O., & Appiagyei, K. (2023). Seven years of United Nations' sustainable development goals in Africa: A bibliometric and systematic methodological review. *Journal of Cleaner Production, 395*, 136422. doi:10.1016/j.jclepro.2023.136422

Jide-Omole, A. A. (2023). Towards Sustainability and Stability: Espousing the Benefits of Space-Based Solar Power Systems in Africa. In Space Fostering African Societies: Developing the African Continent Through Space, Part 4 (pp. 45–58). Springer.

Jun, Y., Craig, A., Shafik, W., & Sharif, L. (2021). Artificial intelligence application in cybersecurity and cyberdefense. *Wireless Communications and Mobile Computing, 2021*, 1–10. doi:10.1155/2021/3329581

Kalinaki, K., Fahadi, M., Alli, A. A., Shafik, W., Yasin, M., & Mutwalibi, N. (2024). Artificial Intelligence of Internet of Medical Things (AIoMT) in Smart Cities: A Review of Cybersecurity for Smart Healthcare. Handbook of Security and Privacy of AI-Enabled Healthcare Systems and Internet of Medical Things, (pp. 271-292). Research Gate.

Lubinga, S., Maramura, T. C., & Masiya, T. (2023). The Fourth Industrial Revolution Adoption: Challenges in South African Higher Education Institutions. *Journal of Culture and Values in Education, 6*(2), 1–17. doi:10.46303/jcve.2023.5

Ma, Y. (2023). Development of the Global Film Industry: Industrial Competition and Cooperation in the Context of Globalization. International Journal of Communication, 17, 3.

Mare, A., Woyo, E., & Amadhila, E. M. (2023). Harnessing the technological dividends in African higher education institutions during and post-COVID-19 pandemic. In *Teaching and Learning with Digital Technologies in Higher Education Institutions in Africa* (pp. 1–24). Routledge.

McCallum, W., & Aziakpono, M. J. (2023). Regulatory sandbox for FinTech regulation: Do the conditions for effective adoption exist in South Africa? *Development Southern Africa, 40*(5), 1–17. doi:10.1080/0376835X.2023.2182759

Mensah, I., Dube, K., & Chapungu, L. (2023). Impact of COVID-19 on Tourism and Prospects of Recovery: An African Perspective. In COVID-19, Tourist Destinations and Prospects for Recovery: Volume Two: An African Perspective (pp. 3–17). Springer.

Modiba, M. (2023). User perception on the utilisation of artificial intelligence for the management of records at the council for scientific and industrial research. *Collection and Curation.*

Ndhlovu, N. J., & Goosen, L. (2023). To What Extent Can Multidisciplinary Artificial Intelligence Applications Enhance Higher Education?: Open and Distance E-Learning in South Africa. In Multidisciplinary Applications of Deep Learning-Based Artificial Emotional Intelligence (pp. 166–185). IGI Global.

Ndzendze, B., & Marwala, T. (2023). Artificial Intelligence and International Relations. In *Artificial Intelligence and International Relations Theories* (pp. 33–54). Springer. doi:10.1007/978-981-19-4877-0_3

Nyholm, S. (2023). Artificial Intelligence, Humanoid Robots, and Old and New Control Problems. In *Social Robots in Social Institutions* (pp. 3–12). IOS Press. doi:10.3233/FAIA220594

Peter, O., Pradhan, A., & Mbohwa, C. (2023). Industry 4.0 concepts within the sub–Saharan African SME manufacturing sector. *Procedia Computer Science, 217*, 846–855. doi:10.1016/j.procs.2022.12.281

Ramnund-Mansingh, A., & Naidoo, K. (2023). Lead the African way! *African Journal of Economic and Management Studies.*

Reynolds, T. W., Biscaye, P. E., Leigh Anderson, C., O'Brien-Carelli, C., & Keel, J. (2023). Exploring the gender gap in mobile money awareness and use: Evidence from eight low and middle income countries. *Information Technology for Development, 29*(2-3), 1–28. doi:10.1080/02681102.2022.2073579

Ruttkamp-Bloem, E. (2023). Epistemic Just and Dynamic AI Ethics in Africa. In Responsible AI in Africa: Challenges and Opportunities (pp. 13–34). Springer International Publishing Cham. doi:10.1007/978-3-031-08215-3_2

Sanusi, I. T., Sunday, K., Oyelere, S. S., Suhonen, J., Vartiainen, H., & Tukiainen, M. (2023). Learning machine learning with young children: Exploring informal settings in an African context. *Computer Science Education*, 1–32. doi:10.1080/08993408.2023.2175559

Shafik, W. (2023). A Comprehensive Cybersecurity Framework for Present and Future Global Information Technology Organizations. In *Effective Cybersecurity Operations for Enterprise-Wide Systems* (pp. 56–79). IGI Global. doi:10.4018/978-1-6684-9018-1.ch002

Shafik, W. (2023). IoT-Based Energy Harvesting and Future Research Trends in Wireless Sensor Networks. Handbook of Research on Network-Enabled IoT Applications for Smart City Services, 282-306.

Shafik, W. (2023). Making Cities Smarter: IoT and SDN Applications, Challenges, and Future Trends. In *Opportunities and Challenges of Industrial IoT in 5G and 6G Networks* (pp. 73–94). IGI Global. doi:10.4018/978-1-7998-9266-3.ch004

Shafik, W. (2023). Cyber Security Perspectives in Public Spaces: Drone Case Study. In *Handbook of Research on Cybersecurity Risk in Contemporary Business Systems* (pp. 79–97). IGI Global. doi:10.4018/978-1-6684-7207-1.ch004

Shafik, W. (2024). Predicting Future Cybercrime Trends in the Metaverse Era. In Forecasting Cyber Crimes in the Age of the Metaverse (pp. 78-113). IGI Global.

Shafik, W. (2024). Wearable Medical Electronics in Artificial Intelligence of Medical Things. Handbook of Security and Privacy of AI-Enabled Healthcare Systems and Internet of Medical Things, 21-40.

Shafik, W., Matinkhah, S. M., & Ghasemzadeh, M. (2020). Internet of things-based energy management, challenges, and solutions in smart cities. *Journal of Communications Technology. Electronics and Computer Science*, 27, 1–11.

Shafik, W., Matinkhah, S. M., & Shokoor, F. (2022). Recommendation system comparative analysis: internet of things aided networks. *EAI Endorsed Transactions on Internet of Things, 8*(29).

Shafik, W., & Tufail, A. (2023). Energy Optimization Analysis on Internet of Things. In *Advanced Technology for Smart Environment and Energy* (pp. 1–16). Springer International Publishing. doi:10.1007/978-3-031-25662-2_1

Shava, E., & Mhlanga, D. (2023). Mitigating bureaucratic inefficiencies through blockchain technology in Africa. *Frontiers in Blockchain*, 6, 1. doi:10.3389/fbloc.2023.1053555

Shokoor, F., Shafik, W., & Matinkhah, S. M. (2022). Overview of 5G & Beyond Security. *EAI Endorsed Transactions on Internet of Things, 8*(30).

Stahl, B. C., Leach, T., Oyeniji, O., & Ogoh, G. (2023). AI Policy as a Response to AI Ethics? Addressing Ethical Issues in the Development of AI Policies in North Africa. In Responsible AI in Africa: Challenges and Opportunities (pp. 141–167). Springer International Publishing Cham. doi:10.1007/978-3-031-08215-3_7

Tompihe, J. G. (2023). Financing Terrorism With FinTechs in West Africa? In Exploring the Dark Side of FinTech and Implications of Monetary Policy (pp. 118–143). IGI Global. doi:10.4018/978-1-6684-6381-9.ch006

Tsvetkova, N. N. (2023). New technologies and countries of Asia and Africa. *Digital Orientalia, 2*(1–2).

Tunjera, N., & Chigona, A. (2023). Mobile Technologies Revolutionizing Teacher Preparation for Effective Education 4.0 Outcomes in Marginalised Communities. *Society for Information Technology & Teacher Education International Conference*, 2302–2315.

Turki, H., Pouris, A., Ifeanyichukwu, F.-A. M., Namayega, C., Taieb, M. A. H., Adedayo, S. A., Fourie, C., Currin, C. B., Asiedu, M. N., & Tonja, A. L. (2023). *Machine Learning for Healthcare: A Bibliometric Study of Contributions from Africa.*

Ukoba, K., Kunene, T. J., Harmse, P., Lukong, V. T., & Chien Jen, T. (2023). The Role of Renewable Energy Sources and Industry 4.0 Focus for Africa: A Review. *Applied Sciences (Basel, Switzerland),* *13*(2), 1074. doi:10.3390/app13021074

Uunona, G. N., & Goosen, L. (2023). Leveraging Ethical Standards in Artificial Intelligence Technologies: A Guideline for Responsible Teaching and Learning Applications. In Handbook of Research on Instructional Technologies in Health Education and Allied Disciplines (pp. 310–330). IGI Global. doi:10.4018/978-1-6684-7164-7.ch014

Uwamahoro, L., Sikubwabo, I., Ndikumana, A., Cyemezo, P. C., & Paix, J. deLa. (n.d.). *IoT and AI for Nature Conservation: Nyungwe forestry management and real time monitoring system.*

van Heerden, J., & Mulumba, M. (2023). Science, Technology and Innovation (STI): Its Role in South Africa's Development Outcomes and STI Diplomacy. In Science, Technology and Innovation Diplomacy in Developing Countries: Perceptions and Practice (pp. 141–154). Springer.

Vernon, D. (n.d.). *Culturally Competent Social Robotics for Africa: A Case for Diversity, Equity, and Inclusion in HRI.*

Wang, Y., Shafik, W., Seong, J. T., Al Mutairi, A., Mustafa, M. S., & Mouhamed, M. R. (2023). Service delay and optimization of the energy efficiency of a system in fog-enabled smart cities. *Alexandria Engineering Journal,* *84*, 112–125. doi:10.1016/j.aej.2023.10.034

Yang, Z., Jianjun, L., Faqiri, H., Shafik, W., Talal Abdulrahman, A., Yusuf, M., & Sharawy, A. M. (2021, May 27). Green Internet of things and big data application in smart cities development. *Complexity,* *2021*, 1–5. doi:10.1155/2021/4922697

Zhao, L., Zhu, D., Shafik, W., Matinkhah, S. M., Ahmad, Z., Sharif, L., & Craig, A. (2022). Artificial intelligence analysis in cyber domain: A review. *International Journal of Distributed Sensor Networks,* *18*(4), 15501329221084882. doi:10.1177/15501329221084882

ADDITIONAL READING

Adam, L., & Wood, F. (1999). An investigation of the impact of information and communication technologies in sub-Saharan Africa. *Journal of Information Science,* *25*(4), 307–318. doi:10.1177/016555159902500407

Afolabi, J. A. (2023). Advancing digital economy in Africa: The role of critical enablers. *Technology in Society,* *75*, 102367. doi:10.1016/j.techsoc.2023.102367

Bouhari, M., & Mathlouthi, Y. (2023). Impact of ICT Diffusion on the Economic Growth and Its Volatility: A Case Study on African and MENA Countries. *European Journal of Science. Innovation and Technology,* *3*(3), 321–342.

Ford, D. M. (2007). Technologizing Africa: On the bumpy information highway. *Computers and Composition*, *24*(3), 302–316. doi:10.1016/j.compcom.2007.05.005

Iddrisu, A. G., & Chen, B. (2022). Economic growth through digitalization in Africa: does financial sector development play a mediating role? *International Journal of Emerging Markets*.

Lawin, L. M. (2023). ICTs Development and Tax Revenue Mobilization in West African Economic and Monetary Union Countries. *American Journal of Economics*, *13*(1), 1–12.

Omotoso, K. O., Adesina, J., & Adewole, O. G. (2020). Exploring gender digital divide and its effect on women's labour market outcomes in South Africa. *African Journal of Gender. Social Development*, *9*(4), 85.

Solomon, E. M., & van Klyton, A. (2020). The impact of digital technology usage on economic growth in Africa. *Utilities Policy*, *67*, 101104. doi:10.1016/j.jup.2020.101104 PMID:32904493

Spyridonis, F., Taylor, S. J., Abbott, P., Barbera, R., Nungu, A., Gustafsson, L. L., Pehrson, B., Oaiya, O., & Banda, T. (2015). A study on the state-of-the-art of e-Infrastructures uptake in Africa. *Palgrave Communications*, *1*(1), 1–7. doi:10.1057/palcomms.2014.7

Yegon, K., Ongus, R., & Njuguna, A. (2014). Comparative Study of Challenges Affecting Adoption of E-Learning for Capacity Building in Public Service Sectors of Kenya and South Africa. *Computer Science and Information Technology (Alhambra, Calif.)*, *2*(5), 249–254. doi:10.13189/csit.2014.020504

KEY TERMS AND DEFINITIONS

Artificial Intelligence: The creation of computer systems with the ability to carry out tasks that normally require human intelligence.

Blockchain: Distributed ledger technology that operates decentralized and transparently across numerous computers to securely record transactions. It provides an impenetrable means to record and verify data without requiring a central authority.

Cryptocurrency Revolution: To the paradigm-shifting change in finance brought about by the rise of decentralized digital currencies, such as Bitcoin, that run on blockchain technology. These currencies pose a threat to established banking institutions and provide new avenues for investment, value exchange, and financial independence.

Digital Era: A time when digital technologies have been widely adopted and integrated, radically changing the ways in which information is produced, accessed, shared, and used in a variety of contexts including daily life, business, and society.

Digital Infrastructure: The foundation of contemporary digital ecosystems, supporting information exchange and technological advancements by encompassing the fundamental systems and components that allow digital technologies to function and be connected. These include networks, hardware, software, data centers, internet services, and communication technologies.

Information and Communications Technology (ICT): Is the umbrella term covering technologies used in networks, hardware, software, and the internet to support data exchange and interaction as well as communication, information processing, and transmission.

Robotics: The design, construction, management, and application of robots to carry out tasks in a range of industries, from manufacturing and healthcare to exploration and beyond.

Socio-Economic Transformation: The essential and frequently substantial alterations to economic institutions, societal norms, and behavior that have a big impact on how opportunities, wealth, and resources are distributed as well as a community's general well-being.

Chapter 8
Exploring AI and Dialogic Education Outcomes From a Learning Sciences Perspective

Gideon Mensah Anapey

https://orcid.org/0000-0001-5534-3818

University of Ghana, Ghana

ABSTRACT

Regardless of the imperatives of the COVID-19 pandemic and the increasing adoption of artificial intelligence (AI) in higher education to meet learning outcomes, little is known about its integration in dialogic learning outcomes in the post-COVID 19 era. From the learning sciences perspective, this chapter explores faculty members' adoption of AI resources for dialogic pedagogy using a participatory research design and social-constructivism theory. Interview data was obtained from 6 faculty members of two of Ghana's teacher education universities. Manual coding in Microsoft Excel yielded themes from the participants' narrative data with voices embedded. The results suggest that generic computer training, social media and internet exposure, data analytics, multimedia capacity, and digital pedagogy are the leading skills required for AI integration for dialogic learning goals among faculty members. In conclusion, capacity building for faculty to effectively deploy AI resources in students' dialogic learning goals requires learning scientists' effort and inputs.

BACKGROUND TO THE STUDY

Emerging concerns about AI's fictional characteristics associated with learning unexpected information from data arrays originated from the West and little algorithmic inputs from the Global South (Kaivo-oja, Roth, & Westerlund, 2017), false logics and abuses non-transparency and data control by users, evaluation bias and heterogeneous definitions have been noted (Westerlund, 2019; Sanderson, 2023) are some contributing factors to low generative AI integration in learning. Tensions also exist between humans and AI decision making, teacher and learner control issues in classrooms, and intellectual copyrights (U.S. Department of Education, 2023). While the optimism behind technology in education is certainly

DOI: 10.4018/978-1-6684-9962-7.ch008

forward-looking for students' achievements and future of work, clear indication of how such AI tools could impact their deep learning outcomes are fuzzy. Certainly, human cognition is required to evaluate AI's generative information and its impact on deep pedagogy as faculty members' professional knowledge about student learning outcomes are important for critical thinking, collaborative and digital algorithm skills, technical communication, conceptual thinking, and global citizenship skills ought to be examined from Learning Scientists' perspective in the Digital Age. It would seem that empirical discourse about generative AI, dialogic pedagogy, and algorithmic skills amongst higher education faculty remains relatively unexamined form Learning Sciences domain in the Global South.

Learning Sciences (LS) is an interdisciplinary field that examines learning across a range of environments such as formal and informal settings, and social groups (Giannakos & Cukurova, 2022); it strives to gain a deeper understanding of the cognitive and social processes that lead to effective learning outcomes (Sawyer, 2006). The sciences of learning encompass diverse fields including cognitive science, educational psychology, computer science, anthropology, sociology, information sciences, neurosciences, education, design studies, and instructional design, amongst others (Lee, 2023). As a nascent discipline, the field of Learning Sciences (LS) is still in the process of defining itself (Dede et al., 2018) and guided by theories of learning such as constructivism, social constructivism, socio-cognitive, and socio-cultural (Sawyer, 2022). While cognitive science, emerging technologies, and interactions in learning ecosystem have potentially impacted knowledge acquisition across life spans (Evans et al., 2016), LS answers critical questions around inclusion and access, inquiry-based pedagogy, and learning environments. Therefore, the role of LS in conceptualisation of instructional outcomes in the wake of educational reforms such as AI's impacts has been advanced (Sawyer, 2006).

As AI programming expands, deep learning outcomes should be championed by professional teachers as most universities students are leapfrogging their faculty members in its adoption in lieu of traditional classroom experiences that rely on regurgitation of information. As digital natives operating in hyper-connectivity world, today's students are increasing using digital devices to access information but they will require pedagogical coaching that aligns with dialogic education goals from instructors (Buabeng et al., 2020). Involvement of LS in digitally mediated learning environments would also mitigate the impact of global health on education as over 229,756 learners dropped out of school (Statistica, 2023), with 93,640 failing in STEM subjects at the senior high school level in Ghana (Bonney, 2023) during COVID-19 pandemic alone. Within the context of Ghana's Education Sector Plan 2018-2030 which seeks improved equitable access and participation in quality, deepen inquiry-based learning outcomes, and achieve Sustainable Development Goal 4, integration of LS principles into AI deployment has the potential to transform higher education in the Global South. Importantly, students are already using AI but they will require pedagogical guidance to connect theory to practice while solving real-world scenarios.

At the governance and policy levels, Ghana has pursued broad goals of improving its education system to align teacher education with modern educational research and practices through the Transforming Teacher Education & Learning (T-TEL) initiative programme under the Ghana Tertiary Education Commission (GTEC) (Ministry of Education, 2017) and the Bachelor in Education degree programmes in 46 public Colleges of Education affiliated to five public universities (Ministry of Education, 2018; University of Ghana, 2023). Probably, these interventions are yet to recognise the impact of AI on dialogic learning outcomes for students' achievements at the pre-tertiary level (Buabeng et al., 2020) where learning is linked with evolving and real-life issues (NaCCA, 2019). Consequently, demands for students' deep learning outcomes using AI algorithms will require empirical findings about faculty members' technology pedagogical content and experiential learning knowledge that support digital learners to navigate today's educational realities.

Technology has always been a fulcrum of human development since the invention of stone monoliths in the history of humanity. Today, artificial intelligence (AI) has been predicted to drive global literacy standards in all sectors of society (Laupichler, Aster, et al., 2023). AI programming is transforming the ways humans interact in synchronous and asynchronous times, work, and live everyday routine (Newman, Mintrom, & O'Neill, 2022), medical diagnostics (Reddy & Fox, 2019; Kim, Lee, Oh, & Chung, 2023), public administration (Noordt & Tangi, 2023), and education (Zhai, et al., 2021). Economically, generative pre-trained (ChatGPT) has been estimated to impact over 80% jobs with significant jobs design facing many industries including education (Rock, et al., 2023). However, the education sector is largely unprepared for the ethical and pedagogical integration of digital innovations as illustrated by only 10% of over 450 schools and universities commitment to institutional policies and formal guidance concerning for generative AI applications (UNESCO, 2023). In spite of the huge impact of AI in education, teacher supervision and student's independent evaluation are required for developing critical thinking and global citizenship.

Adaptivity and personalized features of AI technology have also contributed to growing research in pattern recognition, machine learning, computer vision, algorithm, data mining, natural language procession, control theory, human computer interactivity (HCI), and psycholinguistics between 2010 and 2021 (U.S. Department of Education, 2023). Excluded from the leading publications is the field of Learning Sciences such as psychology, curriculum, and instructional design to examine implications of AI's adaptability and personalization to deep learning approaches. Learning Scientists focus on the core mandate of knowledge propagation and deep learning approaches while embracing innovations while defining knowledge as a progressive representation and interpretation of experience, built constructive and transformative action and discourse (Formenti & Jorio, 2018). Therefore, professionalism that connects theoretical, conceptual, and best practices with AI tools for analytical and conceptual thinking, natural language processing, and algorithmics skills will thrive on multidisciplinary knowledge from Learning Sciences. Therefore, the aim of the study is to explore AI integration experiences and deep learning pedagogy of university faculty members. The following research questions (RQ) guided the study:

RQ 1: *what are faculty members' experiences integrating AI tools into deep learning outcomes? and*
RQ 2: *what are digital skills of faculty to adopt AI resources in higher education?*

LITERATURE REVIEW

Artificial Intelligence in Education

With the hype associated with the ushering in of the year 2000 (Y2K), educational application of computers has been limited to generic skills development for many third world countries. Today, higher education course offerings include AI with anecdotal benefits for differential and adaptive learning, student support services, data analytics, assistive resource mobilisation, and improving students' writing (Lynch, 2018). Recent survey in Ghana has highlighted low ICT access and skills, usage, and digital divide at the household and school levels (National Communication Authority [NCA], 2019). The optimism is that AI would not replace teachers, it will certainly save faculty members' time, minimise workload and repetitive tasks as higher order cognitive skills will be demanded while robotizing the role of the human teacher with lesson planning, preparing materials, providing feedback to students, and assessing assignments (UNESCO, 2023). Indeed, digital innovations are inevitably associated with multiple risks and challenges that can outpace policy debates and regulatory frameworks. Without an empirical approach and integration into learning goals, the potentials of AI to the academe could remain a mirage. Therefore, appreciating the impact of Artificial intelligence's (AI) on education, future of work and Sustainable Development Goal 4 ought to be grounded in scientific data to inform students' dialogic learning outcomes.

First, it is essential to understand AI's constituents and applications in education from Learning Sciences. AI denotes multiple constructs with practitioners adopting eclectic approach to its conceptualisation with nine components such as learning, planning, communication, action, perception, knowledge representation, and reasoning, optimization, automated planning and scheduling, robotics, computer vision, knowledge based systems, machining learning, types, and natural language processing (Regona, et al., 2022). From human reasoning, AI consists of application of theory for the development of computer systems in executing activities usually demanding human cognition including visual perception, speech recognition, learning, decision making and language processing (IEEE-USA Board of Directors, 2017). Others defined it as a computer system with the ability to think and learn like humans in automated processing such as cognition and decision making (Kühl, et al., 2022). An important component of AI's definition with respect to deep learning outcomes is its metacognitive capability with support for students' conceptual and critical thinking, humanism, algorithmic skills, and ethics intricately linked to dialogic education.

Integrating Artificial Intelligence into Dialogic Pedagogy

As evolutionary tales of curriculum reform favours political elites in many societies, an important learning goal that has always dominated educational discourse has been critical thinking skills by students. However, curriculum reforms lack well-articulated strategies to guide the process (Chu, et al., 2017) with cyclical process of educational reforms globally. For instance, reforms aimed at twenty-first century skills development require evaluation strategy for assessing critical dialogic learning outcomes but has eluded education stakeholders over the years. Indeed, digital innovation is an important variable impacting curriculum discourse (Ornstein & Hunkins, 2018). Consequently, AI integration approach will be critical in assessing students' critical thinking skills in the twenty-first century since students' ability to engage with content standards using critical questioning skills will be crucial for sustainable education goals.

Freire has been critical about the passive posture ascribed to students as recipients of information given (Freire, 1993). Rooted in critical and social consciousness and pedagogy of the oppressed, dialogic learning was originally attributed to Paulo Freire, given his disenchantment about colonised schooling systems in developing nations and his call for dialogue amongst students and society (Ornstein & Hunkins, 2018). In reference to monologic education whereby teachers deposit content in the minds of students and which they in turn reproduce in examinations, Freire referred to this structure of pedagogy as 'the banking system' (Mui, 2013). His critique of the banking model of education in colonized societies has impacted real-world problem solving and critical dialogue where learners cultivate empowerment to offer constructive criticisms and question their own existence in the world.

Progressively, dialogic inquiry uses creative approaches that focus on learning outcomes such as conceptual and critical thinking skills, attitudes, and power to speak and engage socially (McLaren & McLaren, 1993). Clearly, semantic constructions are pivotal to dialogic relationship building using psycholinguistics concepts and theories congruent to deep learning didactics. While AI programming also depend on natural language and metacognition processing, it is the considered opinion for Learning Scientist that higher education faculty members have pedagogical responsibility to design higher cognitive learning domains with AI tools that support content-standards; while designing authentic assessment practices to solve real-world problems using interrogative skills in higher education. Surely, outputs from generative pre-determined trained and algorithmic software might seem real but critical consciousness skills based on cognitive psychology and metacognition is essential for decoding AI's benefits. Freire's original views were informed by educational underachievement foisted on colonised people where educational enterprises were regulated by power struggles. Today, many school systems in the Global South are struggling to educate students to develop dialogic learning outcomes but school environments, curriculum reforms, administration, and assessment practices in many higher institutions require dialogic instructional models as a departure from the banking model. Hence, this study posits that the application of Learning Sciences principles and theories to support students dialogic learning goals will be essential for reaping the full benefits of new forms of generative pre-trained algorithmic applications in higher education. Conversely, the failure of education stakeholders to account for students' deep learning needs using digital resources could minimise AI's potential in education.

Promoting Ethical AI in Education

Guided by Learning Sciences approach to intellectual engagement while advancing global skills development of students in the Digital Age, this section raises awareness about the ethical nuances involved with using AI in education for students and faculty members. Teaching, researching, and learning are complete and entangled processes that require adaption to cross-cutting themes guided by ethics but rapid technological innovations are causing disruptions to such already complicated learning environments without equal standardisation and capacity building for learners and teachers (Fenwick & Edwards, 2013). Saddled with overburdening curriculum and low- cost training budgets for developing countries, training needs sometimes receive least attention from senior management. Eminent is weak ethical standards governing technology deployment, which is creating tension between students and faculty members with the use of AI.

As an illustration, education stakeholders warned that deploying AI in educational contexts that are already fragmented with unequal opportunities poses high risks (Turner, 2023). Indeed, several concerns remain over AI's role in supporting students' differential abilities and narrower student learning existing digital resources barriers such as cost, lack of local content, disability, parental and institutional restrictions, connectivity, and lack of internet skills (NCA, 2019). Unlike the US education system that adopted National Educational Technology Standards for students, teachers, and administrators to guide fair and responsible use, application of productivity tools, creativity and innovation, communication and collaboration, research, critical thinking, problem solving, decision making, digital citizenship, and mastery of digital operations and concepts provide a comprehensive framework for advancing learning goals (International Society for Technology in Education [ISTE], 2008). As teachers and students adhere to these national standards, systems are instituted to guide ethical applications of computer technologies in education thereby alleviating the trepidation associated with educational systems with low integration and adoption of AI tools. As discourse on the emergence of AI appears to be that of panic with students considered culprits with little guidance from experienced faculty members to supervise deep learning and dialogic goals using AI, avoidance of use will also exclude key population groups and compromise on fairness, equity, inclusion, and the digitally marginalised in the Global South.

Imperative is the rapidly emerging generative AI systems requiring governments to regulate their use in schools to ensure a human-centred approach in education (UNESCO, 2023). While teachers might be confronted with a duality demand to learn with and about AI, the overarching question remains about how will teachers support student to acquire knowledge using AI? Unfortunately, historicism on educational integration in curriculum has not favoured teachers as technical and programming experts with others arguing for overloaded school curriculum. Teachers' pedagogical knowledge about learner diagnostics, inquiry-based approaches, and assessment of competency-based outcomes will be important to make AI count in today's higher education. With over reliance on traditional teaching approaches in marginalized classrooms, examination focus curriculum, and large class sizes posing challenges to creative pedagogy, students might leapfrog their faculty in the use of AI tools whilst faculty play the catch-up. With this ambivalent position, a student might find support systems in AI resources but it will take faculty to educate students with deep learning principles. Similarly, human computer interactivity (HCI) might provide interactive environment for students using AI but their humanism and dialogic questioning skills that support knowledge acquisition resides with faculty professionalism to align AI models with shared vision for learners, instructional outcomes, and modern learning approaches (U.S. Department of Education, 2023). Learning Scientists' focus on deep learning outcomes using AI to support students' humanistic skills, higher education pedagogy based on dialogic instructional principles and theories will be relevant in the Digital Age.

Social-Constructivism Theory and AI Adoption for Deep Learning

The field of Learning Sciences benefits from an amalgam of theories from curriculum development, psychology, psycholinguistics, instructional design, educational anthropology, measurement and evaluation, and sociology; reflecting its multidisciplinary nature. AI and dialogic pedagogy support depend on the teacher's learning goals and content-standards. Based on metacognitive demands of AI resources and natural language processing, Paulo Freire's critical consciousness model presents intentional approach to engaging higher education students' use of AI in achieving dialogic learning outcomes in the 21st century within the social-constructivism theory for the current study. Anchored in the revolutionary thinking for Vygotsky, the theory has been widely used in tradition academic fields including psychology (Knapp, 2018) and teaching in online learning environments (Deulen, 2013). Learner-centred pedagogy has promoted open-ended strategies, project-based activities and real-world problem solving from experience involving media technologies, video-based laboratory support, virtual reality, flipped learning approach (see Khalid, et al., 2023). Just as psychologists are concerned with interpretation of human behaviour and mental processes with specific environments (Mather, Cacioppo, & Kanwisher, 2013), social-constructivism has been widely used to help learner knowledge development based on environmental determinism with the assumption that thought processes are influenced by cultural contexts (Mitchell, et al., 2002).

Yet, the foundational assumption of social-constructivism can be daunting for untrained faculty members with little technology pedagogical content knowledge. Such limitations unaddressed can impact the realisation of AI benefits and deep learning goals in the Digital Age. Intertwined with centuries of cultural nuances, students engage in meaningful dialogue or social discourse for informed decision making is important skill for evaluation of generative AI tools. Perhaps, social consciousness approach that is required to hold authority figures accountable in democratic society would be endangered today with students' access to AI as well. However, higher educational system failure to incorporate humanism, deep learning goals, and content-standards linked to real-world problem solving will significantly affect students' questioning skills required to decode false data. Therefore, AI adoption in education ought to be grounded in constructivism didactic for the achievement of the Sustainable Development Goal 4 and the objectives of countries' higher education curriculum.

Methods

A participatory research approach that engages participants to construct knowledge through dialogue has been dominant in qualitative studies (Creswell & Clark, 2011; Johnson & Christensen, 2019). Co-produced, adaptative and contextually appropriate methodologies are needed to explore events in emerging fields. Hence, interview was adopted to generate narrative data from six purposefully selected faculties from two universities in Ghana using maximum variation samples (MVS). The aim of MVS is to sample heterogenous group of respondents to enable in-depth exploration of a phenomenon with information-rich cases (Patton, 2002). The sampling approach was particularly adopted to provide detailed account of emerging AI nuances on deep learning principles. Inclusion criteria invoked for the current study included faculties with teaching credentials, supervision of pre-service teachers, and a minimum of 3 years tenure position. Four males and two female teachers also constituted the sample in a face-to-face interview session.

Interview protocol included participants' demographics (academic area of specialisation, sex, tenure, academic area of specialisation) and two overarching questions. Question 1 explored faculty members' AI adoption for deep learning pedagogies while Question 2 examined digital integration skill gaps for the use of generative AIs in higher education. Validity and confirmability procedures were observed with colleague academics with the educational technology and education specialisations. While adhering to ethical standards of data protection, anonymity, and confidentiality, participants' voices were transcribed and coded manually. Subsequently, axial coding techniques were applied to the narrative data for research questions 1 and 2. Eight themes emerged from the assembled transcripts summarising faculty members' experiences with generative AI and deep learning didactic. Embedded voice notes were used to support themes during results presentation.

Results

Generative artificial intelligence for machine learning, digital algorithms natural language processing, and robotics tools impact human routines (Newman, Mintrom, & O'Neill, 2022). Education has been projected to dominate AI utilisation by replacing repetitive and boring curriculum duties (UNESCO, 2023). While optimism on AI's potential to ease learning challenges globally has been expressed, several discussions remain mere anecdotal with paucity of scientific outcomes from the Global South. Grounded in social-constructivism theoretical framework the current study explored faculty members' AI experiences and deep learning outcomes and capacity building needs.

The findings showed faculty members' experiences and integration in curriculum were limited to *Awareness* of AI with students increasing *Usage for Assignments*. Some faculty members indicated that in spite of their awareness, they were unable to incorporate AI into students deep learning goals, while others reported occasional rejection of students' scripts from ChatGPT due to inconsistencies in responses. While respondents acknowledge existence of information and communication technology (ICT) and plagiarism policies in their respective universities, AI education is yet to receive pedagogical attention for higher education in this study. Invariably, participants have acknowledged the increasing adoption of the AI tools to support their academic tasks without faculty intentionality about integrating into creative pedagogical approaches supported by social-constructivism assumptions. In support of the themes, a female faulty member with four years tenure reported, "As for AI, I don't have much knowledge about it. I heard of it. When I give work to students, I am unsure whether they use it [AI] to generate answers or not. I don't simply have in-depth knowledge." These responses illustrate the basal level of technology adoption model proposed by educationists (Hall & Hord, 1987).

Another faculty member was able to detect his students use of AI to generate assignments when he shared this;

AI [,] you realize that it summarizes the information for the student. I realised two of my students the responses they were giving they [sic] were information I needed. I said you! Someone has been doing your work for you. He [student] watched me and laughed. I said if you don't tell me I will take disciplinary action against you. Then he said sir, you I will tell you. Then he said with the help of AI.

On dialogic learning outcome assessments, faculty members acknowledge that critical thinking and content-standards evaluations dominate the competency measurements with a male faculty generalizing;

We don't measure all learning outcomes [including digital literacy]. Apart from the students taking ICT as a subject, I don't have any other assessment of children digital learning experiences in the classroom. They [students] have no way to co-create content by typing, drawing, imagining, recording contents digitally. We use essay questions in examinations and occasionally give project works with term papers in majority instead of real-world problems solving.

The RQ2 explored faculty members' digital skills for AI integration in dialogic learning goals. Sixty-one digital skill deficits (Figure 1) were coded under eight overarching themes. Generic ICT and basic internet and typing skills dominated the narratives on AI integration in dialogic learning outcomes (Critical thinking, conceptual knowledge, communication, and collaborative skills) ; and advanced competencies such as online pedagogy, multimedia design, research skills, database, and data analytics skills featuring in this study.

In support of the above findings, respondents shared insightful experiences about AI integration in deep learning. A male faculty with over five years teaching experience narrates,

While the underpinning philosophy of the dialogic education include teachers' creativity and knowledge in the subject, many faculty [members] tend to rely on prescribed reading lists that could pigeonhole students in the learning process and ignore emerging technology such as AI. Their [students] creativity is limited to what is in the book and they are likely to reproduce same [text] in examinations. To some students and teachers, if it [content] is not in the book, it does not exist.

Figure 1. Faculty digital skill deficits for AI adoption

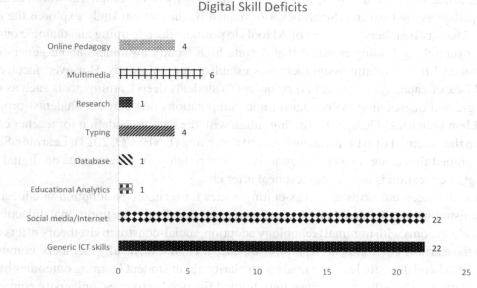

His views cohere with Paulo Freire's banking concept of education where educational institutions might be limiting learners' potential to engage in real-world problem solving and use of social dialogue to question systems and colonial structures (Freire, 1993).

The findings in this study ought to be examined within the context of widening digital divides for developing country like Ghana with marginalised communities, gender, and poor socio-economic backgrounds. Household Survey on ICT showed low level computer skills for Ghanaians (National Communication Authority, 2019) and proportion of citizens with ICT skills depicting regional disparities with Greater Accra (37.9%); Ashanti (26.8%); and Eastern (19.6%) as the top three leaders as leading urban regions. However, skills gap is pronounced in Northern (5.7%); Upper West (6.9%); and Upper East (9%) with less than 10% of the population; urban (30.5%) and rural (10.5%); male (27.8%) and female (15%) dichotomies also exist (Ghana Statistical Service, 2019). Undoubtedly, the emergence of AI will not be an exception (Turner, 2023). By extension, digital skills required for generative AI adoption in Ghana's higher education might not support deep learning didactic from both faculty and students. Implications of the findings for literature, theory, and policy are examined next.

DISCUSSION

The hype and pomp associated with bringing computers to schools appear to have limited success with students' deep learning needs as twenty-first century skills keep expanding. In spite of the essential role received during the COVID-19 pandemic in keeping students from a complete break from school, technology applied to education is not a miracle cure (UNESCO, 2023). Narratives accompanying the nascent generative AI in education is equally associated with futuristic views (Laupichler, et al., 2023; Newman, et al., 2022; Rock, et al., 2023; Kaivo-oja, et al., 2017) without empirical works addressing deep learning pedagogy by Learning Scientists. Consequently, the current study explored the experiences of selected faculty members' adoption of AI tools to promote deep learning and dialogic outcomes in Ghana. The overarching finding revealed that despite high faculty awareness about generative AI, increasingly students' use to submit assignment was established in this study. However, faculty members' indicated lack of capacity to connect AI resources to students deep learning goals such as critical thinking, dialogic and questioning skills, algorithmic computations that connect students' projects to real-world problem scenarios. Though the findings align with the recommendation for teacher capacity building that tap the potential of AI for students' creative learning (UNESCO, 2023), Learning Scientist s' have always argued that bringing technology to schools through policy statements on digital access provision in higher education is not the biggest deal after all.

Theoretical and conceptual skills are cross-cutting issues for technology adoption in education for education administrators, faculty members, and policy makers. Evidently, the traditional didactic model prevails in most classrooms with minimal technology adoption, social-constructivist theory offers experience sharing in the learning environment (Khalid, et al., 2023). Therefore, faculty members' commitment to the adoption of AI and dialogic learning goals with clarity about student learning outcomes has been challenging for participants in this study. Even with limited financial resources, university commitment to achieving AI integration depends on multidisciplinary knowledge of Learning Sciences (LS) to join the technology integration team during policy conceptualisation and implementation; evaluation is important for the realisation of higher education institutions strategic plans focusing on digital integration to promote student's twenty-first century skills.

The outcome of Research Question 2 reflects generic computer skills requirement by participants in this study. The current study confirms the 2019 ICT survey by the National Communication Authority (2019) that revealed typing, basic files management, word processing, and presentation tools as the dominant skills in Ghanaian households. Research Questions 1 and 2 findings are conjoining at pedagogical levels; deep learning teaching that support learners to construct their experiences using digitally mediated platforms such as AI depends on skills to pull online media together. Supporting students to work collaboratively, raise critical questions from content-standards, and finding intelligent and meaningful answers does not exist for samples in this study. Therefore, the awareness level will not lend credence to bringing technology to higher education and these tools will remain at the superficial level with student and teacher interaction still limited to the traditional classroom with the faculty member acting as the sage on the stage even in the wake of generative AI tools for many Global South universities. As tech enthusiasts extol AI's (Newman, et al., 2022) Global discourse on generative AIs can be stepped up with modules with design thinking from Learning Scientists.

CONCLUSION AND RECOMMENDATIONS

Though views expressed by the respondents might lack statistical generalisation, the deployment of maximum variation sampling approach to examine AI and deep learning pedagogies provides theoretical generalisation for dialogic learning experts. Grounded in social-constructivism, AI's capability to use natural language coding, algorithms, machine learning, perception, robotics, and knowledge generation is being adopted by students in Ghana's higher education. While faculty AI awareness is high, intentionality to adopt technology professional development integration into dialogic education is slow. Low technology skills for students and faculty from marginalised communities, barriers including gender gap, poor socio-economic status, and regional digital divides continue to stalk a developing country like Ghana in the 21st century. The present study concludes that higher education institutions in the Global South will continue to be on the fringes of the digital revolution without strategic approach to integration in deep learning pedagogies. While curriculum in advance societies are supporting students to simulate knowledge and build scenarios using digital algorithms in subject-specific learning, it appears that third world higher education institutions are yet to move beyond generic computer skills. In order to reduce the digital algorithm gaps, the current study recommends that Learning Sciences including psychology, educational technology and anthropology, instructional design, sociology, curriculum development, psycholinguistics, machine learning, and psychometrics should be incorporated into dialogic learning outcomes in Ghana's teacher education institutions. Secondly, academic departments ought to progress from generic ICT education to intentional application of AI resources with real-world problem solving scenarios. Finally, deep learning assessment culture with rubrics to measure dialogic competencies such as critical thinking, effective communication skills, conceptual thinking, ethical standards, and team work must be considered.

REFERENCES

Aalst, J., Mu, J., Damsa, C., & Msonde, S. (2022). *Learning sciences research for teaching*. Routledge.

Bonney, E. (2023, February 28). *WASSCE for Private Candidates: More candidates fail Mathematics*. Retrieved October 13, 2023, from Graphic Online: https://www.graphic.com.gh/news/education/wassce-for-private-candidates-more-candidates-fail-mathematics.html

Chu, S. K., Raynolds, R. B., Tavares, N. J., Notari, M., & Lee, C. W. (2017). *21st century skills development through inquiry-based learning: From theory to practice*. Springer. doi:10.1007/978-981-10-2481-8

Dede, C., Richard, J., & Saxberg, B. (2018). *Learning engineering for online education - theoritical context and design-based examples*. Routledge. doi:10.4324/9781351186193

Deulen, A. A. (2013). Social Constructivism and online learning environments: Toward a theological model for christian educators. *ristian Education Journal: Research on Educational Ministry, 10*(1), https//2080/. doi:10.1177/073989131301000107

Evans, M. A., Packer, M. J., & Sawyer, R. K. (2016). *Reflections on the learning sciences: past, present and future*. Cambridge University Press. doi:10.1017/CBO9781107707221

Fenwick, T., & Edwards, R. (2013). Performative ontologies. Sociomaterial approaches to researching adult education and lifelong learning. *RELA European Journal for Research on the Education and Learning of Adults, 4*(1), 49–63. doi:10.3384/rela.2000-7426.rela0104

Formenti, L., & Jorio, F. (2018). Multiple visions, multiple voices: A dialogic methodology for teaching in higher education. *Journal of Transformative Education, 17*(3), https://2080/ doi:10.1177/1541344618796761

Freire, P. (1993). *Pedagogy of the oppressed*. Bloomsbury Inc.

Ghana Statistical Service. (2019). *Ghana multiple indicator cluster survey 2017/18*. Ghana Statistical Service.

Giannakos, M., & Cukurova, M. (2022). The role of learning theory in multimodal learning analytics. *British Journal of Educational Technology*, ●●●, 1–22.

Hall, G. E., & Hord, S. M. (1987). *Changes in schools: Facilitating the process*. State University of New York Press.

IEEE-USA Board of Directors. (2017, February 10). *Artificial intelligence research, development and regulation. IEEE*. Retrieved October 13, 2023, from http://globalpolicy.ieee.org/wp-content/uploads/2017/10/IEEE17003.pdf

International Society for Technology in Education [ISTE]. (2008). *The ISTE national educational technology standards (NETS●T) and performance indicators for teachers*. US: ISTE.

ISLS. (2023). Retrieved July 27, 2023, from About ISLS: https://www.isls.org/about/

Kaivo-oja, J., Roth, S., & Westerlund, L. (2017). Futures of robotics. Human work in digital transformation. *nternational Journal of Technology Management, 4*(73), 176-205.

Khalid, A., Kazim, T., Diaz, K. R., & Iqbal, J. (2023). Breaking barriers in higher education: Implementation of cost-effective social constructivism in engineering education. *International Journal of Mechanical Engineering Education*, https:// 2080/ doi:10.1177/03064190231218123

Kim, K., Lee, J., Oh, S. J., & Chung, M. J. (2023). AI-based computer-aided diagnostic system of chest digital tomography synthesis: Demonstrating comparative advantage with X-ray-based AI systems. *Computer Methods and Programs in Biomedicine, 240*, 107643. Advance online publication. doi:10.1016/j.cmpb.2023.107643 PMID:37348439

Knapp, N. F. (2018). The shape activity: Social Constructivism in the psychology classroom. *Teaching of Psychology, 46*(1), https:// 2080/ doi:10.1177/0098628318816181

Kühl, N., Schemmer, M., Goutier, M., & Satzger, G. (2022). Artificial intelligence and machine learning. *Electronic Markets, 32*(4), 2235–2244. doi:10.1007/s12525-022-00598-0

Laupichler, M. C., Aster, A., Haverkamp, N., & Raupach, T. (2023). Development of the "Scale for the assessment of non-experts' AI literacy" – An exploratory factor analysis. *Computers in Human Behavior Reports, 12*, 100338. Advance online publication. doi:10.1016/j.chbr.2023.100338

Lee, V. (2023). Learning sciences and learning engineering: A naturak or artificial distinction? *Journal of the Learning Sciences, 32*(2), 288–304. doi:10.1080/10508406.2022.2100705

Lynch, M. (2018, December 6). *My vision for the future of artificial intelligene in education*. Retrieved from The Advocate: https://www.theedadvocate.org/vision-future-artificial-intelligence-education/

Mather, M., Cacioppo, J. T., & Kanwisher, N. (2013). How fMRI can inform cognitive theories. *Psychological Science, 27*(2), 108–113. PMID:23544033

McLaren, P., & McLaren, P. (1993). *Paulo Freire: A critical encounter*. Routledge.

Mitchell, R., Busenitz, L., Lant, T., McDougall, P. P., Morse, E. A., & Smith, B. (2002). Towards a theory of entrepreneurial cognition: Rethinking the people side of entrepreneurship research. *Entrepreneurship Theory and Practice, 27*(2), 93–104. doi:10.1111/1540-8520.00001

Mui, M. S. (2013). Dialogic pedagogy in Hong Kong: Introducing art and culture. *Arts and Humanities in Higher Education, 12*(4), 408–423. Advance online publication. doi:10.1177/1474022213481939

National Communication Authority. (2019). *Household survey on ICT in Ghana 2019*. NCA.

Newman, J., Mintrom, M., & O'Neill, D. (2022). Digital technologies, artificial intelligence, and bureaucratic transformation. *Futures, 136*, 102886. Advance online publication. doi:10.1016/j.futures.2021.102886

Noordt, C., & Tangi, L. (2023). The dynamics of AI capability and its influence on public value creation of AI within public administration. *Government Information Quarterly, 40*(4), 101860. Advance online publication. doi:10.1016/j.giq.2023.101860

Ornstein, A. C., & Hunkins, F. P. (2018). *Curriculum: Foundations, principles, and issues*. Pearson Education Ltd.

Patton, M. Q. (2002). Qualitative research and evaluation methods. Thousand Oaks, CA: 2002.: Sage Publications.

Reddy, J., Fox, P. M., & Purohit, M. P. (2019). Artificial intelligence-enabled healthcare delivery. *Journal of the Royal Society of Medicine, 1*(112), 22–28. doi:10.1177/0141076818815510 PMID:30507284

Regona, M. Y., Tan, X., & Bo, L. R. (2022). Opportunities and adoption challenges of AI in the construction industry: A PRISMA review. *Journal of Open Innovation, 8*(45), 45. Advance online publication. doi:10.3390/joitmc8010045

Rock D. Elondou T. Manning S. Mishkin P. (2023, Otober 11). *GPTs are GPTs: An early Look at the labor market impact potential of large language models*. Retrieved from Cornell University: https://arxiv.org/abs/2303.10130

Sawyer, K. R. (2022). An introduction to the learning sciences. In K. R. Sawyer (Ed.), *The Cambridge handbook of the learning sciences* (3rd ed., pp. 1–24). Cambrideg University Press.

Sawyer, R. K. (2006). *The Cambridge handbook of the learning sciences*. Cambridge University Press.

Statistica. (2023). *Number of teachers in secondary education in Ghana from 2010 to 2020*. Retrieved October 2023, from Number of teachers in secondary education in Ghana from 2010 to 2020: https://www.statista.com/statistics/1184183/number-of-teachers-in-secondary-education-in-ghana/

Turner, N. (2023, October 11). *Artificial Intelligence and Future of Teaching and Learning: Insights and Recommendations*, Retrieved from U.S. Department of Education, Office of Educational Technology: https://tech.ed.gov

UNESCO. (2023). *Artificial intelligence in education*. Retrieved January 2024, from Digital learning and transformation of education: https://www.unesco.org/en/digital-education/artificial-intelligence

UNESCO. (2023). *The UNESCO courier: Education in the age of artificial intelligence*. UNESCO.

U.S. Department of Education. (2023, October 11). *Office of Educational Technology, Artificial Intelligence and Future of Teaching and Learning: Insights and Recommendations*. Washington, DC, 2023.: Office of Educational Technology, Retrieved from https://www2.ed.gov/documents/ai-report/ai-report.pdf

Zhai, X., Chu, X., Chai, C. S., Jong, M. S., Istenic, A., Spector, M., Liu, J.-B., Yuan, J., & Li, Y. (2021). A review of artificial intelligence (AI) in education from 2010 to 2020. *Complexity*, *2021*, 1–8. doi:10.1155/2021/8812542

ADDITIONAL READING

Anapey, G. M., & Aheto, S.-P. K. (2022). Distance education tutors' technology pedagogical integration during covid- 19 in Ghana: Implications for development education and instructional design. In O. T. Kwapong, D. Addae, & J. K. Boateng (Eds.), *Reimagining Development Education in Africa* (pp. 155–170). Springer., doi:10.1007/978-3-030-96001-8_9

Evans, M. A., Packer, M. J., & Sawyer, R. K. (2016). *Reflections on the learning sciences: past, present and future*. Cambridge University Press. doi:10.1017/CBO9781107707221

Jonassen, D. H., & Land, S. M. (2017). *Theoretical foundations of learning environments*. Lawrence Erlbaum.

Jukes, I., & Schaaf, R. (2019). *A brief history of the future of education: learning in the age of disruption* (1st ed.). Corwin. doi:10.4135/9781544355061

Kim, J., & Maloney, J. E. (2020). *Learning innovations and the future of higher education* (1st ed.). John Hopkins University Press. doi:10.1353/book.71965

Krüger, J. M., & Bodemer, D. (2022). Application and investigation of multimedia design principles in augmented reality learning environments. *Information (Basel)*, *13*(2), 74. doi:10.3390/info13020074

Mehta, J., & Fine, S. (2019). *In search of deeper learning: The quest to remake the American high school*. Harvard University Press. doi:10.4159/9780674239951

Morrison, G. R., Ross, S. M., & Kemp, J. E. (2019). *Designing effective instruction*. John Wiley & Sons Inc.

Ormrod, J. (2019). *Human learning* (8th ed.). Pearson.

Stone, D. L., & Hart, T. (2019). *Sociocultural psychology and regulatory processes in learning activity: contributions of cultural-historical psychological theory*. Cambridge University Press. doi:10.1017/9781316225226

KEY TERMS AND DEFINITIONS

Artificial Intelligence: (AI) deploys digital algorithmic programming languages including natural languages to mimic human cognitive process in form of applications for diverse functioning. Machine learning, data analytics, perceptual and speech recognition tools are examples of AI gaining traction currently.

Deep Learning Pedagogy: is a departure from traditional static text teaching to more organic process that account for experiences and diagnostics to construct meanings while connecting content-standards to real-world solving and conceptual thinking.

Dialogic Education: is a system of learning originally ascribed to Paulo Freire's pedagogy of the oppressed to denote the use of effective questioning skills and conversation that elicits critical thinking active participation in social settings as opposed to regurgitation of information in colonised communities.

Learning Sciences: (LS) is an interdisciplinary field that draws on areas including cognitive sciences, educational technology, curriculum development, instructional design, educational anthropology, and computational thinking to examine learning environments. Using instructional design, LS theories and concepts support learners to develop global competencies for the twenty-first century.

Chapter 9
Digitalisation of Banking as a Catalyst for Inter–Country Money Transfers in Africa

Ranson Sifiso Gwala

https://orcid.org/0000-0002-1545-2259

University of KwaZulu-Natal, South Africa

Pfano Mashau

https://orcid.org/0000-0003-0490-1925

University of KwaZulu-Natal, South Africa

ABSTRACT

The purpose of this research was to examine how banking digitalisation acts as a catalyst for money transfers and economic development between countries of origin and country of labour migration in Africa. This chapter used desktop research to understand how improvements in banking digitalisation using different platforms is transforming African movement of money and saving money senders a lot of money and time in inter account transfers. M-PESA; Mukuru, supermarket money market transfers, bank transfers have been dominant FinTech innovations transforming and improving quality of life and fostering financial inclusion within the African continent and diaspora. This chapter aids in understanding how digitalisation assists ordinary citizens, especially the poor who need to save every rand or dollar that they can save in order to make meaningful change in their lives and the lives of their loved ones anywhere in Africa and the world under these trying post-COVID 19 economic conditions.

INTRODUCTION

Africa remains the most underdeveloped continent in the world. It is however a continent with some of the world riches that reside under the earth. It is also a mecca for the world tourists as it contains the world greatest game reserves, showing a variety of fauna and flora. Africa still lags behind many continents, long after colonisation ended. Some of the African countries are still riddled by wars, and

DOI: 10.4018/978-1-6684-9962-7.ch009

plunder of economic resources. Many FinTech start-ups that are innovating and transforming financial services are taking disruptive action against the financial sector (Srivastava & Dhamija, 2022; Wewege et al., 2020). Since 1995, the phrase "disruptive innovation" has gained widespread use to describe how several, usually technology, start-up enterprises have conquered the world market (Martínez-Vergara & Valls-Pasola, 2021). FinTech firms are transforming the financial sector through FinTech innovations, upending the financial markets, and aiming to displace already well-established financial firms. FinTech businesses provide services to underserved market niches and were once seen as a minor threat to well-established businesses. Financial institutions that are fully digitalized and give high levels of customer satisfaction at reasonable prices dominate the market (Rahmayati, 2021). Although established financial institutions make an effort to stay up with technological advancements by launching new digital services, their position has become more challenging as a result of the entrance of major technology businesses. To close the technological gap and compete in the market, traditional financial companies frequently devise a strategy of engagement with FinTech firms (Iman, 2023).

THE BACKGROUND

The African banking system ranges from some of the best systems that have been able to survive the recent 2008 recession; the world crunch and the recent COVID-19 pandemic. The banking system in Africa is the pillar that supports the economy of the continent. The economy is critical in ensuring that the growing young population of Africa is able to study and get jobs. Economic growth is critical in job creation under very turbulent conditions. Africa is generally a source of raw materials and not a manufacturer of goods. Although Africa has vast amount of agricultural land, it imports a lot of food and seeds from the west. As changes take place, the banking system is also not exempted. The risk of moving from cash to digital transfers increases the risks of banking from both the banking system and the customers. The digitalisation of the banking system has brought about banking without going to the bank. Many customers are now enjoying the control of their banking and understanding of possibilities in the comfort of their own homes. Africa is charecterised by migrant labour system, moving from neighbouring countries. The likes of Botswana, South Africa, Democratic Republic of Congo, Ghana and Nigeria attract a lot of migrant labour to their informal trade, mines and oil rigs.

THE LITERATURE REVIEW

New evidence suggests that African countries not only suffer from a significant digital divide but also derive fewer advantages from rising levels of digitalization. If Africa wishes to digitalize manufacturing, it needs to have greater access to the internet and other information and communication tools (Gwala & Mashau, 2022). This can be done by implementing robust policies that will alter national conditions and enhance the environment for investment, firm capabilities, national innovation systems, ICT infrastructure, direct financing opportunities, and participation in global value chains, (GVCs) (Banga & te Velde, 2018). The Internet and online technologies have developed and become more widely used over the past few decades, opening up numerous possibilities for business digitalization and the development of new digital business models. Banks are no exception to the trend of businesses around the world being remade and reorganised as a result of the Fourth Industrial Revolution (4IR) (Louw & Nieuwenhuizen,

2020). Since the global financial crisis, banks have faced chances and threats unmatched in history that are primarily fuelled by technology (Blake, 2022). In order to provide customers with a better, more affordable, more convenient, or more efficient value proposition, the Financial Technology, also known as "Fintech disruptors," are actively tapping into their service delivery network (Edwards-Dashti, 2022). Regulators have had to make sure that the pervasiveness of technological disruption does not endanger the soundness of banks and the stability of economies as banks have been forced to think more strategically about how to conduct themselves in light of the impending use of technologies like virtual reality, artificial intelligence, biometrics, and big data (Gwala & Mashau, 2022).

Diffusion of Innovation Model

The diffusion of innovation model suggests the diffusion of innovation theory (DIT) to explain the variables influencing the adoption of new technologies. Innovation should demonstrate an improvement to one's way of doing things (Rogers, 2003). The theory considers the relative advantage, trialability, observability, complexity; and compatibility in diffusion of innovation.

Figure 1. Diffusion innovation model
Source (Rogers, 2003)

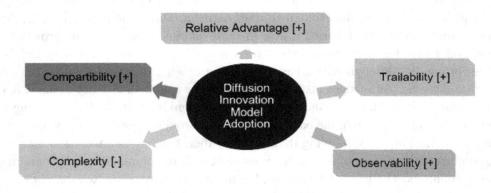

Table 1. Diffusion innovation model (Source: Rogers, 2003)

	Attribute	Definition	Association with adoption
1.	Relative advantage	The degree to which an innovation is perceived beneficial (economic, and health outcomes) over the action, idea, or product it is replacing	The greater the perceived advantage, the more the rapid innovation is likely to be adopted.
2.	Complexity	The degree to which an innovation is perceived as difficult to use or understand.	The greater the complexity, the less likely an innovation is adopted
3.	Comparability	The degree to which an innovation fits with the values and needs of adopters	The greater the perceived compatibility, the more rapid the innovation is likely to be adopted
4.	Trialability	The degree to which an innovation can be experimented with on a limited basis before adopting it more permanently	The greater the perceived trialability, the more rapid the innovation is likely to be adopted.
5.	Observability	The degree to which the results of an innovation are tangible	The greater the perceived observability, the more rapid the innovation is likely to be adopted.

The belief that innovation is superior to the prior idea, practise, or thing is the ***relative advantage***. Innovation's nature and significance to the potential adopters immediately affect the benefit it represents. In his research, Rogers found that some benefits—such as the provision of incentives, the initial cost, and the potential for achieving or gaining social status—contribute significantly to the acceptance of an innovation. This characteristic may be the most important determinant of an invention's adoption when a user seeks to understand the benefits an innovation brings. How it changes their life or makes them in any way better off than they were before will be a key motivator. ***Users' trialability*** is a measure of how willing they are to try out the invention. For FinTech innovations like mobile money to be extensively used as a payment mechanism, one would need to register their mobile number for mobile money. Before someone will be willing to employ an innovation to its utmost potential, they must actually use it. If the innovation is advantageous to one's well-being, whether one makes this determination based on their own experiences or the experiences of others, this feature is essential to the development of that affirmation. The perception of difficulty in using and comprehending the invention by people who accept it is correlated with its ***complexity***. In some particular circumstances, the significance of complexity pales in comparison to the importance of compatibility and relative advantage. The author uses the diffusion of computers as an illustration of how individuals who value technology continue to utilise it despite its challenges because they must in order to satisfy the demands of daily life and several other contexts. However, in the Diffusion of Innovation Theory (DIT), inventions that are acknowledged as being complex in their usage typically struggle with their spread and may even be rejected, employed insufficiently, or replaced over time. The visible outcomes of using the invention are referred to as ***observability***, another feature. Adopters of an innovation are more likely to accept it and aid in the diffusion process if they notice favourable effects from it. In this situation, it is thought that members of a certain social structure are more open to ideas, customs, or products that have previously been embraced by their peers. Rogers uses the diffusion of mobile communication devices as an illustration; these initially expensive items rose in popularity as a result of their obvious application.

Any innovation is worthwhile for people to accept since it is simple to use. It is quite likely that users won't be persuaded to use the invention if it is difficult to use (Sharma & Gandhi, 2023). The idea that an invention is ***compatible*** with the ideas, values, social conventions, prior experiences, and requirements of its potential users is referred to as the compatibility attribute. According to Rogers, there will be less confusion about a new idea's possible benefits and drawbacks if it is more suitable with the context in which it will be used. Generally speaking, any invention must be tailored to the sociocultural values, obviously not at odds with the customs and beliefs. Observing ***compatibility*** with previously established concepts or innovations also lends the innovation under consideration a sense of evolution.

This is a complicated process that is driven by choices, actions, and decisions that gradually define how the innovation is incorporated through time. In this way, the DIT provides a model for the innovation-decision process that includes five more time stages: *knowledge, persuasion, choice, implementation, and confirmation.*

Knowledge: This refers to the pursuit of information regarding the innovation, which can take place in the awareness dimensions (awareness-knowledge), referring to the presence of the invention, use of the innovation (how-to knowledge), and the principles of the innovation (principles-knowledge).

Persuasion: In the DIT's view, persuasion does not refer to a particular kind of induction that differs in the sense of inducing human behaviour to something because the possible adopter will have his or her own autonomy of critical thought, experimentation, and, ultimately, of choosing.

Figure 2. Diffusion innovation model decision process
Source: Rogers, 2003; Self & Roberts, 2019

Decision: It entails making a choice between accepting or rejecting the invention. Adoption refers to the decision to fully and optimally utilise an innovation, whereas rejection refers to the decision not to adopt it.

Implementation: The act of putting an innovation into practise. Until it is institutionalised or adopted by its adopters as a routine practise, implementation may take a long time.

Confirmation: This happens when the adoption unit (individual/group) tries to reaffirm the choice made in the earlier stage.

Unified Theory of Acceptance and Use of Technology (UTAUT)

A variety of industries, including healthcare, e-government, mobile internet enterprise systems, mobile banking, and applications (apps), have been studied using the original and extended Unified Theory of Acceptance and Use of Technology (UTAUT) models (AlHadid et al., 2022). The UTAUT applications showed a significant relationship between the two perception factors—perceived performance and perceived ease of use—and behavioural intention. For instance, the adoption of a clinical decision support system based on pharmacokinetics was studied using the technological acceptance framework (Berge et al., 2023). With the exception of enabling conditions, all constructions had a major impact on intention. These conditions solely affected how the technology was actually used (Berge et al., 2023; Ronaghi & Forouharfar, 2020). The analysis of the factors influencing the adoption of e-government by employees in a state organisation in a developing country revealed that all UTAUT variables were significantly influenced, moderated by gender, with performance and effort expectancy showing the highest effects (Trkman et al., 2023; Zeebaree et al., 2022). Three out of the four predictors of usage intention were found to be significant when the model was applied to investigate the acceptance of ERP software training (Ashrafi et al., 2022). Employees' intentions to use training tools were influenced by effort expectations, performance expectations, and facilitating conditions, but the impact of social influence was unsupported.

Financial Inclusion as Means to Improve Economic Growth

In terms of financial inclusion, Africa comes in last. Given that financial inclusion is closely related to poverty, an increasing number of African nations are developing mobile money programs (using USSD technology) to combat financial exclusion (Kouladoum et al., 2022; Van et al., 2021). Financial inclusion is regarded as a key element of financial development and is a recognised catalyst for economic growth (Liu et al., 2022). There are two ways that financial inclusion and economic expansion can be connected. Similar to this, there are two sorts of indicators for financial inclusion: supply-side indicators and demand-side indicators (Liu & Walheer, 2022). Under demand-side indices of financial inclusion, banks penetration, the availability of bank services, and banking system utilisation are included (Geraldes et al., 2022). On the other hand, supply side factors include having access to savings opportunities and insurance services. Theoretical connections between demand and supply side measures of financial inclusion and economic growth are established in Figure 3 (Ibne Afzal et al., 2023). Greater access to diverse banking services by businesses and people lowers the cost of transactions and information in the economy. The IMF and World Bank have advocated for the need for high financial inclusion as a strategy for sustainable economic development over the past year (Chang et al., 2023). This is because high financial inclusion has been linked to sustainable economic development and growth in developed countries (Huang et al., 2021; Li et al., 2022).

Figure 3. Financial Inclusion Model
Adapted from (Sethi & Acharya, 2018)

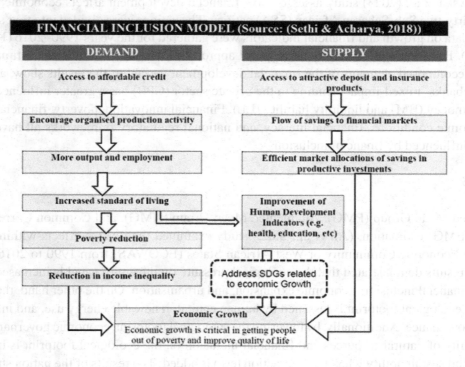

Financial inclusion should be everyone's task. The international monetary organisations should seek to achieve high financial inclusion, not only for profit maximisation but for ensuring that people access services. All services that are linked to an improved quality of life are associated with financial markets, namely the ability to buy and sell goods and services freely at market prices. Consequently, financial inclusion promotes access to education which leads to job creation and employability. These activities become closely linked to each other and under good governance, lead to sustainable economic growth.

SADEC

Financial inclusion initiatives have been created by a number of Southern African Development Community (SADC) member states in an effort to offer financial services to those who are economically disadvantaged. This resulted from a panel discussion that senior-level representatives from the Ministries of Finance, Central Banks, Non-bank Regulators, and the private sector attended during the annual SADC Regional Financial Inclusion Forum in Johannesburg, South Africa. The European Union's Support to Improving the Investment and Business Environment in the SADC Region (SIBE) Programme helps to support the financial inclusion strategies. The majority of policymakers worldwide agree that an inclusive financial system is important, and it is increasingly being prioritised in international policymaking. A financial system that is inclusive ensures equitable access to economic possibilities while also generating new ones. However, many developing nations still view agriculture as a major source of economic growth, therefore it is impossible to undervalue the significance of financial inclusion for the advancement of agriculture.

Kowalewska et al. (2023) study assessed how financial development affects economic growth in a subset of thirty-two Sub-Saharan African (SSA) nations. The nations were divided into four sub-regions, and yearly data on growth and financial indicators were gathered for the years 1990–2016 (Kowalewska et al., 2023). Panel estimation and dynamic panel approaches were employed in the estimate process. Using the decomposed elements of the financial development variables, the results show, among other things, that banks' mixed-impact lending to the private sector (CPB) has a greater influence on growth than broad money (BM) and liquidity liability (LL). Financial innovation, poverty, financial sector stability, economic conditions, financial literacy, and national regulatory frameworks all have an impact on and are influenced by financial inclusion.

ECOWAS

Using Pooled Mean Group (PMG), Augmented Mean Group (AMG), and Common Correlated Mean Group (CCEMG) estimation, (Ali et al., 2022) study examined the diverse effects within the framework of the Economic Community of West African States (ECOWAS) from 1990 to 2016 (Ali et al., 2022). The results demonstrated that the ecological pressure on the entire panel is increased by natural resources, financial inclusion, economic expansion, and urbanisation. On the other hand, the ECOWAS economies' ecological footprint is lessened by human capital, renewable energy use, and institutions of economic governance. Additionally, by lowering the ecological footprint, economic governance between the availability of natural resources and financial inclusion on the ecological footprint is beneficial to environmental sustainability when the interaction term is added. The results of the nation study showed that natural resources have a negative impact on environmental quality in Cameroon, Gambia, Nigeria, and Senegal, but have a positive but negligible effect in other countries. Therefore, financial inclusion accelerates Senegal's and Ghana's environmental imprint. With interdependencies amongst actors that are more dynamic than those found outside of Africa, Ghana's FinTech ecosystem is dynamic and complicated. The actors include traditional financial institutions, telecommunication intermediaries, merchants,

FinTech firms, agents, think tanks and development groups, users, and government actors including the central bank and regulators of the telecommunications industry (Senyo et al., 2022).

The body of research demonstrates that the financial system is crucial to the expansion and advancement of the economy. The financial system's ability to significantly support economic growth and development, however, is questionable if the poorest members of society are left out. Regretfully, current worldwide data on financial inclusion shows that a sizable portion of the populace is now not included in the financial system. Therefore, the purpose of this study is to raise awareness among Nigerian researchers and policymakers regarding the significance of ICT in promoting financial inclusion in the nation (Ogbuabor et al., 2020). When it comes to financial inclusion, developed and developing nations deal with the same problems, while high- and low-income nations have different concerns. However, financial literacy is associated with sophisticated investment behaviour, retirement planning, and macroeconomic implications in high-income nations, whereas it is associated with bank account ownership and insurance take-up in low-income countries.

SUB-SAHARAN AFRICA (CEN –SAD)

The highest rates of mobile money usage in Africa are found in the East Africa area, which includes nations like Kenya, Tanzania, and Uganda. The use of mobile money has increased significantly recently in a number of countries, including Ghana, Rwanda, Madagascar, Mozambique, and Guinea, according to the IMF's Financial Access Survey (FAS) (Coulibaly, 2021; Hellström & Tröften, 2010; Lorenz & Pommet, 2021).The growth of opportunities and choices that people have access to in order to live their lives to the fullest is known as human development. Despite the abundance of natural resources on the continent, human development has always been low in Africa. Fosu and Mwabu's findings, which show that human development in African nations is still lagging behind that of other parts of the world, lend credence to this theory. Encouraging gender equality is one of the Sustainable Development Goals (SDG). Women can achieve gender equality by regaining economic power through access to formal financial services. Gender disparity between men and women, estimated to be 15% in OECD countries and 38% in the Middle East, Sub-Saharan Africa and North Africa, causes the majority of women to be unemployed and unfit for employment, which results in revenue loss (Hansen et al., 2021). Compared to men, more women in developing nations will be able to work for themselves thanks to improved access to financial goods and services. Because of their credit histories or lack of collateral, women pay greater interest rates on loans than men do (Soyemi et al., 2020).

Bringing women into the formal financial system will contribute to closing the gender inequality gap. Interest banking and mobile banking are two examples of digital financial products and services that lessen the risk that women face from theft, asymmetric knowledge, and competitive risk. Matekenya, et al (2021) sought to investigate how financial inclusion affects human development in Sub-Saharan Africa (SSA). Financial services can be accessed and used to manage risk and decrease the impact of financial shocks, invest in health and education, support company start-ups, and generally have a positive impact on human development. The findings demonstrate the beneficial impact of financial inclusion on human development. As a result, it is advised that governments take action to lower the expenses associated with obtaining and using financial services, such as by making infrastructural expenditures and increasing public knowledge of these services.

COMESA

Using annual time series data from 1997 to 2018, a study looked at the roles that digital finance and financial inclusion played in the process of economic growth in nineteen COMESA member nations. The study discovered that digital finance and financial inclusion are significant drivers of growth in the area using the Panel Autoregressive Distributed Lag Model (ARDL) methodology (Manasseh, Nwakoby, et al., 2023; MANASSEH, OKANYA, et al., 2023). The results specifically showed that the number of deposit accounts with commercial banks per 1,000 adults, the number of registered mobile money accounts per 1,000 adults, the number of active mobile money agent outlets, digital card ownership, and financial literacy are important growth predictors. Additionally, the results indicated that automated teller machines, mobile purchases, point of sale, and mobile banking are also important predictors. Additionally, it discovered evidence of a bidirectional causal relationship between the index of digital finance, financial inclusion, and economic growth. This finding raises the possibility that policies aimed at advancing financial inclusion and digital finance could accelerate growth. It discovered that a poor legal system and high macroeconomic volatility can inhibit growth by adjusting for institutional environment and macroeconomic volatility (Alimi & Adediran, 2020; Lemma et al., 2022; Manasseh, Nwakoby, et al., 2023).

THE RESEARCH METHODOLOGY

The research utilised desktop review of literature. Secondary data from a variety of sources (websites, journals, books, and other e-content) were used in this study to accomplish the aforementioned objectives. This was mainly using Google Scholar, Web of Science, Scopus, etc as the source of peer-reviewed articles databases capturing the digitalisation of the higher education sector in Africa. The research methodology is based on the desk study, social survey, comparative analysis and logical construction research methods. The survey of literature with identified terms closely linked to the objectives and the topic of the chapter. The survey of literature is aimed at observing, understanding richness of data to give themes and sub-themes.

The objectives of the study were:

a)   to analyse the extent to which Fintech phenomenon, expansion and use has grown in Africa;
b)   to assess level of digitalisation, and how this has improved digital access, financial inclusion in African continent.

THE DISCUSSION

Africa provides a lot of wealth to the world. The businesses which operate internationally would like to extend their experience and technologies from other continents in order to ensure ease of doing business. There are four emerging themes of intercountry money transfers that were observed. These have enhanced digitalisation and improved the lives of African people. These are:

a) MPESA
b) Mukuru
c) Money Market Transfer- Supermarkets
d) Bank Money Transfer Services

M-PESA, bank money transfer, money market transfers have been widely studied to a varying degrees, whilst Mukuru has been less studied. The expansion of cell phones has made it possible to expand digitalisation. The cell phone has a potential to connect people, whilst the intercountry charges or difference in charges is still a challenge. The cell phone companies have also been a hindrance to transformation and lowering of data. Affordable data is the currency that drives digital access.

M-PESA

Customers' daily lives are getting more and more integrated with virtual engagement. Although not perfect for everyone, a (mostly) cashless world is probably coming in the not-too-distant future. A few instances of how connectivity and mobility enable the possibility for interaction on a mobile platform include eWallets and M-Pesa (Anderson et al., 2021; Granger et al., 2022a). The M-Pesa mobile money transfer service was introduced by mobile operator Safaricom in March 2007. Since then, both those with bank accounts and those without have started using the mobile payment method (Alvarez et al., 2022; Gelb & Mukherjee, 2020). Due to the relative affordability of mobile phones and the mobile banking services they provide, microbusiness operators in Kenya have adopted the use of mobile payments as a method of conducting enterprise. Mobile payments are used for a variety of transactions, including making payments to vendors for products and services, paying bills, sending money to friends and family, getting cash withdrawals, and topping off airtime accounts (Acker & Murthy, 2020; Nan et al., 2021).

The traditional banks in a number of African countries understood that many people don't own a bank account but need and transact on daily basis. Africa has a large informal market economy that does not subscribe to the traditional banking. The taxi (minibus) industry in South Africa dates back to apartheid times where many African people transported other using Valiant cars within townships (Jinnah, 2022). About 65% of South Africans use taxis or minibuses for transportation, and the sector has served as a breeding ground for black entrepreneurship. However, this business is plagued by a history of illegality as a result of apartheid-era legislation that limited black South Africans' access to the economy. This graduated to the current, vibrant taxi industry (Brown et al., 2022). As advancements in geotagging, biometrics, and tokens enhance the protection of parties to transactions from fraudsters, interactional confidence is rising (Granger et al., 2022b). A cashless society might cause the payment industry to consolidate, giving customers visibility into the majority of their payment operations and useful information about their lifestyle, preferences, and wealth generation and management.

Mukuru International Money Transfers

Mukuru is a Fintech company that provides emerging consumers with access to cost-effective and trustworthy financial services (Carvalho, 2022). Our business is based on assisting you with international money transfers so you may move money into, out of, and throughout Africa (Gaschler, 2022; VanZyl, 2020). It has never been simpler to send money for immediate collection, top up a bank account, or use a mobile wallet. From this foundation, we have expanded to offer a wide range of services to meet all of our clients' financial needs. When it comes to money transfers, Mukuru is the market leader in Africa. It also has a leading Next Gen Financial Services Platform that provides rising consumers with cost-effective and dependable financial services (Costa, 2020). The migrant diaspora's needs for safe, convenient money transfers is the core of their business, and as a result, we have developed a wide range of products and services to meet those needs. Cash Transfers and The Mukuru Wallet are only two of the many services offered by Mukuru. Mukuru simplified customer engagement to allow the customers to understand what Mukuru offers (Aderibigbe, 2023). Through WhatsApp, free USSD, the Mukuru App, and the website, Mukuru interacts with its clients. To meet the demands of our clients, their call centre provides customer care in 15 different languages. With 60 agreements and a global presence, Mukuru enables more than 100 brands to offer pay out points. Plans call for growing its Orange Booths and its capacity to receive remittances from within Africa. As a payment partner for WorldRemit remittances in regions where Mukuru has its own booth and branch network, the company partners with WorldRemit (Owuor, 2018). The 2020 FXC Intelligence Incumbents versus Challengers in Cross-Border Payments report lists Mukuru as one of the top 150 worldwide cross-border companies. Mukuru operates in over 16 countries within Africa and four other countries including (India, Bangladesh, China and Pakistan) internationally and expanding (Mugo, 2021).

Mukuru International Money Transfers, a leading African remittance service provider, has been a catalyst for digitalization in the region. Through its innovative approach to money transfers, Mukuru has played a significant role in driving the adoption of digital financial services and transforming the traditional remittance landscape. Here are the ways Mukuru has acted as a catalyst for digitalization:

Mukuru recognized the power of mobile technology in Africa, where mobile phone penetration is high. The company has integrated with popular mobile money platforms such as M-Pesa, EcoCash, and Airtel Money, enabling customers to send and receive money directly to and from their mobile wallets (Davidovic et al., 2020; Niesten, 2023). This integration has facilitated faster, more convenient, and secure transactions, encouraging the adoption of digital payment solutions. Mukuru's digital platform has contributed to financial inclusion by providing access to financial services for unbanked individuals. Many African countries have a significant portion of the population without access to traditional banking services (Castro, 2020). Mukuru's digital platform allows them to send and receive money without needing a bank account, thus expanding financial inclusion and promoting economic empowerment.

Traditional remittance channels are often associated with high fees, which can be a barrier for individuals sending or receiving money. Mukuru's digital platform has brought down the cost of remittances, making it more affordable for users. Lower transaction fees make digital remittances an attractive alternative to traditional methods, encouraging individuals to embrace digitalization (Cirolia et al., 2022). One of the significant advantages of digital remittances is the speed of transactions. Mukuru's platform enables near-instantaneous money transfers, reducing the time taken for funds to reach recipients. This speed is crucial for individuals who rely on remittances for daily expenses or urgent financial needs (MacIsaac, 2023). By offering quick and efficient transactions, Mukuru has accelerated the adoption of digital remittance services.

Mukuru has prioritized providing a seamless and user-friendly experience for its customers. The digital platform offers a range of features such as real-time tracking, notifications, and customer support, ensuring that users have transparency and convenience throughout the remittance process (George et al., 2023). The positive customer experience encourages individuals to embrace digital solutions for their money transfer needs. Mukuru has formed strategic partnerships with various technology providers, payment processors, and financial institutions. These collaborations have enabled the company to leverage cutting-edge technologies and infrastructure, ensuring the reliability, security, and scalability of its digital platform (Kelsall et al., 2021). The partnerships have also facilitated interoperability between different financial service providers, making it easier for customers to access Mukuru's services through multiple channels.

In Kenya, Mukuru has implemented digital identity solutions to enhance security and compliance. By employing technologies such as biometric verification and identity authentication, Mukuru ensures that transactions are secure and aligned with regulatory requirements (Gaschler, 2022; TERENCE, 2022). These digital identity solutions contribute to building trust in digital financial services and pave the way for broader adoption.

Money Market Transfers: Through Supermarkets

Given the significance of banks in the financial system, it is crucial to comprehend the threats and opportunities that FinTech poses to banks, as well as how it will affect the primary roles of financial intermediaries and their participation in contemporary financial service ecosystems (Murinde et al., 2022; Varma et al., 2022). It is particularly unclear if the FinTech revolution will entirely destroy traditional banking or, on the other hand, whether it will strengthen the portfolio of current banking products (Saiz, 2020). A review of the body of knowledge on FinTech and services made possible by technology, there is greater collaboration between banks and supermarkets. In South Africa, Zimbabwe, Nigeria, Namibia, Zambia, Botswana, Swaziland and many other African countries, many banks now support cash withdrawals at supermarkets at relatively lower charges compared to bank withdrawals. This is another FinTech breakthrough that is supported and used by consumers. Many consumers don't see the need to visit traditional bank branches, hence alternatives are welcomed in this field.

Over the past ten years, money market transfers made possible by supermarkets have had a positive impact on the lives of Africans. Numerous advantages have resulted from this novel approach to financial services, including increased financial inclusion and better living standards (Senyo & Osabutey, 2020; Torkelson, 2020). Here are some ways that money market transfers made possible by supermarkets have made life better for Africans:

Convenience and Accessibility: By using supermarkets as money markets, those who might not have easy access to traditional banking infrastructure have more access to financial services. Since supermarkets are frequently situated in densely populated regions, it is simple for customers to obtain essential financial services like cash deposits, withdrawals, and transfers while finishing their daily shopping (Adeosun & Adeosun, 2023; Puspitasari & Zulaikha, 2023).Money market transfers made possible via supermarkets have cut down on the time and expense often involved with traditional banking services. Individuals are not need to go to a different bank branch in order to execute their financial transactions. Particularly for individuals dwelling in remote or underdeveloped locations where banks are few, this saves them time and travel expenses.

The promotion of financial inclusion in Africa has been greatly aided by money market transfers made possible by supermarkets (Mhlanga, 2023). Financial service companies have been able to access underserved communities, including people who might not have a bank account, by utilizing the already-existing grocery networks (Mhlanga, 2023; Pazarbasioglu et al., 2020). This makes it possible for individuals to obtain fundamental financial services, take part in the official financial system, and generally better their financial situation. Money market transfers made through supermarkets sometimes involve staff who can give customers basic financial education and advice. By increasing their financial literacy and giving them the tools to manage their money wisely, this gives people more power. Customers can comprehend budgeting, saving, and other financial concepts better through these interactions.

Money market transfers made through supermarkets now go beyond simple exchanges. Nowadays, a lot of supermarkets provide extra services including microloans, airtime purchases, and bill payments (Guma & Mwaura, 2021). Customers may manage their finances more conveniently and adaptably thanks to these services, which improves their quality of life even more. Supermarkets are frequently regarded as secure local centres where people feel at ease transacting money. This existing trust makes money market transfers through supermarkets more advantageous and gives customers a sense of security and dependability. Particularly in areas where conventional financial institutions might be viewed with suspicion, this trust is essential.

The development of jobs and economic expansion have been aided by money market transfers made through supermarkets. More employees are needed as these services grow in order to handle the transactions and offer customer service. This improves local economies and quality of life by creating employment possibilities, especially for locals. Recently, digital integration has also been used for money market transfers done through supermarkets (Gupta & Kanungo, 2022). Nowadays, many supermarkets provide mobile payment options that enable customers to utilise their phones to make purchases. Combining conventional and digital media increases accessibility and convenience, especially for the younger, more tech-savvy population.

Bank/Online Bank Money Market Transfers

According to a report, automation will soon replace 60% of duties performed by workers today. FinTech, or financial technology, robots, artificial intelligence, and other technical advancements will all be key components of new growth models (Mosteanu & Faccia, 2020; Sharma et al., 2022). According to the studies by (Bakar et al., 2020; Nguyen, 2022), Fintech will result in decreased corporate expenses and profit margins for banks and established financial institutions, for start-ups FinTech companies, this will lower the cost of doing business. The ripple effect of lower cost of doing business will result, in the short term at the increase of start-ups being established. There is a big potential market for Fintech companies because an estimated 38% of the world's population lacks official bank accounts and another 40% is underserved by banks. A number of established FinTech companies have an opportunity to become part of the FinTech revolution by offering their customers some of these products that are offered by the start-up FinTech companies because they will stand a chance to keep some of the customers who would be attracted by low cost of transacting.

A number of African banks have joined in the FinTech revolution, offering low cost transactional banking. In South Africa, there was a financial coalition which lobbied for financial access by the he poor. This led to the introduction of the Mzansi account (South African Account). Banks were under regulatory pressure to offer their banking services to the 18 million unbanked people by the Financial Sector Charter of 2005 (Mushonga, 2018; Ward & Naude, 2018). The banking industry responded by introducing the Mzansi account, which was defined as a "best-effort" endeavour to attract new consumers to the SA banking industry (Shuping, 2021). The Mzansi account seemed successful on paper. By December 2010, there were 4.9 million Mzansi account holders, according to the report. Approximately 15% of the 32 million adult SA citizens were represented by this, up from 13% in 2009 and 11% in 2008 (Ismail & Masinge, 2012; Maity & Sahu, 2022).

IMPLICATIONS FOR DIGITALISATION OF BANKING AS A CATALYST FOR INTER COUNTRY MONEY TRANSFERS IN AFRICA

The digitalization of banking has significant implications for intercountry money transfers in Africa. It has the potential to act as a catalyst for transforming and improving the efficiency, accessibility, and affordability of cross-border financial transactions within the continent. Digitalization enables faster and more efficient intercountry money transfers. Traditional methods of sending money across borders in Africa have often been slow and cumbersome, involving lengthy processes and intermediaries. Digital banking solutions, including online banking and mobile money, streamline the transfer process, allowing funds to be sent and received in real-time or within a matter of minutes. This speed and efficiency enhance financial flows between countries, supporting trade and economic activities.

Digital banking solutions can significantly reduce the costs associated with intercountry money transfers. Traditional methods, such as wire transfers or using remittance service providers, often involve high fees and exchange rate mark-ups. Digital platforms and FinTech companies offer competitive rates, lower transaction fees, and better exchange rates, making cross-border transfers more affordable for individuals and businesses (Bindseil & Pantelopoulos, 2022). Reduced costs contribute to increased remittance flows and improved financial inclusion across countries in Africa. Digitalization of banking promotes accessibility to financial services and fosters financial inclusion for individuals and businesses across borders. Mobile banking and digital payment platforms have expanded access to banking services, allowing individuals without traditional bank accounts to send and receive money internationally. These digital solutions are particularly valuable for migrants, diaspora communities, and small businesses engaged in cross-border trade, facilitating easier and more affordable money transfers.

The digitalization of banking for intercountry money transfers also presents regulatory challenges. National regulators need to establish frameworks that enable seamless and secure cross-border transactions while ensuring compliance with anti-money laundering (AML) and know-your-customer (KYC) regulations. Harmonizing regulations and cooperation between countries can facilitate the growth of digital cross-border payment systems and address potential risks related to financial integrity and consumer protection. Digitalization opens up opportunities for innovation and collaboration among financial institutions, FinTech companies, and other stakeholders involved in intercountry money transfers (Kouchih & Lyoussi, 2022). Partnerships between traditional banks, FinTech start-ups, and mobile network operators can leverage their respective strengths to offer innovative solutions for cross-border transactions. Collaboration can lead to the development of interoperable systems, common standards, and shared infrastructure, further enhancing the efficiency and reach of intercountry money transfers.

The digitalization of intercountry money transfers promotes economic integration and trade facilitation within Africa. Streamlined and efficient cross-border payment systems support regional economic cooperation, cross-border investments, and trade flows. Improved financial connectivity can contribute to the growth of intra-African trade, reducing reliance on external markets and promoting economic resilience and diversification (Warikandwa, 2023).

RECOMMENDATIONS FOR GROWTH OF THE BANKING SECTOR IN AFRICA IN THE FINTECH ERA

In the age of digital financial technology, or FinTech, Africa's banking industry has a chance to change dramatically in ways that will improve financial innovation, efficiency, and inclusiveness (Danladi et al., 2023; Ediagbonya & Tioluwani, 2023). Spend money on initiatives that will raise people's level of digital literacy. Both clients and bank employees are included in this. To use digital financial tools effectively and securely, one must understand them. Grow your mobile banking business to take advantage of Africa's enormous mobile phone penetration (Nan et al., 2021). This can include USSD-based banking services, mobile banking apps, and mobile payment solutions, all of which increase accessibility to financial services. Encourage cooperation with FinTech firms to introduce cutting-edge products to the market. Start-ups frequently have creativity and agility at their heart, and collaborations can give banks access to cutting-edge concepts and technologies.

Boost cybersecurity defences to safeguard bank transactions and customer information. The security of online financial services must be given top priority due to the growing reliance on digital channels.

Examine how blockchain technology can be used to make transactions transparent and safe. Blockchain can decrease fraud, expedite procedures like international payments, and improve the general effectiveness of financial operations. Reach unbanked and underbanked communities by utilising FinTech. Provide solutions that address the particular requirements and difficulties faced by these markets to increase the inclusivity of financial services. Make use of artificial intelligence and data analytics to comprehend consumer behaviour and preferences. By providing individualised banking services based on this data, clients will be more satisfied and loyal. Collaborate with authorities to establish a setting that is favourable for FinTech advancements.

Simplifying legal frameworks can promote the ethical creation and uptake of FinTech products. By automating repetitive and manual processes, Robotic Process Automation (RPA) can lower operating costs and boost productivity (Taj & Zaman, 2022). This frees up banking employees to concentrate on tasks that are more intricate and add value. Accept the idea of "open banking," which permits outside developers to build services and apps centred around financial institutions. This may result in a financial ecosystem that is livelier and more integrated. Considering how quickly technology is developing, make an ongoing training investment for bank employees. This guarantees that they can continue to effectively guide consumers and maintain their proficiency with new technology (Momoh et al., 2023). Use chatbots driven by AI to improve customer support. Chatbots can improve the overall customer experience by offering immediate assistance, responding to questions, and assisting clients with a variety of banking procedures.

CONCLUSION

The use of technology has been improving with every leap in the industrial revolution. The fourth industrial revolution brought about opportunities and threats, but the opportunities outweigh the threats. The banking sector has also ensured that it uses the developing financial technology (Fintech) to advance and leap into the digitalisation of the banking sector. This has allowed banks to tap into untapped markets.

The blue ocean strategy claims that looking for new markets where no new markets have existed before. The expansion of the banking sector reaches new markets and new customers. These customers have options and they can pay as they use for these new services. The uneven development in countries forces those who are lagging behind to catch up. It also allows expansion of the banking sector to include other outlets like shops, supermarkets and other financial service providers to collaborate.

M-PESA, Mukuru International Money Transfers, Money Market Transfer-Supermarkets, and Bank/Online Bank Money Transfer Services have collectively revolutionized the financial landscape in Africa, offering various benefits to individuals and driving financial inclusion. Financial inclusion plays a vital role in improving economic growth in Africa. By providing individuals and businesses with access to affordable and appropriate financial services, it enhances savings, investments, access to credit, productivity, employment, business expansion, and resilience. Financial inclusion fosters formalization, strengthens government efficiency, encourages innovation, and supports technological advancements. Together, these factors contribute to a more inclusive, resilient, and prosperous economy in Africa.

M-PESA, a pioneering mobile money service, has transformed the way people in Africa handle their finances. It has facilitated the adoption of digital financial services, providing convenient and secure mobile money transfers, bill payments, and financial services to millions of users. M-PESA has played a significant role in expanding financial inclusion, particularly among the unbanked population.

Mukuru International Money Transfers has acted as a catalyst for digitalization by leveraging mobile money integration, reducing costs, improving transaction speed, and promoting financial inclusion. With its digital platform, Mukuru has made remittances more affordable, convenient, and accessible, empowering individuals to send and receive money efficiently, even without a bank account.

Money Market Transfer-Supermarkets have brought financial services closer to the people. By offering basic financial transactions, such as deposits, withdrawals, and transfers, through supermarkets, these services have enhanced convenience, accessibility, and cost efficiency. They have played a crucial role in promoting financial inclusion, particularly for individuals residing in underserved areas with limited access to traditional banking services.

Bank/Online Bank Money Transfer Services have evolved to meet the changing needs of customers. With online banking and mobile apps, individuals can conveniently and securely transfer money, make payments, and access various financial services. These services have provided individuals with greater control over their finances, offering features such as real-time transaction tracking, financial insights, and enhanced security measures.

Overall, these financial services—M-PESA, Mukuru International Money Transfers, Money Market Transfer-Supermarkets, and Bank/Online Bank Money Transfer Services—have collectively contributed to financial inclusion, improved accessibility, convenience, cost efficiency, and technological advancement in Africa. They have empowered individuals, supported economic growth, and laid the foundation for a more inclusive and digitally-driven financial ecosystem on the continent.

REFERENCES

Acker, A., & Murthy, D. (2020). What is Venmo? A descriptive analysis of social features in the mobile payment platform. *Telematics and Informatics*, *52*, 101429. doi:10.1016/j.tele.2020.101429

Adeosun, O. T., & Adeosun, O. A. (2023). Agent bankers and customer victimization in Ado City, Nigeria. *Journal of Community Safety & Well-being*, *8*(1), 33–40. doi:10.35502/jcswb.284

Aderibigbe, I. D. (2023). *E-migrant women entrepreneurs: mobile money apps, transnational communication and the maintenance of social practices.* Faculty of Humanities.

AlHadid, I., Abu-Taieh, E., Alkhawaldeh, R. S., Khwaldeh, S., Masa'deh, R., Kaabneh, K., & Alrowwad, A. A. (2022). Predictors for E-government adoption of SANAD App services integrating UTAUT, TPB, TAM, Trust, and perceived risk. *International Journal of Environmental Research and Public Health, 19*(14), 8281. https://mdpi-res.com/d_attachment/ijerph/ijerph-19-08281/article_deploy/ijerph-19-08281. pdf?version=1657159300. doi:10.3390/ijerph19148281 PMID:35886133

Ali, K., Jianguo, D., & Kirikkaleli, D. (2022). Modeling the natural resources and financial inclusion on ecological footprint: The role of economic governance institutions. Evidence from ECOWAS economies. *Resources Policy, 79*, 103115. doi:10.1016/j.resourpol.2022.103115

Alimi, A. S., & Adediran, I. A. (2020). ICT diffusion and the finance–growth nexus: A panel analysis on ECOWAS countries. *Future Business Journal, 6*(1), 1–10. doi:10.1186/s43093-020-00024-x

Alvarez, F. E., Argente, D., & Van Patten, D. (2022). *Are cryptocurrencies currencies? Bitcoin as legal tender in El Salvador.*

Anderson, J., Rainie, L., & Vogels, E. A. (2021). Experts say the 'new normal' in 2025 will be far more tech-driven, presenting more big challenges. Pew Research Center, 18.

Ashrafi, A., Zareravasan, A., Rabiee Savoji, S., & Amani, M. (2022). Exploring factors influencing students' continuance intention to use the learning management system (LMS): A multi-perspective framework. *Interactive Learning Environments, 30*(8), 1475–1497. doi:10.1080/10494820.2020.1734028

Bakar, S., Nordin, N. A., & Amani Nordin, N. (2020). Fintech Investment And Banks Performance In Malaysia, Singapore & Thailand. *European Proceedings of Social and Behavioural Sciences, 100.*

Banga, K., & te Velde, D. W. (2018). *Digitalisation and the Future of Manufacturing in Africa.* ODI London.

Berge, G., Granmo, O., Tveit, T., Munkvold, B., Ruthjersen, A., & Sharma, J. (2023). Machine learning-driven clinical decision support system for concept-based searching: A field trial in a Norwegian hospital. *BMC Medical Informatics and Decision Making, 23*(1), 5. https://bmcmedinformdecismak.biomedcentral. com/counter/pdf/10.1186/s12911-023-02101-x.pdf. doi:10.1186/s12911-023-02101-x PMID:36627624

Bindseil, U., & Pantelopoulos, G. (2022). Towards the holy grail of cross-border payments.

Blake, D. (2022). The Great Game Will Never End: Why the Global Financial Crisis Is Bound to Be Repeated. *Journal of Risk and Financial Management, 15*(6), 245. doi:10.3390/jrfm15060245

Brown, T., Mullins, K., Betzer, C., Ford, S., Freitag, J., Nolan, H., Rattray, A., Sleigh, F., Swanson, S., & Thompson, A. (2022). *The Elusive Rainbow: Racial Reconciliation in South Africa.* Nelson A. Rockefeller Center for Public Policy.

Carvalho, C. E. M. M. d. (2022). *Banking on mobile: financial inclusion through FinTech: the Hidroelétrica de Cahora Bassa: IPO Case Study.* Research Gate.

Castro, C. S. P. (2020). *How can fintech serve the unbanked in Sub-Saharan Africa?* Chang, L., Iqbal, S., & Chen, H. (2023). Does financial inclusion index and energy performance index co-move? *Energy Policy, 174*, 113422.

Cirolia, L. R., Hall, S., & Nyamnjoh, H. (2022). Remittance micro-worlds and migrant infrastructure: Circulations, disruptions, and the movement of money. *Transactions of the Institute of British Geographers, 47*(1), 63–76. doi:10.1111/tran.12467

Costa, J. N. P. P. (2020). *How can fintech serve the unbanked in Sub-Saharan Africa?: Sub-Saharan Africa: land of opportunities for fintech.*

Coulibaly, S. S. (2021). A study of the factors affecting mobile money penetration rates in the West African Economic and Monetary Union (WAEMU) compared with East Africa. *Financial Innovation, 7*(1), 25. doi:10.1186/s40854-021-00238-0

Danladi, S., Prasad, M., Modibbo, U. M., Ahmadi, S. A., & Ghasemi, P. (2023). Attaining Sustainable Development Goals through Financial Inclusion: Exploring Collaborative Approaches to Fintech Adoption in Developing Economies. *Sustainability (Basel), 15*(17), 13039. doi:10.3390/su151713039

Davidovic, S., Soheib, N., Prady, D., & Tourpe, H. (2020). *Beyond the COVID-19 Crisis: A Framework for Sustainable Government-to-person Mobile Money Transfer.* International Monetary Fund.

Ediagbonya, V., & Tioluwani, C. (2023). The role of fintech in driving financial inclusion in developing and emerging markets: Issues, challenges and prospects. *Technological Sustainability, 2*(1), 100–119. doi:10.1108/TECHS-10-2021-0017

Edwards-Dashti, N. (2022). *FinTech Women Walk the Talk: Moving the Needle for Workplace Gender Equality in Financial Services and Beyond.* Springer. doi:10.1007/978-3-030-90574-3

Gaschler, F. O. J. (2022). *Fintech in Africa: how digital payment tech is bringing financial services to the unbanked.* Research Gate.

Gelb, A., & Mukherjee, A. (2020). Digital technology in social assistance transfers for COVID-19 relief: Lessons from selected cases. *CGD Policy Paper, 181*, 1 at 21.

George, A. S., George, A. H., Baskar, T., & Martin, A. G. (2023). An Overview of India's Unified Payments Interface (UPI): Benefits, Challenges, and Opportunities. *Partners Universal International Research Journal, 2*(1), 16–23.

Geraldes, H. S. A., Gama, A. P. M., & Augusto, M. (2022). Reaching financial inclusion: Necessary and sufficient conditions. *Social Indicators Research, 162*(2), 599–617. doi:10.1007/s11205-021-02850-0

Granger, J., de Clercq, B., & Lymer, A. (2022a). 1 Tapping Taxes. *TAXATION IN THE DIGITAL ECONOMY, 21.*

Granger, J., de Clercq, B., & Lymer, A. (2022b). *Tapping taxes–digital disruption and revenue administration responses: Digital Disruption and Revenue Administration Responses.*

Guma, P. K., & Mwaura, M. (2021). Infrastructural configurations of mobile telephony in urban Africa: Vignettes from Buru Buru, Nairobi. *Journal of Eastern African Studies : the Journal of the British Institute in Eastern Africa, 15*(4), 527–545. doi:10.1080/17531055.2021.1989138

Gupta, S., & Kanungo, R. P. (2022). Financial inclusion through digitalisation: Economic viability for the bottom of the pyramid (BOP) segment. *Journal of Business Research, 148*, 262–276. doi:10.1016/j.jbusres.2022.04.070

Gwala, R. S., & Mashau, P. (2022). Corporate governance and its impact on organisational performance in the fourth industrial revolution: a systematic literature review. *Corporate Governance and Organizational Behaviour Review, 6*(1), 98–114. https://doi.org/https://doi.org/10.22495/cgobrv6i1p7

Hansen, N., Huis, M. A., & Lensink, R. (2021). Microfinance services and women's empowerment. *Handbook on ethics in finance*, 161-182.

Hellström, J., & Tröften, P.-E. (2010). *The innovative use of mobile applications in East Africa*. Swedish international development cooperation agency (Sida).

Huang, R., Kale, S., Paramati, S. R., & Taghizadeh-Hesary, F. (2021). The nexus between financial inclusion and economic development: Comparison of old and new EU member countries. *Economic Analysis and Policy, 69*, 1–15. doi:10.1016/j.eap.2020.10.007

Ibne Afzal, M. N., Nayeem Sadi, M. A., & Siddiqui, S. A. (2023). Financial inclusion using corporate social responsibility: A socio-economic demand–supply analysis. *Asian Journal of Economics and Banking, 7*(1), 45–63. doi:10.1108/AJEB-04-2022-0039

Iman, N. (2023). Idiosyncrasies, isomorphic pressures and decoupling in technology platform business. *Journal of Science and Technology Policy Management*.

Ismail, T., & Masinge, K. (2012). Mobile banking: Innovation for the poor. *African Journal of Science, Technology, Innovation and Development, 4*(3), 98–127. https://doi.org/doi:10.10520/EJC132191

Jinnah, Z. (2022). *Informal Livelihoods and Governance in South Africa: The Hustle*. Springer Nature. doi:10.1007/978-3-031-10695-8

Kelsall, T., Mitlin, D., Schindler, S., & Hickey, S. (2021). *Politics, systems and domains: A conceptual framework for the African Cities Research Consortium*.

Kouchih, A., & Lyoussi, D. (2022). *Collaborative Innovation and Its Actors at the Time of Banking Digitalization: Comparative Analysis Between National and International Practice* (2516-2314). Research Gate.

Kouladoum, J.-C., Wirajing, M. A. K., & Nchofoung, T. N. (2022). Digital technologies and financial inclusion in Sub-Saharan Africa. *Telecommunications Policy, 46*(9), 102387. doi:10.1016/j.telpol.2022.102387

Kowalewska, A., Osińska, M., & Szczepaniak, M. (2023). Institutions in the development of Sub-Saharan African countries in 2004–2019. *Ekonomia i Prawo. Economics and Law, 22*(1).

Lemma, A., Parra, M. M., & Naliaka, L. (2022). *The AfCFTA: unlocking the potential of the digital economy in Africa* (Vol. 13). ODI.

Li, N., Pei, X., Huang, Y., Qiao, J., Zhang, Y., & Jamali, R. H. (2022). Impact of financial inclusion and green bond financing for renewable energy mix: Implications for financial development in OECD economies. *Environmental Science and Pollution Research International, 29*(17), 1–12. doi:10.1007/s11356-021-17561-9 PMID:34843047

Liu, D., Xie, Y., Hafeez, M., & Usman, A. (2022). The trade-off between economic performance and environmental quality: Does financial inclusion matter for emerging Asian economies? *Environmental Science and Pollution Research International, 29*(20), 1–10. doi:10.1007/s11356-021-17755-1 PMID:34993792

Liu, F., & Walheer, B. (2022). Financial inclusion, financial technology, and economic development: A composite index approach. *Empirical Economics, 63*(3), 1457–1487. doi:10.1007/s00181-021-02178-1

Lorenz, E., & Pommet, S. (2021). Mobile money, inclusive finance and enterprise innovativeness: An analysis of East African nations. *Industry and Innovation, 28*(2), 136–159. doi:10.1080/13662716.2020.1774867

Louw, C., & Nieuwenhuizen, C. (2020). Digitalisation strategies in a South African banking context: A consumer services analysis. *South African Journal of Information Management, 22*(1), 1–8. doi:10.4102/sajim.v22i1.1153

MacIsaac, S. (2023). Remittance Modality: Unpacking Canadian Money Transfer Mechanism Choices. *The International Migration Review*, 01979183231181564. doi:10.1177/01979183231181564

Maity, S., & Sahu, T. N. (2022). *Financial Inclusion and the Role of Banking System.* Springer. doi:10.1007/978-981-16-6085-6

Manasseh, C. O., Okanya, O. C., Logan, C. S., Ede, K. E., Ejim, E. P., Ozor, S. N., Onuoha, O., & Okiche, E. L. (2023). Digital finance, financial inclusion and economic growth nexus in COMESA: the role of regulatory quality, rule of law and government effectiveness. *Russian Law Journal, 11*(5).

Manasseh, C. O., Nwakoby, I. C., Okanya, O. C., Nwonye, N. G., Odidi, O., Thaddeus, K. J., Ede, K. K., & Nzidee, W. (2023). Impact of digital financial innovation on financial system development in Common Market for Eastern and Southern Africa (COMESA) countries. *Asian Journal of Economics and Banking.*

Martínez-Vergara, S. J., & Valls-Pasola, J. (2021). Clarifying the disruptive innovation puzzle: A critical review. *European Journal of Innovation Management, 24*(3), 893–918. doi:10.1108/EJIM-07-2019-0198

Matekenya, W., Moyo, C., & Jeke, L. (2021). Financial inclusion and human development: Evidence from Sub-Saharan Africa. *Development Southern Africa, 38*(5), 683–700. doi:10.1080/0376835X.2020.1799760

Mhlanga, D. (2023). Block chain technology for digital financial inclusion in the industry 4.0, towards sustainable development? *Frontiers in Blockchain, 6*, 1035405. doi:10.3389/fbloc.2023.1035405

Momoh, I., Adelaja, G., & Ejiwumi, G. (2023). *Analysis of the Human Factor in Cybersecurity: Identifying and Preventing Social Engineering Attacks in Financial Institution.*

Mosteanu, N. R., & Faccia, A. (2020). Digital systems and new challenges of financial management–FinTech, XBRL, blockchain and cryptocurrencies. *Quality - Access to Success, 21*(174), 159–166.

Mugo, J. W. (2021). *Perceived Factors Influencing Performance of Community Based Housing Projects in Urban Informal Settlements: a Case of Mukuru Slums, Nairobi County*. University of Nairobi.

Murinde, V., Rizopoulos, E., & Zachariadis, M. (2022). The impact of the FinTech revolution on the future of banking: Opportunities and risks. *International Review of Financial Analysis*, *81*, 102103. doi:10.1016/j.irfa.2022.102103

Mushonga, M. (2018). *The efficiency and sustainability of co-operative financial institutions in South Africa*. Stellenbosch University.

Nan, W., Zhu, X., & Lynne Markus, M. (2021). What we know and don't know about the socioeconomic impacts of mobile money in Sub-Saharan Africa: A systematic literature review. *The Electronic Journal on Information Systems in Developing Countries*, *87*(2), e12155. doi:10.1002/isd2.12155

Nguyen, V. P. (2022). The Critical Success Factors for Sustainability Financial Technology in Vietnam: A Partial Least Squares Approach. *Human Behavior and Emerging Technologies*, *2022*, 2022. doi:10.1155/2022/2979043

Niesten, H. (2023). *Are Digital and Traditional Financial Services Taxed the Same? A Comprehensive Assessment of Tax Policies in Nine African Countries*.

Ogbuabor, J. E., Eigbiremolen, G., Orji, A., Manasseh, C., & Onuigbo, F. (2020). ICT and financial inclusion in Nigeria: An overview of current challenges and policy options. *Nigerian Journal of Banking and Finance*, *12*(1), 90–96.

Owuor, S. (2018). *HCP report no. 6: the urban food system of Nairobi, Kenya*. Hungry Cities Partnership.

Pazarbasioglu, C., Mora, A. G., Uttamchandani, M., Natarajan, H., Feyen, E., & Saal, M. (2020). Digital financial services. World Bank, 54.

Puspitasari, R., & Zulaikha, E. (2023). Review of Business Actor's Financial Behavior in the Ultra Micro Segment. *IPTEK Journal of Proceedings Series*, *0*(1), 32–36. doi:10.12962/j23546026.y2023i1.16372

Rahmayati, R. (2021). Competition Strategy In The Islamic Banking Industry: An Empirical Review. *International Journal Of Business, Economics, And. Social Development*, *2*(2), 65–71.

Rogers, E. (2003). *Diffusion of innovations*. FL: Free Press.

Ronaghi, M. H., & Forouharfar, A. (2020). A contextualized study of the usage of the Internet of things (IoTs) in smart farming in a typical Middle Eastern country within the context of Unified Theory of Acceptance and Use of Technology model (UTAUT). *Technology in Society*, *63*, 101415. doi:10.1016/j.techsoc.2020.101415

Saiz, A. (2020). Bricks, mortar, and proptech: The economics of IT in brokerage, space utilization and commercial real estate finance. *Journal of Property Investment & Finance*, *38*(4), 327–347. doi:10.1108/JPIF-10-2019-0139

Self, C. C., & Roberts, C. (2019). Credibility. In *An integrated approach to communication theory and research* (pp. 435–446). Routledge. doi:10.4324/9780203710753-36

Senyo, P. K., Karanasios, S., Gozman, D., & Baba, M. (2022). FinTech ecosystem practices shaping financial inclusion: The case of mobile money in Ghana. *European Journal of Information Systems, 31*(1), 112–127. doi:10.1080/0960085X.2021.1978342

Senyo, P. K., & Osabutey, E. L. (2020). Unearthing antecedents to financial inclusion through FinTech innovations. *Technovation, 98*, 102155. doi:10.1016/j.technovation.2020.102155

Sethi, D., & Acharya, D. (2018). Journal of Financial Economic Policy. *Policy, 10*(3), 369–385.

Sharma, A., & Gandhi, A. V. (2023). Consumer adoption study for innovative technology products and services in an emerging economy. *International Journal of Innovation Science.* doi:10.1108/IJIS-06-2022-0106

Shuping, D. K. (2021). *The impact of the effort's standards on legal certainty and the interpretation of contracts.* University of Johannesburg (South Africa).

Soyemi, K. A., Olowofela, O. E., & Yunusa, L. A. (2020). Financial inclusion and sustainable development in Nigeria. *Journal of Economics and Management, 39*(1), 105–131. doi:10.22367/jem.2020.39.06

Srivastava, K., & Dhamija, S. (2022). FinTech: Application of Artificial Intelligence in Indian Banking. Proceedings of International Conference on Communication and Artificial Intelligence: ICCAI 2021, Taj, I., & Zaman, N. (2022). Towards industrial revolution 5.0 and explainable artificial intelligence: Challenges and opportunities. *International Journal of Computing and Digital Systems, 12*(1), 295–320.

Terence, T. (2022). *Developing And Validating A Hybrid Framework For Machine Learning Operationalisation Within FSIS In Developing Countries: A Case For Zimbabwe.* Midlands State University.

Torkelson, E. (2020). Collateral damages: Cash transfer and debt transfer in South Africa. *World Development, 126*, 104711. doi:10.1016/j.worlddev.2019.104711

Trkman, M., Popovič, A., & Trkman, P. (2023). The roles of privacy concerns and trust in voluntary use of governmental proximity tracing applications. *Government Information Quarterly, 40*(1), 101787. doi:10.1016/j.giq.2022.101787

Van, L. T.-H., Vo, A. T., Nguyen, N. T., & Vo, D. H. (2021). Financial inclusion and economic growth: An international evidence. *Emerging Markets Finance & Trade, 57*(1), 239–263. doi:10.1080/1540496X.2019.1697672

VanZyl, K. (2020). *Barriers and enablers for the uptake of Fintech remittance platforms by migrant entrepreneurs in South Africa.* University of Pretoria.

Varma, P., Nijjer, S., Sood, K., Grima, S., & Rupeika-Apoga, R. (2022). Thematic Analysis of Financial Technology (Fintech) Influence on the Banking Industry. *Risks, 10*(10), 186. doi:10.3390/risks10100186

Ward, M., & Naude, R. (2018). *Banking for a Sustainable Economy.*

Warikandwa, T. V. (2023). Financial Inclusion, Intra-African Trade and the AfCFTA: A Law and Economics Perspective. In Financial Inclusion and Digital Transformation Regulatory Practices in Selected SADC Countries: South Africa, Namibia, Botswana and Zimbabwe (pp. 207-228). Springer.

Wewege, L., Lee, J., & Thomsett, M. C. (2020). Disruptions and digital banking trends. *Journal of Applied Finance and Banking*, *10*(6), 15–56.

Zeebaree, M., Agoyi, M., & Aqel, M. (2022). Sustainable adoption of E-Government from the UTAUT perspective. *Sustainability (Basel)*, *14*(9), 5370. doi:10.3390/su14095370

ADDITIONAL READING

Becha, H., Kalai, M., Houidi, S., & Helali, K. (2023, May). The Symmetric and Asymmetric Effects of Digitalization on Economic Growth in African Countries: Evidence from Linear and Non-Linear ARDL Models. In *International Conference on Digital Economy* (pp. 315-345). Cham: Springer International Publishing. 10.1007/978-3-031-42788-6_20

Bongomin, G. O. C., Akol Malinga, C., Amani Manzi, A., & Balinda, R. (2023). Agent liquidity: A catalyst for mobile money banking among the unbanked poor population in rural sub-Saharan Africa. *Cogent Economics & Finance*, *11*(1), 2203435. doi:10.1080/23322039.2023.2203435

Gencer, M. (2011). The mobile money movement: Catalyst to jump-start emerging markets. *Innovations: Technology, Governance, Globalization*, *6*(1), 101–117. doi:10.1162/INOV_a_00061

Gwala, R. S., & Ijaz, S. (2023). The Role of Artificial Intelligence in FinTech as a Catalyst of the Economic Growth Drive in Africa. In *The Impact of AI Innovation on Financial Sectors in the Era of Industry 5.0* (pp. 77–95). IGI Global.

Iwedi, M., Kocha, C., & Wike, C. (2022). Effect of digitalization of banking services on the Nigeria economy. *Contemporary Journal of Banking and Finance*, *2*(1), 1–9.

Komen, L. J. (2024). *Digitization communication and financial independence in East Africa*. Women's Agency and Mobile Communication Under the Radar.

Maigari, M. A., & Yelwa, M. M. (2023). Digital Transaction: A Catalyst for Financial Inclusion and Job Creation. *Journal of Digital Marketing and Halal Industry*, *5*(1), 57–76. doi:10.21580/jdmhi.2023.5.1.15001

Ndung'u, N. (2019). *Digital technology and state capacity in Kenya*.

Siano, A., Raimi, L., Palazzo, M., & Panait, M. C. (2020). Mobile banking: An innovative solution for increasing financial inclusion in Sub-Saharan African Countries: Evidence from Nigeria. *Sustainability (Basel)*, *12*(23), 10130. doi:10.3390/su122310130

Soutter, L., Ferguson, K., & Neubert, M. (2019). Digital payments: Impact factors and mass adoption in sub-saharan Africa. *Technology Innovation Management Review*, *9*(7), 41–55. doi:10.22215/timreview/1254

Chapter 10
Navigating Digital Payments in Ghana's Public Sector:
A Journey to Better Service Delivery

Kwami Ahiabenu
ⓘ https://orcid.org/0000-0002-8254-3214
Global Centre for Fintech Innovations, Canada

ABSTRACT

The adoption of digital payments presents new opportunities for enhancing public sector service delivery. However, little coherent literature exists on the diffusion of public-sector digital payments, including deployment challenges and successes. This chapter reviews the evidence on the evolution of digital payments in Ghana's public sector. It draws upon stakeholder theory to analyze the diffusion of digital payments for public service delivery in Ghana. This chapter gathered qualitative evidence through expert interviews to map the evolution of public sector digital payments. The findings of this chapter reveal that Ghana's public sector finances are digititalized, leading to a significant reduction in the use of physical cash. Government entities are empowered to access public finance data in real time, supporting better revenue collection, disbursement, and judicious utilization of financial resources. This chapter highlights the need to improve stakeholder engagement as a prerequisite to ensuring increased usage of public sector digital payments.

INTRODUCTION

This chapter aims to understand the evolution of digital payments in the public sector in Ghana by highlighting critical issues around its deployment, the role of stakeholders, and key implementation challenges. Digital payments for the public sector refer to the use of electronic or digital methods to facilitate the public sector's financial transactions, revenue collection, and disbursement of funds within government operations. It usually involves transferring money or value from one entity to another, where at least one of the parties is a government entity. For example, digital payments for the public sector can

DOI: 10.4018/978-1-6684-9962-7.ch010

include tax payments, social transfers, salaries, pensions, fees, fines, and procurement payments (The World Bank Group, 2021).

The rollout of digital payments in the public sector can facilitate better fiscal management and enable business growth (The Economist, 2018). Further, digitalizing government payments and receipts can increase tax and non-tax revenue collection without raising tax rates and reduce public sector waste, fraud, corruption, and bribery (Lund et al., 2017). Also, public-sector digital payments can enhance trust between citizens and government while increasing transparency and traceability in public-sector revenue collection (Mtebe & Sausi, 2021). The global COVID-19 pandemic accelerated the need for digitalization of public sector service delivery. Ghana, like most countries during the pandemic, increased its rate of digitalization to ensure public service provision did not suffer disruptions by moving a number of services online (Bawole & Langnel, 2023). However, Eggers et al., (2021), in their survey of 800 government officials globally, suggested 80% of governments have accelerated their digital transformation processes, mostly directed at digitalization of front-end services, but not achieved a fundamental transformation of government operations, processes and systems. Klapper & Singer, (2017) reviewed the evidence on the benefits and challenges faced by governments migrating from cash to digital government-to-person (G2P) payments, and their results pointed out that such migration works best within the framework of an appropriate consumer financial protection framework. In assessing the effectiveness of digital payment for public sector services, Rocheleau & Wu, (2005) suggested that there is a gap between the potential of digital payments in the public sector versus reality given that since usage is relatively low, fees charged on electronic payments may have a negative effect on use.

This chapter poses this main research question: how has the public sector digital payment ecosystem evolved over time? Thus, this chapter seeks to critically analyze the evolution of public sector digital payments in Ghana using the descriptive aspects of stakeholder theory based on the case study approach. The chapter elucidates the value of stakeholders' salience to explain the evolution of Ghana's public sector digital payments. Given that the public sector digital payments system is an essential public policy issue with a lot of interest, the primary motivation for this work is to fill the gap in the literature. The remainder of this chapter is organised into the following sections: literature review, methodology, an overview of public sector digital payments, history, and implementation challenges. The chapter continues with a discussion section, and the last section concludes this chapter by reflecting on the implications of its main findings and recommendations.

LITERATURE REVIEW

The literature on e-payments and public service delivery in developing countries is a diverse and growing field that explores various aspects, such as the drivers, barriers, benefits, risks, and influences of digital payments on government performance, citizen satisfaction, and social outcomes. At a broader level, digitalistion of public service delivery, including the deployment of digital technologies and tools, can significantly improve service delivery (Ofoma, 2021). As Shin & Rakhmatullayev (2019) noted, digital transformation of public services is successful when built on the foundation of successful government administrative reforms. The goal is to build a "single centre" that serves individuals and businesses based on a "single window" that combines payments with service delivery seamlessly. Overall, the potential for digital transformation to improve public service delivery is significant, but it also requires careful consideration of the associated challenges (Curtis, 2019).

In the context of the adoption of digital payments by the public sector, Vaidya and Sharma, (2020), pointed out that citizens in India prefer digital payments over more traditional payment methods because of convenience and factors such as age, education, and profession which have a significant impact in terms of awareness and usage of digital payment platforms in the consumption of public services. Sengupta and Shastri, (2019) noted that the digitalisation of government payments can expedite direct payments while simultaneously facilitating paperless transactions in a secure environment, reducing overall costs and promoting green banking. Also, Simatele, (2021) suggested that e-payment instruments can enhance welfare by reducing costs and improving access to financial services. Rashidov and Rustamov(2021) argue that government identity management systems are critical to enabling trusted and secure digital payments. The digital government payment system supports effective public service delivery at public institutions, especially if this system is integrated with other payment systems(Nyambi and Assey, 2021).

Griffin et al., (2023) aver that there are operational and financial risks related to the adoption of digital payments by the public sector, and these risks can be mitigated by strengthening institutional and technological capacities. Cangiano et al.,(2019) suggest a framework for assessing the readiness and potential of countries to adopt digital payments, and identify the key elements and steps for successful implementation. Ofori et al. (2023) show no significant difference between optimism and discomfort by national and local government implementing units vis-à-vis performance and intention to use the Ghana Electronic Procurement System (GHANEPS). Demuyakor (2021) indicates that Ghana's digital governance initiatives have greatly helped reduce corruption, increase productivity, and facilitate citizens' e-participation in governance. Agyei-Ababio et al. (2023) noted that providing a legal framework for the digitalisation of revenue authority functions plays a vital role in ensuring that the system is used effectively to realize its full benefits. Astudy by Larkotey & Ifinedo (2022) found that factors that can influence the development of digital payment systems are contradictory requirements of stakeholders, lack of technical skills of public sector staff, technical challenges, and rigid software. The literature a general tendency to focus on implementation risks, benefits and framework for digital payments adoption in the public sector, however, the literature on the design of digital payments from stakeholders' perspective is sparse, therefore this chapter contributes to the literature on the digitalization of public sector payments system situated within multifaceted nature of stakeholder theory.

THEORETICAL FRAMEWORK

This chapter relies on the descriptive aspect of stakeholder and salience theory as theoretical underpinnings to situate digital payments in the public sector. Stakeholders' salience theory has been applied e-government studies. For example, Rose et al., (2018) report that e-government initiatives are often initiated, implemented and managed by multiple stakeholders with dynamic complementary or competing values; Axelsson et al., (2013) posit that e-government implementation might experience change in stakeholder's salience over time and how information technology impacts a stakeholder model of governance (Flak & Rose, 2005). The digitalisation of government payments is situated within the framework of innovations since it brings about change and new ways of facilitating digital payments in place of cash.

There are two paths open to organisations when it comes to enabling innovation; either they rely on internal resources and control all aspects of the innovation process without external stakeholders' involvement, known as closed innovation, or the organisation can take the path of open innovation where there are concerted efforts to integrate internal and external resources and new stakeholders in the innovation process. As noted by Chesbrough, (2003), an open approach to innovation stimulates organisations' demand for new ideas, leading them to incorporate new thinking into their organisation. When complexity is high, closed innovation is considered a superior approach (Almirall & Casadesus-Masanell, 2010). Open innovation is complex and therefore requires conditions for success, such as managing a network of internal and external actors, the presence of sufficient capabilities to successfully integrate input from external sources into internal systems, conflict management, facilitating dialogue and relationship management (Gould, 2012).

In considering to take either the path of an open or closed innovation approach, considerations include network effects, the complementary role of each stakeholder, incentives by stakeholders to invest in the relationships and how intellectual property rights are managed. Stakeholder orientation can impact the quality and quantity of innovation. Flammer & Kacperczyk, (2014) argue that paying attention to non-financial aspects of stakeholder orientation can spark innovation by promoting a conducive environment for experimentation and enhancing the interests of various stakeholders. Also, identifying and analysing the contribution, importance and role of stakeholders' stake in any project that straddles multiple actors is critical to understanding each player's functions. The delivery of the digital payments system for the public sector is premised on the collective effort of a number of stakeholders.

To understand the interaction of stakeholders, three values can be considered, namely descriptive, normative and instrumental aspects of the stakeholder model. The descriptive aspect refers to language and concepts to explain what an organisation is, especially how it deals with collaborative and competing interests. The instrumental aspect focuses on the effective management of stakeholders and contributes to the realisation of organisational goals – such as growth, increased profit and sustainability; this requires that the relationship between managing stakeholders and reaching the organisational goal must be established. Normative value describes stakeholders 'inherent value in an organisation based on ethical principles (Carroll et al., 2018). The normative approach is premised on deductions, whereas the descriptive aspect seeks to understand individual cases in terms of inductive and instrumental perspectives focusing on identifying causality (Smaguc, 2022). In summarising the difference between the three stakeholders' approaches, Jones(1995) suggests normative approaches focus on "what should happen", while the descriptive try to answer the question "what happens" and the instrument aspect looks at "what happens if ".

The core of the descriptive approach to stakeholder theory is the description and interpretation of specific characteristics and behaviours of organisations in the usual conditions. It clarifies an organisation as a mixed bag of cooperative and competitive interests. The descriptive model, therefore, provides a framework for describing empirical claims that can be observed about the nature of the firm and how the organisation is managed in reality (Donaldson & Preston, 1995).

Jawahar & McLaughlin(2001) argue that at any point in time in an organisational life cycle (start-up, growth, maturity, decline), specific stakeholders are in a better place to satisfy crucial organisational needs better than others. Invariably, the strategy an organisation applies in its relationship with each stakeholder is a function of how important that stakeholder is. This is because, in each phase of an organisation's life cycle, it may deal with different threats and opportunities in the context of its dealings with stakeholders.

In the literature, salience theory is quite popular in the identification and relevance of stakeholders. Stakeholders' salience is a function of their legitimacy, power and urgency in their relationship with an organisation. Legitimacy focuses on the appropriateness of their involvement, while power connotes the ability of a stakeholder to impose their will in dealing with an organisation, and urgency refers to the need for immediate action by the stakeholders. Therefore, the most salient stakeholders are those who possess all three characteristics (Colvin et al., 2020; Freeman et al., 2020). Mitchell et al., (1997) argue that the value of the stakeholder theory's descriptive aspects is its ability to identify stakeholders and their relative importance, which is salience.

RESEARCH METHODOLOGY AND METHODS

We operationalise digital payments in this paper as any form of electronic or digital payment facilitated by tools such as mobile money, cards (debit and credit), online transfers, online banking, Automated Clearing House (ACH), Society for Worldwide Interbank Financial Telecommunication (SWIFT), Electronic Funds Transfer (EFT) that transfer value from one payment system to another with or without human intermediaries. This chapter is based on a case study, using information from online sources, documents, and expert interviews. Case study research is an important tool for gaining an in-depth understanding of a phenomenon in a life setting using exploratory, explanatory or descriptive approaches (Yin, 2017). According to Darke et al., (1998), case studies can prove useful in newer research areas, especially where there is the need to examine the context and dynamics of a situation. Dobson, (1999) noted that in undertaking in-depth case studies, the researcher needs to select a description approach where an idealist philosophy is adopted or an explanatory path which emphasises a realist approach.

After the choice is made between description or explanation, the next step is to decide on the use of a grounded theory approach, a single theory or multiple theories. Commenting on the use of theory in interpretive studies, Walsham, (1995) noted that the use of theory in interpretive research can be less rigid in comparison to positivist studies, however, theories in interpretive studies can serve as a source of inspiration, take account of previous knowledge and aid in the understanding of complex social situations. This chapter utilises the description approach combined with stakeholder and open innovation theories, which provide the opportunity to enrich the chapter with multiple perspectives.

Although the use of case studies is very popular in social science research to aid in-depth understanding of a phenomenon, it is still controversial. Tellis (1997) and Yin, (2017) argue that it lacks rigour, has little basis for scientific generalisation, dependens on single case exploration and small samples. Hamel et al., (1993) insist that the establishment of research objectives and related parameters is far more important in the use of a case study than relying on a large sample size.

This chapter's data collection process started with selecting the case for this research, which was premised on the research objective. The case selected for Citizens to Government (C2G) and Business to Government (B2G) systems is wwww.eservices.gov.gh, which was later transformed into www.ghana.gov.gh, an e-government service integrated with digital payments. The second element of this case study is the Ghana Integrated Financial Management Information System (GIFMIS), which focuses on the Government to Business(G2B) system.

The second step in the research process was data collection. Data for this study was collected from three main sources: analysis of www.eservices.gov.gh and www.ghana.gov. Though www.eservices.gov.gh is no longer operational, the researcher made use of www.archive.org which is a central internet archive to access content from this non-operational website. Similarly, GIFMIS was analysed. Another important source of data for this chapter is a thorough analysis of published online articles and documents. Also, six expert interviews formed part of the data utilised for this case study. The experts were drawn from the Ministry of Finance, Controller and Accountant-General's Department, Ghana Revenue Authority, National Information Technology Agency (NITA), digital payments providers and independent digital finance experts. This study applied a purposive selection of experts through their qualifications, experience, expertise, and demonstrated track record in digital payments for the public sector.

The last step in the process was data analysis through a largely four-step inductive procedure, which started with familiarization with the research data. Secondly, the process of aggregation of data consisting of interviews and secondary data was undertaken. In the third step, the researcher developed an analytical chronology which describes digital payments in Ghana's public sector, its history, the motivation to set up the government digital payments system, challenges confronting the operationalization of the public sector payment system and some solutions to these problems.

RESULTS

Government-to-Business Digital Payments

Ghana's public financial management saw a number of reforms, such as the Public Financial Management Reform Program (PUFMARP) in 1997 thereafter, the Ghana Integrated Financial Management (GFIMIS) was launched in 2010, and finally, the Public Financial Management Reform Project (PFMRP) was initiated in 2015. PFMRP aims to improve budget management, financial control and reporting of the Government of Ghana. Historically, Ghana's public financial sector was running a largely paper-based system until a major change in 2012 with the introduction of the Oracle E-Business suite to manage government institutions' finances, known as GIFMIS, launched fully in 2014. The overall objective of GFMIS is to facilitate the monitoring of revenue collection, disbursement and judicious utilisation of government revenue, as well as prevention of fraud (Bio-Tchane, 2021; GBN, 2023)

With the introduction of GIFMIS any entity doing work for the government of Ghana needed to be onboarded on the GIFMIS since it became the only way entities can get paid. The public institution does the onboardingso the supplier will transact business with it. For the onboarding the supplier is expected to provide business certificates issued by the Registrar -General's Department, bank account information, contact details and other documents . Since most of these services are for the provision of goods and services, the supplier in question will go through Public Procurement Authority (PPA) approval process; albeit this is yet to be automatically connected to GIFMIS. Thereafter, the public entity in question will send the supplier's information to GIFMIS to complete the onboarding process.

To operationalise GFMIS, all public sector payments are now expected to be processed and paid electronically. Typically, all public institutions hold an account with the Bank of Ghana, previously a paper-based processing system was used, and cheques were issued for payment. Under GIFMIS, the payment process starts with annual budget approval for public institutions by the Parliament of Ghana through submission by the Ministry of Finance. Once the budget is approved, this information is used to set a spending limit for the public entity digitally. Therefore, government ministries, departments and agencies are compelled to spend only within their budget. Another new dimension is the digital payment component, through the use of Electronic Funds Transfer (EFT), Automated Clearing House (ACH) and SWIFT to make payments instead of paper cheques. EFT payments are mainly used for big vendors, whereas ACH is commonly used to pay allowances and other remuneration to individuals such as consultants.

In terms of the Consolidated Fund(Government of Ghana fund established by law into which are paid all revenue and any other monies [receipts and trust monies raised or received on behalf of the government] and from which all lawful disbursements are made on behalf of the government), using the digital payment system, the Chief Cashier or head of the treasury is able to run real-time analysis on the system to generate cash requirement reports. Hitherto, information about cash availability was not timely. To process statutory funds, the public entity in question makes use of internal approval procedures, thereafter, the process continues on GIFMIS using the approval hierarchy per law. Once this stage is completed, payments are made. Donor funds held with the Bank of Ghana also follow designated steps, thereafter, the public entity utilises their internal processes and completes the process within the GIFMIS using the EFT.

The internally generated fund is not controlled solely by the Ministry of Finance's budget since such funds sit with the public entity generating those funds. However, public institutions run their budget based on internally generated funds and other funds using the Budget preparation Management (Oracle Hyperion) system. All government entities generating internal funds are mandated to open a holding account with the Bank of Ghana based on a capping system, and fund inflows are split on a percentage basis. A percentage is assigned to the organization generating the funds, and they retain this portion to finance their operations, and the remainder that is assigned to the central government is transmitted to the Consolidated Fund. Bank of Ghana does not have offices in all the regions; therefore, some of the government entities internally generating funds hold such funds at commercial banks, which means GIFMIS does not capture these funds, creating a challenge of incomplete transactions on the GIFMIS, including creating gaps in the GIFMIS dataset and an inability of the GIFMIS to process such transactions. To solve this problem, the CAGD is working with Ghana Interbank Payment and Settlement Systems (GhiPSS) as the intermediary to make payments while it works on connecting the system to GIFMIS.

Key Stakeholders and Relationships

The Ministry of Finance is the major stakeholder in the public finance ecosystem. It plays a key role as policymakers in the areas of macroeconomics, fiscal and financial policies, provision of oversight over the public purse, and ensuring effective and efficient resource mobilisation and utilisation. Given this mandate, the Ministry is the driver of the digitalisation of Ghana's public finances. The Ministry works hand in hand with the Controller & Accountant-General's Department (CADG), whose main mandate is the management of all public funds. CADG is therefore assigned the role of enabling Integrated Financial Management Information System (IFMIS) and Payroll management. The Public Services Commission, as the entity responsible for public human resource management, plays a key role in public finance management by ensuring there is the right calibre of human resources. Other stakeholders are the Ghana Revenue Authority (GRA), Public Procurement Authority, Internal Audit Agency, Ghana Audit Service and Parliament (CAGD, 2022; Ghana MoF, 2022).

In terms of actual service delivery, the Ministries, Departments and Agencies (MDAs) and Metropolitan, Municipal and District Assemblies (MMDAs), are at the forefront of ensuring policy implementation and resource mobilisation, especially internally generated ones. The National Information Technology Agency (NITA) is the government-mandated agency responsible for the rollout and implementation of technology systems for all government entities. Based on this role, they are an important stakeholder in the public finance digitalisation processes at all levels. Bank of Ghana serves as the main banker for the government and is paramount to the success of public sector payments digitalisation, it works with GhiPSS, an agency under the Bank of Ghana. From the private sector side of the coin, commercial banks and FinTech companies play a key role in the digitalisation of public sector finance. Working together, all these stakeholders contribute to effective and efficient public sector payment digitalisation efforts.

The Effects of G2B Digital Payments

As part of the rollout of the public sector digital payments solution, Expert 1 explained that " All government entites who are subsidised by the consolidated fund, had their cheque books taken from them, to reduce the printing of cheque books and therefore cash in circulation, to facilitate the uptake of electronic means of payments". This directive is in line with government cash lite policy (Finance Ministry Ghana, 2020). After the retrieval of cheque books, one issue that came up was how to deal with cash payments since the cashless option is not entirely possible. Therefore, GHiPSS, in partnership with CAGD is in the process of introducing mobile money as part of its digital options to ensure a better system of cash payments. In this direction, a mobile money wallet will be created and assigned to these entities through Ghana Pay, a mobile money wallet created by banks in Ghana. This is to ensure these entities can make micropayments, which was previously done on a cash basis. Through GIFMIS, the public entities can process a cash request transaction and thereafter transfer the money onto the entity's Ghana Pay mobile wallet. When the said public entity needs to make a cash payment, they visit their bank and make a withdrawal from their Ghana Pay instead of using a cheque for such withdrawals. Also, since the bank issues a receipt for such a withdrawal, they have a proper paper trail of all cash transactions. Further, through the use of the public entity's Ghana Pay mobile money wallet, they can make cash payments for transactions directly through Point of Sales (POS) instead of writing a cheque or carrying cash around. In the past, when the staff of government entities travelled, especially abroad, they had to carry cash to finance their Daily Subsistence Allowance (DSA). Under the new system based on GIFMIS, such DSA are processed electronically, and the staff member is issued with an electronic card, reducing the handling of cash and creating greater accountability.

According to the respondents, overall payment processes, which were taking a more extended period in the past are now done within weeks or days on condition that the entity has funds available for the said activity due to the efficiency brought on board by a digital payment system. Furthermore, the system has contributed to savings of money and time and enabled efficiency in public finance management. The system has significantly reduced the use of paper, improved transparency in terms of budgeting, and entities are able to access their funds quickly to facilitate payments.

Budget preparation is now faster and more efficient due to the use of digital systems. Also, the digital system has introduced several budgetary controls, thereby protecting the integrity of public finance data. Through GIFMIS, all entities can see in real-time cash available for their operation; at the same time CAGD is able to have regular updates on internally generated funds. It is expected that with full integration of all revenue, especially internally generated funds, into GIFMIS, there will be greater transparency of national revenue flows. Expert 2 pointed out that, the introduction of an integrated system means all entities are able to report to CAGD in a timely manner, leading to the production of the final government account on time for submission to the Audit Service.

Challenges of Government to Business Digital Payments

Per its mandate, CAGD is expected to generate a report of all government revenue and expenditure for the whole country, however, there are gaps, such as internally generated funds kept at commercial banks instead of the central bank, Bank of Ghana, as well as a lack of real-time connection of C2G and B2G systems (Ghana.gov) to GIFMIS. That said, steps are underway to connect GIFMIS to Ghana.gov in due course through an interface. There is no clarity on how such an interface will look like, however the goal is to ensure all receivables flow into GIFMIS to strengthen CAGD reporting functions.

There is a lot of scepticism on the part of stakeholders, primarily government entities. This ranges from mistrust of digital payments to a lack of understanding of the systems and some persons assuming the introduction of the system will lead to job losses. Deep stakeholder participation and engagement in the decision-making process could have provided solutions to some of these problems(Flammer & Kacperczyk, 2014). One respondent indicated that CAGD is investing in change management to reduce the level of scepticism.Digital payments systems rely heavily on the internet and communication channels to make them work effectively, however, there are persistent network challenges and reliability issues particularly in areas outside the major city. With no connectivity in place, entities at the local government level struggle to utilise GIFMIS effectively.

Expert 2 stated that investments are being made to improve connectivity through the use of Virtual Private Networks (VPN) and fibre Internet connections. Also, CAGD continually engages Internet Service Providers (ISPs) so that they can increase the uptime of their connection, especially to districts. Since NITA is a key entity supplying internet connectivity to government entities, CAGD works with them to ensure reliable internet access.

Another challenge facing GIFMIS is the relatively low level of usage; a respondent estimated this to be 40%. In order to deal with this challenge, CAGD is working assiduously to increase usage, reduce reliance on cheques and increase payments via digital means. One respondent pointed out that, there are concerns about fraud and cyber security, however, there are no reported breaches so far. The IT department for GIFMIS is constantly working to ensure the system is protected, including constant investment in firewalls, security tools and around-the-clock monitoring of the system.

C2G and B2G Digital Payments System

The History and Evolution of C2G and B2G Digital Payments System

Public facing government sector digital payments started in 2012 when the government of Ghana, through the Ministry of Communication and National Information Technology Agency(NITA), launched http://www.eservices.gov.gh/ as electronic public services in parallel with digital payments. The portal was built by a vendor under the supervision of NITA, with the Ministry of Finance providing guidance for the design and implementation of the platform as the major stakeholder whose mandate comprises oversight over government revenue. At inception, 11 core institutions were piloted, per Ministry of Finance requirements, NITA signed a Service Level Agreement (SLA) with these entities to ensure optimum service provision by NITA. The 11 institutions were selected because of the challenge of signing all government entities due to stakeholder management issues.

The website http://www.eservices.gov.gh/ offers a number of services, namely registrations, renewal, requests for permits and transfers, including birth certificates, marriage licenses, driver's licenses, business permits, passport applications, death certificates, import processing, building permits, vehicle registration security verification (fingerprint check and vetting) etc. Users could also select services offered by all government ministries, departments, and agencies in Ghana. The major challenge with http://www.eservices.gov.gh/ platform was that services were not "talking" to payments, and users could not consume and pay for services online, therefore there were a lot of inconveniences for users attempting to use the service. Also, there was a lack of clarity on the apportionment of funds collected among stakeholders. To solve these problems, the Ministry of Finance revised its strategy and adopted an open innovation Almirall and Casadesus-Masanell(2010); Gould 2012 in contrast to the closed innovation approach used previously. Therefore, it expanded the pool of stakeholders to include a private sector actor through a consortium of Ghanaian FinTechs under Private Public Partnership with the Government of Ghana to deploy the new platform https://www.ghana.gov.gh.

C2G and B2G Digital Payments System New Developments

The http://www.eservices.gov.gh/ website was effectively migrated to https://www.ghana.gov.gh through a re-direct. This new platform was initiated by the Minister of Finance because of the non-performance of the e-services platform, which negatively affected the ability of the government to generate the needed revenue. The main goal of this new platform was to bring onboard private sector stakeholders due to their ability to enhance the system to aggressively generate revenue, which highlights the saliency of stakeholders (Colvin et al., 2020; J. Freeman & Engel, 2007). The new platform was built in conjunction with three local Fintech companies (Hubtel, Expresspay and IT Consortium), collaborating to deploy this portal under a Public Private Partnership (PPP) and a revenue-sharing arrangement between these firms and the government of Ghana. As noted by Expert 4, "The initial setup of Ghana.gov is different from the first attempt, due to the fact that the government partnered with Fintechs to deliver this new service". The platform is managed by the consortium on a day-to-day basis, with NITA as the lead. NITA runs a call centre to receive and process client feedback with a technical team to deal with any technological issues. The system is set up to escalate specific issues to relevant government entities within for resolution.

Ghana.Gov, was launched by the Vice President of Ghana, Dr. Mahamudu Bawumia, on July 14, 2021, with the goal to improve revenue mobilisation. According to Dr Bawumia, "An estimated 10 to 15 per cent of revenue is lost through inefficiencies, theft or other accounting schemes. Going digital means we can improve our revenue collection by an estimated $526 million annually" (Osiakwan, 2021). Also, the government of Ghana estimated that there will be savings of more than $7 million a year from the digitization platforms which combines services offered by Ministries, Departments and Agencies (MDAs) and Metropolitan, Municipal and District Assemblies (MMDAs) as a common platform based on cloud-based technologies, a centralized open architecture connecting all service-flows and workflow systems of participating government entities, thereby creating a single Common Workflow and Services Platform. The common platform, therefore, standardizes all predefined services, payments and transfers (both electronic and cash) while enabling easy monitoring and user management. One of the system's core components is a post-payment workflow management system, customer notification, feedback and service ratings.

The Ghana.Gov platform is designed as a one-stop platform to enable citizens to easily access government services and simplify payments for public services using digital means, thereby promoting transparency of internally generated funds while offering simplicity, convenience and a single point solution for payments. The new platform is offered through the website: www.ghana.gov.gh, mobile phone' Unstructured Supplementary Service Data (USSD) short code: *222# and mobile app.

The platform accepts mobile money, bank cards (debit and credit), GHQR codes, FinTech apps to pay for government service and there is no offline payment option. The deployment of Ghana.Gov is compulsory for all MDAs and MMDAs providing services to the public that require payments. The portal can process all payments and transfers against predefined services offered by Government entities at all levels (Dowuona, 2021).

Rationale for Ghana.Gov

According to NITA, (2023) Ghana's Domestic revenue is mainly made up of tax/non-tax revenue and revenue collections by MMDAs. Due to inefficiencies in revenue collection, the 2017 Auditor-General's report stated that the country lost over GHS2 billion. Currently, there are over 254 MMDAs and 127 public organizations operating more than 2,000 physical points in terms of public services using mostly manual processes, affirming that these inefficiencies are bound to occur. To resolve these inefficiencies and increase revenue collection, Ghana.gov was conceived as a digital service and revenue collection platform, bringing all Government of Ghana services for the public sector under a single roof. The goal for Ghana.gov, therefore, is to harness new technologies to improve revenue collection and customer service, which is aligned with the Government's vision of digitalizing the economy, contributing to the attainment of a cash-lite policy, and modernizing the way the government pays its bills and collects revenue. Further, based on 100% mobile money coverage and over 35% internet penetration, a digital technology platform that facilitates service delivery and payments has a greater chance of working effectively.

Ghana.Gov Use Cases and Services Workflow

There are over 1501 government entities on the government's digital system providing a myriad of services. There are four use cases for Ghana.Gov. First, a user can apply online and make payments, and services are delivered online without any offline component. For example, to pay taxes to Ghana Revenue Authority(GRA), the user starts the processes on https://taxpayersportal.com/auth once the tax payment application process is completed, the user is automatically redirected to www.ghana.gov where they make payment and are redirected to a second portal, https://taxpayersportal.com/auth to complete the process and are given a receipt.

Second, a user applies and makes payment online and thereafter goes to a physical point to consume the service. For example, to apply for a passport, the user applies and makes payment online on Ghana.Gov; then, they must physically visit the passport office to complete the process.

Key Stakeholders and Relationships

The following stakeholders are part of the C2G and B2G digital payments ecosystem, namely; the Ministry of Finance, private sector FinTech consortium (Express Pay, IT Consortium and Hubtel), MDAs, MMDAs, GhiPSS, NITA, Ministry of Communication and Bank of Ghana. The primary holders of content that is service delivery are government entities, with NITA assigned the role of technical partner responsible for the operational management of the platform, whereas the private sector consortium is responsible for handling the processing of digital payments.

The financial model, therefore, is structured to compensate NITA for the management of the technology and private sector FinTech consortium for providing a payment platform. All the funds received are channelled to the entity delivering the services, thereafter, these entities will circle back to the Ministry of Finance since it is the legal entity with oversight responsibilities for government revenue. In order to facilitate stakeholder engagement, a coordination committee was formed as a mechanism to enable all parties to work together.

Expert 6 intimated that " Governmnt issued policy directives and guidelines to all government entities, that all government transactions involving payments should go through the ghana.gov." Based on this directive, NITA took steps to onboard these entities. However, not all government entities are able to follow this government directive largely due to their low level of maturity in digital technology.This directive is important since it collapses various government silo payment platforms into one harmonised platform leading to a more effective and efficient C2G and B2G payments mechanism.The matured entities have to go through a simple application process to be onboarded onto Ghana.Gov. The main requirement for the entity to enrol is the availability of core infrastructure, connectivity and capabilities to deliver services online.

The Effects of (C2G) and (B2G) Digital Payments System

Overall, the introduction of digital payments has made it easier for citizens to transact business with the government in the comfort of their homes or offices without incurring the cost of transportation to a physical service delivery location. Thus, it has contributed significantly to the increase in the availability of public services online, incorporated with digital payments.

According to Table 1, from 2020 to the end of August 2023, the system has served over 78 million users, increasing progressively from 1 million users in 2020 to over 56 million by August 2023. Currently, there are over 1501 government entities on the system,generating over US$14 billion transactions since 2020, growing from US$ 436 millionin 2020 to over US$ 4.9 billion by the end of August 2023. To contextualise this volume of transactions, the current GDP of Ghana as of 2022 stands at US$72.84 billion

Although there is improvement in service delivery efficiencies due to convenience, time and cost savings enabled by digital payments, there is no sufficient data to buttress the notion that the introduction and usage of digital payments can automatically lead to better public service delivery. In assessing key success factors for Ghana.Gov, one respondent noted the following contributory factors to the success of citizens to government payments, namely the "phenomenal growth of mobile money as a digital payments tool, the rise of FinTech companies, digital services offered by banks, the facilitating role of

Table 1. Ghana.Gov progress report

Usage	2020	2021	2022	year 2023 Jan to Aug	Totals
Total Transactions in US $	436 million	3.4 billion	5.4 billion	4.9 billion	14.4 billion
Transactions count (users)	1,611,868	9,845,907	10,051,660	56,923,312	78,432,747.00
Entities					
MDAs onboarded	26	110	33	6	175
MMDAs onboarded	32	0	227	0	259
SOEs onboarded	0	22	11	0	33
Health and Education sectors	0	10	1024	0	1034
Total Agencies onboarded	58	142	1295	6	1501

Source: NITA 2023

GhiPSS especially its interoperability platform, enabling laws and the Government of Ghana policy directive that all payments made to the government for public services delivery should be channelled through Ghana.Gov platform."

Ghana.Gov Challenges

The challenges mitigating the success of Ghana.Gov can be segmented into two areas; issues related to government entities as services providers, and consumers accessing these services. For most government entities, the long years of offering offline services have developed a deep bureaucratic system, which means offering services online requires a huge culture change coupled with a steep learning curve; therefore, the quality of their service delivery is negatively impacted. One respondent noted there is an urgent need to promote a "just-in-time service delivery mindset" as a best practice in order for these entities to deliver exceptional services online to their client base.

Further, there are gaps in the number of services offered by Ghana.Gov due to the inability of some of the entities to be onboarded on the online platform due to their geographical locations as most local government entities located outside major cities, are not offering services on the platform. Some of these local government entities do not have the necessary infrastructure, including an internal computing system, trained staff, or internet connectivity, which adversely impacts their ability to deliver services online. Another key challenge is that most of the entities are not able to offer end-to-end public services delivery online; users can only apply and make payments, whereupon they must go to the physical location of the entity they are consuming services from to complete transactions, which leads to a double amount of time for users as they are not able to consume services exclusively online.

The low level of publicity about Ghana.Gov means a lot more citizens are not aware of how they can utilise the platform to consume public services, leading to relatively low diffusion of this online opportunity. Also, there is no documented evidence of citizens' involvement as a stakeholder in the rollout of Ghana.Gov. In addition to a low level of digital literacy, some persons cannot access the services offered by the online platform because they do not have the requisite devices, such as a smartphone or tablet connected to the Internet. Also, there are a number of times when users cannot access services due to a lack of internet access or the poor nature of internet connectivity. To ameliorate this problem, Ghana.Gov does have a short code, for users using a feature phone that can access the public services delivered on Ghana.gov by going through a series of simple steps. That said, there is the need to provide the service in local languages through voice recognition solutions on mobile phones, where persons who are illiterate can call a number to access these public services.

Also, according to a respondent, "NITA piloted physical access to Ghana.gov at the Central Post Office where we have about 20 computers available for those who do not have access to computers". During the pilot, in addition to computers, there were tellers stationed at this physical point to assist users consume services available on these shared devices connected to Ghana.Gov. Also, the Ghana.Gov physical points were outfitted with printing services to print permits, licenses, etc.

Some users suffer from cyber phobia and, therefore, are not willing and able to consume public services online. This group of persons could be helped through education and support to build trust in leveraging online opportunities. There is also the challenge of users who cannot navigate the online platform, especially how to follow a sequence to apply for a service and pay for it online.

A respondent opinionated that issues related to fraud and security are not a challenge since there has been no incident to date. The system was designed with the best practices and standards in mind, plus there is a robust encryption infrastructure with plans underway to incorporate digital signatures. However, some users may hold the view that there are cyber and fraud risks related to the use of digital services and payments and therefore, make a decision not to consume services on digital payments platforms.

DISCUSSIONS

Stakeholders can positively assist or hinder attempts at innovation, especially when it comes to the digitalisation of public sector payments. Therefore, the nature and level of stakeholder engagement are key success factors in the government of Ghana's efforts to digitalise public sector payments. There is no doubt stakeholder engagement from both private and public sector realms can be complex and unpredictable, especially in the absence of a clear-cut stakeholder engagement strategy. Hence, the success achieved so far by the government in enabling digital payments could have been far greater with a systematic process in place to enable stakeholders' participation. Both at the levels of G2B, C2G and B2G digital payments, the level of usage could be higher if there was systems thinking invested in managing stakeholder expectations and participation. From a theoretical perspective, analysis of the effect of stakeholder salience is at the centre of ensuring better outcomes. Therefore, an explicit plan for stakeholder engagement, elicitation of feedback and participation is a necessary condition for achieving the aims and objectives of effective deployment of digital payments for the public sector.

In assessing the future of digital payments for the public sector, the issue of infrastructure, especially reliable, fast and affordable internet coupled with digital devices, is an important requirement for the rapid growth of public sector digital payments. The issue of reliable infrastructure is crucial for the entities that are providing public services on the one hand and citizens and businesses who consume the services on the other hand. Beyond traditional means of payment such as cards, bank transfers and mobile money, over time, new forms of payment, such as blockchain's Distributed Ledger Technology (DLT) for payment and Central Bank digital currency (CBDC), should be investigated for their incorporation as a channel of digital payments.

Recommendations

Digital payments can thrive when linked to digital service delivery in a robust manner since the value of making payment online can be fully derived when matched with full digital service delivery; therefore, the Government must work to become a truly digital-first entity by continually investing in government digital transformation processes. The government must ensure (G2B) digital payments (GIFMIS) is connected in a more robust manner to (C2G) and (B2G) via Ghana.Gov instead of running the two as silos. Secondly, a lot of citizens still do not have access to reliable internet, plus digital devices such as smartphones or tablets are needed to access public services and pay for them online, therefore, the Government must invest in physical points by relying on Post Offices and Community Information Centers (CIC). This investment in physical access points will enable digital public services and payment facilities for citizens without access. Thirdly, government entities must invest in public education and awareness creation about the benefits of consuming public services online by placing emphasis on how digitalization saves valuable time and money, making consuming public services very convenient and secure. Furthermore, the Government should build confidence in the service by ensuring its reliability and timely delivery while also working to ensure tailored interactions which increase citizens' satisfaction and engagement since most of these platforms inherently enable customization. It is always important for government entities to ensure their digital platforms are user-friendly, the length of time in processing is kept to the minimum, and the processes are simplified to reduce any complexity in the workflow.

Limitations and Directions For Future Research

While this chapter attempts to contribution to theory and practice with respect to public serive delivery and digitalization, it has some limitations, including its inability to establish the relationship between digital payments and improvement in public services.; Future studies could empirically test this relationship. Also, the study could not include the voices of citizens and businesses who consume online public services or receive payments from the government via digital means; thus, future research in this area can investigate users' intention to adopt and rate of usage of online public services combined with digital payments.

CONCLUSION

This chapter set out to investigate the research question: How has the public sector digital payment ecosystem evolved in Ghana? Thus, this chapter critically analyzed the evolution of public sector digital payments using the descriptive aspects of stakeholder theory based on the case study approach. The results show that GIFMIS, the centre of G2B payments, launched in 2014, has supported the digitalisation of public sector finances in Ghana by enabling the capture of all public finances previously scattered across different units, producing a single unified chart of accounts and budget classification; re-engineered government finance management processes and consolidate the reporting of all government finances. The GIFMIS rollout means most government payments for goods and services are made through digital payments using ACH, SWIFT and EFT. In order to actualise the digital payments, all government entities were issued a directive to stop using cheque books. Micro cash payments were facilitated by the use of Ghana Pay, a mobile money wallet created by banks in Ghana.

The deployment of GIFMIS has improved financial data collection, enabling government entities to monitor revenue collection, disbursement and the judicious utilisation of financial resources. Also, the results point to a reduction of the time utilised in processing payments, savings of money and time, and greater efficiency in the management of public finance through the digitalisation of payments. Through GIFMIS, all entities are able to see the funds available for their operation in real-time, leading to better funds management. The results of this chapter indicate that, over time, the digitalisation of public finance contributed significantly to the reduction in the use of physical cash since most payments are now paid through digital means in line with the government's 'cash-lite-society' policy. The chapter results highlight the lack of deep stakeholder engagement in the rollout of GIFMIS, occasioning relatively low usage of the system.

C2G and B2G digital payments started in 2012 through the launch of http://www.eservices.gov.gh/, and in 2021, the platform was relaunched as https://www.ghana.gov.gh. The results of this chapter show stakeholders' salience by private sector provision of digital payments in the ecosystem explains the success of the Ghana.Gov platform. The introduction of digital payments has made it easier for citizens to transact business with the government in the comfort of their homes or offices without having to incur the cost of transportation to a physical service delivery location. The analysis of this chapter shows that the volume of transactions on Ghana.Gov is growing year on year.

Further, the number of entities offering public services is increasing exponentially, based on stakeholder engagements at the level of government entities, thus increasing the range of public services available online for citizens. Although there is improvement in service delivery efficiencies due to convenience, time and cost savings enabled by digital payments, there is no sufficient data to buttress the notion that the introduction and usage of digital payments can automatically lead to better public service delivery.

REFERENCES

Agyei-Ababio, N., Ansong, E., & Assa-Agyei, K. (2023). Digitalization of revenue mobilization in an emerging economy: The new Institutional Theory perspective. *International Journal of Information Systems and Project Management, 11*(2), 5–22. doi:10.12821/ijispm110201

Almirall, E., & Casadesus-Masanell, R. (2010). Open versus closed innovation: A model of discovery and divergence. *Academy of Management Review, 35*(1), 27–47. doi:10.5465/AMR.2010.45577790

Axelsson, K., Melin, U., & Lindgren, I. (2013). Stakeholder salience changes in an e-government implementation project. Lecture Notes in Computer Science (Including Subseries Lecture Notes in Artificial Intelligence and Lecture Notes in Bioinformatics), 8074 LNCS. doi:10.1007/978-3-642-40358-3_20

Bawole, J. N., & Langnel, Z. (2023). Administrative Reforms in the Ghanaian Public Services for Government Business Continuity During the COVID-19 Crisis. *Public Organization Review, 23*(1), 181–196. doi:10.1007/s11115-022-00687-w

Bio-Tchane, Y. (2021). *Information Systems in Public Financial Management Expanding the institutional coverage of a financial management information system: Lessons from Benin, Nigeria and Ghana.*

CAGD. (2022). *The Public Financial Management Reform Project (PFMRP).* CAGD. https://www.cagd.gov.gh/projects/the-public-financial-management-reform-project-pfmrp/

Cangiano, M., Gelb, A., & Goodwin-Groen, R. (2019). Public Financial Management and the Digitalization of Payments. In *DC (Vol. 416).* www.cgdev.orgwww.cgdev.orgwww.cgdev.org

Carroll, A. B., Brown, J. A., & Buchholtz, A. K. (2018). Business & Society: Ethics, Sustainability, and Stakeholder Management. In Business & society : ethics, sustainability, and stakeholder management.

Chesbrough, H. W. (2003). The era of open innovation. *MIT Sloan Management Review, 44*(3).

Colvin, R. M., Witt, G. B., & Lacey, J. (2020). Power, perspective, and privilege: The challenge of translating stakeholder theory from business management to environmental and natural resource management. *Journal of Environmental Management, 271*, 110974. doi:10.1016/j.jenvman.2020.110974 PMID:32579526

Curtis, S. (2019). Digital transformation—The silver bullet to public service improvement? *Public Money & Management, 39*(5), 322–324. doi:10.1080/09540962.2019.1611233

Darke, P., Shanks, G., & Broadbent, M. (1998). Successfully completing case study research: Combining rigour, relevance and pragmatism. *Information Systems Journal, 8*(4), 273–289. doi:10.1046/j.1365-2575.1998.00040.x

Demuyakor, J. (2021). Ghana's Digitization Initiatives: A Survey of Citizens Perceptions on the Benefits and Challenges to the Utilization of Digital Governance Services. *International Journal of Publication and Social Studies, 6*(1), 42–55. doi:10.18488/journal.135.2021.61.42.55

Dobson, P. J. (1999). Approaches to theory use in interpretative case studies - a critical realist perspective. Edith Cowan University.

Donaldson, T., & Preston, L. E. (1995). Stakeholder theory: Concepts, evidence, and implications. *Academy of Management Review, 20*(1), 65. doi:10.2307/258887

Dowuona, S. (2021, May 7). *3 Ghanaian FinTechs build Ghana.GOV to block state revenue leakages.* TechFocus. https://www.techfocus24.com/3-ghanaian-fintechs-build-ghana-gov-to-block-state-revenue-leakages/

Eggers, W. D., Manstof, J., Kamleshkumar Kishnani, P., & Barroca, J. (2021). *Seven pivots for government's digital transformation. How COVID-19 proved the importance of "being" digital.* Deloitte Insights.

Finance Ministry Ghana. (2020). *Toward a Cash-Lite Ghana Building an Inclusive Digital Payments Ecosystem.* MOFEP. https://mofep.gov.gh/sites/default/files/acts/Ghana_Cashlite_Roadmap.pdf

Flak, L. S., & Rose, J. (2005). Stakeholder Governance: Adapting Stakeholder Theory to E-Government. *Communications of the Association for Information Systems, 16.* Advance online publication. doi:10.17705/1CAIS.01631

Flammer, C., & Kacperczyk, A. (2014). The Impact Of Stakeholder Orientation On Innovation: Evidence From A Natural Experiment. *Management Science, 62*(7).

Freeman, J., & Engel, J. S. (2007). California Management Models of Innovation: Startups and Mature Corporations. *California Management Review.*

Freeman, R. E., Phillips, R., & Sisodia, R. (2020). Tensions in Stakeholder Theory. *Business & Society, 59*(2), 213–231. Advance online publication. doi:10.1177/0007650318773750

GBN. (2023, August). *MMDAs urged to ensure strict adherence to GIFMIS.* GBN. https://www.ghana-businessnews.com/2023/08/01/mmdas-urged-to-ensure-strict-adherence-to-gifmis/

Ghana MoF. (2022). *5 years Public Financial Management strategy.* Ghana MoF. https://mofep.gov.gh/sites/default/files/reports/economic/Ghana%27s-2022-2026-Approved-PFM-Strategy.pdf

Gould, R. W. (2012). Open innovation and stakeholder engagement. *Journal of Technology Management & Innovation, 7*(3), 1–11. doi:10.4067/S0718-27242012000300001

Griffin, N., Uña, G., Bazarbash, M., & Verma, A. (2023). Fintech Payments in Public Financial Management: Benefits and Risks. *IMF Working Papers, 2023*(020). doi:10.5089/9798400232213.001

Hamel, J., Dufour, S., & Fortin, D. (1993). *Case Study Methods.* SAGE Publications, Inc., doi:10.4135/9781412983587

Jawahar, I. M., & McLaughlin, G. L. (2001). Toward a descriptive stakeholder theory: An organizational life cycle approach. *Academy of Management Review, 26*(3), 397. Advance online publication. doi:10.2307/259184

Jones, T. M. (1995). INSTRUMENTAL STAKEHOLDER THEORY: A SYNTHESIS OF ETHICS AND ECONOMICS. *Academy of Management Review, 20*(2), 404. doi:10.2307/258852

Klapper, L., & Singer, D. (2017). The opportunities and challenges of digitizing government-to- person payments. *The World Bank Research Observer, 32*(2), 211–226. doi:10.1093/wbro/lkx003

Larkotey, W. O., & Ifinedo, P. (2022). Socioetechnical Factors that Shape E-Government Payment Portal Development in Ghana. *IFIP Advances in Information and Communication Technology, 657 IFIP.* doi:10.1007/978-3-031-19429-0_2

Lund, S., White, O., & Lamb, J. (2017). *The Value of Digitalizing Government Payments in Developing Economies.* Digital Revolutions in Public Finance.

Mitchell, R. K., Agle, B. R., & Wood, D. J. (1997). Toward a theory of stakeholder identification and salience: Defining the principle of who and what really counts. *Academy of Management Review, 22*(4), 853. doi:10.2307/259247

Mtebe, J. S., & Sausi, J. (2021). Revolutionization of Revenue Collection with Government E-Payment Gateway System in Tanzania: A Public Value Creation Perspective. *East African Journal of Science. Technology and Innovation, 2*(3). doi:10.37425/eajsti.v2i3.248

NITA. (2023). *Ghana's Digital Services and Payments Platform.* Ghana. https://www.ghana.gov.gh/

Nyambi, A. B., & Assey, T. (2021). *Assessing the Effectiveness of Digitizing Government Payment Systems on Service Delivery in Public Institution: A Case Study of Arusha Public Institutions.*

Ofoma, C. (2021). Digitalization Driven Public Service And Service Delivery: The Nigeria's Experience. *Journal of Public Administration. Finance and Law, 22.* doi:10.47743/jopafl-2021-22-05

Ofori, D., Light, O., & Ankomah, J. (2023). Adoption intentions of electronic procurement among public sector organisations (PSOs) in Ghana: emerging economy perspective. *Journal of Public Procurement.* doi:10.1108/JOPP-09-2022-0045

Osikwan, E. (2021). Fintechs, SMEs and digitization in Africa – Ghana leads the charge. *The BFT Online.* https://thebftonline.com/2021/08/03/fintechs-smes-and-digitization-in-africa-ghana-leads-the-charge/

Rashidov, R., & Rustamov, A. (2021). THE IMPORTANCE OF DIGITAL PAYMENTS IN THE DIGITAL ECONOMY. *INNOVATIONS IN ECONOMY, 4*(3), 66–72. doi:10.26739/2181-9491-2021-3-9

Rocheleau, B., & Wu, L. (2005). e-Government and Financial Transactions: Potential Versus Reality. *Electronic Journal of EGovernment, 3*(4).

Rose, J., Flak, L. S., & Sæbø, Ø. (2018). Stakeholder theory for the E-government context: Framing a value-oriented normative core. *Government Information Quarterly, 35*(3), 362–374. doi:10.1016/j.giq.2018.06.005

Sengupta, D., & Shastri, N. (2019). Digital payments through PFMS - Facilitating digital inclusion and accelerating transformation to a "Digital Economy. *ACM International Conference Proceeding Series, Part F148155*. ACM. 10.1145/3326365.3326391

Shin, S. C., & Rakhmatullayev, Z. M. (2019). Digital Transformation of the Public Service Delivery System in Uzbekistan. *International Conference on Advanced Communication Technology, ICACT, 2019-February*. ACM. 10.23919/ICACT.2019.8702014

Simatele, M. (2021). E-payment instruments and welfare: The case of Zimbabwe. *The Journal for Transdisciplinary Research in Southern Africa, 17*(1). Advance online publication. doi:10.4102/td.v17i1.823

Smaguc, T. (2022). Comparison of Normative, Instrumental and Descriptive Approaches to Stakeholder Theory. *28th RSEP International Conference on Economics, Finance & Business*. ACM.

Tellis, W. (1997). Introduction to Case Study. *The Qualitative Report*. doi:10.46743/2160-3715/1997.2024

The Economist. (2018). The 2018 Government E-Payments Adoption Ranking. *The Economist Intelligence Unit*.

The World Bank Group. (2021). *Tools for Digitizing Government Payments Learnings from FISF*. The World Bank. https://openknowledge.worldbank.org/server/api/core/bitstreams/064bd45f-73c8-540e-92b8-62857c7d1937/content

Vaidya, M., & Sharma, S. (2020). DIGITAL PAYMENT AS A KEY ENABLER OF E-GOVERNMENT SERVICES: A CASE STUDY OF CHANDIGARH CITY (INDIA). *International Journal of Control and Automation, 13*(1s).

Walsham, G. (1995). Interpretive case studies in IS research: Nature and method. *European Journal of Information Systems, 4*(2), 74–81. Advance online publication. doi:10.1057/ejis.1995.9

Yin, R. K. (2017). Case Study Research and Applications Design and Methods. []. Sage.]. *Journal of Hospitality & Tourism Research (Washington, D.C.), 53*(5).

ADDITIONAL READING

Aimee, H. (2022, October). *Digital payments in sub-Saharan Africa: Trends over the past decade*. Poverty Action Lab. https://www.povertyactionlab.org/blog/10-3-22/digital-payments-sub-saharan-africa-trends-over-past-decade-0

Akolgo, I. A. (2023). On the contradictions of Africa's fintech boom: Evidence from Ghana. *Review of International Political Economy, 30*(5), 1639–1659. doi:10.1080/09692290.2023.2225142

Botta, A., Fjer, A., Gold, E., Amaah, N., Ofusu-Amaah, N. A., & Seshie, E. (2022). *The future of payments in Africa*. McKinsey & Company.

Chiapello, È., Engels, A., & Gonçalves Gresse, E. (2023). *Financializations of Development*. Routledge. doi:10.4324/9781003039679

Domingo, E., & Teevan, C. (2022). *Africa's journey towards an integrated digital payments landscape and how the EU can support it – ECDPM Briefing Note 146.* EU Agenda. https://euagenda.eu/upload/publications/africas-journey-towards-integrated-digital-payments-landscape-how-eu-can-support-ecdpm-briefing-note-146-2022.pdf

Fichers, N., & Naji, L. (2020). *Digitalising person-to-government payments.* GSMA. https://www.gsma.com/publicpolicy/wp-content/uploads/2020/09/GSMA-Digitalising-person-to-government-payments.pdf

KendallJ.SchiffR.SmadjaE. (2013). Sub-Saharan Africa: A Major Potential Revenue Opportunity for Digital Payments. In SSRN. doi:10.2139/ssrn.2298244

Piyush, K., & Armaan, J. (2022). *What Is A Digital Payment and How Does It Work?* Research Gate.

Romina, B., & Sundar, R. (2021). *Developing Inclusive Digital Payment Systems.* Center for Strategic and International Studies.

Tay, L. Y., Tai, H. T., & Tan, G. S. (2022). Digital financial inclusion: A gateway to sustainable development. In Heliyon, 8(6). doi:10.1016/j.heliyon.2022.e09766

KEY TERMS AND DEFINITIONS

Business to Government (B2G) Payments: These payments made by businesses to government entities for various purposes, such as taxes, fees, fines, or contracts.

Central Bank digital currency (CBDC): This is a digital currency issued and regulated by a country's central bank as legal tender, backed by the full faith and credit of the government.

Citizens to Government (C2G) Payments: These are financial transactions from individuals or citizens who pay government entities for various services, fees, taxes, or other obligations.

Cyberphobia: This is an extreme fear of computers or new technologies. People experiencing cyberphobia may feel anxious or panicked when they have to use a computer, a smartphone, or digital devices.

Digital Payments: These refer to the electronic transactions conducted over the internet or other electronic networks facilitating the exchange of value. They could include Card PaymentsOnline Banking Transfer. Mobile Wallets, Contactless Payments, Peer-to-Peer (P2P) Payments and Cryptocurrency Transactions.

Digital Transformation: This refers to integrating digital technologies, processes, and strategies across an organization to drastically change its operations and enable value addition to its audiences.

Distributed Ledger Technology (DLT): This can be described as a digital register that shares information about transactions or events linked to an asset or an item of value. DLT enable multiple parties to process, access, validate and update the same data simultaneously without the role of an intermediary.

Electronic Payments: Sometimes used interchangeably with digital payments, describe various mechanisms which aid the transfer of money or value from one entity to another without using cash or checks. Some key advantages of electronic payments are convenience, speed and security.

Government-to-Person (G2P) Payments: These refer to disbursements made by the government to individuals for various purposes, such as social protection, public service delivery, or financial inclusion

USSD (Unstructured Supplementary Service Data): These messages facilitate users' access to various services or perform other operations based on a simple and interactive menu-based system on mobile devices. Compared to Short Message Service (SMS), USSD operates in real-time and does not store messages it transmits on the users' mobile devices. It is typically a four-digit number.

Chapter 11
Creating the African Digital Platform Play:
A Focus on Ghana

Eric Nsarkoh
Street Streams Ltd., Ghana

ABSTRACT

Fintech infrastructure in Africa has continued to evolve towards more resilient digital forms over the past decade. The chapter reviews various stages of the Ghanaian journey and the disaggregation into the pillars of innovation that the chapter identifies. Fintech is considered as only one of such pillars. The discussion touches briefly on AI, Big Data, Blockchain and other generic elements, which can be considered as arrowheads of change. The conclusion is that Platform Play is enabled by stitching together the various axes and multifaceted domains of digital and other forms of knowledge.

INTRODUCTION

The challenge of the African society appears to be closely coupled with the evolution path of systems and technology. The sheer capacity of households to scale agriculture, tame an environment or steer a cause, would depend on how much tooling is available for activities that defy natural strength. To that end, the prevalence of modern technology in some locations, relative to others, should normally not be associated with shallow determinants like race and geography.

Africa boasts of great civilizations like Great Zimbabwe, Bakongo, Nok Nok, Benin, Ashanti, Akwamu etc. These societies, their systems of government, warfare, farming etc, could not have emanated from instincts and scavenging. The thinking and intellectual enquiry they represent are evident. It would be interesting to identify the causes of the disconnect from that heritage properly, and how those, in turn, pose a challenge to the quality of modern systems in Africa. UNESCO may be making that point partially in the "Policy Document for the Integration of a Sustainable Development Perspective into the Processes of the World Heritage Convention" as adopted by the General Assembly of States Parties to World Heritage Convention at its 20th session (UNESCO, 2015) The document speaks to an "indispens-

DOI: 10.4018/978-1-6684-9962-7.ch011

able requirement for sustainable development and the well-being of present and future generations by "promoting sustainable forms of inclusive and equitable economic development, productive and decent employment and income-generating activities for all"(2015,p.8-9). There is copious intellectual debate around the best methods for coupling the identified heritage and cultural anchors, into the development narrative of a society.

Engineering projects fall on these heritage perspectives, to drive the adoption of technology on a large scale. Engineers will inspire their creative energy by drawing from the springs of culture. Projects of various kinds will be designed to incorporate the granularity of the people, their homes, their markets, and all the nuances of lifestyles and context. These render perfect monuments, infrastructure, production facilities, and technology, which an entire nation can feel a part of.

The converse is when the model on which a design is benchmarked feels alien to the society. In that case, the design does not resonate with, but a distance is created from, the intended recipients. The tale of the telecommunication industry in Ghana, for example, illustrates how the market leader continued to scale many products and propositions, while offerings from competition did not take root. In June 2020, the market leader (MTN) was declared dominant, in a bid to rebalance the market share per operator. It could be safe to say that despite a few years of this effort by the government of Ghana, MTN has widened its lead on major business metrics such as revenue, cash flow, and profits.

When the author was head of Sales and Distribution at MTN from January 2014 to April 2021, the success of the company was very closely linked to the anchors of heritage it invested in across Ghana. The business had achieved a fit between fraud control measures and fraud risk hotspots for example, using real time analytics. Likewise, the investments of the organization, were channeled to the exact locations, where the best returns could be derived from customers. This meant that the radio access network was expanded precisely where population numbers were increasing. The fit was extending to training programs, incentives, promotions, distribution, and sponsorships. Sales teams were deployed where opportunities existed. This knowledge of the terrain and what was required for business was achieved from the ability of analytical reports to resonate with local sentiment. A lot of the salespeople (as is the case worldwide), knew the communities, the channels, the stakeholders, the native customs, and the anchors of immersion into Africa.

These anchors have however not been studied in great enough detail by the corporate professionals, who lead the private sector, and the academics who train them. There is a need for academic immersion into the historical dimensions that have driven change through markets, for example in the change from cowries to currency. The late Sociology professor Nukunya stated in an interview with MTN sales leadership that there was a need for another generation to contextualize the research he did for his book *Tradition and change in Ghana: An introduction to sociology*, in contemporary times. In the absence of published academic research, corporate work today depends on teams that can speak to the various constituencies of culture. A lot of engagement is required with staff at royal palaces, service teams at funerals, elders at traditional gatherings, family heads, court administrators, and the various interfaces to heritage. There is an obligation to be respectful in a consistent way and congenial in a natural way. The chords established by being in flow with the culture and heritage of people entrench brands in a way that is very difficult to alter.

The challenge remains to formalize the science of nuanced interaction and immersion. The work that corporations do will result in higher returns (with respect to profits and commercial metrics) for their brands. Yet out of that, it should be possible to distill research and teaching aids for generations of students who will create the next offerings for the society. This requires adaptive pedagogy and experienced teaching. Academic resources will be required to create a high level of intrinsic motivation for the society, by framing a partnership between innovators and adopters. At MTN, the Centre for Social Policy Studies at the University of Ghana was contracted to publish on the linkages between the work that had gone into the creation of products, such as mobile money, and the history and psychology of the Ghanaian consumer. The conversation between corporate teams and scholars created healthy fulfilment for both sides as well as lasting knowledge content for students and employees. Ideally, a project like that should have spurned the delivery of research content at an increased pace. The absence of spontaneous follow-ups to knowledge-based work is however not entirely unusual.

It could be argued that our society is plagued by an educational system that was socialized around the great postulates of the European Enlightenment and how those feed into the robust limb movements of Western industrialization. Careful examination of the common corollaries in the journey of Western societies point to thought processes that prioritize goals, which in turn enable rational, material, and mundane pursuit of wealth and property. There are many axes for charting this journey. One axis could be the thread through philosophical mindsets over time. This can be traced to the pre-Socratic era, in which modern thinkers have cited less and less in their work. The immediate successor to that era takes us through the era of the Greek philosophers (key among them being Socrates, Plato, and Aristotle). The next millennium featured giants like Augustine at the onset, and the generation of Sir Thomas Aquinas and Ibn Khaldun as it tapered off. In the years that follow, dense philosophical discourse is generated among thinkers ranging (in no particular order) from Machiavelli to others like Calvin and Luther. The era of Enlightenment that followed is associated with René Descartes, Hume, Locke, Zaya Yacob, and scores of others. We do not seek to do a full review of the timelines, but this era of modernism evolved into post-modernism and more lately, a contemporary struggle with social forces like the Internet and Artificial Intelligence.

We must aspire to tap into our heritage to build a better-engineered society. This should be a space that taps into the work of the sages throughout our history and the values entrenched in generations that followed. These principles are evident again in the work that has been done to create some of the more successful system deployments in recent history. This work connected to the giants of African thinking and the work they did. Besides the work of Nukunya (1992), Gyekye (1997) and Wiredu's (1996) radical comments about the centricity of language and culturally embedded cogitation are essential. It puts the African engineer in the right frame of mind to connect the dots.

For example, to deploy mobile money systems, various perspectives of African heritage had to be consciously navigated. MTN, Zain, and many telecommunication players launched products over time (especially the period from 2008 to 2011) in Africa to usher in the territory. However, with the exception of Safaricom in East Africa, scale eluded most. The massive success of Safaricom's MPESA (Amoah, 2014) is well-researched and what followed in East Africa was nearly a subculture of mobile money systems. In West Africa, however, as at 2013, Ghana stood with just about 200,000 users of mobile money every month. Ghana had accepted what we thought was an engineered conclusion that these systems were for a different culture. There was a firm belief that using cards to load airtime onto phones was "the West African way". The talent journey to navigate past our entrapment was formidable. When corporate leaders mustered the courage to start the plunge though, it was swift. It could be argued that the telecommunications market leader in Ghana, MTN, was the arrowhead of seven quick years of innovation that in turn has many lessons of history, philosophy, and culture. At the end of this period, mobile money had reached almost 12 million people, scratch cards had been eliminated, and the company was maturing its systems into a period of gradual, linear growth.

The integration of sales work with engineering projects and system implementations is key to such innovation. In the Ghanaian case described, mastery of the methodology required that local chieftaincy structures were engaged, community-thought leaders in youth mobilization found a role, and the pervasive markets of Ghana took ownership of the journey. These wide structures of work were built over time. The impact became more evident when multiple categories of FINTECH players were given a lease of life with the Payment Systems and Services Act (Act 987) which was promulgated into Law in 2019. Interviews with the founders of the businesses that registered under this law confirm that a common thread for most of them is the difficulty in finding engineers to resource projects and operations. The resource profile calls for more business technology leads, anchored in Engineering and Sales than it does for engineers in the regular mold.

The lack of research into the causes of the talent gaps has left the industry in a lopsided position, where a string of regulatory interventions to protect players has had dismal results. There are multiple possibilities going forward. Africa could see the work done by the big telecom players as part of the puzzle to be unraveled. This would appear to be a surrender of the right to rigorous and infinite inquiry, but it affords the opportunity to travel faster into the future. This would mean the platforms that have been built in Ghana for instance should continue to be tuned into the way of life of artisans, farmers, students, community organizations, religious bodies, etc. New platforms must however be generated to scale the employment base of mobile money and allied technologies. Today, the domestic and international remittance ecosystem has given a wage to hundreds of thousands of agents. The possibilities are much wider in the space of informal digital commerce for example Jiji, Tonaton, Brorno etc. on app stores, as well as content opportunities such as WiFlix. Agritech initiatives such as Agro Innova and CompleteFarmer cast the net even wider. These platforms are being examined by multiple scholars for a new theory of development. The gains from the intellectual interrogation are married to the resilience of these initiatives over time. It is obvious from early results that these are making a big mark in interconnecting Silicon Valley venture capital with Africa. An increasing number of deals (especially in Nigeria) are showing the way towards sustainable fund-raising methods for Africa, which depend on showcasing talent instead of vulnerability.

PLATFORMS-GETTING STARTED

The African development struggle is one that must focus on talent. History is littered with the transformational stories that polymaths such as Einstein, Leonardo da Vinci, Ephraim Amu, Ibn Khaldun and Florence Dolphyne have driven. There is some such momentum in the Ghanaian wind of change in tertiary education, which has seen the lead jobs of the key institutions of learning such as University of Ghana, Kwame Nkrumah University of Science and Technology, and Ashesi University in the hands of very driven female professors. The richness of diversity guarantees success.

Kearney et al. (2019) describe the meteoric growth of platform economy firms, and refer to digital platforms as the levers for the reorganization of ever-greater segments of the contemporary economy. As this occurs, existing firms, jobs, and labor relationships are being reorganized. New tasks and enterprises are emerging, and existing firms are adjusting to the changes wrought by platforms in terms of value creation and logistics.

Platforms present a unique opportunity that does not yet dominate the public media and online narrative in Ghana. Platforms such as Pay TM in India, Rappi in Latin America, MTN MoMo in Ghana, and Mpesa in Kenya create an access point for governments to raise revenue and provide protection to informal workers.

The dearth of theory to support the opportunity around local platforms and the extent to which they determine economic growth for countries like Ghana is reminiscent of Koskella and Howell's (2002) description of the state of the theoretical framework within project management as a state of poverty. There are various elements that make the enrichment of the theoretical foundation urgent. These include:

i.   Technological innovation is a fundamental driver of economic growth and human progress (Broughel and Thierer, 2019). The creation of Electronic Money Issuers (EMIs) under the Payment Systems and Services Act (Act 987, 2019) in Ghana must lend itself to scrutiny within the framework of technological innovation and correlated economic growth.

ii. Models of productivity growth for all industries and specifically EMI impact are required for explanations of growth phenomena, and these must be built for Ghana and Africa, along the lines that Berndt and Christensen (1973), Jorgenson and Fraumeni (1981), and Jorgenson (1984), among others, have done for the USA.

iii. The inability to accurately determine the capability of countries to successfully implement technology, as captured by Pressman (2010), should be countered by formalization of change management models. The work in Africa is particularly urgent.

Given these, and other gaps in the provision of African data sets to contextualize existing theory, there is a need to build the base of research in the area by testing more constructs.Hamel (2002) states that innovation is a significant business challenge. Perhaps more significantly though is that surmounting the challenges that innovation poses is essential for growth. The work envisaged between corporates and academia is vital to the strengthening of the learning process for students, faculty, and employees.

Approximately, 12 percent of the global goods trade is conducted via international e-commerce (Manyika et al., 2016). Even the smallest enterprises can be born global, allowing small firms to compete with large multinationals using digital distribution. However, the phenomenon is not sufficiently exploited in Ghana. According to Internet World Stats (2020), Ghana had over 12m Internet users in 2020. Quarshie and Ami-Narh (2012) revealed that a decade ago only 6% of transactions in Ghana were classified as e-commerce. Statista (2023) estimates penetration as 12.2% (Sasu, 2023). The growing e-commerce space has major corporate actors, social media entrepreneurs, and the digitally native generation to thank for the modest growth. In recent times, the Brorno platform has sought to place the myriads of digitally exclusive petty traders into a technology landscape that fully anticipates the challenges of petty trading. Many such efforts exist to foster development dialogues that leverage technology opportunities. Rochet and Tirole (2003) demonstrated that economic value is created by "interactions" or "transactions" between pairs of end users, buyers, and sellers in platform economic models. They indicated in their work "Two-Sided Markets" that buyers are heterogeneous in that their gross surpluses associated with a transaction differ. Similarly, sellers' gross surplus from a transaction differs. Such transactions are mediated by a platform. The platform's marginal cost of a transaction is usually extremely low.

By the general framework that illustrates the platform above, the MTN Mobile Money platform has by Bank of Ghana statistics been the disproportionately most successful platform in Ghana today. As an Electronic Money Issuer, the enablement this platform provides for economic growth in Ghana requires the balanced theoretical linkages between the models of technology acceptance, starting from Davis (1985) and the economic value creation discourse, starting from Solow (1962).

The scaling of a platform of this size into multiple axes of value creation is central to the societal transformation that Ghana seeks. Agricultural technology lends itself to the work that Complete Farmer, Agro Innova, Farmerline, Sommalife and many corporate actors have done. The educational technology space has also seen Dext, Deaf can Talk, Techaide, ECampus and many more niche players. The story is similar when told of MPharma, MPedigree, Medpharma, and others in the pharmaceutical space. There is hardly a facet of the Ghanaian social space in which economic value creation is not being scaled by the emerging technology platforms. The efficiency they render, the distribution they trigger, and the investment they attract are all key ingredients of our development ambition.

DIGITAL INNOVATION

The pillars of the digital development dialogue could be distinguished along the lines of the major domains of the technology thought process. For easy categorization, these could be grouped as:

- FINTECH
- Artificial Intelligence
- Analytics
- Blockchain
- Digital Commerce
- Talent

These will be discussed separately. This does not in any way zone out the equally vital infrastructure, software development, cloud strategy and other discussions in the space. An exhaustive analysis is however impossible and the compartments are chosen for convenience.

FINTECH

Players in the Ghanaian banking sector have shown tremendous interest in novel agency banking models. ECOBANK has generated tremendous value in the space with an expanding team and growing contributions from its agency banking team. Banks like Fidelity have demonstrated similar prowess while GCB has marketed its GMONEY product as a direct answer to the preponderance of telecom-enabled services in the space. The intended scaling of conventional banking products from banking halls to a wider distribution space has positive implications for development.

It is however interesting to see the adjacent telecommunication sector that has also established itself as the major muscle behind financial inclusion.

The integrated look at the space and what it offers would require a disaggregation into:

- Integration services using Application Programming Interfaces (APIs)
- Products such as lending, remittance, pensions, savings, insurance, etc.
- Partnerships

APIs

The software that allows two or more applications to connect according to defined standards, would broadly fit into the category of APIs. This is increasingly prevalent within the Ghanaian technology landscape and has offered value from banks, aggregators, and many platform owners to partners and agents. Tools for easier integration of APIs have continued to be extended from global giants and the marketplace for API management continues to grow by multiple billions of dollars per year. The ability to create the right value out of FINTECH automation depends on clarity of standards, talent, investment and many variables which a comprehensive policy approach must enable. The innovation component of APIs has no novelty. Integrations have been done for payment of utility bills, validation of IDs, various payments, and an endless list of deployments. What matters though is that the sharing of databases for the creation of platforms is dependent on mastery of the security landscape around APIs.

Discussions for the future architecture of marketplace platforms, for example, will depend on quick evolution of standards for integration to back-office systems, funding partnerships, payments, data repositories, academic databases, and the vast array of sources for boosting platform utility and quality. In Ghana, the aggregation ecosystem still does not have the needed breadth that offers ready price books for complex integrations as well as accessible contracting frameworks.

The inefficiency that results from many startups duplicating each other and making it impossible for the upstream platforms to reconcile their systems presents an opportunity. Large aggregators are needed to automate "the jungle" and strengthen offerings.

Products

The GHC1.2 trillion plus of transaction values from mobile money transactions in Ghana (2022) is indicative of the massive relevance of today's products to the lifestyles of Ghanaians.

Product management skills however are difficult to hone. A product manager is typically a cross breed between hard core technology work and commercial exposure. The education system of Ghana has limited opportunities to cross fertilize curricula from the disparate domains of academia, owing predominantly to the resources of universities and the breadth of faculty. This triggers further challenges with obtaining corporate manpower who can traverse the journey of product formulation, launch, and scaling.

The mobile money ecosystem has created over half a million agent jobs that are mostly tracked on the commission records of large telecommunication giants such as MTN. Considering that this is almost 2% of the population of Ghana and an even larger percentage of the adult population, it is not sufficiently leveraged as the dipstick into the computational general equilibrium model that can profile the space for trading ecosystems. There is an urgent need for economists to model these platform models and inform policy with credible recommendations from rigorous models.

Efforts were made by both MTN and Stanbic Bank at certain points to build funded collaboration partnerships with teams of economists from public universities. Researchers did not show much appetite and the advice from advisors was to seek out hybrid intellectuals with a mix of engineering, private corporate practice, and academia. The search eventually led to resources from outside the continent of Africa (owing also to the fact that the investment in the search was low).

Today, the product portfolios are extensive but grossly inadequate. The aggregated super app experience has been fairly chaotic and continues to deny consumers the thrill of an entire journey in one place.

The ecosystems have relegated Micro, Small and Medium Scale Enterprises (MSMEs) to the penurious elements of platforms, where high transaction fees are extracted and yet scale is not transformational. Products are required to ease the integration of catalogs, applications, data sources, payments, subscriptions, and the full landscape of business commerce. The work to achieve that requires more deliberate planning and resourcing than has been achieved currently.

Partnerships

The journey of platforms is one of partnerships. Today, the ecosystems of the world are mostly consuming the infrastructure that Microsoft, Amazon, Oracle, Google, Huawei, IBM and the cloud hosting giants have built. The mindset of partnership is however tied to legal ecosystems, technology talent and business maturity. The product discussion for the telecommunication industry has been encouraging because of the agility with which financial sector licenses have been leveraged in legal frameworks that allow telecommunication sector distribution to build their relevance. Cross skilling has been commonplace among engineers, lawyers, marketers, and the full base of talent that underpin the complex organizational forms. The partnership conversation in the FINTECH space is the essence of the narrative.

Telecom financial remittance products, for example, sit on the licenses of banks. The banking industry is the best sector to guarantee protection of funds, compliance with regulatory frameworks for managing money and judicious deployment of deposits into safe products that grow value. The complicated nature of banking regulations would imply that a lot of planning is required for the most mundane partnerships to be executed. The journeys for onboarding customers are also complicated by the attachment of systems from across industries in ways that reflect a siloed mindset. In Ghana, the payment of bills for example might require multiple apps, one to confirm the outstanding amount, the other to pay, and in many cases, a completely separate customer service channel, if there is a problem with payment. Many institutions that contract third parties to manage their integration work, do not have an architecture that allows the 3rd parties to offer much assistance to achieve user-friendly customer journeys.

Tools like IBM API Connect that are used when large organizations offer integration to their systems come with extremely expensive support for organizations in Africa. This affects what can be achieved even in the best partnerships. Fortunately, the situation is improving with the time towards a younger generation, who are native to building extended architecture for systems. The impact of simple chatbots to ease the connection of consumers to offerings also raises the stakes for institutions to support the trend towards bigger partnerships. Users prefer to match their needs through fewer apps. That would imply a need to have fewer siloes, fewer fees between them, a smoother journey, and laws that evolve to boost efficiency.

Artificial Intelligence

Owoyemi et al. (2020) flag their concerns about the absence of large datasets for the training of AI platforms in Africa and the deepening of algorithmic biases as a result. In 2023, the Meltwater Entrepreneurial School of Technology (MEST), in Accra, announced that it had funded five new startups. Four of these applied various AI platforms to their innovation. The big challenge that they all expressed was the cost of adopting platforms from richer countries to solve local problems.

The partitioning of the world according to algorithms and cost offerings is a risk to innovation in Africa. The simple task of automatically summarizing a voice survey into text and summarizing findings requires very deliberate parceling of the problem to highly motivated and skilled resources who must collaborate to surmount the obstacles. Innovators in Africa tend to prevail with sheer grit and end up with response accuracy levels for AI that trail the world. Out of frustration, many teams abandon their efforts and capitulate to enticing employee offers from Western corporations.

The future of all platforms, nonetheless, must be that they incorporate AI as the midrib of computation. Maas et al. (2002) speak of a key challenge for neural modeling as the ability to explain how a continuous stream of multimodal input from a rapidly changing environment can be processed by stereotypical recurrent circuits of integrate-and-fire neurons in real time. Though this is the challenge, the fact that it mimics the brain presents massive reference data for today's innovators. It also means that for the first time, Africa gets to use its disadvantages such as low quality of frontline service, to allow live users a window into building datasets. There is a lot of discipline required for trailblazers who must introduce a human review of AI recommendations to fine-tune the AI. There must be a sense of duty about this since the technology resource base offers Africa a shortcut to scalable platforms that serve the citizenry with good quality medical consultation, school tuition, and business training (among many others).

The adoption rates differ among big corporations in Ghana with respect to AI. Google has a major AI center for Africa that is stationed in Accra but has not necessarily been accessible to young entrepreneurs seeking knowledge. United States collaboration still must be facilitated much better for the fledgling ecosystem of hassling startups to assimilate the vital props that are on offer. The same is true of funding for example, where massive support is needed to connect resources like YCombinator, Startupbootcamp, Techstars etc. into the psyche of innovators. The virtuous cycle of ideation, funding, pivoting, scaling and generating returns is insufficiently enabled but yet vital to development and growth.

AI is currently the huge missing link in the Ghanaian platform play. It is costly to integrate despite having much lower accuracy levels than elsewhere in the world. The interest of governments, academia and industry is way too frail to inject buoyancy into the conversation. The traction though is positive among the early enthusiasts who have built remarkably impressive prototypes that will hopefully serve to persuade the custodians of resources to give the required boost to the space.

Big Data Analytics

A lesson we learned in the telecommunication industry was to keep our analytics simple and scalable. Below is an extract from an upcoming book on that era:

One lesson was in the application portfolio. A business intelligence tool called "Business in the Box" from a partner called PBT (very small). There was a trade automation tool from High Tech Synergy in Nigeria. There were open-source tools like Survey 123. These worked wonders for ensuring the visibility that would energize the limbs of the Sales organization. As cash flows strengthened and motivation peaked, the time would come when the more modern systems would be inevitable. Till then though, we had great teams who simplified the alerts we got on our dashboards, participated in the reviews, and most importantly, created the common language across teams. Engineers were not rocket scientists and sales teams were not magicians. In very healthy meeting settings, we agreed that the services to particular communities required the best adaptations possible, and the capital expenditure budgets, required mutual accountability.

It was not as easy as it sounds in retrospect. The simplification of the scaling process required fiefdoms to be broken and resourcing to be different from what was conventional. Open-mindedness, team support and agility, were extremely critical. Great professional equity was built by technical team leads who decided that the priority was to collaborate and support. There was a shared purpose, and the respect for frontline and market teams soared. Various steering committees ensured that the culture of simplicity to scale, was felt across levels. Most issues were resolved without escalation and the bond between team members allowed very candid exchanges to happen. (Nsarkoh, forthcoming)

The datasets we processed through our patchwork of simple technology were massive within the context. Some of the biggest datasets in Ghana would relate to surveys of one kind or the other, whether in the seismic space, Demography, Geographical Information Systems, Imaging or others. We were able to focus on linking these, so, we had a way of tracing all activity to locations. We knew the townships where customer feedback was indicating operational problems. We could also tell where stakeholders had recommendations or complaints. We designed and deployed network infrastructure or investment according to these needs. We purchased a dataset from the Centre for Remote Sensing and Geographical Information Systems (CERSGIS) of the University of Ghana, and this was the basis on which we tracked the adequacy or otherwise of field agents. The analytical models were fit for purpose and scalable.

In the global context, what we did hardly qualifies for discussion under the Big Data Analytics context. When we evolved from the Business in a Box platform, we went to Hadoop, which by then was a time-tested technology in other jurisdictions but very novel and future-proof in our context. Technology debates have tended to cloud the utility of data models. Many changes have been discussed for years and delivered little value on arrival. It is important to get early results and tailor investments to deliver outcomes that make the highest impact. The skills to make this happen are the biggest differentiator. Leadership that engages across disciplines and makes calls on the basis of the reports available is the most vital ingredient for data sets to scale into extensive big data platforms that match the long-term vision.

Platforms are validated by their analytics and the journey into multi-pronged deployments across education, agriculture, medicine, FINTECH, and the full range of domains will depend on how much omnidirectional visibility can be built in.

Blockchain

Ackah (2023) refers to crypto currencies as the principal instantiation of the block chain in Ghana. The general lack of traction in mainstreaming other dimensions of the sprawling distributed ledgers that constitute block chain is akin to the AI challenge in the sense that the datasets that warrant the technology are not widely available. There is, therefore, insufficient interest in forming the critical mass that can mobilize the needed corporate muscle into the space. Legislation is hardly informed by the rapidly growing technology. In the 2023 cohort of Computer Engineering at the University of Ghana, there was no researcher in blockchain technologies at the thesis presentation. This focus on crypto currencies as the essence of the blockchain opportunity remains a misrepresentation of the sector and what it offers.

Early in 2023, Jack Dorsey (co-founder of Twitter), visited a Blockchain conference in Ghana. While a lot was discussed about the payment space and the enablement of cryptocurrencies, there was very little conversation on the issues of dispersed population statistics, and datasets in general that could benefit from the distributed but dependable architecture of blockchain. While the can keeps getting kicked down the road, the myriad of development challenges, which could be addressed by the technology are looming. Anonymized health records for training AI to do disease detection, diagnosis, and treatment remain unavailable. A lot of the public record-keeping challenges could be matched to the solutions that emerge from the blockchain world.

Skills in smart contracting, solidity programming, dispute resolution, and the universe of domains required will require massive rejuvenation to meet the demands of the space.

Digital Commerce

The aggression of e-commerce players over the years has been palpable. In Ghana, brands like Jumia, Jiji, Tonaton, Hubtel, Bolt, Glovo and many more are becoming very visible in communication and advertising. The opportunity for most developed countries is to formalize the informal sector using these as vectors into formal retail.

Recently, the Brorno app was deployed on Google Playstore and the Apple App stores to deal with the obvious gap between retail trade culture and the more conventional solutions. The idea is that the informal, micro retailers who tend to have simpler value chains can transact online with no item catalogues or fixed prices. A reverse auction is initiated by a buyer who requests merchant quotations for an item or cart. The bids are made by merchants who seek to fulfill the buyer's request. A winning bid is then paid for to an escrow account and credited to the merchant when the delivery piece is fulfilled. The well-known gap between formal and informal retail is gradually being filled up by the simple mechanics of homegrown platforms. It is expected that digital commerce is an opportunity for the modernization of the congested physical markets in Ghana and all countries with underdeveloped trading spaces. The social change it ignites allows efficiency, market transformation, and modernization.

As MTN head of Sales and Distribution, I was directly charged with the registration and oversight of Mobile Financial Services between 2013 and 2021. This effort spanned every market center, social meeting point, and community. The trajectory was inspiring in the peak growth years. Mobile money, though, continues to be dominated by remittances and advanced financial service products. The enablement of vibrant trade in goods and services has shown some encouraging growth, but business value chains continue to weaken, in a few senses. The choice of the phrase "informal sector" to describe the numerous verticals that distribute the output from the narrow manufacturing industries of Ghana and similar countries feels very much like a misnomer. The digitization dividend for goods and services is extensive.

The Ghana Union of Traders Associations (GUTA) boasts 2.5 million registered members and 5 million estimated unregistered members. There is an interest in strengthening the Food and Beverages Association and the individual market leadership structures. Out of these, there is a leadership footprint, which responds to investment in the same way as mobile money did. This space requires some staying power from digital platforms, which must possess the necessary agility in design.

Talent

Leaders are needed for the recommendations that have been made. The flow of work will require the enquiring minds of citizens to pry open better ways of doing what we have always accepted. The African way requires customization and nurturing to make the needed strides in innovation and impact. There are definitely many institutions today that continue to train manpower for the continent's problems and the solutions thereof. The real opportunity is to create new disciplines that integrate the individual tracks of learning and anchor them to the foundations of society.

Engineering as a broad category of knowledge domains allows society to synthesize the concepts of basic science into large-scale projects that transform lives. This can be seen in the reach that electrification and telephony, for example, have attained in Ghana. The difficulties experienced with maintenance, quality, resilience, and availability point to a knowledge gap in ancillary fields that would render engineering effective.

On the journey through manufacturing, retail, telecommunication, and banking, we have often encountered the question of pathways to higher efficiency. The missing link has been partnership, collaboration, integrated workflows, and systems mindsets. Many regard the problems as so complex that total mental rewiring is needed before progress can be made. Our submission is that there are systems engineers and architects who are trained for that purpose. The assimilation of global best practices to determine optimal designs for deploying smartphones across Ghana on the dawn of mobile Internet or authentication systems to back telephony did not require an entirely new Ghanaian. The presence of the polymaths has sometimes helped the trajectory of development. The appreciation of the total systems' perspective allows resilient platforms that cannot be unseated by the whims of minor tyrants.

Platform Play will always require the best quality talent that is possible for public leadership and oversight. It is important though that the work does not stop to usher in ideal leadership. It is important to work within the framework of multilateral dialogue among actors. The triangle of academia, financiers, and innovators must recognize how much power they simultaneously generate to influence policy.The question in relation to platforms is not one of generating more talent in individual domains. It requires professionals who know one or two domains well enough, to rewrite the integration rules to others. In essence, we must address quality!

REFERENCES

Ackah, B. (2023). Ghana's blockchain scene on WhatsApp: A space for convergence and divergence. *Journal of Digital Social Research*, *5*(2), 55–79. doi:10.33621/jdsr.v5i2.141

Amoah, L. G. A. (2014). *Impacts of the knowledge society on economic and social growth in Africa*. IGI Global. doi:10.4018/978-1-4666-5844-8

Berndt, E. R., & Christensen, L. R. (1973). The translog function and the substitution of equipment, structures, and labor in US manufacturing 1929-68. *Journal of Econometrics*, *1*(1), 81–113. doi:10.1016/0304-4076(73)90007-9

Broughel, J., & Thierer, A. (2019). Technological innovation and economic growth: A brief report on the evidence. SSRN *Electronic Journal*. https://doi.org/ doi:10.2139/ssrn.3346495

Davis, F. D. (1985). *A technology acceptance model for empirically testing new end-user information systems: Theory and results* [Doctoral dissertation, Massachusetts Institute of Technology].

Fraumeni, B. M., & Jorgenson, D. W. (1981). Capital formation and US productivity growth, 1948–1976. In A. Dogramaci (Ed.), *Productivity analysis: A range of perspectives* (pp. 49–70). Springer. doi:10.1007/978-94-011-7402-2_4

Gyekye, K. (1997). *Tradition and modernity: philosophical reflections on the African experience*. Oxford University Press. doi:10.1093/acprof:oso/9780195112252.001.0001

Hamel, G. (2002). Innovation now! *Fast company*, 114-124.

Internet World Stats. (2020). *Internet Users Statistics for Africa*. Internet World Stats. https://www.internetworldstats.com/stats1.htm

Jorgenson, D. W. (1984). The role of energy in productivity growth. *The Energy Journal (Cambridge, Mass.)*, *5*(3), 11–26. doi:10.5547/ISSN0195-6574-EJ-Vol5-No3-2

Kearney, H., Kliestik, T., Kovacova, M., & Vochozka, M. (2019). The embedding of smart digital technologies within urban infrastructures: Governance networks, real-time data sustainability, and the cognitive internet of things. *Geopolitics, History, and International Relations*, *11*(1), 98–103. doi:10.22381/GHIR11120195

Koskela, L., & Howell, G. (2002). The Underlying Theory of Project Management is Obsolote. *Proceedings of the PMI Research Conference, 2002*. Research Gate. https://www.researchgate.net/publication/44708842_The_Underlying_Theory_of_Project_Management_is_Obsolete

Maass, W., Natschläger, T., & Markram, H. (2002). Real-time computing without stable states: A new framework for neural computation based on perturbations. *Neural Computation*, *14*(11), 2531–2560. doi:10.1162/089976602760407955 PMID:12433288

Manyika, J., Lund, S., Bughin, J., Woetzel, J., Stamenov, K., & Dhingra, D. (2016, February). *Digital globalization: The new era of global flows*. McKinsey Global Institute. https://www.mckinsey.com/capabilities/mckinsey-digital/our-insights/digital-globalization-the-new-era-of-global-flows

Nukunya, G. K. (1992). *Tradition and change in Ghana: An introduction to sociology*. Ghana Universities Press.

Owoyemi, A., Owoyemi, J., Osiyemi, A., & Boyd, A. (2020). Artificial intelligence for healthcare in Africa. *Frontiers in Digital Health*, *2*, 6. doi:10.3389/fdgth.2020.00006 PMID:34713019

Pressman, R. S. (2010). *Software engineering: A practitioner's approach* (7th ed.). McGraw Hill.

Quarshie, H. O., & Ami-Narh, J. (2012). The growth and usage of Internet in Ghana. *Journal of Emerging Trends in Computing and Information Sciences*, *3*(9).

Rochet, J. C., & Tirole, J. (2003). Platform competition in two-sided markets. *Journal of the European Economic Association*, *1*(4), 990–1029. doi:10.1162/154247603322493212

Sasu, D. D. (2023, December). *E-commerce in Ghana - statistics & facts*. Statista. https://www.statista.com/topics/10270/e-commerce-in-ghana/#topicOverview

Solow, R. M. (1962). Technical progress, capital formation, and economic growth. *The American Economic Review*, *52*(2), 76–86.

UNESCO. (2015, February). *Policy document for the integration of a sustainable development perspective into the processes of the World Heritage Convention*. UNESCO. https://whc.unesco.org/document/139146

Wiredu, K. (1996). *Cultural universals and particulars: an African perspective*. Blackwell Publishing.

ADDITIONAL READING

Amoah, L. G. A. (2014). *Impacts of the knowledge society on economic and social growth in Africa*. IGI Global. doi:10.4018/978-1-4666-5844-8

Coleman, D. (2019). Digital colonialism: The 21st century scramble for Africa through the extraction and control of user data and the limitations of data protection laws. *Michigan Journal of Race & Law*, *24*(24.2), 417–439. doi:10.36643/mjrl.24.2.digital

Hassan, Y. (2023). Governing algorithms from the South: A case study of AI development in Africa. *AI & Society*, *38*(4), 1429–1442. doi:10.1007/s00146-022-01527-7

Jin, D.J. (2013). The construction of platform imperialism in the globalization era. *triple*, *11*(1), 145-172.

Jin, D. J., & Curan, J. (2015). *Digital platforms, imperialism, and political culture*. Routledge.

Jutel, O. (2021). Blockchain imperialism in the Pacific. *Big Data & Society*, *8*(1), 1–14. doi:10.1177/2053951720985249

Mayer, M., Carpes, M., & Knoblich, R. (2014). The global politics of science and technology: an introduction. In M. Mayer, M. Carpes, & R. Knoblich (Eds.), *The global politics of science and technology* (Vol. 1, pp. 1–35). Springer. doi:10.1007/978-3-642-55007-2_1

Mhlanga, D. (2020). Industry 4.0 in finance: The impact of artificial intelligence (AI) ondigital financial inclusion. *International Journal of Financial Studies*, *8*(45), 1–14. doi:10.3390/ijfs8030045

Schiller, D. (1999). *Digital capitalism: networking the global market system*. The MIT Press. doi:10.7551/mitpress/2415.001.0001

Zehle, S. (2012). New world information and communication order. In G. Ritzer (Ed.), *The Wiley-Blackwell Encyclopedia of Globalization* (pp. 1–4). Wiley Blackwell. doi:10.1002/9780470670590.wbeog426

KEY TERM AND DEFINITION

Digital Platform Play: This refers to the technology landscape that allows consumers and suppliers to interact across interfaces defined by computing technology. It is jointly defined by fintech, agritech, etc.

Chapter 12
What Influences Citizen Use of a Digital National Property Addressing System?
The Case of Ghana's GhanaPostGps

Eli Fianu

(iD) https://orcid.org/0000-0003-2308-6831
Ghana Communication Technology University, Ghana

Stephen Boateng
University of Mines and Technology, Ghana

Zelda Arku
University of Mines and Technology, Ghana

ABSTRACT

The chapter attempts to unravel the factors that influence citizens' usage of an e-government location-based service, the Ghana Post GPS. The research model comprises a set of relationships between constructs from UTAUT (effort expectancy, performance expectancy, and social influence; age and gender as moderating variables), the model of PC utilization (complexity and affect towards use), TAM2 (output quality, intention to use, and actual usage). A quantitative research design was used for the study. The sample consisted of three hundred and thirty-seven (337) respondents. Data was analysed using PLS-SEM (partial least squares structural equation modelling) via SmartPLS 3. Twelve (12) hypotheses were tested; eight (8) were rejected while four (4) were accepted. The results are thoroughly discussed, and relevant recommendations made.

INTRODUCTION

A profound technological revolution is sweeping the globe altering governance, business and personal lives in unprecedented ways through emerging technologies such as 5G telecommunications, cloud computing, artificial intelligence (AI), geographic information systems (GIS), and Big Data Analytics

DOI: 10.4018/978-1-6684-9962-7.ch012

(Layton-matthews & Landsberg, 2022). Advancements in technology are driving electronic government and digitalization across the public sector. The term "digitalization" refers to the process of enabling or enhancing processes through the use of digital technologies and digitised data (de Mello & Ter-Minassian, 2020). E-government is the use of information and communication technologies (ICTs) to improve revenue mobilisation, promote citizen participation, and access to improved public services (Grigalashvili, 2022). Digitalization of the public sector is a critical priority for many governments worldwide, especially those in developing economies due to immense pressure to provide transparent, effective and efficient public services to citizens (Mensah, 2020). Information and communication technology (ICT) has the potential to transform virtually all facets of governance including health, education, social services, taxation and communication (Nguyen et al., 2020; Utama, 2020).

Within the public sector, the sustainability of e-government initiatives is dependent on citizens' willingness and ability to use the systems provisioned (Li, 2021). A positive synergy between the supply-side (government) and demand-side (citizens) of digitalised government services is critical to its success (Pérez-Morote et al., 2020). Several developing countries such as Kenya, Ghana, Tanzania, Nigeria and Rwanda have deployed ICT for accelerated development (ICT4D) towards advancing the United Nations agenda for sustainable development goals (SDGs) (Othman et al., 2020) and enhancing socio-economic development (Ramadan & Abdel-Fattah, 2022). In Africa, few countries have implemented digital addressing systems to enhance location accuracy and service delivery. For instance, Liberia's National Digital & Postal Addressing System (NDPAS), powered by SnooCODE, provides a unique 5–7-digit alphanumeric address code to every location, significantly improving address-related services across various sectors (Tech Labari, 2023). Similarly, Nigeria introduced the Nigerian Postal Service (NIPOST) aiding in efficient mail delivery and location services (Ogbonne et al., 2021). E-government platform usage is usually plagued with context-specific challenges such as system complexity, performance, quality and failure to ensure value co-creation with stakeholders (Hu et al., 2019). This study explores the usage intentions of a digital property addressing system; an e-government initiative in a developing country.

The Government of Ghana (GoG) is committing enormous efforts and resources towards the advancement of e-government initiatives aimed at establishing the country as a regional hub for digital services (Adjei-Bamfo et al., 2020). Notable among such e-government initiatives is the national digital property address system (NDPAS), also referred to as Ghana-Post GPS. Ghana as a sovereign state hitherto did not have a property addressing system, a situation which created challenges for local, regional and national authorities across the country to effectively locate and coordinate the resources within their jurisdiction (ACET, 2018). The NDPAS was launched in 2017 to assign a unique digital address to each permanent edifice in the country. The NDPAS is expected to alleviate navigation difficulties faced by emergency response and law enforcement institutions, boost revenue mobilisation from registered businesses and promote national development (PwC, 2017). The NDPAS is a catalyst for national development; however, there is a dearth of research on its adoption and usage.

Few studies have investigated e-government applications from the perspective of property and location addressing platforms. The studies on e-government have been conducted from a broad perspective; there is scanty research focusing on specific e-government platform use (see Meiyanti et al., 2019; Mensah et al., 2021; Verkijika & De Wet, 2018). Verkijika and De Wet, (2018, p. 83) in their study on e-government adoption revealed that "performance expectancy, social influence, perceived risk and computer self-efficacy significantly influenced attitudes, while attitudes, facilitating conditions, trust of government and trust of the Internet had a direct significant influence on behavioural intention". Their study was on e-government in general. There is scanty research on e-government property addressing systems. Given the scarcity of research in this area, the current study aims to conduct a study on an e-government application, that is, the Ghana-Post GPS to fill the gap in the literature. A research model is proposed based on the Unified Theory of Acceptance and Use of Technology (UTAUT), Model of PC Utilization (MPCU), and the extended Technology Acceptance Model (TAM 2) to investigate the factors that influence citizens' usage of the Ghana Post GPS. The proposed model comprises a set of relationships between constructs from the UTAUT (Effort Expectancy, Performance Expectancy, and Social Influence; age and gender as moderating variables), the model of PC utilization (Complexity and Affect Towards Use), and TAM2 (Output Quality, Intention to Use and Actual Usage).

This paper is organised as follows: the next section of the paper outlines the theories that underpin the research model, followed by sections on hypotheses development and methodology. Next, the PLS-SEM results are presented, followed by a discussion of the results and conclusion.

THEORETICAL FOUNDATION

This study is underpinned by three IS adoption theories; UTAUT, MPCU and TAM 2. UTAUT is the base model for this study. It helps users to understand their motivations for using an IS (Venkatesh, 2000). UTAUT was created by fusing eight previous models of technology adoption including "Theory of reasoned action" (TRA), "Technology Acceptance Model" (TAM), "Motivational Model" (MM), "Theory of Planned Behaviour" (TPB), "Model Combining Technology Acceptance Model and Theory of Planned Behaviour" (C-TAM-TPB), "Model of PC Utilization" (MPCU), "Innovation Diffusion Theory" (IDT), and "Social Cognitive Theory" (SCT). Venkatesh et al., (2003) put together empirically tested constructs to formulate UTAUT after an extensive systematic literature review. Yu, (2012) affirms that UTAUT has been empirically tested and hence, has superior performance over the eight-constituent model.

MPCU is substantially based on Triandis' (1977) theory of human behaviour. The model proposed by Triandis was later adapted and refined for the field of information systems by Thompson, Higgins and Howell, (1991). Thompson et al., (1991) in the study used the model to predict IS use and acceptance at the individual level. MPCU takes into account affect towards use, facilitating conditions, long-term effects, perceived consequences, societal pressures, complexity, and job fit.

Using TAM as the core (an established model for explaining IS adoption behaviour), Venkatesh and Davis, (2000, p. 187) "formulated TAM2 by incorporating additional theoretical constructs spanning social influence processes (subjective norm, voluntariness, and image) and cognitive instrumental processes (job relevance, output quality, result demonstrability, and perceived ease of use)".

The current study extends UTAUT with two MPCU constructs (affect towards use and complexity) and one construct from TAM2 (output quality).

HYPOTHESIS DEVELOPMENT

Affect Towards Use

Affect is "the feelings of joy, elation, or pleasure, or depression, disgust, displeasure, or hate associated by an individual with a particular act" (Triandis, 1980, p.36). Triandis, (1980) contends that there is a profound relationship between affect and behaviour in the literature. In the current study, affect towards use reflects users' or citizens' affection or disaffection towards the use of NDPAS. Affect is an individual's personal beliefs about engaging in a particular behaviour, whether they be negative or positive. Numerous scholars have argued in the past that affect towards use has a substantial impact on user intention to adopt new technology systems (Anthony Jnr, 2022; Bervell & Umar, 2020). For instance, in their study on learning management systems, Bervell & Umar, (2020) postulated that lecturers' affect towards the use of ICT is critical for blended learning since it encompasses not only their comprehension and experience with blended learning technologies but also their attitude toward its pedagogical applications. Seemingly, affect alters users' viewpoint, implying that a positive attitude has a substantial effect on the intention to use e-government applications (Zahid & Din, 2019). Therefore, the following hypothesis is proposed:

H1: Affect towards use has a significant influence on intention to use the Ghana-Post GPS app

Complexity

According to Rogers and Shoemaker, (1971, p. 154) "complexity is the degree to which an innovation is perceived as relatively difficult to understand and use". Complexity is the time or effort needed to learn a system (Thompson et al., 1991). Complex innovations are adopted less often (Tornatzky and Klein, (1982). Perceived complexity negatively affects intention to use e-government services, according to Riyadh et al., (2018). Mousa, (2020) revealed complexity as a core technological factor for Cloud-based e-government (CBEG) adoption in Libya along with relative advantage and reliability. It is hypothesized that:

H2: Complexity has a significant influence on intention to use the Ghana-Post GPS app

Social Influence

Social influence is the degree to which a user perceives that important others believe the user should use the technology (Blut, Chong, Tsigna, & Venkatesh, 2022). The current study describes social influence as someone's decision to use the Ghana-Post GPS app due to the opinions of his/her social network. Previous research has shown a strong relationship between social influence and usage intention. For instance, Albashrawi and Motiwalla, (2017) state that the uptake of mobile banking services by customers is influenced by social linkages. Ahmad, Markkula, and Oivo, (2013) argue that e-government adoption is influenced by social ties such as family, colleagues, and friends. Abu-Shanab, (2014) indicated that people's willingness to use e-government services is influenced by their social networks. Additionally, Senshaw and Twinomurinzi, (2021) postulated that social influence on the use of digital government innovation is moderated by gender. It is hypothesized that:

H3a: Social influence has a significant influence on intention to use the Ghana-Post GPS app

H3b: Gender has a significant moderating effect on the relationship between Social influence and Usage Intention

Effort Expectancy

Effort expectancy is "the degree of ease associated with the use of a system" (Venkatesh, et al, 2003, p.451). Effort expectancy is defined in the current study as the level of simplicity of the Ghana-Post GPS app. Though Effort expectancy is vast in the IS literature (Fedorko et al., 2021; Gansser & Reich, 2021), very few studies have used it to investigate e-government innovations (Lessa et al., 2011; Senshaw & Twinomurinzi, 2021). Lessa et al., (2011) found that the influence of effort expectancy on WoredaNet (an e-government application) users' behavioral intention is moderated by gender, age, and experience. Regarding e-business platforms, Pahnila, Siponen, Myyry and Zheng (2011) found that effort expectancy has a significant influence on intention to use the Chinese eBay Platform. Additionally, Gansser and Reich, (2021) found that there is an inverse relationship between effort expectancy and the intention to use e-government applications. Based on the review of the literature, it is hypothesized that:

H4a: Effort expectancy has a significant influence on Intention to use the Ghana-Post GPS app

H4b: Gender has a significant moderating effect on the relationship between Effort Expectancy and Usage Intention

H4c: Age has a significant moderating effect on the relationship between Effort Expectancy and Usage Intention

Performance Expectancy

Performance expectancy is defined "as the degree to which an individual believes that the technology provides benefits to users when performing certain activities" (Blut et al., 2022, p.7). It has previously been used to explore how people expect technology to help them with their jobs (Izuagbe et al., 2021; Gao & Zhang, 2015; Owusu Kwateng, Atiemo & Appiah 2019). Owusu Kwateng et al., (2019) researched mobile banking acceptability and use in Ghana and found that performance expectancy affects behavioral intention to use. Gao and Zhang, (2015) found that performance expectancy influences behavioral intention while using location-sharing services on social networks. Younger people and men are more likely to use new technologies (Yousafzai & Yani-de-soriano, 2012). The influence of performance expectancy on intention to use is moderated by gender and age, with a greater effect for men and younger men (Anderson & Schwager, 2004). The authors of this study posit that the Ghana-Post GPS app enhances location identification and thus facilitates business transactions. It is hypothesized that:

H5a: Performance Expectancy has a significant influence on Intention to use the Ghana-Post GPS app

H5b: Gender has a significant moderating effect on the relationship between Performance Expectancy and Usage Intention

H5c: Age has a significant moderating effect on the relationship between Performance Expectancy and Usage Intention

Output Quality

Output quality refers to the degree to which an individual believes that the system performs his or her job tasks well (Venkatesh & Bala, 2008). Izuagbe et al., (2021) state that output quality is about the system's ability to deliver. Cheng, (2018) found that output quality will positively affect the perceived usefulness of cloud ERP. Additionally, Khoa, Ha, Nguyen and Bich, (2020) studied lecturers' adoption of learning management systems and confirmed that output quality has a positive impact on the perceived usefulness of learning management systems. The authors posit that individuals will find the Ghana Post GPS app useful if the output quality of the app is desirable. It is therefore hypothesized that:

H6: Output Quality has a significant influence on Performance Expectancy

Usage Intention and Actual System Usage

The final hypothesis examines the relationship between intention to use and actual use. Intention to use and actual use have been linked in several studies (Alwreikat, Shehata, & Zaid, 2021; Tao, 2009). Tao (2009) hypothesized that the behavior of intending to utilize an e-resource had a major impact on the actual use, and this was found to be true. Alwreikat et al., (2021) found that the desire to utilize IS has a direct impact on the actual use. The authors posit that if a person intends to use the Ghana-Post GPS, they will utilize it. It is hypothesized that:

H7: Intention to use the Ghana-Post GPS has a significant influence on Actual Usage of the Ghana-Post GPS

Figure 1 shows the research model.

Figure 1. The research model

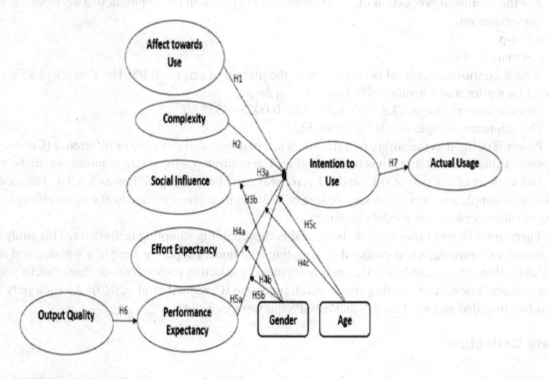

METHODOLOGY

Research Design

The study used a quantitative research design. The quantitative research design was chosen because the researchers wanted to statistically test the influence of independent latent constructs on mediating latent constructs and dependent latent constructs via path analysis.

Sampling

The population for the study comprised citizens of Ghana who had installed and used the GhanaPost GPS app. The Cochran (1963) formula for calculating the sample size for an unknown population size (large populations) was used. The formula is shown below:

$n_0 = Z^2pq/e^2$

where:

n_0 = sample size
Z = the Z score. A z-score describes the position of a raw score in terms of its distance from the mean when measured in standard deviation units
p = the estimated proportion of an attribute that is present in the population. This is also known as the prevalence rate
q = 1-p
e = margin of error
A 95% confidence interval is chosen; thus, the margin of error is 0.05. The Z-score at 95% is 1.96. Based on a pilot study, a value of 0.3 was chosen for p.
From equation (1) n_0 = (3.8416 x 0.3 x 0.6)/ 0.0025 = 322.69
The minimum sample size is therefore 323.
Power is defined as the ability of a statistical test to detect a relationship or difference (Cohen, 1992). A power value is acceptable if it is 0.80 or higher. The minimum sample size required to achieve a power of 0.95 with an effect size of 0.15 and 5% error was calculated using G*Power 3.1.9.4. The calculated minimum sample size was 74. A sample size of 323 will thus give the statistical test the ability to detect relationships between the model constructs.
There are different types of probability and non-probability sampling techniques. This study adopts A purposive sampling, a non-probability sampling technique. Purposive sampling was deemed suitable in that it allows the researcher to use their judgement in selecting respondents or cases that fit a specific criterion and relevant to meeting the research objective (Campbell et al., 2020). As such only people who had installed and used the GhanaPostGPSapp were targeted.

Data Collection

This study relied solely on primary data. The data collection process for this study was done in three distinct steps. That is, survey instrument design, selecting an appropriate channel and administering the questionnaire to respondents. The survey instrument was developed on the basis of theoretical underpinnings for this study and literature review on the topic. This led to the adaptation of previous measurement scales wherever appropriate to suite the current study. Table 1 shows a summary of the research constructs from the proposed conceptual framework, the measurement items, and scholarly sources. An online survey, via google forms was used for data collection. As an ethical consideration, all respondents were assured of confidentiality prior to commencing the survey. Three hundred and thirty-seven (337) valid responses were received.

Table 1. Study constructs and measurement items

Construct	Measurement Items	Adapted Source
User Experience	The GhanaPostGPS app makes my location search more interesting Using the GhanaPostGps app is fun	Thompson et al. (1991)
Complexity	Using the GhanaPostGPS app is complicated. It takes too long to learn how to use the GhanaPostGPS app to make it worth the effort. Using the GhanaPostGPS involves too much time doing technical operations	Thompson et al. (1991)
Social Influence	People who influence my behavior think that I should use the GhanaPostGPS app People who are important to me think that I should use the GhanaPostGPS app Friends and family are helpful in the use of the GhanaPostGPS app In general, friends and family support the use of the GhanaPostGPS app.	Venkatesh et al. (2003)
Effort Expectancy	I believe the GhanaPostGPS app is useful in location search. Using the GhanaPostGPS app enables me to search locations more quickly. Using the GhanaPostGPS app increases my location search productivity	Venkatesh et al. (2003)
Output Quality	If I use the GhanaPostGPS app, I increase my chances of getting better results The quality of the output I get from the app is high I have no problem with the quality of the app's output	Venkatesh and Davies (2000)
App usage intention	I intend to frequently use the GhanaPostGPS app. I predict I will frequently use the GhanaPostGPS app I plan to frequently use the GhanaPostGPS app	Venkatesh et al. (2003)
Actual Usage of the App	I frequently use the GhanaPostGPS app to locate permanent residential addresses. I frequently use the GhanaPostGPS app to locate businesses in permanent structures. I frequently use the GhanaPostGPS app to locate other permanent structures (other than residential and business)	Venkatesh et al. (2003)

DATA ANALYSIS AND RESULTS

Data analysis was done using the partial least squares-structural equation modelling (PLS-SEM) technique via SmartPLS 3. PLS-SEM is appropriate for the non-parametric modelling of complex cause-effect relationships between latent variables (Hair et al., 2012). The two-step approach to PLS-SEM proposed by Chin (1998) is used. The measurement model (outer model) was initially assessed, followed by the assessment of the structural model (inner model). Data cleaning was done before PLS-SEM. The data was checked for missing values and outliers; 331 responses were retained after data cleaning. The demographic profile of the respondents is shown in Table 2.

The measurement model was assessed using reliability, convergent validity, and discriminant validity tests. Reliability was assessed using Cronbach's alpha, composite reliability, and Dijkstra–Henseler's rho. A construct exhibits reliability if Cronbach's alpha, composite reliability, and Dijkstra–Henseler's rho values are 0.7 and above (Hair et al., 2012).

Convergent validity was assessed using the average variance extracted (AVE). A construct exhibits convergent validity if the AVE value is 0.5 and above (Hair et al., 2012). Table 3 shows that all the constructs exhibit reliability and convergent validity.

Discriminant validity was assessed using the heterotrait-monotrait ratio of correlations (HTMT$^{0.90}$). If the HTMT value is below 0.90, discriminant validity has been established between two constructs (Hair et al., 2014). Table 4 shows that all the constructs exhibit discriminant validity.

A bootstrapping procedure was used to assess the structural model to determine the significance of each estimated path. Bootstrapping is the process of drawing a large number of re-samples with replace-

Table 2. Demography of participants

Demographic	Characteristics	No.	(%)
Gender	Female	89	26.4
	Male	248	73.6
	Total	337	100
Age	18- 20	39	11.6
	21-30	226	67.1
	31-40	57	16.9
	41-50	14	4.2
	> 50	1	0.3
	Total	337	100
Education	Diploma	39	11.6
	Doctorate	6	1.8
	First Degree	176	52.2
	Masters	35	10.4
	Other	6	1.8
	Secondary School	75	22.3
	Total	337	100
Employment	Employed	99	29.4
	Partially employed	23	6.8
	Self-employed	25	7.4
	Unemployed	190	56.4
	Total	337	100
Frequency of Use	Occasionally	144	42.7
	Often	32	9.5
	Rarely	143	42.4
	Very often	18	5.3
	Total	337	100
Computer Proficiency	Above average	152	45.1
	Average	177	52.5
	Below average	8	2.4
	Total	337	100

ments from the original sample and then estimating the model parameters for each bootstrap re-sample. The results of the bootstrapping procedure are shown in Table 5. Constructs with p values equal to or less than 0.05 are significant, while constructs with p values greater than 0.05 are not significant. Table 5 shows that four of the hypotheses were supported, that is, H3a, H5a, H6, and H7 while eight hypotheses were not supported, that is, H1, H2, H3b, H4a, H4b, H4c, H5b, and H5c.

The proposed model explained 42.6% of the variance in actual usage, 41.4% of the variance in usage intention, and 40% of the variance in performance expectancy. The R square values are shown in Table

Table 3. Construct reliability and validity

Construct	Cronbach's Alpha	rho_A	Composite Reliability	Average Variance Extracted (AVE)
Actual Usage	0.764	0.850	0.858	0.621
Age	1.000	1.000	1.000	1.000
Complexity	0.778	0.807	0.868	0.687
Effort Expectancy	0.802	0.817	0.883	0.717
Gender	1.000	1.000	1.000	1.000
Intention to Use	0.898	0.900	0.936	0.831
Output Quality	0.759	0.807	0.890	0.802
Performance Expectancy	0.906	0.913	0.934	0.781
Social Influence	0.833	0.847	0.888	0.664
Affect towards use	0.717	0.750	0.874	0.777

Table 4. Heterotrait-monotrait ratio of correlations (HTMT)

	[1]	[2]	[3]	[4]	[5]	[6]	[7]	[8]	[9]	[10]
Actual Usage [1]										
Age [2]	0.066									
Complexity [3]	0.346	0.092								
Effort Expectancy [4]	0.528	0.052	0.515							
Gender [5]	0.124	0.056	0.1	0.019						
Intention to use [6]	0.784	0.093	0.282	0.474	0.129					
Output Quality [7]	0.633	0.054	0.484	0.648	0.013	0.684				
Performance Expectancy [8]	0.669	0.008	0.409	0.69	0.087	0.656	0.74			
Social Influence [9]	0.525	0.047	0.116	0.344	0.16	0.55	0.452	0.524		
Affect towards Use [10]	0.704	0.006	0.388	0.559	0.154	0.587	0.65	0.701	0.603	

5. The standardized root mean square residual (SRMR) was used to assess model fit in SmartPLS. Hu & Bentler (1999) proposed that models that have SRMR values less than 0.08 have a good model fit. Table 5 shows SRMR value of 0.064 which implies the model has a good fit.

DISCUSSION

The current study sought to investigate the factors that influence citizens' usage of an e-government location-based service, the Ghana Post GPS, via the integration of three IS use models. The study showed

Table 5. Hypothesis testing results

Hypothesis	Hypothesized Path	Path Coefficient	t Statistics	P Values	Result
H1	Affect towards Use -> Intention to Use	0.122	1.718	0.086	Not supported
H2	Complexity -> Intention to Use	-0.028	0.564	0.573	Not supported
H3a	Social Influence -> Intention to Use	0.228	4.277	0.000	Supported
H3b	GEND_SOC_INT -> Intention to Use	0.013	0.245	0.807	Not supported
H4a	Effort Expectancy -> Intention to Use	0.048	0.734	0.463	Not supported
H4b	GEND_EFF_INT -> Intention to Use	0.029	0.463	0.643	Not supported
H4c	AGE_EFF_INT -> Intention to Use	-0.005	0.076	0.939	Not supported
H5a	Performance Expectancy -> Intention to Use	0.391	5.304	0.000	Supported
H5b	GEND_PERF_INT -> Intention to Use	0.036	0.533	0.594	Not supported
H5c	AGE_PERF_INT -> Intention to Use	0.011	0.180	0.857	Not supported
H6	Output Quality -> Performance Expectancy	0.629	16.645	0.000	Supported
H7	Intention to Use -> Actual Usage	0.654	18.019	0.000	Supported
	R^2 (Actual Usage) = 0.426				
	R^2 (Usage Intention) = 0.414				
	R^2 (Performance Expectancy) = 0.400				
	SRMR = 0.064				

that intention to use the Ghana Post GPS app is significantly influenced by social influence, performance expectancy, and output quality. Intention to use the app significantly influences actual app usage. Affect towards use, complexity, effort expectancy and the moderating variables (age and gender), were found not to significantly influence intention to use the app.

The non-significance of the relationship between affect towards use and usage intention implies that the nature of the feeling citizens/users experience (pleasure or displeasure) while using the Ghana Post GPS app is not significant in influencing their intention to use the app. There is however a positive relationship between the two constructs which suggests that positive feelings regarding usage will lead to positive usage intentions, and vice versa. The non-significant relationship between affect towards use and usage intention is consistent with Almunawar et al. (2020) who found that affect towards use (hedonic motivation) had a non-significant relationship with user adoption of ride-hailing location-based services. Almunawar et al. (2020) state that early adopters (for instance respondents in Isradila & Indrawati (2015)) are impressed by ride-hailing, thus a positive relationship between affect towards use and intention to use. Almunawar et al. (2020) further state that in the case that respondents are used to the service, it becomes part of their daily lives; using the service has nothing to do with hedonic motivation.

Unlike affect towards use and complexity, our results indicate that social influence is positively associated with intention to use the Ghana Post GPS. This result is consistent with the findings of Graf-Vlachy et al. (2018) who found that social influence profoundly affects human behaviour in general and technology adoption in particular. Our study is also supported by Lee et al. (2017) who reiterated the positive effects of social influence (subjective norms) on the usage intention of location-based applications. This finding implies that family, friends, and peers influence most people in communal cultures with regard to technology usage intention primarily because they are likely to see the positive benefits others obtained by using the Ghana Post GPS (see Babalola, 2019).

The study found that output quality has a positive association with performance expectancy. The finding is supported by Khoa et al. (2020) who found that output quality is a necessary condition for the satisfactory performance and usefulness of learning management systems. This finding implies that for the NDPAS or Ghana Post GPS to hold value for citizens it needs to invariably perform the functions for which it was designed and this can be reflected in the output quality (see Cheng, 2018).

Performance expectancy was found to significantly influence usage intention. It is prevalent in technology adoption research that users' intention to use a new technology is usually influenced by the perception of an expected advantage. This results is consistent with the findings of previous studies (Chao, 2019; Mannan & Haleem, 2017). This finding implies that users intend to use the Ghana Post GPS because they perceive that doing so will generate some positive value or benefit.

The current study found a negative non-significant relationship between complexity and intention to use. This finding suggests the non-significance of complexity in the usage of the Ghana Post GPS. It is likely that users have become used to the app such that they don't find it to be complex. The negative relationship between the constructs suggests that the more complex users find the app, the less their intention to use it, and vice versa.

Effort expectancy was found to have a positive non-significant influence on intention to use the Ghana Post GPS. This result is consistent with Fitriah et al. (2021) who found that there is no significant relationship between effort expectancy and user behavioural intention to use a location-based service. Fitriah et al. (2021) state that the non-significance of complexity means that users do not think much about the application's complexity, including the supporting device. They further state that users will be ready to use a system, regardless of its complexity, if it provides the performance needed to complete a job. The authors affirm the position of Fitriah et al. (2021) because of the significant relationship between performance expectancy and intention to use, in the current study. The effect of effort expectancy may be reduced due to the strong impact of performance expectancy (Aharony, 2015; Fianu et al., 2020; Nair et al., 2015).

Notable among the findings is the non-significance of age and gender as moderating variables. The majority of the respondents were young with ages between 21 and 30, thus, it is anticipated that the effect of age as a moderating variable would be moderate considering the likelihood of technology savviness. Gender on the other hand has been found to have a significant moderating effect on social influence, effort expectancy and performance expectancy (Lee et al., 2019; Rahmi & Frinaldi, 2020). The non-significance of gender as a moderator of this study could be attributed to the disproportionate male respondents over female respondents. This result implies that citizens age and gender do not impact the intention to use the Ghana Post GPS app.

Finally, intention to use was found to significantly influence the actual usage of Ghana Post GPS. Our findings confirm the evidence from previous studies that examined this relationship (Febrianto et al., 2018; Sharma & Sharma, 2019). The results show that a high usage intention will result in increased usage of the Ghana Post GPS application.

CONCLUSION AND RECOMMENDATIONS

This study contributes to the dearth of knowledge on the implementation dynamics of National Digital Property Address systems (NDPAS) from a developing economy context. The findings have shown that whereas social influence and performance expectancy, are constructs that significantly influence the usage of the GhanaPostGPS app, output quality is a significant determinant of performance expectancy. As such managers of NDPAS such as the GhanaPostGPS app in developing economies should give these factors more attention. Regarding performance expectancy, the app should basically be of benefit to users. Managers of the app must engage citizens to find out ways in which the app would be of benefit to them. The relevance of social influence presupposes that there is the need for managers of the app to encourage users to recommend the app to their family, friends, and other people withing their social circle. Managers of the app can use social media and other communication channels to do this. Regarding output quality, user acceptability tests should be conducted to ensure the app has the required output quality. This finding emphasizes the need for extensive testing prior to the implementation of NDPAS apps.

It is also important to note that there are other factors, not studied in this article, that may contribute to either the intention to use or actual use of NDPAS and hence future research can explore other hypothesized factors and relationships. Beyond usage, future research can examine the impact of NDPAS such as the GhanaPostGPS app on both traditional and electronic businesses. This is likely to reveal new insights for post-implementation improvement as well as encourage policy directive for the uptake of NDPAS across Africa and other developing economies.

Conflict of Interest

The authors of this publication declare there is no conflict of interest.

Funding Agency

This research received no specific grant from any funding agency in the public, commercial, or not-for-profit sectors.

REFERENCES

Abu-Shanab, E. (2014). Antecedents of trust in e-government services: An empirical test in Jordan. *Transforming Government: People. Transforming Government*, 8(4), 480–499. doi:10.1108/TG-08-2013-0027

ACET. (2018). *Moving Beyond Aid — Revenue Mobilization G20 Compact with Africa*. ACET. https://www.compactwithafrica.org/content/dam/Compact with Africa/events/BeyondAid_Report2018-1.pdf

Adjei-Bamfo, P., Domfeh, K. A., Bawole, J. N., Ahenkan, A., Maloreh-Nyamekye, T., Adjei-Bamfo, S., & Darkwah, S. A. (2020). An e-government framework for assessing readiness for public sector e-procurement in a lower-middle income country. *Information Technology for Development*, 26(4), 742–761. doi:10.1080/02681102.2020.1769542

Aharony, N. (2015). Factors affecting the adoption of e-books by information professionals. *Journal of Librarianship and Information Science*, 47(2), 131–144. doi:10.1177/0961000614532120

Ahmad, M. O., Markkula, J., & Oivo, M. (2013). Factors affecting e-government adoption in Pakistan: A citizen's perspective. *Transforming Government: People. Transforming Government*, 7(2), 225–239. doi:10.1108/17506161311325378

Albashrawi, M., & Motiwalla, L. (2017). *When IS Success Model Meets UTAUT in a Mobile Banking Context : A Study of Subjective and Objective System Usage. Proceedings of the Southern Association for Information Systems Conference*, St. Simons Island.

Almunawar, M. N., Anshari, M., & Ariff Lim, S. (2020). Customer acceptance of ride-hailing in Indonesia. *Journal of Science and Technology Policy Management, 12*(3), 443–462. doi:10.1108/JSTPM-09-2019-0082

Alwreikat, A., Shehata, A. M. K., & Abu Zaid, M. K. (2021). *Arab scholars' acceptance of informal scholarly communication tools: applying the technology acceptance model 2 (TAM2)*. Global Knowledge, Memory and Communication., doi:10.1108/GKMC-04-2021-0070

Anderson, J. E., & Schwager, P. H. (2004). Association for Information Systems AIS Electronic Library (AISeL) SME Adoption of Wireless LAN Technology: Applying the UTAUT Model SME ADOPTION OF WIRELESS LAN TECHNOLOGY: APPLYING THE UTAUT MODEL. *Association for Information Systems AIS Electronic Library (AISeL), SAIS 2004 Proceedings*. https://aisel.aisnet.org/sais2004%0Ahttp://aisel.aisnet.org/sais2004/6%0Ahttp://aisel.aisnet.org/sais2004%0Ahttp://aisel.aisnet.org/sais2004/6

Anthony, B. Jnr. (2022). An exploratory study on academic staff perception towards blended learning in higher education. *Education and Information Technologies, 27*(3), 3107–3133. doi:10.1007/s10639-021-10705-x

Babalola, S. O. (2019). *Factors influencing behavioral intention to the use of Information and Communication Technology (ICT) among students of Federal Polytechnic, Ilaro.Ogun State*. Library Philosophy and Practice.

Bervell, B., & Umar, I. N. (2020). Blended learning or face-to-face? Does Tutor anxiety prevent the adoption of Learning Management Systems for distance education in Ghana? *Open Learning, 35*(2), 159–177. doi:10.1080/02680513.2018.1548964

Blut, M., Chong, A. Y. L., Tsigna, Z., & Venkatesh, V. (2022). Meta-Analysis of the Unified Theory of Acceptance and Use of Technology (UTAUT): Challenging its Validity and Charting a Research Agenda in the Red Ocean. *Journal of the Association for Information Systems, 23*(1), 13–95. doi:10.17705/1jais.00719

Campbell, S., Greenwood, M., Prior, S., Shearer, T., Walkem, K., Young, S., Bywaters, D., & Walker, K. (2020). Purposive sampling: Complex or simple? Research case examples. *Journal of Research in Nursing, 25*(8), 652–661. doi:10.1177/1744987120927206 PMID:34394687

Chao, C. M. (2019). Factors determining the behavioral intention to use mobile learning: An application and extension of the UTAUT model. *Frontiers in Psychology, 10*(JULY), 1–14. doi:10.3389/fpsyg.2019.01652 PMID:31379679

Cheng, Y. M. (2018). What drives cloud ERP continuance? An integrated view. *Journal of Enterprise Information Management, 31*(5), 724–750. doi:10.1108/JEIM-02-2018-0043

Chin, W. W. (1998). The partial least squares approach to structural equation modeling. *Modern Methods for Business Research, 295*(2), 295–336.

Cochran, W. G. (1963). *Sampling Techniques* (2nd ed.). John Wiley & Sons.

Cohen, J. (1992). Statistical power analysis. *Current Directions in Psychological Science, 1*(3), 98–101. doi:10.1111/1467-8721.ep10768783

de Mello, L., & Ter-Minassian, T. (2020). Digitalisation Challenges and Opportunities for Subnational Governments. *OECD Working Papers on Fiscal Federalism, 31*, 1–24.

Febrianto, G., Hidayatullah, S., & Ardianto, Y. T. (2018). The Effect of Intention to Usage to Actual Usage E-Purchasing Application. *International Journal of Scientific and Engineering Research, 9*(12), 363–370.

Fedorko, I., Bacik, R., & Gavurova, B. (2021). Effort expectancy and social influence factors as main determinants of performance expectancy using electronic banking. *Banks and Bank Systems, 16*(2), 27–37. doi:10.21511/bbs.16(2).2021.03

Fianu, E., Blewett, C., & Ampong, G. O. (2020). Toward the development of a model of student usage of MOOCs. *Education + Training, 62*(5), 521–541. doi:10.1108/ET-11-2019-0262

Fitriah, N., Budi, A., Adnan, H. R., Firmansyah, F., Hidayanto, A. N., Kurnia, S., & Purwandari, B. (2021). Why do people want to use location-based application for emergency situations? The extension of UTAUT perspectives. *Technology in Society, 65*(November 2018), 101480. doi:10.1016/j.techsoc.2020.101480

Gansser, O. A., & Reich, C. S. (2021). A new acceptance model for artificial intelligence with extensions to UTAUT2: An empirical study in three segments of application. *Technology in Society, 65*, 101535. doi:10.1016/j.techsoc.2021.101535

Gao, S., & Zhang, X. (2015). User Adoption of Location Sharing Services on Social Networking Platforms: an experimental study. *Fourteenth Wuhan International Conference on E-Business*, (pp. 333–340). IEEE.

Graf-Vlachy, L., Buhtz, K., & König, A. (2018). Social influence in technology adoption: Taking stock and moving forward. *Management Review Quarterly, 68*(1), 37–76. doi:10.1007/s11301-017-0133-3

Grigalashvili, V. (2022). E-government and E-governance: Various or Multifarious Concepts. *International Journal of Scientific and Management Research, 05*(01), 183–196. doi:10.37502/IJSMR.2022.5111

Hair, J. F., Black, W. C., Babin, B. J., & Anderson, R. E. (2014). *Multivariate data analysis* (7th ed.). Pearson Education International.

Hair, J. F., Sarstedt, M., Pieper, T. M., & Ringle, C. M. (2012). The Use of Partial Least Squares Structural Equation Modeling in Strategic Management Research : A Review of Past Practices and Recommendations for Future Applications. *Long Range Planning, 45*(5–6), 320–340. doi:10.1016/j.lrp.2012.09.008

Hu, G., Yan, J., Pan, W., Chohan, S. R., & Liu, L. (2019). The influence of public engaging intention on value co-creation of e-government services. *IEEE Access : Practical Innovations, Open Solutions, 7*, 111145–111159. doi:10.1109/ACCESS.2019.2934138

Hu, L., & Bentler, P. M. (1999). Cutoff criteria for fit indexes in covariance structure analysis: Conventional criteria versus new alternatives. *Structural Equation Modeling, 6*(1), 1–55. doi:10.1080/10705519909540118

Isradila, ., & Indrawati, . (2015). Analysis of user acceptance towards online transportation technology using UTAUT2 model: a case study in Uber, grab and GO-JEK in Indonesia. *International Journal of Science and Research, 6*(7), 1479–1482.

Izuagbe, R., Olawoyin, O. R., Nkiko, C., Ilo, P. I., Yusuf, F., Iroaganachi, M., Ilogho, J., & Ifijeh, G. I. (2021). Impact analysis of e-Databases' job relevance, output quality and result demonstrability on faculty research motivation. *Library Hi Tech.* doi:10.1108/LHT-03-2020-0050

Khoa, B. T., Ha, N. M., Nguyen, T. V. H., & Bich, N. H. (2020). Lecturers' adoption to use the online Learning Management System (LMS): Empirical evidence from TAM2 model for Vietnam. *Hcmcoujs - Economics and Business Administration, 10*(1), 3–17. doi:10.46223/HCMCOUJS.econ.en.10.1.216.2020

Layton-matthews, B. S., & Landsberg. (2022). *The Fourth Industrial Revolution (4IR) and its Effects on Public Service Delivery in South Africa. 90,* 55–64.

Lee, J., Kim, M., Ham, C. D., & Kim, S. (2017). Do you want me to watch this ad on social media?: The effects of norms on online video ad watching. *Journal of Marketing Communications, 23*(5), 456–472. doi:10.1080/13527266.2016.1232303

Lee, J. M., Lee, B., & Rha, J. Y. (2019). Determinants of mobile payment usage and the moderating effect of gender: Extending the UTAUT model with privacy risk. *International Journal of Electronic Commerce Studies, 10*(1), 43–64. doi:10.7903/ijecs.1644

Lessa, L., Negash, S., & Amoroso, D. L. (2011). Acceptance of WoredaNet e-Government services in Ethiopia: Applying the UTAUT Model. *17th Americas Conference on Information Systems 2011, AMCIS 2011, 2,* (pp. 972–982). AMCIS.

Li, W. (2021). The role of trust and risk in Citizens' E-Government services adoption: A perspective of the extended UTAUT model. *Sustainability (Basel), 13*(14), 7671. doi:10.3390/su13147671

Mannan, B., & Haleem, A. (2017). Understanding major dimensions and determinants that help in diffusion & adoption of product innovation: Using AHP approach. *Journal of Global Entrepreneurship Research, 7*(1), 12. doi:10.1186/s40497-017-0072-4

Meiyanti, R., Utomo, B., Sensuse, D. I., & Wahyuni, R. (2019). E-Government Challenges in Developing Countries: A Literature Review. *2018 6th International Conference on Cyber and IT Service Management.* IEEE. 10.1109/CITSM.2018.8674245

Mensah, I. K. (2020). Impact of Government Capacity and E-Government Performance on the Adoption of E-Government Services. *International Journal of Public Administration, 43*(4), 303–311. doi:10.1080/01900692.2019.1628059

Mensah, R., Cater-Steel, A., & Toleman, M. (2021). Factors affecting e-government adoption in Liberia: A practitioner perspective. *The Electronic Journal on Information Systems in Developing Countries, 87*(3), e12161. doi:10.1002/isd2.12161

Mousa, M. A. S. (2020). Determinants of Cloud Based E-Government in Libya. *Journal of Critical Reviews, 7*(13), 13.

Nair, P. K., Ali, F., & Leong, L. C. (2015). Factors affecting acceptance & use of ReWIND: Validating the extended unified theory of acceptance and use of technology. *Interactive Technology and Smart Education*, *12*(3), 183–201. doi:10.1108/ITSE-02-2015-0001

Nguyen, T. T., Phan, D. M., Le, A. H., & Nguyen, L. T. N. (2020). The determinants of citizens' satisfaction of E-government: An empirical study in Vietnam. *Journal of Asian Finance. Economics and Business*, *7*(8), 519–531. doi:10.13106/jafeb.2020.vol7.no8.519

Ogbonne, I. P., Omeje, A. N., & Omenma, J. T. (2021). Utilisation of information and communication technology among informal traders in the local economies in Nigeria. *International Journal of Entrepreneurship and Small Business*, *44*(3), 211–234. doi:10.1504/IJESB.2021.119228

Othman, M. H., Razali, R., & Nasrudin, M. F. (2020). Key Factors for E-Government towards Sustainable Development Goals. *International Journal of Advanced Science and Technology*, *29*(6s), 2864–2876.

Owusu Kwateng, K., Osei Atiemo, K. A., & Appiah, C. (2019). Acceptance and use of mobile banking: An application of UTAUT2. *Journal of Enterprise Information Management*, *32*(1), 118–151. doi:10.1108/JEIM-03-2018-0055

Pahnila, S., Siponen, M., Myyry, L., & Zheng, X. (2011). the Influence of Individualistic and Collectivistic Values To Utaut: the Case of the Chinese Ebay. *Ecis, 2011*. https://aisel.aisnet.org/ecis2011/45

Pérez-Morote, R., Pontones-Rosa, C., & Núñez-Chicharro, M. (2020). The effects of e-government evaluation, trust and the digital divide in the levels of e-government use in European countries. *Technological Forecasting and Social Change*, *154*(March), 119973. doi:10.1016/j.techfore.2020.119973

PwC. (2017). *Putting Ghana Back to Work*. PWC. https://www.pwc.com/gh/en/assets/pdf/2018-budget-highlights.v2.pdf

Rahmi, Y., & Frinaldi, A. (2020). *The Effect of Performance Expectancy, Effort Expectancy, Social Influence and Facilitating Condition on Management of Communities-Based Online Report Management in Padang Pariaman District*. Atlantis Press. doi:10.2991/assehr.k.200803.059

Ramadan, I. M. M., & Abdel-Fattah, M. A. (2022). a Proposed Model for Enhancing E-Government Services To Achieve the Sustainable Development Goals in Egypt " Case Study. *Journal of Theoretical and Applied Information Technology*, *100*(1), 268–285.

Riyadh, H. A., Alfaiza, S. A., & Sultan, A. A. (2018). The effects of technology, organisational, behavioural factors towards utilization of egovernment adoption model by moderating cultural factors. *Journal of Theoretical and Applied Information Technology*, *97*(8), 2142–2165.

Rogers, E. M., & Shoemaker, F. F. (1971). *Communication of Innovations; A Cross-Cultural Approach* (2nd ed.). The Free Press.

Senshaw, D., & Twinomurinzi, H. (2021). The Moderating Effect of Gender on Adopting Digital Goverment Innovations in Ethopia. *Conference on Implications of Information and Digital Technologies,* (pp. 734–751). IEEE.

Sharma, S. K., & Sharma, M. (2019). Examining the role of trust and quality dimensions in the actual usage of mobile banking services: An empirical investigation. *International Journal of Information Management, 44*(September 2018), 65–75. doi:10.1016/j.ijinfomgt.2018.09.013

Tao, D. (2009). Intention to use and actual use of electronic information resources: further exploring Technology Acceptance Model (TAM). *AMIA ... Annual Symposium Proceedings / AMIA Symposium. AMIA Symposium, 2009*, 629–633.

Tech Labari. (2023). *SnooCODE Partners with Liberian Government to Launch National Digital Postal Addressing System.* Tech Labari. https://techlabari.com/snoocode-partners-with-liberian-government-to-launch-national-digital-postal-addressing-system.

Thompson, R. L., Higgins, C. A., & Howell, J. M. (1991). Personal computing: Toward a conceptual model of utilization. *Management Information Systems Quarterly, 15*(1), 125–142. doi:10.2307/249443

Tornatzky, L. G., & Klein, K. J. (1982). Innovation Characteristics and Innovation Adoption-Implementation: A Meta-Analysis of Findings. *IEEE Transactions on Engineering Management. IEEE Transactions on Engineering Management, 29*(1), 28–45. doi:10.1109/TEM.1982.6447463

Triandis, H. C. (1980). Reflections on trends in cross-cultural research. *Journal of Cross-Cultural Psychology, 11*(1), 35–58. doi:10.1177/0022022180111003

Utama, A. . G. S. (2020). The implementation of e-government in indonesia. *International Journal of Research in Business and Social Science (2147- 4478), 9*(7), 190–196. doi:10.20525/ijrbs.v9i7.929

Venkatesh, V. (2000). Determinants of Perceived Ease of Use: Integrating Control, Intrinsic Motivation, and Emotion into the Technology Acceptance Model. *Information Systems Research, 11*(4), 342–365. doi:10.1287/isre.11.4.342.11872

Venkatesh, V., & Agarwal, R. (2006). Turning visitors into customers: A usability-centric perspective on purchase behavior in electronic channels. *Management Science, 52*(3), 367–382. doi:10.1287/mnsc.1050.0442

Venkatesh, V., & Davis, F. D. (2000). Theoretical extension of the Technology Acceptance Model: Four longitudinal field studies. *Management Science, 46*(2), 186–204. doi:10.1287/mnsc.46.2.186.11926

Venkatesh, V., Morris, M. G., Davis, G. B., & Davis, F. D. (2003). Human Acceptance of Information Technology. *MIS, 27*(3), 425–478. doi:10.1201/9780849375477.ch230

Verkijika, S. F., & De Wet, L. (2018). E-government adoption in sub-Saharan Africa. *Electronic Commerce Research and Applications, 30*(May), 83–93. doi:10.1016/j.elerap.2018.05.012

Yousafzai, S., & Yani-de-Soriano, M. (2012). Understanding customer-specific factors underpinning internet banking adoption. *International Journal of Bank Marketing, 30*(1), 60–81. doi:10.1108/02652321211195703

Yu, C. S. (2012). Factors affecting individuals to adopt mobile banking: Empirical evidence from the utaut model. *Journal of Electronic Commerce Research, 13*(2), 105–121.

Zahid, H., & Din, B. H. (2019). Determinants of intention to adopt e-government services in Pakistan: An imperative for sustainable development. *Resources*, *8*(3), 128. doi:10.3390/resources8030128

ADDITIONAL READING

Acheampong, R. A., Siiba, A., Okyere, D. K., & Tuffour, J. P. (2020). Mobility-on-demand: An empirical study of internet-based ride-hailing adoption factors, travel characteristics and mode substitution effects. *Transportation Research Part C, Emerging Technologies*, *115*, 102638. doi:10.1016/j.trc.2020.102638

Dzisi, E., Obeng, D. A., Tuffour, Y. A., & Ackaah, W. (2023). Digitalization of the paratransit (trotro) using mobility as a service: What are the adoption intentions of operators and operator unions in Ghana? *Research in Transportation Business & Management*, *47*, 100968. doi:10.1016/j.rtbm.2023.100968

Fauzi, A. A., & Sheng, M. L. (2020). Ride-hailing apps' continuance intention among different consumer groups in Indonesia: The role of personal innovativeness and perceived utilitarian and hedonic value. *Asia Pacific Journal of Marketing and Logistics*, *33*(5), 1195–1219. doi:10.1108/APJML-05-2019-0332

He, M., & Liang, X. (2021). An empirical study on the impacts of multi-facet benefits on continued usage intention: Evidence from carsharing services in China. *International Journal of Electronic Business*, *16*(2), 157–185. doi:10.1504/IJEB.2021.115721

Lavuri, R. (2023). Ride-hailing apps' continuance intention among millennials in the indian emerging market: A mediation and moderation analysis. In Exploring Business Ecosystems and Innovation Capacity Building in Global Economics. doi:10.4018/978-1-6684-6766-4.ch012

Ofori, K. S., Chai, J., Adeola, O., Abubakari, A., Ampong, G. O. A., Braimah, S. M., & Boateng, R. (2023). Exploring users' continuance intention towards a peer-to-peer accommodation sharing platform. *Journal of Hospitality and Tourism Technology*, *14*(3), 330–346. doi:10.1108/JHTT-04-2020-0074

Oliveira, T., Barbeitos, I., & Calado, A. (2022). The role of intrinsic and extrinsic motivations in sharing economy post-adoption. *Information Technology & People*, *35*(1), 165–203. doi:10.1108/ITP-01-2020-0007

Tsou, H.-T., Chen, J.-S., Chou, C. Y., & Chen, T.-W. (2019). Sharing economy service experience and its effects on behavioral intention. *Sustainability (Basel)*, *11*(18), 5050. doi:10.3390/su11185050

Tumaku, J., Ren, J., Boakye, K. G., Ofori, K. S., & Abubakari, A. (2023). Interplay between perceived value, trust and continuance intention: Evidence in the sharing economy. *International Journal of Quality and Service Sciences*, *15*(1), 74–96. doi:10.1108/IJQSS-05-2022-0048

Yang, H., & Xia, L. (2022). Leading the sharing economy: An exploration on how perceived value affecting customers' satisfaction and willingness to pay by using DiDi. *Journal of Global Scholars of Marketing Science: Bridging Asia and the World*, *32*(1), 54–76. doi:10.1080/21639159.2020.1808833

KEY TERMS AN DEFINITIONS

Digital Address: A unique alphanumeric address assigned to a permanent structure based on GPS data.

E-Government: Internet-based services (such as websites) provided by the government to provide government services to citizens and organizations (private and government).

Ghana Post GPS: A digital addressing system managed by Ghana Post Company Limited

Global Positioning System (GPS): A system that provides location and time information anywhere on or near the earth. It is a satellite-based navigation system.

Location-Based Services: Applications that use a device's location data, for instance GPS, Wi-Fi, or cellular network information, to offer services or information relevant to the user's location.

Chapter 13
Quantum Leap and Uptake for Technological Advances in Africa in the Era of the COVID–19 Crisis

Emmanuel de-Graft Johnson Owusu-Ansah

iD https://orcid.org/0000-0002-3678-7314

Kwame Nkrumah University of Science and Technology, Ghana

Richard Kodzo Avuglah

iD https://orcid.org/0000-0003-2034-7071

Kwame Nkrumah University of Science and Technology, Ghana

Yaa Adwubi Kyere

Kwame Nkrumah University of Science and Technology, Ghana

ABSTRACT

This chapter explores how the COVID-19 pandemic affected technology in Africa, focusing on technological innovations and uptake. The COVID-19 pandemic has encouraged industrial innovation and digital transformation in Africa. The COVID-19 pandemic has shown that traditional methods are ineffectual, and technology is needed. African nations need digital technology to improve healthcare, education, e-commerce, and governance. Technology narrows the digital divide by improving productivity, access to critical services, and promoting economic development. Telemedicine, e-learning, digital payments, and remote working made Africa resilient in the face of the pandemic. The chapter evaluates African technical problems and potential. Poor infrastructure, internet connectivity, high fees, and digital illiteracy are critical issues that need to be addressed. The chapter suggests that government, industry, and international organizations work together to solve these problems. COVID-19 might boost African technology. Technology may boost African economies and living standards through digital transformation if the aforementioned critical issues are overcome.

DOI: 10.4018/978-1-6684-9962-7.ch013

INTRODUCTION.

In the aftermath of the COVID-19 pandemic's unparalleled worldwide disruption, a narrative of resistance and creativity has arisen, particularly in the context of Africa's technological landscape. While the crisis has presented significant obstacles, it has also served as a stimulus for a quantum jump in the use and integration of technology throughout the continent's diverse industries. This book chapter digs into the pandemic's revolutionary influence on technology advancements in Africa, examining how need has pushed quick adoption and deployment of digital solutions.

As curfews and social isolation became the new normal, there was an urgent need to bridge physical gaps via digital technology. African innovators and governments alike adapted swiftly, understanding that reliable internet and mobile connectivity were no longer a luxury but a need. This period saw a rapid expansion of broadband infrastructure and an endeavor to make internet access more affordable and widespread. The chapter examines how these initiatives have aided in the democratization of information flow and the continuity of education, business, and governance.

As the healthcare system became the front lines in the virus's combat, it was put under great strain. The popularity of telemedicine platforms, AI-powered diagnostic tools, and mobile health applications enable remote patient care and smart resource management. The pandemic emphasized the critical role of technological innovation in improving healthcare resilience, leading to agreements between technology companies, governments, and international organizations to offer healthcare practitioners cutting-edge tools.

Financial technology is a notable area in which Africa has achieved tremendous progress. Due to the scarcity of physical banking, fintech solutions such as contactless payments, mobile money services, and online banking have surged in popularity. Fintech has provided convenience throughout the pandemic and promoted financial inclusion for underserved groups.

Due to the disruption in traditional educational institutions, a quick shift to e-learning platforms was critical. Educational institutions, from elementary schools to universities, have embraced digital technology to encourage lifelong learning and continue to be integrated into traditional learning, sparking numerous online learning and certification avenues for would-be learners and creating additional revenues for educational facilitators through online course content creation.

Moreover, due to the crisis, many people turned to digital platforms to make a living. The emergence of digital entrepreneurship and its consequences for job creation and skill development in Africa's workforce has seen substantial growth over the years, shifting the overdependence on governments for job creation and launching local digital entrepreneurship into the global marketplace, competing with the rest of the world and connecting the globe.

THEORETICAL FRAMEWORK OF TECHNOLOGY UPTAKE.

This study is explained by varied theories, which include the Theory of Reasoned (TR), the Theory of Planned behavior (TPB), the Technology Acceptance Model (TAM), the Enhanced Technology Acceptance Model (TAM2), the Unified Theory of Acceptance and Use of Technology's (UTAUT) and the of Innovation Diffusion Theory. The study of Technology adoption and post-adoption behaviors is deeply rooted in social psychology, with the Theory of Reasoned Action (TRA) and Theory of Planned Behaviour (TPB) playing critical roles in establishing the theoretical framework. These intention-based theories and their applied counterparts, such as the Technological Acceptance Model (TAM), pave the way for a more complex explanation of people's decisions to adopt and use technological innovations and ICT. Adding new theories, such as Innovation Diffusion Theory and Social Cognitive Theory, broadens the theoretical landscape and allows for a more in-depth examination of the complex dynamics of technological innovation adoption that spearhead the quantum lead of technological uptake during the Covid crisis era.

Theory of Reasoned

The Theory of Reasoned Action (TRA), created in 1975 by Fishbein and Ajzen, is a well-known social psychology theory that explains individual action through behavioral purpose. TRA serves as a core theoretical framework in ICT adoption and use research. According to the idea, behavioral intention is determined by an individual's attitude toward the conduct and their impression of subjective norms associated with that behavior. Other dimensions in ICT adoption include satisfaction, image, and perceived usefulness. Researchers have coupled TRA with other theories and models to explain technological adoption dynamics better. Studies by Brown et al. (2002), Karahanna et al. 1999), and Hsieh et al. (2008) have highlighted the pivotal role.

Theory of Planned Behaviour

TPB, like TRA, is a well-established social psychology theory that suggests that distinct salient beliefs influence behavioral intentions and subsequent conduct, as proposed by Ajzen in 1991. Unlike TRA, TPB adds a construct known as Perceived Behavioral Control (PBC), which is defined as one's perceptions about their ability to do a specific action easily.

TPB has been employed as a theoretical framework in several studies on ICT adoption and usage, including works by Hsu and Chiu (2004) and Liao et al. (2007). This research, like TRA studies, has frequently discovered significant relationships between attitude, subjective norm, perceived behavioral control, and behavioral intention. Incorporating PBC in TPB has offered insights into the importance of perceived difficulty in the activity and the individual's perceived ability to carry out the behavior. Research has shown that PBC directly impacts technology adoption intention (Chau & Hu, 2001; Wu & Chen, 2005) and prolonged usage intention (Hsu et al., 2006; Liao et al.,2007). This demonstrates the importance of perceived behavioral control in influencing intentions and subsequent actions related to technology adoption and use.

Technology Acceptance Model

The Theories of Reasoned Action (TRA) and Theory of Planned Behavior (TPB) have had a considerable impact on the Technology Acceptance Model (TAM) and its augmented variants, which are extensively used to research the adoption and use of Information and Communication Technology (ICT). Davis developed TAM in 1989 (Davis, 1989)as a framework for describing the factors that influence end-user computer system adoption. TAM comprises two key constructs: perceived utility (PU) and perceived ease of use (PEOU), influencing the desire to utilize a system (Venkatesh, 2000). TAM has served as the theoretical foundation for several research aimed at better understanding ICT uptake and. It has been demonstrated that PU is positively associated with adoption and future intentions (Thong et al., 2006).

PU has been found to influence satisfaction and attitude toward technology in post-adoption studies. Another TAM component, PEOU, impacts both PU and adoption intent. PEOU has been demonstrated to predict satisfaction, continuation intention, and continuation usage after adoption (Dishaw & Strong, 1999). Despite its significance in analyzing ICT adoption and usage, TAM has been criticized for flaws such as the original model's intended universality and parsimony, failure to account for non-organizational contexts, and failure to account for moderating influences in various ICT adoption and use scenarios. Scholars have identified these limits, sparking continuous discussions about improving TAM to cope with the complexities of technology adoption scenarios (Sun & Zhang, 2006).

Enhance Technology Acceptance Model (TAM2)

To address the inadequacies of the Technology Acceptance Model (TAM), Venkatesh and Davis (2000) created the Extended Technology Acceptance Model (TAM2). TAM2 tried to provide a more detailed account of the factors influencing perceived utility ratings. TAM2 expanded on the original TAM by including social influence processes (subjective norm, voluntaries, image, and experience) as well as cognitive instrumental processes (job relevance, output quality, and outcome demonstrability) (Chan & Lu, 2004; Venkatesh & Davis, 2000). TAM2 focused on the social factors that impact people's judgments of usefulness, focusing on terms such as subjective norm and image. The image was used to investigate subjective norm, a well-known TRA and TPB concept. Image is defined as how individuals prefer to be regarded (Karahanna et al., 1999). Several studies have revealed that appearance influences perceived usefulness and attitude. Despite adding new components to increase explanatory power, TAM2 only described a tiny part of a system's utilization (Lu et al., 2005). In response to this constraint, Venkatesh, Morris, Davis, and Davis established the Unified Theory of Acceptance and Use of Technology (UTAUT) paradigm in 2003. UTAUT attempted to solve the same explanatory challenges mentioned in TAM2 and advanced knowledge of technology acceptance and usage (Venkatesh et al., 2003).

Unified Theory of Acceptance and Use of Technology (UTAUT's)

The Unified Theory of Acceptance and Use of Technology (UTAUT) explains how variables impacting intention and behavior evolve. UTAUT proposes three direct predictors of use behavior (intention and enabling circumstances) and three direct predictors of use intent (performance expectation, effort expectancy, and social influence). Gender, age, experience, and voluntariness of usage all impact these correlations. According to the UTAUT empirical study, there are substantial relationships between performance expectation, effort expectation, and social effect with technical aim. A subsequent study found that social effects (Hong . et al., 2006; Lu, et al., 2005) impact perceived usefulness and ease of usage. However, research on the impact of social influence on continued intention has been contradictory (Hong . et al., 2006; Hong. et al., 2008), with some studies finding substantial linkages ((Chiu & Wang, 2008)) and others finding non-significant ones. UTAUT differentiates itself as a comprehensive theory that includes various individual difference categories as moderating factors, including gender, age, experience, and voluntariness of usage. Despite some contradictions in prior research addressing individual variations, experts have established that gender, age, previous experience, and voluntariness of usage all strongly moderate the correlations indicated in UTAUT. The model's adaptability and applicability in a wide range of technology adoption situations is enhanced by this rigorous examination of individual attributes (Morris et al., 2005; Venkatesh & Morris, 2000; Venkatesh, et al., 2003; Morris & Venkatesh, 2000; Venkatesh & Davis, 1996; Venkatesh, et al., 2003).

Innovation Diffusion Theory

Rogers' Innovation Diffusion Theory (IDT) is used to examine people's technology uptake (Rogers, 2003). IDT attempts to understand innovation adoption by looking at four factors: innovation, time, communication channels, and social systems. Individuals' technology adoption behavior is impacted by their views of relative benefit, compatibility, complexity, trialability, observability, and social norms, according to IDT (Ritu et al., 1997; Brancheau & Wetherbe, 1990).

To explain ICT adoption and use, some research has used IDT as a theoretical framework or coupled it with other theories/models. According to information systems (IS) academics, classical diffusion principles are achievable in end-user computer situations, as well as relative usage intention (Lin et al., 2006). In ICT adoption and usage research, the five basic qualities of IDT—relative benefit, compatibility, complexity, trialability, and observability—have been found to correspond to many metrics significantly. Relative advantage, for example, is positively related to attitude and relative usage intention. Compatibility influences perceived utility, ease of use, attitude, and intent. On the other hand, complexity has a negative relationship with technology adoption intention. These studies emphasize the relevance of perceived advantages, compatibility, and simplicity in changing customers' attitudes and intentions toward adopting new technologies (Hernandez et al., 2010; Lee et al., 2003; Saeed & Muthitacharoen, 2008; Beatty et al., 2001; Son & Benbasat, 2007).

THE CHAPTER'S PURPOSE AND METHODOLOGY

The specific objective and scope are to examine how technology affected numerous aspects of African society during the pandemic and bring to the forefront technological advances. This chapter seeks to present, analyze, and discuss with specific countries' examples the role and significance of technological innovations, advancements, and uptake in Africa in response to the challenges posed by the COVID-19 pandemic, leading to a quantum leap in technology earlier predicted to happen in a decade.

In this study, a comprehensive literature search was undertaken in June 2023 using several academic databases, including Google Scholar, Web of Science, ERIC, Science Direct, PubMed, and the Directory of Open Access Journals. The search was conducted by using the search keywords "Africa AND Innovations AND Coronavirus OR COVID-19 AND Technology OR [Country] AND Coronavirus OR COVID-19 AND TECHNOLOGY" in order to locate any publications that may have been overlooked in the first searches. We included articles that discussed the use of technology in the management of COVID-19 across several nations. The papers used in our study encompassed publications sourced only from scholarly journals, reputable news outlets, governmental entities, and esteemed organizations, including the United Nations and the World Health Organization (WHO). In all, 145 articles comprising of 47 research publications and 98 news items, Civil Society organizations reports, government agencies, independent organizations, and quasi-governmental/international institutions reports. After filtering, 73 articles were classified as irrelevant to the study, leaving 72 for the study; the remaining cut across multiple areas of interest for the study, such as disease prevention technologies, Clinical supplies management, diagnosis of diseases, technological growth, technology for non-pharmaceutical interventions, technology and adoptions, technology regulations and guidelines. The study make use of case study systematic review to analyse the evidential reports in the literature gathered and delve deeper into the results by shedding insight on the various findings of the case studies in the various countries.

AFRICAN TECHNOLOGY ACCESS AND INFRASTRUCTURE DURING THE PANDEMIC

The International Telecommunication Union (ITU) Report 2021 gave an interesting look into Africa's technological access from 2017 to 2020. According to the report (ITU, 2021), the region has shown consistent, albeit moderate, growth in ICT infrastructure, access, and utilization during the last four years. The report indicates that mobile cellular coverage in Africa was 88.4 percent. This figure depicts the percentage of the population that lives within the geographic range of a mobile cellular signal. Moreover, a sizable majority of the population, specifically 77%, can connect to a 3G signal.

Furthermore, 44.3% of people can access a long-term evolution (LTE) mobile broadband signal. The percentage of people who use the Internet increased from 24.8 percent in 2017 to 28.6 percent at the end of 2019. Similarly, home Internet connectivity increased by 0.1 percentage point, rising from 14.2 percent in 2017 to 14.3 percent by the end of 2019.

Over the last four years, there has been a significant expansion in both the fixed and mobile broadband sectors, with the number of active mobile broadband connections now exceeding that of fixed internet subscriptions. However, there is still severe gender disparity and a divide between rural and urban communities. In 2019, the proportion of women who used the Internet was 20.2 percent, while males used the Internet at a greater rate of 37.1 percent.

Likewise, although only 6.3% of rural families had access to Internet connectivity in 2019, metropolitan households had a substantially higher proportion of 28% (Figure 1). According to 2019 data, a sizable proportion of people aged 15 to 24, namely 39.6 percent, used the Internet. This ratio exceeds the regional standard, although it is still much lower than the global average of 69 percent, as seen in figure 1

Technological Access in the face of the Pandemic

The Issue Brief (2023) by Observer Research Foundation contended that, compared to other regions, the pandemic has had a disproportionately devastating impact on the African continent. However, its response has shown a propensity for resourcefulness in the face of adversity. The efficient response to the COVID-19 pandemic in Africa was aided by technological advancements such as remote healthcare access, real-time information distribution, and digital transaction platforms. Implementing a careful and progressive approach to digital transformation was critical for governments, companies, and individuals in light of the pandemic's repercussions. This was especially noteworthy given that the informal sector employs a large share of the population in the region.

Both governments and people have utilized new technologies to improve healthcare service, deepen customer relationships, and increase involvement. Handling the pandemic's impact on public health and the economy required several entities, including the Africa Centre for Disease Control (CDC), to implement coordinated actions.

According to a World Health Organization (WHO) estimate, Africa will see the piloting or acceptance of more than 120 health technology innovations in 2020. These breakthroughs accounted for roughly

Figure 1. Key ICT statistics, Africa region, 2017-2020

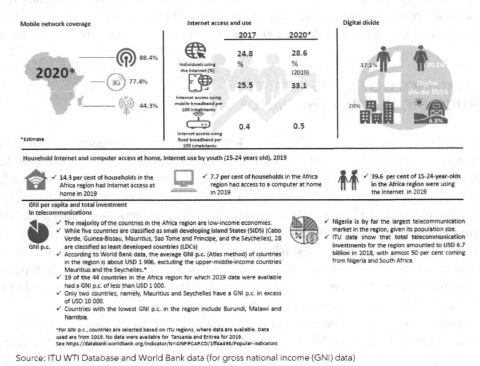

Source: ITU WTI Database and World Bank data (for gross national income (GNI) data)

12.8% of the global output of such technology. The technology in question enhanced many parts of the COVID-19 response, including monitoring, contact tracing, community participation, treatment, laboratory infrastructure, and prevention and control measures, in line with this, South Africa had the highest proportion of inventions, accounting for 13% of all. Kenya came in second with a rate of 10%, while Nigeria and Rwanda had rates of 8% and 6%, respectively. The growing need for digital forms of communication, solid broadband infrastructure, and the usage of financial technology (fintech) is evidence of digital technologies' widespread acceptance across industries. The use of e-commerce platforms and virtual workplaces increased significantly.

The presence and utilization of mobile phones in Africa offered a substantial potential for integrating this technology into healthcare delivery systems. A recent study indicated that rate of mobile phone adoption in Africa reached 44% by the conclusion of 2017, and it is anticipated to increase to 52% by 2025 (Olayiwola et al., 2020). Based on the latest mobile usage data provided by GSMA for several African nations, it is observed that 91% of people in South Africa possess a mobile phone.

Similarly, mobile phone ownership rates are 80% in Ghana, Nigeria, and Kenya, 79% in Senegal, and 75% in Tanzania (GSMA, 2019). GSMA again previously projected that by 2019, about 556 million individuals in Africa, accounting for 54.2% of the population, will have access to a functional fiber optic network. Nevertheless, it is worth noting that numerous African nations continue to have limited bandwidth, namely at 63 kb/s. In stark contrast, G7 and G20 countries, such as the United States, boast significantly higher bandwidth capabilities, reaching up to 270,000 megabits per second (Addo, 2019).

Despite the prevailing issue of limited internet access and the substantial portion of the inhabitants lacking access to broadband technologies and associated services, Governments within the continent are steadfast in their dedication to enhancing internet accessibility for their constituents. This phenomenon is evident in several national telecommunications initiatives (Africa Regional Initiative Report, 2018), exemplified by the broadband plan to achieve widespread and reasonable connectivity and accessibility. It is a relief to note that the successes choked by various were enormous, as more countries saw substantial growth and adoption in the various technological innovations in Africa, as seen in Table 1.

Table 1. Technological uptake of selected african countries during the COVID-19 pandemic, based on various indicators:

Country	Internet Penetration (%)	Mobile Phone Penetration (%)	E-commerce Growth (%)	Mobile Money Growth (%)	Telemedicine Adoption (%)	Online Learning Adoption (%)
Egypt	48	94	25.9	26.1	High	High
Algeria	16	98	20.8	10.5	Medium	Medium
Morocco	58	95	28.3	39.1	High	High
Tunisia	43	123	26.5	8.9	Medium	Medium
Libya	17	127	3.4	2.8	Low	Low
Uganda	19	70	32.5	16.5	High	High
Tanzania	6	76	17.4	3.2	Low	Medium
Ethiopia	15	44	5.5	5.5	Medium	Low
Angola	14	44	25.8	17.5	High	Medium
Ivory Coast	16	85	20.1	17.6	High	Medium
Senegal	28	84	33.3	31.3	High	High
Cameroon	6	50	10.5	5.6	Low	Medium
Democratic Republic of Congo	6	22	6.5	4.1	Low	Low
Burkina Faso	13	73	21.4	18.3	High	Low
Zambia	15	84	27.6	12.7	High	Medium

Sources: • Internet Penetration and Mobile Phone Penetration: GSMA Intelligence, 2021. E-commerce Growth: Statista, 2021, Mobile Money Growth: GSMA, 2020.

Innovations in Healthcare, Education, and Technology

Overview of Healthcare Technological Advancements During COVID-19

Several African nations have employed various technological advancements, including telemedicine, unmanned aerial vehicles (UAVs), and mobile health applications, to enhance their efforts in combating the pandemic. A smartphone application was built in Rwanda with the purpose of monitoring and tracing COVID-19 instances, as well as offering contact details.

Unmanned aerial vehicles (UAVs), commonly called drones, were employed to deliver essential medical resources to geographically isolated regions in South Africa, Rwanda, Malawi, and Ghana. In Kenya, telemedicine services provide patients with remote consultation and diagnosis. African nations have employed e-health technology to support treating individuals affected by infections, monitor the travel history of infected individuals, and gather crucial data necessary for effective and coordinated governance.

There is a prevailing belief among health professionals that utilizing these technologies will benefit them, leading to a faster adoption and integration of digital innovation in the healthcare sector. However, it is worth noting that the actual progress of their implementation on the continent has been slower than anticipated in recent years; somehow, thanks to the pandemic, the uptake has seen astronomical growth (Okereafor et al. 2020),.

Moreover, preceding the onset of the COVID-19 pandemic, using SMS-based communication for health education to distribute valuable information was a prevalent approach. Zimbabwe's Maisha, developed by Econet, and Burkina Faso's Hello Health, developed by AlloLaafia, are currently recognized for effectively utilizing SMS-based communication systems in disseminating viral information. This approach has been particularly beneficial in addressing the challenges posed by the pandemic. Some studies (Ekong et al., 2020) anticipate that SMS-based communication will yield advantages in Africa amidst the pandemic, and it lived to deliver its significance for the past two years.

Moreover, due to its widespread usage and cost-effectiveness (Ekong et al., 2020), the general population utilizes the WhatsApp platform to disseminate health information. According to a survey by GeoPoll in South Africa, Kenya, and Nigeria, WhatsApp emerged as the predominant platform for disseminating viral information (Elliot, 2020). Ensuring the credibility and reliability of information disseminated via these channels was a significant challenge. In the context of the COVID-19 pandemic, there were some pilot implementations of m-health platforms, such as SimMed, to address the issue of medication adherence among patients in countries with insufficient healthcare personnel, like Kenya, Lesotho, and Nigeria (Nyoni & Okumu, 2020). SimMed is an uncomplicated and cost-effective system that operates through SMS technology, necessitating patients to authenticate themselves on a central server whenever they adhere to their prescription regimen. Additionally, it provides reminders to patients in instances where medicine administration has been inadvertently overlooked. When patients deviate from the prescribed medication regimen, the healthcare system notifies the physician, motivating them to arrange subsequent appointments for further evaluation and intervention.

Before the onset of the COVID-19 pandemic, pilot testing of comparable applications in Cape Town (SimMed) and rural southwest Uganda (Wise pill) demonstrated treatment success rates of 94% and 60%, respectively (Chilunjika and Chilunjika A, 2023), according to a report by Newstime (2020), frontline workers in Rwanda credit the successful prevention of the virus to the government's comprehensive technological strategy. Five humanoid robots were implemented to support healthcare personnel at two COVID-19 treatment facilities in Kigali. The purpose of this technological innovation was to aid medical practitioners in maintaining a certain level of physical separation, particularly in scenarios where the utilization of robots was deemed highly advantageous following an evaluation process.

Case Studies of Initiatives in Telemedicine, Health Monitoring, and Contact Tracing

The utilization of telemedicine technology emerged as a prominent aspect within healthcare systems in response to the pandemic (Bokolo, 2020; Kamulegeya et al., 2020). Health authorities such as the

World Health Organization (WHO) have advocated for measures to reduce physical contact and replace it with non-pharmaceutical interventions. As a result, telemedicine emerged as a crucial instrument for mitigating the transmission of the infection. (Nittas, 2020).

The aforementioned technologies encompass videoconferencing, which is live and involves platforms such as Zoom, Skype, and Facebook, as well as communication tools like email. Additionally, digital photography and electronic health records are also included in this list. Telemedicine played a pivotal role in mitigating the impact of Africa's severe scarcity of healthcare professionals. Based on the findings of David and Adebisi (2020), it is seen that of the 54 African countries examined, 31 of them exhibit a patient-to-physician ratio of roughly 1:10,000. In contrast, countries with more economic prosperity, such as Italy, demonstrate a significantly lower ratio of 1:270.

Telemedicine enables patients to engage in real-time communication with healthcare providers located both inside and beyond their geographical region, thereby effectively addressing the challenges associated with staff shortages. Moreover, the authors David and Adebisi (2020) assert that the implementation of telemedicine interventions enables healthcare professionals in Sub-Saharan Africa (SSA) to provide ongoing patient care even in cases of mild symptoms, thereby mitigating the impact of personnel shortages. Various African countries, such as Ghana, Kenya, Zambia, and Zimbabwe, have also implemented comparable technological advancements, thereby offering a temporary resolution to the continent's longstanding issue of severe personnel shortages. Implementing telemedicine has effectively mitigated the geographical divide between healthcare professionals in distant areas and their counterparts in urban centers and various global locations.

Telemedicine provided consistent online training for healthcare professionals in several remote regions of Africa with access to mobile networks during the pandemic (Kamulegeya et al., 2020). Utilizing an artificial intelligence-powered chatbot in Nigeria facilitated providing information and preliminary evaluations of symptoms related to COVID-19 (The Guardian, 2020). This initiative effectively bridged the gap between patients and healthcare professionals, enabling the timely dissemination of relevant information. Several African countries generated a number of medical advances through the utilization of their creativity, which was further facilitated by government policy (Figure 2). Several technologies employed in the efforts to mitigate the impact of COVID-19 in Africa have been developed by African nations, these technologies encompass a range of applications, including those focused on illness prevention, monitoring, and diagnosis, as well as clinical supply and management. (See Table 2 for further details.)

Obstacles and Opportunities in Implementing Healthcare Technology Solutions

Insufficient Financial Resources and the Evaluation of Cost-Effectiveness

The economic efficiency of eHealth technology for Africans remains understudied about alternative health treatments used in the area during the COVID-19 pandemic despite the apparent advantages it offers (Nuwagira & Muzoora, 2020). Due to the recurring issue of inadequate healthcare financing in Africa, assessing the financial efficacy of e-health projects has become a pressing topic. In their research done in Ghana's Amansie-west area, Otsen and Agyei-baffour (2016) examined the cost-effectiveness of creating an e-health clinic compared to a traditional Primary Health Clinic. The findings revealed that developing an e-health clinic costs 4.3% more than constructing a typical Primary Health Clinic. Based on the study's findings, establishing a clinic within a community of 149,437 individuals requires a minimum expenditure of $700,000 to acquire the necessary equipment.

Figure 2. Summary of health innovation, African region, 2020
Sources: Adyasha Maharana et al (2021)

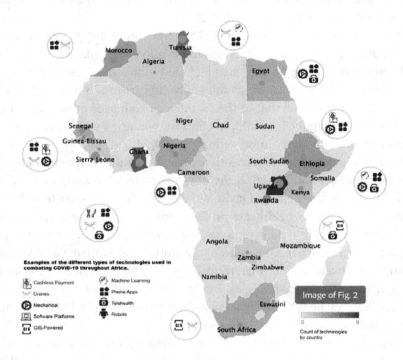

When evaluating the entirety of e-health, it seems implausible, given that most African nations have not fulfilled their commitment, as stated in the 2001 Abuja Declaration, to allocate a minimum of 15% of their yearly budgets to healthcare. Considering the aforementioned circumstances, it is questionable if most African countries will allocate resources toward establishing pandemic-prepared emergency digital health systems. In addition, it is worth noting that in many African countries, like Cameroon Genesis (Telecare), Tanzania's Thamini Uhai, and Kenya's WelTel, e-health test projects were set up before the pandemic.

However, these initiatives failed to achieve widespread community adoption primarily due to their reliance on external funding from Non-Governmental Organizations and private companies. Unfortunately, these entities were compelled to withdraw their support due to financial constraints during the COVID-19 pandemic (Chilunjika S and Chilunjika A, 2023). In Africa, e-health technology implementation relies mainly on grants and donor monies. Conversely, in developed nations, such as the First World, the bulk of e-health initiatives are financed and supervised by governmental entities (Olayiwola et al., 2020). Consequently, during the pandemic, the grants and loan programs accessible to African governments are more inclined towards procuring personal protective equipment (PPE) and essential drugs required by patients and healthcare personnel rather than allocating funds towards e-health technology.

Sustainability of Electronic Health (E-Health) Services

The enduring sustainability of electronic health (e-health) services E-health devices need significant maintenance, which is hindered by the confluence of costly internet fees, limited availability of high-

Table 2. Summary of the different types of technologies used for combating COVID-19 throughout Africa. Diseases prevention, surveillance and diagnosis and clinical supply and management.

Technology	Examples and Usage for Diseases Prevention	Countries of Adoption
DISEASES PREVENTION		
Cashless Payment	Internet-based payment, Electronic pass	Ethiopia, Sierra Leone
Drones	Issue warning, awareness messages and disinfectants	Ghana, Morocco, Rwanda , SierraLeone, SouthAfrica , Tunisia
Mechanical	Contactless soap dispensers, Solar-powered hand washing sink, Thermal imaging, Plastic motorcycle shields	Ethiopia, Ghana, Senegal, Uganda
Software Platforms	Bot for COVID-19 questions	Morocco
GIS-Powered	Ushahidi	Kenya
Low-Tech	SMS & caller ringtones	Guinea
Machine Learning	Text-to-speech radio monitoring	Uganda
DISEASES SURVEILLANCE AND DIAGNOSIS		
Mechanical	Thermal imaging	Uganda
Software Platforms	COVID-19 case dashboards, Tableau dashboard for emergency calls, Vulnerability mapping dashboard using satellite imagery	Ghana, Nigeria, Sierra Leone, Somalia, South Africa , Tunisia
GIS-Powered	GIS-based tracking dashboard, GIS-powered handsets, Hot-spot tracking using additional data sources	Rwanda, South Africa
Low-Tech	Open Data Kit	Rwanda
Machine Learning	text-to-speech radio monitoring of public opinion	Tunisia
Phone Apps	Recording travel info, Checking symptoms, Risk assessment, Contact tracing	Algeria, Ethiopia, Ghana, Nigeria, Sierra Leone Tunisia
Genomics (e.g., Nanopore Sequencing)	Virus sequencing	Gambia, Ghana, Zambia
Tests	Sample pooling, Home-grown swab kits	Rwanda , Uganda , Senegal
CLINICAL SUPPLY AND MANAGEMENT		
Mechanical	3D printing for PPE and ventilators, Indigenous low-cost ventilators	Egypt, Ethiopia, Gambia, Kenya, Nigeria, Sierra Leone, Ethiopia, Gambia , Kenya,
Software Platforms	Information exchange platform for Healthcare professionals, Medical Supplies Platform	South Africa, Benin, Morocco , Nigeria
Low-Tech	Repurposed phone-based HIV self-care	Uganda
Machine Learning	Chest X-rays analysis	Tunisia
Phone Apps	Assisting pregnant women, Ride-hailing apps for providing medical supplies	Egypt, Uganda
Robots	Dr. Car, Police robot, Robot for clinical assistance	Rwanda , Senegal , Tunisia
Telehealth	Video recording, Digital-first care, Triaging	Egypt , Eswatini, Ghana , Libya, Rwanda , Uganda
Miscellaneous	Online training of health professionals	Africa

Source: Adyasha et al (2021)

speed internet in several communities, and unreliable and inadequate electrical infrastructure, hence posing challenges to e-health endeavors in Africa (Africa Regional Initiative Report, 2018).

In a study conducted in 2020 by the Alliance4AffordableInternet (A4AI), it was shown that those residing in Africa have the most elevated internet expenses globally. According to A4AI, affordable internet provides 1GB of mobile broadband data at a cost that does not exceed 2% of an individual's monthly income.

Nevertheless, it is worth noting that the mean expenditure within the Sub-Saharan Africa (SSA) region is around 7.2%, with certain nations surpassing one-fifth of the average income (A4A1 2020). The 40% of the population living in extreme poverty within the SSA region faces significant barriers to using e-health technology due to the unavailability of affordable data (Manyati & Mutsau, 2020). This suggests that online consultations have become reasonably priced, particularly accessible to those belonging to the middle and higher socioeconomic groups in Sub-Saharan Africa. This situation gives rise to worries over the digital divide among the people.

Moreover, studies conducted in developed countries indicate that eHealth technologies are supported by both governmental entities and private health insurance companies (Umeh, 2018). Nevertheless, within the context of the region, health insurance entities primarily cover conventional healthcare services. Even if these organizations were to provide financial assistance for e-health services, the inclination of patients to pay for access to such services tends to be limited (Arize & Onwujekwe, 2017). While some African countries, like South Africa (Discovery Online 2020) and Rwanda (STL partners, 2019), have added telemedicine to their health insurance plans in response to the pandemic, others have not followed suit.

The prevalence of the belief among Africans that successful treatment requires in-person consultation with a trained practitioner may contribute to this phenomenon. Furthermore, countries significantly depend on donor technology, particularly in healthcare (Olayiwola et al., 2020). This reliance on donor funding for implementing e-health systems raises concerns about its long-term sustainability.

Insufficient Information and Communication Technology (ICT) Proficiency, Competency, and Linguistic Hurdles

According to scholarly research conducted by Furusa and Coleman (2018) and Umeh (2018), it has been observed that the implementation of e-health services is hindered by a persistent lack of technical expertise among healthcare personnel and a significant portion of the rural population in Africa. Due to a limited number of African public health institutions offering training in e-health technologies, many African health professionals lack the necessary information and communication technology (ICT) skills and competence to use these innovative solutions effectively in their everyday practice.

Moreover, Chawarura et al. (2019) have identified a deficiency in the African population's understanding of the significance and practicality of e-health, leading to limited acceptance of e-health systems among healthcare professionals and the general people. In addition, the presence of language hurdles poses a hindrance to the successful adoption of electronic health systems in Sub-Saharan Africa. According to Abolade and Durosinmi (2018), a significant barrier to the adoption of e-health in Sub-Saharan Africa (SSA) is the predominance of English as the language of over 80% of internet material.

Firstly, it is important to note that there is a restricted level of proficiency in the English language, mostly concentrated among highly educated and wealthy societies in Africa.

Secondly, there is a lack of easily accessible internet resources in local languages. The potential outcome of this situation might result in a disparity between cultural and technical factors, which may hinder the adoption and use of e-health services at both individual and community levels. Based on the results of this research, it is probable that these circumstances would impede the effective implementation of e-health technologies for delivering services during the pandemic.

Security and Privacy, a Significant Worry in Contemporary Society

Numerous studies conducted on e-health in Africa have consistently encountered challenges stemming from the absence of crucial governance frameworks (Chikuni, 2016), inadequate expertise (Furusa & Coleman, 2018), and insufficient political determination to effectively tackle ethical issues pertaining to data ownership, consent for usage, and safeguarding of patient information (Ekong et al., 2020;).

A study by IIori (2020) asserts that the state of data protection in Africa is rather nascent, as seen by the fact that just 28 out of the 55 African nations have enacted data protection laws, and only 15 have established data protection bodies to oversee its implementation. Safeguarding patient information is widely recognized as a crucial ethical principle in medicine (Furusa & Coleman, 2018). However, the absence of comprehensive legal frameworks to effectively mitigate privacy breaches and the improper utilization of health data continues to impede the extensive adoption of e-health technologies among healthcare professionals and individuals in Africa.

Amidst the ongoing issue, several governments in industrialized countries have undertaken legislative revisions to prohibit the unauthorized use of patient data and establish regulatory frameworks to manage the requirements for e-health implementation. The insufficiency of data privacy and security measures implemented by the majority of governments in Africa, as evidenced by the current state of the 2014 Malabo Convention on data security (Ekong et al., 2020; IIori, 2020). (which has been signed by 14 African Union member states, endorsed by five, and deposited to the African Union Commission by six out of 55 members), could potentially result in resistance from users regarding the extensive utilization of these governments' clinical services in response to the pandemic.

Interoperability of E-Health Systems

Cooperation and interoperability E-health systems function at the intersection of the health and information technology sectors, giving rise to knowledge and coordination gaps that impede advancements in Least Developed Countries (LEDCs) (Chikuni, 2016). Researcher specializing in m-health technologies in Zimbabwe, asserts that various government policies are formulated in isolation from each other.

Given the interdisciplinary nature of e-health, it is essential that it operates in conjunction with other policies and initiatives, such as national information and communication technology (ICT) policies and projects aimed at rural electrification. This collaboration is necessary to facilitate coordination, ensure platform interoperability, and foster the involvement of many stakeholders. According to Adenuga et al. (2020), the rapid implementation and use of e-health in Africa during the pandemic is unlikely to lead to the creation of several interconnected and compatible e-health apps. Consequently, this may make e-health systems ineffective within the context of Africa.

Technology for Remote Work and Education

Remote Work

The COVID-19 pandemic has accelerated the worldwide use of remote work practices, particularly in Africa. Organizations across many industries were compelled to swiftly adapt to remote work arrangements to ensure business continuity while following social distancing protocols.

During this period, technology played a crucial role in facilitating the practice of remote labor. The pandemic has also increased remote work in Africa, with many businesses adopting telecommuting to ensure business continuity. As a result, various remote work solutions, such as video conferencing apps and collaboration tools, have been developed. The option of remote work has become a viable alternative for numerous professionals in countries like Nigeria, where there has been a consistent rise in internet penetration rates. Organizations employ video conferencing platforms like Zoom and Microsoft Teams to facilitate virtual meetings and remote collaboration (Oyelere et al., 2020).

Similarly, companies operating in Ghana have employed cloud-based services such as Google Drive and Dropbox to streamline the process of sharing documents and fostering collaboration among geographically dispersed teams (Agyapong et al., 2021). A video conferencing app in South Africa was developed to allow doctors and patients to consult remotely. An online platform in Kenya was developed to connect freelancers with remote work opportunities. A police robot was deployed to patrol regions of Tunisia's capital. (BBC, 2020) as part of the promotion of remote work by the police. People spotted on the streets must then show their ID and other documents to the robot's camera so that the police in command can check them remotely.

Education

Education has been severely disrupted in Africa due to the pandemic, with school closures affecting millions of students. Conversely, technology has played an essential role in providing alternative learning modes, such as online classes, e-learning platforms, and educational apps.

The government launched a free e-learning platform in Nigeria for primary and secondary school students. In Rwanda, an e-learning platform was developed to provide university students with online classes. Mobile-based learning solutions were introduced in Kenya to reach students with limited internet access in rural areas. In Ghana, the government provided enough support for high schools and universities to move online.

According to a UNICEF report (UNICEF Relies (2021)), the COVID-19 pandemic has substantially impacted the educational access of roughly 40% of African children of primary and secondary school age, rendering them unable to attend school. To reduce the spread of the virus in the future, educational institutions throughout Africa were forced to close early. Kenya declared 2020 a "lost year" for elementary and secondary school students. As a result, the importance of innovation in education has reached unparalleled heights. As a result of the pandemic's urgent requirements, educational establishments, educators, students, and their families faced a limited amount of time to prepare for the continuation of instruction following school closure collaboratively. Students worked hard to maintain their educational progress by utilizing various online learning tools. Angele Messa, a budding entrepreneur, established EduClick, a remote learning platform in Cameroon, to provide educational opportunities to underprivileged children who faced barriers to education due to the pandemic or pre-existing poor conditions prior to the onset of the COVID-19 crisis.

Similarly, the Kisomo SmartLearn program, which was available in Tanzania, provided digital educational resources in the region's native tongue. Furthermore, a considerable majority of students consume educational content via television. Since the initial lockdown measures were implemented, there has been a significant increase of up to 97 percent in young people engaging with instructional online platforms. Over sixty educational technology items were primarily aimed at youngsters. Among Africa's 450 million internet users, around 19 million are youngsters under 14 who use the internet regularly. Over 17 million children watch television programming produced by Ubongo, Africa's most popular educational entertainment company.

Students in South Africa adopted a type of instruction known as blended learning, which includes a variety of instructional resources such as internet platforms, radio broadcasts, and television programs. In Tanzania, implementing an online educational platform known as Shule Direct, which both professors and students use, facilitates the pursuit of higher education. This platform is being used by over 2 million students and 23,000 teachers across the United States. During the COVID-19 epidemic, which lasted from 2020 to 2021, telecommunications service providers provided free access to this website, erasing all restrictions. Similarly, Eneza Education provided high-quality instructional content to 380,000 children in elementary and secondary schools in Kenya, Ghana, and Ivory Coast. This was accomplished through the use of SMS or USSD technology, which allowed students to subscribe on a daily, weekly, or monthly basis.

E-Commerce/Online Marketplaces, and Digital Payments

E-Commerce and Online Marketplaces

The closing of physical retail businesses pushed many to switch to Internet purchasing, hastening the adoption of electronic commerce in Africa. As a result, the popularity of several e-commerce platforms, such as Jumia, Kilimall, and Konga, has increased. The African e-commerce sector expanded significantly. Between 2020 and 2021, the size of the e-commerce market more than doubled (UNCTAD Global Review 2020).

Jumia, a pan-African e-commerce platform, saw its transaction volume increase from $3.1 million to $4.7 million in the first half of 2020 (*TechCrunch, 2022*). Flutterwave, a digital payment service provider, launched in April 2020 to serve the needs of small enterprises. By November 2021, it will have successfully served over 30,000 small businesses (Fluetterwave Report, 2021). Individuals in Kenya procured grocery and food items via online platforms, notably Twiga Foods, an agrotechnology firm (TechCrunch Report, 2022). FarmCrowdy, an agrotech platform, facilitated investment options in small-scale, community-based farms, allowing users to profit-sharing and purchase agricultural produce from a network of over 25,000 farmers (TechCrunch Report).

The adoption of e-commerce solutions in Mauritius saw an increase in user involvement during the first two weeks of the statewide closure in March 2020 (Mauritius Fintech Report (2022)). The use of Internet channels by informal entrepreneurs has increased significantly. In contrast to prior figures, which showed that just 10% of informal enterprises had internet access, the current scenario shows a significant growth in this proportion. Furthermore, informal entrepreneurs' Internet use for supplier searches has increased significantly, with nearly one in every four people engaged in this practice. Approximately 30% of Ghana's informal microenterprises used online services to market and sell their products.

According to research, firms that had incorporated digital technology before the COVID-19 pandemic displayed superior levels of productivity, output, profitability, employment, and earnings, regardless of whether they were formal or informal in type (Cusolito et al, 2020). Furthermore, businesses that used cell phones, digital transactions, and digital management tools like accounting and inventory control/point-of-sale software saw a significant increase in productivity. The use of inventory control/POS software by informal enterprises in Senegal increased revenue by 1.6 times when compared to organizations that did not use such software. Similarly, employment firms that use Internet resources for recruitment have successfully employed more than twice as many employees (Atiyas and Dutz, 2021) as firms that do not use these tools. Additionally, it was discovered that businesses that used digital transactions received 1.5 to 2.4 times more compensation than businesses that did not (World Bank, 2021). AgroCenta, a Ghanaian agrotech enterprise, allows the connecting of 10,000 farmers and buyers, allowing farmers to earn a higher price for their agricultural products. Approximately 22% of Sub-Saharan African firms have begun or increased their use of the Internet, social media, and digital platforms for the provision of services and the execution of financial transactions (World Bank, 2021).

Digital Payments

Digital payment systems in Africa have significantly transformed the monetary transaction methods employed throughout the continent. The pandemic's effects have facilitated the proliferation of mobile money and other digital payment methods in Africa, resulting in a decrease in the use of conventional currency. The proliferation of diverse payment technologies has facilitated the integration of contactless transactions, reduced the risk of COVID-19 transmission, and expedited the establishment of a cashless economic framework.

Based on the results of research conducted by the World Bank in 2020, the advent of digital payment platforms has facilitated the provision of banking services to individuals who previously had challenges accessing traditional financial institutions. The introduction of Kenya's mobile money network, M-Pesa, has substantially influenced the level of financial inclusivity inside the nation, leading to a notable transformation in the economic landscape. The availability of mobile money in Kenya has reached over 80% of the country's adult population, as reported by the World Bank in 2020. This innovation has facilitated secure monetary transactions, access to credit facilities, and participation in e-commerce activities, which have been significantly influenced by the global pandemic. Kenya is a notable illustration of a nation effectively using digital payment systems. The advent of M-Pesa by Safaricom in 2007 significantly impacted the nation's financial landscape. In 2020, the Communications Authority of Kenya (2021) reported that M-Pesa achieved a significant milestone by facilitating around 11 billion transactions, amounting to a total value of 4.35 trillion Kenyan Shillings, equivalent to over 40 billion US Dollars. According to the findings of this research, it was observed that the Kenyan people have shown a propensity to adopt and use digital payment systems during the COVID-19 pandemic.

The Ghanaian government and other financial organizations have advocated the introduction of digital payment methods as a means to mitigate virus transmission by minimizing direct human contact. The Mobile Money Interoperability Report for 2021 indicates an increasing popularity of mobile money services such as MTN Mobile Money, Vodafone Cash, and AirtelTigo Money. The growing societal embrace of contactless payment methods might explain the trend. The Bank of Ghana has implemented measures to enhance interoperability among mobile money service providers, facilitating seamless transmission and receipt of funds across several networks (Bank of Ghana, 2021). These efforts were implemented in order to bolster the prevailing tendency. Furthermore, the government established the COVID-19 National Trust Fund, which serves as a platform for collecting financial contributions through diverse online payment mechanisms (COVID-19 National Trust Fund). The aforementioned modifications were implemented to enhance the accessibility of financial services and support Ghana's transition towards a less cash-dependent society.

Digital payment systems have played a crucial role in facilitating economic progress in African nations. Based on an estimate by McKinsey & Company (2021), integrating digital payment systems in Africa can enhance the continent's Gross Domestic Product (GDP) by as much as 3.7 trillion dollars by 2025. Digital payment solutions enhance the expediency and efficacy of corporate transactions, reducing cash management expenses and augmenting overall operational effectiveness. In addition, digital payment systems facilitate the expansion of clientele and participation in electronic commerce for small and medium-sized firms (SMEs), which are essential components for fostering economic growth and development. In the last several years, there has been a notable surge in the use of digital payment systems in Nigeria, contributing considerably to the country's thriving economy. The Central Bank of Nigeria (2020) reported a significant 47% rise in the value of electronic payment transactions inside the nation during the COVID-19 pandemic. The proliferation of digital payment mechanisms has facilitated the emergence of electronic commerce platforms and empowered businesses to sustain operations despite lockdown measures and limitations on mobility. Due to the aforementioned advancements, it is anticipated that the eNaira platform will be launched in October 2021. This platform is vital to the nation's efforts to enhance its digital payment infrastructure.

During and after the COVID-19 pandemic, South Africa significantly transformed consumer behavior, particularly concerning digital payments. Based on a poll conducted by Visa in 2021, it was found that a significant majority of South African customers, namely 67 percent, showed a rise in their use of contactless payment options amidst the ongoing pandemic. The observed trend indicates a rising inclination towards payment methods that prioritize security and convenience, leading to a surge in the use of digital payment systems. Based on the research mentioned above, a recent survey by Mastercard (2021) indicates that 73 percent of individuals from the African continent surveyed have increased their use of digital payment mechanisms in reaction to the pandemic. The enduring impact of this shift in consumer behavior is anticipated to last far after the conclusion of the pandemic, expediting the acceptance and use of digital payment technology.

POLICY AND REGULATORY STRUCTURES

Legislation and Advisory Committees

In light of the challenges posed by the global pandemic, it is imperative to establish robust legislative and regulatory frameworks that can effectively navigate the evolving technological terrain. Numerous African nations have enacted regulations and legislation aimed at fostering innovation and creating a conducive ecosystem for technology-driven solutions to bolster these advancements in technology. The "COVID-19 Innovation Challenge" has been established by the Ministry of Information, Communication, and Technology in Kenya. This initiative, facilitated by the Kenya COVID-19 ICT Advisory Committee, aims to stimulate local digital enterprises to present innovative proposals addressing the challenges posed by the pandemic (Kenya Ministry of ICT).

In contrast, Rwanda has established a regulatory sandbox framework that enables companies to experiment with innovative technologies without being subjected to burdensome regulatory constraints (Rwanda Development Board). Amidst the epidemic, this particular approach facilitated prompt experimentation and expedited the implementation of technology-driven solutions. Moreover, a number of African nations have recognized the significance of enhancing data protection and privacy measures in order to safeguard the personal information of citizens. The Protection of Personal Information Act (POPIA) in South Africa serves as an illustrative instance of legislative measures designed to safeguard personal data and promote conscientious data utilization (South Africa Government Gazette).

Policy and Regulatory Frameworks After COVID-19

The preservation of technological achievements is critical as Africa enters a post-pandemic change period. It is critical that governments across the continent continue to prioritize the construction of comprehensive legislative and regulatory systems that encourage the progress of innovation, digital inclusion, and economic expansion. The expansion of broadband infrastructure is a critical issue that must be considered. The availability of affordable and consistent internet connectivity is critical in supporting technology adoption and the digital transformation process. Nigeria, like other countries, has recognized the importance of meeting this goal and has implemented efforts to increase broadband penetration, such as the Nigeria Communications Commission's National Broadband Plan. According to the Ministry of Information (2020),

Ghana's Ministry of Communication has recognized the importance of expanding infrastructure to rural areas. A policy framework has been established to do this, expanding on the preceding national broadband policy and implementation strategy of 2012. Furthermore, governments have promoted the development of indigenous technological ecosystems by providing help to new enterprises and innovative individuals. The emergence of innovation centers, incubators, and funding programs has aided in this endeavor. Ghana's National Entrepreneurship and Innovation Plan (NEIP) is an example of a government-driven initiative to strengthen new firms and develop an entrepreneurial culture (Ghana Ministry of Business Development). Furthermore, the partnership of governments, private sector entities, and international organizations has considerably impacted the development of successful policy and regulatory frameworks. The African Union's Digital Transformation Strategy provides a comprehensive framework for boosting regional collaboration in the growth of technology adoption and developing digital skills across the African continent (African Union Commission).

CHALLENGES AND OPPORTUNITIES FOR THE FUTURE

Challenges for Technological Leap and Uptake in Africa

The pandemic exerted a significant global influence, with Africa being no exception to its effects. The continent has encountered many issues, encompassing a decline in economic activity, increased poverty and inequality, and a burden on healthcare systems. The adoption of technology is a crucial factor in Africa's economic recovery and long-term development, however, challenges still exist for the full adoption of some of the technological innovations during the pandemic; these include the following

Restricted Availability of Technological Resources

A prominent barrier hindering the use of technology in Africa is the limited availability of technological resources. A significant portion of the African population, particularly those residing in rural areas, have limited availability and utilization of internet connectivity, cell phones, and other forms of digital technology. According to the International Telecommunication Union (ITU), the internet access rate for Africans in 2020 was estimated to be around 27%, in stark contrast to the far higher rates of 87% in Europe and 95% in North America. The inability of individuals and businesses to fully engage in the digital economy and harness the advantages of technological advancements is mostly attributed to restricted technology accessibility.

The High Cost of Technology

The exorbitant cost associated with technology presents a significant barrier to the widespread adoption of technical advancements in Africa. Many individuals residing in Africa face financial constraints that prevent them from acquiring smartphones, laptop computers, and other electronic gadgets due to their high costs. Based on a survey published by the World Bank, it has been observed that the cost of a basic smartphone exceeds double the average monthly salary in numerous African nations. Consequently, many individuals from Africa, particularly those from economically disadvantaged households, encounter challenges in obtaining technological resources.

Absence of Digital Literacy Skills

One of the barriers to technological adoption in Africa is the absence of digital literacy. A significant proportion of African individuals face a deficiency in the requisite skills and knowledge necessary for proficient utilization of digital technology, constraining their capacity to engage in the digital economy actively. According to an African Development Bank assessment, only 25% of Africans have the requisite digital skills to use technology successfully. The absence of digital literacy is a substantial obstacle to the use of technology, particularly in rural regions characterized by restricted access to education and training opportunities.

Inadequate Infrastructure

Insufficient infrastructure poses a significant barrier to the adoption of technology in Africa. Numerous African nations face a deficiency in the infrastructure required to facilitate the widespread adoption of digital technology, including reliable energy and internet connectivity. According to the African Development Bank, only 20% of Africans have access to reliable energy, and only 30% have access to high-speed internet. Due to infrastructure difficulties, businesses and individuals are finding it challenging to participate in the digital economy.

The Cybersecurity Risks

Cybersecurity concerns provide a significant barrier to the adoption of technology in Africa. The growing adoption of digital technologies among Africans exposes them to heightened susceptibility to cyberattacks and various manifestations of cybercrime. As per the African Union's assessment, cybercrime poses a significant obstacle to advancing digital infrastructure in Africa, with several nations on the continent lack the legal and policy frameworks to combat these vulnerabilities effectively. The absence of robust cybersecurity measures is a significant challenge for organizations and individuals, impeding their ability to place complete trust in and effectively utilize digital technologies.

Opportunities for the Future

Amidst the challenges posed by the pandemic, opportunities also abound for Africa to make strides in the technological uptake to modernize its economy and accelerate growth; among these, we discuss the following, though not exhaustive.

Digital Transformation

The pandemic also accelerated the need for digital transformation throughout Africa's industries. With the adoption of lockdowns and social distancing measures, various institutions, including corporations, governments, and individuals, turned to technology to maintain their operations. The current transformation has drawn attention to the importance of digital infrastructure and connectivity, presenting opportunities for investment in telecommunications networks, internet access, and e-commerce platforms (World Bank, 2020). In reaction to the issue, African countries have implemented measures to facilitate the adoption of digitalization.

The Kenyan government launched the "Digital Economy Blueprint" in 2020 to exploit technological breakthroughs to drive economic growth and provide job opportunities (Government of Kenya, 2020). These programs foster innovation and entrepreneurship, increasing productivity and competitiveness.

E-Learning and Remote Work

The closure of educational institutions in Africa due to the pandemic highlighted the imperative for developing e-learning opportunities in the region. In order to maintain instructional continuity, numerous educational institutions have implemented online platforms. According to UNESCO (2020), implementing this modification can mitigate the digital divide by broadening educational opportunities of superior quality outside the confines of conventional classroom settings.

Likewise, throughout the ongoing pandemic, a considerable number of professionals have come to realize the imperative nature of engaging in distant employment. This phenomenon allows African employees to participate in global labor markets regardless of location. Moreover, it facilitates the ability of enterprises to tap into talent reservoirs across the continent, thus fostering employment opportunities and boosting economic progress (African Development Bank Group, 2020).

Healthcare Innovation

The global health crisis highlighted the significance of solid healthcare systems across Africa. Technological solutions can potentially improve healthcare infrastructure and increase service provision significantly. Telemedicine technologies can give remote consultations and healthcare help, relieving pressure on traditional healthcare institutions (World Health Organization, 2020). Furthermore, the use of digital tools in disease tracking and contact tracing has the potential to minimize the spread of infectious diseases greatly. The current situation provides a favorable environment for African countries to direct their resources on improving and strengthening health information systems and data analytics skills (Africa CDC, 2020).

Financial Inclusion

A significant number of individuals from the African continent continue to encounter obstacles in accessing financial services. On the other hand, the COVID-19 epidemic has expedited the use of digital financial solutions such as mobile money and digital wallets. According to the World Bank (2020), individuals and enterprises can employ these technologies to remotely avail themselves of financial services, execute payments, and engage in transactions.

Through the promotion of financial inclusion, technology can contribute to mitigating poverty and enhancing economic empowerment in Africa. According to the United Nations Capital Development Fund (2020), this technology enables consumers to accumulate savings, access loans, and participate in official economic transactions with enhanced security measures.

CONCLUSION

The COVID-19 crisis has catalyzed technological advancements in Africa, leading to significant advancements across several sectors. The current pandemic has brought attention to the significance of technology in addressing challenges and has accelerated the use of digital solutions throughout the continent. Africa has rapidly embraced technology across several sectors, including healthcare, education, business, and government, facilitating the development of a more inclusive technological landscape for the future.

Advancements in technology have significantly impacted the healthcare industry. The pandemic brought attention to the vulnerabilities of healthcare systems in Africa, leading to the exploration of innovative solutions. Telemedicine and remote healthcare services have seen a surge in popularity, helping individuals obtain medical advice and consultations inside the confines of their residences. Mobile applications and web-based platforms have been developed to distribute information about COVID-19, monitor its transmission, and facilitate the process of contact tracing. The aforementioned improvements have not only enhanced the accessibility of healthcare but have also bolstered the efficiency and efficacy of healthcare provision.

The use of technology has seen a substantial rise within the realm of education. Due to the closure of educational institutions during lockdown periods, e-learning platforms have become imperative for facilitating remote learning. In order to ensure the uninterrupted provision of education, governmental bodies, and educational institutions have collaborated with technology enterprises to provide online learning resources and platforms. The transition towards digital education has expanded the availability of high-quality educational opportunities and facilitated the continuous acquisition of knowledge and skills development throughout one's lifetime.

The COVID-19 crisis had a significant impact on the African economic landscape as a result of advancements in technology. The advent of e-commerce and digital platforms has compelled conventional brick-and-mortar enterprises to either adapt or face extinction, leading to an increasing dependence on these technological advancements. Small and medium-sized firms (SMEs) have embraced online marketplaces and digital payment methods, facilitating the expansion of their client reach and enhancing their competitive edge. Moreover, there has been a significant increase in the use of remote working arrangements as organizations increasingly depend on communication and collaboration technology to ensure the uninterrupted operation of their businesses.

Moreover, the use of technology has significantly contributed to enhancing the efficacy of African governmental institutions and providing public services. Governments have used digital platforms to distribute information, provide updates on COVID-19 actions, and engage people. Digital identification technologies have enhanced the efficiency and transparency of allocating funds for disaster relief and social welfare initiatives. The technological developments have not only enhanced the efficiency of government operations but have also facilitated more openness and accountability.

The COVID-19 crisis has catalyzed technological advancements in Africa, leading to significant advancements across all domains. The global pandemic has expedited the use of digital solutions, resulting in transformative effects on several sectors, such as healthcare, education, business, and government. The increasing reliance on technology has mitigated pressing challenges and paved the way for a more technologically inclusive future in Africa.

REFERENCES

Abolade, T. O., & Durosinmi, A. E. (2018). The benefits and challenges of e-health applications in developing nations: A review. In *Paper presented at the 14th iSTEAMS conference at AL- hikmah university IIrion Kwara state Nigeria.*

Addo, C. P. (2019). Africa has the slowest data speeds. Here's how to accelerate things. *Africa Report.* https://www.theafricareport.com/21516/africa-has-the-slowest-data-speeds-heres-how-to-accelerate-things

Adenuga, K. I., Iahad, T., & Miskon, D. (2020). Telemedicine system: Service adoption and implementation issues in Nigeria. *Indian Journal of Science and Technology*, *13*(12), 1321–1327. doi:10.17485/IJST/v13i12.180

Affordable4Affordable Internet. (2020). *Affordability report.* Affordable4Affordable. https://a4ai. org/affordability-report/report/2020/

Africa C. D. C. (2020). *COVID-19: Digital Solutions for Africa's Response.* Africa CDC. https://africacdc.org/download/covid-19-digital-solutions-for-africas-response/

Africa Regional Initiative Report. (2018). *Buenos aires action plan 2018-2021(WTDC- 17).* ITU.

African Development Bank. (2020). *Digital Transformation in Africa.* African Development Bank. https://www.afdb.org/en/topics/digital-transformation-in-africa

African Development Bank Group. (2020). *COVID-19: Opportunities for Africa's Economic Transformation*. African Development Bank. https://www.afdb.org/en/news-and-events/covid-19-opportunities-africas-economic-transformation-36156

Agarwal, R., & Prasad, J. (1997). The Role of Innovation Characteristics and Perceived Voluntariness in the Acceptance of Information Technologies. *Decision Sciences*, *28*(3), 557–582. doi:10.1111/j.1540-5915.1997.tb01322.x

Agyapong, G. K., Agyapong, E. K., & Asamoah, D. (2021). The Impact of COVID-19 on Remote Work in Ghana: Challenges and Opportunities. *Journal of African Business*, *22*(1), 1–18.

Ajzen, I. (1991). The Theory of Planned Behavior. *Organizational Behavior and Human Decision Processes*, *52*(2), 179–211. doi:10.1016/0749-5978(91)90020-T

Arize, I., & Onwujekwe, O. (2017). Acceptability and willingness to pay for telemedicine services in Enugu state, Southeast Nigeria. *Digital Health*, *3*(1). Advance online publication. doi:10.1177/2055207617715524 PMID:29942606

Atiyas & Dutz (2021). *COVID-19 and the future of work in Africa; emerging Trends in Digital Technology Adoption*. ISSUU. https://issuu.com/world.bank.publications/docs/9781464817144

Bank of Ghana. (2021). *Bank of Ghana Launches Mobile Money Interoperability System*. Bank of Ghana. https://www.bog.gov.gh/news/press-releases/2018/bank-of-ghana-launches-mobile-money-interoperability-system/

Bank of Ghana Report. (2021). Mobile Money Interoperability: A Game Changer for Financial Inclusion in Ghana. *World Bank Blogs*. https://blogs.worldbank.org/digital-development/mobile-money-interoperability-game-changer-financial-inclusion-ghana [https://www.bbc.com/news/world-africa-52148639]

Beatty, R. C., Shim, J. P., & Jones, M. C. (2001). Factors influencing corporate web site adoption: A time-based assessment. *Information & Management*, *38*(6), 337–354. doi:10.1016/S0378-7206(00)00064-1

Bokolo, A. J. (2020). Exploring the adoption of Telemedicine and virtual software for care of outpatients during and after COVID-19 pandemic. *International Journal of Medical Sciences*, 2020. PMID:32642981

Brancheau, J. C., & Wetherbe, J. C. (1990). The Adoption of Spreadsheet Software: Testing Innovation Diffusion Theory in the Context of End-User Computing. *Information Systems Research*, *1*(2), 115–143. doi:10.1287/isre.1.2.115

Brown, S. A., Massey, A. P., Montoya-Weiss, M. M., & Burkman, J. R. (2002). Do I Really Have to? User Acceptance of Mandated Technology. *European Journal of Information Systems*, *11*(4), 283–295. doi:10.1057/palgrave.ejis.3000438

Central Bank of Nigeria. (2020). *Electronic Payment Channels in Nigeria: Post COVID-19 Impact Assessment*. Central Bank of Nigeria. https://www.cbn.gov.ng/Out/2020/CCD/Electronic%20Payment%20Channels%20in%20Nigeria.pdf

Chan, S.-C., & Lu, M. (2004). Understanding Internet Banking Adoption and Use Behavior: A Hong Kong Perspective. *Journal of Global Information Management*, *12*(3), 21–43. doi:10.4018/jgim.2004070102

Chau, P. Y. K., & Hu, P. J. H. (2001). Information Technology Acceptance by Individual Professionals: A Model Comparison Approach. *Decision Sciences*, *32*(4), 699–719. doi:10.1111/j.1540-5915.2001. tb00978.x

Chawarura, T., Stam, G. V., & Van Dijik, J. H. (2019*). E-Health in Zimbabwe, A case of techno-social development*. Research Gate. https://www.researchgate,net/publication/ 332668100.

Chikuni, D. (2016). Potential/preparedness of E-health services in Zimbabwe. *International Journal of Research in IT and Management*, *6*(1), 43–54.

Chilunjika, S., & Chilunjika, A. (2023). Embracing e-health systems in managing the COVID 19 pandemic in Sub-Saharan Africa. *Social Sciences & Humanities Open*, *8*(1), 100556. doi:10.1016/j. ssaho.2023.100556 PMID:37214273

Chiu, C.-M., & Wang, E. T. G. (2008). Understanding Web-based learning continuance intention: The role of subjective task value. *Information & Management*, *45*(3), 194–201. doi:10.1016/j.im.2008.02.003

Communications Authority of Kenya. (2021). *Quarterly Sector Statistics Report Q4 2020/2021*. Community Authority of Kenya. https://ca.go.ke/wp-content/uploads/2021/05/QSS-Report-Q4-2020_21.pdf

COVID-19 National Trust Fund. (2021). Ministry of Finance Ghana. https://www.mofep.gov.gh/covid-19-national-trust-fund

Cusolito, Lederman, & Peña (2020). Wordbank Policy Research Paper; The Effects of Digital-Technology Adoption on Productivity and Factor Demand Firm-level Evidence from Developing Countries. World Bank. https://documents1.worldbank.org/curated/en/829161595512126439/pdf/The-Effects-of-Digital-Technology-Adoption-on-Productivity-and-Factor-Demand-Firm-level-Evidence-from-Developing-Countries.pdf

David, K. B., & Adebisi, Y. A. (2020). Proposed model for hospital and community pharmacy services during COVID-19 pandemic in Nigeria. *International Journal of Pharmacy Practice, 4*(10), 1111/ ijpp/12652. Pub Med.

Davis, F. D. (1989). Perceived Usefulness, Perceived Ease of Use, and User Acceptance in Information Technology. *Management Information Systems Quarterly*, *13*(3), 319–340. doi:10.2307/249008

Dishaw, M. T., & Strong, D. M. (1999). Extending the technology acceptance model with task-technology fit constructs. *Information & Management*, *36*(1), 9–21. doi:10.1016/S0378-7206(98)00101-3

Ekong, I. I., Chukwu, E., & Chukwu, M. (2020). COVID-19 mobile positioning data contact tracing and patient privacy regulations: Exploratory serach of global response strategies and the use of digital tools in Nigeria. JMIR. *mHealth, 8*(4), 1–7.

Elliot, R. (2020). *Coronavirus in sub- saharan Africa: A Geopoll survey report*. International Development research www.geoploo.com/blog/coronavirus-africa/

Fishbein, M., & Ajzen, I. (1975). *Belief, Attitude, Intention, and Behavior*. Addison-Wesley.

Fluetterwave. (2021). *Flutterwave Launches Market, a New E-commerce Service to Scale SME Growth*. FlutterWave. https://flutterwave.com/us/blog/flutterwave-launches-market

Furusa, S. S., & Coleman, A. (2018). Factors influencing E-health implementation by medical doctors in public hospitals in Zimbabwe. *South African Journal of Information Management*, *20*(1), 928–945. doi:10.4102/sajim.v20i1.928

Global Cybersecurity Index, I. T. U. 2018, https:// www. itu. int/ en/ ITU -D/ Cybersecurity/ Pages/ global -cybersecurity -index. aspx ITU WTI Database, ICT indicators.

Government of Kenya. (2020). *Digital Economy Blueprint*. Government of Kenya. https://www.digital.go.ke/digital-economy-blueprint/

GSMA. (2019). The mobile economy in sub saharan. *Africa*. https://www.gs and ma.com/subsaharanafrica/resources/the-mobile-economy-sub-saharan-africa-

Hernandez, B., Jimenez, J., & Martin, M. J. (2010). Business management software in high-tech firms: The case of the IT services sector. *Journal of Business and Industrial Marketing*, *25*(2), 132–146. doi:10.1108/08858621011017750

Hong, S.-J., & Tam, K. Y. (2006). Understanding the Adoption of Multipurpose Information Appliances: The Case of Mobile Data Services. *Information Systems Research*, *17*(2), 162–179. doi:10.1287/isre.1060.0088

Hong, S.-J., Thong, J. Y. L., Moon, J.-Y., & Tam, K.-Y. (2008). Understanding the behavior of mobile data services consumers. *Information Systems Frontiers*, *10*(4), 431–445. doi:10.1007/s10796-008-9096-1

Hsieh, J. J. P.-A., Rai, A., & Keil, M. (2008). Understanding Digital Inequality: Comparing Continued Use Behavioral Models of the Socio-Economically Advantaged and Disadvantaged. *Management Information Systems Quarterly*, *32*(1), 97–126. doi:10.2307/25148830

Hsu, M.-H., & Chiu, C.-M. (2004). Predicting electronic service continuance with a decomposed theory of planned behaviour. *Behaviour & Information Technology*, *23*(5), 359–373. doi:10.1080/0144929041 0001669969

Hsu, M.-H., Yen, C.-H., Chiu, C.-M., & Chang, C.-M. (2006). A longitudinal investigation of continued online shopping behavior: An extension of the theory of planned behavior. *International Journal of Human-Computer Studies*, *64*(9), 889–904. doi:10.1016/j.ijhcs.2006.04.004

Iiori, T. (2020). *Data protection in Africa and the COVID-19 pandemic*. Research Gate.

International Telecommunication Union. (2020). *ICT Data and Statistics*. ITU. https://www.itu.int/net4/statistics/ICTDataAndStatistics.aspx

ITU. (2020). Tech v COVID-29: Managing the crisis. *ITUNews03*. https:// www. itu. int/ en/ myitu/ Publications/ 2020/ 09/ 09/ 13/ 13/ ITU -News -Magazine -No3 -2020

ITU platforms. (2020). *Connect2Recover*. Global Network Resiliency Platform "REG4COVID", the WSIS ICT Case Repository, and CYB4COVID.

Kamulegeya, L. H., Bwanika, J. M., & Musingazi, D. (2020). Continuity of health service delivery during the COVID-19 pandemic: The role of digital health technologies in Uganda. *The Pan African Medical Journal*, *35*(2, Supp 2), 1–3. doi:10.11604/pamj.supp.2020.35.2.23115 PMID:33623568

Karahanna, E., Straub, D. W., & Chervany, N. L. (1999). Information Technology Adoption across Time: A Cross-Sectional Comparison of Pre-Adoption and Post-Adoption Beliefs. *Management Information Systems Quarterly*, *23*(2), 183–213. doi:10.2307/249751

Karahanna, E., Straub, D. W., & Chervany, N. L. (1999). Information Technology Adoption across Time: A Cross-Sectional Comparison of Pre-Adoption and Post-Adoption Beliefs. *Management Information Systems Quarterly*, *23*(2), 183–213. doi:10.2307/249751

Lee, Y., Kozar, K. A., & Larsen, K. R. T. (2003). The Technology Acceptance Model: Past, Present, and Future. *Communications of the Association for Information Systems*, *12*(50), 752–780. doi:10.17705/1CAIS.01250

Liao, C., Chen, J.-L., & Yen, D. C. (2007). Theory of planning behavior (TPB) and customer satisfaction in the continued use of e-service: An integrated model. *Computers in Human Behavior*, *23*(6), 2804–2822. doi:10.1016/j.chb.2006.05.006

Lin, J., Chan, H. C., & Wei, K. K. (2006). Understanding competing application usage with the theory of planned behavior. *Journal of the American Society for Information Science and Technology*, *57*(10), 1338–1349. doi:10.1002/asi.20453

Lu, J., Yao, J. E., & Yu, C.-S. (2005). Personal Innovativeness, Social Influences and Adoption of Wireless Internet Services via Mobile Technology. *The Journal of Strategic Information Systems*, *14*(3), 245–268. doi:10.1016/j.jsis.2005.07.003

Lu, J., Yao, J. E., & Yu, C.-S. (2005). Personal Innovativeness, Social Influences and Adoption of Wireless Internet Services via Mobile Technology. *The Journal of Strategic Information Systems*, *14*(3), 245–268. doi:10.1016/j.jsis.2005.07.003

Maharana, A., Amutorine, M., Sengeh, M. D., & Nsoesie, E. O. (2021). COVID-19 and beyond: Use of digital technology for pandemic response in Africa. *Scientific African*, *14*, e01041. doi:10.1016/j.sciaf.2021.e01041 PMID:34746524

Manyati, T. K., & Mutsau, M. (2020). A systematic review of the factors that hinder the scale up of mobile health technologies in antenatal care programmes in Sub Saharan Africa. *African Journal of Science, Technology, Innovation and Development*, *2020*, 1–17.

Mastercard. (2021). Mastercard New Payments Index: Consumer Appetite for Digital Payments Takes Off. Retrieved from https://newsroom.mastercard.com/mea/files/2021/03/Mastercard-New-Payments-Index.pdf

McKinsey & Company. (2021). *Digital payments in Africa: Unlocking the $3.7 trillion opportunity*. McKinsey.

Morris, M., & Venkatesh, V. (2000). Age differences in technology adoption decisions: Implications for a changing work force. *Personnel Psychology*, *53*(2), 375–403. doi:10.1111/j.1744-6570.2000.tb00206.x

Morris, M. G., Venkatesh, V., & Ackerman, P. L. (2005). Gender and Age Differences in Employee Decisions About New Technology: An Extension to the Theory of Planned Behavior. *IEEE Transactions on Engineering Management*, *52*(1), 69–84. doi:10.1109/TEM.2004.839967

Nigeria Communications Commission. (2021). *National Broadband Plan*. Nigeria Communications Commission. [http://fmcde.gov.ng/wp-content/uploads/2021/12/An_Update_on_Nigerian_National_Broadband_Strategic_Plan_Nigerian_National_Broadband_Council_Secretariat-_May_2017.1.pdf]

Nittas, V. (2020). When e-health goes viral: The strengths and weaknesses of health tech during COVID-19. *Mobile Health News*. https://www.mobihealthnews.com/news/europe/when-ehealth-goes-viral-strangths-weaknesses-of-health-tech-during-COVID-19/

Nuwagira, E., & Muzoora, C. (2020). Is sub-saharan Africa prepared for COVID-19? *Tropical Medicine and Health*, *48*(1), 18–30. doi:10.1186/s41182-020-00206-x PMID:32288543

Nuwagira, E., & Muzoora, C. (2020). Is sub-saharan Africa prepared for COVID-19? *Tropical Medicine and Health*, *48*(1), 18–30. doi:10.1186/s41182-020-00206-x PMID:32288543

Nyoni, T., & Okumu, S. (2020). COVID-19 compliant strategies for supporting treatment adherence among people living with HIV in Sub-Saharan Africa. *AIDS and Behavior*, *25*(1), 2473–2476. doi:10.1007/s10461-020-02888-0 PMID:32333204

Okereafor, K., Adebola, O., & Djehaicher, R. (2020). Exploring the potentials of Telemedicine and other non-contact electronic health technologies in controlling the spread of the Novel COVID-19. *IJITE*, *8*(4), 1–13.

Olayiwola, J. N., Udenyi, E. D., Yusuf, G., Magaña, C., Patel, R., Duck, B., Sajanlal, S., Potapov, A., & Kibuka, C. (2020). Leveraging electronic consultations to address severe subspecialty care access gasps in Nigeria. *Journal of the National Medical Association*, *112*(1), 92–102. doi:10.1016/j.jnma.2019.10.005 PMID:32044103

Olayiwola, J. N., Udenyi, E. D., Yusuf, G., Magaña, C., Patel, R., Duck, B., Sajanlal, S., Potapov, A., & Kibuka, C. (2020). Leveraging electronic consultations to address severe subspecialty care access gasps in Nigeria. *Journal of the National Medical Association*, *112*(1), 92–102. doi:10.1016/j.jnma.2019.10.005 PMID:32044103

Oyelere, R., Oyolola, M., & Olurinola, I. (2020). COVID-19 and the welfare effects of remote work: Evidence from Nigeria. *World Development*, *136*, 105132.

Rogers, E. M. (2003). *Diffusion of Innovations*. Free Press.

Rwanda Development Board. (n.d.). *Regulatory Sandbox Framework*. Rwanda Development Board. [https://www.bnr.rw/laws-and-regulations/regulatory-digest-market-consultation/regulatory-digest/regulatory-sandbox-regulation/]

Saeed, K. A., & Muthitacharoen, A. (2008). To Send or Not to Send: An Empirical Assessment of Error Reporting Behavior. *IEEE Transactions on Engineering Management*, *55*(3), 455–467. doi:10.1109/TEM.2008.922623

Son, J., & Benbasat, I. (2007). Organizational buyers' adoption and use of B2B electronic marketplaces: Efficiency-and legitimacy-oriented perspectives. *Journal of Management Information Systems*, *24*(1), 55–99. doi:10.2753/MIS0742-1222240102

South Africa Government Gazette. (n.d.). Protection of Personal Information Act (POPIA). *South Africa Government Gazette.* [https://popia.co.za/]

Sun, H., & Zhang, P. (2006). The Role of Moderating Factors in User Technology Acceptance. *International Journal of Human-Computer Studies, 64*(2), 53–78. doi:10.1016/j.ijhcs.2005.04.013

TechCrunch. (2022). The E-commerce Boom is Still Afoot in Africa, Jumia's Earnings Indicate. *TechCrunch.* https://techcrunch.com/2022/05/17/the-e-commerce-boom-is-still-afoot-in-africa-jumias-earnings-indicate/

TechCrunch. (2022). *The E-commerce Boom is Still Afoot in Africa.* Jumia's Earnings Indicate.

TechCrunch. (2020). *Farmcrowdy Raises $1M Round to Bring Nigerian Farmers Online and to Market.* TechCrunch. https://techcrunch.com/2017/12/18/1579210/

Thong, J. Y. L., Hong, S.-J., & Tam, K. Y. (2006). The effects of post-adoption beliefs on the expectation-confirmation model for information technology continuance. *International Journal of Human-Computer Studies, 64*(9), 799–810. doi:10.1016/j.ijhcs.2006.05.001

Umeh, C. A. (2018). Challenges toward achieving health coverage in Ghana, Kenya and Tanzania. *The International Journal of Health Planning and Management, 33*, 794–805. doi:10.1002/hpm.2610 PMID:30074646

UNCTAD Global Review. (2020). *Covid-19 and Global Review.* UNCTAD. https://unctad.org/system/files/official-document/dtlstict2020d13_en_0.pdf

UNESCO. (2020). *COVID-19 Educational Disruption and Response.* UNESCO. https://en.unesco.org/covid19/educationresponse

United Nations Capital Development Fund. (2020). *Digital Financial Services for COVID-19 Response and Recovery in Africa.* UNCDF. https://www.uncdf.org/article/5537/digital-financial-services-for-covid-19-response-and-recovery-in-africa

Venkatesh, V. (2000). Determinants of Perceived Ease of Use: Integrating Control, Intrinsic Motivation, and Emotion into the Technology Acceptance Model. *Information Systems Research, 11*(4), 342–365. doi:10.1287/isre.11.4.342.11872

Venkatesh, V., & Davis, F. D. (1996). A Model of the Antecedents of Perceived Ease of Use: Development and Test*. *Decision Sciences, 27*(3), 451–481. doi:10.1111/j.1540-5915.1996.tb01822.x

Venkatesh, V., & Davis, F. D. (2000). A Theoretical Extension of the Technology Acceptance Model: Four Longitudinal Field Studies. *Management Science, 46*(2), 186–204. doi:10.1287/mnsc.46.2.186.11926

Venkatesh, V., Morris, M. G., Davis, G. B., & Davis, F. D. (2003). User Acceptance of Information Technology: Toward a Unified View. *Management Information Systems Quarterly, 27*(3), 425–478. doi:10.2307/30036540

Visa. (2021). *Visa Back to Business Study: South Africa Edition.* Visa. https://www.visa.co.za/dam/VCOM/regional/ap/pdf/south-africa/en/ZAR-visa-back-to-business-study-south-africa-edition.pdf

World Bank. (2020). *Digital Development in Africa*. World Bank. https://www.worldbank.org/en/region/afr/brief/digital-development-in-africa

World Bank. (2020). *Financial Inclusion Data - Global Findex Database*. World Bank. https://databank.worldbank.org/reports.aspx?source=global-findex-database

World Bank. (2020). *The African Continental Free Trade Area: Economic and Distributional Effects*. World Bank. https://openknowledge.worldbank.org/handle/10986/33738

World Bank. (2021). *COVID-19 and the Future of Work in Africa: Emerging Trends in Digital Technology*. World Bank. https://www.worldbank.org/en/publication/africa-pulse/pulse- 2021-sm

World Health Organization. (2020). *Digital Health in the African Region: Opportunities and Challenges*. WHO. https://www.afro.who.int/publications/digital-health-african-region-opportunities-and-challenges

Wu, I.-L., & Chen, J.-L. (2005). An extension of Trust and TAM model with TPB in the initial adoption of on-line tax: An empirical study. *International Journal of Human-Computer Studies*, *62*(6), 784–808. doi:10.1016/j.ijhcs.2005.03.003

ADDITIONAL READING

Abolade, T. O., & Durosinmi, A. E. (2018). The benefits and challenges of e-health applications in developing nations: A review. In *Paper presented at the 14th iSTEAMS conference at AL*. Hikmah University.

Africa C. D. C. (2020). *COVID-19: Digital Solutions for Africa's Response*. Africa CDC. https://africacdc.org/download/covid-19-digital-solutions-for-africas-response/

African Development Bank Group. (2020). *COVID-19: Opportunities for Africa's Economic Transformation*. African Development Bank Group. https://www.afdb.org/en/news-and-events/covid-19-opportunities-africas-economic-transformation-36156

Bokolo, A. J. (2020). Exploring the adoption of Telemedicine and virtual software for care of outpatients during and after COVID-19 pandemic. *International Journal of Medical Sciences*, 2020. PMID:32642981

ITU platforms. (2020). *"Connect2Recover", the Global Network Resiliency Platform "REG4COVID."* WSIS ICT Case Repository, and CYB4COVID.

Maharana, A., Amutorine, M., Sengeh, M. D., & Nsoesie, E. O. (2021). COVID-19 and beyond: Use of digital technology for pandemic response in Africa. *Scientific African*, *14*, e01041. doi:10.1016/j.sciaf.2021.e01041 PMID:34746524

McKinsey & Company. (2021). *Digital payments in Africa: Unlocking the $3.7 trillion opportunity*. McKinsey. https://www.mckinsey.com/~/media/McKinsey/Industries/Financial%20Services/Our%20Insights/Digital%20payments%20in%20Africa%20Unlocking%20the%2037%20trillion%20opportunity/Digital-payments-in-Africa-Unlocking-the-37-trillion-opportunity-vF.pdf

UNESCO. (2020). *COVID-19 Educational Disruption and Response*. UNESCO. https://en.unesco.org/covid19/educationresponse

World Bank. (2020). *Digital Development in Africa*. World Bank. https://www.worldbank.org/en/region/afr/brief/digital-development-in-africa

KEY TERMS AND DEFINITIONS

AI-Powered Diagnostic Tools: These refer to medical or healthcare applications and systems that utilize artificial intelligence (AI) algorithms and technologies to assist in the diagnosis of medical conditions, diseases, or health-related issues. These tools leverage machine learning, deep learning, and other AI techniques to analyze and interpret medical data, such as images, clinical notes, and patient records, to aid healthcare professionals in making accurate and timely diagnoses.

Digital Payments: This refers to financial transactions that are conducted electronically, using digital or electronic platforms and technologies to transfer money or make payments. These transactions replace traditional physical forms of payment, such as cash or checks, with digital methods that are facilitated through electronic devices and online channels.

Digital Transformation: This refers to the process of utilizing digital technologies to reshape or revolutionize the way businesses operate, deliver value to customers, and adapt to the changing demands of the modern digital landscape. It involves the integration of digital technologies into various aspects of an organization, fundamentally altering how it conducts its business, interacts with stakeholders, and delivers products or services.

E-Commerce: short for electronic commerce, refers to the buying and selling of goods and services over the internet or other electronic networks. It involves online transactions between businesses and consumers (B2C), businesses and businesses (B2B), or consumers and consumers (C2C), facilitated through electronic platforms, websites, or online marketplaces.

E-Health (Electronic Health): This refers to the use of information and communication technologies (ICT) to support and enhance healthcare services, delivery, and management. It encompasses a broad range of digital tools, systems, and platforms that contribute to the improvement of healthcare processes, patient care, and overall health outcomes.

E-Learning: short for electronic learning, refers to the use of electronic technologies, primarily the internet, to facilitate and enhance learning and education. It encompasses a broad range of educational activities, materials, and platforms delivered through digital means, allowing learners to access educational content and interact with instructors or peers remotely.

Financial Technology: commonly known as FinTech, refers to the use of innovative technologies to deliver financial services, products, and solutions. FinTech companies leverage advancements in information technology, data analytics, artificial intelligence, blockchain, and other emerging technologies to enhance and automate various aspects of the financial industry.

M-Health (Mobile Health): This refers to the use of mobile devices, such as smartphones, tablets, and wearable devices, in the delivery of healthcare services, information, and health-related applications. M-health leverages the capabilities of mobile technology to support various aspects of healthcare, including remote monitoring, health education, communication between patients and healthcare providers, and the management of health-related data.

Momo: In some regions, particularly in Africa, "momo" is used as a colloquial abbreviation for "mobile money." Mobile money services allow users to make financial transactions, including money transfers and payments, using their mobile phones. M-Pesa, as mentioned earlier, is a well-known example of a mobile money service, and it is sometimes informally referred to as "momo."

M-Pesa: It is a mobile money service that originated in Kenya and has since expanded to various countries in Africa and beyond. The term "M-Pesa" is derived from the Swahili words "mobile" and "pesa" (money), reflecting its nature as a mobile-based financial service. M-Pesa was launched by Safaricom, a leading telecommunications provider in Kenya, in 2007.

Pandemic: is an epidemic of an infectious disease that has spread across a large region, multiple countries, continents, or even worldwide, affecting a substantial number of people. It is commonly used to describe the widespread and sustained impact of a contagious illness that exceeds what is typically expected in a specific geographic area.

Quantum: The term "quantum" has several meanings depending on the context in which it is used: In mathematics, "quantum" is sometimes used as an adjective to describe discrete or discontinuous quantities. For example, a "quantum leap" refers to a sudden and significant change, often used metaphorically to describe abrupt progress or advancement.

Technological Infrastructure: refers to the underlying foundation of hardware, software, networks, and facilities that support and enable the operation of various technologies within a given system, organization, or society. It forms the backbone for the functioning of information technology and communication systems, providing the necessary resources and capabilities for technological services and operations.

Telemedicine: refers to the use of telecommunications technology, such as video calls, phone calls, or secure messaging, to provide healthcare services remotely. It involves the exchange of medical information from one location to another, allowing healthcare professionals to diagnose, treat, and care for patients without the need for in-person visits.

Uptake: Refers to the acceptance and integration of new technologies or innovations within a particular community, industry, or society. For instance, "The rapid uptake of smartphones revolutionized communication globally.

Utilization: refers to the effective or practical use, application, or deployment of something for a specific purpose or function. It involves the extent to which a resource, system, service, or capability is put into operation or applied to fulfill a particular need or achieve a specific goal.

Chapter 14
Utilization of Industry 4.0 Technologies in Nigerian Technical and Vocational Education:
A Conundrum for Educators

Williams Kennedy George
Department of Technical Education, Akwa Ibom State College of Education, Nigeria

Edidiong Isonguyo Silas
Department of Technical Education, Akwa Ibom State College of Education, Nigeria

Digvijay Pandey
iD https://orcid.org/0000-0003-0353-174X
Department of Technical Education, India

Binay Kumar Pandey
iD https://orcid.org/0000-0002-4041-1213
Department of Information Technology, College of Technology, Govind Ballabh University of Agriculture and Technology, Pantnagar, India

ABSTRACT

Technical and vocational education and training (TVET) play a pivotal role in preparing the Nigerian workforce for the demands of a rapidly evolving digital economy. In the wake of the Fourth Industrial Revolution 4.0, the integration of digital competencies in TVET programs has become imperative. This chapter explores the strategies and approaches to foster digital competencies in Nigeria's TVET by leveraging Industrial Revolution 4.0 as an enabling technology. The chapter presents the context of the historical evolution of industry 4.0, its components, design principles, main characteristics, and the TVET approach in Nigeria. Emphasizing the urgency of aligning TVET programs with Industrial Revolution 4.0 requirements, the chapter presents best practices that illustrate successful models of incorporating digital competencies into vocational training. The chapter examines the existing challenges and gaps in integrating digital skills into TVET curriculum in Nigeria, addressing issues related to infrastructure, funding, policy frameworks, and inclusivity. The chapter discusses the role of stakeholders such as government bodies, educational institutions, industry partners, and international organizations in facilitating the implementation of Industrial Revolution 4.0-driven initiatives in Nigerian TVET. Furthermore, the chapter offers actionable recommendations for policymakers, educators, and stakeholders to collaboratively design and implement strategies for integrating Industrial Revolution 4.0 technologies into Nigeria's TVET landscape. By doing so, it advocates for a more agile and future-ready workforce capable of harnessing the transformative power of digital technologies in the Nigerian context.

DOI: 10.4018/978-1-6684-9962-7.ch014

INTRODUCTION

The integration of digital competencies into TVET programs has emerged as a critical imperative for preparing the Nigerian workforce to thrive in an increasingly digitized economy. Developing countries like Nigeria must keep up with technological changes if they are to harness the opportunities offered by Industrial Revolution 4.0 and manage its potential disruption. In Nigeria, this revolution has posed both challenges and opportunities, particularly in Technical and Vocational Education and Training (TVET). This introductory chapter sets the stage for a comprehensive exploration of the strategies, challenges, and potential solutions in developing digital competencies in Nigeria's TVET sector by harnessing Industrial Revolution 4.0 as an enabling technology. It endeavors to shed light on the significance of aligning vocational education with the technological advancements characterizing Industrial Revolution 4.0 and emphasizes the urgency of this alignment in driving sustainable economic growth and fostering inclusive development.

This chapter scrutinizes the current state of TVET in Nigeria, identifying the existing challenges and limitations in equipping students with digital skills requisite for Industrial Revolution 4.0 driven workplaces. It delves into the gaps in the curriculum, teacher training, infrastructure, and policies, which hinder the effective integration of digital competencies into vocational education. Drawing from a range of perspectives, including the current state of technical education in Nigeria, the evolving landscape of industry 4.0 technologies and the challenges encountered by educators in their adoption, this chapter offer pragmatic strategies for educators navigating this transformative era. By acknowledging the complexity involved in proposing viable pathways, the chapter define the core concepts of Industrial Revolution 4.0 and TVET, elucidate the key technological advancements associated with Industrial Revolution 4.0, such as artificial intelligence, robotics, the Internet of Things (IoT), big data analytics, and automation. It outlines their transformative impact on industries globally and underscores the necessity for Nigerian TVET to adapt and integrate these digital competencies into its curriculum to remain relevant and competitive.

The evolution of the Fourth Industrial Revolution 4.0 has triggered a profound transformation across global industries, reshaping the landscape of work and necessitating the acquisition of new skills (Huang, 2017). The word revolution denotes abrupt and radical change. Given that in the era of globalization, industrial organizations are under continuous pressure to innovate, improve their competitiveness and perform better than their competitors in the global market. Every industrial revolution centered on boosting productivity. The last three centuries have seen quantum leaps in the human condition. The First Industrial Revolution began in England in about 1750 - 1760 that lasted between 1820 and 1840; the second revolution started in the late 19th; and the third revolution, taking off in the late 20th century (Schwab, 2016 & Mohajan, 2019). The first three industrial revolutions had a significant impact on industrial operations, allowing for increased productivity and efficiency.

The first industrial revolution ushered in the migration of manual labor performed by people and animals to a more optimized form of labor performed by people through the use of steam powered engines and machine tools (William, 2012; Ionescu, 2018). The second industrial revolution occurred in the United States during the 1850 - 1870s, until the First World War in 1914 with the advent of steel, petroleum and the use of electricity in factories and new transport and communication systems (Flashes Magazine, 2017). The IR3 started in the late 1960's known as the digital revolution (Gordon, 2000), is considered as the movement from mechanical and analogue electronic technology to digital technologies, such as improvement in the communication, the development of the Internet, networks, green buildings, electric cars, and distributed manufacturing (Duarte, Sanches & Dedini 2018). The latest industrial revolution 4.0 or Industry 4.0 has emerged due to the emphasis digital technologies are having on businesses. Schwab (2016) and Pauceanu (2020) maintained that Industrial Revolution 4.0 technological advancements offer a comprehensive, interlinked and holistic approach to manufacturing. It connects the physical and digital technologies, allowing for better collaboration and access to departments, partners, vendors, products and people.

According to Koch et al. (2014) and Surah et al. (2018), Industrial Revolution 4.0 refers to a new phase of revolution that focuses heavily on interconnectivity, automation, machine learning and real time data. It is also referred to as Industrial Internet of Things (IIoT) or Smart Manufacturing/Factories (Hermann et al., 2015). All these revolutions generated changes related to work, education, scientific field, and mostly with the human consumption, which brought the mass production concept. Bock (2014), notes that one of the most essential aspects of Technical and Vocational Education and Training (TVET), is its orientation toward the world of work and the development of transferable skills to students. As an emerging technology, the majority of educational researchers might be unaware of what the Industrial Revolution 4.0 is, and its relevance in TVET. It should be noted that introducing the Industrial Revolution 4.0 into the educational field may trigger several controversial issues that deserve further discussion, calling for a review of the concept, components, design principles, characteristics, opportunities and challenges facing effective integration of Industrial Revolution 4.0 in TVET.

THE CONCEPT OF INDUSTRIAL REVOLUTION 4.0

Industry 4.0 is a concept that emerged for the first time in 2011 at a Hannover Fair in Germany with the objective of characterizing highly digitized manufacturing processes where information flows among machines in a controlled environment so that human intervention is reduced to a minimum (Qin, Liu & Grosvenor, 2016). The concept was developed by German Industrial and Academic communities with the support of the German Government with the intention of framing and developing the country's industrial competencies that have been powered by digitization of the production processes in several industrial sectors (Kagerman, Washler & Helbig, 2013). The idea was adopted by the federal German Government as part of their high-tech strategy for 2020. The management board of the International Organization for Standardization (ISO) announced in the year 2015, the constitution of interdisciplinary strategic consultative line-up focusing on Industry 4.0 in collaboration with the International Electro-Technical Commission (IEC) and the International Telecommunication Union (ITU) in order to produce a concise description or definition of Industry 4.0.

The Fourth Industrial Revolution is characterized by a technological revolution was builds upon the third Industrial Revolution which applied electronics and information technology to automate production (Spottl, 2016). According to Schwab (2016), the Fourth Industrial Revolution includes the emergence of the Digital Economy and use of automation and data exchange in industrial technologies. These technologies include the Internet of Things, synergy between networked machines and human beings in decision-making, and artificial intelligence for computerized technical processes, whereas Spottl (2016), describes Industry 4.0 as a convergence of technologies that cut across the physical, digital, and biological spheres. Pauceanu, Rabie and Moustafa (2020) described industry 4.0 as the relationship between the physical, electronic, and biological spheres is shaped by a collection of technologies that make up the fourth industrial revolution. Industry 4.0 is the process of increasing productivity and service using a management system that focuses on strengthening the use of intelligent systems (smart systems) that are able to communicate between machines with machines and humans with machines.

Industry 4.0 according to Usoro, Ezekiel and Ojobah (2021), was built from advanced technologies, namely: adaptive robots, data computing and artificial intelligence in the form of big data analytics, simulations, embedded systems, communication and industrial internet networks, cloud systems, additive manufacturing, and Augmented Reality all of which would accelerate the development of the modern world (Schwab, 2016; Mustapha, 2021; Usoro, Ezekiel & Ojobah, 2021). These technological advancements are critically required for efficiently improved systems that reduce human imperfections and mediation (Nguyen et al., 2022). The smart products integration with smart production, smart logistics and smart networks and Internet of Things results in the transformation of current value chains and the emergence of new and innovative business models, making the smart factory the key element of future smart infrastructures. This new age of revolution is based on the creation of an integrative and collaborative environment, with the intention to add cyber physical systems and to consider the customer as part of the production process. On this fourth industrial revolution, the analysis and the test of the product are done before it goes to the market, not after, which bring up the opportunity to predict what is going to happen before it happens, improving the management of the investment that is made around the production.

The main input of the fourth industrial revolution was the setup of the Intel industries, where it is not just about data compilation, but keeping in mind the importance of the interaction between all these information, being allowed to connect it with different information sources and being able to create a controlled system with a high speed and flexible kind of production (Duarte, Sanches & Dedini, 2018). The Fourth Industrial Revolution 4.0 has ushered in extraordinary technological advances, fusing boundaries of physical, digital, and biological worlds to create new paradigms in the way we live, work, and interact. These trends have heralded excitement in advancing frontiers of human endeavor and fear of negative repercussions on jobs and rising inequalities. It is the fusion of these technologies and their interaction across the physical, digital and biological domains that make the fourth industrial revolution fundamentally different from previous revolutions. In this revolution, emerging technologies and broad-based innovation are diffusing much faster and more widely than in previous ones, which continue to unfold in some parts of the world (Usoro, Ezekiel & Ojobah, 2021). Figure 1 shows the concepts of the industrial revolution from Industry 1.0 to Industry 4.0.

Figure 1. Industrial revolution from Industry 1.0 to Industry 4.0
Source: Spectral Engines (2018)

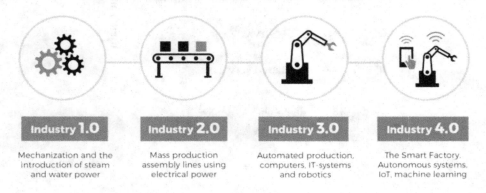

One of the peculiarities of the industry 4.0 is its integration capability. The Koch, Geissbauer and Schrauf, (2014), presented the fundamental and interdependent presence of two value chains, horizontal and vertical. This process involves the integration and proactive control of all internal areas of the company, such as planning, purchasing, production and logistics. The process also includes all external value chain partners who are key participants in meeting customer demand requirements and fulfilling the requested services. Figures 2 and 3 show the horizontal and vertical value chain with its respective members.

Figure 2. Horizontal value chain in Industry 4.0
Source: Koch, et.al., 2014

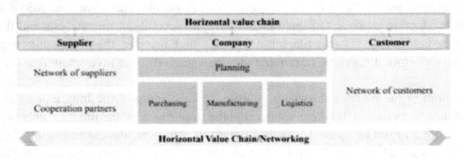

Figure 3. Vertical value chain in Industry 4.0.
Source: Koch, et.al., (2014)

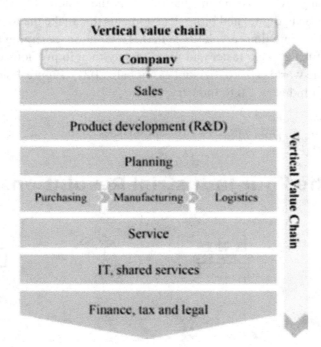

COMPONENTS OF INDUSTRIAL REVOLUTION 4.0 TECHNOLOGIES

The fourth Industrial Revolution (Industry 4.0) framework indicates the creation and intersection of advanced technologies, such as the Internet of Things (IoT), Cyber Physical Systems (CPS), cloud computing, and digital twins, which are pervasive (Ayoade et al, 2022). These technological advancements are critically required for efficiently improved systems that reduce human imperfections and mediation (Nguyen et al., 2022). The main components that form the concept of Industrial Revolution 4.0 according to Schwab (2016), Tay et al., (2018), Soldatos (2019), Oztemel and Gursev (2020) and Ghadge et.al (2020) are:

1. **Additive Manufacturing (AM)**: In Industrial Revolution 4.0 manufacturing environments, these technologies are the best choice for producing small-batch, customized and high-performance products. With AM, some industry segments can switch production of their products using materials that do not come directly from nature, or that are biodegradable, or even edible, for some very specific types of industry. In this way the industry can achieve a more environmentally productive input. The AM can use materials that have been nonconforming or spare in the industry and make them viable to produce new products that integrate them rather than selecting materials to be extracted or prefabricated, eliminating irregular ones causing negative environmental results.

2. **Artificial Intelligence/Cloud Computing**: AI is referred to an area of computer science where intelligent machines/software is created that work or react like humans. AI is a broad term describing machines and software carrying out non-traditional computing tasks. Cloud computing uses the assets and capabilities of the IoT, advanced data analytics, and cognitive technologies such as AI and machine learning to drive improvements in the quality, efficiency, and reliability of manufacturing processes.

3. **Augmented Reality and Simulation:** The augmented reality (AR) works effectively with Industrial Revolution 4.0 enhanced reality in which direct or indirect views of physical real-world environments are augmented with computer-generated visuals projected even in real-time, thus streamlining the decision-making process to perform actions or repairs. With AR, process testing and optimization through simulation permit people to decrease business changeover, risk, setup time, and enhance quality control for future processes and services, even before the implementation of adjustments in the actual physical world. with AR the worker needs no longer to consult paper manuals or phone supports. staff can rather view on-line the repair or service instructions provided by an expert from a remote location.

4. **Big Data/Advanced Analytics (BDA):** Industrial Revolution 4.0 is typically empowered by Big Data technologies for data collection, consolidation and storage, given that industries need to bring together multiple fragmented datasets and to store them in a reliable and cost-effective fashion. Its potential for Industrial Revolution 4.0 is to group, analyze and provide relevant data and information on existing resources, resources used, machine functionality, energy efficiency, waste generation, waste utilization and pollution levels emitted. The BDA can provide historical information on a possible resource already used in the production of the same good, which may be reused. It can also notify, by systems, the lack of a certain resource for production, or even the breakdown of some machine, causing the production process to be interrupted. BDA serves as a warning of opportunities and correction needs, as well as its high capacity for storing data and information.

5. **Machine to Machine (M2M) Communication:** M2M communication refers to the technology that allows direct communication between devices/machinery using wired or wireless communication. Machine-to-machine communication can include personal communications and industrial instrumentation, enabling a sensor or meter to communicate the information it records to software that can use it like adjusting an industrial process based on machine feedback or placing orders to replenish inventory.

6. **Industrial Internet of Things (IIoT):** The IIoT is a concept that combines various technologies, techniques, network of devices, computers and sensors to gather and share data to create a smart manufacturing environment, also known as a smart factory. The data collected is then stored in a centralized cloud-based repository where data is aggregated and shared with end users in a meaningful way. The IIoT allows industries to identify reversible or non-reversible machine and equipment failures, sensor and system problems, production disruption, changing customer demand requirements, stakeholder service opportunities, and many other possibilities.

7. **Cyber Physical System (CPS):** It is the term that describes the unification of digital (cyber) with real (physical) workflows. In general, Cyber means computation, communication, and control that are discrete and logical. When computing and communication systems bridges with the physical world are referred to as Cyber Physical Systems. A Cyber Physical System (CPS) is a mechanism controlled or monitored by computer-based algorithms, integrated with internet and its users. With internet connectivity, the CPS can communicate any changes that need to be made it through notices to computer systems and mobile devices and perform autonomous (when programmed) or allowed (when coordinated by people), the necessary changes in the production process. They provide rapid control and verification of process feedback in order to generate predicted outputs.

8. **Cybersecurity:** Industrial Revolution 4.0 environments include connectivity and communications protocols as well as sophisticated identity and access management systems. These technologies enable manufacturers to provide secure, reliable communications and data flow throughout Industrial Revolution 4.0 systems. Industrial Revolution 4.0 applications introduce several security challenges, given that they are on the verge of IT which pose conflicting requirements from the security viewpoint. Any Industrial Revolution 4.0 solutions should come with strong security features towards protecting datasets, ensuring the trustworthiness of new devices and protecting the deployment for vulnerabilities of IT assets.

9. **Real Time Locating Systems (RTLS):** The location detection is a technology commonly used with the tag system. When the location of machines and equipment, products in the production stage, finished products is known, accuracy, waste generation and pollutants are minimized throughout the industry. The location detection helps resources that should be on the production line be easily located without wasting a lot of time and energy efficiency on running machines. With location detection the industry becomes more agile and accurate, reducing waste generation due to local verification errors. Also, logistics can prevent wrong deliveries and cargoes by mistake in defining the correct location to arrive.

10. **Smart Sensors:** The smart sensors (SS) are a type of technology that informs systems for employee viewing of possible errors or non-conformities whether in materials, products, machines, steps or production lines, and can measure levels of waste or pollution generated. The SS is a technology that can send these notifications to employees through systems on machines, central computers, or mobile devices and can take no further action, or can act, when so programmed, autonomously. The SS may receive an initial configuration of acceptable indices distributed at different scales, and when nonconformity that exceeds such ranges occurs, the SS may notify employees or take action that the production process is not erroneous at any stage, resulting in negative results for the environment.

The challenges facing Industrial Revolution 4.0 technologies according to Carvalho, Carvalho and Carvalho (2020) is presented in table 1.

Table 1. The challenges facing Industrial Revolution 4.0 technologies

S/N	Technologies 4.0	Main Challenges
1.	Cyber-physical systems	Cost considered still high for acquisition
		Installation in suitable places considering space and distance
		Need to connect to all machines throughout the production area
		Need to connect to all systems and sensors in the production area.
		Be connected in real-time to the whole productive area
		Pass by constant and periodic maintenance
2.	Cloud manufacturing	Have ample data and information storage capacity
		Receive, archive and share data and information in real-time
		Be connected in real-time to industry computers, systems and machines
		Be connected in real-time with stakeholder demands
3.	Big Data analytics	Have ample data and information storage capacity
		Receive, combine, analyze, archive and share data and information in real-time
		Be connected in real-time to industry computers, systems and machines
		Have historical information and records of changes made
		Be connected in real-time with the needs and changing demands of stakeholders
4.	Augmented reality	Have interconnected auxiliary devices of adequate amplitude
		Have discipline in strictly necessary uses
		Be connected with systems and sensors for assisted production operations
		Have internet connectivity for use in different parts of the industry or in another location.
5.	Smart sensors	Have space and distance required for correct performance
		Be connected to internet in real-time
		Be connected to systems in real-time
		Be connected to each other and machines in real-time
		Have the machines integrated performance capability
6.	Location detection	Be properly and accurately installed in machinery and equipment
		Be connected to internet in real-time
		Be connected to systems in real-time
		Act together with smart sensors
7.	Industrial Internet of Things	Capacity installation on all machines, sensors and systems
		Be included on all central computers and mobile devices
		Receive, combine, share and notify industry internal and external stimuli
		Be included in partnering and service network systems from other industries
8.	Additive manufacturing	Consider the best materials use option in the manufacture of a product
		Consider the need for resistance of the material to be used in the manufacture of the product
		Consider the use of waste generated as material for manufacturing
		Deliberate the ideal ways of disposing of the product when no longer used
		Control manufacturing according to need and demand, always considering the impacts on the environment

THE INDUSTRIAL REVOLUTION 4.0 DESIGN PRINCIPLES

The Industrial Revolution 4.0 encompasses six design principles in its framework, which are called decentralization, virtualization, interoperability, modularity, real-time capability, and service orientation. These principles are called "design principles" because they contribute to the design or transition process from IR3.0 to Industrial Revolution 4.0 (Hermann & Pentek Otto, 2015). According to Domingo (2016), Yasanur (2018) and Amiron, Latib and Subari (2019) the main Industrial Revolution 4.0 design principles are as follows:

1. **Decentralization:** The first principle known as decentralization is understood in industry 4.0 as the greater ability of companies, specific operations, as well as machines, to make their decisions without interference. Rather than using central computers or passing a decision hierarchically, enabling and allowing local operators to respond to changes and readjust, this principle provides more flexibility and makes it easier to use expertise. However, the principle of decentralization cannot be observed for machines, as it refers to the autonomy granted to people as collaborators in industry 4.0. They have greater freedom to identify aspects, analyze parameters, and carry out decision-making whenever necessary, aiming at the common good for their area of activity in the industry as well as for its fullness.

2. **Virtualization**: The principle of virtualization is that by using machine-to-machine (M2M) monitoring and communication, a virtual twin can be abstracted from the industry. The sensor data is linked to virtual plant models and simulation models. Thus, a virtual copy of the physical world can be created. In case of failure, an employee can be notified. In addition, all necessary information, such as next work steps or security provisions, remains available. The virtualization in industry 4.0 is used by people as highly potential tools to aid human work. This principle streamlines the time, analysis, and decision-making of employees and established teams by providing, sharing, and synthesizing information virtually, quickly, and in real time.

3. **Interoperability:** The principle of interoperability in the industry 4.0 manufacturing environment is that cyber-physical system (CPS) comprises intelligent machines and intelligent storage systems and facilities capable of autonomously exchanging information, initiating actions, and controlling each other independently. The embedded manufacturing systems are vertically connected with business processes internal to industries, and horizontally, with the value chain, by connecting software and programs.

4. **Modularity:** The principle of modularity involves modular systems that can flexibly adapt to changing requirements by replacing or expanding individual production modules, making adding or removing modules much easier. These modular systems can thus simply be adjusted in case of seasonal fluctuations or changes in product production needs, as in the case of including new technologies. Thus, production can always adjust to environmental, systemic, and changing customer demands without error, lost productivity, or customer dissatisfaction.

5. **Real-time capability:** To define the principle of real-time capability, states that in the manufacturing process, intelligent machines with specific software will automatically adapt to the process and decision-making by CPS to the productive needs, thus monitoring the product quality in order to make decisions at every moment of need. This interconnection will minimize misuse of resources, waste, material waste, and increase energy efficiency. The real-time capability principle is one of the most outstanding aspects of industry 4.0 as it is responsible for ensuring that the industry has

the best possible response time to internal and external stimuli by sharing, receiving, and analyzing data and information in real time.

6. **Service orientation:** The principle of service orientation is characterized by the availability, through the Internet, of human, business services, and CPS, which can be used by other stakeholders, facilitating the creation of product-service systems (PSS), also known as product-service. They can be offered internally to and outside the organization. In this way, industry 4.0 preserves its network performance in partnerships with all its stakeholders, whether customers, partner industries, and suppliers, among many others. Everyone can have access to useful services, products, and information about the industry using virtual and digital platforms available at all times.

THE CHARACTERISTICS OF INDUSTRIAL REVOLUTION 4.0

Industry 4.0 is characterized primarily by connection, integration and industrial digitalization, highlighting the possibilities for integrating all components in a value-adding system. The core progress from traditional manufacturing to Industrial Revolution 4.0 are categorized into four key features and characteristics according to Santos, Brittes, Fibian and German (2018), Aoun, Ghandour and Ibrahim (2021) and Karnik, Bora, Bhadri, Kadambi and Dhatra (2021) as follows:

1. **Vertical networking of smart production:** Industry 4.0's first main characteristic is the vertical networking of smart manufacturing systems. Vertical integration in Industry 4.0 establishes a connection between the many levels of the industry, from the manufacturing floor up, via production monitoring, control, and supervision, quality management, operations, product management, processing, and so on. This interconnectedness across all corporate levels provides for a fluid, transparent data flow, allowing for data-driven strategic and tactical choices. Processing data, anomalies, and defects from various processing stages of the manufacturing line are automatically captured and registered, allowing for quick responses to order changes, quality variations, and even machinery breakdowns. As a consequence, waste is decreased, and resource efficiency, notably in terms of material usage, energy consumption, and human resources is improved.

2. **Horizontal networking of smart production:** In the Industry 4.0 concept, horizontal integration refers to the network of diverse processes, companies, and services that make up a product's global value chain. This can be viewed at the production level as a total consolidation of all associated manufacturing processes. If an enterprise owns several production sites, the horizontal integration enables to share inventory levels and unexpected delays, and possibly redistribute work among owned facilities to respond to market demand fluctuations rapidly or increase the efficiency and speed of the production process. The horizontal integration across all the activities creates a transparent value chain that is updated in real-time.

3. **Through-life engineering across the entire value chain:** Industry 4.0 will enable integrated and cross-disciplinary engineering throughout the value chain, as well as throughout product and customer life cycles. Industry 4.0 applications are intended to ensure the traditional domain of product innovation.

4. **The Impact of Exponential Technologies:** Corporate venture capital firms have a strong chance of profiting from disruptive innovation and exponential technology by investing in new trends early on. Corporate venture capital investing in start-ups allows businesses to participate in the develop-

ment of new products and services while also ensuring their long-term competitiveness. This type of investment allows for early and convenient access to new technologies.

INDUSTRIAL REVOLUTION 4.0 TECHNOLOGY IN NIGERIAN TVET

The term National Policy on Education (NPE) in Nigeria is described as an educational constitution policy document that embraces nearly all aspects of Nigerian Education system which serves as a guide to be followed. The policy document came into being as a result of the National Curriculum conference or seminar of experts drawn from a wide range of interest groups within Nigeria that was convened in Lagos in 1973. The first edition of the NPE was published in 1977 and subsequently reviewed in 1981, 1988, 2004, and 2013 (FRN 1981; FRN, 1988; FRN, 2004 & FRN, 2013). In 1977, when the National Policy on Education (NPE) was first published, the issue of acquisition of practical skills to make students more self-reliant was incorporated (FRN, 1977). The 2013 edition of NPE (FRN, 2013) section 3, paragraph 49 and Shikalepo (2019) refers to "those aspects of the educational process involving, in addition to general education, the study of technologies and related sciences and the acquisition of practical skills, attitudes, understanding and knowledge relating to occupations in various sectors of economic and social life as TVET. It is important to note that all the revisions unequivocally stated the importance and the objectives of TVET, though the training program was given different names as Technical Education (TE) in 1981; Polytechnic and Monotechnic Education (PME) in 1988; Technical and Vocational Education in 2004; and Technical and Vocational Education and Training (TVET) in 2013.

Nigerian philosophy of education therefore is based on the development of the individual into a sound and effective citizen; the full integration of the individual into the community; and the provision of equal access to educational opportunities for all citizens of the country at the primary, secondary and tertiary levels both inside and outside the formal school system. For the philosophy to be in harmony with Nigeria's national goals, education has to be geared towards self-realization, better human relationship individual and national efficiency, effective citizenship, national consciousness, national unity, as well as towards social, cultural, economic, political, scientific and technological progress. The national educational goals, which derive from the philosophy, are the training of the mind in the understanding of the world around; and the acquisition of appropriate skills and development of mental, physical an abilities and competencies as equipment for the individual to live in and contribute to the development of the society.

A very important point of view in the era of Industrial Revolution 4.0 is the problem of having work capabilities such as abilities, competencies, skills and willingness employed collaboratively in TVET (Rahim & Shamsudin, 2019). According to Pereira et al. (2017), the quest of applying Industry 4.0 brings diverse technological challenges, with high influences on many dimensions in today's manufacturing industry. The demand of changing the workforce in the era of the industrial revolution 4.0 is a fundamental challenge for Technical Vocational Education and Training (TVET) to quickly and efficiently meet the needs of changing skills. Several studies address the challenges that some countries are facing in preparing TVET graduates in terms of their Industrial Revolution 4.0 job readiness skills. A series of skills mismatches will cause unemployment among graduates, and the cause is due to lack of experience, lack of job market information, and lack of employability skills such as communication skills as well as new skills that have not been found to align with future job market demand (Wang et.al. 2016).

Furthermore, the challenges faced by the industry as a result of the revolution are the lack of digital culture and lack of training, and context-based knowledge of Industry 4.0 (Kot, 2018 & Ślusarczyk, 2018).

There are already emerging jobs and redundant jobs in the era of digital transformation and industrial revolution 4.0 in Nigeria TVET. Currently, there are inadequate Data analysis and Scientists, Big data Specialists, AI and Machine Learning Specialists, Digital Marketing and Strategy Specialists, Renewable Energy Engineers, Process Automation Specialists, Internet of Things Specialists, Digital Transformation Specialists, Business Services and Administration Managers, Business Development Professionals to facilitate the core Industrial Revolution 4.0 skills in TVET in Nigeria. TVET educators and graduates lack core Industrial Revolution 4.0 skills including Analytical thinking and innovation skill; Active learning and learning strategies skill; Creativity, originality and initiative skill; Design and programming technology skill; Critical thinking and analysis skill; Complex problem-solving skill; Leadership and social influence skill; Emotional intelligence skill; reasoning, problem solving and ideational skill; system analysis and evaluation skill. The cost of implementing economic and technological reforms for social benefits is just too high for most African States including Nigeria. This is because most of the technology required to transform society are coming from outside Africa (Usoro, Ezekiel & Ojobah, 2021). Educators are expected to experience challenges as they are teaching the digital generation, who has different learning styles that mostly involve the aid of communication and in addition, this generation gains information from multiple and various sources and channels. The roles and tasks of lecturers have also changed as they are no longer expected to merely lecture but also curate basic knowledge for their students.

Usoro, Ezekiel & Ojobah (2021), noted that collaboration with international partners in the utilization of Industry 4.0 technologies in Nigerian Technical and Vocational Education (TVET) brings various benefits and opportunities in the following ways:

1. **Knowledge Exchange and Expertise Sharing:** International partnerships facilitate the exchange of knowledge, expertise, and best practices in integrating Industry 4.0 technologies. This collaboration allows Nigerian TVET institutions to learn from global experiences, advancements, and successful models.

2. **Access to Advanced Technology and Tools:** Partnering with international institutions or organizations grants access to advanced technologies, software, equipment, and tools. This access enables Nigerian TVET institutions to equip their facilities with state-of-the-art resources for practical training and learning experiences. Offer opportunities for capacity building through specialized training programs, workshops, and seminars conducted by experts in Industry 4.0 technologies. These programs enhance the skills of educators and students, ensuring they are up-to-date with the latest technological trends.

3. **Joint Research and Development Initiatives:** Collaborative research projects between Nigerian TVET institutions and international partners facilitate innovation and the development of new applications for Industry 4.0 technologies. Joint R&D initiatives encourage the creation of solutions relevant to local needs, assists in the enhancement and reform of TVET curricula. Partnering institutions contribute insights and perspectives, aiding in the development of industry-aligned curricula that integrate relevant IR4.0 concepts and skills.

4. **Global Networking and Partnerships:** Collaboration with international partners broadens the network of TVET institutions in Nigeria. It creates opportunities for strategic alliances, fostering relationships with reputable global organizations, universities, and industries, which can result in

future collaborations and exchanges. Partnerships facilitate student exchange programs and internships abroad. Nigerian TVET students get exposure to international work environments, gaining practical experience and cross-cultural understanding, which enriches their learning.

5. **Policy Support and Advocacy:** International partnerships often involve advocating for policy support and funding from global organizations and donor agencies. Such support aids in policy reforms, funding initiatives, and the implementation of projects aimed at integrating Industry 4.0 technologies in TVET.

The complexity of work situations in the industry is steeply increasing and is consequently leading to higher demands in the quality of workforces with special competencies to meet companies' needs (D'Souza & Mudin, 2018; Azman & Ibrahim, 2018; Ibrahim et al., 2018; Shafei, Haris & Hamzah, 2018). Successful implementation of Industrial Revolution 4.0 driven initiatives in Nigerian TVET requires a coordinated effort among government bodies, educational institutions, industry partners, and international organizations. Collaboration, resource-sharing, curriculum alignment, and skill development are key factors in ensuring that TVET graduates are equipped with the skills needed for the evolving job market in the era of Industry 4.0 to facilitating this implementation. Some potential initiatives to integrate IR4.0 technologies into TVET in Nigeria are:

1. **GE Lagos Garage Initiative:** General Electric (GE) launched the Lagos Garage, an innovation hub providing training and resources in advanced manufacturing, technology development, and innovation. While not specifically a TVET program, it aimed to impart skills related to Industry 4.0 technologies to participants.
2. **Siemens Mechatronics Training Center:** Siemens Nigeria initiated plans to establish a Mechatronics Training Center in Nigeria. This center was intended to provide hands-on training in mechatronics, combining mechanical and electrical engineering with automation and IoT, aligning with Industry 4.0 principles.
3. **Partnerships with Industry Leaders**: TVET institutions in Nigeria have been seeking collaborations with industry leaders to create specialized training programs. These collaborations aimed to equip students with skills relevant to Industry 4.0, potentially including sectors such as robotics, IoT applications, and data analytics.
4. **National Automotive Design and Development Council (NADDC):** Initiatives by NADDC aimed to modernize Nigeria's automotive industry by introducing IR4.0 technologies. While not directly linked to TVET, it could pave the way for skill development and training programs related to advanced manufacturing techniques.
5. **Skills Development Programs by Technology Hubs:** Various technology hubs and incubators in Nigeria have been offering skill development programs that might indirectly touch upon IR4.0 technologies. These programs targeted young entrepreneurs and tech enthusiasts, potentially involving aspects of IoT, AI, and digital manufacturing.
6. **Technical Colleges Modernization Efforts:** Some technical colleges and polytechnics in Nigeria have been undergoing modernization efforts, although detailed case studies might not be readily available. These initiatives could encompass updates in curriculum, laboratories, and infrastructure to align with IR4.0 principles.
7. **Nigerian Universities' Collaboration with Tech Companies:** Some Nigerian universities have been collaborating with tech companies on research projects related to Industry 4.0 technologies.

These projects might trickle down to the TVET sector through curriculum updates or knowledge transfer initiatives.

IMPACT OF DEVELOPING INDUSTRIAL REVOLUTION 4.0 IN NIGERIAN TVET

Developing TVET digital competencies in Nigeria is pivotal to ensuring graduates are adequately prepared to meet the demands of a technology-driven job market, fostering employability and contributing to the country's economic development. The integration of Technical Vocational Education and Training (TVET) digital competencies in Nigeria using Industrial Revolution 4.0 as an enabling technology according to Usoro, Ezekiel and Ojobah (2021) has the potential to empower individuals with the digital competencies required for current and future job markets, fostering economic growth, and enhancing the country's global competitiveness as follows:

1. **Enhanced Employability:** Equipping TVET graduates with digital competencies aligned with Industrial Revolution 4.0 technologies increases their employability. These skills are in high demand across various industries, enabling graduates to qualify for a broader range of job opportunities.
2. **Industry Relevance:** By leveraging Industrial Revolution 4.0 as an enabling technology, TVET programs can be tailored to impart skills directly relevant to the needs of industries. This alignment ensures that graduates are equipped with practical skills and knowledge demanded by the evolving industrial landscape. Employers seek candidates proficient in technologies like data analytics, artificial intelligence, robotics, and IoT, making Industrial Revolution 4.0-skilled graduates more desirable in the job market.
3. **Entrepreneurship Opportunities:** Industrial Revolution 4.0 integration in TVET nurtures a generation of entrepreneurs with technological acumen. Graduates possessing digital competencies can create startups or small businesses leveraging these skills, contributing to economic growth and job creation.
4. **Job Creation in Emerging Sectors:** Industrial Revolution 4.0-driven TVET can facilitate the emergence of new job sectors and roles. Graduates proficient in these technologies can spearhead roles in emerging fields like cybersecurity, digital marketing, renewable energy, and smart manufacturing, creating employment opportunities.
5. **Cross-Sector Mobility:** Digital competencies gained through Industrial Revolution 4.0-integrated TVET programs enable graduates to transition across various sectors. These skills are transferable, allowing individuals to adapt to changing job landscapes and explore diverse career paths.
6. **Closing Skills Gap:** Addressing the demand for Industrial Revolution 4.0-related skills in the job market through TVET narrows the existing skills gap. This alignment between education and industry needs ensures a workforce with the requisite skills, reducing unemployment due to skill mismatch.
7. **Global Competitiveness:** A digitally skilled workforce positions Nigeria competitively in the global labor market. Industrial Revolution 4.0-integrated TVET programs produce talent capable of competing internationally, attracting foreign investment and enhancing the country's reputation in technological proficiency.
8. **Upskilling for Existing Workforce:** Incorporating Industrial Revolution 4.0 technologies in TVET also benefits existing workers by offering opportunities for upskilling and reskilling. This enables

the workforce to adapt to technological advancements, ensuring their skills remain relevant in an ever-changing job market.

9. **Social and Economic Empowerment:** The integration of Industrial Revolution 4.0 technologies into TVET has the potential to spur innovation and foster economic growth. It can lead to the creation of tech-savvy entrepreneurs and facilitate the emergence of new industries or the transformation of existing ones. TVET graduates equipped with digital competencies are more empowered economically, contributing positively to socio-economic development. Their employability enhances financial stability and fosters social mobility for individuals and communities.

10. **Fulfilling Industry Demands:** By producing graduates proficient in Industrial Revolution 4.0 technologies, TVET programs can supply industries with a skilled workforce, fulfilling their demands for digital expertise. This fosters a symbiotic relationship between educational institutions and employers.

IMPLEMENTATION OF INDUSTRY 4.0 TECHNOLOGIES IN NIGERIAN TECHNICAL AND VOCATIONAL EDUCATION AND TRAINING

As we know at this moment there are studies in the field of engineering and management teaching and needs of students and of the industrial workforce are changing (Barbara, et al., 2017). The complexity of employment situations in the industry is steeply increasing and is consequently leading to higher demands in the quality of workforces with special competencies to meet companies' needs (Kergroach, 2017). Successful implementation of Industrial Revolution 4.0 driven initiatives in Nigerian TVET requires a coordinated effort among government bodies, educational institutions, industry partners, and international organizations for employability and self-reliance. Collaboration, resource-sharing, curriculum alignment, and skill development are key factors in ensuring that TVET graduates are equipped with the skills needed for the evolving job market in the era of Industry 4.0 (Amornvuthivorn, 2016). According to Amornvuthivorn (2016) and Ebil (2017), diverse perspectives highlight the multi-faceted nature of Industry 4.0 technology integration in Nigerian TVET, emphasizing collaboration, skills acquisition, policy support, and alignment with industry needs to foster a successful transition towards a technology-driven education system as follows:

1. **Government Bodies:** The government views Industry 4.0 as pivotal for Nigeria's economic development and recognizes the need to create policies that support the integration of these technologies into TVET. Government bodies has played a crucial role in formulating policies that support the integration of Industrial Revolution 4.0 technologies into TVET. This involves creating frameworks that encourage investment, innovation, and the adoption of advanced technologies in vocational training programs. Providing financial support, grants, and incentives for TVET institutions to acquire modern equipment, develop curriculum, and train educators in Industrial Revolution 4.0 technologies. Establishing regulations that promote the use of Industrial Revolution 4.0 technologies while ensuring safety, quality standards, and compliance with industry requirements.

2. **Educational Institutions:** TVET institutions need to revamp their curriculum to include Industrial Revolution 4.0 related skills such as data analytics, artificial intelligence, robotics, IoT, etc. These institutions should collaborate with industries to ensure alignment with industry needs. Providing training and upskilling opportunities for instructors to familiarize them with the latest technologies.

This includes workshops, seminars, and partnerships with industries for hands-on training. Investing in infrastructure and laboratories equipped with Industrial Revolution 4.0 tools and machinery for practical learning experiences.

3. **Industry Partners:** Industries seek graduates with practical competencies in Industry 4.0 technologies. They emphasize collaboration with educational institutions to tailor programs that meet industry needs, ensuring graduates possess relevant skills for employment. This ensures that graduates are equipped with skills relevant to industry needs. Offering internship programs, apprenticeships, or industrial attachments to TVET students, allowing them to gain practical experience and exposure to real-world applications of Industrial Revolution 4.0 technologies. Sharing expertise, resources, and providing mentorship to TVET institutions to bridge the gap between academic learning and industry requirements.

4. **International Organizations:** Facilitate partnerships between Nigerian TVET institutions and international counterparts for knowledge exchange, best practices, and access to global networks. Providing technical assistance, training programs, and resources to enhance the capacity of TVET educators and administrators in implementing Industrial Revolution 4.0-driven initiatives. Offering financial support, grants, or aid packages to assist in the acquisition of technology, curriculum development, and capacity building initiatives.

5. **Student's Perspective:** Students desire practical exposure to Industry 4.0 technologies, aiming to acquire skills that enhance their employability. They seek hands-on experiences, internships, and access to modern tools to prepare them for future careers.

6. **Community Perspective:** Communities expect TVET programs to equip youth with skills that enable them to contribute meaningfully to the community's development. They view Industry 4.0 integration as a means to create employment opportunities and reduce youth unemployment.

7. **Technology Providers' Perspective:** Providers aim to collaborate with educational institutions by offering access to cutting-edge technologies, software, and expertise. They see this collaboration as an avenue to promote the adoption of their solutions while supporting educational advancements.

ETHICAL CONSIDERATIONS FOR IMPLEMENTATION OF INDUSTRY 4.0 TECHNOLOGIES IN NIGERIAN TECHNICAL AND VOCATIONAL EDUCATION AND TRAINING

When developing TVET digital competencies in Nigeria using Industrial Revolution 4.0 as an enabling technology, several ethical and legal considerations should be addressed to create a responsible and secure learning environment by TVET institutions and stakeholders in Nigeria while maximizing the benefits of technological advancements in education in the following ways:

1. **Data Privacy and Security:** Protect students' and educators' data privacy and ensuring ethical use of personal information collected during digital training and comply with data protection laws and regulations to safeguard sensitive information collected and stored within educational systems.

2. **Ethical Use of AI and Algorithms:** Ensure transparency, accountability, and fairness in the use of artificial intelligence (AI) algorithms in educational technologies and abiding by laws governing AI use, such as avoiding bias and discrimination in algorithmic decision-making processes.

3. **Intellectual Property Rights:** Respect intellectual property rights, both in content creation and utilization of proprietary technologies and comply with copyright laws when using third-party content and adhering to licensing agreements for software and digital tools.

4. **Inclusive Access and Digital Divide:** Ensure equitable access to digital learning resources and opportunities for all students, regardless of socio-economic status or geographic location and address legal frameworks to bridge the digital divide and provide equal access to technology and education across diverse communities.

5. **Ethical Use of Educational Technologies:** Ensuring that educational technologies are used ethically and responsibly, avoiding over-reliance on technology that might diminish human interaction and personalized learning experiences and comply with regulations concerning the appropriate use of educational technologies within the TVET curriculum.

CHALLENGES FACING THE IMPLEMENTATION OF INDUSTRY 4.0 TECHNOLOGIES IN NIGERIAN TECHNICAL AND VOCATIONAL EDUCATION AND TRAINING

According to Kergroach (2017), Pereira et al. (2017), Minghat, et al. (2020) the quest of applying Industry 4.0 brings diverse technological challenges, with high influences on many dimensions in today's manufacturing industry. Some key challenges related to developing Technical Vocational Education and Training (TVET) digital competencies in Nigeria while utilizing Industrial Revolution 4.0 as an enabling technology are as follows:

1. **Outdated Curriculum and Educational Models:** The current TVET curriculum in Nigeria lack the necessary flexibility and agility to swiftly incorporate rapidly evolving Industrial Revolution 4.0 technologies. There's a challenge in aligning the curriculum with the dynamic needs of industries, resulting in potential skill gaps among students.

2. **Resource Limitations:** Insufficient resources, including funding constraints and inadequate infrastructure, present significant hurdles. Access to up-to-date technological tools, software, and hardware required to effectively teach Industrial Revolution 4.0-related subjects remains a challenge for many institutions.

3. **Inadequate Teacher Training and Capacity Building:** Educators and trainers might lack the requisite skills and knowledge needed to teach Industrial Revolution 4.0-related subjects. There's a need for comprehensive training programs to upskill teachers and instructors, enabling them to effectively impart digital competencies (Bibby & Dehe, 2018).

4. **Limited Industry Collaboration:** Limited collaboration between TVET institutions and industries can hinder the development of relevant and practical curricula. Closer partnerships are necessary to ensure that the skills being taught align closely with the demands and advancements within the industrial landscape.

5. **Inadequate Policy Frameworks:** Inadequate or outdated policies and regulatory frameworks might impede the integration of Industrial Revolution 4.0 technologies into TVET. There's a need for policy reforms that support and encourage the adoption of these technologies within educational settings.

6. **Inadequate Access and Inclusivity:** Rural areas and underserved communities may face challenges in accessing quality TVET programs incorporating Industrial Revolution 4.0 technologies. Ensuring inclusivity and equal access to these educational advancements across regions and social strata remains a critical challenge.

7. **Resistance to Change:** Resistance to change within educational institutions could be a barrier. Traditional teaching methodologies might resist incorporating new technologies, hindering the effective integration of Industrial Revolution 4.0-related subjects into the curriculum (Bonekamp & Sure, 2015; Dhanpat, et al., 2020).

8. **Irrelevant Evaluation and Assessment:** The methods for evaluating and assessing the effectiveness of incorporating digital competencies into TVET remain a challenge. Developing robust evaluation frameworks that measure the impact of these technologies on students' learning outcomes is essential.

9. **Lack of Sustainability and Scalability:** Implementing Industrial Revolution 4.0-enabled TVET initiatives on a broader scale and ensuring their sustainability can be challenging. Strategies need to be devised to scale successful pilot programs to a national level while maintaining quality and relevance.

10. **Inadequate Awareness and Perception:** Finally, raising awareness and changing perceptions among stakeholders about the significance of Industrial Revolution 4.0 technologies in TVET is crucial. Overcoming misconceptions and demonstrating the tangible benefits of integrating these technologies pose a challenge.

STRATEGIES TO IMPLEMENTING INDUSTRIAL REVOLUTION 4.0 IN NIGERIAN TECHNICAL AND VOCATIONAL EDUCATION AND TRAINING

The complexity of work situations in the industry is steeply increasing and is consequently leading to higher demands in the quality of workforces with special competencies to meet companies' needs. Implementing strategies to overcome challenges in developing TVET digital competencies in Nigeria using Industrial Revolution 4.0 as an enabling technology requires a multifaceted approach. By implementing effective strategies, TVET institutions and stakeholders in Nigeria can systematically address the challenges and pave the way for the successful integration of Industrial Revolution 4.0 technologies into vocational education, ensuring a future-ready and digitally skilled workforce in the following ways:

1. **Policy Framework Development:** Policymakers need to formulate comprehensive policy frameworks specifically addressing the integration of digital competencies into TVET. TVET institutions and stakeholders in Nigeria should develop national policies outlining strategies, goals, and standards for integrating digital skills into TVET curricula. Ensure alignment with industry demands and global technological trends.

2. **Infrastructure and Resource Allocation:** Insufficient infrastructure and resources hinder the effective integration of digital competencies in TVET. TVET institutions and stakeholders in Nigeria should allocate adequate funding and resources to upgrade infrastructure, providing modern laboratories, software, internet connectivity, and up-to-date technology tools required for digital skills training.

3. **Curriculum Development and Reforms:** Outdated curricula do not encompass relevant digital competencies required by industries. Facilitate curriculum reforms that embed digital skills across vocational fields. TVET institutions and stakeholders in Nigeria should establish mechanisms for regular reviews and updates to ensure alignment with industry 4.0 trends.
4. **Quality Assurance and Accreditation:** Quality assurance mechanisms are crucial for ensuring the effectiveness and relevance of TVET digital competencies. TVET institutions and stakeholders in Nigeria should implement accreditation standards that evaluate the integration and delivery of digital skills within TVET programs, ensuring quality education and industry relevance.
5. **Teacher Training and Capacity Building**: Educators' skills and capacity need enhancement to effectively teach digital competencies. TVET institutions and stakeholders in Nigeria should develop continuous professional development programs for TVET educators, providing training in digital skills, innovative teaching methodologies, and industry-oriented practices.
6. **Public-Private Partnerships (PPPs):** Collaboration between TVET institutions and industries is vital for practical exposure and skill development. Foster PPPs to provide internships, apprenticeships, and industry-relevant projects. TVET institutions and stakeholders in Nigeria should establish advisory boards comprising industry experts to guide curriculum design and implementation.
7. **Research and Innovation Support:** Limited focus on research and innovation hampers the development of cutting-edge digital skills. TVET institutions and stakeholders in Nigeria should encourage research hubs within TVET institutions, promoting innovation and collaboration with industries to explore new applications and advancements in digital technologies.
8. **Monitoring, Evaluation, and Reporting:** Lack of mechanisms for monitoring and evaluating the effectiveness of digital competency integration. TVET institutions and stakeholders in Nigeria should establish a robust monitoring and evaluation framework to assess the impact of digital skills integration. Regular reporting and feedback mechanisms ensure accountability and continuous improvement.
9. **Inclusivity and Equity:** Inequitable access to digital resources might widen educational disparities. TVET institutions and stakeholders in Nigeria should implement policies ensuring equitable access to digital infrastructure and resources across regions, genders, and socio-economic backgrounds, reducing the digital divide.

CONCLUSION

This chapter presents the context of the historical evolution of Industrial Revolution 4.0, concept, components, design principles, characteristics of Industrial Revolution 4.0, TVET Approach in Nigeria and effective Industrial Revolution 4.0 integration strategies in Nigerian TVET. This discussion of Industrial Revolution 4.0 is a prerequisite for understanding the details of the digital solutions that are presented in subsequent chapters. Organizing TVET in the era of Industrial Revolution 4.0 requires the process of developing capability and employability skills through in-depth knowledge and information on creative skills. To have knowledge and information on work skills, it is increasingly apparent that no larger classes and many teachers are needed. Digital media provides solutions to these needs. Learning with Industrial Revolution 4.0 is a solution for future learning needs. Virtual tour technology in factories, virtual factory planning, virtual reality, virtual tour in planned houses, university to visit, schools to visit, virtual diagnostics on complex systems, virtualization with feedback of senses, language acquisition by computer, medical distance consulting, translation support, learning with digital media, blended learning, neural networking, capture instructions, medical remote diagnosis, automated translation, conducting learning, automated language learning, predictive analysis, automatic recognition and promotion of human thinking, automated presentation of thinking result in multiple languages will all be substitutes for classrooms, laboratories, media education in the classroom, factory settings, and even the replacement of most teachers in Industrial Revolution 4.0.

REFERENCES

Amiron, E., Latib, A. A., & Subari, K. (2019). Industry Revolution 4.0 skills and enablers in Technical and Vocational Education and Training Curriculum. *International Journal of Recent Technology and Engineering*, 8(2), 484–490.

Amornvuthivorn, K. (2016). Public-private partnerships (PPPs) in Technical Vocational Education and Training (TVET): Lessons learned from Singapore and USA and implications for public management in Thailand. *Journal of Public and Private Management*, 23(1), 91–91.

Aoun, A., Ilinca, A., Ghandour, M., & Ibrahim, H. (2021). A review of Industry 4.0 characteristics and challenges, with potential improvements using Blockchain technology. *Computers & Industrial Engineering*, 16(2), 1–11. doi:10.1016/j.cie.2021.107746

Ayoade, I. A., Adedigba, A. P., Adeyemi, O. A., Adeaga, O. A., & Akanbi, O. V. (2022). Trends and prospects of digital twin technologies: A review. *Quantum Journal of engineering, science and technology*, 3(4), 11-24. www.qjoest.com

Azman, Z., & Ibrahim, J. (2018). *The Readiness of Nilai Polytechnic Graduates in Facing the Wave of Industrial Revolution 4.0 (IR 4.0)*. Paper presented at the 8th National Conference in Education – Technical & Vocational Education and Training (CiE-TVET) 2018. IJICC.

Barbara, M., Gabriele, B., Stefano, U., Domenico, S., & Stefano, F. (2017). How will change the future engineers' skills in the Industry 4.0 framework? A questionnaire survey. *27th International Conference on Flexible Automation and Intelligent Manufacturing, FAIM2017*, Modena, Italy.

Bibby, L., & Dehe, B. (2018). Defining and assessing industry 4.0 maturity levels – case of the defense sector. *Production Planning and Control*, 29(12), 1030–1043. doi:10.1080/09537287.2018.1503355

Bock, L. (2014). *An empirical study of the planning and implementation of competency-based education and training in vocational education training centres in Namibia: The case of Namibia Training Authority* [Doctoral dissertation, Polytechnic of Namibia].

Bonekamp, L., & Sure, M. (2015). Consequences of industry 4.0 on human labor and work organisation. *Journal of Business and Media Psychology*, 6(1), 33–40.

Carvalho, A. C. P., Carvalho, A. P. P., & Carvalho, N. G. P. (2020). *Industry 4.0 Technologies: What Is Your Potential for Environmental Management?* Knowledge Unlatched. www.knowledgeunlatched.org

D'Souza, U.J.A., & Mudin, D.K.D. (2018). Industrial revolution 4.0: Role of universities. *Borneo Journal of Medical Sciences*, 12, 1. 1–2.

Dhanpat, N., Buthelezi, Z., Joe, R., Maphela, T., & Shongwe, N. (2020). Industry 4.0: The role of human resource professionals. *SA Journal of Human Resource Management, 18*(1), 1–11. doi:10.4102/sajhrm.v18i0.1302

Duarte, A. Y. S., Sanches, R. A., & Dedini, F. G. (2018). Assessment and technological forecasting in the textile industry: From first industrial revolution to the industry 4.0. *Strategic Design Research Journal., 11*(3), 193–202. doi:10.4013/sdrj.2018.113.03

Ebil, S., Othman, N., Nor, H. N. H. M., Ahmad, M. H., Mujah, O., & Keh, C. W. (2017). Brunei TVET transformation: The development of the Institute of Brunei Technical Education's two key surveys. *Journal for Technical and Vocational Education and Training in Asia, 8,* 1–15.

Federal Republic of Nigeria. (1977). National policy on education. Lagos: Nigerian Educational Research Council (NERDC) Press.

Federal Republic of Nigeria. (1988). National policy on education. Lagos: Nigerian Educational Research Council (NERDC) Press.

Federal Republic of Nigeria. (2004). National policy on education. Lagos: Nigerian Educational Research Council (NERDC) Press.

Federal Republic of Nigeria. (2013). National policy on education. Lagos: Nigerian Educational Research Council (NERDC) Press.

Flashes Magazine. (2017). The first industrial revolution. In: Revue économique, 19(2).

Ghadge, A., Er Kara, M., Moradlou, H., & Goswami, M. (2020). The impact of industry 4.0 implementation on supply chains. *Journal of Manufacturing Technology Management, 31*(4), 157–169. doi:10.1108/JMTM-10-2019-0368

Gordon, R. J. (2000). Does the "New Economy" Measure up to the Great Inventions of the Past? *The Journal of Economic Perspectives, 14*(2), 49–74. doi:10.1257/jep.14.4.49

Hermann, M., Pentek, T., & Otto, B. (2015). Design principles for Industry 4.0 scenarios: A literature review. *HICSS '16 Proceedings of the 2016 49th Hawaii International Conference on System Sciences.* IEEE.

Huang, T. (2017). *Development of Small-scale Intelligent Manufacturing System (SIMS) - A case study at Stella Polaris.* AS UIT Faculty of Engineering Science and Technology the Artic University of Norwya.

Ibrahim, R., Baharuddin, S., & Baharom, H. (2018). Strengthening TVET: Readiness Level Polytechnic Lecturer in Education Transformation National 21st Century as the Industrial Revolution 4.0. *Journal of Technical Education and Training, 12*(3).

Ionescu, I. G. (2018). The first industrial revolution and general features of the world economy between the 16Th century and 1780. *SEA Practical Application of Science, 17*(2), 183–186.

Kagerman, H. Wahlster, W. & Helbig, J. (2013). Securing the Future of German Manufacturing Industry Recommendations for Implementing the Strategic Initiative Industries 4.0 *Final Report of the Industries 4.0 Working Group.*

Karnik, N., Bora, U., Bhadri, K., Kadambi, P., & Dhatrak, P. A. (2021). Comprehensive study on current and future trends towards the characteristics and enablers of industry 4.0. *Journal of Industrial Information Integration*, *10*(10), 82–94.

Kergroach, S. (2017). Industry 4.0: New Challenges and Opportunities for the Labor Market. *Foresight and STI Governance*, *11*(4), 6–8. doi:10.17323/2500-2597.2017.4.6.8

Koch, V., Kuge, S., Geissbauer, R., & Schrauf, S. (2014). Industry 4.0: Opportunities and challenges of the industrial internet. Tech. Rep. TR 2014-2, PWC Strategy GmbH, United States, New York City, New York (NY).

Kot, S. (2018). A Scoping Review on Digital English and Education 4.0 for Industry 4.0. *The Social Science Journal*, *7*, 221–227.

Minghat, A. D., Ana, A., Jamaludin, S., Mustakim, S. S., & Shumov, P. V. (2020). Identification of teaching competencies among TVET instructors towards the realization of 4th industrial revolution. Научный журнал. *Вестник НАН РК*, (5), 233–240.

Mohajan, H. K. (2019). The First Industrial Revolution: Creation of a New Global Human Era. *Journal of Social Sciences and Humanities*, *5*(4), 377–387.

Mustapha, S. F. B. (2021). *Readiness of Industry Revolution 4.0 implementation in Asset Integrity Management (aim)*. [Unpublished Dissertation, Universiti Tunku Abdul Rahman].

Oztemel, E., & Gursev, S. (2020). Literature review of industry 4.0 and related technologies. *Journal of Intelligent Manufacturing*, *31*(1), 127–182. doi:10.1007/s10845-018-1433-8

Pauceanu, A. M., Rabie, N., & Moustafa, A. (2020). Employability in the fourth industrial revolution. *Economia e Sociologia*, *13*(3), 269–283.

Pereira, A. C., & Romero, F. (2017). A review of the meanings and the implications of the industry 4.0 concept. *Procedia Manufacturing*, *13*, 1206–1214. doi:10.1016/j.promfg.2017.09.032

Qin, J., Liu, Y., & Grosvenor, R. (2016). A categorical framework of manufacturing for Industry 4.0 and beyond. *Procedia CIRP*, *52*, 173–178. doi:10.1016/j.procir.2016.08.005

Rahim, M.I., & Shamsudin, S. (2019). Categorization of video lecture designs in MOOC for technical and vocational education and training educators. *Journal of Technical Education and Training*, *11*. 11–17.

Santos, L., Brittes, G., Fabián, N., & Germán, A. (2018). The expected contribution of industry 4.0 technologies for industrial performance. *International Journal of Production Economics*, *13*, 196–204.

Schwab, K. (2016). *The Fourth Industrial Revolution*. World Economic Forum: Geneva.

Shafei, S., Haris, M. H. H., & Hamzah, Z. (2018). The Readiness of POLIMAS Lecturers in the Challenges of Industrial Revolution 4.0. *Paper presented at the 8th National Conference in Education – Technical & Vocational Education and Training (CiE-TVET) 2018*.

Shikalepo, E. E. (2019). Sustainability of Entrepreneurship and Innovation among TVET Graduates in Namibia. *International Journal for Innovation Education and Research*, *7*(5), 133–145. doi:10.31686/ijier.vol7.iss5.1484

Ślusarczyk, B. (2018). Industry 4.0: Are we ready? *Polish Journal of Management Studies*, *17*(1), 58–69. doi:10.17512/pjms.2018.17.1.19

Soldatos, J. (2019). Introduction to Industry 4.0 and the Digital Shopfloor Vision.

Spottl, P. D. (2016). *TVET International Conference 2016*. University of Bremen: Centre of Technology, Work and TVET.

Tay, S. I., Lee, T. C., Hamid, N. Z. A., & Ahmad, A. N. A. (2018). An overview of industry 4.0: Definition, components, and government initiatives. *Journal of Advanced Research in Dynamical and Control Systems*, *10*(14), 1379–1387.

Usoro, A. D., Ezekiel, C. E., & Ojobah, L. O. (2021). The Fourth Industrial Revolution: Discourse and Contexts Shaping Nigeria's Participation. *American Journal of Education and Information Technology*, *5*(2), 106–112. doi:10.11648/j.ajeit.20210502.17

Wang, S., Wan, J., Zhang, D., Li, D., & Zhang, C. (2016). Towards smart factory for industry 4.0: A self-organized multiagent system with big databased feedback and coordination. *Computer Networks*, *101*, 158–168. Advance online publication. doi:10.1016/j.comnet.2015.12.017

William, R. (2012). *The Most Powerful Idea in the World: A Story of Steam, Industry and Invention*. University of Chicago Press.

Yasanur, K. (2018). Sustainability impact of digitization in logistics. *15th Global Conference on Sustainable Manufacturing Procedia Manufacturing*, *21*(7), 782–789.

ADDITIONAL READING

Amiron, E., Latib, A. A., & Subari, K. (2019). Industry Revolution 4.0 skills and enablers in Technical and Vocational Education and Training Curriculum. *International Journal of Recent Technology and Engineering*, *8*(2), 484–490.

Asian Development Bank. (2021). Reaping the benefits of industry 4.0 through skills development in the Philippines. ADB. www.adb.org

Fadel, N. S. M., Ishar, M. I. M., Jabor, M. K., Ahyan, N. A. M., & Janius, N. (2022). Application of Soft Skills Among Prospective TVET Teachers to Face the Industrial Revolution 4.0. [MJSSH]. *Malaysian Journal of Social Sciences and Humanities*, *7*(6), e001562. doi:10.47405/mjssh.v7i6.1562

Intja, N. S., Sindano, G., & Nauyoma, O. S. (2022). The Philosophy of Vocational Education in the Face of 4th Industrial Revolution: A Namibian National Training Authority Perspective. *International Journal of Research and Innovation in Social Science*, *VI*(XI), 247–250.

Ismail, A., Wan, H. W. A. S., Ahmad, F., Affan, Z., & Harun, M. (2020). Students' Readiness in Facing Industrial Revolution 4.0 Among Students of Technical Teacher's Education. *International Journal of Scientific and Technology Research*, *9*(8), 300–305.

Karnik, N., Bora, U., Bhadri, K., Kadambi, P., & Dhatrak, P. A. (2021). Comprehensive study on current and future trends towards the characteristics and enablers of industry 4.0. *Journal of Industrial Information Integration*, *10*(10), 82–94.

Mustapha, S. F. B. (2021). *Readiness of Industry Revolution 4.0 implementation in Asset Integrity Management (aim).* [Unpublished Dissertation, Universiti Tunku Abdul Rahman].

Nurjanah, I., & Ana, A. (2021). Work Readiness of TVET Graduates in the Context of Industry 4.0. Proceedings of the 4th International Conference on Innovation in Engineering and Vocational Education. *Advances in Social Science, Education and Humanities Research, 651.*

Usoro, A. D., Ezekiel, C. E., & Ojobah, L. O. (2021). The Fourth Industrial Revolution: Discourse and Contexts Shaping Nigeria's Participation. *American Journal of Education and Information Technology*, *5*(2), 106–112. doi:10.11648/j.ajeit.20210502.17

Zulnaidi, H., Rahim, S. S. A., & Salleh, U. K. M. (2020). The Readiness of TVET Lecturers in Facing the Intelligence Age IR4.0. *Journal of Technical Education and Training*, *12*(3), 89–96. https://penerbit.uthm.edu.my/ojs/index.php/jtet

KEY TERMS AND DEFINITION

Conundrum: A challenging problem or dilemma that presents difficulties in finding a suitable solution or making decisions, often due to conflicting factors or complex circumstances.

Curriculum Development: The process of designing, planning, and implementing educational programs and courses to meet specific learning objectives and outcomes.

Digital Transformation: The integration and adoption of digital technologies to fundamentally change business or educational processes, operations, and models to enhance efficiency and effectiveness.

Educators: Individuals involved in teaching and facilitating learning within educational institutions, including teachers, instructors, professors, and education administrators.

Industry 4.0: Refers to the fourth industrial revolution characterized by the integration of advanced technologies such as artificial intelligence (AI), robotics, Internet of Things (IoT), big data, cloud computing, and automation in industrial processes.

Partnerships: Collaborative relationships between educational institutions, industry sectors, governmental bodies, and other stakeholders to achieve common goals such as improving education, fostering innovation, and addressing societal needs.

Policy Framework: A set of guidelines, regulations, and principles established by governments or educational institutions to guide decision-making and implementation strategies in education and technology integration.

Skills Gap: The disparity between the skills possessed by individuals and the skills demanded by industries or job markets, often highlighting areas where education and training need improvement.

Technical and Vocational Education: Educational programs designed to equip individuals with practical skills, technical knowledge, and expertise necessary for specific industries or occupations.

Technological Integration: The incorporation and utilization of advanced technologies, tools, and digital resources within educational frameworks to enhance teaching, learning, and skill acquisition.

Chapter 15
Assessing the Rapid Expansion of Technology in Africa:
Challenges and Opportunities for Higher Education

William Chakabwata

ⓘ https://orcid.org/0000-0002-4224-5239

University of South Africa, South Africa

ABSTRACT

The chapter assesses the state of digital technology in Africa as a catalyst for economic growth and development. The chapter also appraises the state of higher education on the continent in order to determine its preparedness to produce professionals who can function in a digital economy. A number of technological diffusion models which include diffusion of innovation (DIO), theory of reasoned action, and technology adoption model (TAM) were used to explore the diffusion of innovation to Africa from developed countries. Although there is a rapid growth in technological penetration in Africa impacting sectors such as agriculture, education, and finance, more investment in technology is still needed to power strides towards optimum levels of economic development. Africa, with its rapidly growing population and ever expanding market, is perceived as the next economic frontier after Asia. Higher education through curriculum models such as Education 5.0 can lead the way to make Africa the next economic frontier.

INTRODUCTION

This chapter explores the rapid expansion of technology in Africa focalising on challenges and opportunities for higher education. The background of the expansion of technology is presented in the light of the growth of education 5.0. The impact of the development of technology in Africa and the opportunities that are presented for higher education in Africa are also examined. The outbreak of COVID-19 seem to have propelled the utilisation of technology in higher education in Africa. The chapter takes parse of the use of Learning Management Systems (LMS) in higher education, use of Artificial Intelligence (AI)

DOI: 10.4018/978-1-6684-9962-7.ch015

and the Blackboard. Opportunities availed by the use of technology are dissected and also the challenges that emerge in higher education, as a consequence of the introduction of technology. The introduction of technology in higher education in Africa is an innovation that is underpinned in this study by Theory of Reasoned Action, Diffusion of Innovation and Technology Adoption Model. The theoretical underpinning are followed by a discussion of the study and then recommendations and conclusions of the study. The methodology that was employed in the construction of this chapter was based on desk review of work. A review of journal articles, thesis and book chapters were explored in order to illuminate this study. The article were selected using Google scholar and other search engines. The inclusion criteria included the selection of articles with words such as opportunities for technology expansion, utilisation of technology in higher education, Learning Management System (LMS), Artificial Intelligence (AI), blended Learning, among many other terms. The articles that were excluded were those that focalised on technology outside Africa, and technology based resources focusing on the business sector and other areas outside higher education.

BACKGROUND

Africa has 54 countries and the landmass is greater than that of China, India,adjoining states to US, and the large part of Europe combined (Giallauraskis, 2023).Giallauraskis (2023) postulated that by 2025, the utilisation of smartphones in Africa is predicted to double by 2025. It is also anticipated that the population of Africa will expand from the current 1,2 billion to 1,7 billion people by 2030. Africa is also experiencing rapid urbanisation and it is predicted that 50% of the population will be residing in urban areas by 2030.

Diestro (2022) averred that the outbreak of the COVID 19 pandemic was associated with new learning modes and pedagogies. Education 5.0 is not merely focussing on ensuring that each learner has access to a gadget that has access to internet, but preparation of learners to function in diverse social and geographical context and to be able to display holistic development. The priority of the education 5.0 is to ensure that the correct pedagogical approaches are utilised that are intended to inspire creativity and motivate learners to learners.

The evolution of educational technology reflects the dynamic nature of the educational system (Wuta,2023;Alharbi,2023).Technological innovations have been conceptualised as evolving in five key stages that include Education 1.0, up to Education 5.0, which is the contemporary focus on education. Alharbi (2023) noted that education 1.0 was the first educational experience which was marked by rote learning, a uniform approach to teaching for all learners, passive learning and absence of technology in teaching. Education 2.0 which superceded Education 2.1 had attributes such as active learning, and constricted use of technology. Education 3.0 is demarcated by complete technological integration, learning engagements that support collaboration and active learning, proactive learning and primacy of student learning. Education 4.0 was marked by a preponderance of the use of technology in education. Education 4.0 was also distinctive of the use of Artificial Intelligence in industry,use of robbotics and interactive technology that promoted learning.

The current way of thinking is encapsulated by Education 5.0, which advocate personalised learning experiences and where administrators, educators, learners are all actively involved in the learning experience. Education 5.0 is summed up Alharbi as constitutive of:

- Provision of personalised learning encounters
- Engagement that promotes collaborative learning
- Individualised learning that is adaptive and takes into account student diversities and experiences
- Technology is central to the learning experience
- Use of analytics in learning
- Use of computer applications that display low latency learning

In spite of the theoretical underpinning of Education 5.0, it has been criticised for being gender blind and failing to take into account the need to offer female students opportunities for advancement (Muchabaiwa & Chauraya, 2022). Other weakness that have been explicated included the way it neglects actual practical skills required in the real world by the manner it adopted a rarefied approach to learning,its association with the industrial revolution, making it an inflexible framework and unable to promote in learners required competencies such as adaptability,collaboration and capacity to generate new ideas. The framework is criticised for placing students under stress by its emphasis on the utilisation of standardised tests, and the way it places less emphasis on academic achievement. It is due to these criticism that some scholars have advocated Education 6.0.

Traore, Ozozco, & Velandia (2021) averred that in 2019, an estimated 58% of the population in Africa, lived in any area that had access to 4G networks, in contrast to 23% in 2015. Between 2015 and 2019, new firms in technology support expanded six times from greater than the global rate. Khan etal.(2021) averred that the eruption of COVID-19 led higher education to reconsider the way higher education is governed and functions. Online learning or blended learning, a didactic approach that consolidate asynchronous and face to face or synchronous learning were widely implemented in higher education. Technology has been employed to ensure access to learning resources and also to facilitate communication among students and also between lecturers and students. The intergration of eLearning culminated in praxis that is termed as blended learning (BL) which encompass face to face instruction with technology enabled virtual learning.

European Investment Bank (2021,p36) averred that Africa's optic fibre network grew to 1 025 000 June 2018 an extension of 8,7% from 2018. The mobile services tends to be a more prevalent form of technology in Africa, with 447 million people connected to mobile services in sub-Sahara Africa, which constitute 45% of the population.A number of learning management systems were introduced in Africa as innovation, which included Moodle, Google Classroom and Canvass. Prasad (2020) explicated learning management system (LMS) as a software that helps to enable the management of digital learning resources. The dominant features of LMS are chronicled as enabling storage of learning resources that students are able to access any time of the day, allowing for management of learning by giving users a facility to register, administration of virtual learning and blended learning, and it allows learning activities to be tracked, grade assessments, create reports, create statistics and issue certificates among many other functions.

The beginning of LMS is traced to Sydney Pressey (1924-1934), who experimented with automation of education (Petrina, 2004). Pressey had worked on a machine that was designed to ensure that students are able to drill and test themselves. The device that Pressey innovated was constructed from a typewriter components and was intended to assess intelligence in about thirty minutes. The next precursor of automated learning was the invention of Milton Ezra Lazerte (1929), a scholar at Alberta of a devise called Problem Cylinder (Maguire, 1989). The machine was employed for problem-solving and responding to multiple choice question. The University of Houston was the first one to run classes remotely with workers learning at home. The immediate precursor of the LMS were SAKI and Programmed Logic for Automatic Teaching Operations (PLATO). SAKI was designed by Gordon Pask and McKinned Wood (1928-1996) and was the first device to offer lessons that were personalised.SAKI offered more personal learning opportunity. This was followed by PLATO which was computer based software that allowed for learning at the student's own pace and also gave students an opportunity to collaborate on learning.

The calculator HP-9100A, was an innovation which had sophisticated features and it could effect computations, find solutions to engineering challenges faster than devices that were available at the time. It paved the way to manner LMS are designed and connected to the internet today. The innovation termed Modular Object-Oriented Dynamic Learning Environment (Moodle), was the first open learning platform. Moodle had functionalities such as the plug in and play which guaranteed that learning became accessible to students speedily and at an affordable cost. Bradley (2021) opined that LMS allow for learning to occur in a blended way using synchronous and asychronous way. Other technologies that have been adopted in higher education are the use of simulation and games (Vlachopoulos & Makri, 2017; Jong, 2019). Higher education in Africa has a mandate to ensure that graduates acquire technological competencies that are needed in the world of work to ensure development in Africa.Technological adoption of eLearning in higher education serves as a driver for technological transformation of Africa in diverse areas such as business, and e-government and governance in general.

Higher education has a key role to play in preparing the people in Africa to utilise technology. Aruleba et al., (2022) observed that information technology has become very pervasive in the education sector across the world. As it was demonstrated in preceding section, African countries are experiencing rapid penetration of technology especially in the aftermath of COVID-19 pandemic. Stosic (2015,p111) averred that " educational technology is a systematic and organised process of applying modern technology to impove the quality of education". Stosic (2015) asserted that the use of technology in education can be encapsulated in three ways:

- Technology as the facilitator of learning
- Technology as a gadget to use for facilitating instruction
- Technology as a learning tool

Aruleba et al.,(2022) explicated the growth in the use of technology in South African Universities during the lockdown imposed by the government to contain the spread of the COVID-19 pandemic. Aruleba et al.,(2022) noted that the government of South Africa introduced lock down level 5 which prohibited gatherings of many people leading to the closure of many universities. In order to salvage the academic semester, most universities decided to migrate to online teaching, which included the use of technologies such as blackboard, Zoom, Google Classroom, moodle and other online platforms. A decision was made by ten universities in South Africa to migrate completely to online courses (Dell, 2020). The next section explores the opportunities and challenges related to the implementation of technology in higher education in Africa.

OPPORTUNITIES RELATED TO EXPANSION OF TECHNOLOGY

The use of technology presents huge opportunities for higher education in Africa. Awoyemi & Olaniyi (2022) avers that creating a class that utilises technology, is interactive and student- centred, can help to build motivation and differentiation in instruction. The use of virtual learning evironment in higher education offers innovative ways to administer varied online assessments that affords students access to online rubrics for each assessments. Technology avails opportunities for students to collaborate on projects using platforms such as the wiki and the discussion forum (Cohen et al.,2004).

Using technology in higher education enables facilitators of learning to meet the needs of diverse groups of learners. Research indicates that the use of technology in higher education can enhance student's achievement (Awoyemi & Olaniyi, 2022). Burke (2014) observed that pundits lack a consensus on the meaning of the term gamification. Gamification is perceived as using game mechanics and experiences to innovate and engage people to realise their goals (Burke, 2014). Gamification encapsulates elements such as:

- Engagement of students with computers, smartphones and other digital devices
- Most games have common elements such as badges and leather boards
- That are able to enhance skills and or to develop innovation (Burke,2014).

Janna (2022) expounded that quizes can be designed into games where content is embedded into the game. Educators in higher education can develop assessments in a way that can immerse students in a learning activity. Games may be employed in the teaching of physics, mathematics, business studies or Engineering courses. The same author indicated that a whole course may be converted into a game, presenting opportunity for motivating students and for turning traditional lessons to innovative teaching.

Kamunya eta al.,(2019) averred that play is acknowledged as contributing to cognitive development. A central feature of the use of games in education involves the focalising of games on education as opposed to entertainment. Gamification involve the use of "patterns, principles and objects,models and methods directly inspired by games as used in education for student motivation and engagement"(Kamunya eta al.,2019,p1). The primary goal of gamification is to increase student's engagement. In a didactic context, gamification and student motivation and engagement are central to learning. Engagement in the context of learning may be perceived as enhancing hidden psychological, neural and biological occurances.

Dhlalisa & Govender (2020) expounded that the use of Learning Management Systems (LMS), offers numerous opportunities for higher education in Africa, which include easy of communication, information that is readily available, flexibility for students who may be employed, and interactivity. LMS are also linked to high motivation among students and facilitators of instruction and creating active and student centred classes. Student centred learning is realised through engaging in activities which include searching for information and also retrieving data for research or assignments. Students are propelled to develop graduate attributes such as critical thinking, lifelong learning and problem -solving by working independently or jointly in online activities.

LMS and use of the Blackboard offers students opportunities to learn in asynchronous environment. There are numerous LMS such as Canvass which can afford students any opportunity to effect changes to their work and resubmit. Moodle is a learning management system that can avails to students opportunities to participant in quizes such as as multiple choice, and which can be graded automatically after submission (Janna, 2022). Some LMS are designed to function as search engines.

Higher education is able to use Virtual Learning technology to enhance learning (Koh, Chapman, & Lam,2022). Virtual Reality (VR), enables facilitators to embed assessments in authentic learning contexts, which assists students to develop capabilities to tackle multifaceted challenges. VR is a computer simulation that enables students to experience a sense of 3 dimensional environment (3D) that makes them feel being contiguous in that environment. VR has the potency to engender multiple learning experiences, and provides a technology driven learning encounter. VR is termed as either high or low immersion. High immersion pertain to the use of head-mounted display (HMDs), by contrast, low immersion connotes the use of desktop, tablet and other digital devices to authentic learning situations. VR makes learning less rarefied, affective and fascinating when compared with the traditional learning environment (Koh,2017).

Damian (2022) explicated the value of teleconferencing using platforms such as Google classroom, Microsoft Teams among many others in enabling remote learning.This presents opportunities for virtual learning in African higher education.Video Conferencing tools can allow students in higher education to learn in a remote setting. The use of video conferencing mainfest a number of benefits which include the ability to interact with other students and also to share learning resources.

Carter & Shakwa (2022) avers that the flipped classroom creates an opportunity for students to engage in face to face learning and simultaneoulsy engaging in online learning. Students who engage in the flipped learning engage in deeper learning and are able display autonomous learning attributes. The University of Science and Technology in Namibia,offers a post graduate degree in higher education and the mode of instruction includes the use of the flipped classroom. Carter & Shakwa (2022) flipped classroom offers facilitators of instruction in higher an opportunity to navigate from traditional teaching to student centred-learning. Research on eLearning displays that students experienced enhanced retention rate, effective use of content, robust engagements and collaboration among students (Khan et al.,2021).

The definition of Artificial Intelligence (AI) has proved to be slippery. Holistic definitions encapsulates elements such as computing systems that can mainfest human like processes which include processing, rectifying,analysing and using sophisticated data (Sodiq, 2020; jaldi, 2023). AI is a vital component of the fouth Industrial Revolution. Many of the AI innovations are being introduced in education are owned by companies that are located in the Silicon Valley in California and Zhogguancon in Beijing. The top African countries in the use of AI are Mauritius, Egypt, Tunisia and Morocco.

The institutions that are involved in the development of AI in Africa are Google,IBM,Facebook have instituted centres for the development of AI in Africa and this effort is supplemented by local research centres such as Deep Learning Indaba, Data Science Africa and African Institute for Mathematical Scientists (AIMS). These research centres are still in the embryonic stage and have provided the basis for the growth of AI networks in Africa.

Sodiq (2020) asserted that Artificial Intelligence (AI) had a rotatory impact in higher education in Africa. AI is perceived as a key to the attainment of Goal 4 and promises the vitality of enhancing access to education. This form of technology holds the opportunity to shift from traditional education and to innovative education, to offer quality education. Al enables students to partake in individualised instruction and also facilitate the setting up of a learning community. It also reinforces the implementation of blended learning. AI offers multiple opportunities for higher education practitioners such as marking of assessments and offering educators flexibility in teaching.

Singh (2023) opines that Generative Pre-Trained Transformer (ChatGPT) is a component of AI and is capable to assisting a user to search for information,synthesise and generate a report. The use of ChatGPT has proved to be very controversial in higher education with some proponents arguing that it is a useful tool, while others perceive it as compromising the integrity of academic research in higher education. ChatGPT belongs to a group of language tools that are available on AI, which are competent to generate solutions to complex phenonemon. ChatGPT was jointly developed by Elon Musk using a platform titled Open AIFoundation IN 2022 and from its inception has garnered a retinue of over 100million subscribers. The use of ChatGPT also creates opportunities for African higher education to as it has capacity to help students to express themselves effectively, assess assignments, assists with translation of documents, and process sophisticated data.

CHALLENGES RELATED TO EXPANSION OF TECHNOLOGY

Although COVID 19, led to an exponential growth in the use of technology in higher education in Africa, there has been some challenges that emerged in many African Higher education institutions. Aruleba et al.,(2022) postulated that some of the challenges experienced in African higher education in South Africa, particularly historically disadvantaged universities, were identified as challenge of training students and lecturers and also constricted infrastructure.Students who come from low socio-economic status tended to experience impediments such as difficulties in adjusting to knew technology, challenges of accessing devices, lack of parental support, creating a digital divide (Khan et al.,2021).

The innovation of using LMS is accompanied with a host of challenges such as apprehension of students and lecturers on using technology,resistant to the innovation and constriction related to digital literacy,inadequate ancillary support to users, inadequate network capability, unstable, weak organisation and coordination and constricted capacity and network (Khan et al.,2021). In the context of South Africa, the same authors underscored that multiple students hail from background of destitution, schools with paucity of resources, and students with a diverse cultural and learning context, who habour multiple and varied educational expectations impacting on their educational outcomes. The majority of students attending schools in South Africa emerge from low socio-economic background and have no access to library infrastructure or digital devices and lack amenities which include electricity. Similar challenges were noted in Ghana and Nigeria where weak infrustructure and unstable connectivity led to challenges to online instruction in the context of rural institutions. Melisew et al.,(2022) asserted that Africa has a challenge of constricted penetration of technology globally which was estimated at 39,3%, which is low in the world in contrast to 62,9% for the rest of the world. Africa also tends to experience a challenge with student's access to devices such as smartphones and tablet. Such restricted technological penetration collaborating with a dearth of technological devices has connotations for learning.

European Investment Bank (2021) noted that although Africa is experiencing a huge digital transformation, there are still an estimated 9 million people who are not yet connected to the internet. In the case of the people who are connected to the internet there are colossal challenges such as high costs of connectivity, and a constricted bandwitdth in many areas. The internet infrustructure is a precondition for the introduction of a digital services in Africa. High speed networks and data centres are needed for instituting digital services (European Investment Bank, 2021). It is imperative to enhance the capacity of transmission in all countries in Africa. The bandwidth connection in Africa rose from 400 million in 2017 and 526 million in 2019. The degree of bandwidth expansion in Africa was at a paltry figure of 39% (European Investment Bank, 2021, p. 36).

World Bank (2023) noted that many governments were not investing adequate amounts of capital in developing digital infrastructure, services, human capital and businesses. AU (2020,p4) SWOT analysis noted the existence of the following impediments in setting digital transformation in Africa:

- Inept coordination among different policy frameworks such as AUDA -NEPAD to utilise resources to the optimum for the effective implementation of the digital agenda.

- Limited management capability to tackle challenges related to cyber-attacks

Carter & Shakwa (2022) in a study at the University of Science and Technology (NUST) identified challenges related to the use of technology in higher education as unreliable technology, enormous class size and paucity of resources that are critical for teaching. Other challenges that was mentioned were the student absentism in a virtual class and students inability to access LMS prior to the onset of the class leading to disruption of the learning plans.

Chinengudu (2022) averred that in Technical and Vocational Education (TEVT) suffer from constrictions such as limited level of digitisation, institutional weaknesses which were foregrounded by the outbreak of COVID-19 and lack of access to internet by numerous students in higher education. Some of the technologies such as Microsoft Teams used for teleconferencing, VR learning and gamifications tends to be very exorbitant for higher educations institutions in middle and low income countries in Africa.In addition utilisation of technology in higher education demands appropriate models, requisite teaching methods and an appropriate learning context (ILO-UNESCO-World Bank, 2021).

Dhlalisa & Govender (2020) and Carter & Shakwa (2022) expounded that facilitators of learning in higher education have displayed a propensity to continue to practice the sage on stage, in spite of the adoption of LMS. Facilitators of instruction who had highly developed skills in the use of computer technology and LMS were more enthusiatic to use the learning platform, in contrast to those with rudimentary skills.

Mukuni (2019) lamented that the use of technology in higher education in sub-Sahara Africa, has led to huge disenchantment due to the astronomical costs related to its implementation. The same author enumerated the impediments related to the use of technology in higher education in Africa as extremely high prohibitive costs, insufficient strategies to expand use of innovation, paucity of appropriate information for users, inadequate standards of internet provision and hostile regulatory regimes. Another study noted additional challenges which include absence of face to face preparatory instruction to students, poor material development, high costs of development of materials, failure to prioritise professional development, rapid and dynamic changes in technology courses,lack of computer skills among students and paltry funding (Afolabi, 2015).

Sodiq (2020) opines that challenges that can be encountered by using AI in schools may be classified into policy, techno-economic and security. The policy dimension requires technical comptence which is not readily available in Africa, and also the lofty costs of utilising the technology. In the short term the economic disparity will sustain previleges among certain communities, while disadvantages others. AI is driven by financial resources and technology it will previlege groups that already have financial resources. There are ethical challenges related to the use of technology such as AI, which include invasion of individual privacy. Sodiq (2020) postulate that structural disparities means that Africa is lagging behind and there is scarcity of skilled workers. It is also asserted that the level of AI skills in the sub-Sahara are the lowest in the world. Kamunya eta al.,(2019) observed that gamification had very restricted success due to the challenges related to dearth of skills in the design of games in education.

The recent innovation in the use of ChatGPT has also been associated with challenges for higher education in Africa which include its potential to generate responses that are incomprehensible and to display fallibility (Singh, 2023). The algorithm used in the construction of application has also been associated with gender bias. The application also has been accused of promoting academic cheating and lack of integrity in higher education.

THEORETICAL UNDERPINNING

This chapter is underpinned by the Theory of Reasoned Action, Diffusion of Innovation and Technology Adoption Model. The Theory of Reasoned Action explores how people make decisions or act on purpose and this is vital for comprehending how different higher education institutions adopted technology for teaching and learning. Diffusion of Innovation dissects how technology related to teaching and learning spread from developed countries to developing states. The Adoption of Technology Model takes parse on how people adopt and embrace technological innovations.

THEORY OF REASONED ACTION

Hagger (2019) averred that the theory of reasoned action has its genesis in the 1970s and was postulated by Martin Fishbein and Icek Ajzen. The theory of reasoned action and reasoned behaviour which in recent times has been termed reasoned action had a very impacful influence on accounting for way people are likely to act or take intentional action. These theories had application in many situations, behaviours and populations. The most primary version of this theory was the theory of reasoned action, which anticipated and explained intentional behaviour. The theory had its roots in social cognitive and attitude theory and sought to explain individual's belief regarding the performance of a given action. The chief tenet of the theory is intention, which is a construct that explained intention as the highest motivation of behaviour.

Intention is conceptualised as a construct of two key constructs which are attitude and subjective norms. Attitudes are conceptualised as either negative or positive evaluation of displaying the behaviour in future, while subjective norms reflect the attitude that significant others would expect them to display the action in future.

DIFFUSION OF INNOVATION

Evidence from the industrialisation of western nations supports the view that United States and other states were able to catch up with Britain due to the successul diffusion of ideas and technology. Ensuring that innovation spread from the western nations to Africa is not an easy process, athough the use of technology has many merits (Rogers, 2003). It is for that reason that diffusion of new concepts such as use of technology takes many years to become a reality in Africa. The concern for multiple organisation is to ensure that new ideas spread rapidly in order to ensure that innovation becomes readily available. Rogers (2003,p 26) averred that diffusion "is the process in which an innovation is communicated through certain channels over time among the members of a social system". Diffusion of technology for Africa refers to the way technology spreads from developed to developing nations (de Souza Ferreira et al.,2022).

Rogers (2003) asserted that diffusion involves the exchange of information through communication and it eventually culminate in a transformationn of a social system. This has application in Africa where governance and business systems are undergoing transformation due to technological changes. Rogers (2003,p30) postulated that diffusion depends on factors that include " a process by which an innovation is spread through certain channels,overtime,among members of a social system". An innovation is encapsulated as a concept, practice or item that is viewed as novel by an individual or organisation. When a new idea or object is introduced, the number of individuals who embrace it multiply and this diminishes the risk associated with that innovation as the patrons of that object or idea multiplies. Vejgaard (2019) averred that one of the chief preoccupation of diffusion of Innovation is the question of what influences the rate of adoption of innovation, in the context of this chapter technological innovation.

Makovhololo (2017) averred that Diffusion of Innovation (DOI) refers to the process by which an innovation is disseminated through certain channels to individuals within a social system. Diffusion of Innovation was preocupied with the desire to determine the rate at which diffusion spread in a culture or system. The theory is constructed on the premise that the acceptance of an innovation depends on the attitudes of the members to that innovation. Communities or organisation have an option to embrace or resist an innovation. Diffusion of Innovation is foregrounded on terms such as "relative advantage,compartibility, complexity,triability, and observability" (Comer & Kendall, 2013, p. 121).

Potential adopters assess the innovation and opt to embrace or reject the innovation. The DOI has been used in academia and also organisations to account for the way novel ideas spread through a social system. The DOI can be used to explain the way technology diffuses from the developed nations to Africa. The theory has been used widely in academia, due its flexibility and adaptability in different contexts. New innovation creates a sense of precariousness in the people and for that reason the theory seeks to diminish that sense of uncertainty. In decisions that have to be made to embrace an innovation, it is vital to know the key decision makers and their motivations.

Vejgaard (2019) explained that culture when taken in the context of Rodgers theory refers to the interlinkages that occur within a person's social system, and this could be at village level. Studies have also shown that interlinkages can occur at national level constituting a culture. The factors that influence diffusion of innovations are a multitude, although research has tended to focus on factors which include economic indicators, social factors such as level of education and a nation's ideology on investment The next section explores technology adoption model to explain diffusion of technology to Africa.

TECHNOLOGY ADOPTION MODEL

Zaineldeen et al.,(2020) averred that Technology Adoption Model (TAM) was mooted by Davies etaal who sought to create a model for computer technology acceptance. From its inception it is acknowledged that TAM had affinity with the theory of reasoned action.ATM has become a dominant theory that has wide acceptance when it comes to account for the way people adopt innovation. The TAM model was introduced by Davis (1989) and it explains the acceptance,adoption, and use of information technology. As a matter of fact TAM is constitutive of the following variables disposition towards behaviour, behaviour that demontrates intention, real use of the technology, and the perception that users have on the easy of use of the innovation.

Each of these factors may not be perceived in isolation because they tend to interplay on each other for instance "actually usage of the system is instantly affected by behavioural intention, which is impacted by an equal attitude towards behaviour and perceived usefulness. Attitude towards behaviour is straightly impacted by perceived ease of use in addition to perceived usefulness" (Zaineldeen et al., 2020, p. 5062). Davis (1989) submitted that technology has a colosal potential to enhance workplace performance. This improvement in performance is premised on the ability of the user to adopt technology in the workplace. Zaineldeen et al.,(2020) model is foregrounded on the following premises which are perceived ease of use and perceived ease of use.

TAM explores the factors that make people to either adopt or reject new technology. The first criteria that is postulated by Davis is termed perceived usefulness, which connotes that people are likely to use technology depending on the degree to which they perceive that it will enhance their work performance. If the technology is difficult to use then the people may become reluctant to use it. This leads to the second factor that Davis termed perceived ease of use, which is the thoughts that users have towards the technology. Venkatesh & Davis (2000) expounded the principles of TAM to include social influences and cognitive processess. TAM sought to analyse why the challenge of technological adoption continue to vex many organisations long after innovations have been identified.

The extended model by Venkatesh & Davis (2000) (Venkatesh & Davis, 2000) explicate some components of perceived useful have been undermined in literature on technological innovation social influence. The social influence is further unpacked as "subjective norm, voluntariness and image" (Venkatesh & Davis, 2000, p. 187). The next section explores the issues that have been discussed in this chapter and then proceeds to offer recommendations and conclusion.

DISCUSSION

It is noteworthy that although technology has been available in Africa, it received a great impetus in use in tertiary institutions in Africa, due to COVID-19 (Aruleba et al.,2022). Many institutions ended up migrating courses to online platforms due to the imposition of national lockdown that were designed to limit public gathering in order to reduce the risk of new infections. The technological innovations were not only apparent in tertiary institutions, but also through the economies in Africa. Tertiary institutions are also anticipated to take a lead in providing the skills that professionals require for using technology. This may be realised by equipping universities with an appropriate curriculum and also reducing the digital divide based on students' socio economic status.

Technological innovation holds the potential for assisting Africa in realizing the much need economic growth. European Investment Bank (2017) averred that in order to realise digital transformation of Africa, it is important to take into account the inclusion of groups that are marginalised such as women. The following section explores action that may need to be taken to address challenges Africa has with adopting technology. The study noted that there are multiple technologies that were implemented in Africa as innovations during the outbreak of COVID-19, such as LMS, AI and teleconferencing applications (Alharbi, 2023; Afolabi, 2015; Bradley, 2021). These technologies provides opportunities for students in higher education to use active learning, develop graduate attributes and also to collaborate with other students. However, the use of these technologies have also been associated with challenges that are related to infrustructure deficit, connectivity challenges and limited access to digital gadgets. In the light of these challenges and opportunities identified this chapter suggest the recommendations in the next section.

RECOMMENDATIONS

Evidence from research demonstrates that there is a growing penetration of technology in Africa. This penetration would require an increase in connectivity and also broadband width. It is therefore recommended that government in Africa in collaboration with stakeholders work on increasing digital infrastructure in Africa in order to increase access to technology for groups that are marginalized such as women and other groups.

The study acknowledges the central place of technology in Africa's economic growth. It also acknowledges the primary role that can be played by tertiary institutions in ensuring economic growth. Based on these observations the chapter recommended that governments in Africa prioritise investment in infrastructure for technology particularly the institution of the optic fiber network that can render access to internet affordable to the majority of the people. Government must also work towards the reduction of the digital divide within countries by increasing access to marginalized groups such as women. The recommendations made by Carter & Shakwa (2022) in reference to NUST are relevant to this study. The appropriate departments in higher education must ensure that there is a dependable access to LMS for students and facilitators of instruction. Higher Education institutions have to institute better server facilities and also enhance the bandwidth for ensuring better access to internet resources. Professional development of facilitators of learning must be prioritised as well for the students to ensure that the innovation is adopted in higher education in Africa. Higher education institutions could levy students in order to help fund acqusition of digital devices and also to finance improved internet connectivity.

The recommendations proferred by Mukuni, (2019) are also relevant to this study and they include:

- Training of educators in higher education in the use of online teaching and development of quality learning resources
- Engaging in continuous improvement of online teaching by seeking feedback from students and also extracting data from LMS.
- Experimenting with innovation of reducing costs related to online instruction without compromising the quality of instruction.
- Enacting legislative framework that secure the operations of internet service providers and also offering them incentives when they offer services to higher education institutions.
- Enhancing IT infrastructure and improving flow of network traffic.
- Improving funding for ICT programmes in higher education
- Offering incentives to suppliers of ICT devices such as laptops and softwares

CONCLUSION

The chapter assessed the expansion of technological innovation in Africa. The study noted that technological innovation is expanding rapidly in Africa transforming the business and educational landscape in Africa. However the rate of expanding is not rapid enough to meet the required developmental needs of Africa. Technological innovations are impacting Education in Africa in the form of Education 5.0.

REFERENCES

Afolabi, A. (2015). *Availability of online learningtools and the readiness of teachers and students towards it in Adekunle Ajasin University, Akunegba-Akoko*. Ondo State Nigeria: Procedia-Social and Behavioral Sciences.

African Union. (2020). *Digital Transformation Strategy for Africa (2020-2030).* African Union.

Alharbi, A. (2023). Implementation of Education 5.0 in Developed and Developing Countries: A Comparative Study. *Creative Education, 14*(5), 914–942. doi:10.4236/ce.2023.145059

Arthur, P., Hanson, K., & Ruplampu, K. (2020). *Disruptive Technologies, Innovation and development in Africa.* Palgrave MacMillan. doi:10.1007/978-3-030-40647-9

Aruleba, K., Jere, N., & Matarirano, O. (2022). Technology Adoption Readiness in Disadvantaged Universities during COVID-19 Pandemic in South Africa. *International Journal of Higher Education, 11*(2), 172–180. doi:10.5430/ijhe.v11n2p172

Awoyemi, R., & Olaniyi, E. (2022). Using Technology to Support Inclusive Classroom-Based Instruction. In J. Keengwe (Ed.), *Handbook of Research on Promoting Global Citizenship Education* (pp. 195–208). IGI Global.

Bradley, V. M. (2021). Learning Management System (LMS) Use with Online Instruction. *International Journal of Technology in Education, 4*(1), 68–92. doi:10.46328/ijte.36

Burke, B. (2014). *Gamify: How Gamification enables People to do Extraordinary Things.* Gartner Inc.

Carter, K., & Shakwa, G. (2022). Flipping the Post-COVID online Classroom in a Professional Development Programme at the Namibia University of Science and Technology. In J. Keengwe (Ed.), *Handbook for Research on Transformative and Innovative Pedagogies in Education* (pp. 93–111). IGI Global. doi:10.4018/978-1-7998-9561-9.ch006

Chemma, N. (2021). Disruptive innovation in a dynamic environment: A winning strategy? An illustration through the analysis of the yoghurt industry in Algeria. *Journal of Innovation and Entrepreneurship, 10*(34), 1–19. doi:10.1186/s13731-021-00150-y

Chinengudu, T. (2022). Simulated-Work Based Learning in Technical and Vocational Education and Training: An Innovative Pedagogy. In J. Keengwe (Ed.), *Handbook of Research Transformative and Innovative Pedagogies in Education* (pp. 112–129). IGI Global. doi:10.4018/978-1-7998-9561-9.ch007

Christensen, C. (1997). *The innovators dilemma: When new technologies cause great firms to fail.* Harvard Business School Press.

Cohen, L., Manion, L., Morrison, K., & Wyse, D. (2004). *A Guide to Teaching Practice.* Routledge.

Comer, J., & Kendall, P. (2013). *The Oford handbook of research strategies for clinical psychology.* Oxford University Press.

Damian, M. (2022). Connecting Students on Hospital Wards to Hospital Classrooms and the Community Using Video Conferencing Technologies. In J. Keengwe (Ed.), *Handbook of Research on Transformative and Innovative Pedagogies in Education* (pp. 76–92). IGI Global.

Lalima:Dangwal, K. (2017). Blended Learning An Innovative Approach. *Universal Journal of Educational Research, 5*(1), 129–136. doi:10.13189/ujer.2017.050116

Davis, F. (1989). Perceived usefulness, perceived ease of use and user acceptance of information technology. *Management Information Systems Quarterly, 13*(3), 319–340. doi:10.2307/249008 de Souza Ferreira, W., Vale, G. M., & Correa, V. (2022). Diffusion of Innovation in Technological Platforms: The Uber Case. *Brazilian Administration Review*, *19*(3), 1–32.

Dell, S. (2020). *Universities prepare for online teaching and learning*. University Wo.

Dhlalisa, F., & Govender, G. (2020). Challenges of acceptance and usage of a Learning Management System amongst Academics. *International Journal of eBusiness and eGovernment Studies, 12*.

Diestro, D. (2022). Learning readiness in education 5.0 as influenced by value creation and academic productivity. *EPRA International Journal of Research and Development (IJRD)*, *7*(8), 179-184.

Dube, T., Van Eck, R., & Zuva, T. (2020). The Review of Technology Adoption Models and Theories to Measure Readiness and Acceptable Use of Technology in a Business Organisation. *Journal of Information Technology and Digital World*, *02*(04), 207–212. doi:10.36548/jitdw.2020.4.003

European Investment Bank. (2017). *Banking in sub-Sahara Africa: Interim report on digital financial inclusion*. European Investment Bank.

European Investment Bank. (2021). *The rise of Africa's digital economy*. European Investment Bank.

Flavin, M. (2017). *Disruptive Technology enhanced learning: The use and misuse of technology enhanced learning in higher education*. Palgrave MacMillan. doi:10.1057/978-1-137-57284-4

Fomunyam, K. (2020). Towards enhancing Science and Technology, Enginering and Mathsmatics (STEM) Education: A case for higher education in Africa. *International Journal of Engineering Research & Technology (Ahmedabad)*, *13*(7), 1516–1524. doi:10.37624/IJERT/13.7.2020.1516-1524

Fox, L., & Signe, L. (2022). *From subsistence to disruptive innovation: Africa's the Fouth Industrial Revolution and the future of jobs*. Brookings. https://www.brookings.edu/articles/from-subsistence-to-disruptive-innovation-africa-the-fourth-industrial-revolution-and-the-future-of-jobs/

Giallauraskis, A. (2023). *Africa on the cusp of an innovation revolution*. Business Sweden.

Hagger, M. (2019). The reasoned action approach and theories of reasoned action and planned behaviour. In D. Dunn (Ed.), *Oxford Bibliography in Psychology* (pp. 1–30). Oxford University Press.

ILO-UNESCO-World Bank. (2021). *Skills Development in the time of COVID -19:Takingstock of the intial responses in technical and vocational education and training*. International Labour Office.

Jaldi, A. (2023). *Artificial Intelligence Revolution in Africa: Economic Opportunities and Legal Challenges*. Morocco: Policy Centre for the New South .

Janna, J. (2022). Epic Boss Battles: How to Addict Your Students by Creating Asynchronous Course-Based Games. In J. Keengwe (Ed.), *Handbook of Research on Transformative and Innovative Technologies in Education* (pp. 1–17). IGI Global.

Jong, T. (2019). Moving towards engaged learning in STEM domains; there is no simple answer, but clearly a road ahead. *Journal of Computer Assisted Learning*, *35*(2), 153–167. doi:10.1111/jcal.12337

Kamunya, S., Maina, E., & Onoko, R. (2019). Gamification Model for eLearning Platforms. *IST-Africa 2019 Conference Proceedings* (pp. 1-9). Kenya: IIMC International Information Management Corporation.

Khan, N., Erasmus, T., Jali, N., Mthiyane, P., & Ronne, S. (2021). Is blended learning the way forward? Students' perceptions and attitudes at a South African university. *AJHPE, 13(*4), 219-222.

Koh, K. (2017). Authentic Assessment. In G. Noblit (Ed.), *Oxford Research Encylopedia of Education*. Oxford University Press. doi:10.1093/acrefore/9780190264093.013.22

Koh, K., Chapman, O., & Lam, L. (2022). An intergration of Virtual Reality into the Design of Authentic Assessment for STEM Learning. In J. Keengwe (Ed.), *The Handbook of Research on Transformative and Innovative Pedagogies in Education* (pp. 18–35). IGI Global. doi:10.4018/978-1-7998-9561-9.ch002

Lai, P. (2020). The literature Review of Technology Adoption Models and Theories of Novelty technology. *Journal of Information Systems and Technology Management, 02*.

Leavy, B. (2018). Value innovation and how to successfully incubate "blue ocean" initiatives. *Strategy and Leadership*, *46*(3), 10–20. doi:10.1108/SL-02-2018-0020

Maguire, T. (1989). Educational Problems Revisited. Commentary on and Reprint of "M. E. LaZerte: Pioneer Educational Innovator," by George H. Buck, originally published in 1989. *The Alberta Journal of Educational Research*, *40*(4), 499–510.

Makovhololo, P. (2017). Diffusion of Innovation Theory for Information technology decision making in organisational strategy. *Journal of Contemporary Management*, *14*, 461–481.

Melisew, D. L., Ngutuku, E., Emeka, E., & Siebert, A. (2022). Information and Communication Technology in Africa: Challenges from the COVID Pandemic. *Africa Knowledge Series*, *1*(3), 1–20.

Muchabaiwa, W., & Chauraya, E. (2022). *The gender blindness of the education 5.0 framework: An obstruction to promotion opportunities for female academics in Zimbabwe*. Sage. doi:10.1177/08920206221126640

Mukuni, J. (2019). Challenges of Educational Digital Infrustructure in Africa: A tale of hope and disillusionment. *J. Afr. Stud. Dev. Vol*, *11*(5), 59–63. doi:10.5897/JASD2019.0539

Muxtorjonovna, A. (2020). Significance Of Blended Learning In Education System. *The American Journal of Social Science and Education Innovations*, *2*(8), 507–511. doi:10.37547/tajssei/Volume02Issue08-82

Nyakito, C., Amino, C., & Allida, V. (2021). Challenges of intergrating Information and Communication Technology in Teaching among National National Teachers' Colleges in Uganda. *East African Journal of Education and Social Sciences*.

Petrina, S. (2004). Sidney Pressey and the Automation of Education, 1924-1934. *Technology and Culture*, *45*(2), 305–330. doi:10.1353/tech.2004.0085

Prasad, R. (2020). *eLearning Industry*. A brief History of the LMS. https://elearningindustry.com/brief-lms-history

PWC. (2023, 10 6). *Disrupting Africa: Riding the wave of the digital revolution*. PWC Global. https://www.pwc.com/gx/en/archive/industries/technology/disrupting-africa--riding-the-wave-of-the-digital-revolution.html#:~:text=The%20power%20and%20potential

Rogers, E. (2003). *Diffusion of innovation*. Free Press.

Russo-Spena, T., Mele, C., & Marzullo, M. (2019). Practicing value innovation through artificial intelligence: The IBM Watson Case. *Journal of Creating*, *5*(1), 11–24.

Sang, H., & Tsai, D. (2009). Analysing strategies of integrating ICT into teaching activities using innovation diffusion theory. *NCM 09. Fifth International Joint Conference* (pp. 1876-1878). Seoul Korea: NCM.

Singh, G. H. (2023). Maintaning the Integrity ofSouth African University: The Impact of CHATGPT on plagiarism and scholarly Writing. *South African Journal of Higher Education*, *37*(5), 203–220. doi:10.20853/37-5-5941

Sodiq, O. (2020). Teaching and Learning in the Cloud: Prospects and Challenges of Artificial Intelligence for Education in Africa. Nigeria: Financial Institutions Training Centre (FITC) Lagos.

Stosic, L. (2015). The importance of Educational Technology in Teaching. *(IJCRSEE) International Journal of Cognitive Research in Science. Engineering and EducationVol.*, *3*(1), 111–114.

Traore, B., Ozozco, J., & Velandia, J. (2021). *Digital drivers of inclusive growth in Africa and Latin America and Carribean*. OECD.

Vejgaard, H. (2019). *Culture as a determinant in innovation diffusion*. IntechOpen. doi:10.5772/intechopen.80806

Venkatesh, V., & Davis, F. (2000). A Theoretical Extension of the Technology Acceptance Model: Four Longitudinal Field Studies. *Management Science*, *46*(2), 186–204. doi:10.1287/mnsc.46.2.186.11926

Vlachopoulos, D., & Makri, A. (2017). The effect of games and simulations on higher education: A systematic literature review. *International Journal of Education*, *14*(22), 1–33.

Wuta, R. (2023). Extendibility of the Education 5.0 Concept to Zimbabwe's Secondary School System as Encapsulated in Curriculum Framework 2015-2022. *Indiana Journal of Humanities and Social Sciences, 03*(5), 914-942.

Zaineldeen, S., Hongbo, L., Koffi, A., & Hassam, B. (2020). Technology Acceptance Model's Concepts, Contribution and Limitation, Adoption in Education. *Universal Journal of Educational Research*, *8*(11), 5061–5071. doi:10.13189/ujer.2020.081106

KEY TERMS AND DEFINITIONS

Disrupt: To disturb processes or practices in affirm in a way that brings about radical changes and new services or products.

Disruptive Technologies: Technologies that are adopted by firms which are cheaper, easy to use and adaptable and have potential to transform business practices in a radical way.

ELearning: Digital platforms that are used to support learning in a virtual or face to face session

Inclusion: A policy that ensures that all people are a part of a policy, project or programme.

Innovation: A new or novel idea, device or strategy for doing business

Latency: When using a computer, the delay that occurs before a transfer of data occurs.

Sustaining Technologies: These are technologies that have the capacity to make business practice better but do not lead to completely new products.

Compilation of References

Aalst, J., Mu, J., Damsa, C., & Msonde, S. (2022). *Learning sciences research for teaching*. Routledge.

Abdelwahap, M., Elfarash, M., & Eltanboly, A. (2021). Applications Of Natural Language Processing In Healthcare Systems. *The International Undergraduate Research Conference*. Research Gate.

Abimbola, O., Aggad, F., & Ndzendze, B. (2021). What is Africa's Digital Agenda?. *Africa Policy Research Institute (APRI), 23*.

Abolade, T. O., & Durosinmi, A. E. (2018). The benefits and challenges of e-health applications in developing nations: A review. In *Paper presented at the 14th iSTEAMS conference at AL- hikmah university IIrion Kwara state Nigeria*.

Abu-Shanab, E. (2014). Antecedents of trust in e-government services: An empirical test in Jordan. *Transforming Government: People. Transforming Government, 8*(4), 480–499. doi:10.1108/TG-08-2013-0027

ACET. (2018). *Moving Beyond Aid — Revenue Mobilization G20 Compact with Africa*. ACET. https://www.compactwithafrica.org/content/dam/Compact with Africa/events/BeyondAid_Report2018-1.pdf

Ackah, B. (2023). Ghana's blockchain scene on WhatsApp: A space for convergence and divergence. *Journal of Digital Social Research, 5*(2), 55–79. doi:10.33621/jdsr.v5i2.141

Acker, A., & Murthy, D. (2020). What is Venmo? A descriptive analysis of social features in the mobile payment platform. *Telematics and Informatics, 52*, 101429. doi:10.1016/j.tele.2020.101429

Acs, Z. J., & Preston, L. (1997). Small and medium-sized enterprises, technology, and globalization: Introduction to a special issue on small and medium-sized enterprises in the global economy. *Small Business Economics, 9*(1), 1–6. doi:10.1023/A:1007945327618

Adam, L. (2010). *Ethiopia ICT sector performance review 2009/2010?* (Policy Paper No.9). Research ICT Africa. https://www.researchictafrica.net/publications/ICT_Sector_Performance_Reviews_2010/Vol%202%20Paper%209%20-%20Ethiopia%20ICT%20Sector%20Performance%20Review%202010.pdf

Adams, R. (2021). Can artificial intelligence be decolonized? *Interdisciplinary Science Reviews, 46*(1-2), 176–197. doi:10.1080/03080188.2020.1840225

Addo, C. P. (2019). Africa has the slowest data speeds. Here's how to accelerate things. *Africa Report*. https://www.theafricareport.com/21516/africa-has-the-slowest-data-speeds-heres-how-to-accelerate-things

Adebisi, Y. A., Nwogu, I. B., Alaran, A. J., Badmos, A. O., Bamgboye, A. O., Rufai, B. O., Okonji, O. C., Malik, M. O., Teibo, J. O., Abdalla, S. F., Lucero-Prisno, D. E. III, Samai, M., & Akande-Sholabi, W. (2022). Revisiting the issue of access to medicines in Africa: Challenges and recommendations. *Public Health Challenges, 1*(2), e9. doi:10.1002/puh2.9

Ade-Ibijola, A., & Okonkwo, C. (2023). Artificial Intelligence in Africa: Emerging Challenges. In Responsible AI in Africa: Challenges and Opportunities (pp. 101–117). Springer International Publishing Cham.

Ade-Ibijola, A., & Okonkwo, C. (2023). Artificial Intelligence in Africa: Emerging Challenges. In D. O. Eke & ... (Eds.), *Responsible AI in Africa: Challenges and Opportunities* (pp. 101–117). Springer International Publishing. doi:10.1007/978-3-031-08215-3_5

Adenuga, K. I., Iahad, T., & Miskon, D. (2020). Telemedicine system: Service adoption and implementation issues in Nigeria. *Indian Journal of Science and Technology*, *13*(12), 1321–1327. doi:10.17485/IJST/v13i12.180

Adeosun, O. T., & Adeosun, O. A. (2023). Agent bankers and customer victimization in Ado City, Nigeria. *Journal of Community Safety & Well-being*, *8*(1), 33–40. doi:10.35502/jcswb.284

Aderibigbe, I. D. (2023). *E-migrant women entrepreneurs: mobile money apps, transnational communication and the maintenance of social practices*. Faculty of Humanities.

Adesina, O. S. (2017). Foreign policy in an era of digital diplomacy. *Cogent Social Sciences*, *3*(1), 13. doi:10.1080/23311886.2017.1297175

Adesina, O. S. (2022). *Africa and the future of digital diplomacy*. Brookings Institution.

Adjei-Bamfo, P., Domfeh, K. A., Bawole, J. N., Ahenkan, A., Maloreh-Nyamekye, T., Adjei-Bamfo, S., & Darkwah, S. A. (2020). An e-government framework for assessing readiness for public sector e-procurement in a lower-middle income country. *Information Technology for Development*, *26*(4), 742–761. doi:10.1080/02681102.2020.1769542

Affordable4Affordable Internet. (2020). *Affordability report*. Affordable4Affordable. https://a4ai. org/affordability-report/report/2020/

Afolabi, A. (2015). *Availability of online learningtools and the readiness of teachers and students towards it in Adekunle Ajasin University, Akunegba-Akoko*. Ondo State Nigeria: Procedia-Social and Behavioral Sciences.

Africa C. D. C. (2020). *COVID-19: Digital Solutions for Africa's Response*. Africa CDC. https://africacdc.org/download/covid-19-digital-solutions-for-africas-response/

Africa Regional Initiative Report. (2018). *Buenos aires action plan 2018-2021(WTDC- 17)*. ITU.

African Development Bank Group. (2020). *COVID-19: Opportunities for Africa's Economic Transformation*. African Development Bank. https://www.afdb.org/en/news-and-events/covid-19-opportunities-africas-economic-transformation-36156

African Development Bank. (2020). *Digital Transformation in Africa*. African Development Bank. https://www.afdb.org/en/topics/digital-transformation-in-africa

African Union. (2020). *Digital Transformation Strategy for Africa (2020-2030)*. African Union.

African Union. (2020). *Digital transformation strategy for Africa (2020-2030)*. African Union. https://au.int/sites/default/files/documents/38507-doc-dts-english.pdf

African Union. (2022). *Digital education strategy and implementation plan*. African Union. https://au.int/en/documents/20221125/digital-education-strategyand-implementation-plan

Agance France Presse. (2022, June 06). *Ethiopia Shows off Combat Drone at Military Ceremony*. Garowe Online. https://www.garoweonline.com/en/world/africa/ethiopia-

Agarwal, R., & Prasad, J. (1997). The Role of Innovation Characteristics and Perceived Voluntariness in the Acceptance of Information Technologies. *Decision Sciences*, *28*(3), 557–582. doi:10.1111/j.1540-5915.1997.tb01322.x

Agbebi, M. (2022, February 1). China's Digital Silk Road and Africa's technological future. *Council on Foreign Relations*. https://www.cfr.org/sites/default/files/pdf/Chinas%20Digital%20Silk%20Road%20and%20Africas%20Technological%20Future_FINAL.pdf

Agyapong, G. K., Agyapong, E. K., & Asamoah, D. (2021). The Impact of COVID-19 on Remote Work in Ghana: Challenges and Opportunities. *Journal of African Business*, *22*(1), 1–18.

Agyei-Ababio, N., Ansong, E., & Assa-Agyei, K. (2023). Digitalization of revenue mobilization in an emerging economy: The new Institutional Theory perspective. *International Journal of Information Systems and Project Management*, *11*(2), 5–22. doi:10.12821/ijispm110201

Aharony, N. (2015). Factors affecting the adoption of e-books by information professionals. *Journal of Librarianship and Information Science*, *47*(2), 131–144. doi:10.1177/0961000614532120

Ahmad, M. O., Markkula, J., & Oivo, M. (2013). Factors affecting e-government adoption in Pakistan: A citizen's perspective. *Transforming Government: People. Transforming Government*, *7*(2), 225–239. doi:10.1108/17506161311325378

Ahuja, S., & Chan, Y. E. (2016). Digital platforms for innovation in frugal ecosystems. In S. Tanja (Ed.), *Academy of management proceedings* (pp. 1700–17007). Academy of Management. doi:10.5465/ambpp.2016.17007abstract

Aigbavboa, C., Ebekozien, A., & Mkhize, N. (2023). A qualitative approach to investigate governance challenges facing South African airlines in the fourth industrial revolution technologies era. *Social Responsibility Journal*.

Ajzen, I. (1991). The Theory of Planned Behavior. *Organizational Behavior and Human Decision Processes*, *52*(2), 179–211. doi:10.1016/0749-5978(91)90020-T

Aker, J. C., & Mbiti, I. M. (2010). Mobiles phones and economic development in Africa. *The Journal of Economic Perspectives*, *24*(3), 207–232. doi:10.1257/jep.24.3.207

Akogo, D., Samori, I. A., Jimah, B. B., Anim, D. A., Mensah, Y. B., & Sarkodie, B. D. (2022). MinoHealth. AI: A Clinical Evaluation of Deep Learning Systems for the Diagnosis of Pleural Effusion and Cardiomegaly in Ghana, Vietnam, and the United States of America. *arXiv preprint arXiv:2211.00644*.

Alami, H., Rivard, L., Lehoux, P., Hoffman, S. J., Cadeddu, S. B. M., Savoldelli, M., Samri, M. A., Ag Ahmed, M. A., Fleet, R., & Fortin, J.-P. (2020). Artificial intelligence in health care: Laying the Foundation for Responsible, sustainable, and inclusive innovation in low-and middle-income countries. *Globalization and Health*, *16*(1), 1–6. doi:10.1186/s12992-020-00584-1 PMID:32580741

Alaziz, S. N., Albayati, B., El-Bagoury, A. A. A. H., & Shafik, W. (2023). Clustering of COVID-19 Multi-Time Series-Based K-Means and PCA With Forecasting. [IJDWM]. *International Journal of Data Warehousing and Mining*, *19*(3), 1–25. doi:10.4018/IJDWM.317374

Albashrawi, M., & Motiwalla, L. (2017). *When IS Success Model Meets UTAUT in a Mobile Banking Context : A Study of Subjective and Objective System Usage. Proceedings of the Southern Association for Information Systems Conference*, St. Simons Island.

AlHadid, I., Abu-Taieh, E., Alkhawaldeh, R. S., Khwaldeh, S., Masa'deh, R., Kaabneh, K., & Alrowwad, A. A. (2022). Predictors for E-government adoption of SANAD App services integrating UTAUT, TPB, TAM, Trust, and perceived risk. *International Journal of Environmental Research and Public Health*, *19*(14), 8281. https://mdpi-res.com/d_attachment/ijerph/ijerph-19-08281/article_deploy/ijerph-19-08281.pdf?version=1657159300. doi:10.3390/ijerph19148281 PMID:35886133

Alharbi, A. (2023). Implementation of Education 5.0 in Developed and Developing Countries: A Comparative Study. *Creative Education, 14*(5), 914–942. doi:10.4236/ce.2023.145059

Ali, K., Jianguo, D., & Kirikkaleli, D. (2022). Modeling the natural resources and financial inclusion on ecological footprint: The role of economic governance institutions. Evidence from ECOWAS economies. *Resources Policy, 79*, 103115. doi:10.1016/j.resourpol.2022.103115

Alimi, A. S., & Adediran, I. A. (2020). ICT diffusion and the finance–growth nexus: A panel analysis on ECOWAS countries. *Future Business Journal, 6*(1), 1–10. doi:10.1186/s43093-020-00024-x

Allman, J. (2008). Nuclear imperialism and the Pan-African struggle for peace and freedom: Ghana 1959-1962. *Souls, 10*(2), 83–102. doi:10.1080/10999940802115419

Allman, J. (2013). Phantoms of the archive: Kwame Nkrumah, a Nazi pilot named Hanna, and the contingencies of postcolonial history-writing. *The American Historical Review, 118*(1), 104–129. doi:10.1093/ahr/118.1.104

Almirall, E., & Casadesus-Masanell, R. (2010). Open versus closed innovation: A model of discovery and divergence. *Academy of Management Review, 35*(1), 27–47. doi:10.5465/AMR.2010.45577790

Almunawar, M. N., Anshari, M., & Ariff Lim, S. (2020). Customer acceptance of ride-hailing in Indonesia. *Journal of Science and Technology Policy Management, 12*(3), 443–462. doi:10.1108/JSTPM-09-2019-0082

Alnssyan, B., Ahmad, Z., Malela-Majika, J. C., Seong, J. T., & Shafik, W. (2023). On the identifiability and statistical features of a new distributional approach with reliability applications. *AIP Advances, 13*(12), 125211. doi:10.1063/5.0178555

Alvarez, F. E., Argente, D., & Van Patten, D. (2022). *Are cryptocurrencies currencies? Bitcoin as legal tender in El Salvador.*

Alwreikat, A., Shehata, A. M. K., & Abu Zaid, M. K. (2021). *Arab scholars' acceptance of informal scholarly communication tools: applying the technology acceptance model 2 (TAM2).* Global Knowledge, Memory and Communication., doi:10.1108/GKMC-04-2021-0070

Amiron, E., Latib, A. A., & Subari, K. (2019). Industry Revolution 4.0 skills and enablers in Technical and Vocational Education and Training Curriculum. *International Journal of Recent Technology and Engineering, 8*(2), 484–490.

Amoah, L. G. A. (2014). *Impacts of the knowledge society on economic and social growth in Africa.* IGI Global. doi:10.4018/978-1-4666-5844-8

Amoah, L. G. A. (2019). Six decades of Ghanaian statecraft and Asia relations: strategies, strains and successes. In J. R. Ayee (Ed.), *Politics, governance, and development in Ghana* (pp. 147–166). Lexington Books.

Amornvuthivorn, K. (2016). Public-private partnerships (PPPs) in Technical Vocational Education and Training (TVET): Lessons learned from Singapore and USA and implications for public management in Thailand. *Journal of Public and Private Management, 23*(1), 91–91.

Anderson, J. E., & Schwager, P. H. (2004). Association for Information Systems AIS Electronic Library (AISeL) SME Adoption of Wireless LAN Technology: Applying the UTAUT Model SME ADOPTION OF WIRELESS LAN TECHNOLOGY: APPLYING THE UTAUT MODEL. *Association for Information Systems AIS Electronic Library (AISeL), SAIS 2004 Proceedings.* https://aisel.aisnet.org/sais2004%0Ahttp://aisel.aisnet.org/sais2004/6%0Ahttp://aisel.aisnet.org/sais2004%0Ahttp://aisel.aisnet.org/sais2004/6

Anderson, J., Rainie, L., & Vogels, E. A. (2021). Experts say the 'new normal' in 2025 will be far more tech-driven, presenting more big challenges. Pew Research Center, 18.

Anh, P. Q. (2021). Shifting the focus to East and Southeast Asia: A critical review of regional game research. *Fudan Journal of the Humanities and Social Sciences*, *14*(2), 173–196. doi:10.1007/s40647-021-00317-7

Anthony, B. Jnr. (2022). An exploratory study on academic staff perception towards blended learning in higher education. *Education and Information Technologies*, *27*(3), 3107–3133. doi:10.1007/s10639-021-10705-x

Aoun, A., Ilinca, A., Ghandour, M., & Ibrahim, H. (2021). A review of Industry 4.0 characteristics and challenges, with potential improvements using Blockchain technology. *Computers & Industrial Engineering*, *16*(2), 1–11. doi:10.1016/j.cie.2021.107746

Arakpogun, E. O., Elsahn, Z., Olan, F., & Elsahn, F. (2021). Artificial Intelligence in Africa: Challenges and Opportunities. In A. Hamdan, A. E. Hassanien, A. Razzaque, & B. Alareeni (Eds.), *The Fourth Industrial Revolution: Implementation of Artificial Intelligence for Growing Business Success. Studies in Computational Intelligence. 935* (pp. 375–388). Springer.

Arize, I., & Onwujekwe, O. (2017). Acceptability and willingness to pay for telemedicine services in Enugu state, Southeast Nigeria. *Digital Health*, *3*(1). Advance online publication. doi:10.1177/2055207617715524 PMID:29942606

Armah, K. (2004). *Peace without power: Ghana's foreign policy 1957-1966*. Ghana Universities Press.

Arthur, P., Hanson, K., & Ruplampu, K. (2020). *Disruptive Technologies, Innovation and development in Africa*. Palgrave MacMillan. doi:10.1007/978-3-030-40647-9

Aruleba, K., Jere, N., & Matarirano, O. (2022). Technology Adoption Readiness in Disadvantaged Universities during COVID-19 Pandemic in South Africa. *International Journal of Higher Education*, *11*(2), 172–180. doi:10.5430/ijhe.v11n2p172

Arza, V. (2010). Channels, benefits and risks of public-private interactions for knowledge transfer: Conceptual framework inspired by Latin America. *Science & Public Policy*, *37*(7), 473–484. doi:10.3152/030234210X511990

Asare, K. (1996). Ghana communications: private players push slowly into the market. *ISP News*. http://www.ipsnews.net/1996/08/ghana-communications-private-players-push-slowly-into-the-market/

Ashrafi, A., Zareravasan, A., Rabiee Savoji, S., & Amani, M. (2022). Exploring factors influencing students' continuance intention to use the learning management system (LMS): A multi-perspective framework. *Interactive Learning Environments*, *30*(8), 1475–1497. doi:10.1080/10494820.2020.1734028

Asumadu-Sarkodie, S., & Owusu, P. A. (2016). Forecasting Nigeria's energy use by 2030, an econometric approach. *Energy Sources. Part B, Economics, Planning, and Policy*, *11*(10), 990–997. doi:10.1080/15567249.2016.1217287

Atiyas & Dutz (2021). *COVID-19 and the future of work in Africa; emerging Trends in Digital Technology Adoption*. ISSUU. https://issuu.com/world.bank.publications/docs/9781464817144

Audretsch, D. B., Lehmann, E. E., & Wright, M. (2014). Technology transfer in a global economy. *The Journal of Technology Transfer*, *39*(3), 301–312. doi:10.1007/s10961-012-9283-6

Awoyemi, R., & Olaniyi, E. (2022). Using Technology to Support Inclusive Classroom-Based Instruction. In J. Keengwe (Ed.), *Handbook of Research on Promoting Global Citizenship Education* (pp. 195–208). IGI Global.

Axelsson, K., Melin, U., & Lindgren, I. (2013). Stakeholder salience changes in an e-government implementation project. Lecture Notes in Computer Science (Including Subseries Lecture Notes in Artificial Intelligence and Lecture Notes in Bioinformatics), 8074 LNCS. doi:10.1007/978-3-642-40358-3_20

Ayoade, I. A., Adedigba, A. P., Adeyemi, O. A., Adeaga, O. A., & Akanbi, O. V. (2022). Trends and prospects of digital twin technologies: A review. *Quantum Journal of engineering, science and technology*, *3*(4), 11-24. www.qjoest.com

Azman, Z., & Ibrahim, J. (2018). *The Readiness of Nilai Polytechnic Graduates in Facing the Wave of Industrial Revolution 4.0 (IR 4.0).* Paper presented at the 8th National Conference in Education – Technical & Vocational Education and Training (CiE-TVET) 2018. IJICC.

Babalola, S. O. (2019). *Factors influencing behavioral intention to the use of Information and Communication Technology (ICT) among students of Federal Polytechnic, Ilaro.Ogun State.* Library Philosophy and Practice.

Baguma, R., Mkoba, E., Nahabwe, M., Mubangizi, M. G., Amutorine, M., & Wanyama, D. (2022). Towards an Artificial Intelligence Readiness Index for Africa. In: Ndayizigamiye, P., Twinomurinzi, H., Kalema, B., Bwalya, K., Bembe, M. (Eds.) *Digital-for-Development: Enabling Transformation, Inclusion and Sustainability Through ICTs. IDIA 2022. Communications in Computer and Information Science. 1774. International Development Informatics Association Conference* (pp. 285-303): Springer.

Baguma, R., Mkoba, E., Nahabwe, M., Mubangizi, M. G., Amutorine, M., & Wanyama, D. (2023). *Towards an Artificial Intelligence Readiness Index for Africa.* Digital-for-Development: Enabling Transformation, Inclusion and Sustainability Through ICTs: *12th International Development Informatics Association Conference, IDIA 2022,* Mbombela, South Africa.

Bainomugisha, E., Ujakpa, M. M., Nakatumba-Nabende, J., Lawrence, N., Kihoza, P., & Annette, I. (2023). *Computer Science Education in Selected Countries from Sub-Saharan Africa.*

Bakar, S., Nordin, N. A., & Amani Nordin, N. (2020). Fintech Investment And Banks Performance In Malaysia, Singapore & Thailand. *European Proceedings of Social and Behavioural Sciences, 100.*

Banfi, R. (2023). Gaming I, II, and III: Arcades, video game systems, and modern game streaming services. *Games and Culture, 0*(0), 1–38. doi:10.1177/15554120231186634

Banga, K., & te Velde, D. W. (2018). *Digitalisation and the Future of Manufacturing in Africa.* ODI London.

Bank of Ghana Report. (2021). Mobile Money Interoperability: A Game Changer for Financial Inclusion in Ghana. *World Bank Blogs.* https://blogs.worldbank.org/digital-development/mobile-money-interoperability-game-changer-financial-inclusion-ghana [https://www.bbc.com/news/world-africa-52148639]

Bank of Ghana. (2021). *Bank of Ghana Launches Mobile Money Interoperability System.* Bank of Ghana. https://www.bog.gov.gh/news/press-releases/2018/bank-of-ghana-launches-mobile-money-interoperability-system/

Barbara, M., Gabriele, B., Stefano, U., Domenico, S., & Stefano, F. (2017). How will change the future engineers' skills in the Industry 4.0 framework? A questionnaire survey. *27th International Conference on Flexible Automation and Intelligent Manufacturing, FAIM2017,* Modena, Italy.

Bawole, J. N., & Langnel, Z. (2023). Administrative Reforms in the Ghanaian Public Services for Government Business Continuity During the COVID-19 Crisis. *Public Organization Review, 23*(1), 181–196. doi:10.1007/s11115-022-00687-w

Beatty, R. C., Shim, J. P., & Jones, M. C. (2001). Factors influencing corporate web site adoption: A time-based assessment. *Information & Management, 38*(6), 337–354. doi:10.1016/S0378-7206(00)00064-1

Beijing International Studies University. (2018, April 28). *Beijing International Studies University held the 2018 International Youth Innovation and Entrepreneurship Program (known as the Vine Program) international student internship and the African session.* BISU. UNESCO. https://www.bisu.edu.cn/art/2018/4/28/art_1424_173269.html

Bell, G., & Dourish, P. (2006). Yesterday's tomorrows: Notes on ubiquitous computing's dominant vision. *Personal and Ubiquitous Computing, 11*(2), 133–143. doi:10.1007/s00779-006-0071-x

Bennett, W. L., & Segerberg, A. (2013). *The logic of connective action: Digital media and the personalization of contentious politics.* Cambridge University Press. doi:10.1017/CBO9781139198752

Berge, G., Granmo, O., Tveit, T., Munkvold, B., Ruthjersen, A., & Sharma, J. (2023). Machine learning-driven clinical decision support system for concept-based searching: A field trial in a Norwegian hospital. *BMC Medical Informatics and Decision Making*, *23*(1), 5. https://bmcmedinformdecismak.biomedcentral.com/counter/pdf/10.1186/s12911-023-02101-x.pdf. doi:10.1186/s12911-023-02101-x PMID:36627624

Berndt, E. R., & Christensen, L. R. (1973). The translog function and the substitution of equipment, structures, and labor in US manufacturing 1929-68. *Journal of Econometrics*, *1*(1), 81–113. doi:10.1016/0304-4076(73)90007-9

Bervell, B., & Umar, I. N. (2020). Blended learning or face-to-face? Does Tutor anxiety prevent the adoption of Learning Management Systems for distance education in Ghana? *Open Learning*, *35*(2), 159–177. doi:10.1080/02680513.2018.1548964

Bhagwan, N., & Evans, M. (2023). A review of industry 4.0 technologies used in the production of energy in China, Germany, and South Africa. *Renewable & Sustainable Energy Reviews*, *173*, 113075. doi:10.1016/j.rser.2022.113075

Bibby, L., & Dehe, B. (2018). Defining and assessing industry 4.0 maturity levels – case of the defense sector. *Production Planning and Control*, *29*(12), 1030–1043. doi:10.1080/09537287.2018.1503355

Bindseil, U., & Pantelopoulos, G. (2022). Towards the holy grail of cross-border payments.

Bio-Tchane, Y. (2021). *Information Systems in Public Financial Management Expanding the institutional coverage of a financial management information system: Lessons from Benin, Nigeria and Ghana.*

Birhane, A. (2020). Algorithmic colonization of Africa. *Script-ed*, *17*(2), 389–409. doi:10.2966/scrip.170220.389

Bjola, C., & Holmes, M. (Eds.). (2015). *Digital Diplomacy: Theory and Practice.* Routledge. doi:10.4324/9781315730844

Bjola, C., & Manor, I. (2018). *From digital tactics to digital strategies: Practicing digital PD.* CPD Blog.

Bjola, C., & Manor, I. (2022). The rise of hybrid diplomacy: From digital adaptation to digital adoption. *International Affairs*, *98*(2), 471–491. doi:10.1093/ia/iiac005

Blackwell, A. F., Damena, A., & Tegegne, T. (2022). Inventing artificial intelligence in Ethiopia. *Interdisciplinary Science Reviews*, *46*(3), 363–385. doi:10.1080/03080188.2020.1830234

Blake, D. (2022). The Great Game Will Never End: Why the Global Financial Crisis Is Bound to Be Repeated. *Journal of Risk and Financial Management*, *15*(6), 245. doi:10.3390/jrfm15060245

Blut, M., Chong, A. Y. L., Tsigna, Z., & Venkatesh, V. (2022). Meta-Analysis of the Unified Theory of Acceptance and Use of Technology (UTAUT): Challenging its Validity and Charting a Research Agenda in the Red Ocean. *Journal of the Association for Information Systems*, *23*(1), 13–95. doi:10.17705/1jais.00719

Bock, L. (2014). *An empirical study of the planning and implementation of competency-based education and training in vocational education training centres in Namibia: The case of Namibia Training Authority* [Doctoral dissertation, Polytechnic of Namibia].

Bokolo, A. J. (2020). Exploring the adoption of Telemedicine and virtual software for care of outpatients during and after COVID-19 pandemic. *International Journal of Medical Sciences*, 2020. PMID:32642981

Bonaccorsi, A., & Piccaluga, A. (1994). A theoretical framework for the evaluation of university-industry relationships. *R & D Management*, *24*(3), 229–247. doi:10.1111/j.1467-9310.1994.tb00876.x

Bonekamp, L., & Sure, M. (2015). Consequences of industry 4.0 on human labor and work organisation. *Journal of Business and Media Psychology*, *6*(1), 33–40.

Bonney, E. (2023, February 28). *WASSCE for Private Candidates: More candidates fail Mathematics*. Retrieved October 13, 2023, from Graphic Online: https://www.graphic.com.gh/news/education/wassce-for-private-candidates-more-candidates-fail-mathematics.html

Borenstein, J., & Howard, A. (2021). Emerging challenges in AI and the need for AI ethics education. *AI and Ethics*, *1*(1), 61–65. doi:10.1007/s43681-020-00002-7

Borokini, F., Wakunuma, K., & Akintoye, S. (2023). The Use of Gendered Chatbots in Nigeria: Critical Perspectives. In Responsible AI in Africa: Challenges and Opportunities (pp. 119–139). Springer International Publishing Cham.

Bradley, V. M. (2021). Learning Management System (LMS) Use with Online Instruction. *International Journal of Technology in Education*, *4*(1), 68–92. doi:10.46328/ijte.36

Bradshaw, S. (2015). Digital diplomacy-# not diplomacy. *Canadá: Centre of international governance innovation.*

Braman, S. (2012). Internationalization of the internet by design: The first decade. *Global Media and Communication*, *8*(1), 27–45. doi:10.1177/1742766511434731

Brancheau, J. C., & Wetherbe, J. C. (1990). The Adoption of Spreadsheet Software: Testing Innovation Diffusion Theory in the Context of End-User Computing. *Information Systems Research*, *1*(2), 115–143. doi:10.1287/isre.1.2.115

Braun, V., & Clarke, V. (2006). *Thematic Analysis*. Psych. http;//www.psych.auckland.ac.nz

Brock, A. (2011). "When Keeping it Real Goes Wrong": Resident Evil 5, Racial Representation, and Gamers. *Games and Culture*, *6*(5), 429–452. doi:10.1177/1555412011402676

Broughel, J., & Thierer, A. (2019). Technological innovation and economic growth: A brief report on the evidence. SSRN *Electronic Journal*. https://doi.org/ doi:10.2139/ssrn.3346495

Brown, T., Mullins, K., Betzer, C., Ford, S., Freitag, J., Nolan, H., Rattray, A., Sleigh, F., Swanson, S., & Thompson, A. (2022). *The Elusive Rainbow: Racial Reconciliation in South Africa*. Nelson A. Rockefeller Center for Public Policy.

Brown, S. A., Massey, A. P., Montoya-Weiss, M. M., & Burkman, J. R. (2002). Do I Really Have to? User Acceptance of Mandated Technology. *European Journal of Information Systems*, *11*(4), 283–295. doi:10.1057/palgrave.ejis.3000438

Brunton, B. G. (1988). Institutional Origins of the Military-Industrial Complex. *Journal of Economic Issues*, *22*(2), 599–606. doi:10.1080/00213624.1988.11504790

Bukharin, N. (1972). *Imperialism and world economy*. Merlin.

Burke, B. (2014). *Gamify: How Gamification enables People to do Extraordinary Things*. Gartner Inc.

Butcher, N., Wilson-Strydom, M., & Baijnath, M. (2021). *Artificial intelligence capacity in sub-Saharan Africa: Compendium report*. Artificial Intelligence for Development Africa.

CAGD. (2022). *The Public Financial Management Reform Project (PFMRP)*. CAGD. https://www.cagd.gov.gh/projects/the-public-financial-management-reform-project-pfmrp/

Calabrese, A., Costa, R., Tiburzi, L., & Brem, A. (2023). Merging two revolutions: A human-artificial intelligence method to study how sustainability and Industry 4.0 are intertwined. *Technological Forecasting and Social Change*, *188*, 122265. doi:10.1016/j.techfore.2022.122265

Calderon, C., Cantu, C., & Chuhan-Pole, P. (2018). Infrastructure development in Sub-Saharan Africa: a scorecard. *World Bank Policy Research Working Paper*, (8425), 1-47.

Campbell-Kelly, M., & Garcia-Swartz, D. D. (2013). The history of the internet: The missing narratives. *Journal of Information Technology*, *28*(1), 18–33. doi:10.1057/jit.2013.4

Campbell, S., Greenwood, M., Prior, S., Shearer, T., Walkem, K., Young, S., Bywaters, D., & Walker, K. (2020). Purposive sampling: Complex or simple? Research case examples. *Journal of Research in Nursing*, *25*(8), 652–661. doi:10.1177/1744987120927206 PMID:34394687

Cangiano, M., Gelb, A., & Goodwin-Groen, R. (2019). Public Financial Management and the Digitalization of Payments. In *DC* (*Vol. 416*). www.cgdev.orgwww.cgdev.orgwww.cgdev.org

Capacity Building Seminar. (n.d.). *International Centre for Higher Education Innovation under the Auspices of UNESCO*. UNESCO. https://en.ichei.org/dist/index.html#/buildingIntro

Carr, K. (2017). *Early African Board Games and Toys – History of Games*. Quatr. https://quatr.us/history/african-games-history.htm

Carroll, A. B., Brown, J. A., & Buchholtz, A. K. (2018). Business & Society: Ethics, Sustainability, and Stakeholder Management. In Business & society : ethics, sustainability, and stakeholder management.

Carter, K., & Shakwa, G. (2022). Flipping the Post-COVID online Classroom in a Professional Development Programme at the Namibia University of Science and Technology. In J. Keengwe (Ed.), *Handbook for Research on Transformative and Innovative Pedagogies in Education* (pp. 93–111). IGI Global. doi:10.4018/978-1-7998-9561-9.ch006

Carvalho, A. C. P., Carvalho, A. P. P., & Carvalho, N. G. P. (2020). *Industry 4.0 Technologies: What Is Your Potential for Environmental Management?* Knowledge Unlatched. www.knowledgeunlatched.org

Carvalho, C. E. M. M. d. (2022). *Banking on mobile: financial inclusion through FinTech: the Hidroelétrica de Cahora Bassa: IPO Case Study*. Research Gate.

Casely-Hayford, J. E. (2004). *Ethiopia Unbound*. Lushena Books.

Cassell, C. A., Drake, M. S., & Dyer, T. A. (2018). Auditor litigation risk and the number of institutional investors. *Audit.: J. Pract. Theory*, *37*(3), 71–90.

Castaneda, J., Jover, A., Calvet, L., Yanes, S., Juan, A. A., & Sainz, M. (2022). Dealing with gender bias issues in data-algorithmic processes: A social-statistical perspective. *Algorithms*, *15*(9), 1–16. doi:10.3390/a15090303

Castro, C. S. P. (2020). *How can fintech serve the unbanked in Sub-Saharan Africa?* Chang, L., Iqbal, S., & Chen, H. (2023). Does financial inclusion index and energy performance index co-move? *Energy Policy*, *174*, 113422.

Central Bank of Nigeria. (2020). *Electronic Payment Channels in Nigeria: Post COVID-19 Impact Assessment*. Central Bank of Nigeria. https://www.cbn.gov.ng/Out/2020/CCD/Electronic%20Payment%20Channels%20in%20Nigeria.pdf

Chan, M. (2018). *Ten Years in Public Health 2007-2017: Report by Dr Margaret Chan Director-General World Health Organization*. World Health Organization.

Chan, S. (2017). *Mediations on diplomacy: Comparative cases in diplomatic practice and foreign policy*. E-International Relations Publishing.

Chan, S.-C., & Lu, M. (2004). Understanding Internet Banking Adoption and Use Behavior: A Hong Kong Perspective. *Journal of Global Information Management*, *12*(3), 21–43. doi:10.4018/jgim.2004070102

Chao, C. M. (2019). Factors determining the behavioral intention to use mobile learning: An application and extension of the UTAUT model. *Frontiers in Psychology*, *10*(JULY), 1–14. doi:10.3389/fpsyg.2019.01652 PMID:31379679

Chauke, K. R., Mamokere, J., & Mabeba, S. J. (2023). Reflection on the Proliferation of the Fourth Industrial Revolution and Its Implications on Rural Areas in South Africa. *International Journal of Social Science Research and Review*, *6*(1), 214–226. doi:10.47814/ijssrr.v6i1.890

Chau, P. Y. K., & Hu, P. J. H. (2001). Information Technology Acceptance by Individual Professionals: A Model Comparison Approach. *Decision Sciences*, *32*(4), 699–719. doi:10.1111/j.1540-5915.2001.tb00978.x

Chawarura, T., Stam, G. V., & Van Dijik, J. H. (2019*). E-Health in Zimbabwe, A case of techno-social development.* Research Gate. https://www.researchgate,net/publication/ 332668100.

Chemma, N. (2021). Disruptive innovation in a dynamic environment: A winning strategy?An illustration through the analysis of the yoghurt industry in Algeria. *Journal of Innovation and Entrepreneurship*, *10*(34), 1–19. doi:10.1186/s13731-021-00150-y

Chen, E. Y. (1994). The evolution of university-industry technology transfer in Hong Kong. *Technovation*, *14*(7), 449–459. doi:10.1016/0166-4972(94)90003-5

Cheng, Y. M. (2018). What drives cloud ERP continuance? An integrated view. *Journal of Enterprise Information Management*, *31*(5), 724–750. doi:10.1108/JEIM-02-2018-0043

Chen, R. J., Wang, J. J., Williamson, D. F., Chen, T. Y., Lipkova, J., Lu, M. Y., Sahai, S., & Mahmood, F. (2023). Algorithmic fairness in artificial intelligence for medicine and healthcare. *Nature Biomedical Engineering*, *7*(6), 719–742. doi:10.1038/s41551-023-01056-8 PMID:37380750

Chesbrough, H. W. (2003). The era of open innovation. *MIT Sloan Management Review*, *44*(3).

Chia, Y. M. (2008). Game Developer's Local Arm Launched Debut Title. *Strait Times*.

Chikuni, D. (2016). Potential/preparedness of E-health services in Zimbabwe. *International Journal of Research in IT and Management*, *6*(1), 43–54.

Childs, G. T. (2003). *An introduction to African languages* (Vol. 1). John Benjamins Publishing. doi:10.1075/z.121

Chilunjika, S., & Chilunjika, A. (2023). Embracing e-health systems in managing the COVID 19 pandemic in Sub-Saharan Africa. *Social Sciences & Humanities Open*, *8*(1), 100556. doi:10.1016/j.ssaho.2023.100556 PMID:37214273

Chinengudu, T. (2022). Simulated-Work Based Learning in Technical and Vocational Education and Training: An Innovative Pedagogy. In J. Keengwe (Ed.), *Handbook of Research Transformative and Innovative Pedagogies in Education* (pp. 112–129). IGI Global. doi:10.4018/978-1-7998-9561-9.ch007

Chin, W. W. (1998). The partial least squares approach to structural equation modeling. *Modern Methods for Business Research*, *295*(2), 295–336.

Chiu, C.-M., & Wang, E. T. G. (2008). Understanding Web-based learning continuance intention: The role of subjective task value. *Information & Management*, *45*(3), 194–201. doi:10.1016/j.im.2008.02.003

Christensen, C. (1997). *The innovators dilemma: When new technologies cause great firms to fail.* Harvard Business School Press.

Chu, S. K., Raynolds, R. B., Tavares, N. J., Notari, M., & Lee, C. W. (2017). *21st century skills development through inquiry-based learning: From theory to practice.* Springer. doi:10.1007/978-981-10-2481-8

Cirillo, D., Catuara-Solarz, S., Morey, C., Guney, E., Subirats, L., Mellino, S., Gigante, A., Valencia, A., Rementeria, M. J., Chadha, A. S., & Mavridis, N. (2020). Sex and gender differences and biases in artificial intelligence for biomedicine and healthcare. *NPJ Digital Medicine*, *3*(1), 81. doi:10.1038/s41746-020-0288-5 PMID:32529043

Cirolia, L. R., Hall, S., & Nyamnjoh, H. (2022). Remittance micro-worlds and migrant infrastructure: Circulations, disruptions, and the movement of money. *Transactions of the Institute of British Geographers*, *47*(1), 63–76. doi:10.1111/tran.12467

Cochran, W. G. (1963). *Sampling Techniques* (2nd ed.). John Wiley & Sons.

Cohen, J. (1992). Statistical power analysis. *Current Directions in Psychological Science*, *1*(3), 98–101. doi:10.1111/1467-8721.ep10768783

Cohen, L., Manion, L., Morrison, K., & Wyse, D. (2004). *A Guide to Teaching Practice*. Routledge.

Cohen, R. (1998). *Reflections on the new global diplomacy* [Innovation in diplomatic practice, studies in diplomacy]. MacMillan Press Ltd.

Cole, B., & Wolfe. (2018). Twiplomacy Study 2018.

Coleman, D. (2019). Digital colonialism: The 21st century scramble for Africa through the extraction and control of user data and the limitations of data protection laws. *Michigan Journal of Race & Law*, *24*(24.2), 417–439. doi:10.36643/mjrl.24.2.digital

Collins, J. (2005). A social history of Ghanaian popular entertainment since independence. *Transactions of the Historical Society of Ghana*, *9*, 17–40. https://www.jstor.org/stable/41406722

Collins, J. (1989). The early history of West African Highlife music. *Popular Music*, *8*(3), 221–230. doi:10.1017/S0261143000003524

Colvin, R. M., Witt, G. B., & Lacey, J. (2020). Power, perspective, and privilege: The challenge of translating stakeholder theory from business management to environmental and natural resource management. *Journal of Environmental Management*, *271*, 110974. doi:10.1016/j.jenvman.2020.110974 PMID:32579526

Comer, J., & Kendall, P. (2013). *The Oford handbook of research strategies for clinical psychology*. Oxford University Press.

Communications Authority of Kenya. (2021). *Quarterly Sector Statistics Report Q4 2020/2021*. Community Authority of Kenya. https://ca.go.ke/wp-content/uploads/2021/05/QSS-Report-Q4-2020_21.pdf

Cooper, A., Heine, J., & Thakur, R. (2013). Introduction: the challenges of 21st-century diplomacy.

Cornelius, M. (1986). An historical background to some mathematical games. *Mathematics in School*, *15*(1), 47–49.

Costa, J. N. P. P. (2020). *How can fintech serve the unbanked in Sub-Saharan Africa?: Sub-Saharan Africa: land of opportunities for fintech*.

Coulibaly, S. S. (2021). A study of the factors affecting mobile money penetration rates in the West African Economic and Monetary Union (WAEMU) compared with East Africa. *Financial Innovation*, *7*(1), 25. doi:10.1186/s40854-021-00238-0

COVID-19 National Trust Fund. (2021). Ministry of Finance Ghana. https://www.mofep.gov.gh/covid-19-national-trust-fund

Crist, W. (2019). Passing from the Middle to the New Kingdom: A *Senet* Board in the Rosicrucian Egyptian Museum. *The Journal of Egyptian Archaeology*, *105*(1), 107–113. https://www.jstor.org/stable/26949436. doi:10.1177/0307513319896288

Cull, N. J. (2020). The future of digital diplomacy after COVID-19. *Place Branding and Public Diplomacy*, *16*(3), 135–139.

Curtis, S. (2019). Digital transformation—The silver bullet to public service improvement? *Public Money & Management*, *39*(5), 322–324. doi:10.1080/09540962.2019.1611233

Cusolito, Lederman, & Peña (2020). Wordbank Policy Research Paper; The Effects of Digital-Technology Adoption on Productivity and Factor Demand Firm-level Evidence from Developing Countries. World Bank. https://documents1.worldbank.org/curated/en/829161595512126439/pdf/The-Effects-of-Digital-Technology-Adoption-on-Productivity-and-Factor-Demand-Firm-level-Evidence-from-Developing-Countries.pdf

D'Este, P., & Patel, P. (2007). University-industry linkages in the UK: What are the factors underlying the variety of interactions with industry? *Research Policy*, *36*(9), 1295–1313. doi:10.1016/j.respol.2007.05.002

Damian, M. (2022). Connecting Students on Hospital Wards to Hospital Classrooms and the Community Using Video Conferencing Technologies. In J. Keengwe (Ed.), *Handbook of Research on Transformative and Innovative Pedagogies in Education* (pp. 76–92). IGI Global.

Daniels, C., Erforth, B., & Teevan, C. (2023). Digitalisation for Transformation: New Frontiers for Africa–Europe Co-operation. In Africa–Europe Cooperation and Digital Transformation (pp. 1–16). Routledge.

Danladi, S., Prasad, M., Modibbo, U. M., Ahmadi, S. A., & Ghasemi, P. (2023). Attaining Sustainable Development Goals through Financial Inclusion: Exploring Collaborative Approaches to Fintech Adoption in Developing Economies. *Sustainability (Basel)*, *15*(17), 13039. doi:10.3390/su151713039

Danquah, J. B. (1997). *The Ghanaian Establishment*. Ghana Universities Press.

Darke, P., Shanks, G., & Broadbent, M. (1998). Successfully completing case study research: Combining rigour, relevance and pragmatism. *Information Systems Journal*, *8*(4), 273–289. doi:10.1046/j.1365-2575.1998.00040.x

Dastin, J. (2022). Amazon scraps secret AI recruiting tool that showed bias against women. In *Ethics of data and analytics* (pp. 296–299). Auerbach Publications. doi:10.1201/9781003278290-44

David, K. B., & Adebisi, Y. A. (2020). Proposed model for hospital and community pharmacy services during COVID-19 pandemic in Nigeria. *International Journal of Pharmacy Practice, 4*(10), 1111/ijpp/12652. Pub Med.

Davidovic, S., Soheib, N., Prady, D., & Tourpe, H. (2020). *Beyond the COVID-19 Crisis: A Framework for Sustainable Government-to-person Mobile Money Transfer*. International Monetary Fund.

Davis, F. D. (1985). *A technology acceptance model for empirically testing new end-user information systems: Theory and results* [Doctoral dissertation, Massachusetts Institute of Technology].

Davis, F. D. (1989). Perceived Usefulness, Perceived Ease of Use, and User Acceptance in Information Technology. *Management Information Systems Quarterly*, *13*(3), 319–340. doi:10.2307/249008

de Mello, L., & Ter-Minassian, T. (2020). Digitalisation Challenges and Opportunities for Subnational Governments. *OECD Working Papers on Fiscal Federalism*, *31*, 1–24.

de Souza Ferreira, W., Vale, G. M., & Correa, V. (2022). Diffusion of Innovation in Technological Platforms: The Uber Case. *Brazilian Administration Review*, *19*(3), 1–32.

Dede, C., Richard, J., & Saxberg, B. (2018). *Learning engineering for online education - theoritical context and design-based examples*. Routledge. doi:10.4324/9781351186193

de-Lima-Santos, M.-F., & Ceron, W. (2021). Artificial intelligence in news media: current perceptions and future outlook. *Journalism and media*, *3*(1), 13-26.

Dell, S. (2020). *Universities prepare for online teaching and learning*. University Wo.

Demuyakor, J. (2021). Ghana's Digitization Initiatives: A Survey of Citizens Perceptions on the Benefits and Challenges to the Utilization of Digital Governance Services. *International Journal of Publication and Social Studies, 6*(1), 42–55. doi:10.18488/journal.135.2021.61.42.55

Deos, S. A. (2015). *Digital diplomacy & social capital*. University of Otago.

Deulen, A. A. (2013). Social Constructivism and online learning environments: Toward a theological model for christian educators. *ristian Education Journal: Research on Educational Ministry, 10*(1), https//2080/. doi:10.1177/073989131301000107

Dhanpat, N., Buthelezi, Z., Joe, R., Maphela, T., & Shongwe, N. (2020). Industry 4.0: The role of human resource professionals. *SA Journal of Human Resource Management, 18*(1), 1–11. doi:10.4102/sajhrm.v18i0.1302

Dhlalisa, F., & Govender, G. (2020). Challenges of acceptance and usage of a Learning Management System amongst Academics. *International Journal of eBusiness and eGovernment Studies, 12.*

Diestro, D. (2022). Learning readiness in education 5.0 as influenced by value creation and academic productivity. *EPRA International Journal of Research and Development (IJRD), 7*(8), 179-184.

Digital Skills Gap Index 2021: Your tool to determine global digital skills levels. (n.d.). John Wiley & Sons, Inc. https://dsgi.wiley.com/

Dishaw, M. T., & Strong, D. M. (1999). Extending the technology acceptance model with task-technology fit constructs. *Information & Management, 36*(1), 9–21. doi:10.1016/S0378-7206(98)00101-3

Dobson, P. J. (1999). Approaches to theory use in interpretative case studies - a critical realist perspective. Edith Cowan University.

Donaldson, T., & Preston, L. E. (1995). Stakeholder theory: Concepts, evidence, and implications. *Academy of Management Review, 20*(1), 65. doi:10.2307/258887

Dowuona, S. (2021, May 7). *3 Ghanaian FinTechs build Ghana.GOV to block state revenue leakages*. TechFocus. https://www.techfocus24.com/3-ghanaian-fintechs-build-ghana-gov-to-block-state-revenue-leakages/

D'Souza, U.J.A., & Mudin, D.K.D. (2018). Industrial revolution 4.0: Role of universities. *Borneo Journal of Medical Sciences, 12*, 1. 1–2.

Duarte, A. Y. S., Sanches, R. A., & Dedini, F. G. (2018). Assessment and technological forecasting in the textile industry: From first industrial revolution to the industry 4.0. *Strategic Design Research Journal., 11*(3), 193–202. doi:10.4013/sdrj.2018.113.03

Dube, T., Van Eck, R., & Zuva, T. (2020). The Review of Technology Adoption Models and Theories to Measure Readiness and Acceptable Use of Technology in a Business Organisation. *Journal of Information Technology and Digital World, 02*(04), 207–212. doi:10.36548/jitdw.2020.4.003

Ebil, S., Othman, N., Nor, H. N. H. M., Ahmad, M. H., Mujah, O., & Keh, C. W. (2017). Brunei TVET transformation: The development of the Institute of Brunei Technical Education's two key surveys. *Journal for Technical and Vocational Education and Training in Asia, 8*, 1–15.

Ediagbonya, V., & Tioluwani, C. (2023). The role of fintech in driving financial inclusion in developing and emerging markets: Issues, challenges and prospects. *Technological Sustainability, 2*(1), 100–119. doi:10.1108/TECHS-10-2021-0017

Edwards-Dashti, N. (2022). *FinTech Women Walk the Talk: Moving the Needle for Workplace Gender Equality in Financial Services and Beyond*. Springer. doi:10.1007/978-3-030-90574-3

Egbetokun, A. A. (2015). Interactive learning and firm-level capabilities in latecomer settings: The Nigerian manufacturing industry. *Technological Forecasting and Social Change*, *99*, 231–241. doi:10.1016/j.techfore.2015.06.040

Eggers, W. D., Manstof, J., Kamleshkumar Kishnani, P., & Barroca, J. (2021). *Seven pivots for government's digital transformation. How COVID-19 proved the importance of "being" digital*. Deloitte Insights.

Eguegu, O. (2022). The Digital Silk Road: Connecting Africa with new norms of digital development. *Asia Policy*, *29*(3), 30–39. doi:10.1353/asp.2022.0049

Eke, D. O., Chintu, S. S., & Wakunuma, K. (2023). Towards Shaping the Future of Responsible AI in Africa. In Responsible AI in Africa: Challenges and Opportunities (pp. 169–193). Springer International Publishing Cham. doi:10.1007/978-3-031-08215-3_8

Eke, D. O., Wakunuma, K., & Akintoye, S. (2023). Introducing Responsible AI in Africa. In Responsible AI in Africa: Challenges and Opportunities (pp. 1-11). Springer International Publishing Cham. doi:10.1007/978-3-031-08215-3_1

Ekekwe, N. (2018). How new technologies could transform Africa's health care system. *Harvard Business Review*, 6.

Ekong, I. I., Chukwu, E., & Chukwu, M. (2020). COVID-19 mobile positioning data contact tracing and patient privacy regulations: Exploratory serach of global response strategies and the use of digital tools in Nigeria. JMIR. *mHealth*, *8*(4), 1–7.

Elliot, R. (2020). *Coronavirus in sub- saharan Africa: A Geopoll survey report*. International Development research www.geoploo.com/blog/coronavirus-africa/

Etori, N., Temesgen, E., & Gini, M. (2023). What We Know So Far: Artificial Intelligence in African Healthcare. *arXiv preprint arXiv:2305.18302*.

Etzkowitz, H., & Leydesdorff, L. (2000). The dynamics of innovation: From National Systems and "Mode 2" to a Triple Helix of university-industry-government relations. *Research Policy*, *29*(2), 109–123. doi:10.1016/S0048-7333(99)00055-4

Etzkowitz, H., Webster, A., Gebhardt, C., & Terra, B. R. C. (2000). The future of the university and the university of the future: Evolution of ivory tower to entrepreneurial paradigm. *Research Policy*, *29*(2), 313–330. doi:10.1016/S0048-7333(99)00069-4

European Investment Bank. (2017). *Banking in sub-Sahara Africa: Interim report on digital financial inclusion*. European Investment Bank.

European Investment Bank. (2021). *The rise of Africa's digital economy*. European Investment Bank.

European Navigator. (n.d.). *Final communiqué of the Asian-African conference of Bandun*. ENA. https://www.ena.lu/final_communique_asian_african_conference_bandung_24_april_ 1955-2-1192.

Evans, M. A., Packer, M. J., & Sawyer, R. K. (2016). *Reflections on the learning sciences: past, present and future*. Cambridge University Press. doi:10.1017/CBO9781107707221

Fahim, K. E., Kalinaki, K., & Shafik, W. (2024). Electronic Devices in the Artificial Intelligence of the Internet of Medical Things (AIoMT). In *Handbook of Security and Privacy of AI-Enabled Healthcare Systems and Internet of Medical Things* (pp. 41–62). CRC Press.

Febrianto, G., Hidayatullah, S., & Ardianto, Y. T. (2018). The Effect of Intention to Usage to Actual Usage E-Purchasing Application. *International Journal of Scientific and Engineering Research*, *9*(12), 363–370.

Federal Republic of Nigeria. (1977). National policy on education. Lagos: Nigerian Educational Research Council (NERDC) Press.

Federal Republic of Nigeria. (1988). National policy on education. Lagos: Nigerian Educational Research Council (NERDC) Press.

Federal Republic of Nigeria. (2004). National policy on education. Lagos: Nigerian Educational Research Council (NERDC) Press.

Federal Republic of Nigeria. (2013). National policy on education. Lagos: Nigerian Educational Research Council (NERDC) Press.

Fedorko, I., Bacik, R., & Gavurova, B. (2021). Effort expectancy and social influence factors as main determinants of performance expectancy using electronic banking. *Banks and Bank Systems, 16*(2), 27–37. doi:10.21511/bbs.16(2).2021.03

Fehner, T. R. (1986). *National responses to technological innovations in weapons systems, 1815 to the present.* Booz-Allen and Hamilton Incorporated. doi:10.21236/ADA268480

Fenwick, T., & Edwards, R. (2013). Performative ontologies. Sociomaterial approaches to researching adult education and lifelong learning. *RELA European Journal for Research on the Education and Learning of Adults, 4*(1), 49–63. doi:10.3384/rela.2000-7426.rela0104

Fianu, E., Blewett, C., & Ampong, G. O. (2020). Toward the development of a model of student usage of MOOCs. *Education + Training, 62*(5), 521–541. doi:10.1108/ET-11-2019-0262

Finance Ministry Ghana. (2020). *Toward a Cash-Lite Ghana Building an Inclusive Digital Payments Ecosystem.* MOFEP. https://mofep.gov.gh/sites/default/files/acts/Ghana_Cashlite_Roadmap.pdf

Fishbein, M., & Ajzen, I. (1975). *Belief, Attitude, Intention, and Behavior.* Addison-Wesley.

Fitriah, N., Budi, A., Adnan, H. R., Firmansyah, F., Hidayanto, A. N., Kurnia, S., & Purwandari, B. (2021). Why do people want to use location-based application for emergency situations? The extension of UTAUT perspectives. *Technology in Society, 65*(November 2018), 101480. doi:10.1016/j.techsoc.2020.101480

Flak, L. S., & Rose, J. (2005). Stakeholder Governance: Adapting Stakeholder Theory to E-Government. *Communications of the Association for Information Systems, 16*. Advance online publication. doi:10.17705/1CAIS.01631

Flammer, C., & Kacperczyk, A. (2014). The Impact Of Stakeholder Orientation On Innovation: Evidence From A Natural Experiment. *Management Science, 62*(7).

Flashes Magazine. (2017). The first industrial revolution. In: Revue économique, 19(2).

Flavin, M. (2017). *Disruptive Technology enhanced learning: The use and misuse of technology enhanced learning in higher education.* Palgrave MacMillan. doi:10.1057/978-1-137-57284-4

Fleming, D. (1996). *Toys as popular culture.* Manchester University Press.

Fletcher, A. (2002). France enters the information age: A political history of Minitel. *History and Technology, 18*(2), 103–107. doi:10.1080/07341510220150315

Fluetterwave. (2021). *Flutterwave Launches Market, a New E-commerce Service to Scale SME Growth.* FlutterWave. https://flutterwave.com/us/blog/flutterwave-launches-market

Focus Group Discussion 1. (2021). Focus Group Discussion (FGD) with AIS team of experts. Addis Ababa, Ethiopia.

Focus Group Discussion 2. (2021). Focus Group Discussion (FGD) with AIS team of experts. Addis Ababa, Ethiopia.

Focus Group Discussion 3. (2021). Focus Group Discussion (FGD) with AIS team of experts. Addis Ababa, Ethiopia.

Focus Group Discussion 4. (2021). Focus Group Discussion (FGD) with AIS team of experts. Addis Ababa, Ethiopia.

Focus Group Discussion 5. (2021). Focus Group Discussion (FGD) with AIS team of experts. Addis Ababa, Ethiopia.

Focus Group Discussion 6. (2021). Focus Group Discussion (FGD) with AIS team of experts. Addis Ababa, Ethiopia.

Fomunyam, K. (2020). Towards enhancing Science and Technology, Enginering and Mathsmatics (STEM) Education: A case for higher education in Africa. *International Journal of Engineering Research & Technology (Ahmedabad), 13*(7), 1516–1524. doi:10.37624/IJERT/13.7.2020.1516-1524

Forcucci, L. (2023). Laser Nomad: Roadmaps for Art and Science Research into Ancestral Knowledge. *Leonardo, 56*(4), 1–10. doi:10.1162/leon_a_02354

Formenti, L., & Jorio, F. (2018). Multiple visions, multiple voices: A dialogic methodology for teaching in higher education. *Journal of Transformative Education, 17*(3), https://2080/ doi:10.1177/1541344618796761

Foster, L., Szilagyi, K., Wairegi, A., Oguamanam, C., & de Beer, J. (2023). Smart farming and artificial intelligence in East Africa: Addressing indigeneity, plants, and gender. *Smart Agricultural Technology, 3*, 100132. doi:10.1016/j.atech.2022.100132

Fox, L., & Signe, L. (2022). *From subsistence to disruptive innovation: Africa's the Fouth Industrial Revolution and the future of jobs.* Brookings. https://www.brookings.edu/articles/from-subsistence-to-disruptive-innovation-africa-the-fourth-industrial-revolution-and-the-future-of-jobs/

Fraumeni, B. M., & Jorgenson, D. W. (1981). Capital formation and US productivity growth, 1948–1976. In A. Dogramaci (Ed.), *Productivity analysis: A range of perspectives* (pp. 49–70). Springer. doi:10.1007/978-94-011-7402-2_4

Freeman, J., & Engel, J. S. (2007). California Management Models of Innovation: Startups and Mature Corporations. *California Management Review*.

Freeman, R. E., Phillips, R., & Sisodia, R. (2020). Tensions in Stakeholder Theory. *Business & Society, 59*(2), 213–231. Advance online publication. doi:10.1177/0007650318773750

Freire, P. (1993). *Pedagogy of the oppressed.* Bloomsbury Inc.

Furusa, S. S., & Coleman, A. (2018). Factors influencing E-health implementation by medical doctors in public hospitals in Zimbabwe. *South African Journal of Information Management, 20*(1), 928–945. doi:10.4102/sajim.v20i1.928

Gaffney, M., Adams, R., & Shyllon, O. (2022). Artificial Intelligence. *African Insight*. A Research Summary of the Ethical and Human Rights Implications of AI in Africa. HSRC & Meta AI and Ethics Human Rights Research Project for Africa – Synthesis Report.

Gajjala, R. and Birzescu, A. (2011). Digital imperialism through online social/financial networks. 46(13), 95-102.

Ganasegeran, K., & Abdulrahman, S. A. (2020). Artificial intelligence applications in tracking health behaviors during disease epidemics. *Human Behaviour Analysis Using Intelligent Systems*, 141-155.

Gansser, O. A., & Reich, C. S. (2021). A new acceptance model for artificial intelligence with extensions to UTAUT2: An empirical study in three segments of application. *Technology in Society, 65*, 101535. doi:10.1016/j.techsoc.2021.101535

Gao, S., & Zhang, X. (2015). UserAdoption of Location Sharing Services on Social Networking Platforms: an experimental study. *Fourteenth Wuhan International Conference on E-Business*, (pp. 333–340). IEEE.

Gaschler, F. O. J. (2022). *Fintech in Africa: how digital payment tech is bringing financial services to the unbanked.* Research Gate.

GBN. (2023, August). *MMDAs urged to ensure strict adherence to GIFMIS*. GBN. https://www.ghanabusinessnews.com/2023/08/01/mmdas-urged-to-ensure-strict-adherence-to-gifmis/

Gelb, A., & Mukherjee, A. (2020). Digital technology in social assistance transfers for COVID-19 relief: Lessons from selected cases. *CGD Policy Paper, 181*, 1 at 21.

George, A. S., George, A. H., Baskar, T., & Martin, A. G. (2023). An Overview of India's Unified Payments Interface (UPI): Benefits, Challenges, and Opportunities. *Partners Universal International Research Journal, 2*(1), 16–23.

Geraldes, H. S. A., Gama, A. P. M., & Augusto, M. (2022). Reaching financial inclusion: Necessary and sufficient conditions. *Social Indicators Research, 162*(2), 599–617. doi:10.1007/s11205-021-02850-0

Ghadge, A., Er Kara, M., Moradlou, H., & Goswami, M. (2020). The impact of industry 4.0 implementation on supply chains. *Journal of Manufacturing Technology Management, 31*(4), 157–169. doi:10.1108/JMTM-10-2019-0368

Ghana MoF. (2022). *5 years Public Financial Management strategy*. Ghana MoF. https://mofep.gov.gh/sites/default/files/reports/economic/Ghana%27s-2022-2026-Approved-PFM-Strategy.pdf

Ghana Statistical Service. (2019). *Ghana multiple indicator cluster survey 2017/18*. Ghana Statistical Service.

Giallauraskis, A. (2023). *Africa on the cusp of an innovation revolution*. Business Sweden.

Giannakos, M., & Cukurova, M. (2022). The role of learning theory in multimodal learning analytics. *British Journal of Educational Technology*, ●●●, 1–22.

Global Cybersecurity Index, I. T. U. 2018, https:// www. itu. int/ en/ ITU -D/ Cybersecurity/ Pages/ global -cybersecurity -index. aspx ITU WTI Database, ICT indicators.

Gonsalves, A. H., Thabtah, F., Mohammad, R. M. A., & Singh, G. (2019). Prediction of coronary heart disease using machine learning: An experimental analysis. Proceedings of the 2019 3rd International Conference on Deep Learning Technologies.

Gordon, R. J. (2000). Does the "New Economy" Measure up to the Great Inventions of the Past? *The Journal of Economic Perspectives, 14*(2), 49–74. doi:10.1257/jep.14.4.49

Gould, R. W. (2012). Open innovation and stakeholder engagement. *Journal of Technology Management & Innovation, 7*(3), 1–11. doi:10.4067/S0718-27242012000300001

Government of Ghana (n.d.) *Seven-Year Development Plan for national reconstruction and development*. Office of the Planning Commission: Accra.

Government of Kenya. (2020). *Digital Economy Blueprint*. Government of Kenya. https://www.digital.go.ke/digital-economy-blueprint/

Graf-Vlachy, L., Buhtz, K., & König, A. (2018). Social influence in technology adoption: Taking stock and moving forward. *Management Review Quarterly, 68*(1), 37–76. doi:10.1007/s11301-017-0133-3

Granger, J., de Clercq, B., & Lymer, A. (2022a). 1 Tapping Taxes. *TAXATION IN THE DIGITAL ECONOMY*, 21.

Granger, J., de Clercq, B., & Lymer, A. (2022b). *Tapping taxes–digital disruption and revenue administration responses: Digital Disruption and Revenue Administration Responses*.

Griffin, N., Uña, G., Bazarbash, M., & Verma, A. (2023). Fintech Payments in Public Financial Management: Benefits and Risks. *IMF Working Papers, 2023*(020). doi:10.5089/9798400232213.001

Grigalashvili, V. (2022). E-government and E-governance: Various or Multifarious Concepts. *International Journal of Scientific and Management Research*, *05*(01), 183–196. doi:10.37502/IJSMR.2022.5111

GSMA. (2019). The mobile economy in sub saharan. *Africa*. https://www.gs and ma.com/subsaharanafrica/resources/the-mobile-economy-sub-saharan-africa-

Guerin, D. (1973). *Fascism and Big Business*. Pathfinder Press.

Guma, P. K., & Mwaura, M. (2021). Infrastructural configurations of mobile telephony in urban Africa: Vignettes from Buru Buru, Nairobi. *Journal of Eastern African Studies : the Journal of the British Institute in Eastern Africa*, *15*(4), 527–545. doi:10.1080/17531055.2021.1989138

Guo, S., Xie, C., Li, J., Lyu, L., & Zhang, T. (2022). *Threats to pre-trained language models: Survey and taxonomy*.

Gupta, A., & Katarya, R. (2020). Social media based surveillance systems for healthcare using machine learning: A systematic review. *Journal of Biomedical Informatics*, *108*, 103500. doi:10.1016/j.jbi.2020.103500 PMID:32622833

Gupta, S., & Kanungo, R. P. (2022). Financial inclusion through digitalisation: Economic viability for the bottom of the pyramid (BOP) segment. *Journal of Business Research*, *148*, 262–276. doi:10.1016/j.jbusres.2022.04.070

Gwala, R. S., & Mashau, P. (2022). Corporate governance and its impact on organisational performance in the fourth industrial revolution: a systematic literature review. *Corporate Governance and Organizational Behaviour Review*, *6*(1), 98–114. https://doi.org/https://doi.org/10.22495/cgobrv6i1p7

Gwala, R. S., & Mashau, P. (2023). COVID-19 and SME adoption of social media in developing economies in Africa. In S. Qalati, D. Ostic, & R. Bansal (Eds.), *Strengthening SME performance through social media adoption and usage* (pp. 133–152). doi:10.4018/978-1-6684-5770-2.ch008

Gyekye, K. (1997). *Tradition and modernity: philosophical reflections on the African experience*. Oxford University Press. doi:10.1093/acprof:oso/9780195112252.001.0001

Gyimah, P., Appiah, K. O., & Appiagyei, K. (2023). Seven years of United Nations' sustainable development goals in Africa: A bibliometric and systematic methodological review. *Journal of Cleaner Production*, *395*, 136422. doi:10.1016/j.jclepro.2023.136422

Hagerty, A., & Rubinov, I. (2019). Global AI ethics: a review of the social impacts and ethical implications of artificial intelligence. *arXiv preprint arXiv:1907.07892*.

Hagger, M. (2019). The reasoned action approach and theories of reasoned action and planned behaviour. In D. Dunn (Ed.), *Oxford Bibliography in Psychology* (pp. 1–30). Oxford University Press.

Hair, J. F., Black, W. C., Babin, B. J., & Anderson, R. E. (2014). *Multivariate data analysis* (7th ed.). Pearson Education International.

Hair, J. F., Sarstedt, M., Pieper, T. M., & Ringle, C. M. (2012). The Use of Partial Least Squares Structural Equation Modeling in Strategic Management Research : A Review of Past Practices and Recommendations for Future Applications. *Long Range Planning*, *45*(5–6), 320–340. doi:10.1016/j.lrp.2012.09.008

Hall, G. E., & Hord, S. M. (1987). *Changes in schools: Facilitating the process*. State University of New York Press.

Hamel, G. (2002). Innovation now! *Fast company*, 114-124.

Hamel, J., Dufour, S., & Fortin, D. (1993). *Case Study Methods*. SAGE Publications, Inc., doi:10.4135/9781412983587

Hansen, N., Huis, M. A., & Lensink, R. (2021). Microfinance services and women's empowerment. *Handbook on ethics in finance*, 161-182.

Hassan, Y. (2023). Governing algorithms from the South: A case study of AI development in Africa. *AI & Society*, *38*(4), 1429–1442. doi:10.1007/s00146-022-01527-7

Haula, K., & Agbozo, E. (2020). A systematic review on unmanned aerial vehicles in Sub-Saharan Africa: A socio-technical perspective. *Technology in Society*, *63*, 1–17. doi:10.1016/j.techsoc.2020.101357

Headrick, D. (1991). *The invisible weapon: telecommunications and international politics, 1851-1945*. Oxford University Press. doi:10.1093/oso/9780195062731.001.0001

Headrick, R. D. (1981). *The tools of empire: technology and European imperialism in the nineteenth century*. Oxford University Press.

Hedderich, M. A., Lange, L., Adel, H., Strötgen, J., & Klakow, D. (2020). A survey on recent approaches for natural language processing in low-resource scenarios. *arXiv preprint arXiv:2010.12309*.

Hellström, J., & Tröften, P.-E. (2010). *The innovative use of mobile applications in East Africa*. Swedish international development cooperation agency (Sida).

Hermann, M., Pentek, T., & Otto, B. (2015). Design principles for Industry 4.0 scenarios: A literature review. *HICSS '16 Proceedings of the 2016 49th Hawaii International Conference on System Sciences*. IEEE.

Hernandez, B., Jimenez, J., & Martin, M. J. (2010). Business management software in high-tech firms: The case of the IT services sector. *Journal of Business and Industrial Marketing*, *25*(2), 132–146. doi:10.1108/08858621011017750

Hilferding, R. (1981). *Finance capital: a study of the latest phase of capitalism*. Routledge and Kegan Paul Ltd.

Hocking, B., & Melissen, J. (2015). *Diplomacy in the digital age. Clingendael*. Netherlands Institute of International Relations.

Holden, P. (2004). Modernity's body: Kwame Nkrumah's Ghana. *Postcolonial Studies*, *7*(3), 313–332. doi:10.1080/1368879042000311106

Holmes, M. (2015). *The future of digital diplomacy. Digital diplomacy: Theory and Practice*. Routledge.

Hong, S.-J., & Tam, K. Y. (2006). Understanding the Adoption of Multipurpose Information Appliances: The Case of Mobile Data Services. *Information Systems Research*, *17*(2), 162–179. doi:10.1287/isre.1060.0088

Hong, S.-J., Thong, J. Y. L., Moon, J.-Y., & Tam, K.-Y. (2008). Understanding the behavior of mobile data services consumers. *Information Systems Frontiers*, *10*(4), 431–445. doi:10.1007/s10796-008-9096-1

Hong, Y. (2015). Colonial legacies and peripheral strategies: Social-spatial logic of China's communications development since 1840. *Global Media and Communication*, *11*(2), 89–102. doi:10.1177/1742766515588415

Howson, P. (2020). Climate crises and crypto-colonialism: Conjuring value on the blockchain frontiers of the Global South. *Front. Blockchain*, *3*, 22. doi:10.3389/fbloc.2020.00022

Hsieh, J. J. P.-A., Rai, A., & Keil, M. (2008). Understanding Digital Inequality: Comparing Continued Use Behavioral Models of the Socio-Economically Advantaged and Disadvantaged. *Management Information Systems Quarterly*, *32*(1), 97–126. doi:10.2307/25148830

Hsu, M.-H., & Chiu, C.-M. (2004). Predicting electronic service continuance with a decomposed theory of planned behaviour. *Behaviour & Information Technology*, *23*(5), 359–373. doi:10.1080/01449290410001669969

Hsu, M.-H., Yen, C.-H., Chiu, C.-M., & Chang, C.-M. (2006). A longitudinal investigation of continued online shopping behavior: An extension of the theory of planned behavior. *International Journal of Human-Computer Studies*, *64*(9), 889–904. doi:10.1016/j.ijhcs.2006.04.004

Hu, S., Zhou, L., Dong, N., Zhou, Y., Gao, Z., Xu, J., & Liang, Z. (2016). The design and implementation of the privacy protection system of a Regional Health Information Platform. *2016 IEEE International Conference on Bioinformatics and Biomedicine (BIBM)*. IEEE.

Huang, R., Kale, S., Paramati, S. R., & Taghizadeh-Hesary, F. (2021). The nexus between financial inclusion and economic development: Comparison of old and new EU member countries. *Economic Analysis and Policy*, *69*, 1–15. doi:10.1016/j.eap.2020.10.007

Huang, T. (2017). *Development of Small-scale Intelligent Manufacturing System (SIMS) - A case study at Stella Polaris*. AS UIT Faculty of Engineering Science and Technology the Artic University of Norwya.

Huawei. (2021, June 1). AUU launch the first Huawei ICT Practice Center in Ethiopia. *Addis Standard*. https://addis-standard.com/2021/news-huawei-aau-launch-the-first-huawei-ict-practice-center-in-ethiopia/

Huawei. (2021, June 8). Ministry extend agreement to open more ICT academies. *Ethiopia Monitor*. https://ethiopianmonitor.com/2021/06/08/huawei-ministry-extend-agreement-to-open-more-ict-academies/#:~:text=Huawei%2C%20Ministry%20Extend%20Agreement%20to%20Open%20More%20ICT,industry%2C%20and%20the%20nurturing%20of%20highly%20skilled%20labor

Hu, G., Yan, J., Pan, W., Chohan, S. R., & Liu, L. (2019). The influence of public engaging intention on value co-creation of e-government services. *IEEE Access : Practical Innovations, Open Solutions*, *7*, 111145–111159. doi:10.1109/ACCESS.2019.2934138

Hu, L., & Bentler, P. M. (1999). Cutoff criteria for fit indexes in covariance structure analysis: Conventional criteria versus new alternatives. *Structural Equation Modeling*, *6*(1), 1–55. doi:10.1080/10705519909540118

Ibne Afzal, M. N., Nayeem Sadi, M. A., & Siddiqui, S. A. (2023). Financial inclusion using corporate social responsibility: A socio-economic demand–supply analysis. *Asian Journal of Economics and Banking*, *7*(1), 45–63. doi:10.1108/AJEB-04-2022-0039

Ibrahim, R., Baharuddin, S., & Baharom, H. (2018). Strengthening TVET: Readiness Level Polytechnic Lecturer in Education Transformation National 21st Century as the Industrial Revolution 4.0. *Journal of Technical Education and Training, 12*(3).

IEEE-USA Board of Directors. (2017, February 10). *Artificial intelligence research, development and regulation. IEEE*. Retrieved October 13, 2023, from http://globalpolicy.ieee.org/wp-content/uploads/2017/10/IEEE17003.pdf

Iiori, T. (2020). *Data protection in Africa and the COVID-19 pandemic*. Research Gate.

ILO-UNESCO-World Bank. (2021). *Skills Development in the time of COVID -19:Takingstock of the intial responses in technical and vocational education and training*. International Labour Office.

Iman, N. (2023). Idiosyncrasies, isomorphic pressures and decoupling in technology platform business. *Journal of Science and Technology Policy Management*.

Innis, H. (1950). *Empire and communication*. Clarendon Press.

International Finance Corporation and L.E.K Consulting. (2019). *Digital skills in Sub-Saharan Africa spotlight on Ghana*. IFC. https://www.ifc.org/wps/wcm/connect/ed6362b3-aa34-42ac-ae9f-c739904951b1/Digital+Skills_Final_WEB_5-7-19.pdf?MOD=AJPERES

International Society for Technology in Education [ISTE]. (2008). *The ISTE national educational technology standards (NETS•T) and performance indicators for teachers.* US: ISTE.

International Telecommunication Union. (2020). *ICT Data and Statistics.* ITU. https://www.itu.int/net4/statistics/ICT-DataAndStatistics.aspx

Internet World Stats. (2020). *Internet Users Statistics for Africa.* Internet World Stats. https://www.internetworldstats.com/stats1.htm

Interview 1. (2021). Field interview with Artificial Intelligence Service (AIS) expert. Addis Ababa, Ethiopia.

Ionescu, I. G. (2018). The first industrial revolution and general features of the world economy between the 16Th century and 1780. *SEA Practical Application of Science, 17*(2), 183–186.

ISLS. (2023). Retrieved July 27, 2023, from About ISLS: https://www.isls.org/about/

Ismail, T., & Masinge, K. (2012). Mobile banking: Innovation for the poor. *African Journal of Science, Technology, Innovation and Development, 4*(3), 98–127. https://doi.org/doi:10.10520/EJC132191

Isradila, ., & Indrawati, . (2015). Analysis of user acceptance towards online transportation technology using UTAUT2 model: a case study in Uber, grab and GO-JEK in Indonesia. *International Journal of Science and Research, 6*(7), 1479–1482.

ITU platforms. (2020). *Connect2Recover.* Global Network Resiliency Platform "REG4COVID", the WSIS ICT Case Repository, and CYB4COVID.

ITU. (2020). Tech v COVID-29: Managing the crisis. *ITUNews03.* https:// www. itu. int/ en/ myitu/ Publications/ 2020/ 09/ 09/ 13/ 13/ ITU -News -Magazine -No3 -2020

Izuagbe, R., Olawoyin, O. R., Nkiko, C., Ilo, P. I., Yusuf, F., Iroaganachi, M., Ilogho, J., & Ifijeh, G. I. (2021). Impact analysis of e-Databases' job relevance, output quality and result demonstrability on faculty research motivation. *Library Hi Tech.* doi:10.1108/LHT-03-2020-0050

Jaldi, A. (2023). *Artificial Intelligence Revolution in Africa: Economic Opportunities and Legal Challenges.* Morocco: Policy Centre for the New South .

Janna, J. (2022). Epic Boss Battles: How to Addict Your Students by Creating Asynchronous Course-Based Games. In J. Keengwe (Ed.), *Handbook of Research on Transformative and Innovative Technologies in Education* (pp. 1–17). IGI Global.

Jawahar, I. M., & McLaughlin, G. L. (2001). Toward a descriptive stakeholder theory: An organizational life cycle approach. *Academy of Management Review, 26*(3), 397. Advance online publication. doi:10.2307/259184

Jide-Omole, A. A. (2023). Towards Sustainability and Stability: Espousing the Benefits of Space-Based Solar Power Systems in Africa. In Space Fostering African Societies: Developing the African Continent Through Space, Part 4 (pp. 45–58). Springer.

Jin, D.J. (2013). The construction of platform imperialism in the globalization era. *triple, 11*(1), 145-172.

Jin, D. J., & Curan, J. (2015). *Digital platforms, imperialism, and political culture.* Routledge.

Jinnah, Z. (2022). *Informal Livelihoods and Governance in South Africa: The Hustle.* Springer Nature. doi:10.1007/978-3-031-10695-8

Jones, T. M. (1995). INSTRUMENTAL STAKEHOLDER THEORY: A SYNTHESIS OF ETHICS AND ECONOMICS. *Academy of Management Review, 20*(2), 404. doi:10.2307/258852

Jong, T. (2019). Moving towards engaged learning in STEM domains; there is no simple answer, but clearly a road ahead. *Journal of Computer Assisted Learning, 35*(2), 153–167. doi:10.1111/jcal.12337

Jorgenson, D. W. (1984). The role of energy in productivity growth. *The Energy Journal (Cambridge, Mass.), 5*(3), 11–26. doi:10.5547/ISSN0195-6574-EJ-Vol5-No3-2

Jun, Y., Craig, A., Shafik, W., & Sharif, L. (2021). Artificial intelligence application in cybersecurity and cyberdefense. *Wireless Communications and Mobile Computing, 2021*, 1–10. doi:10.1155/2021/3329581

Jutel, O. (2021). Blockchain imperialism in the Pacific. *Big Data & Society, 8*(1), 1–14. doi:10.1177/2053951720985249

Kagerman, H. Wahlster, W. & Helbig, J. (2013). Securing the Future of German Manufacturing Industry Recommendations for Implementing the Strategic Initiative Industries 4.0 *Final Report of the Industries 4.0 Working Group.*

Kaivo-oja, J., Roth, S., & Westerlund, L. (2017). Futures of robotics. Human work in digital transformation. *nternational Journal of Technology Management, 4*(73), 176-205.

Kalinaki, K., Fahadi, M., Alli, A. A., Shafik, W., Yasin, M., & Mutwalibi, N. (2024). Artificial Intelligence of Internet of Medical Things (AIoMT) in Smart Cities: A Review of Cybersecurity for Smart Healthcare. Handbook of Security and Privacy of AI-Enabled Healthcare Systems and Internet of Medical Things, (pp. 271-292). Research Gate.

Kamen, L. & A. (2013). The digital diplomacy potential. *KMWorld, 22*(6).

Kamulegeya, L. H., Bwanika, J. M., & Musingazi, D. (2020). Continuity of health service delivery during the COVID-19 pandemic: The role of digital health technologies in Uganda. *The Pan African Medical Journal, 35*(2, Supp 2), 1–3. doi:10.11604/pamj.supp.2020.35.2.23115 PMID:33623568

Kamunya, S., Maina, E., & Onoko, R. (2019). Gamification Model for eLearning Platforms. *IST-Africa 2019 Conference Proceedings* (pp. 1-9). Kenya: IIMC International Information Management Corporation.

Karahanna, E., Straub, D. W., & Chervany, N. L. (1999). Information Technology Adoption across Time: A Cross-Sectional Comparison of Pre-Adoption and Post-Adoption Beliefs. *Management Information Systems Quarterly, 23*(2), 183–213. doi:10.2307/249751

Karnik, N., Bora, U., Bhadri, K., Kadambi, P., & Dhatrak, P. A. (2021). Comprehensive study on current and future trends towards the characteristics and enablers of industry 4.0. *Journal of Industrial Information Integration, 10*(10), 82–94.

Katsakioris, C. (2021). Nkrumah's Elite: Ghanaian students in the Soviet Union in the Cold War. *Paedagogica Historica, 57*(3), 260–276. doi:10.1080/00309230.2020.1785516

Kaul, V., Enslin, S., & Gross, S. A. (2020). History of artificial intelligence in medicine. *Gastrointestinal Endoscopy, 92*(4), 807–812. doi:10.1016/j.gie.2020.06.040 PMID:32565184

Kaur, P., Mack, A. A., Patel, N., Pal, A., Singh, R., Michaud, A., & Mulflur, M. (2023). *Unlocking the Potential of Artificial Intelligence (AI) for Healthcare.* IEEE.

Kearney, H., Kliestik, T., Kovacova, M., & Vochozka, M. (2019). The embedding of smart digital technologies within urban infrastructures: Governance networks, real-time data sustainability, and the cognitive internet of things. *Geopolitics, History, and International Relations, 11*(1), 98–103. doi:10.22381/GHIR11120195

Kelsall, T., Mitlin, D., Schindler, S., & Hickey, S. (2021). *Politics, systems and domains: A conceptual framework for the African Cities Research Consortium.*

Kenu, E., Frimpong, J., & Koram, K. (2020). Responding to the COVID-19 pandemic in Ghana. *Ghana Medical Journal, 54*(2), 72–73. doi:10.4314/gmj.v54i2.1 PMID:33536675

Kergroach, S. (2017). Industry 4.0: New Challenges and Opportunities for the Labor Market. *Foresight and STI Governance*, *11*(4), 6–8. doi:10.17323/2500-2597.2017.4.6.8

Khalid, A., Kazim, T., Diaz, K. R., & Iqbal, J. (2023). Breaking barriers in higher education: Implementation of cost-effective social constructivism in engineering education. *International Journal of Mechanical Engineering Education*, https:// 2080/ doi:10.1177/03064190231218123

Khan, N., Erasmus, T., Jali, N., Mthiyane, P., & Ronne, S. (2021). Is blended learning the way forward? Students' perceptions and attitudes at a South African university. *AJHPE, 13*(4), 219-222.

Khoa, B. T., Ha, N. M., Nguyen, T. V. H., & Bich, N. H. (2020). Lecturers' adoption to use the online Learning Management System (LMS): Empirical evidence from TAM2 model for Vietnam. *Hcmcoujs - Economics and Business Administration, 10*(1), 3–17. doi:10.46223/HCMCOUJS.econ.en.10.1.216.2020

Kiely, R. (2010). *Rethinking imperialism*. Palgrave, Macmillan. doi:10.1007/978-1-137-08870-3

Kiemde, S. M. A., & Kora, A. D. (2020). The challenges facing the development of AI in Africa. In *2020 IEEE International Conference on Advent Trends in Multidisciplinary Research and Innovation (ICATMRI)* (pp. 1-6). IEEE.

Kilaba, E. J. M., & Manasseh, E. C. (2020). Telecom Revolution in Africa, The journey thus far and the journey ahead. *Africa and Middle East Journal*, *1*, 29–33.

Kim, K., Lee, J., Oh, S. J., & Chung, M. J. (2023). AI-based computer-aided diagnostic system of chest digital tomography synthesis: Demonstrating comparative advantage with X-ray-based AI systems. *Computer Methods and Programs in Biomedicine*, *240*, 107643. Advance online publication. doi:10.1016/j.cmpb.2023.107643 PMID:37348439

King, D. L., Delfabbro, P. H., & Mark, D. Griffiths. (2013). Video Game Addiction. In P. M. Miller (Ed.), Principles of Addiction (pp. 819-825). London, San Diego and Massachusetts: Academic Press.

Klapper, L., & Singer, D. (2017). The opportunities and challenges of digitizing government-to- person payments. *The World Bank Research Observer*, *32*(2), 211–226. doi:10.1093/wbro/lkx003

Kline, S. (1993). *Out of the Garden: Toys and Children's Culture in the Age of TV Marketing*. Verso.

Kluver, R., & Banerjee, I. (2013). *Digital diplomacy: Theory and practice*. Routledge.

Knapp, N. F. (2018). The shape activity: Social Constructivism in the psychology classroom. *Teaching of Psychology*, *46*(1), https:// 2080/ doi:10.1177/0098628318816181

Koch, V., Kuge, S., Geissbauer, R., & Schrauf, S. (2014). Industry 4.0: Opportunities and challenges of the industrial internet. Tech. Rep. TR 2014-2, PWC Strategy GmbH, United States, New York City, New York (NY).

Koene, A., Clifton, C., Hatada, Y., Webb, H., & Richardson, R. (2019). *A governance framework for algorithmic accountability and transparency*.

Koh, K. (2017). Authentic Assessment. In G. Noblit (Ed.), *Oxford Research Encyclopedia of Education*. Oxford University Press. doi:10.1093/acrefore/9780190264093.013.22

Koh, K., Chapman, O., & Lam, L. (2022). An intergration of Virtual Reality into the Design of Authentic Assessment for STEM Learning. In J. Keengwe (Ed.), *The Handbook of Research on Transformative and Innovative Pedagogies in Education* (pp. 18–35). IGI Global. doi:10.4018/978-1-7998-9561-9.ch002

Kong, L. (2000). Cultural policy in Singapore: Negotiating economic and socio-cultural agendas. *Geoforum*, *31*(4), 409–424. doi:10.1016/S0016-7185(00)00006-3

Koskela, L., & Howell, G. (2002). The Underlying Theory of Project Management is Obsolete. *Proceedings of the PMI Research Conference, 2002*. Research Gate. https://www.researchgate.net/publication/44708842_The_Underlying_Theory_of_Project_Management_is_Obsolete

Kot, S. (2018). A Scoping Review on Digital English and Education 4.0 for Industry 4.0. *The Social Science Journal*, 7, 221–227.

Kouchih, A., & Lyoussi, D. (2022). *Collaborative Innovation and Its Actors at the Time of Banking Digitalization: Comparative Analysis Between National and International Practice* (2516-2314). Research Gate.

Kouladoum, J.-C., Wirajing, M. A. K., & Nchofoung, T. N. (2022). Digital technologies and financial inclusion in Sub-Saharan Africa. *Telecommunications Policy*, 46(9), 102387. doi:10.1016/j.telpol.2022.102387

Kowalewska, A., Osińska, M., & Szczepaniak, M. (2023). Institutions in the development of Sub-Saharan African countries in 2004–2019. *Ekonomia i Prawo. Economics and Law, 22*(1).

Krajnc, P. K. (2004). Public Diplomacy: Basic Concepts and Trends. Teorija in praksa –. *Theory into Practice*, *41*(3-4), 643–658.

Kruss, G., Adeoti, J., & Nabudere, D. (2012). Universities and knowledge-based development in sub-Saharan Africa: Comparing university-firm interaction in Nigeria, Uganda and South Africa. *The Journal of Development Studies*, 48(4), 516–530. doi:10.1080/00220388.2011.604410

Kruss, G., & Visser, M. (2017). Putting university-industry interaction into perspective: A differentiated view from inside South African universities. *The Journal of Technology Transfer*, 42(4), 884–908. doi:10.1007/s10961-016-9548-6

Kühl, N., Schemmer, M., Goutier, M., & Satzger, G. (2022). Artificial intelligence and machine learning. *Electronic Markets*, 32(4), 2235–2244. doi:10.1007/s12525-022-00598-0

Kvangraven, I. H. (2020). Beyond the stereotype: Restating the relevance of the Dependency Research Programme. *Development and Change*, 52(1), 76–112. doi:10.1111/dech.12593

Kyule, M. (2016). The bao: a board game in Africa's antiquity. In A.-M. Deisser & M. Njuguna (Eds.), *Conservation of Natural and Cultural Heritage in Kenya: A Cross-Disciplinary Approach* (1st ed., pp. 93–107). UCL Press. doi:10.2307/j.ctt1gxxpc6.13

Lai, P. (2020). The literature Review of Technology Adoption Models and Theories of Novelty technology. *Journal of Information Systems and Technology Management, 02*.

Lalima:Dangwal, K. (2017). Blended Learning An Innovative Approach. *Universal Journal of Educational Research*, 5(1), 129–136. doi:10.13189/ujer.2017.050116

Lallani, S. S. (2023). Virtual empire: Performing colonialism in the MMORPG *Runescape. Games and Culture*, 18(5), 539–558. doi:10.1177/15554120221109130

LaPensée, E. (2021). *When Rivers Were Trails*: Cultural expression in an indigenous video game. *International Journal of Heritage Studies*, 27(3), 281–295. doi:10.1080/13527258.2020.1746919

Larkotey, W. O., & Ifinedo, P. (2022). Socioetechnical Factors that Shape E-Government Payment Portal Development in Ghana. *IFIP Advances in Information and Communication Technology, 657 IFIP*. doi:10.1007/978-3-031-19429-0_2

Larsson, S. (2020). On the governance of artificial intelligence through ethics guidelines. *Asian Journal of Law and Society*, 7(3), 437–451. doi:10.1017/als.2020.19

Laupichler, M. C., Aster, A., Haverkamp, N., & Raupach, T. (2023). Development of the "Scale for the assessment of non-experts' AI literacy" – An exploratory factor analysis. *Computers in Human Behavior Reports, 12*, 100338. Advance online publication. doi:10.1016/j.chbr.2023.100338

Layton-matthews, B. S., & Landsberg. (2022). *The Fourth Industrial Revolution (4IR) and its Effects on Public Service Delivery in South Africa. 90*, 55–64.

Leavy, B. (2018). Value innovation and how to successfully incubate "blue ocean" initiatives. *Strategy and Leadership, 46*(3), 10–20. doi:10.1108/SL-02-2018-0020

Lee, C.-S., & Wang, M.-H. (2010). A fuzzy expert system for diabetes decision support application. *IEEE Transactions on Systems, Man, and Cybernetics. Part B, Cybernetics, 41*(1), 139–153. PMID:20501347

Lee, J. M., Lee, B., & Rha, J. Y. (2019). Determinants of mobile payment usage and the moderating effect of gender: Extending the UTAUT model with privacy risk. *International Journal of Electronic Commerce Studies, 10*(1), 43–64. doi:10.7903/ijecs.1644

Lee, J., Kim, M., Ham, C. D., & Kim, S. (2017). Do you want me to watch this ad on social media?: The effects of norms on online video ad watching. *Journal of Marketing Communications, 23*(5), 456–472. doi:10.1080/13527266.2016.1232303

Lee, V. (2023). Learning sciences and learning engineering: A naturak or artificial distinction? *Journal of the Learning Sciences, 32*(2), 288–304. doi:10.1080/10508406.2022.2100705

Lee, Y., Kozar, K. A., & Larsen, K. R. T. (2003). The Technology Acceptance Model: Past, Present, and Future. *Communications of the Association for Information Systems, 12*(50), 752–780. doi:10.17705/1CAIS.01250

Leite, F. O., Cochat, C., Salgado, H., da Costa, M. P., Queirós, M., Campos, O., & Carvalho, P. (2016). Using Google Translate^© in the hospital: A case report. *Technology and Health Care, 24*(6), 965–968. doi:10.3233/THC-161241 PMID:27447408

Lemma, A., Parra, M. M., & Naliaka, L. (2022). *The AfCFTA: unlocking the potential of the digital economy in Africa* (Vol. 13). ODI.

Lenin, V. I. (1950). *Imperialism, the highest stage of capitalism.* Foreign Languages Publishing House.

Lessa, L., Negash, S., & Amoroso, D. L. (2011). Acceptance of WoredaNet e-Government services in Ethiopia: Applying the UTAUT Model. *17th Americas Conference on Information Systems 2011, AMCIS 2011, 2*, (pp. 972–982). AMCIS.

Leydesdorff, L., & Etzkowitz, H. (1996). Emergence of a Triple Helix of university-industry-government relations. *Science & Public Policy, 23*(5), 279–286.

Leydesdorff, L., & Etzkowitz, H. (1996). Emergence of a Triple Helix of university—industry—government relations. *Science & Public Policy, 23*(5), 279–286.

Li, W., Badr, Y., & Biennier, F. (2012). Digital ecosystems: challenges and prospects. In proceedings of the international conference on management of Emergent Digital EcoSystems (pp. 117-122). doi:10.1145/2457276.2457297

Liamputtong, P. (2019). *Qualitative research methods.* Oxford University Press.

Liao, C., Chen, J.-L., & Yen, D. C. (2007). Theory of planning behavior (TPB) and customer satisfaction in the continued use of e-service: An integrated model. *Computers in Human Behavior, 23*(6), 2804–2822. doi:10.1016/j.chb.2006.05.006

Li, I., Li, Y., Li, T., Alvarez-Napagao, S., Garcia-Gasulla, D., & Suzumura, T. (2020). What are we depressed about when we talk about covid-19: Mental health analysis on tweets using natural language processing. *Artificial Intelligence XXXVII: 40th SGAI International Conference on Artificial Intelligence, AI 2020,* Cambridge, UK.

Li, N., Pei, X., Huang, Y., Qiao, J., Zhang, Y., & Jamali, R. H. (2022). Impact of financial inclusion and green bond financing for renewable energy mix: Implications for financial development in OECD economies. *Environmental Science and Pollution Research International*, *29*(17), 1–12. doi:10.1007/s11356-021-17561-9 PMID:34843047

Lin, J., Chan, H. C., & Wei, K. K. (2006). Understanding competing application usage with the theory of planned behavior. *Journal of the American Society for Information Science and Technology*, *57*(10), 1338–1349. doi:10.1002/asi.20453

Liu, D., Xie, Y., Hafeez, M., & Usman, A. (2022). The trade-off between economic performance and environmental quality: Does financial inclusion matter for emerging Asian economies? *Environmental Science and Pollution Research International*, *29*(20), 1–10. doi:10.1007/s11356-021-17755-1 PMID:34993792

Liu, F., & Walheer, B. (2022). Financial inclusion, financial technology, and economic development: A composite index approach. *Empirical Economics*, *63*(3), 1457–1487. doi:10.1007/s00181-021-02178-1

Li, W. (2021). The role of trust and risk in Citizens' E-Government services adoption: A perspective of the extended UTAUT model. *Sustainability (Basel)*, *13*(14), 7671. doi:10.3390/su13147671

Lorenz, E., & Pommet, S. (2021). Mobile money, inclusive finance and enterprise innovativeness: An analysis of East African nations. *Industry and Innovation*, *28*(2), 136–159. doi:10.1080/13662716.2020.1774867

Louw, C., & Nieuwenhuizen, C. (2020). Digitalisation strategies in a South African banking context: A consumer services analysis. *South African Journal of Information Management*, *22*(1), 1–8. doi:10.4102/sajim.v22i1.1153

Lubinga, S., Maramura, T. C., & Masiya, T. (2023). The Fourth Industrial Revolution Adoption: Challenges in South African Higher Education Institutions. *Journal of Culture and Values in Education*, *6*(2), 1–17. doi:10.46303/jcve.2023.5

Lu, J., Yao, J. E., & Yu, C.-S. (2005). Personal Innovativeness, Social Influences and Adoption of Wireless Internet Services via Mobile Technology. *The Journal of Strategic Information Systems*, *14*(3), 245–268. doi:10.1016/j.jsis.2005.07.003

Lund, S., White, O., & Lamb, J. (2017). *The Value of Digitalizing Government Payments in Developing Economies*. Digital Revolutions in Public Finance.

Lunze, K., Higgins-Steele, A., Simen-Kapeu, A., Vesel, L., Kim, J., & Dickson, K. (2015). Innovative approaches for improving maternal and newborn health-A landscape analysis. *BMC Pregnancy and Childbirth*, *15*(1), 1–19. doi:10.1186/s12884-015-0784-9 PMID:26679709

Lynch, M. (2018, December 6). *My vision for the future of artificial intelligene in education*. Retrieved from The Advocate: https://www.theedadvocate.org/vision-future-artificial-intelligence-education/

Ma, Y. (2023). Development of the Global Film Industry: Industrial Competition and Cooperation in the Context of Globalization. International Journal of Communication, 17, 3.

Maass, W., Natschläger, T., & Markram, H. (2002). Real-time computing without stable states: A new framework for neural computation based on perturbations. *Neural Computation*, *14*(11), 2531–2560. doi:10.1162/089976602760407955 PMID:12433288

MacIsaac, S. (2023). Remittance Modality: Unpacking Canadian Money Transfer Mechanism Choices. *The International Migration Review*, 01979183231181564. doi:10.1177/01979183231181564

Maguire, T. (1989). Educational Problems Revisited. Commentary on and Reprint of "M. E. LaZerte: Pioneer Educational Innovator," by George H. Buck, originally published in 1989. *The Alberta Journal of Educational Research*, *40*(4), 499–510.

Maharana, A., Amutorine, M., Sengeh, M. D., & Nsoesie, E. O. (2021). COVID-19 and beyond: Use of digital technology for pandemic response in Africa. *Scientific African*, *14*, e01041. doi:10.1016/j.sciaf.2021.e01041 PMID:34746524

Mahomed, S. (2018). Healthcare, artificial intelligence and the Fourth Industrial Revolution: Ethical, social and legal considerations. *South African Journal of Bioethics and Law*, *11*(2), 93–95. doi:10.7196/SAJBL.2018.v11i2.664

Maity, S., & Sahu, T. N. (2022). *Financial Inclusion and the Role of Banking System*. Springer. doi:10.1007/978-981-16-6085-6

Makovhololo, P. (2017). Diffusion of Innovation Theory for Information technology decision making in organisational strategy. *Journal of Contemporary Management*, *14*, 461–481.

Mammo, Y. (2016). Analysis of Ethiopia's national ICT policy and strategy: Insights into policy issues and policy goals. *Ethiopian Journal of Education and Sciences*, *11*(2), 75–89.

Manasseh, C. O., Nwakoby, I. C., Okanya, O. C., Nwonye, N. G., Odidi, O., Thaddeus, K. J., Ede, K. K., & Nzidee, W. (2023). Impact of digital financial innovation on financial system development in Common Market for Eastern and Southern Africa (COMESA) countries. *Asian Journal of Economics and Banking*.

Manasseh, C. O., Okanya, O. C., Logan, C. S., Ede, K. E., Ejim, E. P., Ozor, S. N., Onuoha, O., & Okiche, E. L. (2023). Digital finance, financial inclusion and economic growth nexus in COMESA: the role of regulatory quality, rule of law and government effectiveness. *Russian Law Journal, 11*(5).

Mannan, B., & Haleem, A. (2017). Understanding major dimensions and determinants that help in diffusion & adoption of product innovation: Using AHP approach. *Journal of Global Entrepreneurship Research*, *7*(1), 12. doi:10.1186/s40497-017-0072-4

Manyati, T. K., & Mutsau, M. (2020). A systematic review of the factors that hinder the scale up of mobile health technologies in antenatal care programmes in Sub Saharan Africa. *African Journal of Science, Technology, Innovation and Development*, *2020*, 1–17.

Manyika, J., Lund, S., Bughin, J., Woetzel, J., Stamenov, K., & Dhingra, D. (2016, February). *Digital globalization: The new era of global flows*. McKinsey Global Institute. https://www.mckinsey.com/capabilities/mckinsey-digital/our-insights/digital-globalization-the-new-era-of-global-flows

Mare, A., Woyo, E., & Amadhila, E. M. (2023). Harnessing the technological dividends in African higher education institutions during and post-COVID-19 pandemic. In *Teaching and Learning with Digital Technologies in Higher Education Institutions in Africa* (pp. 1–24). Routledge.

Martin, A. (2019). Mobile money platform surveillance. *Surveillance & Society*, *17*(1/2), 213–222. doi:10.24908/ss.v17i1/2.12924

Martínez-Vergara, S. J., & Valls-Pasola, J. (2021). Clarifying the disruptive innovation puzzle: A critical review. *European Journal of Innovation Management*, *24*(3), 893–918. doi:10.1108/EJIM-07-2019-0198

Martinus, L., & Abbott, J. Z. (2019). A focus on neural machine translation for african languages. *arXiv preprint arXiv:1906.05685*.

Mastercard. (2021). Mastercard New Payments Index: Consumer Appetite for Digital Payments Takes Off. Retrieved from https://newsroom.mastercard.com/mea/files/2021/03/Mastercard-New-Payments-Index.pdf

Matekenya, W., Moyo, C., & Jeke, L. (2021). Financial inclusion and human development: Evidence from Sub-Saharan Africa. *Development Southern Africa*, *38*(5), 683–700. doi:10.1080/0376835X.2020.1799760

Mather, M., Cacioppo, J. T., & Kanwisher, N. (2013). How fMRI can inform cognitive theories. *Psychological Science*, *27*(2), 108–113. PMID:23544033

Matthew, U. O., Kazaure, J. S., Onyebuchi, A., Daniel, O. O., Muhammed, I. H., & Okafor, N. U. (2021). Artificial intelligence autonomous unmanned aerial vehicle (UAV) system for remote sensing in security surveillance. In *2020 IEEE 2nd International Conference on Cyberspace (CYBER NIGERIA)* (pp. 1-10). IEEE.

Mayer, M., Carpes, M., & Knoblich, R. (2014). The global politics of science and technology: an introduction. In M. Mayer, M. Carpes, & R. Knoblich (Eds.), *The global politics of science and technology* (Vol. 1, pp. 1–35). Springer. doi:10.1007/978-3-642-55007-2_1

Mbunge, E., Muchemwa, B., & Batani, J. (2022). Are we there yet? Unbundling the potential adoption and integration of telemedicine to improve virtual healthcare services in African health systems. *Sensors International*, *3*, 100152. doi:10.1016/j.sintl.2021.100152 PMID:34901894

McCallum, W., & Aziakpono, M. J. (2023). Regulatory sandbox for FinTech regulation: Do the conditions for effective adoption exist in South Africa? *Development Southern Africa*, *40*(5), 1–17. doi:10.1080/0376835X.2023.2182759

McGlinchey, S. (Ed.). (2017). *International Relations*. E-International Relations Publishing.

McKinsey & Company. (2021). *Digital payments in Africa: Unlocking the $3.7 trillion opportunity*. McKinsey.

McLaren, P., & McLaren, P. (1993). *Paulo Freire: A critical encounter*. Routledge.

McLuhan, M. (1964). *Understanding media*. Routledge & Kegan Paul.

Meiyanti, R., Utomo, B., Sensuse, D. I., & Wahyuni, R. (2019). E-Government Challenges in Developing Countries: A Literature Review. *2018 6th International Conference on Cyber and IT Service Management*. IEEE. 10.1109/CITSM.2018.8674245

Melisew, D. L., Ngutuku, E., Emeka, E., & Siebert, A. (2022). Information and Communication Technology in Africa: Challenges from the COVID Pandemic. *Africa Knowledge Series*, *1*(3), 1–20.

Melissen, J. (2013). Public diplomacy. In A. Cooper, J. Heine, & R. Thakur (Eds.), *The oxford handbook of modern diplomacy* (pp. 436–452). Oxford University Press.

Mensah, I., Dube, K., & Chapungu, L. (2023). Impact of COVID-19 on Tourism and Prospects of Recovery: An African Perspective. In COVID-19, Tourist Destinations and Prospects for Recovery: Volume Two: An African Perspective (pp. 3–17). Springer.

Mensah, I. K. (2020). Impact of Government Capacity and E-Government Performance on the Adoption of E-Government Services. *International Journal of Public Administration*, *43*(4), 303–311. doi:10.1080/01900692.2019.1628059

Mensah, R., Cater-Steel, A., & Toleman, M. (2021). Factors affecting e-government adoption in Liberia: A practitioner perspective. *The Electronic Journal on Information Systems in Developing Countries*, *87*(3), e12161. doi:10.1002/isd2.12161

Metz, T. (2010). African and Western moral theories in a bioethical context. *Developing World Bioethics*, *10*(1), 49–58. doi:10.1111/j.1471-8847.2009.00273.x PMID:19961513

Mhlanga, D. (2020). Industry 4.0 in finance: The impact of artificial intelligence (AI) on digital financial inclusion. *International Journal of Financial Studies.*, *8*(45), 1–14. doi:10.3390/ijfs8030045

Mhlanga, D. (2023). Block chain technology for digital financial inclusion in the industry 4.0, towards sustainable development? *Frontiers in Blockchain*, *6*, 1035405. doi:10.3389/fbloc.2023.1035405

Miedzian, M. (1992). *Boys Will Be Boys*. Virago.

Miles, M. B., Huberman, A. M., & Saldaña, J. (2020). *Qualitative data analysis: A methods sourcebook* (4th ed.). Sage.

Military Africa. (2022, December 11). Military Drones in Africa: The New Arms Race. Military Africa. https://www.military.africa/2022/12/military-drones-in-africa-the-new-arms-race

Minghat, A. D., Ana, A., Jamaludin, S., Mustakim, S. S., & Shumov, P. V. (2020). Identification of teaching competencies among TVET instructors towards the realization of 4th industrial revolution. Научный журнал. *Вестник НАН РК*, (5), 233–240.

Ministry of Foreign Affairs. (2006, November 16). *Forum on China-Africa Cooperation-Beijing Action Plan.* Ministry of Foreign Affairs. http://www.focac.org/eng/zywx_1/zywj/200611/t20061116_7933564.htm

Ministry of Foreign Affairs. (2009, September 25). *Forum on China-Africa Cooperation-Addis Ababa Action Plan.* Ministry of Foreign Affairs. http://www.focac.org/eng/zywx_1/zywj/200909/t20090925_7933568.htm

Ministry of Foreign Affairs. (2020, June 17). *Joint Statement of the Extraordinary China-Africa Summit on Solidarity Against COVID-19.* Ministry of Foreign Affairs. https://www.fmprc.gov.cn/eng/wjdt_665385/2649_665393/202006/t20200617_679628.html

Ministry of Foreign Affairs. (2021, August 24). *China will work with Africa to formulate and implement a China-Africa partnership plan on digital innovation.* Ministry of Foreign Affairs. https://www.fmprc.gov.cn/mfa_eng/wjbxw/202108/t20210825_9134687.html

Ministry of Foreign Affairs. (2021, December 22). *Forum on China-Africa Cooperation Dakar Action Plan (2022-2024).* FOCAC. http://www.focac.org/eng/zywx_1/zywj/202201/t20220124_10632444.htm

Ministry of Innovation and Technology. (2020). *Digital Ethiopia 2025: A digital strategy for Ethiopia inclusive prosperity.* Government of Ethiopia.

Mitchell, R. K., Agle, B. R., & Wood, D. J. (1997). Toward a theory of stakeholder identification and salience: Defining the principle of who and what really counts. *Academy of Management Review*, 22(4), 853. doi:10.2307/259247

Mitchell, R., Busenitz, L., Lant, T., McDougall, P. P., Morse, E. A., & Smith, B. (2002). Towards a theory of entrepreneurial cognition: Rethinking the people side of entrepreneurship research. *Entrepreneurship Theory and Practice*, 27(2), 93–104. doi:10.1111/1540-8520.00001

Mo, Z. (2018, October 12). Shenzhen boosts Ethiopia's entrepreneurs. *China Daily*. https://global.chinadaily.com.cn/a/201810/12/WS5bc0115aa310eff303282044.html

Modiba, M. (2023). User perception on the utilisation of artificial intelligence for the management of records at the council for scientific and industrial research. *Collection and Curation*.

Mohajan, H. K. (2019). The First Industrial Revolution: Creation of a New Global Human Era. *Journal of Social Sciences and Humanities*, 5(4), 377–387.

Momoh, I., Adelaja, G., & Ejiwumi, G. (2023). *Analysis of the Human Factor in Cybersecurity: Identifying and Preventing Social Engineering Attacks in Financial Institution.*

Morris, M. G., Venkatesh, V., & Ackerman, P. L. (2005). Gender and Age Differences in Employee Decisions About New Technology: An Extension to the Theory of Planned Behavior. *IEEE Transactions on Engineering Management*, 52(1), 69–84. doi:10.1109/TEM.2004.839967

Morris, M., & Venkatesh, V. (2000). Age differences in technology adoption decisions: Implications for a changing work force. *Personnel Psychology*, 53(2), 375–403. doi:10.1111/j.1744-6570.2000.tb00206.x

Mosteanu, N. R., & Faccia, A. (2020). Digital systems and new challenges of financial management–FinTech, XBRL, blockchain and cryptocurrencies. *Quality - Access to Success*, *21*(174), 159–166.

Mousa, M. A. S. (2020). Determinants of Cloud Based E-Government in Libya. *Journal of Critical Reviews*, *7*(13), 13.

Moyo, S., Doan, T. N., Yun, J. A., & Tshuma, N. (2018). Application of machine learning models in predicting length of stay among healthcare workers in underserved communities in South Africa. *Human Resources for Health*, *16*(1), 1–9.

Mpehongwa, G. (2013). Academia-industry-government linkages in Tanzania: trends, challenges and prospects. *Global Journal of Education Research*, *1*(1), 084-091.

Mtebe, J. S., & Sausi, J. (2021). Revolutionization of Revenue Collection with Government E-Payment Gateway System in Tanzania: A Public Value Creation Perspective. *East African Journal of Science. Technology and Innovation*, *2*(3). doi:10.37425/eajsti.v2i3.248

Muchabaiwa, W., & Chauraya, E. (2022). *The gender blindness of the education 5.0 framework: An obstruction to promotion opportunities for female academics in Zimbabwe*. Sage. doi:10.1177/08920206221126640

Mugo, D., Njagi, K., Chemwei, B., & Motanya, J. (2017). The technology acceptance model (TAM) and its application to the utilization of mobile learning technologies. *British Journal of Mathematics & Computer Science*, *20*(4), 1–8. doi:10.9734/BJMCS/2017/29015

Mugo, J. W. (2021). *Perceived Factors Influencing Performance of Community Based Housing Projects in Urban Informal Settlements: a Case of Mukuru Slums, Nairobi County*. University of Nairobi.

Muhammad, A., Umar, U. A., & Adam, F. L. (2023). The Impact of Artificial Intelligence and Machine learning on workforce skills and economic mobility in developing countries: A case study of Ghana and Nigeria. *Journal of Technology Innovations and Energy*, *2*(1), 55–61. doi:10.56556/jtie.v2i1.466

Mui, M. S. (2013). Dialogic pedagogy in Hong Kong: Introducing art and culture. *Arts and Humanities in Higher Education*, *12*(4), 408–423. Advance online publication. doi:10.1177/1474022213481939

Mukuni, J. (2019). Challenges of Educational Digital Infrustructure in Africa: A tale of hope and disillusionment. *J. Afr. Stud. Dev. Vol*, *11*(5), 59–63. doi:10.5897/JASD2019.0539

Muller, H. R. (1930). Warri: A West African game of skill. *Journal of American Folklore*, *43*(169), 313–316. doi:10.2307/534943

Murdoch, B. (2021). Privacy and artificial intelligence: Challenges for protecting health information in a new era. *BMC Medical Ethics*, *22*(1), 1–5. doi:10.1186/s12910-021-00687-3 PMID:34525993

Murinde, V., Rizopoulos, E., & Zachariadis, M. (2022). The impact of the FinTech revolution on the future of banking: Opportunities and risks. *International Review of Financial Analysis*, *81*, 102103. doi:10.1016/j.irfa.2022.102103

Murkherjee, S. (2018). Playing subaltern: Video games and postcolonialism. *Games and Culture*, *13*(5), 504–520. doi:10.1177/1555412015627258

Murkherjee, S. (2018). *Videogames and postcolonialism: empire plays back*. Springer.

Mushonga, M. (2018). *The efficiency and sustainability of co-operative financial institutions in South Africa*. Stellenbosch University.

Mustapha, S. F. B. (2021). *Readiness of Industry Revolution 4.0 implementation in Asset Integrity Management (aim)*. [Unpublished Dissertation, Universiti Tunku Abdul Rahman].

Muxtorjonovna, A. (2020). Significance Of Blended Learning In Education System. *The American Journal of Social Science and Education Innovations*, 2(8), 507–511. doi:10.37547/tajssei/Volume02Issue08-82

Naicker, S., Plange-Rhule, J., Tutt, R. C., & Eastwood, J. B. (2009). Shortage of healthcare workers in developing countries—Africa. *Ethnicity & Disease*, 19, 60–64. PMID:19484878

Nair, P. K., Ali, F., & Leong, L. C. (2015). Factors affecting acceptance & use of ReWIND: Validating the extended unified theory of acceptance and use of technology. *Interactive Technology and Smart Education*, 12(3), 183–201. doi:10.1108/ITSE-02-2015-0001

Nance, M. (2016). *The plot to hack America: How Putin's cyberspies and WikiLeaks tried to steal the 2016 election.* Simon and Schuster.

Nan, W., Zhu, X., & Lynne Markus, M. (2021). What we know and don't know about the socioeconomic impacts of mobile money in Sub-Saharan Africa: A systematic literature review. *The Electronic Journal on Information Systems in Developing Countries*, 87(2), e12155. doi:10.1002/isd2.12155

National Communication Authority. (2019). *Household survey on ICT in Ghana 2019*. NCA.

Natsoulas, A. (1995). The game of mancala with reference to commonalities among the peoples of Ethiopia and in comparison to other African peoples: Rules and strategies. *Northeast African Studies*, 2(2), 7–24. doi:10.1353/nas.1995.0018

Natsumi, K. (2023). *Nintendo's Mario mission: grab IP limelight as Switch sales dim.* Nikkei.

Nayebare, M. (2019). Artificial intelligence policies in Africa over the next five years. *XRDS: Crossroads. The ACM Magazine for Students.*, 26(2), 50–54.

Ndhlovu, N. J., & Goosen, L. (2023). To What Extent Can Multidisciplinary Artificial Intelligence Applications Enhance Higher Education?: Open and Distance E-Learning in South Africa. In Multidisciplinary Applications of Deep Learning-Based Artificial Emotional Intelligence (pp. 166–185). IGI Global.

Ndukwe, I. (2021). *Ghana basks in Twitter's surprise choice as Africa HQ.* BBC. https://www.bbc.com/news/world-africa-56860658

Ndukwe, I. (2022). *Twitter lays off staff at its only Africa office in Ghana.* BBC. https://www.bbc.com/news/world-africa-63569525

Ndzendze, B., & Marwala, T. (2023). Artificial Intelligence and International Relations. In *Artificial Intelligence and International Relations Theories* (pp. 33–54). Springer. doi:10.1007/978-981-19-4877-0_3

Nelson, G. S. (2019). Bias in artificial intelligence. *North Carolina Medical Journal*, 80(4), 220–222. doi:10.18043/ncm.80.4.220 PMID:31278182

Newell, A., & Simon, H. A. (1972). *Human problem solving* (Vol. 104). Prentice-hall Englewood Cliffs.

Newman, J., Mintrom, M., & O'Neill, D. (2022). Digital technologies, artificial intelligence, and bureaucratic transformation. *Futures*, 136, 102886. Advance online publication. doi:10.1016/j.futures.2021.102886

Nguyen, T. T., Phan, D. M., Le, A. H., & Nguyen, L. T. N. (2020). The determinants of citizens' satisfaction of E-government: An empirical study in Vietnam. *Journal of Asian Finance. Economics and Business*, 7(8), 519–531. doi:10.13106/jafeb.2020.vol7.no8.519

Nguyen, V. P. (2022). The Critical Success Factors for Sustainability Financial Technology in Vietnam: A Partial Least Squares Approach. *Human Behavior and Emerging Technologies*, 2022, 2022. doi:10.1155/2022/2979043

Niesten, H. (2023). *Are Digital and Traditional Financial Services Taxed the Same? A Comprehensive Assessment of Tax Policies in Nine African Countries.*

Nigeria Communications Commission. (2021). *National Broadband Plan.* Nigeria Communications Commission. [http://fmcde.gov.ng/wp-content/uploads/2021/12/An_Update_on_Nigerian_National_Broadband_Strategic_Plan_Nigerian_National_Broadband_Council_Secretariat-_May_2017.1.pdf]

NITA. (2023). *Ghana's Digital Services and Payments Platform.* Ghana. https://www.ghana.gov.gh/

Nittas, V. (2020). When e-health goes viral: The strengths and weaknesses of health tech during COVID-19. *Mobile Health News.* https://www.mobihealthnews.com/news/europe/when-ehealth-goes-viral-strangths-weaknesses-of-health-tech-during-COVID-19/

Nkrumah, K. (1964). *Laying of the foundation stone of Ghana's Atomic Reactor: speech delivered by Kwame Nkrumah on the occasion of the laying of the foundation stone of Ghana's Atomic Reactor at Kwabenya.* Ministry of Information and Broadcasting. https://www.ghanaweb.com/GhanaHomePage/NewsArchive/Nkrumah-lays-foundation-for-atomic-reactor-in-1964-122255

Nkrumah, K. (2004). *Neo-colonialism: the last stage of imperialism.* Panaf.

Nobles, C. (2023). Offensive Artificial Intelligence in Cybersecurity: Techniques, Challenges, and Ethical Considerations. In D. N. Burrell (Ed.), *Real-World Solutions for Diversity. Strategic Change, and Organizational Development: Perspectives in Healthcare, Education, Business, and Technology* (pp. 348–363). IGI Global. doi:10.4018/978-1-6684-8691-7.ch021

Noordt, C., & Tangi, L. (2023). The dynamics of AI capability and its influence on public value creation of AI within public administration. *Government Information Quarterly, 40*(4), 101860. Advance online publication. doi:10.1016/j.giq.2023.101860

Norori, N., Hu, Q., Aellen, F. M., Faraci, F. D., & Tzovara, A. (2021). Addressing bias in big data and AI for health care: A call for open science. *Patterns (New York, N.Y.), 2*(10), 100347. doi:10.1016/j.patter.2021.100347 PMID:34693373

Nsanzumuhire, S. U., Groot, W., Cabus, S. J., & Bizimana, B. (2021). Understanding the extent and nature of academia-industry interactions in Rwanda. *Technological Forecasting and Social Change, 170*, 120913. doi:10.1016/j.techfore.2021.120913

Nsanzumuhire, S. U., Groot, W., Cabus, S. J., Ngoma, M. P., & Masengesho, J. (2023). Assessment of industry's perception of effective mechanisms to stimulate academia-industry collaboration in sub-Saharan Africa. *Industry and Higher Education, 37*(3), 409–432. doi:10.1177/09504222221131695

Nukunya, G. K. (1992). *Tradition and change in Ghana: An introduction to sociology.* Ghana Universities Press.

Nutbeam, D. (2000). Health literacy as a public health goal: A challenge for contemporary health education and communication strategies into the 21st century. *Health Promotion International, 15*(3), 259–267. doi:10.1093/heapro/15.3.259

Nuwagira, E., & Muzoora, C. (2020). Is sub-saharan Africa prepared for COVID-19? *Tropical Medicine and Health, 48*(1), 18–30. doi:10.1186/s41182-020-00206-x PMID:32288543

Nwaneri, S., & Ugo, H. (2022). Development of a graphical user interface software for the prediction of chronic kidney disease. *Nigerian Journal of Technology, 41*(1), 175–183-175–183.

Nyakito, C., Amino, C., & Allida, V. (2021). Challenges of intergrating Information and Communication Technology in Teaching among National National Teachers' Colleges in Uganda. *East African Journal of Education and Social Sciences.*

Nyambi, A. B., & Assey, T. (2021). *Assessing the Effectiveness of Digitizing Government Payment Systems on Service Delivery in Public Institution: A Case Study of Arusha Public Institutions.*

Nyholm, S. (2023). Artificial Intelligence, Humanoid Robots, and Old and New Control Problems. In *Social Robots in Social Institutions* (pp. 3–12). IOS Press. doi:10.3233/FAIA220594

Nyoni, T., & Okumu, S. (2020). COVID-19 compliant strategies for supporting treatment adherence among people living with HIV in Sub-Saharan Africa. *AIDS and Behavior*, *25*(1), 2473–2476. doi:10.1007/s10461-020-02888-0 PMID:32333204

O'Driscoll, M. (2009). Explosive challenge. *Journal of Cold War Studies*, *11*(1), 28–56. doi:10.1162/jcws.2009.11.1.28

Obeng, L. E. (2018). *Anthology of a lifetime.* Goldsear.

Obeng, S. (2009). *Selected speeches of Kwame Nkrumah.* Afram Publications.

Ofoma, C. (2021). Digitalization Driven Public Service And Service Delivery: The Nigeria's Experience. *Journal of Public Administration. Finance and Law*, *22*. doi:10.47743/jopafl-2021-22-05

Ofori, D., Light, O., & Ankomah, J. (2023). Adoption intentions of electronic procurement among public sector organisations (PSOs) in Ghana: emerging economy perspective. *Journal of Public Procurement*. doi:10.1108/JOPP-09-2022-0045

Ogbonne, I. P., Omeje, A. N., & Omenma, J. T. (2021). Utilisation of information and communication technology among informal traders in the local economies in Nigeria. *International Journal of Entrepreneurship and Small Business*, *44*(3), 211–234. doi:10.1504/IJESB.2021.119228

Ogbuabor, J. E., Eigbiremolen, G., Orji, A., Manasseh, C., & Onuigbo, F. (2020). ICT and financial inclusion in Nigeria: An overview of current challenges and policy options. *Nigerian Journal of Banking and Finance*, *12*(1), 90–96.

Okereafor, K., Adebola, O., & Djehaicher, R. (2020). Exploring the potentials of Telemedicine and other non-contact electronic health technologies in controlling the spread of the Novel COVID-19. *IJITE*, *8*(4), 1–13.

Olayiwola, J. N., Udenyi, E. D., Yusuf, G., Magaña, C., Patel, R., Duck, B., Sajanlal, S., Potapov, A., & Kibuka, C. (2020). Leveraging electronic consultations to address severe subspecialty care access gasps in Nigeria. *Journal of the National Medical Association*, *112*(1), 92–102. doi:10.1016/j.jnma.2019.10.005 PMID:32044103

Oleribe, O. O., Momoh, J., Uzochukwu, B. S., Mbofana, F., Adebiyi, A., Barbera, T., Williams, R., & Taylor-Robinson, S. D. (2019). Identifying key challenges facing healthcare systems in Africa and potential solutions. *International Journal of General Medicine*, *12*, 395–403. doi:10.2147/IJGM.S223882 PMID:31819592

Olson, W. C. (1991). *The theory and practice of international relations.* Prentice Hall.

Onu, C. C., Lebensold, J., Hamilton, W. L., & Precup, D. (2019). Neural transfer learning for cry-based diagnosis of perinatal asphyxia. *arXiv preprint arXiv:1906.10199*. doi:10.21437/Interspeech.2019-2340

Organization, W. H. (2016). Health workforce requirements for universal health coverage and the sustainable development goals. *Human Resources For Health Observer, 17*.

Orlikowski, W., & Barrett, M. (2014). Digital innovation in emerging markets: A case study of mobile money. *MIT Center for Information Systems, 14*(6). https://cisr.mit.edu/publication/2014_0601_DigitalInnovationVodafone

Ornstein, A. C., & Hunkins, F. P. (2018). *Curriculum: Foundations, principles, and issues.* Pearson Education Ltd.

Osikwan, E. (2021). Fintechs, SMEs and digitization in Africa – Ghana leads the charge. *The BFT Online*. https://thebftonline.com/2021/08/03/fintechs-smes-and-digitization-in-africa-ghana-leads-the-charge/

Osseo-Asare, A. D. (2019). *Atomic Junction: nuclear power in Africa after independence.* Cambridge University Press. doi:10.1017/9781108557955

Othman, M. H., Razali, R., & Nasrudin, M. F. (2020). Key Factors for E-Government towards Sustainable Development Goals. *International Journal of Advanced Science and Technology, 29*(6s), 2864–2876.

Owoyemi, A., Owoyemi, J., Osiyemi, A., & Boyd, A. (2020). Artificial intelligence for healthcare in Africa. *Frontiers in Digital Health, 2,* 6. doi:10.3389/fdgth.2020.00006 PMID:34713019

Owuor, S. (2018). *HCP report no. 6: the urban food system of Nairobi, Kenya.* Hungry Cities Partnership.

Owusu Kwateng, K., Osei Atiemo, K. A., & Appiah, C. (2019). Acceptance and use of mobile banking: An application of UTAUT2. *Journal of Enterprise Information Management, 32*(1), 118–151. doi:10.1108/JEIM-03-2018-0055

Oyebode, O., & Orji, R. (2018). Likita: a medical chatbot to improve healthcare delivery in Africa. *HCI Across Borders (HCIxB).*

Oyelere, R., Oyolola, M., & Olurinola, I. (2020). COVID-19 and the welfare effects of remote work: Evidence from Nigeria. *World Development, 136,* 105132.

OziliP. K.ArunT. (2020). Spillover of COVID-19: Impact on the global economy. Available at SSRN 3562570. doi:10.2139/ssrn.3562570

Oztemel, E., & Gursev, S. (2020). Literature review of industry 4.0 and related technologies. *Journal of Intelligent Manufacturing, 31*(1), 127–182. doi:10.1007/s10845-018-1433-8

Pahnila, S., Siponen, M., Myyry, L., & Zheng, X. (2011). the Influence of Individualistic and Collectivistic Values To Utaut: the Case of the Chinese Ebay. *Ecis, 2011.* https://aisel.aisnet.org/ecis2011/45

Panch, T., Mattie, H., & Atun, R. (2019). Artificial intelligence and algorithmic bias: Implications for health systems. *Journal of Global Health, 9*(2), 010318. doi:10.7189/jogh.09.020318 PMID:31788229

Pankhurst, R. (1971). History and principles of Ethiopian chess. *Journal of Ethiopian Studies, 9*(2), 149–172. https://www.jstor.org/stable/41967474

Pansiri, J. (2005). Pragmatism: A methodological approach to researching strategic alliances in tourism. *Tourism and Hospitality Planning & Development, 2*(3), 191–206. doi:10.1080/14790530500399333

Patil, S., & Davies, P. (2014). Use of Google Translate in medical communication: Evaluation of accuracy. *BMJ (Clinical Research Ed.), 349*(dec15 2), 349. doi:10.1136/bmj.g7392 PMID:25512386

Patton, M. Q. (2002). Qualitative research and evaluation methods. Thousand Oaks, CA: 2002.: Sage Publications.

Patton, M. Q. (2002). Qualitative research and evaluation methods. *Sage (Atlanta, Ga.).*

Pauceanu, A. M., Rabie, N., & Moustafa, A. (2020). Employability in the fourth industrial revolution. *Economia e Sociologia, 13*(3), 269–283.

Pazarbasioglu, C., Mora, A. G., Uttamchandani, M., Natarajan, H., Feyen, E., & Saal, M. (2020). Digital financial services. World Bank, 54.

Pereira, A. C., & Romero, F. (2017). A review of the meanings and the implications of the industry 4.0 concept. *Procedia Manufacturing, 13,* 1206–1214. doi:10.1016/j.promfg.2017.09.032

Pérez-Morote, R., Pontones-Rosa, C., & Núñez-Chicharro, M. (2020). The effects of e-government evaluation, trust and the digital divide in the levels of e-government use in European countries. *Technological Forecasting and Social Change*, *154*(March), 119973. doi:10.1016/j.techfore.2020.119973

Peter, O., Pradhan, A., & Mbohwa, C. (2023). Industry 4.0 concepts within the sub–Saharan African SME manufacturing sector. *Procedia Computer Science*, *217*, 846–855. doi:10.1016/j.procs.2022.12.281

Petrina, S. (2004). Sidney Pressey and the Automation of Education, 1924-1934. *Technology and Culture*, *45*(2), 305–330. doi:10.1353/tech.2004.0085

Pickard, V. (2007). Neoliberal visions and revisions in global communications policy from NWICO to WSIS. *The Journal of Communication Inquiry*, *31*(2), 118–139. doi:10.1177/0196859906298162

Plano C., V. L. & Ivankova, N. V. (2016). *Mixed methods research. A guide to the field.*

Polacheck, H. (1997). Before the ENIAC [weapons firing table calculations]. *IEEE Annals of the History of Computing*, *19*(2), 25–30.

Postman, N. (1994). *The disappearance of childhood.* Vintage.

Powers, S. M., & Jablonski, M. (2015). The Real Cyber War: the Political Economy of Internet Freedom. Urbana, Chicago, and Springfield: University of Illinois Press. doi:10.5406/illinois/9780252039126.001.0001

Powles, J. (2018). *The seductive diversion of 'solving' bias in artificial intelligence.*

Prasad, R. (2020). *eLearning Industry.* A brief History of the LMS. https://elearningindustry.com/brief-lms-history

Pressman, R. S. (2010). *Software engineering: A practitioner's approach* (7th ed.). McGraw Hill.

Provenzo, E. F. (1991). Video Kids: Making Sense of Nintendo. Cambridge, Mass., Harvard: University Press. doi:10.4159/harvard.9780674422483

Pursell, C. (1972). *The military–industrial complex.* Harper & Row Publishers.

Puspitasari, R., & Zulaikha, E. (2023). Review of Business Actor's Financial Behavior in the Ultra Micro Segment. *IPTEK Journal of Proceedings Series*, *0*(1), 32–36. doi:10.12962/j23546026.y2023i1.16372

PwC. (2017). *Putting Ghana Back to Work.* PWC. https://www.pwc.com/gh/en/assets/pdf/2018-budget-highlights.v2.pdf

PWC. (2023, 10 6). *Disrupting Africa: Riding the wave of the digital revolution.* PWC Global. https://www.pwc.com/gx/en/archive/industries/technology/disrupting-africa--riding-the-wave-of-the-digital-revolution.html#:~:text=The%20power%20and%20potential

Qin, J., Liu, Y., & Grosvenor, R. (2016). A categorical framework of manufacturing for Industry 4.0 and beyond. *Procedia CIRP*, *52*, 173–178. doi:10.1016/j.procir.2016.08.005

Quarshie, H. O., & Ami-Narh, J. (2012). The growth and usage of Internet in Ghana. *Journal of Emerging Trends in Computing and Information Sciences*, *3*(9).

Quayson, A. (2002). Obverse denominations: Africa? *Public Culture*, *14*(3), 585-588.

Quayson, A. (2021). Tragedy and postcolonial literature. Cambridge, New York, Melbourne, New Dehli, Singapore: Cambridge University Press. doi:10.1017/9781108921992

Rahim, M.I., & Shamsudin, S. (2019). Categorization of video lecture designs in MOOC for technical and vocational education and training educators. *Journal of Technical Education and Training*, *11*. 11–17.

Rahmayati, R. (2021). Competition Strategy In The Islamic Banking Industry: An Empirical Review. *International Journal Of Business, Economics, And. Social Development*, *2*(2), 65–71.

Rahmi, Y., & Frinaldi, A. (2020). *The Effect of Performance Expectancy, Effort Expectancy, Social Influence and Facilitating Condition on Management of Communities-Based Online Report Management in Padang Pariaman District*. Atlantis Press. doi:10.2991/assehr.k.200803.059

Ramadan, I. M. M., & Abdel-Fattah, M. A. (2022). a Proposed Model for Enhancing E-Government Services To Achieve the Sustainable Development Goals in Egypt " Case Study. *Journal of Theoretical and Applied Information Technology*, *100*(1), 268–285.

Ramnund-Mansingh, A., & Naidoo, K. (2023). Lead the African way! *African Journal of Economic and Management Studies*.

Rashica, V. (2018). The benefits and risks of digital diplomacy. *See Review*, *13*(1), 75–89. doi:10.2478/seeur-2018-0008

Rashidov, R., & Rustamov, A. (2021). THE IMPORTANCE OF DIGITAL PAYMENTS IN THE DIGITAL ECONOMY. *INNOVATIONS IN ECONOMY*, *4*(3), 66–72. doi:10.26739/2181-9491-2021-3-9

Rauniar, R., Rawski, G., Yang, J., & Johnson, B. (2014). Technology acceptance model (TAM) and social media usage: An empirical study on Facebook. *Journal of Enterprise Information Management*, *27*(1), 6–30. doi:10.1108/JEIM-04-2012-0011

Reddy, J., Fox, P. M., & Purohit, M. P. (2019). Artificial intelligence-enabled healthcare delivery. *Journal of the Royal Society of Medicine*, *1*(112), 22–28. doi:10.1177/0141076818815510 PMID:30507284

Regona, M. Y., Tan, X., & Bo, L. R. (2022). Opportunities and adoption challenges of AI in the construction industry: A PRISMA review. *Journal of Open Innovation*, *8*(45), 45. Advance online publication. doi:10.3390/joitmc8010045

Restrepo, J., & Christiaans, H. (2004). Problem structuring and information access in design. *Journal of Desert Research*, *4*(2), 218–236. doi:10.1504/JDR.2004.009842

Reynolds, T. W., Biscaye, P. E., Leigh Anderson, C., O'Brien-Carelli, C., & Keel, J. (2023). Exploring the gender gap in mobile money awareness and use: Evidence from eight low and middle income countries. *Information Technology for Development*, *29*(2-3), 1–28. doi:10.1080/02681102.2022.2073579

Riyadh, H. A., Alfaiza, S. A., & Sultan, A. A. (2018). The effects of technology, organisational, behavioural factors towards utilization of egovernment adoption model by moderating cultural factors. *Journal of Theoretical and Applied Information Technology*, *97*(8), 2142–2165.

Roberts, W. R. (2007). What is public diplomacy? Past practices, present conduct, possible future. *Mediterranean Quarterly*, *18*(4), 36–52. doi:10.1215/10474552-2007-025

Rocheleau, B., & Wu, L. (2005). e-Government and Financial Transactions: Potential Versus Reality. *Electronic Journal of EGovernment, 3*(4).

Rochet, J. C., & Tirole, J. (2003). Platform competition in two-sided markets. *Journal of the European Economic Association*, *1*(4), 990–1029. doi:10.1162/154247603322493212

RockD.ElondouT.ManningS.MishkinP. (2023, Otober 11). *GPTs are GPTs: An early Look at the labor market impact potential of large language models*. Retrieved from Cornell University: https://arxiv.org/abs/2303.10130

Rogers, E. (2003). *Diffusion of innovation*. Free Press.

Rogers, E. (2003). *Diffusion of innovations*. FL: Free Press.

Rogers, E. M. (2003). *Diffusion of Innovations*. Free Press.

Rogers, E. M., & Shoemaker, F. F. (1971). *Communication of Innovations; A Cross-Cultural Approach* (2nd ed.). The Free Press.

Ronaghi, M. H., & Forouharfar, A. (2020). A contextualized study of the usage of the Internet of things (IoTs) in smart farming in a typical Middle Eastern country within the context of Unified Theory of Acceptance and Use of Technology model (UTAUT). *Technology in Society, 63*, 101415. doi:10.1016/j.techsoc.2020.101415

Rose, J., Flak, L. S., & Sæbø, Ø. (2018). Stakeholder theory for the E-government context: Framing a value-oriented normative core. *Government Information Quarterly, 35*(3), 362–374. doi:10.1016/j.giq.2018.06.005

Roselli, D., Matthews, J., & Talagala, N. (2019). Managing bias in AI. In Liu & White (Eds) *Companion Proceedings of the 2019 World Wide Web Conference* (pp. 539-544). 10.1145/3308560.3317590

Rose, N., & Miller, P. (1992). Political power beyond the state: Problematics of government. *The British Journal of Sociology, 43*(2), 173–205. doi:10.2307/591464 PMID:20092498

Russo Spena, T., Tregua, M., & Bifulco, F. (2021). Future Internet and Digital Ecosystems. In T. Russo Spena & F. Bifulco (Eds.), *Digital Transformation in the Cultural Heritage Sector* (pp. 17–38). Springer. doi:10.1007/978-3-030-63376-9_2

Russo-Spena, T., Mele, C., & Marzullo, M. (2019). Practicing value innovation through artificial intelligence: The IBM Watson Case. *Journal of Creating, 5*(1), 11–24.

Ruttkamp-Bloem, E. (2023). Epistemic Just and Dynamic AI Ethics in Africa. In Responsible AI in Africa: Challenges and Opportunities (pp. 13–34). Springer International Publishing Cham. doi:10.1007/978-3-031-08215-3_2

Rwanda Development Board. (n.d.). *Regulatory Sandbox Framework*. Rwanda Development Board. [https://www.bnr.rw/laws-and-regulations/regulatory-digest-market-consultation/regulatory-digest/regulatory-sandbox-regulation/]

Saeed, K. A., & Muthitacharoen, A. (2008). To Send or Not to Send: An Empirical Assessment of Error Reporting Behavior. *IEEE Transactions on Engineering Management, 55*(3), 455–467. doi:10.1109/TEM.2008.922623

Saggi, K. (2002). Trade, foreign direct investment, and international technology transfer: A survey. *The World Bank Research Observer, 17*(2), 191–235. doi:10.1093/wbro/17.2.191

Saiz, A. (2020). Bricks, mortar, and proptech: The economics of IT in brokerage, space utilization and commercial real estate finance. *Journal of Property Investment & Finance, 38*(4), 327–347. doi:10.1108/JPIF-10-2019-0139

Sallstrom, L., Morris, O., & Mehta, H. (2019). Artificial intelligence in Africa's healthcare: Ethical considerations. *ORF Issue Brief,* (312).

Sampene, A. K., Agyeman, F. O., Robert, B., & Wiredu, J. (2022). Artificial intelligence as a pathway to Africa's Transformation. [JMEST]. *Journal of Multidisciplinary Engineering Science and Technology, 9*(1), 14939–14951.

Sang, H., & Tsai, D. (2009). Analysing strategies of integrating ICT into teaching activities using innovation diffusion theory. *NCM 09.Fifth International Joint Conference* (pp. 1876-1878). Seoul Korea: NCM.

Santoro, M. D., & Gopalakrishnan, S. (2000). The institutionalization of knowledge transfer activities within industry-university collaborative ventures. *Journal of Engineering and Technology Management, 17*(3-4), 299–319. doi:10.1016/S0923-4748(00)00027-8

Santos, L., Brittes, G., Fabián, N., & Germán, A. (2018). The expected contribution of industry 4.0 technologies for industrial performance. *International Journal of Production Economics, 13*, 196–204.

Sanusi, I. T., Sunday, K., Oyelere, S. S., Suhonen, J., Vartiainen, H., & Tukiainen, M. (2023). Learning machine learning with young children: Exploring informal settings in an African context. *Computer Science Education*, 1–32. doi:1 0.1080/08993408.2023.2175559

Sasu, D. D. (2023, December). *E-commerce in Ghana - statistics & facts*. Statista. https://www.statista.com/topics/10270/e-commerce-in-ghana/#topicOverview

Sawyer, K. R. (2022). An introduction to the learning sciences. In K. R. Sawyer (Ed.), *The Cambridge handbook of the learning sciences* (3rd ed., pp. 1–24). Cambrideg University Press.

Sawyer, R. K. (2006). *The Cambridge handbook of the learning sciences*. Cambridge University Press.

Schiller, D. (1999). *Digital capitalism: networking the global market system*. The MIT Press. doi:10.7551/mitpress/2415.001.0001

Schiller, D. (2001). World communications in today's age of capital. *Emergences*, *11*(1), 51–68. doi:10.1080/10457220120044666

Schiller, H. I. (1975). Genesis of the free flow of information principles: The imposition of communication domination. *Instant Research on Peace and Violence*, *5*(2), 75–86.

Schoeman, W., Moore, R., Seedat, Y., & Chen, J. Y. J. (2021). Artificial intelligence: Is South Africa ready? Accenture, 1-22.

Schwab, K. (2016). *The Fourth Industrial Revolution*. World Economic Forum: Geneva.

Seib, P. (2013). *Real-Time Diplomacy: Politics and power in the social media era*. Speech.

Sejnowski, T. J. (2018). *The deep learning revolution*. MIT press. doi:10.7551/mitpress/11474.001.0001

Self, C. C., & Roberts, C. (2019). Credibility. In *An integrated approach to communication theory and research* (pp. 435–446). Routledge. doi:10.4324/9780203710753-36

Sengupta, D., & Shastri, N. (2019). Digital payments through PFMS - Facilitating digital inclusion and accelerating transformation to a "Digital Economy. *ACM International Conference Proceeding Series, Part F148155*. ACM. 10.1145/3326365.3326391

Senshaw, D., & Twinomurinzi, H. (2021). The Moderating Effect of Gender on Adopting Digital Goverment Innovations in Ethopia. *Conference on Implications of Information and Digital Technologies*, (pp. 734–751). IEEE.

Senyo, P. K., Karanasios, S., Gozman, D., & Baba, M. (2022). FinTech ecosystem practices shaping financial inclusion: The case of mobile money in Ghana. *European Journal of Information Systems*, *31*(1), 112–127. doi:10.1080/096008 5X.2021.1978342

Senyo, P. K., & Osabutey, E. L. (2020). Unearthing antecedents to financial inclusion through FinTech innovations. *Technovation*, *98*, 102155. doi:10.1016/j.technovation.2020.102155

Sethi, D., & Acharya, D. (2018). Journal of Financial Economic Policy. *Policy*, *10*(3), 369–385.

Sey, A., & Mudongo, O. (2021, July 20). *Case studies on AI skills capacity building and AI in workforce development in Africa*. Africa Portal. https://africaportal.org/publication/case-studies-ai-skills-capacity-building-and-ai-workforce-development-africa/

Shafei, S., Haris, M. H. H., & Hamzah, Z. (2018). The Readiness of POLIMAS Lecturers in the Challenges of Industrial Revolution 4.0. *Paper presented at the 8th National Conference in Education – Technical & Vocational Education and Training (CiE-TVET) 2018.*

Shafik, W. (2023). IoT-Based Energy Harvesting and Future Research Trends in Wireless Sensor Networks. Handbook of Research on Network-Enabled IoT Applications for Smart City Services, 282-306.

Shafik, W. (2024). Predicting Future Cybercrime Trends in the Metaverse Era. In Forecasting Cyber Crimes in the Age of the Metaverse (pp. 78-113). IGI Global.

Shafik, W. (2024). Wearable Medical Electronics in Artificial Intelligence of Medical Things. Handbook of Security and Privacy of AI-Enabled Healthcare Systems and Internet of Medical Things, 21-40.

Shafik, W., Matinkhah, S. M., & Shokoor, F. (2022). Recommendation system comparative analysis: internet of things aided networks. *EAI Endorsed Transactions on Internet of Things, 8*(29).

Shafik, W. (2023). A Comprehensive Cybersecurity Framework for Present and Future Global Information Technology Organizations. In *Effective Cybersecurity Operations for Enterprise-Wide Systems* (pp. 56–79). IGI Global. doi:10.4018/978-1-6684-9018-1.ch002

Shafik, W. (2023). Cyber Security Perspectives in Public Spaces: Drone Case Study. In *Handbook of Research on Cybersecurity Risk in Contemporary Business Systems* (pp. 79–97). IGI Global. doi:10.4018/978-1-6684-7207-1.ch004

Shafik, W. (2023). Making Cities Smarter: IoT and SDN Applications, Challenges, and Future Trends. In *Opportunities and Challenges of Industrial IoT in 5G and 6G Networks* (pp. 73–94). IGI Global. doi:10.4018/978-1-7998-9266-3.ch004

Shafik, W., Matinkhah, S. M., & Ghasemzadeh, M. (2020). Internet of things-based energy management, challenges, and solutions in smart cities. *Journal of Communications Technology. Electronics and Computer Science, 27*, 1–11.

Shafik, W., & Tufail, A. (2023). Energy Optimization Analysis on Internet of Things. In *Advanced Technology for Smart Environment and Energy* (pp. 1–16). Springer International Publishing. doi:10.1007/978-3-031-25662-2_1

Sharma, S. K., & Sharma, M. (2019). Examining the role of trust and quality dimensions in the actual usage of mobile banking services: An empirical investigation. *International Journal of Information Management, 44*(September 2018), 65–75. doi:10.1016/j.ijinfomgt.2018.09.013

Sharma, A., & Gandhi, A. V. (2023). Consumer adoption study for innovative technology products and services in an emerging economy. *International Journal of Innovation Science.* doi:10.1108/IJIS-06-2022-0106

Shava, E., & Mhlanga, D. (2023). Mitigating bureaucratic inefficiencies through blockchain technology in Africa. *Frontiers in Blockchain, 6*, 1. doi:10.3389/fbloc.2023.1053555

Shikalepo, E. E. (2019). Sustainability of Entrepreneurship and Innovation among TVET Graduates in Namibia. *International Journal for Innovation Education and Research, 7*(5), 133–145. doi:10.31686/ijier.vol7.iss5.1484

Shin, S. C., & Rakhmatullayev, Z. M. (2019). Digital Transformation of the Public Service Delivery System in Uzbekistan. *International Conference on Advanced Communication Technology, ICACT, 2019-February.* ACM. 10.23919/ICACT.2019.8702014

Shokoor, F., Shafik, W., & Matinkhah, S. M. (2022). Overview of 5G & Beyond Security. *EAI Endorsed Transactions on Internet of Things, 8*(30).

Shuping, D. K. (2021). *The impact of the effort's standards on legal certainty and the interpretation of contracts.* University of Johannesburg (South Africa).

Silberg, J., & Manyika, J. (2019). Notes from the AI frontier: Tackling bias in AI (and in humans). *McKinsey Global Institute, 1*(6), 1–8.

Simatele, M. (2021). E-payment instruments and welfare: The case of Zimbabwe. *The Journal for Transdisciplinary Research in Southern Africa*, *17*(1). Advance online publication. doi:10.4102/td.v17i1.823

Singh, G. H. (2023). Maintaning the Integrity ofSouth African University: The Impact of CHATGPT on plagiarism and scholarly Writing. *South African Journal of Higher Education*, *37*(5), 203–220. doi:10.20853/37-5-5941

Šisler, V. (2008). Digital Arabs: Representation in video games. *European Journal of Cultural Studies*, *11*(2), 203–220.

Ślusarczyk, B. (2018). Industry 4.0: Are we ready? *Polish Journal of Management Studies*, *17*(1), 58–69. doi:10.17512/pjms.2018.17.1.19

Smaguc, T. (2022). Comparison of Normative, Instrumental and Descriptive Approaches to Stakeholder Theory. *28th RSEP International Conference on Economics, Finance & Business*. ACM.

Snow, N., & Taylor, P. M. (2009). *Routledge handbook of public diplomacy*. Routledge.

Sodiq, O. (2020). Teaching and Learning in the Cloud: Prospects and Challenges of Artificial Intelligence for Education in Africa. Nigeria: Financial Institutions Training Centre (FITC) Lagos.

Soldatos, J. (2019). Introduction to Industry 4.0 and the Digital Shopfloor Vision.

Solow, R. M. (1962). Technical progress, capital formation, and economic growth. *The American Economic Review*, *52*(2), 76–86.

Son, J., & Benbasat, I. (2007). Organizational buyers' adoption and use of B2B electronic marketplaces: Efficiency-and legitimacy-oriented perspectives. *Journal of Management Information Systems*, *24*(1), 55–99. doi:10.2753/MIS0742-1222240102

Sotiriu, S. (2015). *Digital diplomacy: Between promises and reality. Digital diplomacy: Theory and practice*. Routledge.

South Africa Government Gazette. (n.d.). Protection of Personal Information Act (POPIA). *South Africa Government Gazette*. [https://popia.co.za/]

Soyemi, K. A., Olowofela, O. E., & Yunusa, L. A. (2020). Financial inclusion and sustainable development in Nigeria. *Journal of Economics and Management*, *39*(1), 105–131. doi:10.22367/jem.2020.39.06

Spady, J. G. (1989). Dr. Cheikh Anta Diop and the background of scholarship on Black interest in Egyptology and Nile Valley civilizations. *Presence Africaine (Paris, France)*, (149/150), 292–312. doi:10.3917/presa.149.0292

Spottl, P. D. (2016). *TVET International Conference 2016*. University of Bremen: Centre of Technology, Work and TVET.

Srinivasan, R., & Chander, A. (2021). Biases in AI systems. *Communications of the ACM*, *64*(8), 44–49.

Srivastava, K., & Dhamija, S. (2022). FinTech: Application of Artificial Intelligence in Indian Banking. Proceedings of International Conference on Communication and Artificial Intelligence: ICCAI 2021, Taj, I., & Zaman, N. (2022). Towards industrial revolution 5.0 and explainable artificial intelligence: Challenges and opportunities. *International Journal of Computing and Digital Systems*, *12*(1), 295–320.

Stahl, B. C., Leach, T., Oyeniji, O., & Ogoh, G. (2023). AI Policy as a Response to AI Ethics? Addressing Ethical Issues in the Development of AI Policies in North Africa. In Responsible AI in Africa: Challenges and Opportunities (pp. 141–167). Springer International Publishing Cham. doi:10.1007/978-3-031-08215-3_7

Statistica. (2023). *Number of teachers in secondary education in Ghana from 2010 to 2020*. Retrieved October 2023, from Number of teachers in secondary education in Ghana from 2010 to 2020: https://www.statista.com/statistics/1184183/number-of-teachers-in-secondary-education-in-ghana/

Stosic, L. (2015). The importance of Educational Technology in Teaching. *(IJCRSEE) International Journal of Cognitive Research in Science. Engineering and EducationVol.*, *3*(1), 111–114.

Sun, H., & Zhang, P. (2006). The Role of Moderating Factors in User Technology Acceptance. *International Journal of Human-Computer Studies*, *64*(2), 53–78. doi:10.1016/j.ijhcs.2005.04.013

Talented Young Scientist Program. (2015, November 24). *China Science and Technology Exchange Center.* CISTC. http://www.cistc.gov.cn/scientist/details.asp?column=919&id=89345

Tao, D. (2009). Intention to use and actual use of electronic information resources: further exploring Technology Acceptance Model (TAM). *AMIA ... Annual Symposium Proceedings / AMIA Symposium. AMIA Symposium, 2009*, 629–633.

Tay, S. I., Lee, T. C., Hamid, N. Z. A., & Ahmad, A. N. A. (2018). An overview of industry 4.0: Definition, components, and government initiatives. *Journal of Advanced Research in Dynamical and Control Systems*, *10*(14), 1379–1387.

Tech Labari. (2023). *SnooCODE Partners with Liberian Government to Launch National Digital Postal Addressing System.* Tech Labari. https://techlabari.com/snoocode-partners-with-liberian-government-to-launch-national-digital-postal-addressing-system.

TechCrunch. (2020). *Farmcrowdy Raises $1M Round to Bring Nigerian Farmers Online and to Market.* TechCrunch. https://techcrunch.com/2017/12/18/1579210/

TechCrunch. (2022). The E-commerce Boom is Still Afoot in Africa, Jumia's Earnings Indicate. *TechCrunch.* https://techcrunch.com/2022/05/17/the-e-commerce-boom-is-still-afoot-in-africa-jumias-earnings-indicate/

TechCrunch. (2022). *The E-commerce Boom is Still Afoot in Africa.* Jumia's Earnings Indicate.

Teixeira, A. A. C., & Mota, L. (2012). A bibliometric portrait of the evolution, scientific roots and influence of literature on university-industry links. *Scientometrics*, *93*(3), 719–743. doi:10.1007/s11192-012-0823-5

Tellis, W. (1997). Introduction to Case Study. *The Qualitative Report.* doi:10.46743/2160-3715/1997.2024

Terence, T. (2022). *Developing And Validating A Hybrid Framework For Machine Learning Operationalisation Within FSIS In Developing Countries: A Case For Zimbabwe.* Midlands State University.

The Economist. (2018). The 2018 Government E-Payments Adoption Ranking. *The Economist Intelligence Unit.*

The World Bank Group. (2021). *Tools for Digitizing Government Payments Learnings from FISF.* The World Bank. https://openknowledge.worldbank.org/server/api/core/bitstreams/064bd45f-73c8-540e-92b8-62857c7d1937/content

Thompson, R. L., Higgins, C. A., & Howell, J. M. (1991). Personal computing: Toward a conceptual model of utilization. *Management Information Systems Quarterly*, *15*(1), 125–142. doi:10.2307/249443

Thompson, T., Sowunmi, O., Misra, S., Fernandez-Sanz, L., Crawford, B., & Soto, R. (2017). An expert system for the diagnosis of sexually transmitted diseases–ESSTD. *Journal of Intelligent & Fuzzy Systems*, *33*(4), 2007–2017. doi:10.3233/JIFS-161242

Thong, J. Y. L., Hong, S.-J., & Tam, K. Y. (2006). The effects of post-adoption beliefs on the expectation-confirmation model for information technology continuance. *International Journal of Human-Computer Studies*, *64*(9), 799–810. doi:10.1016/j.ijhcs.2006.05.001

Thrift, N. (2003). Closer to the machine? Intelligent environments, new forms of possession and the rise of the supertoy. *Cultural Geographies*, *10*(4), 389–407. doi:10.1191/1474474003eu282oaa

Tignor, R. L. (2006). *Arthur Lewis and the birth of development economics.* Princeton University Press. doi:10.1515/9780691204246

Tompihe, J. G. (2023). Financing Terrorism With FinTechs in West Africa? In Exploring the Dark Side of FinTech and Implications of Monetary Policy (pp. 118–143). IGI Global. doi:10.4018/978-1-6684-6381-9.ch006

Topol, E. (2019). *Deep medicine: how artificial intelligence can make healthcare human again.*

Torkelson, E. (2020). Collateral damages: Cash transfer and debt transfer in South Africa. *World Development, 126,* 104711. doi:10.1016/j.worlddev.2019.104711

Tornatzky, L. G., & Klein, K. J. (1982). Innovation Characteristics and Innovation Adoption-Implementation: A Meta-Analysis of Findings. *IEEE Transactions on Engineering Management. IEEE Transactions on Engineering Management, 29*(1), 28–45. doi:10.1109/TEM.1982.6447463

Townsend, B. A., Sihlahla, I., Naidoo, M., Naidoo, S., Donnelly, D.-L., & Thaldar, D. W. (2023). Mapping the regulatory landscape of AI in healthcare in Africa. *Frontiers in Pharmacology, 14,* 14. doi:10.3389/fphar.2023.1214422 PMID:37693916

Tran, B. X., Vu, G. T., Ha, G. H., Vuong, Q.-H., Ho, M.-T., Vuong, T.-T., La, V.-P., Ho, M.-T., Nghiem, K.-C. P., Nguyen, H. L. T., Latkin, C., Tam, W., Cheung, N.-M., Nguyen, H.-K., Ho, C., & Ho, R. (2019). Global evolution of research in artificial intelligence in health and medicine: A bibliometric study. *Journal of Clinical Medicine, 8*(3), 360. doi:10.3390/jcm8030360 PMID:30875745

Traore, B., Ozozco, J., & Velandia, J. (2021). *Digital drivers of inclusive growth in Africa and Latin America and Carribean.* OECD.

Triandis, H. C. (1980). Reflections on trends in cross-cultural research. *Journal of Cross-Cultural Psychology, 11*(1), 35–58. doi:10.1177/0022022180111003

Trkman, M., Popovič, A., & Trkman, P. (2023). The roles of privacy concerns and trust in voluntary use of governmental proximity tracing applications. *Government Information Quarterly, 40*(1), 101787. doi:10.1016/j.giq.2022.101787

Tsvetkova, N. N. (2023). New technologies and countries of Asia and Africa. *Digital Orientalia, 2*(1–2).

Tugendhat, H., & Voo, J. (2021). *China's Digital Silk Road in Africa and the future of internet governance* (Working Paper No. 2021/50). China Africa Research Initiative (CARI). https://static1.squarespace.com/static/5652847de4b033f56d2bdc29/t/61084a3238e7ff4b666b9ffe/1627933235832/WP+50+-+Tugendhat+and+Voo+-+China+Digital+Silk+Road+Africa.pdf

Tunjera, N., & Chigona, A. (2023). Mobile Technologies Revolutionizing Teacher Preparation for Effective Education 4.0 Outcomes in Marginalised Communities. *Society for Information Technology & Teacher Education International Conference,* 2302–2315.

Turki, H., Pouris, A., Ifeanyichukwu, F.-A. M., Namayega, C., Taieb, M. A. H., Adedayo, S. A., Fourie, C., Currin, C. B., Asiedu, M. N., & Tonja, A. L. (2023). *Machine Learning for Healthcare: A Bibliometric Study of Contributions from Africa.*

Turner, N. (2023, October 11). *Artificial Intelligence and Future of Teaching and Learning: Insights and Recommendations,* Retrieved from U.S. Department of Education, Office of Educational Technology: https://tech.ed.gov

Tylor, E. B. (1880). Remarks on the geographical distribution of games. *Journal of the Anthropological Institute of Great Britain and Ireland, 9,* 23–30. doi:10.2307/2841865

U.S. Department of Education. (2023, October 11). *Office of Educational Technology, Artificial Intelligence and Future of Teaching and Learning: Insights and Recommendations.* Washington, DC, 2023.: Office of Educational Technology, Retrieved from https://www2.ed.gov/documents/ai-report/ai-report.pdf

Ukoba, K., Kunene, T. J., Harmse, P., Lukong, V. T., & Chien Jen, T. (2023). The Role of Renewable Energy Sources and Industry 4.0 Focus for Africa: A Review. *Applied Sciences (Basel, Switzerland), 13*(2), 1074. doi:10.3390/app13021074

Umeh, C. A. (2018). Challenges toward achieving health coverage in Ghana, Kenya and Tanzania. *The International Journal of Health Planning and Management, 33,* 794–805. doi:10.1002/hpm.2610 PMID:30074646

UNCTAD Global Review. (2020). *Covid-19 and Global Review.* UNCTAD. https://unctad.org/system/files/official-document/dtlstict2020d13_en_0.pdf

UNESCO. (2015, February). *Policy document for the integration of a sustainable development perspective into the processes of the World Heritage Convention.* UNESCO. https://whc.unesco.org/document/139146

UNESCO. (2020). *COVID-19 Educational Disruption and Response.* UNESCO. https://en.unesco.org/covid19/educationresponse

UNESCO. (2023). *Artificial intelligence in education.* Retrieved January 2024, from Digital learning and transformation of education: https://www.unesco.org/en/digital-education/artificial-intelligence

UNESCO. (2023). *The UNESCO courier: Education in the age of artificial intelligence.* UNESCO.

UNESCO-China Funds-in-Trust Project. (n.d.). Harnessing technology for quality teacher training in Africa" phase I conclusion and phase II launch meeting. *United Nations Educational, Scientific and Cultural Organization.* UNESCO. https://en.unesco.org/events/unesco-china-funds-trust-project-harnessing-technology-quality-teacher-training-africa-phase

Union, A. (2014). African Union convention on cyber security and personal data protection. *African Union, 27.*

United Nations Capital Development Fund. (2020). *Digital Financial Services for COVID-19 Response and Recovery in Africa.* UNCDF. https://www.uncdf.org/article/5537/digital-financial-services-for-covid-19-response-and-recovery-in-africa

United Nations Conference on Trade and Development (2002). *Investment policy review: Tanzania.* United Nations.

United Nations Development Program. (2021). *Analyzing long-term socioeconomic impacts of COVID-19 across diverse African contexts.* UNDP Regional Bureau for Africa. https://www.undp.org/sites/g/files/zskgke326/files/migration/africa/f5a32ba0e2fb380796e3596e0857ab63f2acb1300c5bb17aad9847e13f941c43.pdf

United Nations Economic Commission for Africa. (2021). *Building forward for an African green recovery.* United Nations Economic Commission for Africa. https://hdl.handle.net/10855/43948

United Nations Educational, Scientific and Cultural Organization. (2018). *Improving the quality of teacher education in Sub-Saharan Africa: Lessons learned from a UNESCO-China Funds-in-Trust project.* UNESCO.

United Nations Educational, Scientific and Cultural Organization. (2023, July 24). *China Funds-in-Trust phase III (CFIT III) in higher education.* UN. https://www.unesco.org/en/articles/china-funds-trust-phase-iii-cfit-iii-higher-education

Usoro, A. D., Ezekiel, C. E., & Ojobah, L. O. (2021). The Fourth Industrial Revolution: Discourse and Contexts Shaping Nigeria's Participation. *American Journal of Education and Information Technology, 5*(2), 106–112. doi:10.11648/j.ajeit.20210502.17

Utama, A. . G. S. (2020). The implementation of e-government in indonesia. *International Journal of Research in Business and Social Science (2147- 4478), 9*(7), 190–196. doi:10.20525/ijrbs.v9i7.929

Uunona, G. N., & Goosen, L. (2023). Leveraging Ethical Standards in Artificial Intelligence Technologies: A Guideline for Responsible Teaching and Learning Applications. In Handbook of Research on Instructional Technologies in Health Education and Allied Disciplines (pp. 310–330). IGI Global. doi:10.4018/978-1-6684-7164-7.ch014

Uwamahoro, L., Sikubwabo, I., Ndikumana, A., Cyemezo, P. C., & Paix, J. deLa. (n.d.). *IoT and AI for Nature Conservation: Nyungwe forestry management and real time monitoring system.*

Vadrot, A. B., Langlet, A., Tessnow-von Wysocki, I., Tolochko, P., Brogat, E., & Ruiz, S. C. (2021). Marine biodiversity negotiations during COVID-19: A new role for digital diplomacy? *Global Environmental Politics*, *21*(3), 169–186. doi:10.1162/glep_a_00605

Vaidya, M., & Sharma, S. (2020). DIGITAL PAYMENT AS A KEY ENABLER OF E-GOVERNMENT SERVICES: A CASE STUDY OF CHANDIGARH CITY (INDIA). *International Journal of Control and Automation*, *13*(1s).

van Heerden, J., & Mulumba, M. (2023). Science, Technology and Innovation (STI): Its Role in South Africa's Development Outcomes and STI Diplomacy. In Science, Technology and Innovation Diplomacy in Developing Countries: Perceptions and Practice (pp. 141–154). Springer.

Van Rheenen, D. (2012). A century of historical change in the game preferences of American children. *Journal of American Folklore*, *125*(498), 411–443. doi:10.5406/jamerfolk.125.498.0411

Van, L. T.-H., Vo, A. T., Nguyen, N. T., & Vo, D. H. (2021). Financial inclusion and economic growth: An international evidence. *Emerging Markets Finance & Trade*, *57*(1), 239–263. doi:10.1080/1540496X.2019.1697672

VanZyl, K. (2020). *Barriers and enablers for the uptake of Fintech remittance platforms by migrant entrepreneurs in South Africa*. University of Pretoria.

Varma, P., Nijjer, S., Sood, K., Grima, S., & Rupeika-Apoga, R. (2022). Thematic Analysis of Financial Technology (Fintech) Influence on the Banking Industry. *Risks*, *10*(10), 186. doi:10.3390/risks10100186

Vejgaard, H. (2019). *Culture as a determinant in innovation diffusion*. IntechOpen. doi:10.5772/intechopen.80806

Venkatesh, V. (2000). Determinants of Perceived Ease of Use: Integrating Control, Intrinsic Motivation, and Emotion into the Technology Acceptance Model. *Information Systems Research*, *11*(4), 342–365. doi:10.1287/isre.11.4.342.11872

Venkatesh, V., & Agarwal, R. (2006). Turning visitors into customers: A usability-centric perspective on purchase behavior in electronic channels. *Management Science*, *52*(3), 367–382. doi:10.1287/mnsc.1050.0442

Venkatesh, V., & Davis, F. D. (1996). A Model of the Antecedents of Perceived Ease of Use: Development and Test*. *Decision Sciences*, *27*(3), 451–481. doi:10.1111/j.1540-5915.1996.tb01822.x

Venkatesh, V., & Davis, F. D. (2000). Theoretical extension of the Technology Acceptance Model: Four longitudinal field studies. *Management Science*, *46*(2), 186–204. doi:10.1287/mnsc.46.2.186.11926

Venkatesh, V., Morris, M. G., Davis, G. B., & Davis, F. D. (2003). Human Acceptance of Information Technology. *MIS*, *27*(3), 425–478. doi:10.1201/9780849375477.ch230

Venkatesh, V., Morris, M. G., Davis, G. B., & Davis, F. D. (2003). User Acceptance of Information Technology: Toward a Unified View. *Management Information Systems Quarterly*, *27*(3), 425–478. doi:10.2307/30036540

Verkijika, S. F., & De Wet, L. (2018). E-government adoption in sub-Saharan Africa. *Electronic Commerce Research and Applications*, *30*(May), 83–93. doi:10.1016/j.elerap.2018.05.012

Vernon, D. (n.d.). *Culturally Competent Social Robotics for Africa: A Case for Diversity, Equity, and Inclusion in HRI.*

Verrekia, B. (2017). *Digital diplomacy and its effect on international relations*. Sage Publications.

Visa. (2021). *Visa Back to Business Study: South Africa Edition*. Visa. https://www.visa.co.za/dam/VCOM/regional/ap/pdf/south-africa/en/ZAR-visa-back-to-business-study-south-africa-edition.pdf

Vlachopoulos, D., & Makri, A. (2017). The effect of games and simulations on higher education: A systematic literature review. *International Journal of Education*, *14*(22), 1–33.

von Neuman, J. (1993). First draft of the report on EDVAC. *IEEE Annals of the History of Computing*, *15*(4), 27–43. doi:10.1109/85.238389

Vukadinović, R. (1994). *Diplomacija. strategija političnih pogajanj (Diplomacy. strategy of political negotations)*. Arah Consulting.

Wahl, B., Cossy-Gantner, A., Germann, S., & Schwalbe, N. R. (2018). Artificial intelligence (AI) and global health: How can AI contribute to health in resource-poor settings? *BMJ Global Health*, *3*(4), e000798. doi:10.1136/bmjgh-2018-000798 PMID:30233828

Walsham, G. (1995). Interpretive case studies in IS research: Nature and method. *European Journal of Information Systems*, *4*(2), 74–81. Advance online publication. doi:10.1057/ejis.1995.9

Wang, R., Bar, F., & Hong, Y. (2020). ICT aid flows from China to African countries: A communication network perspective. *International Journal of Communication*, *14*, 1498–1523.

Wang, S., Wan, J., Zhang, D., Li, D., & Zhang, C. (2016). Towards smart factory for industry 4.0: A self-organized multiagent system with big databased feedback and coordination. *Computer Networks*, *101*, 158–168. Advance online publication. doi:10.1016/j.comnet.2015.12.017

Wang, Y., Shafik, W., Seong, J. T., Al Mutairi, A., Mustafa, M. S., & Mouhamed, M. R. (2023). Service delay and optimization of the energy efficiency of a system in fog-enabled smart cities. *Alexandria Engineering Journal*, *84*, 112–125. doi:10.1016/j.aej.2023.10.034

Wang, Y., Su, Z., Zhang, N., Xing, R., Liu, D., Luan, T. H., & Shen, X. (2022). A survey on metaverse: Fundamentals, security, and privacy. *IEEE Communications Surveys and Tutorials*, *25*(1), 319–352. doi:10.1109/COMST.2022.3202047

Ward, M., & Naude, R. (2018). *Banking for a Sustainable Economy*.

Warikandwa, T. V. (2023). Financial Inclusion, Intra-African Trade and the AfCFTA: A Law and Economics Perspective. In Financial Inclusion and Digital Transformation Regulatory Practices in Selected SADC Countries: South Africa, Namibia, Botswana and Zimbabwe (pp. 207-228). Springer.

Weisser, M. (1991). The computer for the twenty-first century. *Scientific American*, *265*(3), 94–104. doi:10.1038/scientificamerican0991-94

Wekesa, B., Turianskyi, Y., & Ayodele, O. (2021). Introduction to the special issue: Digital diplomacy in Africa. *South African Journal of International Affairs*, *28*(3), 335–339. doi:10.1080/10220461.2021.1961606

Westad, O. A. (2007). *The global Cold War third world interventions and the making of our times*. Cambridge University Press.

Wewege, L., Lee, J., & Thomsett, M. C. (2020). Disruptions and digital banking trends. *Journal of Applied Finance and Banking*, *10*(6), 15–56.

White, E. (2003). Kwame Nkrumah: Cold war modernity, Pan-African ideology and the geopolitics of development. *Geopolitics*, *8*(2), 99–124. doi:10.1080/714001035

William, R. (2012). *The Most Powerful Idea in the World: A Story of Steam, Industry and Invention*. University of Chicago Press.

Wiredu, K. (1996). *Cultural universals and particulars: an African perspective*. Blackwell Publishing.

Woods, E. M. (2005). *Empire of capital*. Verso.

Woods, E. M. (2007). A reply to critics. *Historical Materialism, 15*(3), 143–170. doi:10.1163/156920607X225915

World Bank. (2020). *Digital Development in Africa*. World Bank. https://www.worldbank.org/en/region/afr/brief/digital-development-in-africa

World Bank. (2020). *Financial Inclusion Data - Global Findex Database*. World Bank. https://databank.worldbank.org/reports.aspx?source=global-findex-database

World Bank. (2020). *The African Continental Free Trade Area: Economic and Distributional Effects*. World Bank. https://openknowledge.worldbank.org/handle/10986/33738

World Bank. (2021). *COVID-19 and the Future of Work in Africa: Emerging Trends in Digital Technology*. World Bank. https://www.worldbank.org/en/publication/africa-pulse/pulse- 2021-sm

World Health Organization. (2020). *Digital Health in the African Region: Opportunities and Challenges*. WHO. https://www.afro.who.int/publications/digital-health-african-region-opportunities-and-challenges

Wu, I.-L., & Chen, J.-L. (2005). An extension of Trust and TAM model with TPB in the initial adoption of on-line tax: An empirical study. *International Journal of Human-Computer Studies, 62*(6), 784–808. doi:10.1016/j.ijhcs.2005.03.003

Wuta, R. (2023). Extendibility of the Education 5.0 Concept to Zimbabwe's Secondary School System as Encapsulated in Curriculum Framework 2015-2022. *Indiana Journal of Humanities and Social Sciences, 03*(5), 914-942.

Yang, Z., Jianjun, L., Faqiri, H., Shafik, W., Talal Abdulrahman, A., Yusuf, M., & Sharawy, A. M. (2021, May 27). Green Internet of things and big data application in smart cities development. *Complexity, 2021*, 1–5. doi:10.1155/2021/4922697

Yasanur, K. (2018). Sustainability impact of digitization in logistics. *15th Global Conference on Sustainable Manufacturing Procedia Manufacturing, 21*(7), 782–789.

Ye, W. (2023). *China's education aid to Africa: Fragmented soft power*. Routledge. doi:10.4324/9781003361961

Yilma, K. (2023). In Search for a Role: The African Union and Digital Policies in Africa. *Digital Society : Ethics, Socio-Legal and Governance of Digital Technology, 2*(2), 1–12. doi:10.1007/s44206-023-00047-1

Yin, R. K. (2004). *Case Study Research: Design and Methods* (2nd ed.). Sage.

Yin, R. K. (2017). Case Study Research and Applications Design and Methods. []. Sage.]. *Journal of Hospitality & Tourism Research (Washington, D.C.), 53*(5).

Yousafzai, S., & Yani-de-Soriano, M. (2012). Understanding customer-specific factors underpinning internet banking adoption. *International Journal of Bank Marketing, 30*(1), 60–81. doi:10.1108/02652321211195703

Yu, C. S. (2012). Factors affecting individuals to adopt mobile banking: Empirical evidence from the utaut model. *Journal of Electronic Commerce Research, 13*(2), 105–121.

Zaharna, R. S. (2010). *Battles to bridges: US strategic communication and public diplomacy after 9/11*. Palgrave Macmillan. doi:10.1057/9780230277922

Zahid, H., & Din, B. H. (2019). Determinants of intention to adopt e-government services in Pakistan: An imperative for sustainable development. *Resources*, *8*(3), 128. doi:10.3390/resources8030128

Zaineldeen, S., Hongbo, L., Koffi, A., & Hassam, B. (2020). Technology Acceptance Model's Concepts, Contribution and Limitation, Adoption in Education. *Universal Journal of Educational Research*, *8*(11), 5061–5071. doi:10.13189/ujer.2020.081106

Zavale, N. C., & Langa, P. V. (2018). University-industry linkages' literature on Sub-Saharan Africa: Systematic literature review and bibliometric account. *Scientometrics*, *116*(1), 1–49. doi:10.1007/s11192-018-2760-4 PMID:29527070

Zavale, N. C., & Macamo, E. (2016). How and what knowledge do universities and academics transfer to industry in African low-income countries? Evidence from the stage of university-industry linkages in Mozambique. *International Journal of Educational Development*, *49*, 247–261. doi:10.1016/j.ijedudev.2016.04.001

Zavale, N. C., & Schneijderberg, C. (2021). Academics' societal engagement in ecologies of knowledge: A case study from Mozambique. *Science & Public Policy*, *48*(1), 37–52. doi:10.1093/scipol/scaa055

Zeebaree, M., Agoyi, M., & Aqel, M. (2022). Sustainable adoption of E-Government from the UTAUT perspective. *Sustainability (Basel)*, *14*(9), 5370. doi:10.3390/su14095370

Zehle, S. (2012). New world information and communication order. In G. Ritzer (Ed.), *The Wiley-Blackwell Encyclopedia of Globalization* (pp. 1–4). Wiley Blackwell. doi:10.1002/9780470670590.wbeog426

Zhai, X., Chu, X., Chai, C. S., Jong, M. S., Istenic, A., Spector, M., Liu, J.-B., Yuan, J., & Li, Y. (2021). A review of artificial intelligence (AI) in education from 2010 to 2020. *Complexity*, *2021*, 1–8. doi:10.1155/2021/8812542

Zhang, Y. (2021, January 11). State Councilor and Foreign Minister Wang Yi's media interview upon concluding his visit to five African countries. *China Daily*. https://cn.chinadaily.com.cn/a/202101/11/WS5ffba980a3101e7ce973a014.html

Zhao, L., Zhu, D., Shafik, W., Matinkhah, S. M., Ahmad, Z., Sharif, L., & Craig, A. (2022). Artificial intelligence analysis in cyber domain: A review. *International Journal of Distributed Sensor Networks*, *18*(4), 15501329221084882. doi:10.1177/15501329221084882

Zhu, X., & Chikwa, G. (2021). An exploration of China-Africa cooperation in higher education: Opportunities and challenges in open distance learning. *Open Praxis*, *13*(1), 7–19. doi:10.5944/openpraxis.13.1.1154

About the Contributors

Isaac Adjaye Aboagye was born in Accra, Ghana. He received an MSc and PhD in Information and Communication Engineering from the University of Electronic Science and Technology of China. Since December 2019, He has been a lecturer at the Department of Computer Engineering, University of Ghana. He is currently a senior lecturer. His research focus is on Several next-generation modulation formats for high-speed and robust long-haul optical fiber transmission systems that will significantly impact the design of transmission systems in the foreseeable future. He also has a strong interest in computer networks. He is a reviewer for the Photonic Network Communication Journal.

Josephine Aboagye is a post graduate student with a masters in International Studies at the Centre for African and International Studies, University of Cape Coast, Ghana. Her research interests covers digital diplomacy, foreign policy analysis, women in politics and diplomacy. Her recent research on digital diplomacy highlights on how globally, AI and other technologies have come to stay relevant in the world. She also obtained a bachelor's degree in French from the University of Cape Coast, Ghana in 2017.

Rachel Adams is an Associate Fellow of the Leverhulme Centre for the Future of Intelligence at the University of Cambridge; a Research Associate of the Information Law and Policy Centre at the Institute of Advanced Legal Studies, University of London; and Research Associate at the Tayarisha: African Centre of Excellence for Digital Governance, University of Witwatersrand. She currently serves as the Editor-in-Chief of the South African Journal on Human Rights. Rachel has published widely on issues relating to AI policy, decolonisation, gender and human rights, with a particular focus on the African region. She is the author of Transparency: New Trajectories in Law (2020), and the lead author of Human Rights and the Fourth Industrial Revolution in South African (2021). Her work has featured in, amongst others, the New York Times, The Guardian, Marie Clare and La Croix.

Kwami Ahiabenu is the FinTech Innovations Faculty Director at the Global Centre For FinTech Innovations. He completed his doctoral degree in Business Administration from Ghana Communication Technology University/CASS, majoring in Banking Innovations. He is an accomplished leader with a diverse background in the non-profit, government, and private sectors. He is renowned for his expertise in using technology to drive change and human-centred development, with extensive experience in digital transformation, business strategy, and ICTs. He served as a member of Postal, Communication, and IT policies for Ghana and provided leadership for the Government of Ghana Assisted PC Program. His research interest includes Fintech, digital payments and technological innovations in the banking sector.

Eyram Tawia is the co-founder and CEO of Leti Arts. As an experienced game developer, Eyram believes that Africa can make a salient contribution to the world of game development and preserve culture through this. He has pioneered developing the gaming industry in Africa with Leti Arts. Eyram believes preserving cultural diversity through gaming and entertainment is very important and aims to prove this by creating world class games and comics using African talent. He has been the lead consultant on several gamification projects with USAID, JHPIEGO, UNDP, GIZ and many global NGOS implementing serious games in Africa. He's won several awards for his work in the African video game development space, a frequent speaker at game conferences globally and a Lecturer of Game Design at Ashesi University and an author with his book Uncompromising Passion documenting his Journey as an African video game developer.

Gideon Mensah Anapey (PhD) has over 20 years of experience integrating edtech in standards-based education in the Global South. He is a Lecturer in Learning Sciences and a Licensed Counselling Psychologist at the School of Continuing and Distance Education, University of Ghana. He has consulted for many global partners, a policy advocate, and a life coach. Gideon's research areas include deep learning, development education, standards-based pedagogy, machine learning, psychometrics and diagnostics assessment, and EdTech integration. Gideon has MPhil (MUCG) and doctorate (Winneba) degrees in Counselling Psychology, MBA in Human Resource Management (Cape Coast); Master of Education (Ohio, Athens); and B.A. (Hons.) Psychology with Archaeology (Ghana).

Zelda Arku is an assistant lecturer at the University of Mines and Technology and a PhD student in information systems at the University of Ghana. She holds an MPhil in Management Information Systems from the University of Ghana. Her research interest are electronic learning, cloud computing, enterprise resource planning, internet of things and digitalization.

Srinivasan Balapangu has research interest in Biophysics and Bioinstrumentation. He is working as Lecturer in the Department of Biomedical Engineering and Laboratory Technologist at West African center for cell biology of infectious pathogen. University of Ghana.

Elefelious Belay is an Assistant Professor at School of Engineering and Information Technology, Addis Ababa Institute of Technology, Addis Ababa University. He earned his Ph.D. in Information Technology from Addis Ababa University in 2017. He held a Postdoc at the University of Millan from 2018 to 2019. He has published over 18 articles in various Journals and conference proceedings. His ongoing studies focuses on HCI, Software Engineering, AI, and Data Analytics.

William Chakabwata holds a Master of Education Degree in Curriculum and Arts Education, which he earned from University of Zimbabwe. He has taught at Midlands State University in Namibia and also at Namibia University of Science and Technology(NUST). He is currently, studying for a PhD, in curriculum and Instruction with University of South Africa.

Eli Fianu is a Lecturer, and Managing Director of Liscious Services Ltd. He has over seven years' experience as a Lecturer. He also has over seven years' experience in the banking industry and over a decade experience in the telecommunications industry. Dr Eli Fianu has a PhD in Information Systems and Technology from the University of KwaZulu-Natal in South Africa and a MSc in Management Information Systems from Coventry University in the United Kingdom. He has a specialty in Educational Technology. His research interests are in the areas of technology adoption, e-learning, social media, learning analytics and business analytics. He has co-authored several published articles in these areas. Dr Eli Fianu is an advocate of blended learning and strives to conduct research that facilitates the development of effective e-learning models.

Ranson Sifiso Gwala holds a Doctor of Business Administration (DBA) from the University of KwaZulu Natal (UKZN). He has co-published several peer-reviewed articles. He also attended and presented papers at the international conferences starting in 2022. His interests are corporate governance, marketing, leadership, and leadership development in both the public and private sectors. He believes that academia should be an integral part of supporting the public sector to deliver services and improve the lives of people. Academia is at a vantage point to provide meaningful developmental imperatives for all sectors of society. He was born in Ndwedwe, KwaZulu-Natal, but now resides between Durban and Pietermaritzburg, South Africa

George W. Kennedy is a Nigerian, researcher and lecturer in the Department of Technical Education at Akwa Ibom State College of Education, Nigeria. George W. Kennedy has published several paper in reputable peer review international Journals across the global. He has delivered lectures and speech at several national and international conferences and and professional organizations.

Samuel Kojo Kwofie has research interest in artificial intelligence, machine learning, bioinformatics, drug discovery and diagnostics. He is currently the Head of Department of Biomedical Engineering, University of Ghana.

Pfano Mashau is an academic at the University of KwaZulu-Natal, School of Entrepreneurship and Management. He holds a PhD in Management. He also has various non-degree career development certificates acquired from short programmes (Locally and Internationally). As an academic, he is involved in lecturing at the undergraduate and postgraduate levels. His research focus is on Small Business Development, Innovation, Business Management, Entrepreneurship and Agglomeration Economies. Prior to working as an academic, he worked for JET Education Services, BioRegional and a few small businesses. Prof Mashau has published over 40 research articles, supervised eight doctoral theses to completion, and over 20 Masters dissertations. Some of the research work has been presented in international conferences. He has been an editor for a journal and a book. He is a member of the Pan African Research Council and the Institute of Business Advisors. He was briefly appointed as eThekwini Municipality City Planning Commissioner. Prof Mashau aspires to see researchers conducting impactful and life-changing research studies. Prof Mashau interests outside work are cycling, skateboarding and jogging.

Getachew Hailemariam Mengesha is an Assistant Professor of Information Systems at Addis Ababa University, Ethiopia. He earned his PhD in Information Technology from Addis Ababa University in 2015. He served as Fulbright Visiting Scholar, Terry College of Business, University of Georgia, and Athens, GA from September 2018 to May 2019. He has published over sixteen articles in internationally reputed journals and conference proceedings. Further, he is a certified management consultant and has successfully completed over 25 small and bigger consultancy projects. His current research projects focus on technical, legal, and social implications of Artificial intelligence, Data Science and Machine learning, Social Media Use and Socio Economic Implications, Participatory Design, and Inclusive Innovation.

Eric Nsarkoh is a business executive and engineer who has worked for several leading telecommunications and banking companies in Africa. He is currently the founder and CEO of Street Streams Ltd, an innovation hub with a flagship e-commerce product, Brorno, and a Portfolio Advisor at MEST Africa, an organization supporting African entrepreneurs. He has a wealth of experience and expertise in Africa's technology space. He has over 20 years of experience leading multinational organizations across Africa, including Millicom (Tigo Ghana), Airtel Ghana, and MTN Ghana. He has a passion for digital transformation and innovation in Africa.

Isaac Nunoo (PhD.) is a lecturer at the Centre for African and International Studies, University of Cape Coast (UCC), Prior to joining the UCC, he worked with the Ghana National Chamber of Commerce and Industry as the organisation's public relations officer; he has taught in multiple schools in Ghana. His research interest covers: international relations, political economy, foreign policy analysis, conflict management and security, diplomacy, communications and African studies.

Emmanuel de-Graft Johnson Owusu-Ansah is a risk analyst, statistician, and machine learning faculty member at the Physical and Computational Sciences, College of Science, Kwame Nkrumah University of Science and Technology (KNUST), Kumasi, Ghana. He completed his degree in mathematics at KNUST and continued his education in Technical University of Denmark, the University of Copenhagen, Michigan State University, and Cranfield University for postgraduate studies and professional certificates. He has consulted for several global firms, and he is renowned for his expertise in technological integration in risk application and automation of statistical tools. His research interests span quantitative modeling, risk assessment, technological integration, uncertainty quantification, and statistical decision support.

Binay Kumar Pandey currently working as an Assistant Professor in Department of Information Technology of Govind Ballabh Pant University of Agriculture and Technology Pantnagar Uttrakhand, India. He obtained his M. Tech with Specialization in Bioinformatics from Maulana Azad National Institute of Technology Bhopal M. P. India, in 2008 . He obtained his First Degree B. Tech at the IET Lucknow (Uttar Pradesh Technical University, Uttar Pradesh and Lucknow) India, in 2005. In 2010, he joined Department of Information Technology of College of Technology in Govind Ballabh Pant University of Agriculture and Technology Pantnagar as an Assistant Professor and worked for various UG and PG projects till date. He has more than ten years of experience in the field of teaching and research. He has more than 40 publications in reputed peer journal reputed journal Springer,Inderscience,(sci and socopus indexed journal and others) and 3 patent.He has many awards such PM Scholarship etc . He session chair in IEEE International Conference on Advent Trends in Multidisciplinary Research and Innovation (ICATMRI-2020) on December 30, 2020 organized by Pankaj Laddhad Institute of Technology and Management Studies; Buldhana, Maharashtra, India

Margaret Richardson Ansah (Ph.D.) is an Electrical/Electronic and Computer Engineer with a Ph.D. in Computer Engineering from the University of Ghana and an MSc in Communication and Information Engineering from Jiangsu University, China. She is currently a Post-doctoral Fellow at the

University of Alicante, Spain, and a lecturer in the Computer Engineering department at the University of Ghana. Her current research is on Precision agriculture, Smart City, and Climate and Environmental monitoring, Security in Cloud and Serverless / Federated computing. Her research focuses on Cyber-physical systems and IA-enabled Industrial IoT, Wireless Communications, Cybersecurity, and intelligent systems in achieving socioeconomic and sustainable development in emerging economies. Margaret is also an Edtech enthusiast and STEM mentor who supports the development of youth, especially girls and women, in her role as an Arm Developer Program Ambassador and a Google Women TechMakers Ambassador. She is also an IT consultant.

Wasswa Shafik (Member, IEEE) received the Bachelor of Science degree in information technology engineering with a minor in mathematics from Ndejje University, Kampala, Uganda, and the Master of Engineering degree in information technology engineering (MIT) from Yazd University, Yazd, Iran. He pursued a Ph.D. degree in computer science with the School of Digital Science, Universiti Brunei Darussalam, Brunei Darussalam. He is also the Founder and a Principal Investigator of the Dig Connectivity Research Laboratory (DCRLab) after serving as a Research Associate at Network Interconnectivity Research Laboratory, Yazd University. Prior to this, he worked as a Community Data Analyst at Population Services International (PSI-Uganda), Community Data Officer at Programme for Accessible Health Communication (PACE-Uganda), Research Assistant at the Socio-Economic Data Centre (SEDC-Uganda), Prime Minister's Office, Kampala, Uganda, an Assistant Data Officer at TechnoServe, Kampala, IT Support at Thurayya Islam Media, Uganda, and Asmaah Charity Organization. He has more than 60 publications in renowned journals and conferences. His research interests include computer vision, AI-enabled IoT/IoMTs, smart Cities, cyber security, and privacy.

Nii Longdon Sowah is a Senior Lecturer at the University of Ghana Computer Engineering Department. He holds a PhD in Information and Communication Engineering from the University of Electronic Science and Technology of China, Chengdu China. His research interests include artificial intelligence, robotics, multiple object detection, and tracking. He is a reviewer for the CBAS Science and Development Journal. He has authored and co-authored several papers.

Hannah Chimere Ugo is a lecturer in the Department of Biomedical Engineering at Afe Babalola University, Nigeria. Her current research interests include Rehabilitation Engineering, Artificial intelligence, and Biomechanics. She is also passionate about teaching and mentoring students in the field of Biomedical Engineering.

Index

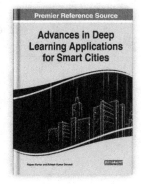
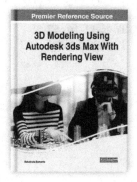

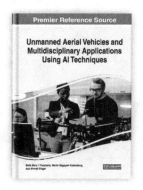

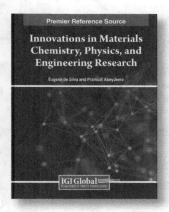
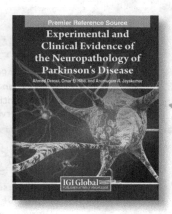
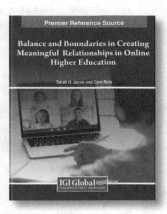

Submit an Open Access Book Proposal

Have Your Work Fully & Freely Available Worldwide After Publication

Seeking the Following Book Classification Types:

Authored & Edited Monographs • Casebooks • Encyclopedias • Handbooks of Research

Gold, Platinum, & Retrospective OA Opportunities to Choose From

Easily Track Your Work in Our Advanced Manuscript Submission System With **Rapid Turnaround Times**

Double-Blind Peer Review by Notable Editorial Boards (*Committee on Publication Ethics* (COPE) Certified

Publications Adhere to All **Current OA Mandates & Compliances**

Affordable APCs *(Often 50% Lower Than the Industry Average)* Including Robust Editorial Service Provisions

Direct Connections with **Prominent Research Funders** & OA Regulatory Groups

Institution Level OA Agreements Available (Recommend or Contact Your Librarian for Details)

Join a **Diverse Community of 150,000+ Researchers Worldwide** Publishing With IGI Global

Content Spread Widely to Leading Repositories (AGOSR, ResearchGate, CORE, & More)

Premier Reference Source

Food Sustainability, Environmental Awareness, and Adaptation and Mitigation Strategies for Developing Countries

Premier Reference Source

New Models of Higher Education
Unbundled, Rebundled, Customized, and DIY

Handbook of Research on

The Global View of Open Access and Scholarly Communications

Retrospective Open Access Publishing

You Can Unlock Your Recently Published Work, Including Full Book & Individual Chapter Content to Enjoy All the Benefits of Open Access Publishing

Learn More

Printed in the United States
by Baker & Taylor Publisher Services